Generative AI and Stochastic Thermodynamics

Originating from lectures delivered at the African Institute of Mathematical Sciences, this book presents a unifying perspective on traditional and modern methods in generative AI and stochastic thermodynamics. By relating the core topics in machine learning to the notion of (variational) free energy, a bridge is built between methods such as latent variable models, variational autoencoders, optimal control, optimal transport, normalizing flows, and diffusion models and concepts such as entropy production and fluctuation theorems in stochastic thermodynamics.

Structured into three main parts, the book commences by setting up the required mathematical and statistical physics preliminaries needed to make it broadly accessible. The largest part of the book then focuses on building intuition of major advances in generative AI by considering discrete-time processes and their relationship to topics in stochastic thermodynamics. Finally, the authors take a short excursion to the continuous-time domain for the more advanced learner.

Max Welling is the co-founder and Chief Technology Officer of the startup CuspAI, and a Full Professor of Machine Learning at the University of Amsterdam. He is a member of the Dutch Royal Academy of Sciences and the Canadian Institute for Advanced Research, and a fellow of the European Lab for Learning and Intelligent Systems. Professor Welling received the ECCV Koenderink Prize in 2010, the 2021 ICML Test of Time Award, and the 2024 ICLR Test of Time Award.

Sirui Lu is a doctoral researcher at the Max Planck Institute of Quantum Optics, Germany. His research focuses on the intersection of (quantum) physics and artificial intelligence. He previously earned his master's and bachelor's degrees in physics from the Technical University of Munich and Tsinghua University, Beijing, respectively.

Lars Holdijk is a PhD student at the University of Oxford. His research focuses on the intersection of generative artificial intelligence, computational biochemistry, and statistical physics.

"Just as thermodynamics proved key to understanding the age of steam, stochastic thermodynamics will prove key to understanding the age of AI. This book is the first comprehensive guide to the principles of stochastic thermodynamics and how they relate to modern AI. It is much needed and will be widely read."

Neil Lawrence, University of Cambridge

"In *Generative AI and Stochastic Thermodynamics*, Max Welling achieves something rare and thrilling: a beautiful marriage of two deep and historically separate fields, weaving together the principles of modern AI with the elegant formalism of statistical physics. Complex ideas are presented with remarkable clarity and care, never sacrificing mathematical rigor for the sake of accessibility, yet remaining wonderfully approachable throughout. This book is an essential read for anyone working at the intersection of AI and the physical sciences, and I have no doubt it will inspire a new generation of cross-disciplinary thinking."

Rose Yu, UC San Diego

"Generative AI and statistical physics keep rediscovering each other's ideas under different names. This book presents both fields in the same framework and is the most interesting textbook I have read this year. It taught me new things about areas I thought I knew well. I strongly recommend it for anyone interested in AI and physics."

Jascha Sohl-Dickstein, Anthropic

Generative AI and Stochastic Thermodynamics

A Tale of Free Energies

MAX WELLING
CuspAI and University of Amsterdam

SIRUI LU
Max-Planck-Institut für Quantenoptik

LARS HOLDIJK
University of Oxford

CAMBRIDGE
UNIVERSITY PRESS

CAMBRIDGE
UNIVERSITY PRESS

Shaftesbury Road, Cambridge CB2 8EA, United Kingdom

One Liberty Plaza, 20th Floor, New York, NY 10006, USA

477 Williamstown Road, Port Melbourne, VIC 3207, Australia

314-321, 3rd Floor, Plot 3, Splendor Forum, Jasola District Centre, New Delhi - 110025, India

Cambridge University Press is part of Cambridge University Press & Assessment, a department of the University of Cambridge.

We share the University's mission to contribute to society through the pursuit of education, learning and research at the highest international levels of excellence.

www.cambridge.org
Information on this title: www.cambridge.org/9781009709064
DOI: 10.1017/9781009709071

When citing this work, please include a reference to the DOI 10.1017/9781009709071

First published 2026

Cover illustration: Molecules (left): tharrison/DigitalVision Vectors/Getty Images Abstract Network Structure (right): AMNART JORNPIBUN/ iStock / Getty Images Plus

A catalogue record for this publication is available from the British Library.

A Cataloging-in-Publication data record for this book is available from the Library of Congress

ISBN 978-1-009-70906-4 Hardback
ISBN 978-1-009-70903-3 Paperback

To the brilliant students at AIMS

Contents

Preface

We have all experienced the situation where the solution to a problem presents itself while riding a bike, taking a shower, walking home, "relaxing" in the washroom, waking up in the morning, etc. Importantly, it did not appear while banging your head against the problem in a conscious effort to solve it, staring at the equations on a piece of paper. In fact, I would claim that my most decisive progress has occurred while taking a break and "relaxing out of the problem". Greek philosophers walked in circles when thinking about a problem, yet most of us stare at a computer screen all day. The purpose of this preface is to make you more aware of where your creative mind is located and to interact with it in a fruitful manner.

Our general thesis is that, contrary to popular belief, creative thinking is not performed by conscious thinking. It is rather an interplay: your conscious mind prepares the seeds to be planted into the unconscious part of your mind, which will "munch" on the problem "out of sight" and return promising paths to solutions to your consciousness at rather random times. This process iterates until the conscious mind decides the problem is sufficiently solved, intractable, or plain dull and moves on to the next. It may be a little unsettling to learn that at least part of your thinking goes on in a part of your mind (or gut?) that seems inaccessible and has a very limited interface with what you think of as yourself. But it is undeniable that it is there and that it plays a role in the creative thought process.

To become a creative thinker, one should learn how to play this game better. To do so, we should think about the language in which to represent knowledge that is most effective in terms of communication with our unconscious mind. In other words, what type of "interface" between our conscious and unconscious mind should we use? It is probably not a good idea to memorize all the details of a complicated equation or problem. Instead, we should extract the abstract idea and capture its essence in a picture. This could be a movie with colors and other baroque features or a more "dull" representation, whatever works for you. Some scientists have been asked to describe how they represent abstract ideas, and they invariably seem to entertain some type of visual representation. A beautiful account of this in the case of mathematicians can be found in the marvelous book *An Essay on the Psychology of Invention in the Mathematical Field* by Hadamard (1945).

By building accurate visual representations of abstract ideas, we create a database of knowledge in the unconscious mind. This collection of ideas forms the basis for what we call intuition. One can often find oneself listening to a talk and feeling uneasy about what is presented. The reason seems to be that the abstract idea one is trying t capture from the talk clashes with a similar idea that has already been stored. This, i turn, can be a sign that one either misunderstood the idea and needs to update it, o that there is actually something wrong with what is being presented. In a similar way one can easily detect that some idea is a small perturbation of what one already kne (one feels happily bored), or something entirely new (one feels intrigued and slightl frustrated). While the novice is continuously challenged and often feels overwhelmed the more experienced researcher feels at ease 90% of the time because the “new” ide was already in their database, which therefore needs no or very little updating.

Somehow, our unconscious mind can also manipulate existing abstract ideas int new ones. This is what we usually think of as creative thinking. One can stimulate thi by seeding the mind with a problem. This is a conscious effort and usually involve a combination of detailed mathematical derivations and building an intuitive pictur or metaphor for the thing one is trying to understand. If you focus enough time an energy on this process and walk home for lunch, you’ll find that you’ll still be thinkin about it in a much more vague fashion: You review and create visual representations o the problem. Then you get your mind off the problem altogether, and when you wal back to work, suddenly parts of the solution surface into consciousness. Somehow your unconscious mind took over and kept working on your problem. The essence i that you created visual representations as the building blocks for the unconscious min to work with.

In any case, whatever the details of this process are (I am no psychologist), suspect that any good explanation should include both an intuitive part – includin examples, metaphors, and visualizations – and a precise mathematical part wher every equation and derivation is properly explained. This, then, is the challenge w have set for ourselves. It will be your task to insist on understanding the abstract ide that is being conveyed and to build your own personalized visual representations. will try to assist in this process, but it is ultimately you who will have to do the har work. Good luck, and above all, have fun!

Max Welling

Acknowledgments

The roots of this book go all the way back to October 2023 when I (MW) went on a trip with my spouse Marga through my favorite country Italy. Each morning, while staying at some random Airbnb in the Italian countryside I would enjoy my cappuccino and write a few pages of this book. Therefore, the first person to thank is Marga for her patience with me spending half of the time during this trip writing this book.

The work continued during our two months visit in January and February 2024 in Pasadena as part of my Merkin Distinguished Professor appointment. I would like to thank Pietro Perona in particular, without whom the visit would not have been possible.

The part of the book that was finished by March 2024 was the basis for a lectures series that was delivered at the African Institute of Mathematical Sciences (AIMS) in Muizenberg, South Africa. I thank the organization of AIMS, and in particular Ulrich Paquet and Claire David, for their generous support of this visit. Most importantly, however, I wish to thank the brilliant students at AIMS who attended our lecture series and enthusiastically engaged as we collectively tried to unravel the relationships that formed the basis of this book. Without their insightful questions this book would truly never have been here.

During the writing of this book the authors benefited from discussions with Sandeep Suresh Cranganore on the definition of work, heat, and entropy in (co-)moving frames of reference.

The book was test-read by Ulrich Paquet and Miranda Cheng, whom I thank for their valuable feedback.

Why Stochastic Thermodynamics of Machine Learning?

In probabilistic machine learning, graphical models, or generative artificial intelligence (AI), we entertain probabilities to express our uncertainty about the many degrees of freedom in the world that we do not explicitly model. The world is simply too complex and chaotic to track all of them. Instead, we introduce coarse-grained and stochastic (random) variables and design probability models to describe them.

The situation is analogous in physics. To describe a large system of molecules, it is completely impossible to track all degrees of freedom of the constituent atoms and electrons. Instead, physicists have developed theories such as thermodynamics and statistical physics to describe these systems approximately through probability distributions. In that framework, we can compute expected (average) quantities and their fluctuations without tracking every individual atom.

In machine learning (ML), we are well aware that probabilities are more like beliefs: They express our belief that the world is in a particular state with a certain probability. There is nothing "real" or ontological about these probabilities; rather, they reflect our lack of knowledge.

Similarly in physics, there is nothing physical about entropy. It is a computational tool that tells us how much information we are missing in our description of the world. Not knowing the precise locations and velocities of particles has real consequences, though, as we are prevented from performing work. That is why we subtract the entropy from the energy and call the result "free energy", as it is the energy that is still free to perform work.

This concept was beautifully illustrated in Maxwell's demon, who used its knowledge of the positions and velocities of particles to move them all to one side of a box with a slider by opening a small door precisely at the right time. Once all the particles are on one side, the demon closes the door, unlocks the slider – which will now move due to the pressure difference – and, as a result, perform work. So a lack of knowledge has real consequences for how much energy we can extract from a system.

Perhaps the first time variational inference was used in ML was by Peterson and Anderson (1987). The concept of a free energy was (to the best of our knowledge) first introduced by Hinton and colleagues (Hinton and Zemel, 1993; Hinton and van Camp, 1993) in the context of Bayesian learning and the minimum description length. Structured variational approximations were developed in a series of papers from Jordan's lab (Jaakkola and Jordan, 1996; Saul et al., 1996; Ghahramani and Jordan, 1997; Jaakkola and Jordan, 1997; Jordan et al., 1999). Another landmark paper was by Neal and Hinton (1998), where the relation between free energy and the expectation maxi mization principle was studied. Today, people often know the free energy formulatio of variational inference as the ELBO (Evidence Lower Bound, Blei et al., 2017), term first coined in Braun and McAuliffe (2010). The ELBO played a key role in th development of variational autoencoders (Kingma and Welling, 2014; Rezende et al 2014) and subsequent hierarchical versions, such as modern diffusion models (Sohl Dickstein et al., 2015; Ho et al., 2020; Song et al., 2021; Kingma et al., 2021; Huan et al., 2021).

In this book, we will dig a bit deeper into this relation between thermodynamics an generative AI. But while thermodynamics and statistical mechanics describe physica systems in equilibrium, generative AI is really described by systems that are out c equilibrium (and live in your computer). For instance, we will find that a learning ste is very similar to performing work in a physical system. Similarly, inference is bes compared with a physical system that settles towards equilibrium.

Perhaps the most beautiful connection between the two is found in modern diffusio models (Sohl-Dickstein et al., 2015; Ho et al., 2020; Song et al., 2021), where a data case is subjected to the second law of thermodynamics and deconstructed into noise Generative AI now inverts this process and learns to turn noise back into structure This is like the proverbial unscrambling of an omelet!

Processes which turn structure into noise, and increase the total entropy in th process, are all around us in the physical world. They happen when an egg falls t the ground, when your body returns to "dust" after you die, and when the univers eventually turns into low-energy photons. But while the second law of thermodynamic says that the total entropy must never decrease, this does not mean that locally we cann decrease entropy. And that is precisely what happens during learning: It happens whe we learn a generative model by inverting the noising process, it happens when lif grows on Earth by using energy from the Sun, and it happens when evolution produce new species that roam the Earth.

This book is meant to bridge the gap between ML (Bishop, 2006) and nonequilibriu thermodynamics (Zwanzig, 2001) (or stochastic thermodynamics: Sekimoto, 201(Van den Broeck and Esposito, 2013; Peliti and Pigolotti, 2021; Shiraishi, 2021). W aim to help students and researchers in both ML and the natural sciences:

- make the connection between these two seemingly so different scientific discipline
- understand that the ELBO is a kind of free energy;
- understand that the variational expectation maximization algorithm can be inte preted in terms of work, heat, and entropy maximization;
- understand that a variational autoencoder and its hierarchical cousin, the diffusio model, are really learning physical systems out of equilibrium;
- understand that inference in these models, either through variational methods (through Markov chain Monte Carlo methods, is very similar to physical system relaxing to equilibrium.

In fact, we will even show that we can think of optimal control and reinforceme learning as a controlled physical system described by a free energy.

We are willing to go as far as saying that there is no real difference between these theories. Probabilistic ML, graphical models, generative AI, or whatever you want to call these approaches, including their learning algorithms and controlled versions, can be described by the same mathematics as nonequilibrium thermodynamics and, in fact, can be fruitfully viewed as a type of physical system that lives in your computer.

The book consists of three parts. In the first part we introduce some mathematical tools, such as probabilities, symmetries, and convex optimization. We also provide a self-contained introduction to deep learning. Finally, we discuss the fundamentals of statistical physics and thermodynamics.

Part II is the core of the book, where we use discrete-time evolution to describe evolving systems out of equilibrium. We introduce the most fundamental concept of this book: the variational free energy. This free energy functional is used both in physics to describe thermodynamical systems out of equilibrium and in ML to provide a learning objective for probabilistic models with latent variables. In this book we argue that these two free energies are very closely related, implying that we can think of inference as a physical system that is relaxing to its lowest free energy state and learning as performing work on a physical system.

This part of the book attempts to relate many concepts in ML to concepts in physics. For instance, we interpret the (variational) expectation maximization algorithm from statistics as minimizing the free energy over the variational posterior distribution (generating heat) and the model parameters (performing work). We show how belief propagation, which is used both in physics and ML, is just another algorithm to minimize the variational free energy. We discuss generative models such as variational autoencoders (VAEs), normalizing flows (NFs) and diffusion models, and how they relate to free energies and thermodynamical concepts.

In Part II we also give a rather comprehensive overview of the concepts of stochastic thermodynamics as viewed from a physicist's perspective, including the famous fluctuation theorems that describe exact relations between thermodynamic quantities such as work, heat and entropy for systems out of equilibrium. To understand these fluctuation theorems deeply, we include a chapter on time reversal symmetries, the breaking of which is related to entropy production. We also add a chapter on free energy estimation methods because of their popularity in the pharmaceutical and chemistry industry, for example in computing how well drugs bind to proteins.

It turns out that fluctuation theorems are deeply related to ideas from the Markov chain sampling literature such as "annealed importance sampling" and other sequential Monte Carlo methods. Markov chain Monte Carlo (MCMC) sampling represents an alternative family of methods for performing inference and (Bayesian) learning. Markov chains are systems that converge to a target distribution of interest and follow the same mathematics as physical systems relaxing to equilibrium. The book has chapters on MCMC and sequential importance sampling.

The most successful class of generative models to date are diffusion models, which were the inspiration for writing this book as they map almost perfectly to the math of nonequilibrium thermodynamics. We go one step further and also show in detail that hybrid methods such as stochastic normalizing flows and SurVAE flows find thei counterpart in physics as escorted free energy methods.

Finally in Part II, we discuss relations between stochastic (nonequilibrium) thermo dynamic systems and concepts such as Schrödinger bridges, generative flow networks and optimal control.

Part III is an introduction to a continuous-time formulation of stochastic thermody namics in terms of Fokker–Planck equations. There are beautiful connections betwee counterdiabatic driving of a physical system and optimal transport theory which w try to explain in this part of the book. And that brings us right back to ML in the forr of flow-based methods.

We end in Part IV with a chapter "Free Energy is All You Need" to emphasize tha all concepts in this book are glued together by the almighty free energy.

This book is based on lectures taught at the African Institute for Mathematica Sciences in Muizenberg, South Africa in March and April 2024. It is by no mean a comprehensive account of all connections between the fields of nonequilibriur thermodynamics and machine learning. We restricted ourselves mostly to discrete time systems and only discuss continuous-time descriptions based on the Fokker Planck equation in the last chapters. We have completely avoided in this book th stochastic differential equation description based on the Langevin and path integra equations. The main reason is that their mathematics can get quite sophisticated, an we thought it unnecessary for a first encounter with the subject. Moreover, the discrete time formulation is the easiest one to directly connect to the ML literature. We definitel intend to write another book (or a later edition of this book) that includes this broade set of theories.

We do hope that this book will help students and researchers from both the ML an natural science communities bridge the chasm between these fields and benefit fro the progress that has been made on the other side.

Part I

Preliminaries

In this part, we build the common language we use throughout the book. Chapter 1 introduces the probabilistic basics we need for latent variables and stochastic processes, Chapter 2 introduces neural networks as function approximators, and Chapter 3 gives an introduction to statistical physics, where concepts like energy, entropy, and partition functions are explained. We highlight here symmetries, gradients, and flows so you can see how they reappear across the discrete- and continuous-time developments that follow.

1 Mathematical Preliminaries

1.1 Introduction

In this chapter we will discuss some mathematical concepts that are useful to familiarize yourself with before you start reading Parts II and III of the book. In particular, we will discuss various aspects of probability theory, including fundamental concepts such as Bayes' rule, and information-theoretic concepts such as entropy. We will introduce you to the concept of symmetries in physics, such as the fundamental concept of time-reversal symmetry. Next, we will provide a comprehensive introduction to convex optimization where you will learn how Lagrange multipliers can help you enforce constraints. Finally, we will say a few words about the difference between the Eulerian and Lagrangian views, which describes the difference between fixed and comoving frames of reference.

1.2 Probabilities

1.2.1 Probability Mass and Density Functions

Probability distributions for a random variable X come in two flavors: probability mass functions (PMFs) and probability density functions (PDFs). The former is defined on discrete states $x = i,\ i = 1, \ldots, N$, while the latter is defined on a continuous space: $x \in \mathbb{R}$. A PMF is defined by a set of non-negative numbers that sum to 1:

$$p(X = x) \geq 0 \text{ for all } x, \quad \sum_x p(X = x) = 1. \tag{1.1}$$

A PDF is a more complicated object due to the presence of a volume element. It consists of a non-negative function that integrates to 1:

$$p(X = x) \geq 0 \text{ for all } x, \quad \int \mathrm{d}x\, p(X = x) = 1. \tag{1.2}$$

Note that for a PMF, all $p(x)$ must be less than or equal to 1; otherwise, they cannot sum to 1 as required by (1.1). This constraint, however, does not necessarily apply to a PDF due to the volume element $\mathrm{d}x$ in (1.2). In fact, we can have $p(x) > 1$ for a PDF as long as the integral over the entire domain equals 1. We will see an example of this shortly when we discuss Gaussian distributions.

For simplicity, we will often write $p(X = x)$ using subscript notation as $p_X(x)$. However, if the context is clear, we will omit specifying the random variable entirely in the following chapters.

A PMF is often described by a categorical distribution, which assigns probabilities to each discrete state x:

$$p(x = i) = \pi_i, \quad \pi_i \geq 0 \text{ for all } i, \quad \sum_i \pi_i = 1. \tag{1.3}$$

Here, we consider π_i to be parameters of the model. To enforce the positivity constraint, we can parameterize the categorical distribution using an exponential form:

$$\pi_i = \frac{1}{Z}\exp(-\varepsilon_i), \quad Z = \sum_i \exp(-\varepsilon_i), \tag{1.4}$$

where ε_i can be interpreted as the energy for state i, and Z is the normalization constant.

There are many examples of PDFs, but one of the most commonly used is the Gaussian (or normal) distribution. We denote a Gaussian distribution with mean μ and standard deviation σ by $G(\mu, \sigma)$, which has the probability density function:

$$p(x) = \frac{1}{\sqrt{2\pi}\sigma}\exp\left(-\frac{1}{2\sigma^2}(x-\mu)^2\right). \tag{1.5}$$

This distribution is illustrated in Figure 1.1. One can check that

$$\mathbb{E}_p[x] = \mu, \quad \mathbb{E}_p[(x-\mu)^2] = \sigma^2, \tag{1.6}$$

$$Z = \int \mathrm{d}x \, \exp\left(-\frac{1}{2\sigma^2}(x-\mu)^2\right) = \sqrt{2\pi}\sigma, \tag{1.7}$$

where $\mathbb{E}_p[\cdot]$ denotes the expectation with respect to the distribution p, defined as

$$\mathbb{E}_p[f(x)] = \int \mathrm{d}x \, p(x) f(x), \tag{1.8}$$

for any function $f(x)$. In the limit of $\sigma \to 0^+$, the Gaussian distribution $G(\mu, \sigma)$ tends to a Dirac delta function,

$$\lim_{\sigma \to 0^+} G(\mu, \sigma) = \delta(x - \mu), \tag{1.9}$$

which has the property that

$$\int \mathrm{d}x \, \delta(x-\mu) f(x) = f(\mu). \tag{1.10}$$

The value of $\delta(x - \mu)$ approaches infinity at $x = \mu$ and zero elsewhere in such a way that the integral remains well defined and equals 1. This confirms our earlier assertion following from (1.2) that for PDFs, the values of $p(x)$ can indeed exceed 1!

The high-dimensional generalization of the Gaussian distribution, (1.5), known as the multivariate Gaussian (or normal) distribution, is given by

$$p(\mathbf{x}) = \frac{1}{(2\pi)^{d/2}|\det(\mathbf{\Sigma})|^{1/2}}\exp\left(-\frac{1}{2}(\mathbf{x}-\boldsymbol{\mu})^\top \mathbf{\Sigma}^{-1}(\mathbf{x}-\boldsymbol{\mu})\right), \tag{1.11}$$

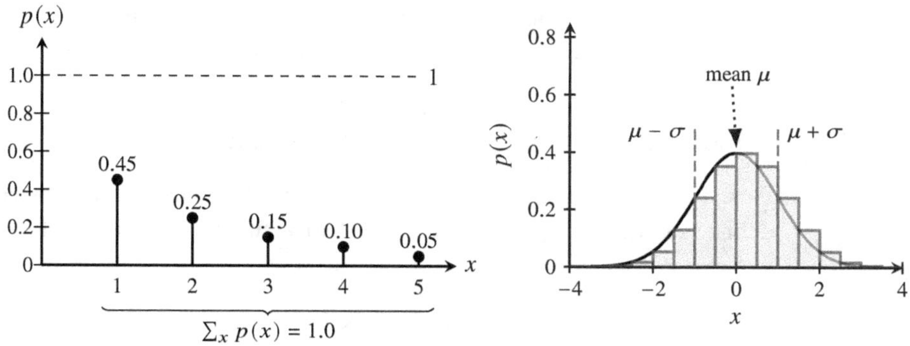

Figure 1.1 (a) A probability mass function assigns probabilities to discrete values that must sum to 1. Each vertical line with a dot represents the probability of a specific outcome, with explicit probability values shown. (b) A Gaussian probability density function with standard deviation $\sigma = 1$. Vertical dashed guides at $\mu - \sigma$ and $\mu + \sigma$ mark the interval that contains approximately 68% of the probability mass, and the histogram bars illustrate how discrete samples from a Gaussian distribution approximate the continuous probability density function.

with mean vector $\boldsymbol{\mu}$ and covariance matrix $\boldsymbol{\Sigma}$. The moments of the multivariate Gaussian distribution are

$$\mathbb{E}_p[\mathbf{x}] = \boldsymbol{\mu}, \quad \mathbb{E}_p[(\mathbf{x} - \boldsymbol{\mu})(\mathbf{x} - \boldsymbol{\mu})^\top] = \boldsymbol{\Sigma}, \tag{1.12}$$

$$Z = \int \mathrm{d}\mathbf{x} \, \exp\left(-\frac{1}{2}(\mathbf{x} - \boldsymbol{\mu})^\top \boldsymbol{\Sigma}^{-1}(\mathbf{x} - \boldsymbol{\mu})\right) = (2\pi)^{d/2} |\det(\boldsymbol{\Sigma})|^{1/2}. \tag{1.13}$$

The above examples are part of a larger family of distributions with nice properties, known as the exponential family (Wainwright and Jordan, 2007). It can be defined as

$$p(x) = \frac{1}{Z} \exp\left(-\sum_k \theta_k f_k(x)\right), \tag{1.14}$$

where θ_k are parameters and f_k are features or sufficient statistics (functions of the random variable x). The function $F(\boldsymbol{\theta}) = -\log Z(\boldsymbol{\theta})$ plays a special role in the exponential family, as it generates the centralized moments (or cumulants) of the distribution:

$$\nabla_{\theta_k} F(\boldsymbol{\theta}) = \mathbb{E}_p[f_k], \tag{1.15}$$

$$\nabla_{\theta_j} \nabla_{\theta_k} F(\boldsymbol{\theta}) = \mathbb{E}_p[f_j]\mathbb{E}_p[f_k] - \mathbb{E}_p[f_j f_k] = -\operatorname*{Cov}_p[f_j, f_k], \tag{1.16}$$

and so on. Many other common distributions, such as the Bernoulli and Poisson, also belong to the exponential family. For example, the Bernoulli distribution, which models binary random variables, can be written as

$$p(x) = \mu^x (1 - \mu)^{1-x} = \exp\left(x \log \frac{\mu}{1 - \mu} + \log(1 - \mu)\right), \tag{1.17}$$

where μ is the probability of success (i.e., $x = 1$). Comparing (1.17) with (1.14), we can identify $f(x) = x$, $\theta = -\log \frac{\mu}{1-\mu}$, and $\log Z(\theta) = \log(1 + e^{-\theta})$.

1.2.2 Conditional Distributions and Bayes' Rule

Focusing on PDFs, the probability of two events occurring simultaneously can be defined as a non-negative function of two arguments that integrates to 1 over all variables:

$$p(x, y) \geq 0 \text{ for all } x, \text{ for all } y, \qquad \iint \mathrm{d}x\, \mathrm{d}y\; p(x, y) = 1. \tag{1.18}$$

This is referred to as the *joint distribution* of X and Y. The previously discussed higher-dimensional generalization of the Gaussian distribution is an example of this, where the different dimensions represent different variables. We can retrieve the single-variable PDF by integrating over all other variables:

$$p(x) = \int \mathrm{d}y\; p(x, y). \tag{1.19}$$

When derived from a joint distribution, $p(x)$ is referred to as the marginal distribution of $p(x, y)$. The marginal distribution still obeys the constraint $\int \mathrm{d}x\; p(x) = 1$.

Instead of marginalizing out y, we can also consider the case where the value of y is fixed. We refer to this as the *conditional distribution* of x given y, obtained as

$$p(x|y) = \frac{p(x, y)}{p(y)}. \tag{1.20}$$

The conditional distribution is also a valid PDF and thus satisfies $\int \mathrm{d}x\; p(x|y) = 1$ for all y.

Bayes' Rule

We can relate the conditional distributions for x given y and y given x as

$$p(y|x) = \frac{p(x|y)p(y)}{p(x)}, \tag{1.21}$$

which is known as *Bayes' theorem* or Bayes' rule (named after Thomas Bayes).

Bayes' rule is an example of a (detailed) balance equation, which we will encounter in various forms throughout the later chapters of this book. If we write it as

$$p(y|x)p(x) = p(x|y)p(y), \tag{1.22}$$

it states that the total flow of probability between any two points x and y is the same, and as such, the marginal probabilities p_X and p_Y will remain the same. The conditional distributions $p(y|x)$ and $p(x|y)$ act as transition probabilities for these flows. We can say that Bayes' rule expresses that the systems described by p_X and p_Y are in relative *equilibrium*.

Bayes' theorem plays a crucial role in machine learning, where it is used to update our beliefs given new evidence. In this context, we refer to $p(y)$ as our *prior probability*, reflecting our original beliefs about a system without having observed any data

Correspondingly, $p(y|x)$ is referred to as the *posterior distribution*, representing our belief about the system after observing x. The denominator in Bayes' theorem,

$$p(x) = \int \mathrm{d}y \; p(x|y)p(y), \tag{1.23}$$

is known as the *evidence*. Because it requires marginalization over the entire space of y, this can be computationally very expensive.

(Conditional) Independence Conditions

Two random variables x and y are said to be *independent* if observing one does not affect the probability of observing the other. For example, consider flipping two fair coins. Observing heads on the first coin does not affect the probability of heads on the second coin, and as such, we can consider these two events to be independent of each other.

More formally, we state that two variables x and y are independent (denoted as $x \perp y$) if and only if their joint probability distribution factorizes; that is,

$$p(x, y) = p(x)p(y), \tag{1.24}$$

which also implies $p(x|y) = p(x)$ and $p(y|x) = p(y)$. Moreover, $\mathbb{E}[xy] = \mathbb{E}[x]\mathbb{E}[y]$.

Additionally, two random variables x and y are said to be *conditionally independent* given a third random variable z (written $x \perp y|z$) if x and y are independent given z,

$$p(x, y|z) = p(x|z)p(y|z). \tag{1.25}$$

As an example, consider flipping two fair coins. If we are told that at least one of the coins landed on heads, the outcomes of the two coins become conditionally dependent given this information. For instance, knowing the first coin is tails now makes it certain the second coin is heads (to satisfy the condition). Knowing the outcome of one coin provides information about the other under this condition. In this scenario, the two coin flips are *marginally independent* but *conditionally dependent* given the information about the combined outcome.

.2.3 Entropy

An important property of a probability distribution, beyond its cumulants, that we will consider in this book is its entropy. In information-theoretic terms, entropy defines an average measure of surprise or uncertainty encoded by the distribution. Formally, it is defined as

$$\mathcal{S}[p] = -\int \mathrm{d}\mathbf{x} \; p(\mathbf{x}) \log p(\mathbf{x}), \tag{1.26}$$

where $S[p](\mathbf{x}) = -\log p(\mathbf{x})$ is known as the *surprisal* (or *unexpectedness*) value for an individual value $\mathbf{x}$. Depending on the context, the base of the logarithm can vary. For example, in information theory, base 2 is often used, in which case the entropy has units of *bits*. In the remainder of this book, however, we will use base e and use *nats* as our unit (Winter, 2021). One nat is $\log_2 e \approx 1.44$ bits.

In the case of a joint distribution of two independent variables, the entropy is give by the sum of their marginal entropies

$$\mathcal{S}[p_{X,Y}] = \mathcal{S}[p_X] + \mathcal{S}[p_Y]. \tag{1.27}$$

For continuous distributions supported on the entire real line, the Gaussian distributio introduced earlier serves as a canonical example. Its entropy can be computed as

$$\begin{aligned}
\mathcal{S}[p] &= \mathbb{E}_p[-\log p(x)] && (1.28)\\
&= \mathbb{E}_p\left[-\log\left(\frac{1}{\sqrt{2\pi}\sigma}\exp\left(-\frac{1}{2\sigma^2}(x-\mu)^2\right)\right)\right] && (1.29)\\
&= \log(\sqrt{2\pi}\sigma) + \frac{1}{2\sigma^2}\mathbb{E}_p[(x-\mu)^2] && (1.30)\\
&= \log(\sqrt{2\pi}\sigma) + \frac{1}{2}. && (1.31)
\end{aligned}$$

This shows that the entropy of the Gaussian distribution depends only on the standar deviation and not on the mean of the distribution.

1.2.4 Comparing Distributions

The Kullback–Leibler (KL) divergence is a nonsymmetric measure of the differenc between two probability distributions. Given two different distributions $p(x)$ and $q(x$ the KL divergence is defined as

$$D_{\mathrm{KL}}[p\|q] = \int \mathrm{d}x\, p(x)\log\frac{p(x)}{q(x)}. \tag{1.32}$$

Intuitively, the KL divergence represents the amount of information lost when express ing a system described by p in terms of the probability distribution q. This informatio loss interpretation becomes clear when expressing the KL divergence as

$$\begin{aligned}
D_{\mathrm{KL}}[p\|q] &= \int \mathrm{d}x\, p(x)\left(\log p(x) - \log q(x)\right) && (1.33)\\
&= -\mathcal{S}[p] + \mathcal{S}[p\|q], && (1.34)
\end{aligned}$$

where $\mathcal{S}[p\|q] = -\int \mathrm{d}x\, p(x)\log q(x)$ is known as the cross-entropy. In this interpre tation, the KL divergence is also known as the relative entropy. When using the K divergence, it is important to note that it is only properly defined when q has the sam support as p; that is, $q(x) \neq 0$ for all x, where $p(x) \neq 0$.

As an example, consider two univariate Gaussian distributions $p(x) = G(\mu_1, \sigma_1)$ and $q(x) = G(\mu_2, \sigma_2)$. The KL divergence between them is given by

$$D_{\mathrm{KL}}[p\|q] = \log\frac{\sigma_2}{\sigma_1} + \frac{\sigma_1^2 + (\mu_1-\mu_2)^2}{2\sigma_2^2} - \frac{1}{2}. \tag{1.35}$$

As mentioned, the KL divergence is nonsymmetric ($D_{\mathrm{KL}}[p\|q] \neq D_{\mathrm{KL}}[q\|p]$) an therefore not a true metric. This nonsymmetry has important implications in machin learning regarding which direction of divergence to use, as illustrated in Figure 1.

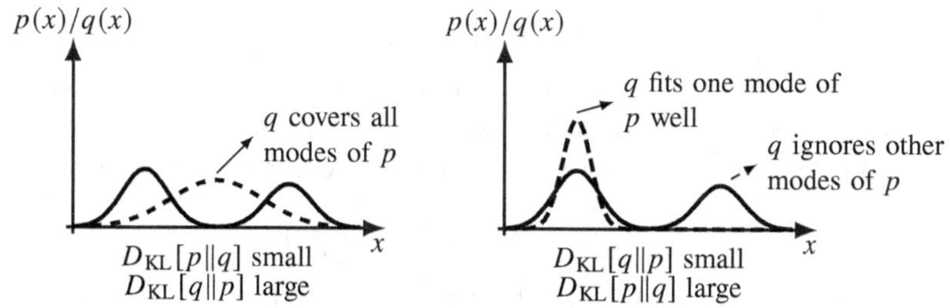

Figure 1.2 Asymmetry of the KL divergence. Let p be the true (bimodal) distribution and q be the approximation. Minimizing the "forward" KL divergence $D_{\mathrm{KL}}[p\|q]$ encourages q to be nonzero wherever p is nonzero, leading to a broad, mode-covering approximation (left). Minimizing the "reverse" KL divergence $D_{\mathrm{KL}}[q\|p]$ penalizes q for being nonzero where p is zero, leading to a focused, mode-seeking approximation that may ignore some modes of p (right).

Furthermore, it does not necessarily satisfy the triangle inequality. However, it is non-negative and satisfies $D_{\mathrm{KL}}[p\|q] = 0$ only if $p = q$ almost everywhere, and can therefore be considered a *divergence* (hence the name).

A useful decomposition of a KL divergence over two (or more) random variables X and Y is given by

$$D_{\mathrm{KL}}[p_{X,Y}\|q_{X,Y}] = D_{\mathrm{KL}}[p_X\|q_X] + \mathbb{E}_{p_X}\left[D_{\mathrm{KL}}[p_{Y|X}\|q_{Y|X}]\right]. \tag{1.36}$$

One can think of this as "Bayes' rule" for KL divergences.

While we will primarily consider the KL divergence in the rest of this book, various other divergences and approaches for measuring the difference between distributions are available. Most notable among these are the χ^2 divergence, mutual information, and the Wasserstein distance (Cover and Thomas, 2006).

1.3 Approximating Expectations

As we can see, many problems surrounding probabilities resolve to solving integrals in the form of expectations,

$$\mathbb{E}_p[f(x)] = \int \mathrm{d}x\; p(x) f(x). \tag{1.37}$$

Achieving this efficiently will be a central theme of this book and, as such, it makes sense to spend some time on the basics of this.

As seen, in the case of a Gaussian this can often be done tractably, but this is not the case in general. Therefore, approximations are required.

1.3.1 Monte Carlo Approximation

Monte Carlo methods are widely used for estimating probabilities and expectations b drawing samples from a target distribution. In regular sampling, we draw N independer and identically distributed (i.i.d.) samples from the target distribution $p(\mathbf{x})$:

$$\mathbf{x}_n \sim p(\mathbf{x}), \quad n = 1, \ldots, N, \tag{1.38}$$

where the notation $\mathbf{x}_n \sim p(\mathbf{x})$ means that each sample $\mathbf{x}_n$ is drawn randomly from th distribution $p(\mathbf{x})$. Given these samples, the expected value of a function $f(\mathbf{x})$, (1.8 can be approximated by the Monte Carlo estimate

$$\mathbb{E}_p[f(\mathbf{x})] \simeq \langle f \rangle = \frac{1}{N} \sum_{n=1}^{N} f(\mathbf{x}_n). \tag{1.39}$$

The law of large numbers ensures that as N increases, the Monte Carlo estimate $\langle f$ converges to the true expected value $\mathbb{E}_p[f(\mathbf{x})]$. This property is known as *consistenc*

The Monte Carlo estimate $\langle f \rangle$ is also an *unbiased* estimator of $\mathbb{E}_p[f(\mathbf{x})]$:

$$\mathbb{E}[\langle f \rangle] = \frac{1}{N} \sum_{n=1}^{N} \mathbb{E}_p[f(\mathbf{x}_n)] = \mathbb{E}_p[f(\mathbf{x})], \tag{1.40}$$

where we used the linearity of expectation and the fact that each sample is drawn fro the same distribution $p(\mathbf{x})$.

Estimator Variance

The expected error of the Monte Carlo estimate can be quantified by its varianc defined as

$$\mathbb{V}[x] = \mathbb{E}\left[(x - \mathbb{E}[x])^2\right]. \tag{1.41}$$

Using this definition, and noting that the samples are independent (s $\mathrm{Cov}(f(\mathbf{x}_n), f(\mathbf{x}_m)) = 0$ for $n \neq m$), we can derive the variance of $\langle f \rangle$ as follows:

$$\begin{aligned}
\mathbb{V}[\langle f \rangle] &= \mathbb{E}\left[(\langle f \rangle - \mathbb{E}_p[f(\mathbf{x})])^2\right] = \mathbb{V}\left(\frac{1}{N}\sum_{n=1}^{N} f(\mathbf{x}_n)\right) \\
&= \frac{1}{N^2} \sum_{n=1}^{N} \sum_{m=1}^{N} \mathrm{Cov}(f(\mathbf{x}_n), f(\mathbf{x}_m)) \\
&= \frac{1}{N^2} \sum_{n=1}^{N} \mathbb{V}(f(\mathbf{x}_n)) \\
&= \frac{1}{N} \mathbb{V}_p(f(\mathbf{x})).
\end{aligned} \tag{1.42}$$

The key insight from this derivation is that the variance of the Monte Carlo estima decreases as $1/N$, where N is the number of samples. This means that increasin the number of samples reduces the expected error of the estimate, with the standar deviation of the error decreasing as $O(1/\sqrt{N})$.

Importance Sampling

As seen, doing a Monte Carlo approximation requires drawing i.i.d. samples from the target distribution $p(\mathbf{x})$. In the next section, as well as at various other points in this book, we will be exploring different methods for doing this, but it is important to note that in many cases this remains intractable within a given compute budget. Importance sampling (IS) in this scenario provides a useful alternative.

Importance sampling uses the identity that we can relate two distributions $p(\mathbf{x})$ and $q(\mathbf{x})$ through the ratio $w(\mathbf{x}) = p(\mathbf{x})/q(\mathbf{x})$. This allows us to rewrite the expectation of the target distribution $p(\mathbf{x})$ in terms of an alternative distribution $q(\mathbf{x})$ as

$$\mathbb{E}_p[f(\mathbf{x})] = \int \mathrm{d}\mathbf{x}\, p(\mathbf{x})f(\mathbf{x}) = \int \mathrm{d}\mathbf{x}\, q(\mathbf{x})\frac{p(\mathbf{x})}{q(\mathbf{x})}f(\mathbf{x}) = \mathbb{E}_q\left[w(\mathbf{x})f(\mathbf{x})\right]. \tag{1.43}$$

If we define the alternative distribution, often referred to as the *proposal distribution*, $q(\mathbf{x})$ such that we can easily draw samples from it, we can use the weights $w(\mathbf{x})$ to obtain an unbiased and consistent estimate of the expectation of the target distribution $p(\mathbf{x})$ as

$$\mathbb{E}_p[f(\mathbf{x})] \simeq \langle f\rangle_{\mathrm{IS}} = \frac{1}{N}\sum_{n=1}^{N} w(\mathbf{x}_n)f(\mathbf{x}_n), \qquad \text{where } \mathbf{x}_n \sim q(\mathbf{x}). \tag{1.44}$$

Both unbiasedness and consistency can similarly be proven using the linearity of expectation and the fact that the samples are i.i.d., as done for the Monte Carlo estimate.

Self-Normalized Importance Sampling

However, while importance sampling allows us to obtain an unbiased estimate of the expectation without requiring direct samples from the distribution, it does require us to be able to compute the ratio $p(\mathbf{x})/q(\mathbf{x})$ for all $\mathbf{x}$. This is often not possible because the normalization constant Z_p of the target distribution $p(\mathbf{x})$ is unknown. If we let $p(x) = \frac{1}{Z_p}\tilde{p}(x)$, then we can rewrite the importance sampling estimate as

$$\mathbb{E}_p[f(\mathbf{x})] = \int \mathrm{d}\mathbf{x}\,\frac{1}{Z_p}\tilde{p}(\mathbf{x})f(\mathbf{x}) = \frac{1}{Z_p}\int \mathrm{d}\mathbf{x}\, q(\mathbf{x})\frac{\tilde{p}(\mathbf{x})}{q(\mathbf{x})}f(\mathbf{x}) = \frac{1}{Z_p}\mathbb{E}_q\left[\tilde{w}(\mathbf{x})f(\mathbf{x})\right], \tag{1.45}$$

where we now have the unnormalized weights $\tilde{w}(\mathbf{x}) = \frac{\tilde{p}(\mathbf{x})}{q(\mathbf{x})}$. Fortunately, it turns out that if we now take the expectation of the unnormalized weights over the proposal distribution $q(\mathbf{x})$, we obtain

$$\mathbb{E}_q[\tilde{w}(\mathbf{x})] = \int \mathrm{d}\mathbf{x}\, q(\mathbf{x})\tilde{w}(\mathbf{x}) = \int \mathrm{d}\mathbf{x}\, q(\mathbf{x})\frac{\tilde{p}(\mathbf{x})}{q(\mathbf{x})} = \int \mathrm{d}\mathbf{x}\, \tilde{p}(\mathbf{x}) = Z_p. \tag{1.46}$$

As such, we can combine these to construct the *self-normalized importance sampling* (SNIS) estimator:

$$\mathbb{E}_p[f(\mathbf{x})] \simeq \langle f\rangle_{\mathrm{SNIS}} = \frac{\frac{1}{N}\sum_{n=1}^{N}\tilde{w}(\mathbf{x}_n)f(\mathbf{x}_n)}{\frac{1}{N}\sum_{n=1}^{N}\tilde{w}(\mathbf{x}_n)}. \tag{1.47}$$

While this is a very useful result, it is important to note that the SNIS estimate i no longer unbiased (i.e., $\mathbb{E}_q[\langle f \rangle_{\text{SNIS}}] \neq \mathbb{E}_p[f(\mathbf{x})]$) due to the fact that the ratio c two expectations is not equal to the expectation of the ratio. It is, however, bot asymptotically unbiased and consistent: the bias vanishes ($\mathbb{E}_q[\langle f \rangle_{\text{SNIS}}] \to \mathbb{E}_p[f(\mathbf{x})]$) and $\langle f \rangle_{\text{SNIS}} \to \mathbb{E}_p[f(\mathbf{x})]$ as $N \to \infty$.

We will further discuss importance sampling at various points throughout the boo For example, we will see that it plays a central role in defining the ELBO in th chapter on VAEs (Chapter 7), and in Chapter 12 we will extend it further to be define over an extended space of distributions as part of the annealed importance samplin framework. This chapter is also where we will discuss the variance of the IS and SNI estimators in more detail.

1.3.2 Sampling Methods

In the previous section, we saw that obtaining a Monte Carlo estimation of an expec tation $\mathbb{E}_p[f(\mathbf{x})]$ requires drawing N independent and identically distributed sample from the distribution $p(\mathbf{x})$. This, however, is in itself a nontrivial problem; som chapters in the book are dedicated to methods that try to achieve this; for exampl Chapter 11 uses Markov chain Monte Carlo methods. We now highlight two gener approaches, based on either using a deterministic transformation to transform a sim ple distribution into a target distribution, or by accepting or rejecting samples from proposal distribution.

Invertible Transformation Methods

When a distribution $p(\mathbf{x})$ is linked to some other less complex distribution $q(\mathbf{z})$ throug some deterministic transformation $\mathbf{x} = g(\mathbf{z})$, we can exploit this relationship to defin a sampling method for $p(\mathbf{x})$ by sampling from $q(\mathbf{z})$ and then transforming the sample to $\mathbf{x}$ using g.

Notably, the exact relationship between $p(\mathbf{x})$ and $q(\mathbf{z})$ in this case is given by th change of variables formula:

$$p(\mathbf{x}) = q(g^{-1}(\mathbf{x})) \left| \det \frac{\partial g^{-1}(\mathbf{x})}{\partial \mathbf{x}} \right|. \tag{1.4}$$

The Jacobian determinant $\left|\det \frac{\partial g^{-1}(\mathbf{x})}{\partial \mathbf{x}}\right|$ represents how infinitesimal volume elemen from the simpler distribution $q(\mathbf{z})$ are scaled when transformed into samples fro $p(\mathbf{x})$ via g. This formula will appear again in detail in the chapter on normalizing flo (Chapter 8).

Example: Box–Muller Transform

A classic example of this is the Box–Muller transform, which transforms a pair independent uniform random variables $\mathbf{u} = (u_1, u_2)$ into a pair of independent standa normal random variables $\mathbf{x} = (x_1, x_2)$ through the transformation

$$x_1 = \sqrt{-2\log u_1}\cos(2\pi u_2), \qquad x_2 = \sqrt{-2\log u_1}\sin(2\pi u_2). \tag{1.4}$$

Example: Inverse CDF

Formally, a PDF is characterized by its cumulative distribution function (CDF) $F(x) = \int_{-\infty}^{x} \mathrm{d}x'\ p(x')$. If this CDF is invertible, we can use it to define a sampling method for $p(x)$ by drawing a uniform random number $u \sim \text{Unif}(0, 1)$ and setting $x = F^{-1}(u)$. This simple approach is limited to distributions that have an invertible CDF and gets complicated for high-dimensional distributions.

Rejection Sampling

A second approach, which does not rely on the existence of an invertible deterministic transformation, is accept–reject sampling. Given our target distribution $p(\mathbf{x})$, accept–reject sampling uses a proposal distribution $q(\mathbf{x})$ to sample from, but instead of transforming the samples $\mathbf{x}$, it accepts them with a probability proportional to the ratio $p(\mathbf{x})/(Mq(\mathbf{x}))$, where M is a constant such that $p(\mathbf{x}) \leq Mq(\mathbf{x})$ for all $\mathbf{x}$. The collection of accepted samples is then distributed according to $p(\mathbf{x})$.

The efficiency of this method is determined by the choice of proposal distribution $q(\mathbf{x})$ and the constant M. The closer the proposal distribution $q(\mathbf{x})$ is to the target distribution $p(\mathbf{x})$, the more efficient the sampling will be. For high-dimensional distributions, accept–reject sampling is often not practical as the acceptance rate is typically very low.

1.4 Symmetries

Symmetries play a very important role throughout physics. They have unified electric and magnetic fields through Lorentz transformations between observers, and they are at the root of general relativity by formulating all physical laws covariant with respect to arbitrary invertible coordinate transformations, which led to the unification of gravity and acceleration as two sides of the same coin. They also organize elementary particles into families related to each other by symmetry transformations.

In this book, we will encounter one very fundamental symmetry in particular: *time reversal symmetry*. This is the idea that the laws of physics should remain the same if we run the "movie" forward or backward in time. If you watch a bunch of molecules jumping around, you cannot tell whether the movie is being played normally or in reverse. This is in sharp contrast to everyday life, where you will never see an omelet unscramble itself. We say that time reversal symmetry is broken at the macroscopic scale for thermodynamical systems that are not in equilibrium. Time reversal symmetry is restored in equilibrium.

The importance of time reversal symmetry (or its breaking) is that concepts such as heat production and entropy production, both macroscopic concepts that have no real analogy at the microscopic level, can be directly tied to it. In loose terms, the total amount of asymmetry between forward and backward dynamics determines the amount of entropy production in the system. This is made more precise in the famous fluctuation theorems of Crooks and Jarzynski (Jarzynski, 2011; Seifert, 2012).

In this section, we will provide some background on the mathematics of symmetries.

Let us assume we have a vector field $\mathbf{v}(\mathbf{x})$ and we want to understand what happens if we rotate the vector field. To describe the rotated vector field, we add a prime: $\mathbf{v}'(\mathbf{x})$. We now ask, how is the new vector field related to the old vector field? After some thinking, we find

$$\mathbf{v}'(\mathbf{x}) = R\mathbf{v}(r^{-1}\mathbf{x}), \tag{1.50}$$

where we use the representation r of the rotation group to rotate the location $\mathbf{x}$ and the representation R to rotate the tangent vector $\mathbf{v}$. These can be different in general, but in this example, you may assume that they are the same. In words, this equation says that in order to get the new vector $\mathbf{v}'$ at position $\mathbf{x}$, you need to rotate $\mathbf{x}$ back to the position $r^{-1}\mathbf{x}$ before the rotation, and then rotate that vector by an amount R. A similar rule applies to matrices and higher-order tensors:

$$\mathbf{M}'(\mathbf{x}) = R\mathbf{M}(r^{-1}\mathbf{x})R^{\top} \;\Rightarrow\; M'_{i,j}(\mathbf{x}) = \sum_{i'j'} R_{i,i'}R_{j,j'}M_{i',j'}(r^{-1}\mathbf{x}), \tag{1.51}$$

$$T'(\mathbf{x}) = R \otimes R \otimes \cdots \otimes R\, T(r^{-1}\mathbf{x}) \;\Rightarrow$$

$$T'_{i_1,i_2,\ldots,i_d}(\mathbf{x}) = \sum_{i'_1,i'_2,\ldots,i'_d} R_{i_1,i'_1}R_{i_2,i'_2}\cdots R_{i_d,i'_d}\, T_{i'_1,i'_2,\ldots,i'_d}(r^{-1}\mathbf{x}). \tag{1.52}$$

These transformations often have the structure of a group. A group consists of elements that compose into new group elements: a sequence of two rotations is another rotation. Other properties of group transformations include that there is an identity transformation, an inverse transformation for every group element, and that group transformations are associative.

The particular form in which they act on a vector space depends on the space's dimension. This form is called the representation. Representations need to respect the group structure, in the sense that if $M(g)$ is a representation of a group element g, then $M(g)\cdot M(h) = M(g \circ h)$. We call this a homomorphism.

The group structure for time inversion is very simple indeed; it is an *involution*. Namely, applying time reversal Ω twice gets you back where you started:

$$\Omega^2 = \mathbb{1}. \tag{1.53}$$

Physical variables transform under certain "symmetry transformations." For involutions there are two types of such variables, even- and odd-parity variables, where the latter switch sign under time reversal. For a trajectory $(\mathbf{x}(\tau), \mathbf{p}(\tau))$ over a time interval $[0, \tau_f]$, the time-reversed trajectory, denoted by a tilde, is defined as

$$\tilde{\mathbf{x}}(\tau) = \Omega\mathbf{x}(\tilde{\tau}) = \mathbf{x}(\tau_f - \tau), \tag{1.54}$$

$$\tilde{\mathbf{p}}(\tau) = \Omega\mathbf{p}(\tilde{\tau}) = -\mathbf{p}(\tau_f - \tau). \tag{1.55}$$

For both cases we indeed have that applying time reversal twice will give us back the original variables.

A symmetry is now "something" that is invariant under group transformations. A circle is invariant under rotations of the circle. We are interested in probability distributions that are invariant and in physical laws that are invariant. At the microscopic

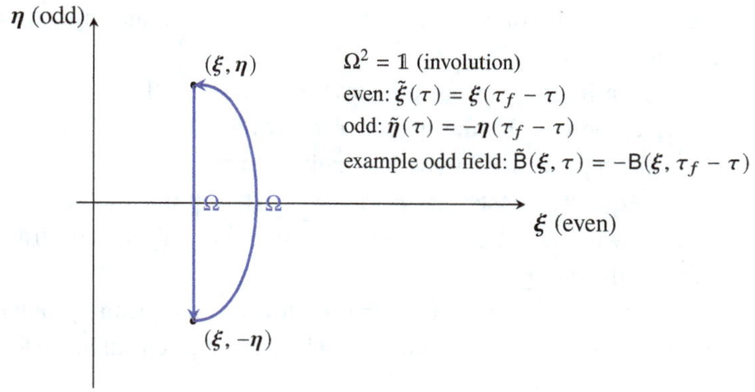

Figure 1.3 Time reversal parity in phase space. Positions (even variables) remain unchanged under time reversal, while momenta (odd variables) flip sign: $\Omega\colon (\xi, \eta) \mapsto (\xi, -\eta)$. The operator Ω is an involution: $\Omega^2 = \mathbb{1}$.

level all physical laws are believed to be invariant under joint charge–parity–time reversal transformations. In this book we consider parity and time reversal. For instance, Hamilton's equations are invariant under time reversal, in the sense that a trajectory that starts at $\mathbf{x}(0), \mathbf{p}(0)$ and ends in the state $\mathbf{x}(\tau_f), \mathbf{p}(\tau_f)$ has, under Hamilton's equations of motion, a dual path that starts at $\mathbf{x}(\tau_f), -\mathbf{p}(\tau_f)$ and evolves under the same equations back to the initial state (with flipped momenta) $\mathbf{x}(0), -\mathbf{p}(0)$; see Figure 1.3.

In thermodynamics, the situation is more complex. The stochastic Brownian-like motion is not invertible in general because, thanks to collisions, we are losing information about the system. That means that the usual stochastic equations of motion are not time-reversal symmetric. The degree by which we lose information is measured by the entropy increase in the system. When the system is in equilibrium, time reversal symmetry is restored and no more entropy is produced (we have lost all the information there is to lose that is consistent with macroscopic variables such as average energy, temperature, and pressure).

.5 Essentials of Convex Optimization

.5.1 The Primal Problem

A constrained optimization problem can be formally expressed as

$$\min_{\mathbf{x}} \quad f_0(\mathbf{x})$$

$$\text{subject to: } \begin{cases} f_i(\mathbf{x}) \leq 0, & \text{for all } i \\ h_j(\mathbf{x}) = 0, & \text{for all } j. \end{cases} \tag{1.56}$$

Here, we have an objective function $f_0(\mathbf{x})$ that we want to minimize, subject to inequality constraints $f_i(\mathbf{x}) \leq 0$ and equality constraints $h_j(\mathbf{x}) = 0$. The goal is to find the optimal solution $\mathbf{x}^*$ that satisfies all the constraints while minimizing the objective function.

To gain intuition about this problem, consider the analogy of a ball rolling down a surface defined by the objective function $f_0(\mathbf{x})$. The ball's motion is constrained by walls, represented by the inequality constraints $f_i(\mathbf{x}) \leq 0$, and tracks, represented by the equality constraints $h_j(\mathbf{x}) = 0$. The optimal solution $\mathbf{x}^*$ corresponds to the position where the ball comes to rest, satisfying all the constraints while minimizing its potential energy.

In convex optimization, (1.56) is known as the primal problem. We now write the primal Lagrangian of this problem, which will be helpful in the following development

$$\mathcal{L}_\mathrm{P}(\mathbf{x}, \boldsymbol{\lambda}, \boldsymbol{\nu}) = f_0(\mathbf{x}) + \sum_i \lambda_i f_i(\mathbf{x}) + \sum_j \nu_j h_j(\mathbf{x}), \tag{1.57}$$

where $\boldsymbol{\lambda} = (\lambda_1, \lambda_2, \ldots)$ and $\boldsymbol{\nu} = (\nu_1, \nu_2, \ldots)$ are Lagrange multipliers associated with the inequality and equality constraints, respectively. The Lagrange multipliers can be interpreted as the "price" or "cost" of violating the constraints. In the ball analogy, λ_i represents the reaction force exerted by the wall on the ball when it is in contact with the wall, and ν_j represents the force exerted by the track on the ball to keep it on the track. We will assume in the following that $\lambda_i \geq 0$ for all i.

1.5.2 The Dual Problem

The primal problem, (1.56), can be transformed into an alternative formulation called the dual problem. From the primal Lagrangian, we can define the dual function as

$$\mathcal{L}_\mathrm{D}(\boldsymbol{\lambda}, \boldsymbol{\nu}) = \inf_{\mathbf{x}} \mathcal{L}_\mathrm{P}(\mathbf{x}, \boldsymbol{\lambda}, \boldsymbol{\nu}). \tag{1.58}$$

Here, "inf" denotes the infimum, which is the greatest lower bound of a set. For optimization problems, we often use inf instead of min when we cannot guarantee that the minimum is actually achieved within the feasible set. Similarly, "sup" denotes the supremum, which is the least upper bound of a set. In this context, it represents the lowest value of the primal Lagrangian $\mathcal{L}_\mathrm{P}$ over all possible values of $\mathbf{x}$, for fixed values of $\boldsymbol{\lambda}$ and $\boldsymbol{\nu}$. This objective can actually become $-\infty$ for certain values of its arguments. We will call parameters $\boldsymbol{\lambda} \geq 0, \boldsymbol{\nu}$ for which $\mathcal{L}_\mathrm{D}(\boldsymbol{\lambda}, \boldsymbol{\nu}) > -\infty$ *dual feasible*.

It is important to note that the dual Lagrangian, (1.58), is a concave function of $\boldsymbol{\lambda}, \boldsymbol{\nu}$ because it is a pointwise infimum of a family of linear functions in $\boldsymbol{\lambda}, \boldsymbol{\nu}$. Hence even if the primal problem, (1.56), is not convex, the dual is always concave (Boyd and Vandenberghe, 2004)!

It is not hard to show that

$$\mathcal{L}_\mathrm{D}(\boldsymbol{\lambda}, \boldsymbol{\nu}) \leq p^*, \tag{1.59}$$

where p^* is the primal optimal value. This follows because for any primal feasible point $\mathbf{x}$, we have $f_i(\mathbf{x}) \leq 0$ and $h_j(\mathbf{x}) = 0$. With $\lambda_i \geq 0$, the sum $\sum_i \lambda_i f_i(\mathbf{x}) + \sum_j \nu_j h_j(\mathbf{x}) \leq 0$. Therefore, $\mathcal{L}_\mathrm{P}(\mathbf{x}, \boldsymbol{\lambda}, \boldsymbol{\nu}) \leq f_0(\mathbf{x})$ for any feasible $\mathbf{x}$. Taking the infimum over all $\mathbf{x}$ on the left and the minimum over feasible $\mathbf{x}$ on the right gives $\mathcal{L}_\mathrm{D}(\boldsymbol{\lambda}, \boldsymbol{\nu}) \leq p^*$.

Thus, the dual problem always provides a lower bound to the primal problem, as seen in (1.59). The tightest lower bound can be found by solving the dual problem,

$$\begin{aligned} &\max_{\lambda,\nu} \quad \mathcal{L}_{\mathrm{D}}(\lambda,\nu) \\ &\text{subject to:} \quad \lambda_i \geq 0 \text{ for all } i, \end{aligned} \tag{1.60}$$

which is therefore a convex optimization problem.

1.5.3 Weak and Strong Duality

If we denote by d^* the dual optimal value, we always have

$$d^* = \mathcal{L}_{\mathrm{D}}(\lambda^*,\nu^*) \leq p^*, \tag{1.61}$$

where λ^* and ν^* are the optimal solutions to the dual problem. This property is known as *weak duality*. The difference between the primal and dual optimal values, $p^* - d^*$, is called the *duality gap*.

Strong duality holds when $p^* = d^*$; that is, when the duality gap is zero. Strong duality is particularly useful, especially if we can express the primal solution $\mathbf{x}^*$ in terms of the dual solution λ^*, ν^*. In such cases, we can simply solve the dual problem, (1.60), and convert the answer to the primal domain, knowing that the solution must be optimal. Often, the dual problem is easier to solve.

So when does strong duality hold? Up to some mathematical details, the answer is: *if the primal problem,* (1.56), *is convex and the equality constraints are affine* (Boyd and Vandenberghe, 2004). This means that $f_0(\mathbf{x})$ and $\{f_i(\mathbf{x})\}$ are convex functions and $h_j(\mathbf{x}) = A_j \cdot \mathbf{x} - b_j$.

The primal problem, (1.56), can be written as

$$p^* = \inf_{\mathbf{x}} \sup_{\lambda\geq 0,\nu} \mathcal{L}_{\mathrm{P}}(\mathbf{x},\lambda,\nu). \tag{1.62}$$

This can be understood by noting that $\sup_{\lambda\geq 0,\nu} \mathcal{L}_{\mathrm{P}}(\mathbf{x},\lambda,\nu) = f_0(\mathbf{x})$ when $\mathbf{x}$ is feasible but ∞ otherwise. To see this, first observe that by violating one of the constraints, you can find a choice of λ, ν that makes the Lagrangian, (1.57), infinite. Also, when all the constraints are satisfied, the best we can do is maximize the additional terms to be zero, which is always possible. For instance, we can simply set all λ, ν to zero, even though this is not necessary if the constraints themselves vanish.

The dual problem by definition is given by

$$d^* = \sup_{\lambda\geq 0,\nu} \inf_{\mathbf{x}} \mathcal{L}_{\mathrm{P}}(\mathbf{x},\lambda,\nu). \tag{1.63}$$

Hence, the "sup" and "inf" can be interchanged if strong duality holds, so the optimal solution is a saddle point. It is important to realize that the order of maximization and minimization matters for arbitrary functions (but not for convex–concave functions, as the minimax theorem guarantees). Imagine a "V-shaped" valley running diagonally across the coordinate system. If we first maximize over one direction, keeping the other direction fixed, and then minimize the result, we end up with the lowest point on the rim. If we reverse the order, we end up with the highest point in the valley.

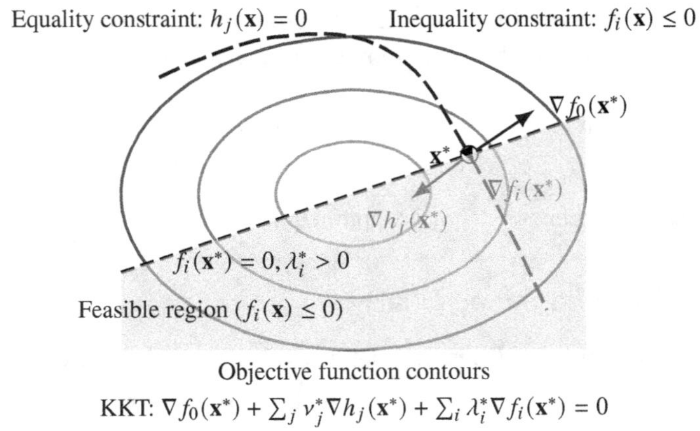

Figure 1.4 Geometric interpretation of constrained optimization and KKT conditions. The optimal point $\mathbf{x}^*$ lies where the long-dashed equality contour $h_j(\mathbf{x}) = 0$ intersects the dashed inequality-constraint boundary $f_i(\mathbf{x}) \leq 0$. The gradient vectors at $\mathbf{x}^*$ illustrate the stationarity condition: $\nabla f_0(\mathbf{x}^*)$ is perpendicular to the objective contour, while the gradients of the constraints oppose motion into infeasible regions. Their weighted sum balances to zero, and the hatched wedge marks the feasible set.

1.5.4 Karush–Kuhn–Tucker Conditions

The Karush–Kuhn–Tucker (KKT) conditions are a set of necessary conditions th hold for problems with zero duality gap. These conditions turn out to be sufficient fc convex optimization problems (Boyd and Vandenberghe, 2004). The KKT condition illustrated in Figure 1.4, are given by

$$\nabla f_0(\mathbf{x}^*) + \sum_i \lambda_i^* \nabla f_i(\mathbf{x}^*) + \sum_j \nu_j^* \nabla h_j(\mathbf{x}^*) = 0, \quad (1.64)$$

$$f_i(\mathbf{x}^*) \leq 0, \quad (1.65)$$

$$h_j(\mathbf{x}^*) = 0, \quad (1.66)$$

$$\lambda_i^* \geq 0, \quad (1.67)$$

$$\lambda_i^* f_i(\mathbf{x}^*) = 0. \quad (1.68)$$

The first condition, (1.64), known as the stationarity condition, can be easily derive from (1.62), which states that $p^* = \inf_{\mathbf{x}} \mathcal{L}_{\mathrm{P}}(\mathbf{x}, \boldsymbol{\lambda}^*, \boldsymbol{\nu}^*)$. This implies that all the deriva tives of the Lagrangian with respect to $\mathbf{x}$ must vanish at the optimal point $\mathbf{x}^*$. Th condition has a nice interpretation as a "balancing of forces." Imagine a ball rollin down a surface defined by $f_0(\mathbf{x})$ (i.e., you are doing gradient descent to find the mini mum). The ball gets blocked by a wall, which is the constraint surface. If the surfac and constraint are convex, then at the point where the ball does not move, we hav reached the optimal solution. At that point, the forces on the ball must balance. Th first term represents the force of the ball against the wall due to gravity (the ball still on a slope). The second term represents the reaction force of the wall in the op posite direction. The λ_i^* represents the magnitude of the reaction force, which neec to be higher if the surface slopes more. We say that this constraint is "active". Other constraints which do not exert a force are "inactive" and have $\lambda_i^* = 0$.

The final KKT condition, (1.68), known as *complementary slackness*, states that either $f_i(\mathbf{x}^*) = 0$ (the constraint is saturated and hence active), in which case λ_i^* is allowed to take on a nonzero value, or if the constraint is inactive ($f_i(\mathbf{x}^*) < 0$), so λ_i^* must vanish.

Complementary slackness, (1.68), can be derived as follows:

$$\begin{aligned} f_0(\mathbf{x}^*) &= \mathcal{L}_\mathrm{D}(\boldsymbol{\lambda}^*, \boldsymbol{\nu}^*) && (1.69)\\ &= \inf_{\mathbf{x}} \left(f_0(\mathbf{x}) + \sum_i \lambda_i^* f_i(\mathbf{x}) + \sum_j \nu_j^* h_j(\mathbf{x}) \right) && (1.70)\\ &\le f_0(\mathbf{x}^*) + \sum_i \lambda_i^* f_i(\mathbf{x}^*) + \sum_j \nu_j^* h_j(\mathbf{x}^*) && (1.71)\\ &\le f_0(\mathbf{x}^*). && (1.72) \end{aligned}$$

Here, (1.69) follows from strong duality, (1.70) is the definition of the dual Lagrangian, (1.71) holds because the infimum is always less than or equal to the value at any point $\mathbf{x}^*$, and (1.72) follows from the feasibility of $\mathbf{x}^*$ – (1.65) and (1.66) – and the non-negativity of λ_i^*, (1.67). Since the first and final expressions in this derivation are equal, all the inequalities must be tight, which implies that each term $\lambda_i^* f_i(\mathbf{x}^*)$ must be zero, yielding the complementary slackness condition.

By solving the KKT conditions, we can find the optimal primal and dual solutions, $\mathbf{x}^*$ and $(\boldsymbol{\lambda}^*, \boldsymbol{\nu}^*)$, respectively.

.5.5 Canonical Ensemble from the Maximum Entropy Principle

A principle proposed by E. T. Jaynes for both physical systems and information systems is that in the absence of information (measured by entropy), the best solution to a problem with some given observations is the one that is consistent with the observations but otherwise maximizes entropy over the remaining degrees of freedom (Jaynes, 1957a,b). In some sense, the system assumes as little as possible about things it does not know. This is sometimes called Occam's razor in Bayesian statistics (Jaynes, 2003).

For a canonical ensemble, we assume that the average energy of the system is known and equal to some value E. The maximum entropy (MaxEnt) problem can then be formulated as

$$\begin{aligned} \rho^{\mathrm{eq}} &= \operatorname*{argmax}_{\rho} \ \mathcal{L}_\mathrm{P}(\rho, \beta, \lambda) && (1.73)\\ &= \operatorname*{argmax}_{\rho} \left[S[\rho] - \beta\left(\int \mathrm{d}\zeta\, \rho(\zeta)\mathcal{H}(\zeta) - E \right) - \lambda\left(\int \mathrm{d}\zeta\, \rho(\zeta) - 1 \right) \right], && (1.74) \end{aligned}$$

where $\rho(\zeta)$ is the probability distribution over microstates ζ, $S[\rho]$ is the entropy functional, and $\mathcal{H}(\zeta)$ is the Hamiltonian of the system. Here, we have two constraints enforced by the Lagrange multipliers β and λ, ensuring that the average energy of the system is equal to E and the probability distribution is normalized. Taking (functional) derivatives of the primal Lagrangian $\mathcal{L}_P$ with respect to ρ and setting it to zero give the stationarity condition in the KKT conditions:

$$\frac{\delta \mathcal{L}_P}{\delta \rho} = -\log \rho(\zeta) - 1 - \beta \mathcal{H}(\zeta) - \lambda = 0, \tag{1.75}$$

which is solved by

$$\rho^{\text{eq}}(\zeta) = \exp(-\beta \mathcal{H}(\zeta) - \lambda - 1) = \frac{1}{Z} \exp(-\beta \mathcal{H}(\zeta)), \quad \lambda = \log Z - 1. \tag{1.76}$$

The Lagrange multiplier λ is easily solved in terms of the normalization constant Z. The other Lagrange multiplier, β, is identified with the inverse temperature $1/(k_B T)$, with k_B being the Boltzmann constant and T the temperature of the heat bath. Note that we could have added a separate inequality constraint to enforce $\rho \geq 0$, but thanks to the exponential form of the solution, this constraint is automatically satisfied. We set $k_B = 1$ in what follows.

The next step is to insert the solution (1.76) of the KKT condition (1.75) back into the primal Lagrangian, (1.73), giving the dual Lagrangian:

$$\mathcal{L}_D(\beta, \lambda) = \beta E + \lambda + \int \mathrm{d}\zeta \; \exp(-\beta \mathcal{H}(\zeta) - \lambda - 1). \tag{1.77}$$

Defining $\tilde{\lambda} = \lambda + 1$ and solving for $\tilde{\lambda}$ to normalize the distribution, we get

$$\tilde{\lambda}^* = \log Z(\beta) = \log \int \mathrm{d}\zeta \; \exp(-\beta \mathcal{H}(\zeta)), \tag{1.78}$$

which leads to

$$\mathcal{L}_D(\beta, \lambda^*) = \beta E + \log Z(\beta) = \beta(E - F(\beta)) = S(\beta), \tag{1.79}$$

where we have used the definition of the equilibrium free energy as $F = -T \log Z$ and the definition of the entropy from $F = E - TS$. We note that this is the entropy at equilibrium as it is a function of β only and not of ρ. This is a nice result! The dual Lagrangian, (1.77), of the (nonequilibrium) maximum entropy problem, (1.73), is an expression for the entropy of the Boltzmann distribution at equilibrium, which we can now maximize over β. Since we know the dual Lagrangian is always concave, this should be a tractable optimization problem. Computing derivatives of $\mathcal{L}_D$ with respect to β, we get

$$\frac{\partial \mathcal{L}_D}{\partial \beta} = E - \mathbb{E}_{\rho^{\text{eq}}(\beta)}[\mathcal{H}]. \tag{1.80}$$

We can perform iterative gradient ascent updates on $\mathcal{L}_D$ until we reach the maximum. The resulting β^* is the inverse temperature of the system that corresponds to an average energy of E.

Since the original problem, (1.73), was convex, we have strong duality which means the primal and dual optimal values are equal; that is, $p^* = d^*$. This ensures that our solution is indeed the global optimum.

To conclude, Jaynes' maximum entropy principle neatly provides us with a derivation of the canonical ensemble, (1.76), or the Boltzmann distribution, through the method of Lagrange multipliers with the interpretation of the inverse temperature β as the Lagrange multiplier that enforces the average energy constraint.

1.6 The Lagrangian versus Eulerian View

In both stochastic thermodynamics and machine learning, we often need to track how probability distributions evolve over time. There are two complementary perspectives for performing such calculations: the Eulerian view, where we observe the system from a fixed reference frame in space, and the Lagrangian view, where we follow individual particles (or samples) as they move. In the fixed Eulerian reference frame, we define space-time coordinates $(\zeta, \tau) = (\xi, \eta, \tau)$ in phase space and fields as functions of these fixed coordinates; that is, we may have a Hamiltonian $\mathcal{H}(\zeta, \tau)$. In general we will write $\mathbf{h}(\zeta, \tau)$ for such functions, which can be scalars, vectors ("fields") or even matrices and higher-order tensors. The particle density is described by the density field $\rho(\zeta, \tau)$, which satisfies the following continuity equation:

$$\partial_\tau \rho(\zeta, \tau) = -\nabla_\zeta \cdot (\rho(\zeta, \tau)\mathbf{v}(\zeta, \tau)) = -\mathbf{div}(\rho(\zeta, \tau)\mathbf{v}(\zeta, \tau)), \tag{1.81}$$

for some vector field $\mathbf{v}$. This is just the continuum expression for what is known as a push-forward (deterministic) transformation of some density along the vector field $\mathbf{v}$. When we compute an average we compute

$$\int \mathrm{d}\zeta\, \rho(\zeta, \tau)\, \mathbf{h}(\zeta, \tau). \tag{1.82}$$

In the above we note that $\rho(\zeta, \tau)$ is a different (transformed) distribution than $\rho(\zeta, 0)$. If this density transforms under a deterministic (push-forward) transformation $\zeta_0 \to \zeta_\tau = g(\zeta_0, \tau)$ for all ζ_0, then we have the following relation:

$$\rho(\zeta_\tau, \tau) = \rho(g(\zeta_0, \tau), \tau) = \rho(\zeta_0, 0) \left|\det\left(\frac{\partial g(\zeta_0, \tau)}{\partial \zeta_0}\right)\right|^{-1}. \tag{1.83}$$

Note that the measure will remain invariant:

$$\rho(\zeta_\tau, \tau)\, \mathrm{d}\zeta_\tau = \rho(\zeta_0, 0)\, \mathrm{d}\zeta_0. \tag{1.84}$$

When we compute an average we can thus do the following:

$$\begin{aligned}
&\int \mathrm{d}\zeta\, \rho(\zeta, \tau)\, \mathbf{h}(\zeta, \tau) \\
&= \int \mathrm{d}\zeta_\tau\, \rho(\zeta_\tau, \tau)\mathbf{h}(\zeta_\tau, \tau) \quad (\zeta \text{ is a dummy integration variable}) \\
&= \int \mathrm{d}\zeta_0\, \rho(\zeta_0, 0)\, \mathbf{h}(g(\zeta_0, \tau), \tau) \quad (\text{invariance of measure}) \\
&= \iint \mathrm{d}\zeta_0\, \mathrm{d}\zeta_\tau\, \rho(\zeta_0, 0)\delta(\zeta_\tau - g(\zeta_0, \tau))\, \mathbf{h}(\zeta_\tau, \tau),
\end{aligned} \tag{1.85}$$

where we can define

$$\rho(\zeta_\tau, \zeta_0) = \rho(\zeta_\tau | \zeta_0)\rho(\zeta_0) = \rho(\zeta_0, 0)\delta(\zeta_\tau - g(\zeta_0, \tau)). \tag{1.86}$$

In the first two lines we consider ζ_0 as a random variable over which we need t integrate. Moreover, both the density $\rho(\zeta, \tau)$ and the function $\mathbf{h}(\zeta, \tau)$ are considere functions of τ. We call this the Eulerian view as the random variables are fixed. I the third line, however, we consider a fixed measure $\rho(\zeta_0, 0)\, \mathrm{d}\zeta_0$, which is the initia measure from which we sample ensemble points. Now the function $\mathbf{h}(\zeta_\tau, \tau)$ depend on time in two ways: first explicitly, but also implicitly through $\zeta_\tau = g(\zeta_0, \tau)$. We ca this the Lagrangian view. This result is also exploited in the reparameterization tric in VAEs.

Let us compute the time derivative of the expression above:

$$
\begin{aligned}
&\frac{\mathrm{d}}{\mathrm{d}\tau} \int \mathrm{d}\zeta\, \rho(\zeta, \tau)\, \mathbf{h}(\zeta, \tau) \\
&= \int \mathrm{d}\zeta\, \partial_\tau \rho(\zeta, \tau)\, \mathbf{h}(\zeta, \tau) + \rho(\zeta, \tau)\, \partial_\tau \mathbf{h}(\zeta, \tau) \\
&= \int \mathrm{d}\zeta\, \boldsymbol{\nabla}_\zeta \cdot (-\rho(\zeta, \tau)\mathbf{v}(\zeta, \tau))\, \mathbf{h}(\zeta, \tau) + \rho(\zeta, \tau)\, \partial_\tau \mathbf{h}(\zeta, \tau) \\
&= \int \mathrm{d}\zeta\, \rho(\zeta, \tau)\, (\mathbf{v}(\zeta, \tau) \cdot \boldsymbol{\nabla}_\zeta \mathbf{h}(\zeta, \tau) + \partial_\tau \mathbf{h}(\zeta, \tau)) \\
&= \int \mathrm{d}\zeta_\tau\, \rho(\zeta_\tau, \tau)\, (\mathbf{v}(\zeta_\tau, \tau) \cdot \boldsymbol{\nabla}_{\zeta_\tau} \mathbf{h}(\zeta_\tau, \tau) + \partial_\tau \mathbf{h}(\zeta_\tau, \tau)) \\
&= \int \mathrm{d}\zeta_0\, \rho(\zeta_0, 0)\, (\mathbf{v}(\zeta_\tau, \tau) \cdot \boldsymbol{\nabla}_{\zeta_\tau} \mathbf{h}(\zeta_\tau, \tau) + \partial_\tau \mathbf{h}(\zeta_\tau, \tau)); \quad \zeta_\tau = g(\zeta_0, \tau) \\
&= \int \mathrm{d}\zeta_0\, \rho(\zeta_0, 0)\, \frac{\mathrm{d}}{\mathrm{d}\tau} \mathbf{h}(\zeta_\tau, \tau); \quad \zeta_\tau = g(\zeta_0, \tau) \\
&= \frac{\mathrm{d}}{\mathrm{d}\tau} \int \mathrm{d}\zeta_0\, \rho(\zeta_0, 0)\, \mathbf{h}(\zeta_\tau, \tau); \quad \zeta_\tau = g(\zeta_0, \tau).
\end{aligned} \tag{1.87}
$$

The equality of the first line with the final line is consistent with the results abov on the Eulerian and Lagrangian views of computing an average. In the first line w need to take two partial derivatives because both ρ and $\mathbf{h}$ depend on τ. However, ζ is just an integration variable and does not depend on τ. In the last line, we take th time derivative in the Lagrangian view, where ρ is now fixed (the initial distributior while $\mathbf{h}$ depends on τ in two ways, explicitly and implicitly through ζ_τ. The tot derivative of $\mathbf{h}$ is sometimes called the "material" or "comoving" derivative. We no that to connect the two views we needed the continuity equation and partial integratio

2 Neural Network Preliminaries

2.1 Introduction

In this chapter, we will provide a brief overview of the most relevant neural network (NN) architecture. In some sense this is background reading to make sure you are up to speed with the latest developments in deep learning. In the remainder of the book we often mention that we will train an NN but then do not expand on the details of that NN. For instance, when we train a diffusion model we need to use a score network, and you can choose one of the architectures described in this chapter for that purpose. Examples include multilayer perceptrons, convolutional NNs, residual networks, or transformers. The last section of this chapter provides an alternative view of backpropagation, which is the workhorse for training these models from data. For a complete discussion of NNs, we refer to the standard textbooks by Goodfellow et al. (2016), Murphy (2012), and Bishop (2006).

2.2 Multilayer Perceptrons

Multilayer perceptrons (MLPs) are one of the earliest forms of *deep* neural network architectures and a specific type of feedforward neural network. In feedforward neural networks, the complexity induced by stacking multiple simple functions is exploited to solve complex tasks. As the name suggests, the simple building block functions for MLPs are called *perceptrons*:

$$\mathbf{f}_l(\mathbf{x}_{l-1}; \boldsymbol{\theta}_l) = \phi(\mathbf{W}_l \mathbf{x}_{l-1} + \mathbf{b}_l), \tag{2.1}$$

where $\boldsymbol{\theta}_l = (\mathbf{W}_l, \mathbf{b}_l)$ is our set of parameters for the lth layer, $\phi\colon \mathbb{R}^{d_l} \to \mathbb{R}^{d_l}$ is a nonlinear activation function applied element-wise, $\mathbf{W}_l \in \mathbb{R}^{d_l \times d_{l-1}}$ is the weight matrix, and $\mathbf{b}_l \in \mathbb{R}^{d_l}$ is the bias vector. Here, $\mathbf{x}_{l-1} \in \mathbb{R}^{d_{l-1}}$ is the input to layer l, which is the output from the previous layer, and d_{l-1} and d_l are the input and output dimensions of the layer, respectively. As illustrated in Figure 2.1, all nodes (features in each layer) within a single MLP layer are connected to all nodes in the subsequent layer through the weights $\mathbf{W}_l$. It is for this reason that MLPs are also sometimes referred to as *fully connected* neural networks.

Using a nonlinear activation function ϕ introduces nonlinearity into the model, so that stacking layers increases expressive capacity rather than collpasing to a single

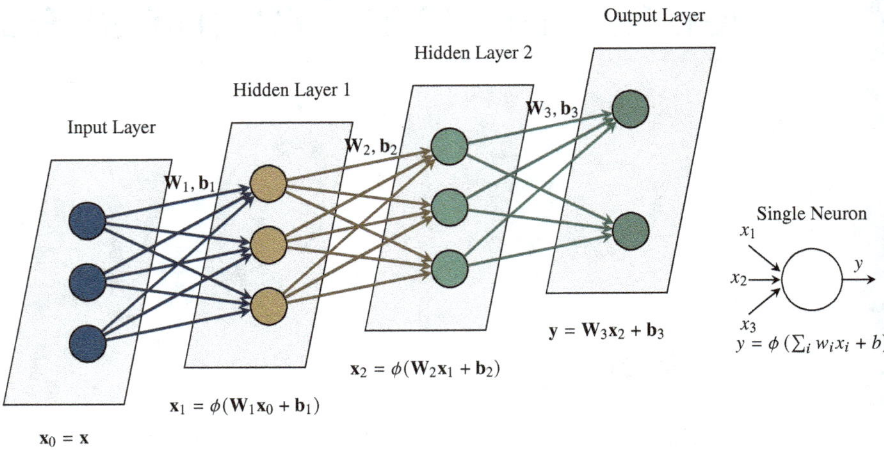

Figure 2.1 Multilayer perceptron with two hidden layers. Each layer is represented as a slante rectangle, with neurons shown as colored circles. The connections between layers (represente by arrows) form weight matrices $\mathbf{W}_1$, $\mathbf{W}_2$, and $\mathbf{W}_3$. Each layer also includes a bias vector $\mathbf{b}_1$, $\mathbf{b}_2$, and $\mathbf{b}_3$. The mathematical operations for each layer are shown. The inset gives a zoomed-i view of how inputs are combined and processed through an activation function ϕ in a single neuron.

linear map. Without activation functions, the network would essentially be a linea model, regardless of the network's depth. Some of the most commonly used activatio functions are:

Sigmoid

The sigmoid (or logistic) function is defined as:

$$\phi(x) = \frac{1}{1 + \exp(-x)}. \qquad (2.2$$

The sigmoid function squashes the input to a value between 0 and 1, which is useful fo binary classification problems and can be interpreted as a probability. Historically, th sigmoid function was popular due to its smoothness and differentiability. However, suffers from the vanishing gradient problem in deep networks, as the sigmoid functio *saturates* at 1 and 0 for large and small input values, respectively. Its gradient $\phi'(x)$ $\phi(x)(1 - \phi(x))$ becomes very small for large positive or negative inputs, slowing dow learning.

Rectified Linear Unit

The rectified linear unit (ReLU) is one of the most popular activation functions use in modern NNs. First introduced by Fukushima (1969), but popularized in the 201((Glorot et al., 2011), the ReLU function is a nonsaturating activation function define as

$$\phi(x) = \text{ReLU}(x) = \max(0, x). \qquad (2.$$

The derivative of a ReLU is 1 if $x > 0$ and 0 when $x \leq 0$, allowing gradients to flow efficiently through the network for positive activations. Variants of ReLU such as leaky ReLU (Maas et al., 2013) have been proposed to address issues like the "dying ReLU" problem, where neurons can become permanently inactive if they consistently output zero.

Softmax

The softmax function is commonly used in the output layer of MLPs for multiclass classification problems or for modeling the probabilities of several discrete outcomes. It maps an input vector $\mathbf{x} \in \mathbb{R}^K$ to a probability distribution over K classes:

$$\text{Softmax}(\mathbf{x})_k = \frac{\exp(x_k)}{\sum_{j=1}^{K} \exp(x_j)}, \quad \text{for } k = 1, \ldots, K. \tag{2.4}$$

The softmax function ensures that the outputs sum to 1 and can be interpreted as probabilities. It does so by exponentiating the input scores and normalizing them by the sum of the exponentiated scores. In supervised learning, the softmax output is often used in conjunction with the cross-entropy loss function to train the network.

In probabilistic models, the softmax function is used to parameterize categorical distributions. For instance, the probability of class k given input $\mathbf{x}_0$ is modeled as

$$p(y = k|\mathbf{x}_0) = \text{Softmax}(f(\mathbf{x}_0))_k = \frac{\exp(f_k(\mathbf{x}_0))}{\sum_{j=1}^{K} \exp(f_j(\mathbf{x}_0))}, \tag{2.5}$$

where $\mathbf{f}(\mathbf{x}_0) = [f_1(\mathbf{x}_0), \ldots, f_K(\mathbf{x}_0)]^\top$ is the output of the network before activation (often referred to as the logits).

While it has been shown that an MLP with *one hidden layer* is a universal function approximator (Hornik et al., 1989), meaning it can approximate any continuous function on compact sets to arbitrary accuracy given sufficient width, this theoretical result doesn't imply practical efficiency. In practice, deeper networks with appropriate architectures that consider the specific modalities and structure of the data are more parameter-efficient and generalize better. We will discuss the primary example of such models, the convolutional neural network, next.

2.3 Convolutional Neural Networks

In our discussion of the MLP earlier, we didn't make any assumptions on the type of data $\mathbf{x}$ provided to the model. However, in most applications of neural networks, the data has a specific *structure* which describes how different features in a single sample are related. The most obvious case of this is in image data, where images are represented as two-dimensional arrays of pixel values. These pixel values have a well-defined structural relationship with nearby pixel values being correlated.

Convolutional neural networks (CNNs) exploit this structure in the data by applying *convolutional layers* (Conv-Layers) (LeCun et al., 1998) (see Figure 2.2 for an illus tration). In contrast to fully-connected layers where every node in the output layer i connected to every node in the previous layers, Conv-Layers only take into account small patch (referred to as the receptive field) of the previous layer for each outpu This property, known as *locality*, allows CNNs to capture local patterns and buil hierarchical representations of the input data.

CNNs can be thought of as glorified feature extractors. As illustrated in Figure 2.2 the convolution operation slides a filter across the patches of the input. At each positior the inner product between the filter and the corresponding area of the input is compute and the result is stored in the output. Mathematically, the discrete convolution operatio for a 2D input $\mathbf{x} \in \mathbb{R}^{H \times W \times C_{\text{in}}}$ and a filter $\mathbf{w} \in \mathbb{R}^{k \times k \times C_{\text{in}} \times C_{\text{out}}}$ can be expressed as

$$\mathbf{f}_l(\mathbf{x}; \boldsymbol{\theta}_l)_{i,j,c} = (\text{Conv}\,\mathbf{x})_{i,j,c} = (\mathbf{x} * \mathbf{w})_{i,j,c} = \sum_{m=0}^{k-1} \sum_{n=0}^{k-1} \sum_{c'=1}^{C_{\text{in}}} x_{i+m,j+n,c'} w_{m,n,c',c} + b_c, \quad (2.6$$

where H and W are the height and width of the input, and C_{in} and C_{out} are the numbe of input and output channels, respectively. Here, the parameters $\boldsymbol{\theta}_l = \{\mathbf{w}, \mathbf{b}\}$ are th learnable parameters (filter weights and bias), and k determines the size of the receptiv field. The indices i and j represent the spatial position in the output feature map, whil m and n index the local neighborhood around (i, j) in the input. The index c represen the output channel, and c' represents the input channel.

This process detects specific patterns or features in the inputs. For example, particular filter might act as an edge detector, detecting edges in the input. It als reduces the number of parameters compared to fully connected layers. The use c multiple filters allows the network to detect various features at each layer, building hierarchical representation of the input data.

Another useful property for the convolutional layers to have is *parameter sharin* The same filter $\mathbf{w}$ is applied to every patch of pixels in the input, forming a *feature ma* of values $\mathbf{f}_l(\mathbf{x}; \boldsymbol{\theta}_l)_{i,j,c}$. This feature map defines the response to the filter for every pix patch. By applying the same filter across the entire input (instead of having individu weights for each input variable like a fully connected layer), CNNs achieve translatio equivariance: when the input is translated by a small amount, the output feature ma will equivalently translate.

Equivariance and Symmetries

Mathematically, a function f is equivariant to a transformation T if $f(T(\mathbf{x})) = T(f(\mathbf{x})$ In CNNs, translational equivariance means that if the input image is translated, th output feature map will be translated by the same amount. This property is partic larly useful in image processing tasks, as it allows the network to recognize patter regardless of their position in the image.

More symmetries, such as rotational or reflectional symmetry, can also be incorp rated into NN architectures to improve their performance and generalization abilit Examples include group equivariant CNNs (Cohen and Welling, 2016) and spheric

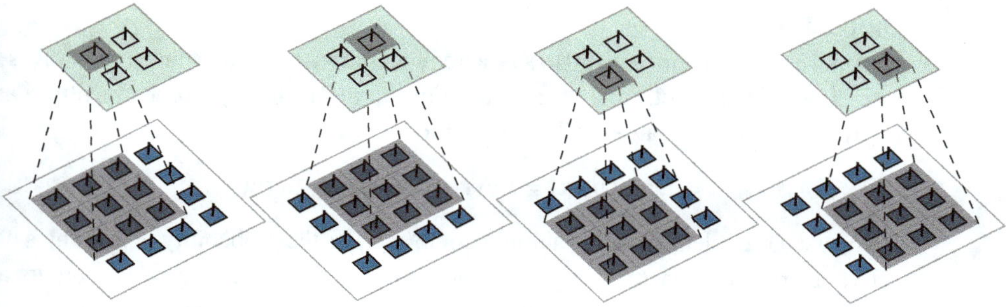

Figure 2.2 Convolutional operation (no padding, unit strides). Bottom grid: input; top grid: output feature map. Shaded 3×3 squares: 3×3 local receptive field at different positions. Corresponding output shown for each position. Illustrates locality (output depends on local input) and parameter sharing (same filter applied across positions). Each vector has an index (outgoing arrows) indicating different input or output channels.

CNNs (Cohen et al., 2018), which extend equivariance to other types of transformations and spherical data, respectively.

Compared to MLPs, CNNs are significantly more efficient for structured data like images. For an image of size $n \times n$ with c channels, an MLP would require $O(n^2c)$ parameters per neuron, while a CNN with a filter size $k \times k$ only needs $O(k^2c)$ parameters per filter, regardless of the image size. This reduction in parameters makes CNNs especially useful for large inputs.

In addition to the Conv-Layer, modern CNNs contain a number of other layers that are important for their functioning, which we describe now.

Pooling Layers

Barring padding questions, Conv-Layers retain the dimensions of the input and therefore require additional layers to reduce the dimension of the model's output. Pooling layers are the most commonly used method for this and work by again taking a patch of the input, but instead of applying a dimension-preserving function, they apply a simple aggregation function, such as taking the maximum (max-pooling) or the average (average-pooling) (Scherer et al., 2010). For max pooling over a $K \times K$ region with stride s

$$f_{\text{pool}}(\mathbf{x})_{i,j,c} = \max_{0 \le m,n \le K-1} x_{si+m,sj+n,c}, \tag{2.7}$$

where i, j are the spatial indices of the output, c is the channel index, K is the pooling window size, and s is the stride (usually equal to K).

Pooling layers help to reduce the spatial dimensions of the feature maps. They also introduce a degree of translation invariance, as small shifts in the input will not significantly affect the pooled output.

Dropout

Dropout (Srivastava et al., 2014) is a regularization technique that randomly sets a fraction of the input units to zero during training to help prevent overfitting and improves the generalization ability of the model:

$$\text{Dropout}(\mathbf{x}) = \mathbf{x} \odot \mathbf{r}, \quad \text{where } r_i \sim \text{Bern}(p). \tag{2.8}$$

Here, $\odot$ denotes element-wise multiplication, and p is the probability of keeping a unit active. During inference, dropout is turned off, and the remaining units' outputs are scaled by p to maintain the same expected output as during training.

Normalization Layers

Normalization layers are used to stabilize and accelerate the training of neural networks by normalizing the activations. Two widely used techniques are batch normalization and layer normalization.

Batch Normalization

Given a mini-batch of inputs $\{\mathbf{x}_n\}_{n=1}^{N}$, batch normalization (Ioffe and Szegedy, 2015) normalizes each feature dimension c as:

$$\text{BatchNorm}(\mathbf{x}_n)_c = \gamma_c \frac{x_{n,c} - \mu_c}{\sqrt{\sigma_c^2 + \varepsilon}} + \beta_c, \tag{2.9}$$

$$\mu_c = \frac{1}{N}\sum_{n=1}^{N} x_{n,c}, \quad \sigma_c^2 = \frac{1}{N}\sum_{n=1}^{N}(x_{n,c} - \mu_c)^2, \tag{2.10}$$

where γ_c, β_c are learnable parameters for each feature dimension c, and ε is a small constant to prevent division by zero.

Layer Normalization

Layer normalization (Ba et al., 2016) normalizes the activations across the features within each individual sample, rather than across the batch. For an input $\mathbf{x} \in \mathbb{R}^d$, LayerNorm computes

$$\text{LayerNorm}(\mathbf{x})_i = \gamma_i \frac{x_i - \mu}{\sqrt{\sigma^2 + \varepsilon}} + \beta_i,$$
$$\mu = \frac{1}{d}\sum_{j=1}^{d} x_j, \quad \sigma^2 = \frac{1}{d}\sum_{j=1}^{d}(x_j - \mu)^2, \tag{2.11}$$

where γ_i, β_i are learnable parameters for each feature dimension i, and ε is a small constant.

BatchNorm is more frequently used in computer vision tasks, where large and consistent batch sizes are common, and the spatial dimensions of images can benefit from batch-wise statistics. By leveraging the statistics across the batch, BatchNorm can regularize the model and improve generalization. On the other hand, LayerNorm is more useful in natural language processing (NLP) tasks, particularly in models like transformers (Vaswani et al., 2017), where sequences have variable lengths and batch sizes may be small. In NLP, models often process one sequence at a time, making BatchNorm less effective. LayerNorm helps to stabilize the activations in such settings by normalizing across the feature dimensions.

2.4 Modern CNN Architectures

Building upon the basic CNN structure, several advanced architectures have been developed to address specific challenges and improve performance across various tasks. We will not provide a complete review here but will discuss two particularly influential architectures: ResNets and U-Nets.

ResNets

Residual networks (ResNets) (He et al., 2016) introduce skip connections that allow the gradient to flow directly through the layers, making it easier to train very deep networks. The key idea is to learn residual functions with reference to the layer inputs,

$$\mathbf{x}_{l+1} = \mathbf{x}_l + F(\mathbf{x}_l; \boldsymbol{\theta}_l), \tag{2.12}$$

where F is the residual mapping to be learned, typically composed of multiple convolutional layers and nonlinearities, and $\mathbf{x}_l$ is the input to the lth layer. The function F and the input $\mathbf{x}_l$ must have the same dimensions for the addition to be valid.

The skip connections in ResNets provide a "shortcut" for the gradient to flow back to earlier layers, easing the vanishing gradient problem that can occur in very deep networks. This seemingly very simple idea makes training extremely deep networks (e.g., with hundreds of layers) more feasible. ResNets have been widely adopted in various computer vision tasks and have also been used in some diffusion models, demonstrating their versatility and effectiveness.

U-Nets

U-Nets (Ronneberger et al., 2015) are a popular CNN architecture that has found widespread use in diffusion models (as discussed in Chapter 13). The U-Net architecture consists of an encoder path that captures context and a symmetric decoder path that enables precise localization, with skip connections between them. The encoder path typically consists of repeated applications of convolutions followed by batch normalization, ReLU activation, and max pooling for downsampling. Each downsampling step doubles the number of feature channels. Mathematically, for the lth layer in the encoder,

$$\mathbf{x}_{l+1} = \mathrm{MaxPool}(\mathrm{ReLU}(\mathrm{BatchNorm}(\mathrm{Conv}(\mathbf{x}_l)))), \tag{2.13}$$

$$\mathrm{ReLU}(x) = \max(0, x), \tag{2.14}$$

$$\mathrm{MaxPool}(\mathbf{x}) = \max_{\text{over } 2\times 2\text{window}} (\mathbf{x}). \tag{2.15}$$

The decoder path consists of upsampling followed by concatenation with the cor responding encoder layer output, and further convolutions. For the lth layer in th decoder

$$\mathbf{x}_{l+1} = \text{ReLU}(\text{BatchNorm}(\text{Conv}(\text{Concat}(\text{Upsample}(\mathbf{x}_l), \text{Skip}(\mathbf{x}_l))))), \quad (2.16$$

where Upsample$(\mathbf{x})$ is typically a transposed convolution or interpolation, and Skip$(\mathbf{x}_l$ is the corresponding encoder layer output.

The skip connections in U-Net play a crucial role in preserving fine-grained spati information. Mathematically, they can be expressed as

$$\mathbf{x}_l^{\text{decoder}} = [\text{Upsample}(\mathbf{x}_{l-1}^{\text{decoder}}), \mathbf{x}_{L-l}^{\text{encoder}}], \quad (2.17$$

where L is the total number of layers, and $[\cdot, \cdot]$ denotes concatenation along the chann dimension.

These skip connections allow the network to combine high-level features fro the decoder path with low-level features from the encoder path, enabling precis localization. In the context of diffusion models, this architecture allows the model t effectively combine information at different scales and noise levels during the denoisin process.

2.5 Transformers

Transformers (Vaswani et al., 2017) are a type of NN architecture that has gaine significant attention in recent years, particularly in NLP and, more recently, in visio tasks and diffusion models, with models like Vision Transformers (ViTs) (Dosovitski et al., 2021) and the Diffusion Transformer (DiT) (Peebles and Xie, 2023).

The core of the transformer architecture is the self-attention mechanism. For a input sequence $\mathbf{X} = [\mathbf{x}_1, \ldots, \mathbf{x}_n]^\top \in \mathbb{R}^{n \times d}$, where n is the sequence length and d i the feature dimension, self-attention is computed as:

$$\text{Attention}(\mathbf{Q}, \mathbf{K}, \mathbf{V}) = \text{Softmax}\left(\frac{\mathbf{Q}\mathbf{K}^\top}{\sqrt{d_k}}\right)\mathbf{V}, \quad (2.18$$

where $\mathbf{Q} = \mathbf{X}\mathbf{W}^Q$, $\mathbf{K} = \mathbf{X}\mathbf{W}^K$, and $\mathbf{V} = \mathbf{X}\mathbf{W}^V$ are the query, key, and value matrice respectively, with $\mathbf{W}^Q, \mathbf{W}^K \in \mathbb{R}^{d \times d_k}$ and $\mathbf{W}^V \in \mathbb{R}^{d \times d_v}$. Here, d_k is the dimensio of the keys and queries, and d_v is the dimension of the values. The intuition behin self-attention is that it allows the model to weigh the importance of different parts c the input when processing each element. The dot product $\mathbf{Q}\mathbf{K}^\top$ measures the similarit between queries and keys, determining how much each value contributes to the outpu

Multi-head attention extends this by applying multiple attention operations in pa allel:

$$\text{MultiHead}(\mathbf{X}) = \text{Concat}(\text{head}_1, \ldots, \text{head}_h)\mathbf{W}^O, \quad (2.19$$

$$\text{head}_i = \text{Attention}(\mathbf{X}\mathbf{W}_i^Q, \mathbf{X}\mathbf{W}_i^K, \mathbf{X}\mathbf{W}_i^V), \quad (2.20$$

where $\mathbf{W}^O \in \mathbb{R}^{hd_v \times d}$ and h is the number of attention heads.

A full transformer block consists of multihead attention followed by a feed-forward network (FFN) with residual connections:

$$\mathbf{Z} = \text{LayerNorm}(\mathbf{X} + \text{MultiHead}(\mathbf{X})), \tag{2.21}$$

$$\text{FFN}(\mathbf{Z}) = \text{ReLU}(\mathbf{Z}\mathbf{W}_1 + \mathbf{b}_1)\mathbf{W}_2 + \mathbf{b}_2, \tag{2.22}$$

$$\text{Output} = \text{LayerNorm}(\mathbf{Z} + \text{FFN}(\mathbf{Z})), \tag{2.23}$$

where $\mathbf{W}_1 \in \mathbb{R}^{d \times d_{\text{FFN}}}$, $\mathbf{W}_2 \in \mathbb{R}^{d_{\text{FFN}} \times d}$, $\mathbf{b}_1 \in \mathbb{R}^{d_{\text{FFN}}}$, and $\mathbf{b}_2 \in \mathbb{R}^{d}$ are the parameters of the feed-forward network. Here, d_{FFN} is the dimension of the inner layer of the feed-forward network. The structure of a transformer block and the multihead attention mechanism is illustrated in Figure 2.3.

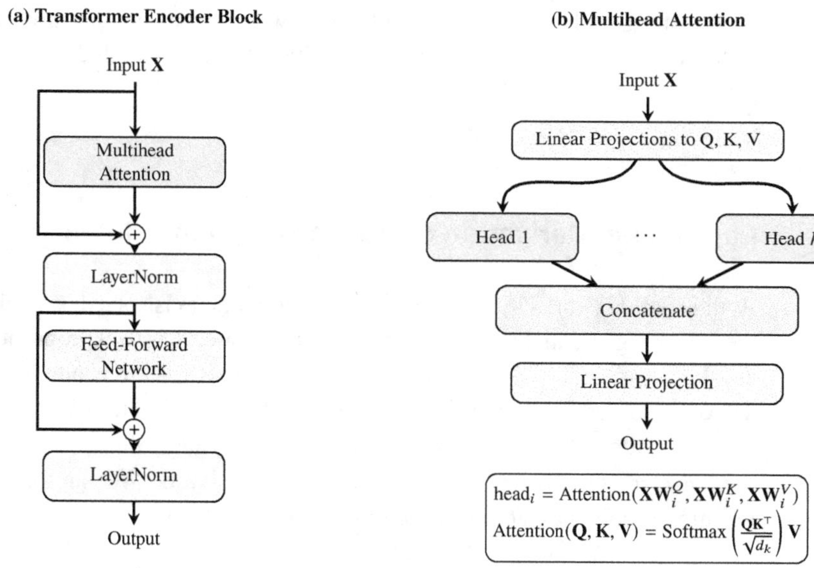

Figure 2.3 The transformer architecture. (a) A single transformer encoder block. Transformer models are typically built by stacking N such blocks. Each block consists of a multihead attention layer and a feed-forward network. The output of each sublayer is added to its input via a residual connection, and the result is then passed through layer normalization. (b) The multihead attention mechanism. The input is linearly projected to create queries ($\mathbf{Q}_i$), keys ($\mathbf{K}_i$), and values ($\mathbf{V}_i$) for multiple parallel "heads". Each head computes scaled dot-product attention. The outputs are then concatenated and passed through a final linear projection.

To incorporate positional information, transformers use positional encodings. For position pos and dimension i of the d_{model}-dimensional embedding, we have

$$\text{PE}_{(\text{pos},2i)} = \sin\left(\frac{\text{pos}}{10000^{2i/d_{\text{model}}}}\right), \tag{2.24}$$

$$\text{PE}_{(\text{pos},2i+1)} = \cos\left(\frac{\text{pos}}{10000^{2i/d_{\text{model}}}}\right). \tag{2.25}$$

Vision Transformers

Vision transformers adapt the transformer architecture for image tasks. The key idea i to treat an image as a sequence of patches. Given an image $\mathbf{X} \in \mathbb{R}^{H \times W \times C}$, it is divide into N patches $\mathbf{x}_p \in \mathbb{R}^{P^2 C}$, where (P, P) is the resolution of each patch. These patche are then linearly embedded and processed by a standard transformer encoder:

$$\mathbf{z}_0 = [\mathbf{x}_{\text{class}}; \mathbf{x}_p^1\mathbf{E}; \mathbf{x}_p^2\mathbf{E}; \ldots; \mathbf{x}_p^N\mathbf{E}] + \mathbf{E}_{\text{pos}}, \tag{2.26}$$

$$\mathbf{z}_l = \text{TransformerEncoder}(\mathbf{z}_{l-1}), \quad l = 1, \ldots, L, \tag{2.27}$$

where $\mathbf{x}_{\text{class}} \in \mathbb{R}^D$ is a learnable classification token, $\mathbf{E} \in \mathbb{R}^{P^2 C \times D}$ is the patc embedding projection, and $\mathbf{E}_{\text{pos}} \in \mathbb{R}^{(N+1) \times D}$ are learnable position embeddings. Her D is the dimension of the transformer's hidden layers.

Transformers have been adapted to work with image data in diffusion models. Fo instance, the diffusion transformer (DiT) (Peebles and Xie, 2023) operates on laten patches.

2.6 Lagrangian Derivation of Backpropagation Rules

With neural networks in hand, only half of the problem is solved: we still need to trai them. The algorithm that has won the "hardware lottery" is backpropagation. While th usual derivation is based on the chain rule of calculus, there is another, more elega derivation based on convex optimization developed by Yann LeCun in his 1987 Ph thesis (LeCun, 1987) and his subsequent paper (LeCun, 1988).

Consider a feedforward neural network with L layers. We can formulate the opt mization problem as a constrained optimization problem:

$$\begin{aligned} &\min_{\{\theta_l, \mathbf{x}_l\}} \quad C(\mathbf{x}_L, \mathbf{y}) \\ &\text{subject to:} \quad \mathbf{x}_l = \mathbf{f}_l(\mathbf{x}_{l-1}; \boldsymbol{\theta}_l), \quad \text{for } l = 1, \ldots, L. \end{aligned} \tag{2.28}$$

Here, $C(\mathbf{x}_L, \mathbf{y})$ is the loss function comparing the network output $\mathbf{x}_L$ with the target $\boldsymbol{\theta}_l \in \mathbb{R}^{d_l \times d_{l-1}}$ are the weights of the lth layer, $\mathbf{x}_l \in \mathbb{R}^{d_l}$ are the activations of the l layer, and $\mathbf{f}_l : \mathbb{R}^{d_{l-1}} \times \mathbb{R}^{d_l \times d_{l-1}} \to \mathbb{R}^{d_l}$ is the layer-wise transformation (for example, a affine transformation followed by a nonlinear activation function).

We introduce Lagrange multipliers $\boldsymbol{\lambda}_l \in \mathbb{R}^{d_l}$ for each layer constraint, forming th Lagrangian:

$$\mathcal{L}[\{\boldsymbol{\theta}_l, \mathbf{x}_l, \boldsymbol{\lambda}_l\}] = C(\mathbf{x}_L, \mathbf{y}) + \sum_{l=1}^{L} \boldsymbol{\lambda}_l^\top (\mathbf{x}_l - \mathbf{f}_l(\mathbf{x}_{l-1}; \boldsymbol{\theta}_l)). \tag{2.29}$$

Applying the KKT conditions (as discussed in Section 1.5), we set the derivativ of the Lagrangian to zero:

$$\frac{\partial \mathcal{L}}{\partial \mathbf{x}_L} = \frac{\partial C(\mathbf{x}_L, \mathbf{y})}{\partial \mathbf{x}_L} + \boldsymbol{\lambda}_L = 0, \tag{2.30}$$

$$\frac{\partial \mathcal{L}}{\partial \mathbf{x}_l} = \boldsymbol{\lambda}_l^\top - \boldsymbol{\lambda}_{l+1}^\top \frac{\partial \mathbf{f}_{l+1}}{\partial \mathbf{x}_l} = 0, \quad \text{for } l = 1, \ldots, L-1, \tag{2.31}$$

$$\frac{\partial \mathcal{L}}{\partial \boldsymbol{\theta}_l} = -\boldsymbol{\lambda}_l^\top \frac{\partial \mathbf{f}_l}{\partial \boldsymbol{\theta}_l} = 0, \quad \text{for } l = 1, \ldots, L. \tag{2.32}$$

From (2.30), we identify $\boldsymbol{\lambda}_L = -\frac{\partial C(\mathbf{x}_L, \mathbf{y})}{\partial \mathbf{x}_L}$, which gives the starting point for the backward pass. Rearranging (2.31) and taking the transpose on both sides, we derive a recursive relation for the Lagrange multipliers:

$$\begin{aligned} \boldsymbol{\lambda}_l &= \left(\frac{\partial \mathbf{f}_{l+1}}{\partial \mathbf{x}_l}\right)^\top \boldsymbol{\lambda}_{l+1} \\ &= \left(\frac{\partial \mathbf{f}_{l+1}}{\partial \mathbf{x}_l}\right)^\top \left(\frac{\partial \mathbf{f}_{l+2}}{\partial \mathbf{x}_{l+1}}\right)^\top \cdots \left(\frac{\partial \mathbf{f}_L}{\partial \mathbf{x}_{L-1}}\right)^\top \boldsymbol{\lambda}_L. \end{aligned} \tag{2.33}$$

This is the backpropagation step, where the Lagrange multipliers (i.e., the error signals) are propagated backwards from the final layer through the network by successive matrix multiplications with the Jacobians of the layer transformations.

Finally, (2.32) states that $\{\boldsymbol{\theta}_l\}$ is a stationary point of $\mathcal{L}$, which is equivalent to finding the minimum of the output loss function $C(\mathbf{x}_L, \mathbf{y})$ while satisfying the constraints. The most straightforward way of doing that is to update the weights using a gradient descent algorithm. For that, we can derive the gradient of the loss with respect to the parameters using (2.32):

$$\begin{aligned} \frac{\partial \mathcal{L}}{\partial \boldsymbol{\theta}_l} &= -\boldsymbol{\lambda}_l^\top \frac{\partial \mathbf{f}_l}{\partial \boldsymbol{\theta}_l} \\ &= -\left(\left(\frac{\partial \mathbf{f}_{l+1}}{\partial \mathbf{x}_l}\right)^\top \cdots \left(\frac{\partial \mathbf{f}_L}{\partial \mathbf{x}_{L-1}}\right)^\top \boldsymbol{\lambda}_L\right)^\top \frac{\partial \mathbf{f}_l}{\partial \boldsymbol{\theta}_l}. \end{aligned} \tag{2.34}$$

The full backpropagation algorithm is given in Algorithm 2.1. Then we update the weights using a gradient descent algorithm:

$$\boldsymbol{\theta}_l \leftarrow \boldsymbol{\theta}_l - \eta \frac{\partial C}{\partial \boldsymbol{\theta}_l}, \tag{2.35}$$

where η is the learning rate. For deep learning problems, the learning rate η is usually chosen to be adaptive (e.g., using the Adam optimizer,Kingma and Ba, 2014) and the gradients are estimated on a batch of data sampled from the training set (called stochastic gradient descent).

Algorithm 2.1 Backpropagation Algorithm

Forward pass: Compute $\mathbf{x}_l = \mathbf{f}_l(\mathbf{x}_{l-1}; \boldsymbol{\theta}_l)$ for $l = 1, \ldots, L$
Compute output gradient: $\boldsymbol{\lambda}_L = -\frac{\partial C(\mathbf{x}_L, \mathbf{y})}{\partial \mathbf{x}_L}$
Compute $\frac{\partial C}{\partial \boldsymbol{\theta}_L}$ **using** $\frac{\partial C}{\partial \boldsymbol{\theta}_L} = -\boldsymbol{\lambda}_L^\top \frac{\partial \mathbf{f}_L}{\partial \boldsymbol{\theta}_L}$ (2.34)
for $l = L-1, \ldots, 1$ **do**
    Compute $\boldsymbol{\lambda}_l$ from $\boldsymbol{\lambda}_{l+1}$ **using** $\boldsymbol{\lambda}_l = \left(\frac{\partial \mathbf{f}_{l+1}}{\partial \mathbf{x}_l}\right)^\top \boldsymbol{\lambda}_{l+1}$ (2.33)
    Compute $\frac{\partial C}{\partial \boldsymbol{\theta}_l}$ **using** $\frac{\partial C}{\partial \boldsymbol{\theta}_l} = -\boldsymbol{\lambda}_l^\top \frac{\partial \mathbf{f}_l}{\partial \boldsymbol{\theta}_l}$ (2.34)
end for

3 Physics Preliminaries

3.1 Introduction

In this chapter, we aim to provide a short overview of statistical physics and thermodynamics. Both are major fields within physics on which numerous books have been written (Landau and Lifshitz, 1980; Huang, 1987). Attempting to come even close to full coverage of these topics here would be futile and unnecessary. Rather, we will focus on topics most relevant to highlighting the similarities between the physics of these fields and the methods of generative AI that we will cover in the remainder of the book. In particular, we will discuss important concepts such as the Hamiltonian that drives the evolution of physical systems through Hamiltonian dynamics. We discuss various thermodynamic ensembles, first formalized by J. Willard Gibbs (1902), such as the microcanonical ensemble (NVE ensemble), the canonical ensemble (NVT ensemble) and grand canonical ensemble (μVT ensemble). We discuss essential thermodynamic quantities such as temperature, entropy, free energy, work, and heat, and briefly discuss the first and second laws of thermodynamics. We end the chapter by resolving a bit of a paradox, namely why the heat that is generated by a system must be proportional to the increase of entropy of the heat bath, a result that is used many times in Parts II and III of the book.

3.2 Fundamentals of Statistical Mechanics

Statistical physics is the branch of physics that deals with large ensembles of particles whose collective behavior is too complex to model from first principles. It bridges the microscopic laws of physics (classical or quantum) with the macroscopic observables of the system that we can measure. As the name suggests, the language used for achieving this is that of statistics.

The central idea behind statistical physics is that even when we can completely define the microscopic state of a physical system, containing all possible degrees of freedom needed to describe the particles it contains (positions, momenta, mass, spin, etc.), this is hardly of much use due to the system always being in constant motion. As such, when we want to infer any measurable macroscopic observables of a material or an object, such as its energy E or volume V, considering a single microstate will only give an instantaneous, fleeting indication. Instead, we need to know all possible state the system could reside in, and how long they will remain in each state.

For this purpose, statistical mechanics aims to describe the system in terms of th probability distribution over microscopic states $\rho(\zeta)$, where $\zeta = (\xi, \eta)$ represent the state of the system in phase space, with ξ denoting the positions and η denotin the momenta. Brushing over some fundamental discussion about time and ensembl averages, we consider this probability to represent the fraction of time spent in the give microscopic state. Given $\rho(\zeta)$ and a function defining the macroscopic property $O(\zeta$ for each microstate, the macroscopic observable can then be defined as the expectatio under this distribution:

$$O[\rho] = \int \mathrm{d}\zeta\, \rho(\zeta) O(\zeta). \qquad (3.1$$

Defining the probability distribution $\rho(\zeta)$ is a question of central interest in statist cal physics, and it can also be seen as a statistical inference problem! According to th information-theoretic interpretation pioneered by E. T. Jaynes (1957a,b), this probabi ity distribution represents our subjective knowledge or beliefs about the microscopi state of the system, given the macroscopic information available.

The primary form for these distributions – the Boltzmann distribution – was derive in Chapter 1 as the maximum entropy distribution for a given average energy. In th following sections, we will derive it again via an approach that clarifies why it describe a system in contact with a fixed-temperature heat bath.

To do so, we will first need to discuss the more restrictive, but fundamental, proba bility distribution $\rho(\zeta)$ that corresponds to an isolated system instead of one in conta with a heat bath. But before that, we introduce the primary macroscopic observabl of interest for the remainder of the chapter, internal energy $\mathcal{U}$, and its correspondin microscopic function, the Hamiltonian $\mathcal{H}$.

3.2.1 Energy and the Hamiltonian

Given a microscopic state $\zeta = (\xi, \eta) = \{\xi_1, \ldots, \xi_N, \eta_1, \ldots, \eta_N\}$ with (ξ_i, η_i) repre senting the three-dimensional coordinates and momenta of particle i, we consider th dynamics of the system to be governed by the Hamiltonian $\mathcal{H}(\zeta)$ via

$$\frac{\mathrm{d}\xi}{\mathrm{d}t} = \frac{\partial \mathcal{H}}{\partial \eta}, \quad \frac{\mathrm{d}\eta}{\mathrm{d}t} = -\frac{\partial \mathcal{H}}{\partial \xi}. \qquad (3.2$$

We can think of the Hamiltonian as a function that computes the total energy of system in microscopic configuration ζ, while also encoding how the positions an momenta evolve over time. It generally takes the form

$$\mathcal{H}(\zeta) = \sum_{i=1}^{N} \frac{1}{2m} \|\eta_i\|^2 + V(\xi), \qquad (3.3$$

where m is the mass of the particles and $V(\xi)$ is the potential energy function. The fir term represents the kinetic energy of the particles, while the second term represen the potential energy due to interactions among the particles and external forces. Most physical theories are formulated as local theories, so the interactions between particles are typically local. For example, molecules interact with each other through a Lennard–Jones potential (the $-r^{-6}$ tail models the attractive van der Waals interaction) that decays with distance,

$$V(\xi) = \sum_{i<j} 4V_0 \left[\left(\frac{\sigma}{|\xi_i - \xi_j|} \right)^{12} - \left(\frac{\sigma}{|\xi_i - \xi_j|} \right)^{6} \right], \tag{3.4}$$

where V_0 is the depth of the potential well, and σ is the distance at which the interparticle potential is zero. Most physical systems also exhibit symmetries, such as the invariance of (3.4) under the exchange of particles.

Averaged over all possible microstates the system can be in, the Hamiltonian gives the average energy of the system, referred to as the internal energy:

$$\mathcal{U}[\rho] = \int \mathrm{d}\zeta\, \rho(\zeta)\mathcal{H}(\zeta). \tag{3.5}$$

Conservation of Phase Space Volume

An important property of Hamiltonian dynamics is that it preserves the volume in phase space. Consider a small volume element $\mathrm{d}V_0$ in the phase space at time $\tau = 0$, which evolves into a new volume element $\mathrm{d}V_\tau$ at time τ (see Figure 3.1). The relationship between these volume elements is given by the Jacobian determinant,

$$\mathrm{d}V_\tau = \left| \frac{\partial(\xi_\tau, \eta_\tau)}{\partial(\xi_0, \eta_0)} \right| \mathrm{d}V_0, \tag{3.6}$$

where $\frac{\partial(\xi_\tau, \eta_\tau)}{\partial(\xi_0, \eta_0)}$ is the Jacobian matrix of the transformation from (ξ_0, η_0) to (ξ_τ, η_τ). The absolute value of the Jacobian determinant gives the ratio of the volumes.

To show that the Jacobian determinant is equal to 1, note that the divergence of the Hamiltonian vector field $(\dot{\xi}, \dot{\eta})$ vanishes by the Hamilton equations and equality of mixed partial derivatives. This result, together with $\mathbf{J}_0 = 1$, implies volume preservation – Liouville's theorem from classical mechanics (Landau and Lifshitz, 1976). Mathematically, this means that the divergence of the Hamiltonian vector field $(\dot{\xi}, \dot{\eta})$ is zero:

$$\frac{\partial \dot{\xi}}{\partial \xi} + \frac{\partial \dot{\eta}}{\partial \eta} = \frac{\partial}{\partial \xi}\frac{\partial \mathcal{H}}{\partial \eta} + \frac{\partial}{\partial \eta}\left(-\frac{\partial \mathcal{H}}{\partial \xi} \right) = 0. \tag{3.7}$$

Using this property and the fact that the Jacobian matrix at $\tau = 0$ is the identity matrix, it can be shown that the Jacobian determinant remains equal to 1 for all τ. Applying the matrix identity $\frac{\mathrm{d}}{\mathrm{d}\tau}\log|\mathbf{J}_\tau| = \mathrm{tr}(\mathbf{J}_\tau^{-1}\frac{\mathrm{d}\mathbf{J}_\tau}{\mathrm{d}\tau})$ to the Jacobian $\mathbf{J}_\tau = \frac{\partial(\xi_\tau,\eta_\tau)}{\partial(\xi_0,\eta_0)}$ gives

$$\begin{aligned}\frac{\mathrm{d}}{\mathrm{d}\tau}\log|\mathbf{J}_\tau| &= \mathrm{tr}\left(\mathbf{J}_\tau^{-1}\frac{\mathrm{d}\mathbf{J}_\tau}{\mathrm{d}\tau}\right)\\ &= \mathrm{tr}\left(\frac{\partial(\xi_\tau,\eta_\tau)}{\partial(\xi_0,\eta_0)}^{-1}\frac{\mathrm{d}}{\mathrm{d}\tau}\frac{\partial(\xi_\tau,\eta_\tau)}{\partial(\xi_0,\eta_0)}\right)\\ &= \mathrm{tr}\left(\frac{\partial(\xi_0,\eta_0)}{\partial(\xi_\tau,\eta_\tau)}\frac{\partial(\dot\xi_\tau,\dot\eta_\tau)}{\partial(\xi_0,\eta_0)}\right)\\ &= \mathrm{tr}\left(\frac{\partial(\dot\xi_\tau,\dot\eta_\tau)}{\partial(\xi_\tau,\eta_\tau)}\right)\\ &= \frac{\partial\dot\xi_\tau}{\partial\xi_\tau}+\frac{\partial\dot\eta_\tau}{\partial\eta_\tau}. \end{aligned} \tag{3.8}$$

Then

$$\frac{\mathrm{d}}{\mathrm{d}\tau}\left|\frac{\partial(\xi_\tau,\eta_\tau)}{\partial(\xi_0,\eta_0)}\right| = \left(\frac{\partial\dot\xi_\tau}{\partial\xi_\tau}+\frac{\partial\dot\eta_\tau}{\partial\eta_\tau}\right)\left|\frac{\partial(\xi_\tau,\eta_\tau)}{\partial(\xi_0,\eta_0)}\right| = 0 \tag{3.9}$$

$$\Rightarrow \left|\frac{\partial(\xi_\tau,\eta_\tau)}{\partial(\xi_0,\eta_0)}\right| = \text{const} = \left|\frac{\partial(\xi_0,\eta_0)}{\partial(\xi_0,\eta_0)}\right| = 1. \tag{3.10}$$

Therefore, the volume of a phase space element remains constant: $\mathrm{d}V_\tau = \mathrm{d}V_0$.

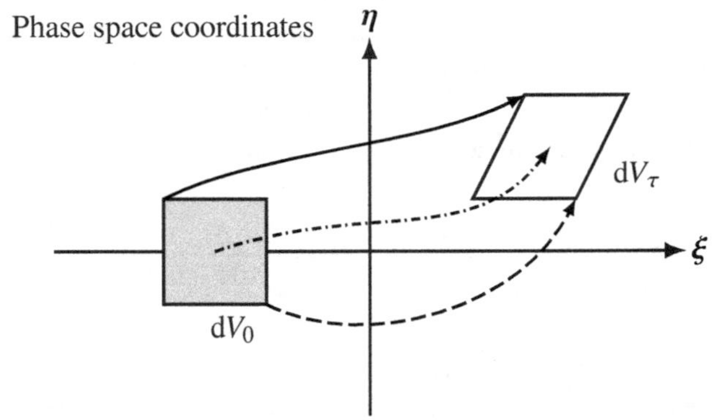

Figure 3.1 Conservation of phase space volume in Hamiltonian dynamics. The hatched rectangle $\mathrm{d}V_0$ is sheared into the cross-hatched parallelogram $\mathrm{d}V_\tau$ with equal area. The three curves (solid, long-dashed, and short-dashed) are trajectories of points in phase space.

3.2.2 Microcanonical Ensemble: Systems with Constant Energy

We first consider systems with constant internal energy $\mathcal{U}$ (the macroscopic observable); that is, the internal energy in (3.5) has zero variance. Such a system is referred to as an isolated system to indicate that there is no energy exchange with any other system that might result in fluctuations in the energy. The universe is the most straightforward example, sitting at constant energy.

Despite being isolated, the system is not static. The microscopic configuration describing the system is always changing, due to the particles moving around and bumping into each other. However, within these fluctuations, particles only exchange energy among themselves, and any gain in energy in one part of the system is the result of energy loss in another part of the system. In other words, for any change $\zeta \to \zeta'$, we have that $\mathcal{H}(\zeta) = \mathcal{H}(\zeta') = E$.

As such, given a macroscopic observed quantity for the energy E at a given time, the system has a nonzero probability of being in each microscopic state ζ for which $\mathcal{H}(\zeta) = E$. However, to determine how the probability mass is distributed across these microscopic states, we need to make one final fundamental assumption:

In an isolated system, all accessible microscopic states are equally likely.

This leads to the probability distribution for an isolated system:

$$\rho(\zeta) = \begin{cases} \frac{1}{\Omega(E)} & \text{if } \mathcal{H}(\zeta) = E, \\ 0 & \text{otherwise,} \end{cases} \tag{3.11}$$

where $\Omega(E)$ is the number of states with energy E.[1] This is referred to as the *microcanonical ensemble*.

Alternatively, the microcanonical ensemble can also be derived using Jaynes's maximum entropy principle (see Section 1.5.5) with only one constraint on the normalization of the probability distribution. The result will be the same.

Entropy

In Section 1.2.3, we discussed entropy as a property of probability distributions. Now that we have defined our system as a probability distribution over states, we can apply this definition here as well. As we will see in the section on equilibrium thermodynamics, entropy will turn out to be one of the most fundamental concepts in physics.

For the microcanonical ensemble, the entropy is given by

$$\begin{aligned} S[\rho] &= -k_{\mathrm{B}} \int \mathrm{d}\zeta \, \rho(\zeta) \log \rho(\zeta) \\ &= -k_{\mathrm{B}} \int \mathrm{d}\zeta \, \frac{\delta(\mathcal{H}(\zeta) - E)}{\Omega(E)} \log \frac{1}{\Omega(E)} \\ &= k_{\mathrm{B}} \log \Omega(E), \end{aligned} \tag{3.12}$$

where we have introduced the Dirac delta function $\delta(\mathcal{H}(\zeta) - E)$ to select only the states with energy E. This entropy is a function of the macroscopic observable energy E. In case you wonder where this dependency is hidden on the left-hand side of the equation, remember that ρ is actually conditioned on E, as discussed earlier.

Notably, we observe that physical entropy and informational entropy are equivalent up to an additional constant k_{B} that we have sneaked into the definition of entropy. This

[1] More faithfully, we should have denoted this distribution as a conditional $\rho(\zeta|E)$, but this is hardly ever done.

constant is known as the Boltzmann constant and will keep popping up throughou statistical mechanics. Its value is approximately 1.380649×10^{-23} J/K. While it i of physical importance, we will often simply set its value to 1 for simplicity in th remainder of this book.

What this clearly shows is that entropy in a physical sense is nothing more than th logarithm of the number of microscopic states that correspond to a given macroscopi observation of the system. In information-theoretic terms, the physical entropy thu describes the amount of missing information – the uncertainty we have – due t describing the system in terms of its macroscopic observables instead of the actu microscopic states.

The deep connection between physics and information has been a subject of gre interest in recent decades. This idea is famously summarized in John Wheeler's mott "it from bit".

According to E. T. Jaynes (1957a), the entropy in physics is not just a property c the physical system but also represents our ignorance about the system's microscopi state, or the microscopic degrees of freedom of that system. Therefore, somewh controversially, we can think of the entropy as a subjective quantity that depends o our knowledge about the system. This subjective view of entropy and modeling is als shared by Bayesian inference, where probabilities represent our degree of belief abo the system rather than the objective frequency of a given event.

Temperature

Moving beyond the philosophical nature of entropy, we now look at an equally im portant concept derived from it: temperature. Temperature, as a concept, differs fro concepts such as entropy because we all have an intuitive understanding of what tem perature means. We can even sense it: On a summer day at Muizenberg Beach, w can feel it being hot. The temperature, as we would describe it in that case, is hig Conversely, in the winter, sitting in a poorly insulated library in Oxford, we feel col The temperature, as we would describe it then, is low.

The easiest way to think of temperature is as (twice) the average energy per degre of freedom stored in the random kinetic motion of the particles. To derive that, we us the "equipartition theorem", which states that the kinetic energy of a system is equal divided among all its degrees of freedom. Recall that for a monatomic ideal gas th internal energy is $E = \frac{3}{2}Nk_{\mathrm{B}}T$. Setting $k_{\mathrm{B}} = 1$ for simplicity, we see that the averag kinetic energy per degree of freedom is $\varepsilon = \frac{1}{2}T$, or $T = 2\varepsilon$ as stated above. The abo can be easily derived by assuming a Hamiltonian with the standard form

$$\mathcal{H}(\boldsymbol{\xi}, \boldsymbol{\eta}) = \frac{1}{2m} \sum_{i=1}^{N} \|\boldsymbol{\eta}_i\|^2 + V(\boldsymbol{\xi}) \tag{3.13}$$

and computing the average kinetic energy under the equilibrium (Boltzmann) distr bution

$$\mathbb{E}[E_{\mathrm{kin}}] = \int \mathrm{d}\boldsymbol{\xi}\, \mathrm{d}\boldsymbol{\eta}\, \frac{1}{Z} \exp(-\beta \mathcal{H}(\boldsymbol{\xi}, \boldsymbol{\eta}))\, \frac{1}{2m} \sum_{i=1}^{N} \|\boldsymbol{\eta}_i\|^2 = \frac{3}{2} NT \tag{3.14}$$

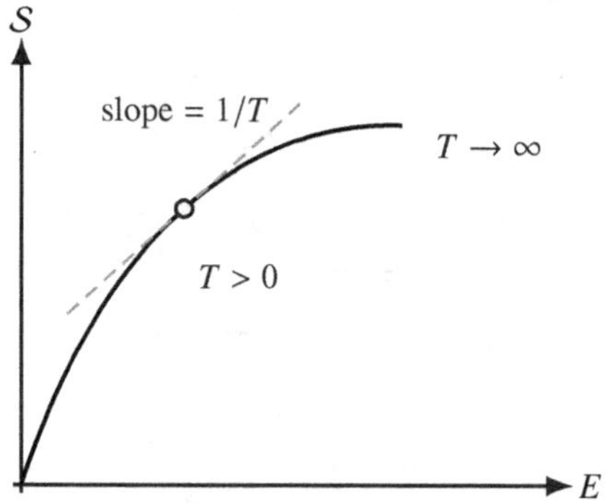

Figure 3.2 Entropy–energy relationship and temperature. The curve $S(E)$ is shown together with a tangent illustrating that the reciprocal slope $1/T$ sets the rate at which entropy grows with energy. As E increases, the tangent flattens, corresponding to ever-higher temperatures.

There is also a thermodynamical definition of temperature:

$$\frac{1}{T} = \frac{\partial S(E)}{\partial E}. \tag{3.15}$$

In words, temperature is defined as the rate at which the entropy changes with respect to energy, evaluated at a specific energy (see Figure 3.2 for an illustration). To make it rigorous, we need to hold some other quantities constant, such as the number of particles N and volume $\mathcal{V}$, when taking the partial derivative. With energy being defined in joules and entropy in J/K (due to the inclusion of the Boltzmann constant), we thus find that temperature is measured in the convenient units of kelvin.

We observe that because T is proportional to the kinetic energy per degree of freedom in the system, and S counts the number of bits required to describe all these hidden degrees of freedom, their product represents something like the total energy represented in these bits. In the definition of the Helmholtz free energy (see Section 3.2.4) we are required to subtract that quantity from the total (average) energy to get to a quantity of energy that is "free" to use.

3.2.3 Canonical Ensemble: Systems with Constant Temperature

So far, while the discussion of entropy and temperature has been universal, we have only considered isolated systems sitting at a constant internal energy. This, however, is practically a very limiting definition for a system. Any system, aside from the universe (perhaps), will itself be part of a larger system and will inevitably be interacting with that system. Through these interactions, the system of interest might be pushed into microscopic configurations which no longer have the same value $\mathcal{H}(\zeta)$. The probability distribution over possible microscopic states ζ of the system can now reach a wider set of possible configurations, no longer all with the same value of $\mathcal{H}(\zeta)$. Crucially, the internal energy in (3.5) now no longer has zero variance.

The way this is formally modeled in statistical mechanics is by considering the

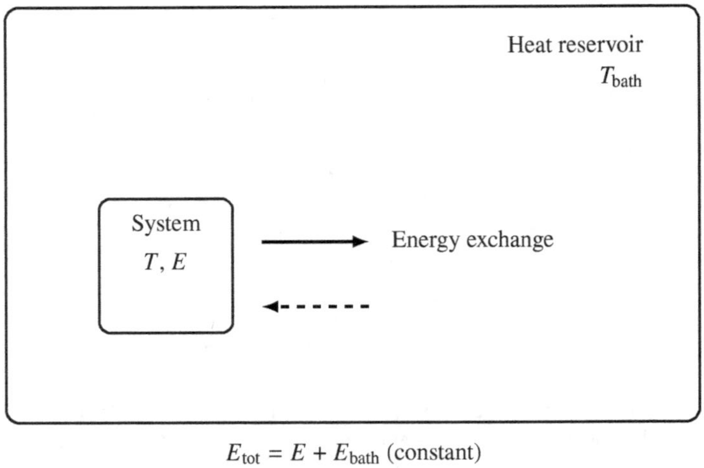

Figure 3.3 System–reservoir coupling. The reservoir remains much larger than the system so that exchanging energy leaves T_{bath} unchanged while keeping the combined energy E_{tot} constant. Opposing arrows show heat exchange.

system of interest being part of a much larger isolated system with a constant interna energy E_{tot} (as illustrated in Figure 3.3). The remaining degrees of freedom of thi isolated system ζ_{bath}, which are not part of the system of interest, are referred to a the heat bath or heat reservoir, a large system in thermal equilibrium with a constan temperature, with which our system of interest can exchange energy. By exchangin energy with this reservoir, $\mathcal{H}(\zeta)$ can now fluctuate while the energy of the total syster remains the same, $E_{tot} = \mathcal{H}(\zeta, \zeta_{bath}) = \mathcal{H}(\zeta) + \mathcal{H}_{bath}(\zeta_{bath})$.[2] Crucially, we assum that the reservoir is several orders of magnitude larger than the system of interest suc that the fluctuations in $\mathcal{H}_{bath}(\zeta_{bath})$ are negligible. As a result, we can assume th temperature of the reservoir T_{bath} to be constant for all possible configurations of th system of interest.

To derive the probability distribution $\rho(\zeta)$ for such a system, we consider th combined system (our system of interest plus the heat reservoir) as an isolated syster with total energy E_{tot}. The probability distribution for the combined system is

$$\rho_{tot}(\zeta, \zeta_{bath}) = \begin{cases} \dfrac{1}{\Omega_{tot}(E_{tot})}, & \text{if } \mathcal{H}(\zeta) + \mathcal{H}_{bath}(\zeta_{bath}) = E_{tot}, \\ 0, & \text{otherwise,} \end{cases} \tag{3.16}$$

where ζ_{bath} represents the microstate of the reservoir.

[2] Energy is for this reason referred to as an *extensive* quantity, meaning that it scales linearly with the siz of the system and therefore characterizes it at the macroscopic level.

Marginalizing over the reservoir states, we obtain:

$$\begin{aligned}\rho(\zeta) &= \int d\zeta_{\text{bath}}\, \rho_{\text{tot}}(\zeta, \zeta_{\text{bath}}) \\ &= \frac{1}{\Omega_{\text{tot}}(E_{\text{tot}})} \int d\zeta_{\text{bath}}\, \delta(E_{\text{tot}} - \mathcal{H}(\zeta) - \mathcal{H}_{\text{bath}}(\zeta_{\text{bath}})) \\ &= \frac{\Omega_{\text{bath}}(E_{\text{tot}} - \mathcal{H}(\zeta))}{\Omega_{\text{tot}}(E_{\text{tot}})},\end{aligned} \tag{3.17}$$

where $\Omega_{\text{bath}}(E_{\text{bath}})$ is the number of microstates of the bath with energy $E_{\text{bath}} = E_{\text{tot}} - \mathcal{H}(\zeta)$.

To proceed, we observe that for a fixed energy level, $\mathcal{H}(\zeta) = E$, we can again assume equipartition of the states within that energy level, and rewrite Ω_{bath} using the definition of entropy for an isolated system in (3.12):

$$\Omega_{\text{bath}}(E_{\text{tot}} - \mathcal{H}(\zeta)) = \exp\left(\frac{\mathcal{S}_{\text{bath}}(E_{\text{tot}} - \mathcal{H}(\zeta))}{k_B}\right). \tag{3.18}$$

Now we make a crucial assumption: The reservoir is much larger than the system of interest. This allows us to use a Taylor expansion of $\mathcal{S}_{\text{bath}}$ around E_{tot}:

$$\begin{aligned}\mathcal{S}_{\text{bath}}(E_{\text{tot}} - \mathcal{H}(\zeta)) &= \mathcal{S}_{\text{bath}}(E_{\text{tot}}) - \left.\frac{\partial \mathcal{S}_{\text{bath}}}{\partial E}\right|_{E_{\text{tot}}} \mathcal{H}(\zeta) + O\left(\frac{\mathcal{H}(\zeta)^2}{E_{\text{tot}}^2}\right), \\ &\approx \mathcal{S}_{\text{bath}}(E_{\text{tot}}) - \frac{\mathcal{H}(\zeta)}{T_{\text{bath}}},\end{aligned} \tag{3.19}$$

where in the first line we expanded the entropy to first order in $\mathcal{H}(\zeta)$. The higher-order terms $O(\mathcal{H}(\zeta)^2/E_{\text{tot}}^2)$ can be neglected since the reservoir is much larger than the system, so $\mathcal{H}(\zeta)/E_{\text{tot}} \ll 1$. This is a common approximation in statistical mechanics when dealing with large systems. In the second line, we used the definition of temperature from (3.15).

Substituting this back into our expression for $\rho(\zeta)$:

$$\begin{aligned}\rho(\zeta) &= \frac{1}{\Omega_{\text{tot}}(E_{\text{tot}})} \exp\left(\frac{\mathcal{S}_{\text{bath}}(E_{\text{tot}})}{k_B}\right) \exp\left(-\frac{\mathcal{H}(\zeta)}{k_B T_{\text{bath}}}\right) \\ &= \frac{1}{Z} \exp\left(-\frac{\mathcal{H}(\zeta)}{k_B T_{\text{bath}}}\right) = \rho^{\text{eq}}(\zeta),\end{aligned} \tag{3.20}$$

where we have absorbed the first exponential term into the normalization constant Z, since $\mathcal{S}_{\text{bath}}(E_{\text{tot}})$ is constant and does not depend on ζ. We have thus included all terms independent of ζ in the normalization constant Z, known as the partition function:

$$Z = \int d\zeta \, \exp\left(-\frac{\mathcal{H}(\zeta)}{k_B T_{\text{bath}}}\right). \tag{3.21}$$

This is the famous Boltzmann distribution, or canonical ensemble, that we found in Section 1.5.5. The parameter $\beta = 1/k_B T_{\text{bath}}$ is known as the inverse temperature, and also gives a physical interpretation to the Lagrange multiplier introduced in Section 1.5.5 as the inverse temperature of the heat reservoir. The normalization constant Z is called the partition function and plays a central role in statistical mechanics, as we will see shortly. It encodes how the probability is distributed among the differer energy levels.

Note that we have dropped the dependence on the total energy E_{tot} of the combine system. The only remaining influence is the temperature of the reservoir T_{bath}, whic at thermal equilibrium equals the temperature T of the system of interest.

3.2.4 From Partition Function to Thermodynamic Quantities

The partition function Z plays a central role in statistical mechanics. It encodes a the thermodynamic information about the system and serves as a generating functio for various thermodynamic quantities. Note that implicitly Z is a function of th temperature T here, or equivalently a function of the inverse temperature $\beta = 1/(k_B T$

We now derive expressions for the three most important thermodynamic quantitie for our purposes in terms of Z: internal energy, entropy, and free energy.

Internal Energy

In (3.5) we defined the internal energy of a system as the expectation of the Hamiltonia over all possible states of the system. We can similarly express this definition in term of the partition function:

$$
\begin{aligned}
E = -\frac{\partial}{\partial \beta} \log Z &= \frac{1}{Z} \int \mathrm{d}\zeta \, \exp(-\beta \mathcal{H}(\zeta)) \mathcal{H}(\zeta), \\
&= \int \mathrm{d}\zeta \, \rho^{\text{eq}}(\zeta) \mathcal{H}(\zeta).
\end{aligned} \quad (3.2
$$

Entropy

The entropy can also be expressed in terms of the partition function:

$$
\begin{aligned}
S = k_B \frac{\partial}{\partial T}(T \log Z) &= k_B \left(\log Z + T \frac{\partial \log Z}{\partial T} \right) \\
&= k_B \log Z + k_B T \left(\frac{\partial \log Z}{\partial \beta} \frac{\partial \beta}{\partial T} \right) \\
&= k_B \log Z + \frac{1}{T} E \\
&= k_B \int \mathrm{d}\zeta \, \frac{1}{Z} \exp\left(-\frac{\mathcal{H}(\zeta)}{k_B T} \right) \left(\log Z + \frac{\mathcal{H}(\zeta)}{k_B T} \right) \\
&= -k_B \int \mathrm{d}\zeta \, \rho^{\text{eq}}(\zeta) \log \rho^{\text{eq}}(\zeta).
\end{aligned} \quad (3.2
$$

In the first line, we applied the product rule to differentiate $T \log Z$ with respect to T. the second line, we introduced the inverse temperature $\beta = \frac{1}{k_B T}$ and used the chain rul where $\frac{\partial \beta}{\partial T} = -\frac{1}{k_B T^2}$ and $\frac{\partial \log Z}{\partial \beta} = -E$. Substituting these into the expression, we obta the entropy in terms of the internal energy E and the partition function Z. Finally, w recognized that $\rho^{\text{eq}}(\zeta) = \frac{1}{Z} \exp(-\beta \mathcal{H}(\zeta))$ and retrieved the familiar integral form the entropy.

Free Energy

Lastly, we consider the Helmholtz free energy F, which is defined as the internal energy minus the product of temperature and entropy:

$$F = E - TS. \tag{3.24}$$

We can again express this in terms of the partition function:

$$\begin{aligned}F &= -\frac{\partial}{\partial\beta}\log Z - k_B T\frac{\partial}{\partial T}(T\log Z)\\ &= k_B T^2\frac{\partial}{\partial T}\log Z - k_B T\frac{\partial}{\partial T}(T\log Z)\\ &= -k_B T\log Z.\end{aligned} \tag{3.25}$$

What is important to note here is that all three quantities expressed in terms of the partition function are only valid when ρ is the Boltzmann distribution; that is, at equilibrium $\rho = \rho^{\mathrm{eq}}$. For other, nonequilibrium, distributions only the original definitions for the quantities hold – (3.22), (3.23), and (3.24) – and we can indeed define the variational free energy:

$$\mathcal{F}[\rho] = \mathcal{U}[\rho] - T\mathcal{S}[\rho] \geq F. \tag{3.26}$$

The notion of free energy is very closely related to most generative AI methods, as you will see throughout the remainder of this book.[3]

Minimum of Free Energy at Equilibrium

It can be shown that the free energy $\mathcal{F}[\rho]$ attains its minimum value at equilibrium; that is, when $\rho = \rho^{\mathrm{eq}}$. We can prove this as follows using the non-negativity of the Kullback–Leibler divergence.

Consider a system at constant temperature T with a probability distribution $\rho(\zeta)$ that may differ from the equilibrium Boltzmann distribution $\rho^{\mathrm{eq}}(\zeta)$. The free energy difference between this distribution and the equilibrium distribution is given by:

$$\begin{aligned}\mathcal{F}[\rho] - F &= \mathcal{U}[\rho] - T\mathcal{S}[\rho] - (-k_B T\log Z),\\ &= \int d\zeta\,\rho(\zeta)\mathcal{H}(\zeta) + k_B T\int d\zeta\,\rho(\zeta)\log\rho(\zeta) + k_B T\log Z\\ &= k_B T\int d\zeta\,\rho(\zeta)\left(\frac{\mathcal{H}(\zeta)}{k_B T} + \log\rho(\zeta) + \log Z\right)\\ &= k_B T\int d\zeta\,\rho(\zeta)\log\left(\frac{\rho(\zeta)}{\rho^{\mathrm{eq}}(\zeta)}\right)\\ &= k_B T D_{\mathrm{KL}}[\rho\|\rho^{\mathrm{eq}}] \geq 0.\end{aligned} \tag{3.27}$$

Thus, the free energy is minimized when $\rho = \rho^{\mathrm{eq}}$; that is, at equilibrium. This means that for a system at constant temperature, any spontaneous change will on average

[3] In particular, the variational free energy is central to the development of variational inference methods, such as the variational autoencoder, to be discussed in Chapter 7.

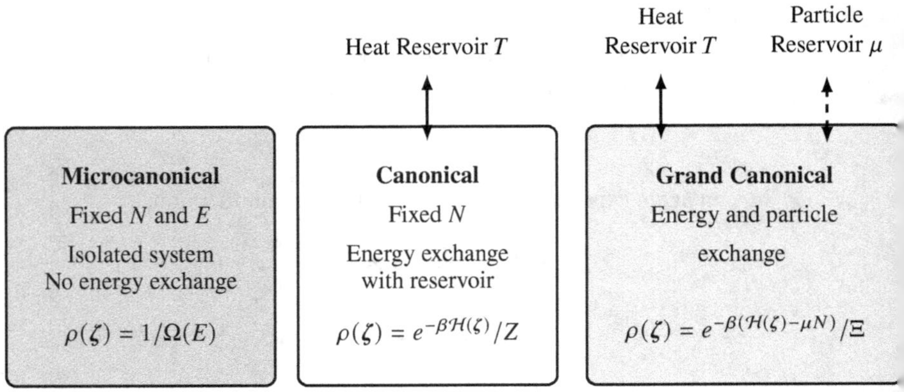

Figure 3.4 Comparison of microcanonical, canonical, and grand canonical ensembles: isolated system (fixed N, E), system with heat exchange (fixed N), and system with heat and particle exchange. Probability distributions, system characteristics, and reservoir interactions are shown for each ensemble.

always be in the direction of decreasing (variational) free energy, and the system will continue to evolve until it reaches the state of minimum (variational) free energy.

It also provides a variational principle for equilibrium: the equilibrium state is the one that minimizes the variational free energy.

3.2.5 Other Macroscopic Quantities

Before moving to the next topic, we need to make a short note on the focus on temperature and internal energy in this chapter. Internal energy is obviously not the only macroscopic observable of a system that could be interesting to study. In fact, if you go through other lecture notes and books on statistical mechanics, you will find that while energy is often treated as a favorite child, it is hardly ever considered in isolation from other macroscopic quantities such as volume and number of particles. The reason for this is mostly due to how they were originally treated in classical thermodynamics before it was given its more formal treatment through statistical physics.

We choose here to deliberately focus on only one macroscopic quantity for our discussion of macroscopic observables and how they define the microcanonical and canonical ensembles. The choice of energy here is purely for convenience as it is most closely aligned with the idea of thermodynamics, but any other macroscopic quantity or combinations of them could have been chosen (see Figure 3.4).

For example, instead of just using energy, we could have considered our system to not only be able to exchange energy with the reservoir in Section 3.2.3 but also particles themselves. If we follow the same reasoning as before, we will now find that our probability distribution is given by:

$$\rho(\zeta) = \frac{1}{\Xi}\exp\big(-\beta(\mathcal{H}(\zeta) - \mu N(\zeta))\big), \tag{3.28}$$

where $\Xi = \int \mathrm{d}\zeta\ \exp(-\beta(\mathcal{H}(\zeta) - \mu N(\zeta)))$ is the partition function of the *grand canonical ensemble* and $N(\zeta)$ counts the number of particles in the configuration ζ. The chemical potential μ plays a similar role for the number of particles as temperature T does for energy. In fact, it is also defined by differentiating the entropy, but this time with respect to the number of particles:

$$\mu = -T \left.\frac{\partial S}{\partial N}\right|_{E,\mathcal{V}}, \tag{3.29}$$

where the subscripts E and $\mathcal{V}$ indicate that the partial derivative is taken at constant energy and volume.

Quantities such as μ and T are referred to as *thermodynamic forces*. These are *intensive* variables – they do not scale with system size, unlike the corresponding *extensive* quantities (number of particles N and energy E) whose exchange between the system and the reservoir they govern. The chemical potential μ drives the flow of particles into or out of the system, similar to how temperature T drives the flow of energy.

Following the same reasoning as for the canonical ensemble, we can equivalently define the internal energy, (internal) number of particles, entropy, and free energy using this definition of ρ. The free energy in this case is instead referred to as the *grand potential*,[4] in correspondence with the grand canonical ensemble. Another often-discussed ensemble is the *isothermal–isobaric* ensemble, which also allows the system to exchange volume with the reservoir (keeping the pressure constant) and uses the *Gibbs free energy*.

As you can see in the case of the grand canonical ensemble (but this is also true for the other ensembles), ρ always takes the same exponential form:

$$\rho(\zeta) = \frac{1}{Z}\exp(-\beta\Phi(\zeta)), \tag{3.30}$$

$$\Phi(\zeta) = \mathcal{H}(\zeta) - \mu N(\zeta) + \cdots, \tag{3.31}$$

where the generalized Hamiltonian $\Phi(\zeta)$ is a function of the extensive quantities (energy, number of particles, volume, etc.) characterizing the system.

Notably, we always include the inverse temperature β here by convention, but we could just as well have used the chemical potential μ or any other thermodynamic force. What this highlights is that we can abstract away from the specific macroscopic potentials and instead consider a generalized Hamiltonian Φ with a corresponding thermodynamic force β.

Macroscopic Potentials in Classical Thermodynamics

Macroscopic observables also play an important role in classical thermodynamics, but as you will see, we will also try to abstract away from the fine details here. Most notably, this will be in the definition of work. Instead of considering individual macroscopic observables and their different mechanisms for performing work, we will

[4] Note that for the canonical ensemble the free energy is actually referred to as the *Helmholtz free energy*.

instead consider a more general definition where work is simply considered to be an change in the generalized Hamiltonian of the system.

3.3 Basics of Thermodynamics

Following our discussion of the fundamentals of statistical mechanics, we now discus the basics of classical thermodynamics (Feynman et al., 1963; Kittel and Kroeme 1980; Callen, 1985). In the previous section, we saw how under minimal assump tions (the only assumption we made was that for an isolated system all accessibl microstates are equally likely) we can derive the microcanonical ensemble and th canonical ensemble. In doing so, we have, however, considered these systems as bein in equilibrium – neither the distributions nor the macroscopic properties they describ change with time.

There are, however, various ways in which we can interact with a system such th its macroscopic observables change. For example:

(i) We can raise the temperature of the heat bath or bring the system into contact wit a different heat bath at a different temperature.
(ii) We can apply an electric current to the system.
(iii) We can change the volume of the box containing the system.
(iv) We can add extra particles to the system.

Whatever way we choose to interact with the system, the originally defined distributio describing the system, based on the given temperature and Hamiltonian, is no longe correct. The system is no longer in equilibrium with respect to the original temperatu and Hamiltonian, but will eventually converge to another equilibrium distribution.

Thermodynamics is a theory that describes systems at equilibrium and small pe turbations around equilibrium. In particular, thermodynamic stability requires that th free energy is at a minimum with respect to small perturbations, ensuring that th system returns to equilibrium after a small disturbance. There are other branches (physics such as kinetic theory, transport theory, and transition state theory that als look at larger changes to the system or at systems out of equilibrium.

In the following we will further explain some core concepts related to classic thermodynamics, while in Chapter 10 we will study stochastic thermodynamics, theory that also describes out-of-equilibrium systems in the presence of a heat bat and at the level of individual trajectories.

3.3.1 First Law of Thermodynamics

The first law of thermodynamics describes the possible ways we can change th macroscopic observables of a system. It states:

$$\Delta \mathcal{U} = Q + \mathcal{W}, \tag{3.3}$$

where $\Delta\mathcal{U}$ refers to the change in the macroscopic observable of interest, in our case the internal energy, Q is the heat added to the system, and $\mathcal{W}$ is the work done on the system.

The infinitesimal version of the first law is written as[5]

$$\mathrm{d}\mathcal{U} = \mathrm{đ}Q + \mathrm{đ}\mathcal{W}. \tag{3.33}$$

Note that we put bars on $\mathrm{đ}Q$ and $\mathrm{đ}\mathcal{W}$ because they are inexact differentials, indicating that heat and work are path-dependent quantities, while $\mathrm{d}\mathcal{U}$ is an exact differential, meaning that internal energy is a state function. However, in this book we will sometimes wear the physicist's hat and use δ to perform calculations with infinitesimal variations.

What do heat and work represent intuitively? We can think of heat as the kinetic energy stored in the random fluctuations of the constituent particles that we exchange with a heat bath (or the environment). Because we have no information on the locations and momenta of these particle movements, we cannot directly extract energy from them. But note that this is again a function of the precision of our devices: with more precise measurement devices that can "couple" very precisely to each particle, we could, in principle, extract much more energy from the system. This is exactly what Maxwell's demon (see page 52) achieves because it has access to information one usually does not have. Work is the part of the energy that is stored in one or very few "accessible" macroscopic degrees of freedom. For instance, we can extract work by letting a gas apply pressure to a movable divider, because we can build a device that can use that pressure to, say, lift a mass against the gravitational field. We therefore conclude that, like entropy, the division between heat and work is "subjective" in the sense that it depends on one's ability to build devices to extract the energy stored in the movement of the particles.

To further clarify the distinction between heat and work, consider the definition of internal energy and its change:

$$\mathcal{U} = \int \mathrm{d}\zeta\, \rho(\zeta)\mathcal{H}(\zeta), \tag{3.34}$$

$$\delta\mathcal{U} = \int \mathrm{d}\zeta\, \delta\rho(\zeta)\mathcal{H}(\zeta) + \int \mathrm{d}\zeta\, \rho(\zeta)\delta\mathcal{H}(\zeta). \tag{3.35}$$

The first term corresponds to heat (change in ρ while keeping $\mathcal{H}$ fixed), while the second corresponds to work (change in $\mathcal{H}$ while keeping ρ fixed). This equation also holds for out-of-equilibrium systems when ρ could change because it relaxes to equilibrium.

Now let us have a look at an equilibrium system described by the Boltzmann

[5] You may remember $\mathrm{d}U = \mathrm{đ}Q - \mathrm{đ}W$ from your physics class, where their $\mathrm{đ}W$ is the work done by the system on the environment, the negative of the work done on the system.

distribution where we apply a small change to the temperature T:

$$\rho(\zeta) = \frac{1}{Z}\exp(-\beta\mathcal{H}(\zeta)), \tag{3.36}$$

$$\delta\rho(\zeta) = -\rho(\zeta)(\mathcal{H}(\zeta)\delta\beta + \delta\log Z). \tag{3.37}$$

Substituting this into the first term of our expression for $\delta\mathcal{U}$, and observing tha $\delta\log Z = -\delta\beta\mathbb{E}_\rho[\mathcal{H}]$ we obtain

$$\begin{aligned}
\delta\mathcal{U} &= -\delta\beta\mathbb{E}_\rho[\mathcal{H}^2] - \mathbb{E}_\rho[\mathcal{H}]\delta\log Z \\
&= -\delta\beta\mathbb{E}_\rho[\mathcal{H}^2] - \mathbb{E}_\rho[\mathcal{H}]\cdot(-\delta\beta\mathbb{E}_\rho[\mathcal{H}]) \\
&= -\delta\beta\left(\mathbb{E}_\rho[\mathcal{H}^2] - \mathbb{E}_\rho[\mathcal{H}]^2\right) = -\frac{\partial\beta}{\partial T}\delta T\mathbb{V}_\rho[\mathcal{H}] \\
&= \beta^2\delta T\mathbb{V}_\rho[\mathcal{H}] = C_\mathcal{V}\delta T.
\end{aligned} \tag{3.38}$$

The term $\mathbb{V}_\rho[\mathcal{H}] = \mathbb{E}_\rho[\mathcal{H}^2] - \mathbb{E}_\rho[\mathcal{H}]^2$ is the variance of the Hamiltonian and i related to the heat capacity, defined as $C_\mathcal{V} = \left(\frac{\partial\mathcal{U}}{\partial T}\right)_\mathcal{V}$ for a system at constant volume The heat capacity measures how much energy is required to raise the temperature of system by one unit. It can be derived from the partition function as follows:

$$C_\mathcal{V} = \left(\frac{\partial\mathcal{U}}{\partial T}\right)_\mathcal{V} = \frac{\partial}{\partial T}\left(-\frac{\partial}{\partial\beta}\log Z\right) = \beta^2\mathbb{V}_\rho[\mathcal{H}]. \tag{3.39}$$

Alternatively, you will sometimes also see the first law stated as

$$\mathrm{d}\mathcal{U} = T\,\mathrm{d}\mathcal{S} - p\,\mathrm{d}\mathcal{V}, \tag{3.40}$$

where p is pressure and $\mathcal{V}$ is volume. This form originates historically from the stud of ideal gases and mechanical systems, where work is performed through volum changes against pressure. However, the first law can be generalized to any conjugat pairs of intensive and extensive variables, which will be more relevant for our M context. In this form, temperature T and pressure p are the intensive variables (the do not depend on system size), while entropy $\mathcal{S}$ and volume $\mathcal{V}$ are the correspondin extensive variables (they scale with the system).

The derivation proceeds from substituting definitions of entropy and energy. For a equilibrium distribution $\rho = \frac{1}{Z}e^{-\beta\mathcal{H}}$ we have

$$\begin{aligned}
\mathrm{d}\mathcal{U} &= T\,\mathrm{d}\mathcal{S} - p\,\mathrm{d}\mathcal{V} \\
&= -k_\mathrm{B}T\int \mathrm{d}\zeta\;[\mathrm{d}\rho(\zeta)\log\rho(\zeta) + \mathrm{d}\rho(\zeta)] + \int \mathrm{d}\zeta\;\rho(\zeta)\frac{\partial\mathcal{H}(\zeta,\mathcal{V})}{\partial\mathcal{V}}\,\mathrm{d}\mathcal{V} \\
&= \int \mathrm{d}\zeta\;\mathrm{d}\rho(\zeta)\,\mathcal{H}(\zeta,\mathcal{V}) - k_\mathrm{B}T(1+\log Z)\int \mathrm{d}\zeta\;\mathrm{d}\rho(\zeta) \\
&\quad + \int \mathrm{d}\zeta\;\rho(\zeta)\frac{\partial\mathcal{H}(\zeta,\mathcal{V})}{\partial\mathcal{V}}\,\mathrm{d}\mathcal{V} \\
&= \int \mathrm{d}\zeta\;\mathrm{d}\rho(\zeta)\,\mathcal{H}(\zeta,\mathcal{V}) + \int \mathrm{d}\zeta\;\rho(\zeta)\partial_\mathcal{V}\mathcal{H}(\zeta,\mathcal{V})\,\mathrm{d}\mathcal{V},
\end{aligned}$$

where we have used the normalization condition $\int \mathrm{d}\zeta\;\mathrm{d}\rho(\zeta) = 0$, and the definitic of the pressure p as the negative expectation value of the volume derivative of the Hamiltonian:

$$p \equiv -\int \mathrm{d}\zeta\, \rho(\zeta) \frac{\partial \mathcal{H}(\zeta, \mathcal{V})}{\partial \mathcal{V}}. \tag{3.41}$$

3.3.2 Second Law of Thermodynamics

As stated earlier, whatever type of interaction we perform on the system to change the internal energy, be it a change in temperature or in the Hamiltonian, the original distribution is no longer correct. The system is no longer in equilibrium and will eventually transform into another equilibrium distribution. The first law of thermodynamics helped us understand what the effect of these changes is on other macroscopic observables, but it did not tell us why the system would actually change distribution. This is what the second law describes:

$$\Delta \mathcal{S}_{\text{tot}} \geq 0. \tag{3.42}$$

This is a fundamental principle of nature: In any natural process, the total entropy of an isolated system always increases or remains constant. This increase in entropy can be interpreted as an increase in the disorder (randomness) of the system, or our uncertainty or missing information in the spirit of Jaynes.

Consider a system that starts in a highly ordered state (low entropy). As it evolves, the system will naturally evolve towards more probable states, which are generally more disordered (high entropy), and our uncertainty about the exact microscopic state generally increases.

What this effectively states is that when we fix any macroscopic observables, the other macroscopic observables will transition to those values that maximize the entropy of the system. For example, when we defined the Boltzmann distribution, we used the temperature of the reservoir T_{bath}, but did not say anything about the temperature of the system itself. We can now define this temperature by fixing the temperature of the reservoir T_{bath}. Consider the total system's entropy as the sum of the entropy of the two subsystems:

$$\mathcal{S}_{\text{tot}} = \mathcal{S}_{\text{sys}} + \mathcal{S}_{\text{bath}}. \tag{3.43}$$

According to the second law, the system will settle into a state that maximizes $\mathcal{S}_{\text{tot}}$, at which point we will have $\mathrm{d}\mathcal{S}_{\text{tot}}/\mathrm{d}E = 0$. Using the definition of temperature, (3.15), and from energy conservation, $\mathrm{d}E = -\mathrm{d}E_{\text{bath}}$, we find

$$0 = \frac{\mathrm{d}\mathcal{S}_{\text{tot}}}{\mathrm{d}E} = \frac{\mathrm{d}\mathcal{S}_{\text{sys}}}{\mathrm{d}E} + \frac{\mathrm{d}\mathcal{S}_{\text{bath}}}{\mathrm{d}E} = \frac{\mathrm{d}\mathcal{S}_{\text{sys}}}{\mathrm{d}E} - \frac{\mathrm{d}\mathcal{S}_{\text{bath}}}{\mathrm{d}E_{\text{bath}}} \tag{3.44}$$

$$\Rightarrow \frac{1}{T_{\text{sys}}} = \frac{1}{T_{\text{bath}}}. \tag{3.45}$$

This state of the system is also referred to as *thermal equilibrium*. This result shows that at thermal equilibrium, the temperature of the system equals the temperature of the reservoir, a direct consequence of the second law. It means that your cup of coffee will, after some time, assume the same temperature as the temperature in the room.

An apparent violation of the second law of thermodynamics is known as Maxwell's demon. This thought experiment involves a room full of gas molecules with a divider. A demon is placed in the box, and controls a gate letting only the fastest molecules pass through while blocking the slower ones. This would cause the temperature of the gas on one side of the box to increase and the temperature on the other side to decrease over time, in contradiction to the second law of thermodynamics. The resolution to this paradox, as pointed out by Landauer and Bennett (Landauer, 1961; Bennett, 1982) is that the demon must acquire, store, and erase information in order to operate, and this process will always increase entropy by an amount greater than or equal to the entropy decrease in the system being observed. The synergy between information and thermodynamics is a fascinating and active topic of research to this day (Parrondo et al., 2015).

We will further expand on the second law of thermodynamics in the chapter on stochastic thermodynamics (Chapter 10). There we will discuss two alternative formulations of the second law: The Clausius statement and the Kelvin statement.

Why is $đQ = T\,\mathrm{d}\mathcal{S}_{\text{bath}}$?

In this book, we will use this equation quite a few times to claim that the heat $đQ$ generated in the system, for example by relaxing to equilibrium, will increase the entropy of the heat bath $\mathcal{S}_{\text{bath}}$ proportionally. In fact, this will prove key to deriving the second law of thermodynamics.

However, this statement is not entirely obvious. As we are considering a heat bath the temperature of the bath, T, will be assumed constant. Since we are not changing the Hamiltonian of the bath, and the bath is assumed to be in equilibrium, how can the equilibrium distribution, and therefore the entropy, even change? Recall that the Boltzmann distribution is entirely determined by the Hamiltonian and the temperature. Furthermore, intuitively, if we are adding energy to the bath in the form of heat, we expect the temperature – which is, after all, related to the average kinetic energy of thermal fluctuations – to increase, not remain strictly constant. So let us see what is happening. Assume the temperature shifts from T to $T' = T + \mathrm{d}T$ after we transfer an infinitesimal amount of heat $đQ$ to the bath. If we take $k_{\mathrm{B}} = 1$, then $\beta = 1/T$ is the inverse temperature; it will change to

$$\beta' = \beta - \beta^2\,\mathrm{d}T. \tag{3.40}$$

We can perform a Taylor expansion of the logarithm of the Boltzmann distribution of the bath up to first order in $\mathrm{d}T$:

$$\begin{aligned}\log \rho'_{\text{bath}}(\zeta, T') &= \log \rho_{\text{bath}}(\zeta, T) + \frac{\partial \log \rho_{\text{bath}}(\zeta, T)}{\partial T}\,\mathrm{d}T + O(\mathrm{d}T^2)\\ &= \log \rho_{\text{bath}}(\zeta, T) + \beta^2\left(\mathcal{H}_{\text{bath}}(\zeta) - \mathbb{E}_{\rho_{\text{bath}}}[\mathcal{H}_{\text{bath}}]\right)\mathrm{d}T,\end{aligned} \tag{3.41}$$

where we have used $\frac{\partial \log \rho_{\text{bath}}}{\partial T} = \beta^2\left(\mathcal{H}_{\text{bath}} - \mathbb{E}_{\rho_{\text{bath}}}[\mathcal{H}_{\text{bath}}]\right)$, and $\mathbb{E}_{\rho_{\text{bath}}}[\cdot]$ denotes the expectation value with respect to ρ_{bath} at temperature T. Similarly, we can expand the internal energy of the bath:

$$\begin{aligned}\mathcal{U}_{\text{bath}}(T') &= \mathcal{U}_{\text{bath}}(T) + \frac{\partial \mathcal{U}_{\text{bath}}}{\partial T}\,\mathrm{d}T + O(\mathrm{d}T^2)\\ &= \mathcal{U}_{\text{bath}}(T) + \beta^2 \mathbb{V}_{\rho_{\text{bath}}}[\mathcal{H}_{\text{bath}}]\,\mathrm{d}T,\end{aligned} \tag{3.48}$$

where $\mathbb{V}_{\rho_{\text{bath}}}[\mathcal{H}_{\text{bath}}] = \mathbb{E}_{\rho_{\text{bath}}}\left[\left(\mathcal{H}_{\text{bath}} - \mathbb{E}_{\rho_{\text{bath}}}[\mathcal{H}_{\text{bath}}]\right)^2\right]$ is the variance of the Hamiltonian in the bath. The entropy of the bath can be expanded similarly:

$$\begin{aligned}\mathcal{S}_{\text{bath}}(T') &= \mathcal{S}_{\text{bath}}(T) + \frac{\partial \mathcal{S}_{\text{bath}}}{\partial T}\,\mathrm{d}T + O(\mathrm{d}T^2)\\ &= \mathcal{S}_{\text{bath}}(T) + \beta^3 \mathbb{V}_{\rho_{\text{bath}}}[\mathcal{H}_{\text{bath}}]\,\mathrm{d}T.\end{aligned} \tag{3.49}$$

From this exercise in Taylor expansions, we immediately read out that

$$\mathrm{d}\mathcal{U}_{\text{bath}}(T) = T\,\mathrm{d}\mathcal{S}_{\text{bath}}(T). \tag{3.50}$$

Since the change in internal energy of the bath is equal to the amount of transferred heat, $đQ = \mathrm{d}\mathcal{U}_{\text{bath}}$, we obtain the desired result:

$$đQ = T\,\mathrm{d}\mathcal{S}_{\text{bath}}(T). \tag{3.51}$$

From (3.48), we can also derive an expression for the change in temperature:

$$\mathrm{d}T = \frac{T^2 đQ}{\mathbb{V}_{\rho_{\text{bath}}}[\mathcal{H}_{\text{bath}}]}. \tag{3.52}$$

This equation tells us that the change in temperature is proportional to T^2 times the amount of transferred heat divided by the variance of the bath's Hamiltonian. Since the bath consists of a very large number of particles N, the Hamiltonian of the bath, $\mathcal{H}_{\text{bath}}$, is effectively a sum over N randomly fluctuating terms. Of course, there are also many interaction terms between the atoms, but this will not impact the argument below. The variance of a sum of N independent random variables grows as $O(N)$. For example, if X is the sum of N independent coin flips with probability p of coming up heads, then $\mathbb{V}[X] = Np(1-p)$.

Therefore, as $N \to \infty$, the variance $\mathbb{V}_{\rho_{\text{bath}}}[\mathcal{H}_{\text{bath}}]$ grows without bound, and the change in temperature $\mathrm{d}T$ approaches zero:

$$\mathrm{d}T \approx \frac{T^2 đQ}{O(N)} \to 0. \tag{3.53}$$

This explains why we can assume that the temperature of the bath remains effectively constant, even when energy is transferred to it.

The resolution of the apparent paradox is that the transferred heat creates an infinitesimal rise in the temperature that is needed to increase the number of microstates accessible to the bath, which are responsible for the rise in the entropy of the bath. However, the derived relation between heat and bath entropy holds even if we let $\mathrm{d}T \to 0$ in the thermodynamic limit as $N \to \infty$.

Part II

Discrete-Time Stochastic Dynamics

In this part, we turn ingredients into recipes. Chapter 4 and Chapter 5 use latent-variable factorizations and variational free energy to make inference workable. Chapter 6 and Chapter 7 push those ideas into message passing and amortized inference, and Chapter 8 develops the discrete flow maps. Chapter 9 and Chapter 10 consider stochastic processes rooted in physics. Chapters 11 and 12 show how samplers are used and connected with inference and physics, while Chapters 13 and 14 present concrete machine learning models inspired by physics. Chapter 15 links control to inference, and Chapter 16 explains generative flow networks. From Chapters 17 we show how the fluctuation relations are used to tighten free energy estimators (Chapter 18). Chapter 19 parallels those estimates with escorted paths that mirror the stochastic normalizing flows in Chapter 20, while also broadening the flow perspective beyond bijections.

4 Latent Variable Models and Graphical Models

4.1 Introduction

Throughout this book you will find that we will be discussing generative AI models by relating their core principles back to notions found within the fields of statistical physics and thermodynamics. A key aspect of this connection, explored in this chapter, is the similarity between the use of observable and latent variables in both fields, and the way that abstracting away information introduces uncertainty.

In physics, observable variables describe the macroscopic quantities that we can measure with sensors (e.g., temperature and pressure). In contrast, unobserved latent variables describe the microscopic state of a system, which we cannot measure directly, but which we can infer. That is, we can infer them when we have full knowledge of the mapping between the microscopic and macroscopic states. Inference then takes the form of a posterior probability that describes the likelihood that the system is in a state given the observations we have access to.

In generative AI we similarly have observed variables that we can measure with sensors (e.g., images, audio, text, etc.) and latent variables that we have no direct knowledge of (the many degrees of freedom of the world that we do not track but gave rise to the observed images, audio, text, etc.). Learning the mapping between these observed and latent variables is the core of generative machine learning. The general language in which this is described is that of latent variable models and their structured extension in the form of graphical models.

This chapter provides an introduction to the field of graphical models: structured probabilistic models between latent and observed variables. Examples include directed models such as hidden Markov models and undirected models such as Markov random fields. In this chapter we study the learning algorithm that can train these models effectively, called the variational expectation maximization (VEM) algorithm. The objective is called the evidence lower bound (ELBO), which happens to have a very strong connection to the free energies in physics. We finish the chapter by applying this framework to Bayesian learning where model parameters are also treated as random variables.

4.2 Latent Variable Models

A latent variable model (LVM) is defined as follows:

$$p_X(\mathbf{x}) = \sum_{\mathbf{z}} p_{X,Z}(\mathbf{x}, \mathbf{z}) = \sum_{\mathbf{z}} p_{X|Z}(\mathbf{x}|\mathbf{z})\ p_Z(\mathbf{z}), \tag{4.1}$$

where $p_X(\mathbf{x})$ is the *marginal (likelihood)* of the observed variables $\mathbf{x}$, $p_{X,Z}$ is the *joint* distribution of the observed and latent variables, $p_{X|Z}(\mathbf{x}|\mathbf{z})$ is the conditional distribution of the observed variables given the latent variables, known as the *likelihood*, and $p_Z(\mathbf{z})$ is the *prior* distribution of the latent variables. While simple in its definition, due to the marginal distribution p_X being given as a marginalization over $\mathbf{z}$ (a mixture over $\mathbf{z}$) this model class is very expressive!

For simplicity, we will assume in this chapter that the latent variables are discrete but the same reasoning can be applied to the case of continuous variables. In this case we can rewrite (4.1) as

$$p(\mathbf{x}) = \int p(\mathbf{x}|\mathbf{z})\ p(\mathbf{z})\ d\mathbf{z}, \tag{4.2}$$

where we now integrate over all possible values of the latent variables $\mathbf{z}$. Note that we have omitted the subscripts X and Z here for brevity, as we will also do in most of the remainder of this chapter, and indeed book.

Using Bayes' rule, we can also derive the distribution of the latent variables given the observed variables:

$$p(\mathbf{z}|\mathbf{x}) = \frac{p(\mathbf{x}|\mathbf{z})\ p(\mathbf{z})}{p(\mathbf{x})}, \tag{4.3}$$

which is known as the posterior distribution of the latent variables. We can interpret this model as factor analysis, where the factors of variation are given by $\mathbf{z}$, and the posterior will tell us which factors explain most of the signal in the observations $\mathbf{x}$.

Connecting back to statistical physics, we can see that the posterior distribution of the latent variables is often the distribution of interest. For example, in the canonical ensemble, the posterior distribution over microscopic states at inverse temperature β is the Boltzmann distribution.

Gaussian Example

As an example, consider a model where the prior p_Z is given by a Gaussian density and the conditionals are also Gaussian:

$$p(\mathbf{z}) = G(\mathbf{0}, \mathbf{I}), \quad p(\mathbf{x}|\mathbf{z}) = G(\mathbf{W}\mathbf{z}, \boldsymbol{\Sigma}). \tag{4.4}$$

You can now compute the joint distribution:

$$p(\mathbf{x}, \mathbf{z}) = G(\mathbf{0}, \boldsymbol{\Gamma}), \tag{4.5}$$

$$\boldsymbol{\Gamma}^{-1} = \begin{bmatrix} \boldsymbol{\Sigma}^{-1} & -\boldsymbol{\Sigma}^{-1}\mathbf{W} \\ -\mathbf{W}^\top\boldsymbol{\Sigma}^{-1} & \mathbf{I} + \mathbf{W}^\top\boldsymbol{\Sigma}^{-1}\mathbf{W} \end{bmatrix}. \tag{4.6}$$

From this joint distribution, we can derive the posterior distribution by "completing squares":

$$p(\mathbf{z}|\mathbf{x}) = G(\mu, \mathbf{\Lambda}), \tag{4.7}$$

$$\mathbf{\Lambda}^{-1} = \mathbf{I} + \mathbf{W}^\top \mathbf{\Sigma}^{-1} \mathbf{W}, \tag{4.8}$$

$$\mu = \mathbf{\Lambda} \mathbf{W}^\top \mathbf{\Sigma}^{-1} \mathbf{x}. \tag{4.9}$$

As an exercise, we encourage you to derive (4.8) and (4.9) from (4.4) and (4.6).

4.3 Graphical Models

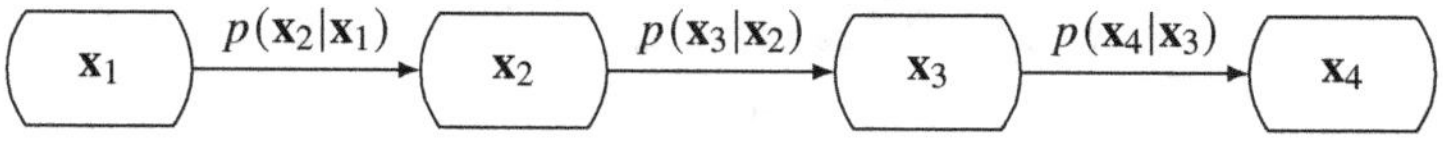

Figure 4.1 Graphical model of a Markov chain representing the probability distribution $p(\mathbf{x}_1, \mathbf{x}_2, \mathbf{x}_3, \mathbf{x}_4) = p(\mathbf{x}_1) \prod_{t=2}^{4} p(\mathbf{x}_t|\mathbf{x}_{t-1})$. Rounded nodes represent observed variables. The arrows indicate the sequential dependency between variables in a simple linear progression. This structure has the Markov property that each variable depends only on the immediately preceding variable.

We can now start to impose structure on these models. The field that deals with structured (latent variable) models is called graphical models (Koller and Friedman, 2009). In a graphical model (GM), nodes represent random variables, and edges represent the probabilistic dependencies between these variables. The structure of the graph encodes the conditional independence assumptions made by the model.

To give an example that we will encounter frequently in this book, let us consider Markov models (MM) given by the structured distribution

$$p(\mathbf{x}_0, \mathbf{x}_1, \ldots, \mathbf{x}_{t_f}) = p_0(\mathbf{x}_0) \prod_{t=1}^{t_f} p_t(\mathbf{x}_t|\mathbf{x}_{t-1}), \tag{4.10}$$

where each conditional distribution $p_t(\mathbf{x}_t|\mathbf{x}_{t-1})$ can be different for every time step. Figure 4.1 illustrates a simple Markov chain, which is a type of MM.

Each GM makes certain assumptions about the (conditional) independence between random variables. In the MM above, the assumption is that $\mathbf{x}_t \perp \mathbf{x}_0, \ldots, \mathbf{x}_{t-2} \mid \mathbf{x}_{t-1}$ for all t. In words: The variable $\mathbf{x}_t$ is statistically independent of all variables in the past of $\mathbf{x}_t$ given the value of $\mathbf{x}_{t-1}$. A simple example proof for a homogeneous MM is as follows:

$$\begin{aligned} p(\mathbf{x}_t, \mathbf{x}_{t-2}|\mathbf{x}_{t-1}) &= \frac{p(\mathbf{x}_t|\mathbf{x}_{t-1})p(\mathbf{x}_{t-1}|\mathbf{x}_{t-2})p(\mathbf{x}_{t-2})}{p(\mathbf{x}_{t-1})} \\ &= p(\mathbf{x}_t|\mathbf{x}_{t-1})p(\mathbf{x}_{t-2}|\mathbf{x}_{t-1}), \end{aligned} \tag{4.11}$$

where we have marginalized out all the variables $\mathbf{x}_0, \ldots, \mathbf{x}_{t-3}, \mathbf{x}_{t+1}, \ldots, \mathbf{x}_{t_f}$ and applied Bayes' rule to get to the last equation. The result states precisely the conditional independence relation as claimed: the joint conditional distribution over $\mathbf{x}_t$ and $\mathbf{x}_{t-2}$ factorizes if we are given $\mathbf{x}_{t-1}$.

Hidden Markov Model

An example of a Markov model with latent variables is given by the hidden Marko model (Rabiner, 1989):

$$p(\mathbf{x}_0, \ldots, \mathbf{x}_{t_f}, \mathbf{z}_0, \ldots, \mathbf{z}_{t_f}) = p_0(\mathbf{z}_0) \prod_{t=1}^{t_f} p_t(\mathbf{z}_t|\mathbf{z}_{t-1}) \prod_{t=0}^{t_f} p(\mathbf{x}_t|\mathbf{z}_t), \quad (4.12$$

where $\mathbf{z}_t$ are latent variables and $\mathbf{x}_t$ are observed variables at time step t. You ca draw a node for every variable and an arrow for every conditional distribution, whic visualizes the structure of the model (as drawn in Figure 4.2) and from which you ca read off all the conditional independence relations.

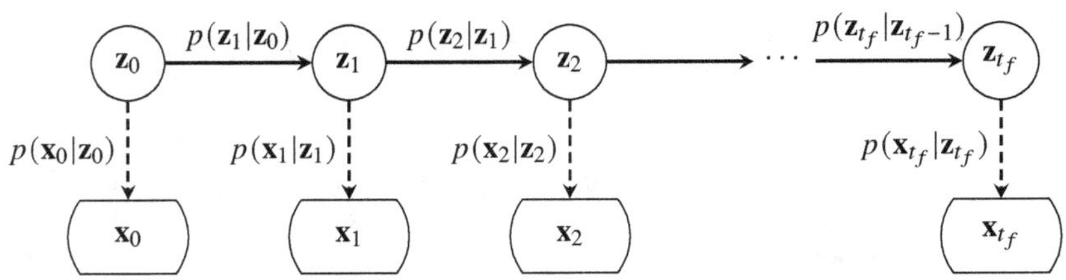

Figure 4.2 Graphical model representation of a homogeneous hidden Markov model (HMM). The model structure is defined by the probability distribution $p(\mathbf{x}_0, \ldots, \mathbf{x}_{t_f}, \mathbf{z}_0, \ldots, \mathbf{z}_{t_f}) = p_0(\mathbf{z}_0) \prod_{t=1}^{t_f} p(\mathbf{z}_t|\mathbf{z}_{t-1}) \prod_{t=0}^{t_f} p(\mathbf{x}_t|\mathbf{z}_t)$. Solid arrows connect th latent states (filled circles) and encode transition probabilities, while dashed arrows link each latent state to its corresponding observed variable through the emission distribution.

Markov Random Fields

A final example that will be very useful for us is the Markov random field (Kinderman and Snell, 1980). A Markov random field (MRF) is defined in terms of potenti functions over subsets of variables (both observed and unobserved). These potentia are typically defined locally in some space; that is, they specify which variables a neighbors in that space. If we introduce cluster $\mathcal{G}_\alpha$ as the cluster indexed by α, an $\mathbf{x}_\alpha = \{\mathbf{x}_{\alpha(1)}, \mathbf{x}_{\alpha(2)}, \ldots, \mathbf{x}_{\alpha(n_\alpha)}\}$ as the subset of variables that participate in th cluster, we can define the following probability distribution:

$$p(\mathbf{x}_1, \mathbf{x}_2, \ldots, \mathbf{x}_N) = \frac{1}{Z} \exp\left(- \sum_\alpha \Psi_\alpha(\mathbf{x}_\alpha) \right), \quad (4.1$$

where $\Psi_\alpha(\mathbf{x}_\alpha)$ are the potential functions defined over the clusters, and Z is the no malization constant. Equivalently, we can also use the definition $p(\mathbf{x}_1, \mathbf{x}_2, \ldots, \mathbf{x}_N)$ $\prod_\alpha \Phi_\alpha(\mathbf{x}_\alpha)/Z$. We call this an undirected GM as we do not have conditional probabi ity distributions but rather a type of Boltzmann distribution with structured potentia We note that the exact same definition is used when we use a mix of latent variables and observed variables $\mathbf{x}$. An example of an MRF is shown in Figure 4.3.

The conditional independence relations implied by the models are as follows. Firs draw an (undirected) edge between a variable $\mathbf{x}_i$ and all the variables that are in the san

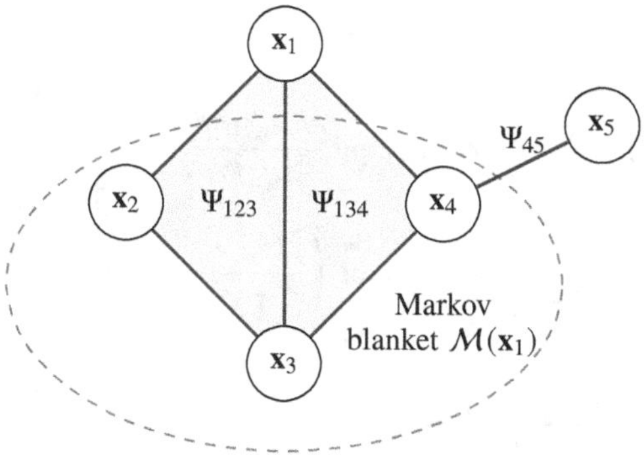

Figure 4.3 Markov random field (MRF) model representing the factorization of the probability distribution into products of potentials over maximal cliques $p(\mathbf{x}) \propto \exp(-\Psi_{123}(\mathbf{x}_1, \mathbf{x}_2, \mathbf{x}_3) - \Psi_{134}(\mathbf{x}_1, \mathbf{x}_3, \mathbf{x}_4) - \Psi_{45}(\mathbf{x}_4, \mathbf{x}_5))$. The Markov blanket of $\mathbf{x}_1$ is $\mathcal{M}(\mathbf{x}_1) = \{\mathbf{x}_2, \mathbf{x}_3, \mathbf{x}_4\}$. The Markov blanket shields $\mathbf{x}_1$ from the influence of $\mathbf{x}_5$, resulting in the conditional independence relation $\mathbf{x}_1 \perp \mathbf{x}_5 \mid \mathcal{M}(\mathbf{x}_1)$.

argument of some potential. Call this set the Markov blanket (MB) $\mathcal{M}(i)$ of variable i. We now have the conditional independence: $\mathbf{x}_i \perp \mathbf{x}_{\setminus\{i \cup \mathcal{M}(i)\}} \mid \mathbf{x}_{\mathcal{M}(i)}$. In words: $\mathbf{x}_i$ is independent of all other variables in the MRF outside the MB if we condition on the variables in the MB; that is, the MB shields $\mathbf{x}_i$ from statistical dependencies of the rest of the variables. The MB of a node is also the smallest set of nodes needed to make $\mathbf{x}_i$ independent of all the other nodes.

4.4 Variational Expectation–Maximization Algorithm

Once we have defined a GM, we need to learn it from data. A dataset consists of N data cases, where each data case assigns values to all of the observed variables in the GM. The marginal log-likelihood that we want to maximize is given by

$$\mathcal{L}(X, \boldsymbol{\theta}) = \sum_{n=1}^{N} \log p(\mathbf{x}_n) = \sum_{n=1}^{N} \log \sum_{\mathbf{z}_n} p(\mathbf{x}_n, \mathbf{z}_n). \tag{4.14}$$

We can derive a lower bound on the log-likelihood using using the non-negativity of the KL divergence and introducing variational distributions $q_n(\mathbf{z}_n)$ for each data case n:

$$\begin{aligned}\mathcal{L}(X,\boldsymbol{\theta}) &= \sum_{n=1}^{N}\sum_{\mathbf{z}_n} q_n(\mathbf{z}_n)\log\frac{p(\mathbf{x}_n)q_n(\mathbf{z}_n)}{q_n(\mathbf{z}_n)} \\ &= \sum_{n=1}^{N}\sum_{\mathbf{z}_n} q_n(\mathbf{z}_n)\log\left(\frac{p(\mathbf{x}_n|\mathbf{z}_n)p(\mathbf{z}_n)q_n(\mathbf{z}_n)}{p(\mathbf{z}_n|\mathbf{x}_n)q_n(\mathbf{z}_n)}\right) \\ &= \sum_{n=1}^{N}\sum_{\mathbf{z}_n} q_n(\mathbf{z}_n)(\log p(\mathbf{x}_n,\mathbf{z}_n) - \log q_n(\mathbf{z}_n)) + \sum_{n=1}^{N} D_{\mathrm{KL}}[q_n(\mathbf{z}_n)\|p(\mathbf{z}_n|\mathbf{x}_n)] \\ &\geq -\sum_{n=1}^{N}\mathcal{F}[q_n,p] \equiv -\mathcal{F}[q_1,\ldots,q_N,p]. \end{aligned} \quad (4.15)$$

Here, the transition from the first to the second line is true because $p(\mathbf{x}_n) = p(\mathbf{x}_n|\mathbf{z}_n)p(\mathbf{z}_n)/p(\mathbf{z}_n|\mathbf{x}_n)$ is true for every value of $\mathbf{z}_n$. We have introduced the free energy (also equivalent to the negative ELBO) for each data case:

$$\mathcal{F}[q_n,p] = \sum_{\mathbf{z}_n} q_n(\mathbf{z}_n)\left(\log q_n(\mathbf{z}_n) - \log p(\mathbf{x}_n,\mathbf{z}_n)\right). \quad (4.16)$$

If we define the entropy $\mathcal{S}[q_n] = -\sum_{\mathbf{z}_n} q_n(\mathbf{z}_n)\log q_n(\mathbf{z}_n)$ and the data-case-specific Hamiltonian $\mathcal{H}_n(\mathbf{z}_n,\mathbf{x}_n) \equiv -\log p(\mathbf{x}_n,\mathbf{z}_n)$, we can write $\mathcal{F}[q_n,p] = \mathbb{E}_{q_n}[\mathcal{H}_n] - \mathcal{S}[q_n]$. This has exactly the same $U - TS$ structure as the nonequilibrium Helmholtz free energy at $T = 1$ (or, equivalently, in units where $k_BT = 1$), which explains the terminology "(variational) free energy". The thermodynamic connection will be developed further in the next chapter.

We conclude that the log-likelihood, which is the natural objective to maximize, is lower bounded by $-\mathcal{F}$, which can be interpreted as the negative of the total free energy of the system of N data cases.

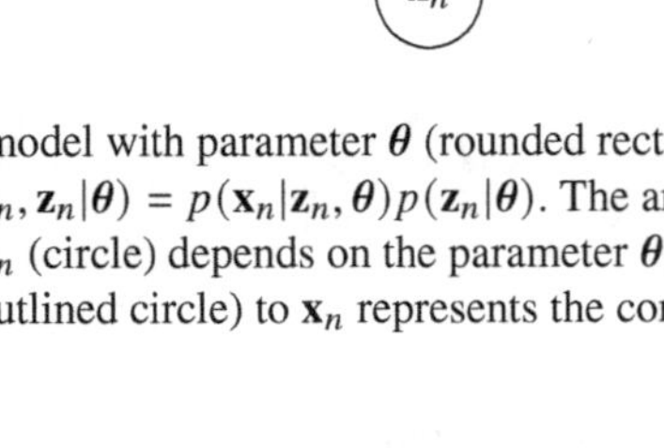

Figure 4.4 Latent variable model with parameter $\boldsymbol{\theta}$ (rounded rectangle), representing the probability distribution $p(\mathbf{x}_n,\mathbf{z}_n|\boldsymbol{\theta}) = p(\mathbf{x}_n|\mathbf{z}_n,\boldsymbol{\theta})p(\mathbf{z}_n|\boldsymbol{\theta})$. The arrow from $\boldsymbol{\theta}$ to $\mathbf{x}_n$ indicates that the observed variable $\mathbf{x}_n$ (circle) depends on the parameter $\boldsymbol{\theta}$, while the arrow from the latent variable $\mathbf{z}_n$ (double-outlined circle) to $\mathbf{x}_n$ represents the conditional probability $p(\mathbf{x}_n|\mathbf{z}_n,\boldsymbol{\theta})$.

4.4.1 VE-Step

To maximize $\mathcal{L}$, we now iterate two steps. First, we minimize $\mathcal{F}$ over the distributions $\{q_n\}$. One can choose to do partial minimizations:, for example, only minimize over a subset of the $\{q_n\}$ or minimize for only a few steps. We call this the VE-step of the inference algorithm and note for future reference that this is like relaxing a physical system that is out of equilibrium towards equilibrium. Assume we have parameterized the inference distributions with data-case-specific parameters, φ_n: $q_n(\mathbf{z}_n|\varphi_n)$. We can then take the derivative of $\mathcal{F}$ with respect to φ_n to get

$$\begin{aligned}\nabla_{\varphi_n}\mathcal{F} &= \sum_{\mathbf{z}_n} \nabla_{\varphi_n} q_n(\mathbf{z}_n|\varphi_n)\left(\log q_n(\mathbf{z}_n|\varphi_n) - \log p(\mathbf{x}_n,\mathbf{z}_n)\right)\\ &\quad + \sum_{\mathbf{z}_n} q_n(\mathbf{z}_n|\varphi_n)\nabla_{\varphi_n}\log q_n(\mathbf{z}_n|\varphi_n)\\ &= \sum_{\mathbf{z}_n} q_n(\mathbf{z}_n|\varphi_n)\nabla_{\varphi_n}\log q_n(\mathbf{z}_n|\varphi_n)\left(\log q_n(\mathbf{z}_n|\varphi_n) - \log p(\mathbf{x}_n,\mathbf{z}_n) + 1\right)\\ &= \sum_{\mathbf{z}_n} q_n(\mathbf{z}_n|\varphi_n)\nabla_{\varphi_n}\log q_n(\mathbf{z}_n|\varphi_n)\left(\log q_n(\mathbf{z}_n|\varphi_n) - \log p(\mathbf{x}_n,\mathbf{z}_n)\right)\\ &\approx \frac{1}{S}\sum_{s:\mathbf{z}_{sn}\sim q_n} \nabla_{\varphi_n}\log q_n(\mathbf{z}_{sn}|\varphi_n)\left[\log q_n(\mathbf{z}_{sn}|\varphi_n) - \log p(\mathbf{x}_n,\mathbf{z}_{sn})\right],\end{aligned} \tag{4.17}$$

where in the last line we replace the sum with Monte Carlo samples drawn from q_n, and in-between we used the following tricks:

$$\nabla_{\varphi_n} q_n(\mathbf{z}_n|\varphi_n) = q_n(\mathbf{z}_n|\varphi_n)\nabla_{\varphi_n}\log q_n(\mathbf{z}_n|\varphi_n), \tag{4.18}$$

$$\sum_{\mathbf{z}_n} q_n(\mathbf{z}_n)\nabla_{\varphi_n}\log q_n(\mathbf{z}_n) = \sum_{\mathbf{z}_n}\nabla_{\varphi_n} q_n(\mathbf{z}_n) = \nabla_{\varphi_n}\sum_{\mathbf{z}_n} q_n(\mathbf{z}_n) = \nabla_{\varphi_n} 1 = 0. \tag{4.19}$$

This is known as the REINFORCE estimator (Williams, 1992). Unfortunately, it has very high variance if you use a Monte Carlo estimate by sampling from q_n to compute the gradient.

Reparameterization Trick

For some distributions, there is a very nice trick to reduce the variance of this estimator called the reparameterization trick (Kingma and Welling, 2014). This works as follows (see Figure 4.5 for an illustration of how it transforms the computation graph to enable efficient gradient calculation). Suppose we want to compute the derivative with respect to θ of an integral of the form

$$\nabla_\theta \int \mathrm{d}z\, q(z|\theta) f(z), \tag{4.20}$$

and imagine performing a change of variables $z = g(\varepsilon, \theta)$ such that

$$\int \mathrm{d}z\, q(z|\theta) = \int \mathrm{d}\varepsilon\, p(\varepsilon), \tag*{(4.2}$$

$$\int \mathrm{d}z\, q(z|\theta) f(z) = \int \mathrm{d}\varepsilon\, p(\varepsilon) f(g(\varepsilon, \theta)), \tag*{(4.2:}$$

$$\nabla_\theta \int \mathrm{d}z\, q(z|\theta) f(z) = \int \mathrm{d}\varepsilon\, p(\varepsilon) \frac{\partial f}{\partial g}(g(\varepsilon, \theta)) \nabla_\theta g(\varepsilon, \theta), \tag*{(4.2}$$

with p being an easy-to-sample-from standard distribution. The key idea is to mo the source of randomness from the distribution $q(z|\theta)$ to an auxiliary variable ε wi a fixed distribution $p(\varepsilon)$.

For example, consider a Gaussian distribution:

$$\int \mathrm{d}z\, G(z|\mu, \sigma) f(z) = \int \mathrm{d}\varepsilon\, G(\varepsilon|0, 1) f(\mu + \sigma \cdot \varepsilon), \tag*{(4.2}$$

$$z = g(\varepsilon, \mu, \sigma) = \mu + \sigma \cdot \varepsilon. \tag*{(4.2}$$

In one dimension, this can always be achieved, but in higher dimensions, it may hard to identify the transformation. We can now rewrite:

$$\begin{aligned} \nabla_\theta \int \mathrm{d}z\, q(z|\theta) f(z) &= \int \mathrm{d}\varepsilon\, G(\varepsilon|0, 1) \frac{\partial f}{\partial g}(g(\varepsilon, \theta)) \nabla_\theta g(\varepsilon, \theta) \\ &\approx \frac{1}{S} \sum_{s=1}^{S} \frac{\partial f}{\partial g}(g(\varepsilon_s, \theta)) \nabla_\theta g(\varepsilon_s, \theta), \quad \varepsilon_s \sim G(0, 1). \end{aligned} \tag*{(4.2}$$

This estimator has much better variance properties!

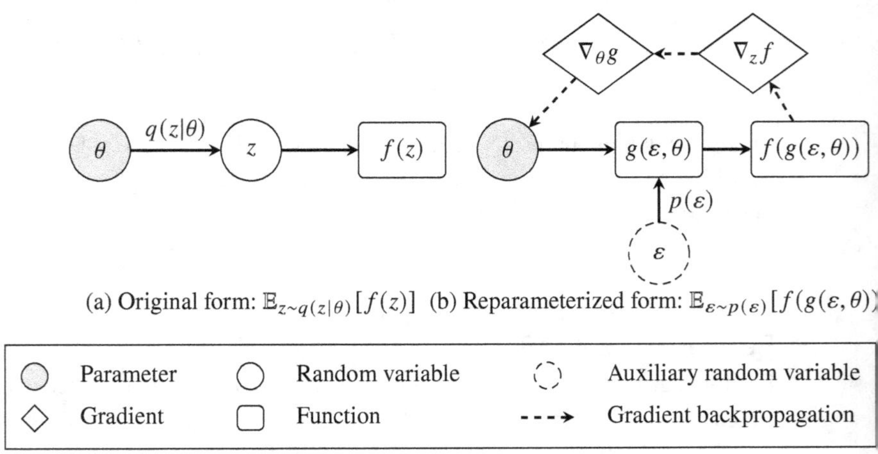

Figure 4.5 Illustration of the reparameterization trick. (a) Original form: expectation over $q(z|\theta)$. (b) Reparameterized form: randomness moved to auxiliary variable $\varepsilon \sim p(\varepsilon)$. Backpropagation of gradients from $f(g(\varepsilon, \theta))$ to θ, enabling direct optimization. The gradi is computed as $\nabla_\theta f(g(\varepsilon, \theta)) = \frac{\partial f}{\partial g} \cdot \nabla_\theta g(\varepsilon, \theta)$.

4.4.2 VM-Step

After the (partial) VE-step is over, we now switch to minimizing $\mathcal{F}$ over P. Here, P is our GM model which is parameterized by parameters $\boldsymbol{\theta}$. In this VM-step we keep q fixed and update these parameters. One can take the gradient of $\mathcal{F}$ with respect to $\boldsymbol{\theta}$ and find

$$\begin{aligned} -\nabla_{\theta}\mathcal{F} &= \sum_{n=1}^{N}\sum_{\mathbf{z}_n} q_n(\mathbf{z}_n)\nabla_{\theta}\log p(\mathbf{x}_n,\mathbf{z}_n|\boldsymbol{\theta}) \\ &\approx \frac{1}{S}\sum_{n=1}^{N}\sum_{s:\mathbf{z}_{sn}\sim q_n}\nabla_{\theta}\log p(\mathbf{x}_n,\mathbf{z}_{sn}|\boldsymbol{\theta}) \\ \Rightarrow\ \boldsymbol{\theta}_{t+1} &= \boldsymbol{\theta}_t - \eta_t\nabla_{\theta_t}\mathcal{F}[q_1,q_2,..,q_N,p_{\theta_t}]. \end{aligned} \tag{4.27}$$

We can iterate VE- and VM-steps in arbitrary order to reach convergence, as illustrated in Figure 4.6. Notably, we can think of $\mathcal{H}_n(\mathbf{z}_n,\mathbf{x}_n) = -\log p(\mathbf{z}_n,\mathbf{x}_n|\boldsymbol{\theta})$ as the Hamiltonian of system n. Indeed, with this identification we can write

$$\mathcal{F} = \sum_n \mathbb{E}_{q_n}[\mathcal{H}_n] - \mathcal{S}[q_n] = \mathbb{E}_q[\mathcal{H}] - \mathcal{S}[q], \tag{4.28}$$

$$q = \prod_n q_n,\quad \mathcal{H} = \sum_n \mathcal{H}_n,\quad \mathcal{S}[q] = \sum_n \mathcal{S}[q_n]. \tag{4.29}$$

As we will see in the next chapters, the M-step is related to performing "work" on a physical system.

An important consideration is that we have separate variational distributions q_n for every datapoint. This means we can have separate parameters $\boldsymbol{\varphi}_n$ to optimize for each q_n. This is a very flexible set of variational distributions. It has, however, the disadvantage that for new (test) data cases one will have to introduce a new distribution q_n and parameters $\boldsymbol{\varphi}_n$ and perform an optimization. This is slow! In a variational autoencoder (Kingma and Welling, 2014; Rezende et al., 2014), as we will see in Chapter 7, we introduce an "amortized" variational distribution which is a (stochastic) function $q(\mathbf{z}|\mathbf{x})$ from $\mathbf{x}$ to $\mathbf{z}$, given by a neural network. For any new data case, we can simply execute this function $q(\mathbf{z}_n|\mathbf{x}_n)$ to find the (variational) posterior. This is much faster (if the time to execute the neural network is shorter than iterative inference over q_n).

If the true posterior $p(\mathbf{z}_n|\mathbf{x}_n)$ can be perfectly approximated by $q_n(\mathbf{z}_n)$, then the optimal distribution q_n^* is given by this posterior: $q_n^*(\mathbf{z}_n) = p(\mathbf{z}_n|\mathbf{x}_n)$. As an exercise, we encourage you to prove that the bound given in (4.15) saturates (equality is attained) precisely when $q_n^*(\mathbf{z}_n) = p(\mathbf{z}_n|\mathbf{x}_n)$ for all n.

Mean-Field Approximation

To keep things tractable, it is sometimes useful to introduce a family of distributions for q_n that is not flexible enough to fully approximate the posterior. In this case, there will always remain a gap: $\mathcal{L} \geq -\mathcal{F}$. Yet, at convergence, we do find the best possible approximation subject to this restriction. For instance, we could use the Gaussian family of distributions and adapt their means and variances to approximate the true posteriors. Or, we could use a decoupled set of distributions:

$$q_n(\mathbf{z}_n) = \prod_i q_{ni}(z_{ni}). \tag{4.30}$$

We call this a mean-field (MF) approximation (Parisi, 1988).

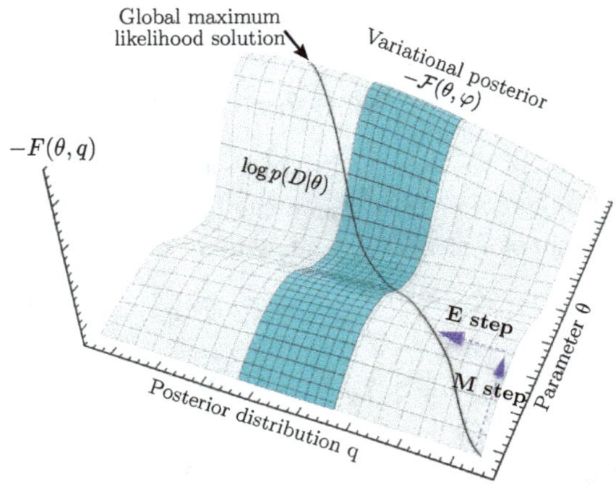

Figure 4.6 Visualization of the expectation-maximization algorithm [inspired by, and recreated from, Figure 2 of Dayan et al. (1995)]. The surface represents the negative free energy $-\mathcal{F}(\theta, q)$ as a function of the model parameter θ and the posterior distribution q. The log-likelihood function $\log p(D|\theta)$ is shown as a curve on the surface. The blue-shaded region represents the variational posterior $-F(\theta, \varphi)$, which is directly related to the ELBO in (4.15). The global maximum likelihood solution is indicated at the peak. The EM algorithm iteratively maximizes the likelihood by alternating between updating the posterior distribution (E-step) and optimizing the model parameters (M-step). The VE-step and VM-step of the algorithm are illustrated as movements along the q and θ axes, respectively.

4.5 Variational Bayes

So far, we have treated latent variables as different from parameters: latent variables are random variables, and they are labeled with the data case, $\mathbf{z}_n$. This means that for every data case, they can take different values. Parameters are treated as deterministic numbers. However, nothing prevents us from treating parameters as random variables as well! We just need to specify probability distributions over them. We note that parameters are not specified for a single data case, but rather at the level of the model. So parameters are not indexed by data cases.

When we treat parameters as random variables, we enter the domain of Bayesian statistics (Jaynes, 2003; Gelman et al., 2013). In Bayesian statistics, we specify a prior distribution $p(\boldsymbol{\theta})$ reflecting our belief of what we think are reasonable values. This is subjective! (This subjectivity is why some prefer frequentist approaches, arguing that science should be objective.) Instead of optimizing a likelihood over parameters $\boldsymbol{\theta}$, a Bayesian is interested in computing the posterior of the parameters given all the evidence they have seen so far. Let D_N be a dataset of N data cases. Then

$$p(\boldsymbol{\theta}|D_N) = \frac{p(D_N|\boldsymbol{\theta})p(\boldsymbol{\theta})}{p(D_N)} \propto p(\boldsymbol{\theta}) \prod_{n=1}^{N} p(\mathbf{x}_n|\boldsymbol{\theta}), \tag{4.31}$$

$$p(D_N) = \int \mathrm{d}\boldsymbol{\theta}\; p(D_N|\boldsymbol{\theta})p(\boldsymbol{\theta}). \tag{4.32}$$

The marginal likelihood, $p(D_N)$, which is the normalization constant (cf. partition function!), plays an important role in model selection. For instance, if we have multiple models $\mathcal{M}$ to choose from, we have

$$p(\mathcal{M}|D_N) = \frac{p(D_N|\mathcal{M})p(\mathcal{M})}{p(D_N)} \qquad \text{(model selection)}, \tag{4.33}$$

$$p(D_N) = \sum_{\mathcal{M}} p(D_N|\mathcal{M})p(\mathcal{M}) \qquad \text{(evidence)}, \tag{4.34}$$

$$p(D_N|\mathcal{M}) = \int \mathrm{d}\boldsymbol{\theta}\; p(D_N|\boldsymbol{\theta},\mathcal{M})p(\boldsymbol{\theta}|\mathcal{M}) \qquad \text{(model evidence)}. \tag{4.35}$$

The model with the highest posterior probability is the one we favor (see Figure 4.7).

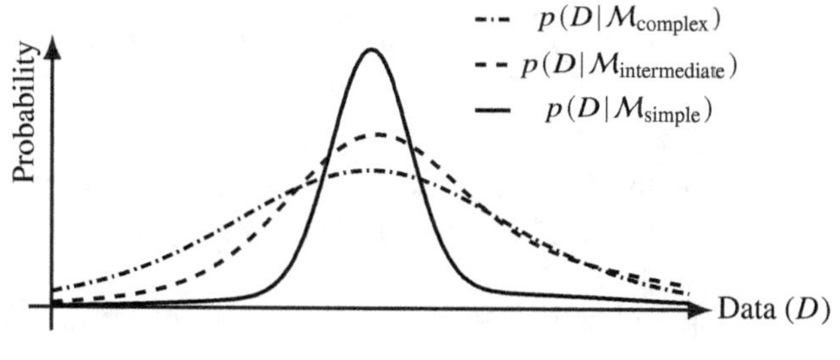

Figure 4.7 Model complexity and marginal likelihood in Bayesian model selection. Simple models have higher peak probabilities but narrower coverage, while complex models have lower peak probabilities but wider coverage. The symbol $\mathcal{M}$ denotes the model class.

Learning is now replaced with inference over $\boldsymbol{\theta}$ and possibly also $\{\mathbf{z}_n\}$ (see Figure 4.4). To perform this inference, we can use Markov chain Monte Carlo algorithms to sample from the posterior, a topic we will explore in Chapter 11. For now, we want to show that this once again can be formulated as a free energy minimization problem over a larger space (see Figure 4.8 for an illustration). Introduce variational inference distributions $q(\mathbf{z}_1, \ldots, \mathbf{z}_N, \boldsymbol{\theta})$. To keep the notation simple, we will write this as $q(Z, \boldsymbol{\theta})$. We can now derive the bound, writing $X \equiv D_N$ for brevity:

$$
\begin{aligned}
-F = \log p(D_N) &= \log \int \mathrm{d}\boldsymbol{\theta} \sum_Z p(X, Z, \boldsymbol{\theta}) \\
&= \log \int \mathrm{d}\boldsymbol{\theta} \sum_Z q(Z, \boldsymbol{\theta}) \frac{p(X, Z, \boldsymbol{\theta})}{q(Z, \boldsymbol{\theta})} \\
&\geq \int \mathrm{d}\boldsymbol{\theta} \sum_Z q(Z, \boldsymbol{\theta}) \log \frac{p(X, Z, \boldsymbol{\theta})}{q(Z, \boldsymbol{\theta})} = -\mathcal{F}[q], \qquad (4.36)
\end{aligned}
$$

where we have applied Jensen's inequality in the third line and used $p(X, Z, \boldsymbol{\theta}) = p(X|Z, \boldsymbol{\theta}) p(Z|\boldsymbol{\theta}) p(\boldsymbol{\theta})$.

In variational Bayesian (VB) inference (Hinton and van Camp, 1993), we make a key simplifying assumption: $q(Z, \boldsymbol{\theta}) = q(\boldsymbol{\theta}) \prod_n q_n(\mathbf{z}_n)$. While it would be reasonable to assume independence of the latent variables given the parameters – that is, $q(Z, \boldsymbol{\theta}) = \prod_n q_n(\mathbf{z}_n|\boldsymbol{\theta}) q(\boldsymbol{\theta})$ – VB makes the much more radical assumption that Z and $\boldsymbol{\theta}$ are completely independent. This is generally not true, as changing the model affects the latent variables. However, for computational reasons this assumption is convenient and using that assumption we can once again define a variational EM (VEM) "learning" scheme. In particular, we can simplify the free energy and the corresponding bound as

$$
\begin{aligned}
\mathcal{F}_{\mathrm{VB}}[q] = \int \mathrm{d}\boldsymbol{\theta}\, q(\boldsymbol{\theta}) \Big[& \log q(\boldsymbol{\theta}) - \log p(\boldsymbol{\theta}) + \\
& \sum_n \sum_{\mathbf{z}_n} q_n(\mathbf{z}_n) \left(\log q_n(\mathbf{z}_n) - \log p(\mathbf{x}_n, \mathbf{z}_n|\boldsymbol{\theta}) \right) \Big] \qquad (4.37) \\
= \sum_n \sum_{\mathbf{z}_n} & q_n(\mathbf{z}_n) \log q_n(\mathbf{z}_n) + \int \mathrm{d}\boldsymbol{\theta}\, q(\boldsymbol{\theta}) \log \frac{q(\boldsymbol{\theta})}{p(\boldsymbol{\theta})} \\
& - \sum_n \int \mathrm{d}\boldsymbol{\theta}\, q(\boldsymbol{\theta}) \sum_{\mathbf{z}_n} q_n(\mathbf{z}_n) \log p(\mathbf{x}_n, \mathbf{z}_n|\boldsymbol{\theta}), \qquad (4.38)
\end{aligned}
$$

where $p(\mathbf{x}_n, \mathbf{z}_n, \boldsymbol{\theta}) = p(\mathbf{x}_n|\mathbf{z}_n, \boldsymbol{\theta}) p(\mathbf{z}_n|\boldsymbol{\theta}) p(\boldsymbol{\theta})$.

Therefore, the free energy decomposes into terms involving $q_n(\mathbf{z}_n)$ and $q(\boldsymbol{\theta})$. The variational Bayesian EM (Beal, 2003) updates are now given by

$$
\text{VBE-step: } q_n^{t+1}(\mathbf{z}_n) = \frac{1}{Z_z} \exp\left(\int \mathrm{d}\boldsymbol{\theta}\, q^t(\boldsymbol{\theta}) \log[p(\mathbf{x}_n|\mathbf{z}_n, \boldsymbol{\theta}) p(\mathbf{z}_n|\boldsymbol{\theta}) p(\boldsymbol{\theta})] \right), \qquad (4.39)
$$

$$
\text{VBM-step: } q^{t+1}(\boldsymbol{\theta}) = \frac{1}{Z(\boldsymbol{\theta})} p(\boldsymbol{\theta}) \exp\left(\sum_n \sum_{\mathbf{z}_n} q_n^{t+1}(\mathbf{z}_n) \log p(\mathbf{x}_n, \mathbf{z}_n|\boldsymbol{\theta}) \right). \qquad (4.40)
$$

While this looks complicated, the only change we have made is to promote parameters to random variables and treat them consistently within the free energy framework. Learning has been entirely replaced with inference. We have created a super-system consisting of many smaller systems (one per data case) where we maximize entropy over $\mathbf{z}_n$ given a single observational constraint $\mathbf{x}_n$. Additionally, we have constructed a much larger system that couples together all these smaller systems through interactions mediated by parameters $\boldsymbol{\theta}$. This larger system is also trying to maximize entropy b is constrained by the entire dataset. We can imagine all these systems evolving under dynamics that maximize entropy (or minimize free energy) while making sure the constraints provided by the data are respected. This is the stochastic thermodynamics view of Bayesian machine learning!

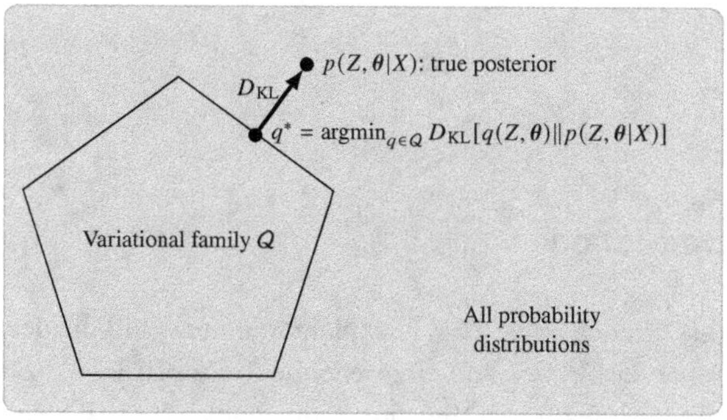

Figure 4.8 Illustration of variational inference: the true posterior is approximated by a distribution in the variational family Q. The light-gray background region represents the space of all candidate probability distributions, while the pentagon represents the variational family Q. The marked dot q^* is the optimal variational distribution that minimizes the KL divergence to the true posterior $p(Z, \theta|X)$ (black point). The arrow indicates the KL divergence being minimized.

5 Thermodynamics of Probabilistic Machine Learning

5.1 Introduction

In this brief chapter, we will explain in more detail the deep connections between fre energies in physics and 'free energies' (i.e., ELBOs) in machine learning. In som sense, this idea lies at the core of this book! We will also connect changes in the fre energy between the two fields. When the free energy changes in physics, it is eithe due to the system relaxing to equilibrium, which we associate with entropy change and heat generation; or because we change the Hamiltonian, for example, because w want to control the system – which we associate with performing work. In ML, thes processes can be mapped to inference and learning.

5.2 Connecting Free Energies in Thermodynamics and ML

The expression for the variational free energy in (nonequilibrium) thermodynamics i given by

$$\mathcal{F}_{\mathrm{TD}}[q] = \mathcal{U}[q] - T\mathcal{S}[q] = \mathbb{E}_q[\mathcal{H}] + T\mathbb{E}_q[\log q], \tag{5.1}$$

which is the expected energy term $\mathcal{U}[q]$ minus the temperature times the entropy.

In ML, we have also derived the variational free energy of the latent variable mod p for a datapoint $\mathbf{x}$,

$$\mathcal{F}_{\mathrm{ML}}[q] = \mathbb{E}_q[-\log p] + \mathbb{E}_q[\log q], \tag{5.2}$$

with $p(\mathbf{x}, \mathbf{z})$ representing the joint distribution over $\mathbf{x}$ and $\mathbf{z}$ and $q(\mathbf{z}|\mathbf{x})$ being th variational distribution.

Comparing the thermodynamic and ML free energies, we see a direct analogy if w identify the Hamiltonian $\mathcal{H}$ with the negative log-joint probability $-\log p(\mathbf{x}, \mathbf{z})$ an set the temperature $T = 1$. In the ML context, there is no explicit heat bath, so it i conventional to work with dimensionless quantities where the temperature is absorbe into the definition of the energy. We will adopt this convention ($T = 1$, or invers temperature $\beta = 1$) for the remainder of the discussion. This means that quantitie analogous to free energy, heat, and work in ML are measured in units of informatic (nats or bits) rather than units of energy (joules). Some researchers have considere reintroducing a temperature-like parameter in ML models, as discussed in Higgins et al. (2017).

In thermodynamics, there are a few ways through which the free energy $\mathcal{F}$ can change, and we will now relate those to the variational expectation-maximization (VEM) updates in ML.

First, let's study the contributions to perturbations of the internal (expected) energy of a system:

$$\begin{aligned} \delta\mathcal{U}(\mathbf{x}) &= \delta \sum_{\mathbf{z}} q(\mathbf{z}|\mathbf{x})\mathcal{H}(\mathbf{z},\mathbf{x}) \\ &= \sum_{\mathbf{z}} \mathcal{H}(\mathbf{z},\mathbf{x})\delta q(\mathbf{z}|\mathbf{x}) + \sum_{\mathbf{z}} q(\mathbf{z}|\mathbf{x})\delta\mathcal{H}(\mathbf{z},\mathbf{x}), \end{aligned} \tag{5.3}$$

where we can identify

$$\text{Heat:}\quad \delta Q(\mathbf{x}) = \sum_{\mathbf{z}} \mathcal{H}(\mathbf{z},\mathbf{x})\delta q(\mathbf{z}|\mathbf{x}) \quad \text{s.t.} \sum_{\mathbf{z}} \delta q(\mathbf{z}|\mathbf{x}) = 0, \tag{5.4}$$

$$\text{Work:}\quad \delta\mathcal{W}(\mathbf{x}) = \sum_{\mathbf{z}} q(\mathbf{z}|\mathbf{x})\delta\mathcal{H}(\mathbf{z},\mathbf{x}). \tag{5.5}$$

In other words: the system generates "heat" when the distribution $q(\mathbf{z}|\mathbf{x})$ changes (e.g., relaxes after a perturbation) at constant Hamiltonian, and the system performs work when the distribution is fixed but the Hamiltonian is changed (e.g., controlled to achieve a certain goal). For now, we will take these as definitions.

When we use the definitions for the Hamiltonian in probabilistic models, we can associate heat and work with inference and learning. Let $\boldsymbol{\theta}$ and $\boldsymbol{\varphi}$ denote the parameters of the joint distribution $p(\mathbf{x},\mathbf{z}|\boldsymbol{\theta})$ and the approximate posterior distribution $q(\mathbf{z}|\mathbf{x},\boldsymbol{\varphi})$, respectively. The parameter $\boldsymbol{\theta}$ typically represents the model parameters that we want to learn, while $\boldsymbol{\varphi}$ represents the parameters of the approximate posterior that we use for inference. Thus:

$$\text{Heat:}\quad \delta Q(\mathbf{x}) = -\sum_{\mathbf{z}} \log p(\mathbf{x},\mathbf{z}|\boldsymbol{\theta}) \frac{\partial q(\mathbf{z}|\mathbf{x},\boldsymbol{\varphi})}{\partial \boldsymbol{\varphi}} \delta\boldsymbol{\varphi}, \tag{5.6}$$

$$\text{Work:}\quad \delta\mathcal{W}(\mathbf{x}) = -\sum_{\mathbf{z}} q(\mathbf{z}|\mathbf{x},\boldsymbol{\varphi}) \frac{\partial \log p(\mathbf{x},\mathbf{z}|\boldsymbol{\theta})}{\partial \boldsymbol{\theta}} \delta\boldsymbol{\theta}. \tag{5.7}$$

This connection allows us to identify the E-step (inference) in the VEM algorithm as relaxing the free energy to the ground state and generating heat and entropy in the process. Also, the M-step (learning) can be identified as performing work on the system to improve its performance:

$$\text{E-step:}\quad \delta\mathcal{F}(\mathbf{x}) = \delta Q(\mathbf{x}) - \delta\mathcal{S}(\mathbf{x}) \quad \text{for all } \mathbf{x}, \tag{5.8}$$

$$\text{M-step:}\quad \delta\mathcal{F} = \sum_{n} \delta\mathcal{W}(\mathbf{x}_n). \tag{5.9}$$

We also observe that the equilibrium distribution is reached when q has minimized the free energy, which we call the Boltzmann distribution. To see this, we set the variation of the free energy to zero:

$$\delta\mathcal{F}(\mathbf{x}) = 0 \Rightarrow \delta Q(\mathbf{x}) - \delta\mathcal{S}(\mathbf{x}) = 0 \Rightarrow \delta Q(\mathbf{x}) = \delta\mathcal{S}(\mathbf{x}). \tag{5.10}$$

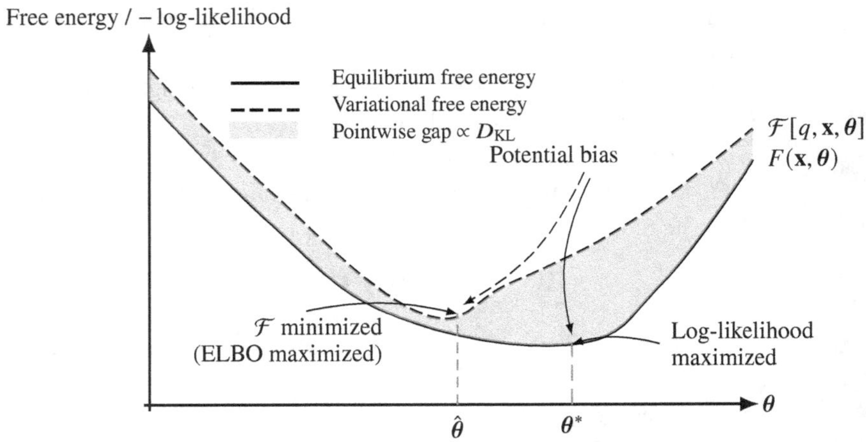

Figure 5.1 Comparison of variational and equilibrium free energies in machine learning. The solid black curve shows the equilibrium free energy $F(\mathbf{x}, \boldsymbol{\theta})$ (negative log-likelihood), while the dashed black curve represents the variational free energy $\mathcal{F}[q, \mathbf{x}, \boldsymbol{\theta}]$ (negative ELBO). The shaded gray area indicates the pointwise difference between the variational free energy and the equilibrium free energy, which equals the KL divergence between the approximate posterior and the true posterior. Note the distinct minima: $\hat{\boldsymbol{\theta}}$ maximizes the ELBO, while $\boldsymbol{\theta}^*$ maximizes the log-likelihood, showing the potential bias in variational methods. This bias stems from the approximation in variational inference and can lead to suboptimal parameter estimates. The pointwise difference (gray area) quantifies the quality of the variational approximation.

Minimizing the free energy with respect to $q(\mathbf{z}|\mathbf{x})$ under the normalization constraint $\sum_{\mathbf{z}} q(\mathbf{z}|\mathbf{x}) = 1$, we get

$$0 = \frac{\partial}{\partial q(\mathbf{z}|\mathbf{x})} \left[\sum_{\mathbf{z}} q(\mathbf{z}|\mathbf{x}) \mathcal{H}(\mathbf{z}, \mathbf{x}) + \sum_{\mathbf{z}} q(\mathbf{z}|\mathbf{x}) \log q(\mathbf{z}|\mathbf{x}) - \lambda \left(\sum_{\mathbf{z}} q(\mathbf{z}|\mathbf{x}) - 1 \right) \right]$$
$$= \mathcal{H}(\mathbf{z}, \mathbf{x}) + (\log q(\mathbf{z}|\mathbf{x}) + 1) - \lambda. \tag{5.11}$$

Solving for $q(\mathbf{z}|\mathbf{x})$, we find

$$q(\mathbf{z}|\mathbf{x}) = \frac{1}{Z(\mathbf{x})} \exp\left(-\mathcal{H}(\mathbf{z}, \mathbf{x})\right) = \frac{1}{p(\mathbf{x})} p(\mathbf{x}, \mathbf{z}) = p(\mathbf{z}|\mathbf{x}), \tag{5.12}$$

where $Z(\mathbf{x}) = \sum_{\mathbf{z}} \exp\left(-\mathcal{H}(\mathbf{z}, \mathbf{x})\right) = p(\mathbf{x})$. The equilibrium free energy is then

$$F(\mathbf{x}) = -\log Z(\mathbf{x}) = -\log p(\mathbf{x}). \tag{5.13}$$

Equipped with the above relations, we finish this section by making the analogy between the definition of the nonequilibrium free energy of stochastic thermodynamics and the definition of the evidence lower bound in machine learning very explicit. In physics, we have:

$$D_{\mathrm{KL}}[q \| p_{\mathrm{B}}] = \beta \sum_{\mathbf{z}} q(\mathbf{z}) \left[\mathcal{H}(\mathbf{z}, \boldsymbol{\theta}) \right] - \mathcal{S}[q] + \log Z(\boldsymbol{\theta}), \tag{5.14}$$

where $p_{\mathrm{B}}(\mathbf{z}) = \frac{1}{Z(\boldsymbol{\theta})} e^{-\beta \mathcal{H}(\mathbf{z}, \boldsymbol{\theta})}$ is the Boltzmann distribution. Since $D_{\mathrm{KL}}[q \| p_{\mathrm{B}}] \geq 0$

we have

$$\begin{aligned} F(\boldsymbol{\theta}) &\equiv -\beta^{-1}\log Z(\boldsymbol{\theta}) \\ &\leq \mathbb{E}_q[\mathcal{H}(\mathbf{z},\boldsymbol{\theta})] - \beta^{-1}\mathcal{S}[q] \equiv \mathcal{F}[q,\boldsymbol{\theta}]. \end{aligned} \tag{5.15}$$

Similarly, in the case of ML (illustrated in Figure 5.1), we condition explicitly on some observations and write

$$D_{\mathrm{KL}}[q_{Z|X}\|p_{Z|X}] = \sum_{\mathbf{z}} q(\mathbf{z}|\mathbf{x})[-\log p(\mathbf{x},\mathbf{z}|\boldsymbol{\theta})] - \mathcal{S}[q_{Z|X}] + \log p(\mathbf{x}|\boldsymbol{\theta}). \tag{5.16}$$

Since $D_{\mathrm{KL}}[q_{Z|X}\|p_{Z|X}] \geq 0$, we have

$$\begin{aligned} F(\mathbf{x},\boldsymbol{\theta}) &\equiv -\log p(\mathbf{x}|\boldsymbol{\theta}) \\ &\leq \mathbb{E}_q[-\log p(\mathbf{x},\mathbf{z}|\boldsymbol{\theta})] - \mathcal{S}[q_{Z|X}] \equiv \mathcal{F}[q,\mathbf{x},\boldsymbol{\theta}]. \end{aligned} \tag{5.17}$$

These derivations reveal a fascinating correspondence between thermodynamic quantities and negative log-probabilities over different probability distributions in machine learning. We should identify $q(\mathbf{z}) \leftrightarrow q(\mathbf{z}|\mathbf{x})$, implying that there are different free energies for every observation $\mathbf{x}$. The Hamiltonian for each of these systems must be identified as $\mathcal{H}(\mathbf{z},\mathbf{x},\boldsymbol{\theta}) = -\log p(\mathbf{x},\mathbf{z}|\boldsymbol{\theta})$, and the equilibrium free energy as $F(\mathbf{x},\boldsymbol{\theta}) = -\log p(\mathbf{x}|\boldsymbol{\theta})$. Additionally, one can define the entropy of the approximate posterior as $\mathcal{S}[q_{Z|X}] = -\sum_{\mathbf{z}} q(\mathbf{z}|\mathbf{x})\log q(\mathbf{z}|\mathbf{x})$ (or $\mathcal{S}[q^{\varphi}_{Z|X}] = -\sum_{\mathbf{z}} q(\mathbf{z}|\mathbf{x},\boldsymbol{\varphi})\log q(\mathbf{z}|\mathbf{x},\boldsymbol{\varphi})$ if we have variational parameters $\boldsymbol{\varphi}$).

6 Belief Propagation

6.1 Belief Propagation and its Extensions

We have seen that probabilistic inference can be viewed as free energy minimization over a variational distribution Q. We have also seen that Bayesian inference, which combines inference over latent variables and model parameters, is a form of probabilistic inference. So probabilistic inference is a very general problem. Unfortunately, in most but the simplest settings the problem is very hard to solve. This has led to approximations that minimize the free energy over a restricted set of variational distributions resulting in an upper bound on the free energy and an approximate distribution Q.

Let us briefly review the mean-field approximation, where we choose $Q(\mathbf{z}) = \prod_k q_k(z_k)$. The variational free energy in this case takes the form:

$$\mathcal{F}[Q] = -\sum_{\mathbf{z}} \left[\prod_k q_k(z_k) \right] \log P(\mathbf{x}, \mathbf{z}) + \sum_k \sum_{z_k} q_k(z_k) \log q_k(z_k). \tag{6.1}$$

Now, let us assume that the model P can be written as a product of terms, each depending on a subset of the latent variables:

$$-\log P(\mathbf{x}, \mathbf{z}) = \sum_\alpha \Psi_\alpha(\mathbf{z}_\alpha; \mathbf{x}), \tag{6.2}$$

with α indexing a possibly overlapping subset of variables $\mathcal{V}_\alpha$ of $\mathbf{z}$, where $\mathcal{V}_\alpha \subseteq \{1, \ldots, K\}$ of the K total variables. This factorization assumption now gives:

$$\mathcal{F}[Q] = \sum_\alpha \sum_{\mathbf{z}_\alpha} \left[\prod_{k \in \mathcal{V}_\alpha} q_k(z_k) \right] \Psi_\alpha(\mathbf{z}_\alpha; \mathbf{x}) + \sum_k \sum_{z_k} q_k(z_k) \log q_k(z_k), \tag{6.3}$$

which leads to the mean-field update:

$$q_k(z_k) \leftarrow \frac{1}{Z_k} \exp\left(- \sum_{\alpha : k \in \mathcal{V}_\alpha} \sum_{\mathbf{z}_\alpha \backslash z_k} \left[\prod_{j \in \mathcal{V}_\alpha \backslash k} q_j(z_j) \right] \Psi_\alpha(\mathbf{z}_\alpha; \mathbf{x}) \right). \tag{6.4}$$

Here, $\mathbf{z}_\alpha \backslash z_k$ denotes the set of variables in $\mathbf{z}_\alpha$ excluding z_k, and $\mathcal{V}_\alpha \backslash k$ denotes the corresponding set of indices. In words: The new estimate for q_k is proportional to the exponential of the negative sum over all the expectations of the energy factors that contain the variable z_k.

While MF is tractable, it is not very accurate due to the severe assumption that all variables are independent. It turns out that there is a much better approximation, called belief propagation (BP). In BP, we make two approximations: first, we approximate the entropy term using a cumulant expansion (see below), and second, we optimize over a space of mutually consistent marginal densities $\{q_\alpha, q_k\}$. By "mutually consistent," we mean that:

$$\sum_{\mathbf{z}_\alpha \backslash z_k} q_\alpha(\mathbf{z}_\alpha) = q_k(z_k), \quad \text{for all } \alpha,\ k \in \mathcal{V}_\alpha. \tag{6.5}$$

The reason this is an approximation is that it is not guaranteed that any set of consistent marginals is consistent with a global distribution $q(\mathbf{z})$; in other words, there may simply not exist a global distribution that has these "marginal distributions" as its true marginals.

The case we will treat here is a special case of an even more general scheme called the cluster variation method (Morita, 1990) or generalized belief propagation (Yedidia et al., 2005). In these more general approaches, we can define clusters of arbitrary subsets of variables and all their intersections and intersections of intersections, which we then make all consistent. In this chapter, we will treat the slightly simpler case called factor graph BP.

Let us first write the approximation to the entropy, known as the Bethe entropy:

$$\mathcal{S}[Q] \approx \sum_\alpha \mathcal{S}_\alpha[q_\alpha] - \sum_k (N_k - 1)\, \mathcal{S}_k[q_k], \tag{6.6}$$

where

$$\mathcal{S}_\alpha[q_\alpha] = -\sum_{\mathbf{z}_\alpha} q_\alpha(\mathbf{z}_\alpha) \log q_\alpha(\mathbf{z}_\alpha), \tag{6.7}$$

$$\mathcal{S}_k[q_k] = -\sum_{z_k} q_k(z_k) \log q_k(z_k). \tag{6.8}$$

Here, N_k is the number of clusters α in which variable z_k participates. One can understand this from an overcounting argument. The entropy is an extensive quantity: the entropy of the union of two disjoint (independent) subsets should add. However, some of these clusters overlap, so we should subtract the amount of overcounting due to including certain variables in multiple clusters. For example, if the clusters are disjoint, every variable participates precisely once in each cluster, and there are no corrections (that is, $N_k = 1$ for all k). If a variable sits in two clusters, we need to subtract its contribution once (that is, $N_k = 2$), and so on.

We also note that on a tree of overlapping clusters, this entropy approximation is exact. The easiest way to visualize this is to draw a factor graph, which is a bipartite graph with clusters α on one side and variable nodes k on the other. If a variable participates in a cluster Ψ_α, you connect the factor node to the variable node. If this factor graph has no cycles, the exact probability distribution can be written as

$$Q(\mathbf{z}) = \prod_\alpha q_\alpha(\mathbf{z}_\alpha) \prod_k q_k(z_k)^{1-N_k}, \tag{6.9}$$

which results in the entropy of (6.6). The Bethe entropy approximation is then motivate by the fact that it is exact on trees and provides a reasonable approximation fo loopy graphs by correcting for the overcounting of variables. Equation (6.6) is jus an approximation.

If we had exact marginals, the energy could be computed exactly because it factorize into the factors. In that case, we could write the following approximation to the fre energy:

$$\mathcal{F}_{\text{BP}}[\{q_\alpha, q_k\}] = \sum_\alpha \sum_{\mathbf{z}_\alpha} q_\alpha(\mathbf{z}_\alpha)\Psi_\alpha(\mathbf{z}_\alpha;\mathbf{x}) - \sum_\alpha \mathcal{S}_\alpha[q_\alpha] + \sum_k (N_k - 1)\,\mathcal{S}_k[q_k] \tag{6.10}$$

$$\text{subject to} \sum_{\mathbf{z}_\alpha \backslash z_k} q_\alpha(\mathbf{z}_\alpha) = q_k(z_k), \quad \text{for all } \alpha,\ k \in \mathcal{V}_\alpha. \tag{6.11}$$

Our task is now to find the "ground state" of this free energy by minimizing $\mathcal{F}_{\text{BP}}$ ove $\{q_\alpha, q_k\}$ subject to consistency constraints.

From Chapter 1, we know how to handle equality constraints: Lagrange multipliers For every constraint, we introduce a Lagrange multiplier $\lambda_{\alpha,k}$ and write the Lagrangiar

$$\begin{aligned}\mathcal{L}&[\{q_\alpha, q_k, \lambda_{\alpha,k}\}] \\ &= \mathcal{F}_{\text{BP}}[\{q_\alpha, q_k\}] + \sum_\alpha \sum_{k\in\mathcal{V}_\alpha} \sum_{z_k} \lambda_{\alpha,k}(z_k)\left[\sum_{\mathbf{z}_\alpha\backslash z_k} q_\alpha(\mathbf{z}_\alpha) - q_k(z_k)\right].\end{aligned} \tag{6.12}$$

We should also add multipliers for the constraints that the distributions q_α and q_k ar normalized and non-negative. It turns out that, by construction, the non-negativity cor straint will be satisfied and normalization can be easily achieved afterwards. Becaus of this, we will omit these multipliers for simplicity.

Taking derivatives with respect to q_α and q_k, we get

$$\frac{\partial \mathcal{L}}{\partial q_\alpha(\mathbf{z}_\alpha)} = \Psi_\alpha(\mathbf{z}_\alpha;\mathbf{x}) + \log q_\alpha(\mathbf{z}_\alpha) + \sum_{k\in\mathcal{V}_\alpha} \lambda_{\alpha,k}(z_k) + c_1, \tag{6.13}$$

$$\frac{\partial \mathcal{L}}{\partial q_k(z_k)} = (1 - N_k)\log q_k(z_k) - \sum_{\alpha:k\in\mathcal{V}_\alpha} \lambda_{\alpha,k}(z_k) + c_2, \tag{6.14}$$

with c_1 and c_2 constants that will be absorbed in the normalization. The notatic $\alpha : k \in \mathcal{V}_\alpha$ means a cluster α where the variable-node k is in its domain. Solving fo q gives

$$q_\alpha(\mathbf{z}_\alpha) = \frac{1}{Z_\alpha}\exp\left(-\Psi_\alpha(\mathbf{z}_\alpha;\mathbf{x}) - \sum_{k\in\mathcal{V}_\alpha} \lambda_{\alpha,k}(z_k)\right), \tag{6.15}$$

$$q_k(z_k) = \frac{1}{Z_k}\exp\left(-\frac{1}{N_k - 1}\sum_{\alpha:k\in\mathcal{V}_\alpha} \lambda_{\alpha,k}(z_k)\right). \tag{6.16}$$

We now define messages as follows:

$$n_{k\to\alpha}(z_k) \equiv \exp\left(-\lambda_{\alpha,k}(z_k)\right) \equiv \prod_{\beta:k\in\mathcal{V}_\beta\setminus\alpha} m_{\beta\to k}(z_k). \tag{6.17}$$

From this, one can derive that:

$$\begin{aligned} q_\alpha(\mathbf{z}_\alpha) &= \frac{1}{Z_\alpha}\exp\left(-\Psi_\alpha(\mathbf{z}_\alpha;\mathbf{x})\right)\prod_{k\in\mathcal{V}_\alpha} n_{k\to\alpha}(z_k) \\ &= \frac{1}{Z_\alpha}\exp\left(-\Psi_\alpha(\mathbf{z}_\alpha;\mathbf{x})\right)\prod_{k\in\mathcal{V}_\alpha}\prod_{\beta:k\in\mathcal{V}_\beta\setminus\alpha} m_{\beta\to k}(z_k), \end{aligned} \tag{6.18}$$

$$q_k(z_k) = \frac{1}{Z_k}\prod_{\alpha:k\in\mathcal{V}_\alpha}\left[n_{k\to\alpha}(z_k)\right]^{\frac{1}{N_k-1}} = \frac{1}{Z_k}\prod_{\alpha:k\in\mathcal{V}_\alpha} m_{\alpha\to k}(z_k). \tag{6.19}$$

In terms of these definitions, we thus see that the approximate marginals on factors are given by the product of the incoming messages $n_{k\to\alpha}$ times any factors living on that factor node. The marginals of a variable node are simply given by the product of incoming messages $m_{\alpha\to k}$. Figure 6.1 illustrates this message passing scheme on a simple factor graph.

The Lagrange multipliers in (6.12) can be solved by ensuring that the local consistency equations in (6.11) on marginals are satisfied. Since we have reparameterized the Lagrange multipliers as messages, we solve for the messages instead:

$$\frac{1}{Z_\alpha}\sum_{\mathbf{z}_\alpha\setminus z_k}\exp\left(-\Psi_\alpha(\mathbf{z}_\alpha;\mathbf{x})\right)\prod_{j\in\mathcal{V}_\alpha}\prod_{\beta:j\in\mathcal{V}_\beta\setminus\alpha} m_{\beta\to j}(z_j) = \frac{1}{Z_k}\prod_{\gamma:k\in\mathcal{V}_\gamma} m_{\gamma\to k}(z_k), \tag{6.20}$$

which, after canceling terms that appear on both sides, leads to a fixed-point update for messages:

$$\begin{aligned} m^{\text{new}}_{\alpha\to k}(z_k) &\propto \sum_{\mathbf{z}_\alpha\setminus z_k}\exp\left(-\Psi_\alpha(\mathbf{z}_\alpha;\mathbf{x})\right)\prod_{j\in\mathcal{V}_\alpha\setminus k} n_{j\to\alpha}(z_j) \\ &= \sum_{\mathbf{z}_\alpha\setminus z_k}\exp\left(-\Psi_\alpha(\mathbf{z}_\alpha;\mathbf{x})\right)\prod_{j\in\mathcal{V}_\alpha\setminus k}\prod_{\beta:j\in\mathcal{V}_\beta\setminus\alpha} m_{\beta\to j}(z_j). \end{aligned} \tag{6.21}$$

We now iterate these fixed-point equations until convergence. On a tree-structured (factor) graph, this is guaranteed to converge in such a way that if we then compute the marginals q_α and q_k using (6.18) and (6.19), we are guaranteed to get the exact result. This can be derived from the fact that there are no approximations to the energy and entropy terms in the free energy in that case. The magic aspect is that even when we iterate these equations in the case where the (factor) graph has loops, the equations often still converge to a fixed point, and the approximate marginals tend to be very good approximations.

There are a few practical tricks to improve convergence and avoid numerical errors. First, note that we have omitted any normalization constants in the update. The reason

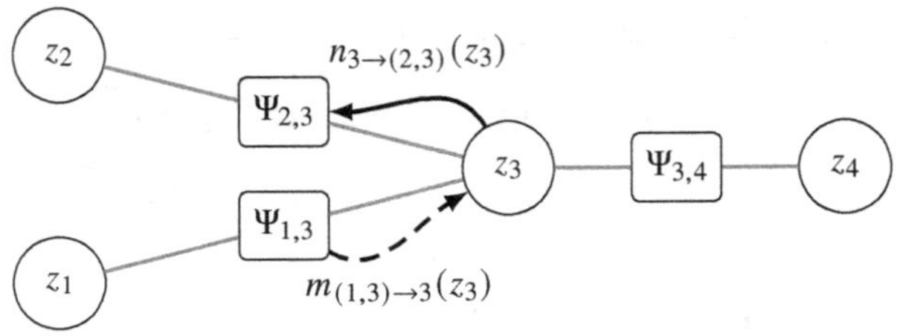

Figure 6.1 Belief propagation on a factor graph. Circular nodes represent variables (z_i), and rounded rectangles represent factors (Ψ_α). Long-dashed arrows show messages $m_{\alpha\to k}(z_k)$ from factors to variables, and solid arrows show messages $n_{k\to\alpha}(z_k)$ from variables to factors. The messages are passed iteratively until convergence.

is that they do not play a role in the final estimates for the marginals, which ge normalized separately anyway (and they only affect these estimates multiplicatively) However, it is good practice to keep the largest values of the messages within bound to prevent numerical overflow.

As a second practicality, one might find that the message update equations do no actually converge for a loopy factor graph. In that case, one can apply (geometric damping by updating the messages as follows:

$$m'_{\alpha\to k}(z_k) = \sum_{\mathbf{z}_\alpha \setminus z_k} \exp\left(-\Psi_\alpha(\mathbf{z}_\alpha;\mathbf{x})\right) \prod_{j\in\mathcal{V}_\alpha\setminus k} \prod_{\beta: j\in\mathcal{V}_\beta\setminus\alpha} m_{\beta\to j}(z_j), \qquad (6.22)$$

$$m^{\text{new}}_{\alpha\to k}(z_k) = \left[m_{\alpha\to k}(z_k)\right]^{1-\eta}\left[m'_{\alpha\to k}(z_k)\right]^{\eta}, \quad \eta\in(0,1], \qquad (6.23)$$

where η is the damping factor. Finally, one needs to initialize the messages, and usuall initializing them to be all ones works well.

It was proven by Yedidia et al. (2005) that even in the case of loopy (factor) graph the fixed points of "loopy belief propagation" (LBP) described above correspond t stationary points of the (approximate) Bethe free energy. It was not shown there tha these are global minima of this free energy. Heskes (2002) subsequently showed tha the *stable* fixed points of LBP are local minima of the Bethe free energy.

LBP has made an enormous impact in the error correction decoding communit as some of the best codes, like turbo codes and low density parity check (LDPC codes, are based on it. Furthermore, as an approximate inference algorithm, LBP an its generalization to Bayesian inference called expectation propagation (Minka, 2001 are still some of the best-performing approximate inference algorithms today.

6.2 A Markov Chain Example

We now apply BP to a Markov chain, which is relevant to the focus of this book an will be used in Chapter 15.

A Markov chain with observations has the joint distribution (see Figure 6.2 for th

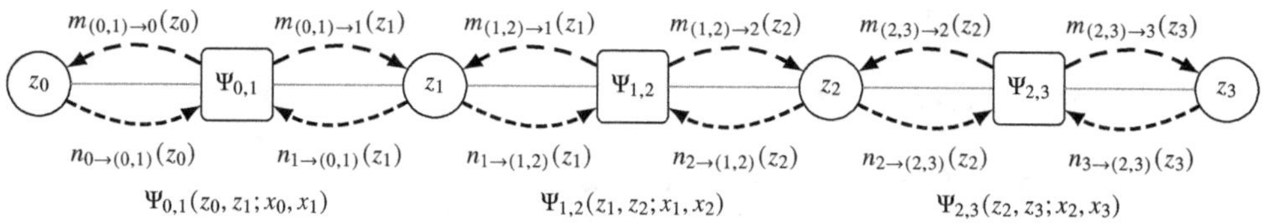

Figure 6.2 Belief propagation on a Markov chain. Circular nodes represent hidden states (z_t), and rounded rectangles represent factors ($\Psi_{t-1,t}$). Long-dashed curves indicate forward messages from factors to variables ($m_{(t-1,t)\to t}(z_t)$), while short-dashed curves show the backward messages from variables to factors ($n_{t\to(t-1,t)}(z_t)$).

graphical model representation):

$$\begin{aligned} P(\mathbf{x}, \mathbf{z}) &= p_0(z_0)p_0(x_0|z_0)\prod_{t=1}^{t_f} p(z_t|z_{t-1})p(x_t|z_t) \\ &= \prod_{t=1}^{t_f} \exp(-\Psi_{t-1,t}(z_{t-1}, z_t; x_t)), \end{aligned} \tag{6.24}$$

with

$$\Psi_{0,1}(z_0, z_1; x_0, x_1) = -\log\left(p_0(z_0)p_0(x_0|z_0)p(z_1|z_0)p(x_1|z_1)\right), \tag{6.25}$$

$$\Psi_{t-1,t}(z_{t-1}, z_t; x_t) = -\log\left(p(z_t|z_{t-1})p(x_t|z_t)\right), \quad \text{for } t > 1. \tag{6.26}$$

Due to the chain structure, each variable z_t participates in exactly two factors (except for the endpoints), so $N_k = 2$ for internal nodes. The relation between the n and m messages simplifies from (6.17) to

$$n_{t\to(t-1,t)}(z_t) = m_{(t,t+1)\to t}(z_t), \tag{6.27}$$

$$n_{t\to(t,t+1)}(z_t) = m_{(t-1,t)\to t}(z_t), \tag{6.28}$$

with clusters α now always of the form $(t, t+1)$.

We initialize all messages to be all ones, and execute (6.21) both from the left and the right:

$$m^{\text{new}}_{(0,1)\to 1}(z_1) = \sum_{z_0} \exp\left(-\Psi_{0,1}(z_0, z_1; x_0, x_1)\right), \tag{6.29}$$

$$m^{\text{new}}_{(t,t+1)\to t+1}(z_{t+1}) = \sum_{z_t} \exp\left(-\Psi_{t,t+1}(z_t, z_{t+1}; x_{t+1})\right) m_{(t-1,t)\to t}(z_t), \tag{6.30}$$

$$m^{\text{new}}_{(t_f-1,t_f)\to t_f-1}(z_{t_f-1}) = \sum_{z_{t_f}} \exp\left(-\Psi_{t_f-1,t_f}(z_{t_f-1}, z_{t_f}; x_{t_f})\right), \tag{6.31}$$

$$m^{\text{new}}_{(t-1,t)\to t-1}(z_{t-1}) = \sum_{z_t} \exp\left(-\Psi_{t-1,t}(z_{t-1}, z_t; x_t)\right) m_{(t,t+1)\to t}(z_t), \tag{6.32}$$

and finally the marginals are computed as:

$$q_{t,t+1}(z_t, z_{t+1})$$
$$= \frac{1}{Z_{t,t+1}} \exp\left(-\Psi_{t,t+1}(z_t, z_{t+1}; x_{t+1})\right) m_{(t-1,t)\to t}(z_t) m_{(t+1,t+2)\to t+1}(z_{t+1}), \quad (6.33)$$
$$q_t(z_t) = \frac{1}{Z_t} m_{(t-1,t)\to t}(z_t) m_{(t,t+1)\to t}(z_t). \quad (6.34)$$

We note that for systems with large state spaces, z_t, the summations required to ru LBP even on a chain will be prohibitive, and additional approximations will be needec

7 The Variational Autoencoder

7.1 Introduction

We are now ready to apply what we learned in the previous chapters about graphical models, and the VEM learning algorithm based on the ELBO objective to a specific model architecture: the variational autoencoder. The VAE has an explicit encoder NN to infer the distribution over latent variables given an observation, and a generative decoder model that turns a random sample from a prior distribution over latent variables into a generated data sample. The core idea of the VAE is that we can accelerate inference by learning a model (the encoder) to predict the outcome of inference using an NN. This core principle is called "amortized inference."

7.2 The Free Energy in Machine Learning

As discussed in the previous chapter, the fundamental quantity used in probabilistic ML is the *evidence lower bound*, or ELBO (Blei et al., 2017). To formulate it, we introduce observed variables $\mathbf{x}$ and unobserved, or latent, variables $\mathbf{z}$. We will sometimes refer to latent variables as hidden variables, but unlike hidden variables in a deep neural network, which are deterministic functions of the observed variables, we will assume here that hidden variables are stochastic in nature.

We formulate two probability distributions over these variables:

$$p(\mathbf{x}, \mathbf{z}) = p(\mathbf{x}|\mathbf{z})p(\mathbf{z}), \tag{7.1}$$

$$q(\mathbf{z}, \mathbf{x}) = q(\mathbf{z}|\mathbf{x})q(\mathbf{x}). \tag{7.2}$$

For reasons that will become clear later, we will call q the *forward model*, *encoder*, or *inference model*, and p the *backward model*, *decoder*, or *generative model*. The term $q(\mathbf{x})$ is often the data distribution, while $p(\mathbf{z})$ is the prior over the latent variables. If we know $q(\mathbf{z}|\mathbf{x})$, we can perform (approximate) inference over the latent factors that have generated the data. If we know $p(\mathbf{x}|\mathbf{z})$, we can (approximately) sample from the data distribution.

It makes sense to make the difference between these two models small. Since we really only care about the data distribution, one objective is to minimize

$$D_{\mathrm{KL}}[q_X \| p_X] = \sum_{\mathbf{x}} q(\mathbf{x}) \left(\log q(\mathbf{x}) - \log p(\mathbf{x})\right), \tag{7.3}$$

$$p(\mathbf{x}) = \sum_{\mathbf{z}} p(\mathbf{x}|\mathbf{z}) p(\mathbf{z}), \tag{7.4}$$

where $q(\mathbf{x})$ is the data distribution.[1] If $p(\mathbf{x})$ depends on some parameters $\boldsymbol{\theta}$ – that is $p(\mathbf{x}|\boldsymbol{\theta})$ – then the objective to minimize becomes

$$\mathcal{L}(\boldsymbol{\theta}, \mathbf{x}) = -\sum_{\mathbf{x}} q(\mathbf{x}) \log p(\mathbf{x}|\boldsymbol{\theta}) \approx -\sum_{n} \log p(\mathbf{x}_n|\boldsymbol{\theta}), \tag{7.5}$$

known as the *maximum likelihood principle* (Bishop, 2006).

Since $p(\mathbf{x})$ involves an intractable integral over the latent variables, this optimization is typically very hard. Instead, we use the following decomposition of the KL divergence between the joint distributions:

$$D_{\mathrm{KL}}[q_{Z,X} \| p_{X,Z}] = D_{\mathrm{KL}}[q_X \| p_X] + \mathbb{E}_{q_X}\left[D_{\mathrm{KL}}[q_{Z|X} \| p_{Z|X}]\right], \tag{7.6}$$

$$D_{\mathrm{KL}}[q_X \| p_X] = D_{\mathrm{KL}}[q_{Z,X} \| p_{X,Z}] - \mathbb{E}_{q_X}\left[D_{\mathrm{KL}}[q_{Z|X} \| p_{Z|X}]\right], \tag{7.7}$$

$$\Rightarrow D_{\mathrm{KL}}[q_X \| p_X] \leq D_{\mathrm{KL}}[q_{Z,X} \| p_{X,Z}]. \tag{7.8}$$

This leads to the inequalities

$$\sum_{\mathbf{x}} q(\mathbf{x}) \log p(\mathbf{x}) \geq \sum_{\mathbf{x}} q(\mathbf{x}) \sum_{\mathbf{z}} q(\mathbf{z}|\mathbf{x}) \left(\log p(\mathbf{x}, \mathbf{z}) - \log q(\mathbf{z}|\mathbf{x})\right), \tag{7.9}$$

$$\mathbb{E}_{q_X}[-\log p(\mathbf{x})] \leq \mathbb{E}_{q_X}\left[\mathbb{E}_{q_{Z|X}}[-\log p(\mathbf{x}, \mathbf{z}) + \log q(\mathbf{z}|\mathbf{x})]\right], \tag{7.10}$$

where we can identify the free energy F, the expected energy $\mathcal{H}$, the entropy $\mathcal{S}$, and the variational free energy $\mathcal{F}$ in the process. In fact, since the bound holds for any $q(\mathbf{x})$, we can choose it to be a delta function on one specific $\mathbf{x}$, implying that the bound holds conditionally for every $\mathbf{x}$:

$$F(\mathbf{x}) = -\log p(\mathbf{x}), \tag{7.11}$$

$$\leq \mathbb{E}_{q_{Z|X}}[\mathcal{H}(\mathbf{x}, \mathbf{z})] - \mathcal{S}(\mathbf{x}) \equiv \mathcal{F}(\mathbf{x}), \tag{7.12}$$

$$\mathcal{H}(\mathbf{x}, \mathbf{z}) = -\log p(\mathbf{x}, \mathbf{z}), \tag{7.13}$$

$$\mathcal{S}(\mathbf{x}) = -\sum_{\mathbf{z}} q(\mathbf{z}|\mathbf{x}) \log q(\mathbf{z}|\mathbf{x}). \tag{7.14}$$

From this, it becomes clear that there is a close connection with physics, which we will be exploring in this book.

[1] Formally, we should always write $q_X(\mathbf{x})$, and so forth, to indicate the distribution and its argument. However, we often leave out the subscripts when we explicitly write the arguments (e.g., $q(\mathbf{x})$) because there can be no confusion. Also, when we write functionals like the KL divergence, we should not write the argument, and so we add the subscript.

7.3 Variational Expectation Maximization

Learning a parameterized model $p(\mathbf{x}|\boldsymbol{\theta})$ can now proceed by iterating the following two steps, which we called the VEM algorithm (Neal and Hinton, 1998) in previous chapters. First, assume that we also equip the variational posterior $q_{Z|X,\varphi}$ with some parameters $\boldsymbol{\varphi}$. Then, we iterate:

$$\text{E-Step:}\quad \varphi^{t+1} = \underset{\varphi}{\text{argmin}}\, D_{\text{KL}}[q_{Z,X|\varphi} \| p_{X,Z|\theta^t}], \tag{7.15}$$

$$\text{M-Step:}\quad \theta^{t+1} = \underset{\theta}{\text{argmin}}\, D_{\text{KL}}[q_{Z,X|\varphi^{t+1}} \| p_{X,Z|\theta}]. \tag{7.16}$$

As in Chapter 4, we could have separated parameters φ_n for every value of $\mathbf{x}_n$ that we observe in the dataset. However, it is much more efficient if we perform *amortized* inference; that is, we share the parameters of the encoder $q_{Z|X,\varphi}$ across all the data cases generated by q_X. This algorithm is the basis for the variational autoencoder (Kingma and Welling, 2014; Rezende et al., 2014).

The gradients for optimization can be easily computed, but the standard gradients with respect to q (often computed using the "REINFORCE" estimator; see Williams (1992)) will have high variance; see (4.19). As in Chapter 4, we can apply the *reparameterization trick* to reduce this variance. The key idea is again to express the random variable $\mathbf{z}$ as a deterministic function of the input $\mathbf{x}$ and an auxiliary noise variable $\boldsymbol{\epsilon}$. For a Gaussian $q(\mathbf{z}|\mathbf{x})$ with mean $\boldsymbol{\mu}(\mathbf{x})$ and standard deviation $\sigma(\mathbf{x})$,

$$\mathbf{z} = \boldsymbol{\mu}(\mathbf{x}) + \sigma(\mathbf{x}) \cdot \boldsymbol{\epsilon}, \quad \boldsymbol{\epsilon} \sim G(\mathbf{0}, \mathbf{I}). \tag{7.17}$$

This allows us to estimate the variational free energy (or the negative ELBO) for each data case $\mathbf{x}$ using Monte Carlo sampling:

$$\mathcal{F}(\mathbf{x}) = \mathbb{E}_{\boldsymbol{\epsilon}\sim G(\mathbf{0},\mathbf{I})}\left[-\log p(\mathbf{x}, \mathbf{z}(\boldsymbol{\epsilon})) + \log q(\mathbf{z}(\boldsymbol{\epsilon})|\mathbf{x})\right] \tag{7.18}$$

$$\approx \frac{1}{S}\sum_{s=1}^{S}\left(-\log p(\mathbf{x}, \mathbf{z}_s) + \log q(\mathbf{z}_s|\mathbf{x})\right), \quad \mathbf{z}_s = \boldsymbol{\mu}(\mathbf{x}) + \sigma(\mathbf{x}) \cdot \boldsymbol{\epsilon}_s, \tag{7.19}$$

with S samples collected as $\boldsymbol{\epsilon}_s \sim G(\mathbf{0}, \mathbf{I})$.

Since $G(\boldsymbol{\epsilon}; \mathbf{0}, \mathbf{I})$ does not depend on any parameters, unlike $G(\mathbf{z}; \boldsymbol{\mu}(\mathbf{x}), \sigma(\mathbf{x}))$, the samples will not depend on these parameters either. This allows for safely moving derivatives with respect to parameters through the sum and applying them directly to the terms inside the expectation. The variational autoencoder (VAE) learning algorithm now consists of sampling a data case $\mathbf{x}_n$, drawing one or more samples $\boldsymbol{\epsilon}_{sn}$ from a standard normal distribution, and then performing gradient updates on the reparameterized expression of the free energy in (7.18).

7.4 Hierarchical VAE

In the standard VAE architecture, we use an NN to map an input $\mathbf{x}$ to a distribution $q_{Z|X}$ by predicting the mean and (co)variance of a normal distribution:

$$q_\varphi(\mathbf{z}|\mathbf{x}) = G(\mathbf{z}; \boldsymbol{\mu}(\mathbf{x}), \sigma(\mathbf{x})), \tag{7.20}$$

$$\boldsymbol{\mu}(\mathbf{x}), \sigma(\mathbf{x}) = \mathrm{NN}_\varphi(\mathbf{x}). \tag{7.21}$$

However, it is much more powerful to introduce multiple layers of stochastic variables (illustrated in Figure 7.1) and build a hierarchical model to learn features at various levels of abstraction. We define:

$$\mathbf{z}_{0:t_f} = \{\mathbf{z}_0, \mathbf{z}_1, \ldots, \mathbf{z}_{t_f}\}, \tag{7.22}$$

where we will use $\mathbf{z}_0$ to indicate the random variable that can be conditioned on data case $\mathbf{x}$. We define both the encoder and decoder as Markov chains. The decoder (generative model) is given by sampling from the prior $p(\mathbf{z}_{t_f})$ and then sequentially sampling $\mathbf{z}_{t-1}$ conditioned on $\mathbf{z}_t$, and finally $\mathbf{z}_0 = \mathbf{x}$ conditioned on $\mathbf{z}_1$:

$$p(\mathbf{z}_{0:t_f}) = p(\mathbf{z}_{t_f}) \prod_{t=1}^{t_f} p_t(\mathbf{z}_{t-1}|\mathbf{z}_t). \tag{7.23}$$

The encoder (inference model) can be factorized in two ways (Kingma et al., 2016):

$$\text{Top-down: } q(\mathbf{z}_{1:t_f}|\mathbf{z}_0 = \mathbf{x}) = q(\mathbf{z}_{t_f}|\mathbf{z}_0 = \mathbf{x}) \prod_{t=1}^{t_f-1} q_t(\mathbf{z}_t|\mathbf{z}_{t+1}, \mathbf{z}_0 = \mathbf{x}), \tag{7.24}$$

$$\text{Bottom-up: } q(\mathbf{z}_{1:t_f}|\mathbf{z}_0 = \mathbf{x}) = \prod_{t=1}^{t_f} q_t(\mathbf{z}_t|\mathbf{z}_{t-1}, \mathbf{z}_0 = \mathbf{x}). \tag{7.25}$$

In top-down factorization, the posterior starts from the highest level latent variable and conditions each lower level on the level above and the data $\mathbf{x}$, while bottom-up factorization builds up the latent representation from the data, propagating from upwards through the hierarchy.

As indicated in Figure 7.1, we can also include labels $\mathbf{y}$ in the generative and inference processes. In the inference model we usually condition on this information if it is observed as part of the data (or generate them if they are unobserved). In the generative process we can choose to pick a label at random from some prior distribution (generate them) or condition on them if we want to generate examples in a specific category.

We note that the bound (7.12) still holds, as it does not depend on the number of latent variables or how they are structured. This hierarchical VAE also forms the basis for diffusion models (Sohl-Dickstein et al., 2015; Ho et al., 2020), which we will discuss in Chapter 13.

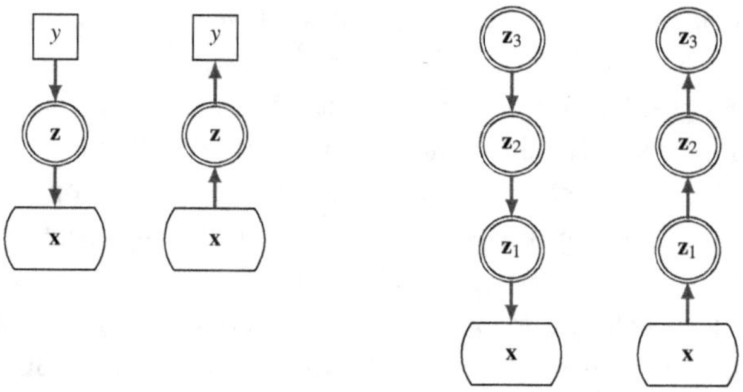

(a) Class-conditional VAEs (b) Hierarchical VAEs

Figure 7.1 Hierarchical extensions of variational autoencoders (VAEs). (a) Class-conditional VAEs introduce a class variable y (square) that influences the latent variable $\mathbf{z}$ (double-outlined circle), which in turn generates the observed data $\mathbf{x}$ (rounded rectangle). The left column shows the generative model (arrows pointing downward), while the right column shows the inference model (arrows pointing upward). (b) Hierarchical VAEs stack multiple layers of latent variables ($\mathbf{z}_1, \mathbf{z}_2, \mathbf{z}_3$), forming a Markov chain in both the generative (left column) and inference (right column) models. The generative process flows top-down, while the inference process flows bottom-up. This hierarchical structure allows for more complex and expressive latent representations, capturing different levels of abstraction in the data.

8 Normalizing Flows

8.1 Introduction

In the previous chapters, we discussed latent variable models that map a latent variabl $\mathbf{z}$ to an observed variable $\mathbf{x}$ using (a series of) stochastic transformations $p_{X|Z}(\mathbf{x}|\mathbf{x}$ By considering the map to be stochastic, methods such as the discussed variationa autoencoder (Kingma and Welling, 2014, 2019) can easily change the dimensionalit of the latent space: adding dimensions is done by mixing in noise random variables while reducing dimensions is achieved through contractive maps like pooling. Th probabilistic framework makes this easy to handle. However, on the flip side, whe using stochastic mapping, the log-likelihood is not tractable and thus optimizing using MLE is only possible through a bound (the ELBO).

In this chapter, we will discuss the normalizing flow, a generative model which, i contrast to VAEs, uses deterministic mappings instead. This allows for exact log likelihood computation and optimization. But, as we will see, it comes with th downside that the mapping must be bijective, which makes the model more complex Figure 8.1 illustrates this transformation process, showing how a simple Gaussian dis tribution can be mapped to a complex multimodal distribution through an invertibl nonlinear function.

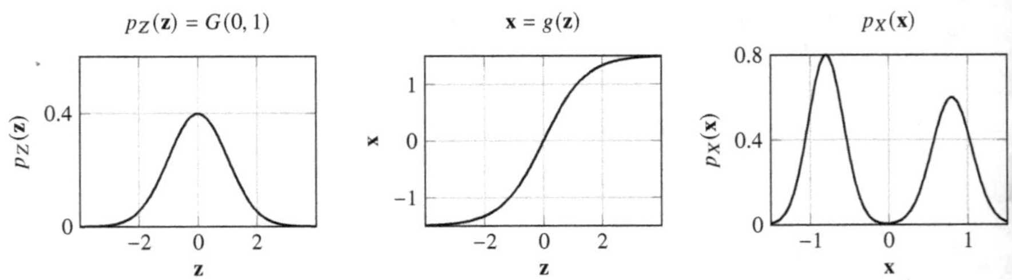

Figure 8.1 Visualization of a normalizing flow transformation. Left: A standard Gaussian pri $p_Z(\mathbf{z}) = G(0, 1)$. Center: A nonlinear invertible transformation g mapping $\mathbf{z}$ to $\mathbf{x}$. Right: The resulting transformed distribution $p_X(\mathbf{x})$, which exhibits a bimodal structure despite the unimodal prior, demonstrating how normalizing flows can model complex distributions.

8.2 Transforming Probability Distributions

Before discussing the normalizing flow, we first recall some of the general rules for transforming probability distributions. One crucial property of probability distributions is that they are normalized, that is, the total probability mass is one, and as such, when we transform the distribution, we need to ensure that mass is conserved:

$$p_X(\mathbf{x})\,\mathrm{d}\mathbf{x} = p_Z(\mathbf{z})\,\mathrm{d}\mathbf{z}. \tag{8.1}$$

In the special case of an invertible deterministic transformation $\mathbf{z} = \mathbf{z}(\mathbf{x})$ we can rewrite this conservation law in terms of the Jacobian of the transformation:

$$p_X(\mathbf{x}) = p_Z(\mathbf{z}(\mathbf{x}))\,|\det \mathbf{J}_\mathbf{z}(\mathbf{x})|\,, \tag{8.2}$$

where we have overloaded the symbol $\mathbf{z}$ to be both a variable in $\mathbb{R}^d$ and a function $\mathbf{z}\colon \mathbb{R}^d \to \mathbb{R}^d$. Equation (8.2) is known as the change of variables formula. It is important to stress here that the function $\mathbf{z}(\mathbf{x})$ must be invertible for this to hold; that is, $\mathbf{x} = \mathbf{x}(\mathbf{z}) = \mathbf{z}^{-1}(\mathbf{z})$.

The final factor is the absolute value of the determinant of the Jacobian matrix $\mathbf{J}$ of the transformation:

$$\mathbf{J}_\mathbf{z}(\mathbf{x}) = \left(\frac{\partial \mathbf{z}(\mathbf{x})}{\partial \mathbf{x}}\right) = \begin{pmatrix} \frac{\partial \mathbf{z}_1(\mathbf{x})}{\partial \mathbf{x}_1} & \cdots & \frac{\partial \mathbf{z}_1(\mathbf{x})}{\partial \mathbf{x}_d} \\ \vdots & \ddots & \vdots \\ \frac{\partial \mathbf{z}_d(\mathbf{x})}{\partial \mathbf{x}_1} & \cdots & \frac{\partial \mathbf{z}_d(\mathbf{x})}{\partial \mathbf{x}_d} \end{pmatrix}. \tag{8.3}$$

The Jacobian is associated with the local expansion or shrinkage of volume in the transformed space (see Figure 8.2). When a map $\mathbf{z}(\mathbf{x})$ is locally contractive, the absolute value of the Jacobian determinant is smaller than 1, while conversely, if the map is locally expansive, it is larger than 1.

Example: Linear Transformation

To build intuition, consider a standard normal distribution $p_Z(z) = G(z; 0, 1)$ to which we apply a linear transformation $x = az + b$. This transformation is invertible, with the inverse given by $z = (x - b)/a$.

We can derive the explicit form of the resulting distribution by considering the change of variables formula. Being a single-variable transformation, the Jacobian is given as the derivative of the transformation; that is, $\mathbf{J}_\mathbf{z}(\mathbf{x}) = \frac{\partial z}{\partial x} = \frac{1}{a}$. Inserting this into the change of variables formula, we get

$$p_X(x) = G\left(\frac{x-b}{a}; 0, 1\right)\frac{1}{|a|} = G(x; b, a). \tag{8.4}$$

This is again a normal distribution with mean b and variance a^2.

This illustrates the role of the Jacobian determinant in the change of variables

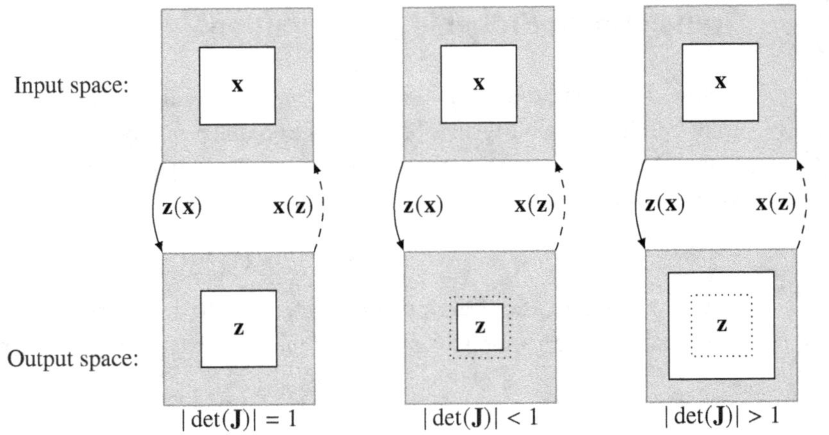

(a) Volume-preserving (b) Volume-shrinking (contraction) (c) Volume-enlarging

Figure 8.2 Invertible transformations between input space **x** and output space **z** in normalizin flows: (a) Volume-preserving transformation where the Jacobian determinant equals 1. (b) Volume-shrinking transformation (contraction) where the Jacobian determinant is less than 1. (c) Volume-enlarging transformation where the Jacobian determinant is greater than 1

formula: it renormalizes the distribution to ensure that the total probability mass i conserved. Depending on the value of a, the variance of the distribution will eithe shrink or expand and thus affect the volume of the distribution. If $|a| > 1$, th is a contractive map with $|\det(\mathbf{J})| < 1$. Otherwise, this map expands the volum The parameter b, on the other hand, only shifts the mean of the distribution an therefore does not change the volume, as exemplified by not occurring in the Jacobia determinant.

8.2.1 Jacobian in Latent Variable Models

We can relate this back to latent variable models and the ELBO by asking what th analogous expression is for the Jacobian in the stochastic setting.

For this purpose, consider the general definition of a latent variable model as w introduced it in Chapter 4:

$$p_X(\mathbf{x}) = \sum_{\mathbf{z}} p_{X|Z}(\mathbf{x}|\mathbf{z})\, p_Z(\mathbf{z}) \qquad (8.5)$$

which, as we saw in the derivation of the ELBO, we can rewrite as

$$p_X(\mathbf{x}) = \sum_{\mathbf{z}} q_{Z|X}(\mathbf{z}|\mathbf{x})\, \frac{p_{X|Z}(\mathbf{x}|\mathbf{z}) p_Z(\mathbf{z})}{q_{Z|X}(\mathbf{z}|\mathbf{x})}, \qquad (8.6)$$

by introducing the variational distribution $q_{Z|X}(\mathbf{z}|\mathbf{x})$. With $z(\mathbf{x})$ being a determinist transformation, we can write the variational distribution $q_{Z|X}(\mathbf{z}|\mathbf{x})$ as a delta functic

$q_{Z|X}(\mathbf{z}|\mathbf{x}) = \delta(\mathbf{z} - \mathbf{z}(\mathbf{x}))$. Plugging this into the expression above, we get:

$$p_X(\mathbf{x}) = \sum_{\mathbf{z}} \delta(\mathbf{z} - \mathbf{z}(\mathbf{x})) \frac{p_{X|Z}(\mathbf{x}|\mathbf{z}) p_Z(\mathbf{z})}{q_{Z|X}(\mathbf{z}|\mathbf{x})}$$
$$= p_Z(\mathbf{z}(\mathbf{x})) \frac{p_{X|Z}(\mathbf{x}|\mathbf{z}(\mathbf{x}))}{q_{Z|X}(\mathbf{z}(\mathbf{x})|\mathbf{x})}. \tag{8.7}$$

Comparing this to the change of variables formula in (8.2), we see that the Jacobian term is given by

$$|\det(\mathbf{J}_{\mathbf{z}}(\mathbf{x}))| = \frac{p_{X|Z}(\mathbf{x}|\mathbf{z}(\mathbf{x}))}{q_{Z|X}(\mathbf{z}(\mathbf{x})|\mathbf{x})}. \tag{8.8}$$

8.3 Normalizing Flows

Having developed the necessary background to transform probability distributions for invertible transformations, we can now use it to build a generative model. For this purpose, let us first consider the case of a single transformation.

We now build a hierarchical model from many layers of these transformations (as illustrated in Figure 8.3), called a *normalizing flow* (Rezende and Mohamed, 2015). Unlike VAEs, normalizing flows use deterministic, bijective transformations (as shown in Figure 8.5(b)). Defining $\mathbf{z}_2 = \mathbf{z}_2(\mathbf{z}_1) = \mathbf{z}_2(\mathbf{z}_1(\mathbf{x}))$, we have

$$\log p_{Z_1}(\mathbf{z}_1) = \log p_{Z_2}(\mathbf{z}_2(\mathbf{z}_1)) + \log \left| \det \left(\frac{\partial \mathbf{z}_2(\mathbf{z}_1)}{\partial \mathbf{z}_1} \right) \right|. \tag{8.9}$$

Therefore, we can write:

$$\log p_X(\mathbf{x}) = \log p_{Z_1}(\mathbf{z}_1(\mathbf{x})) + \log \left| \det \left(\frac{\partial \mathbf{z}_1(\mathbf{x})}{\partial \mathbf{x}} \right) \right|,$$
$$= \log p_{Z_2}(\mathbf{z}_2(\mathbf{z}_1(\mathbf{x}))) + \log \left| \det \left(\frac{\partial \mathbf{z}_2(\mathbf{z}_1(\mathbf{x}))}{\partial \mathbf{z}_1} \right) \right| + \log \left| \det \left(\frac{\partial \mathbf{z}_1(\mathbf{x})}{\partial \mathbf{x}} \right) \right|. \tag{8.10}$$

If we generalize this to many layers of transformations, we get

$$\log p_X(\mathbf{x}) = \log p_{Z_{t_f}} \left(\mathbf{z}_{t_f} \circ \mathbf{z}_{t_f - 1} \circ \cdots \circ \mathbf{z}_1(\mathbf{x}) \right)$$
$$+ \sum_{t=1}^{t_f} \log \left| \det \left(\frac{\partial \mathbf{z}_t(\mathbf{z}_{t-1})}{\partial \mathbf{z}_{t-1}} \right) \right|_{\mathbf{z}_{t-1} = \mathbf{z}_{t-1} \circ \cdots \circ \mathbf{z}_1(\mathbf{x})}. \tag{8.11}$$

To make this a trainable generative model, we parameterize the transformations, choose a simple distribution $p_{Z_{t_f}}$ (e.g., standard normal), and maximize the log-likelihood over a dataset:

$$\sum_n \log p_X(\mathbf{x}_n) = \sum_n \Bigg[\log p_{Z_{t_f}} \left(\mathbf{z}_{t_f}^{\theta_{t_f}} \circ \mathbf{z}_{t_f-1}^{\theta_{t_f-1}} \circ \cdots \circ \mathbf{z}_1^{\theta_1}(\mathbf{x}_n) \right) + \sum_{t=1}^{t_f} \log \left| \det \left(\frac{\partial \mathbf{z}_t^{\theta_t}(\mathbf{z}_{t-1})}{\partial \mathbf{z}_{t-1}} \right) \right|_{\mathbf{z}_{t-1} = \mathbf{z}_{t-1}^{\theta_{t-1}} \circ \cdots \circ \mathbf{z}_1^{\theta_1}(\mathbf{x}_n)} \Bigg]. \quad (8.12$$

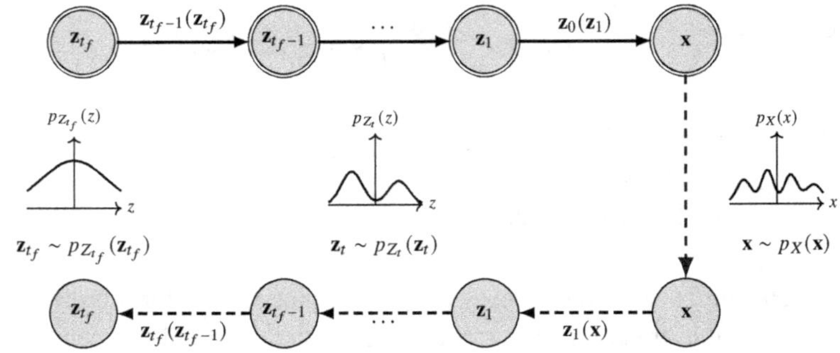

Figure 8.3 Normalizing flow composed of multiple invertible layers. The top row (solid arrows shows the forward transformation from a simple Gaussian distribution $p_{Z_{t_f}}(\mathbf{z}_{t_f})$ to a complex multimodal distribution $p_X(\mathbf{x})$ through a series of invertible transformations. The bottom row (dashed arrows) shows the reverse transformation from the observed data distribution $\mathbf{x}$ back t the simple distribution $\mathbf{z}_{t_f}$. The plots show the evolution of the probability density in the flow from the initial simple distribution gradually towards more complex ones.

8.4 Training

To make this a trainable generative model, we parameterize the transformations, choos a simple distribution $p_{Z_{t_f}}$ (e.g., standard normal), and maximize the log-likelihood ove a dataset. For convenience, we denote the parameterized transformations as $\mathbf{z}_t^{\theta_t}(\mathbf{z}_{t-1}$ where $\boldsymbol{\theta}_t$ are the parameters for the tth transformation. We also define the compose transformation as $\mathbf{z}(\mathbf{x};\boldsymbol{\theta}) = \mathbf{z}_{t_f}^{\theta_{t_f}} \circ \mathbf{z}_{t_f-1}^{\theta_{t_f-1}} \circ \cdots \circ \mathbf{z}_1^{\theta_1}(\mathbf{x})$, where $\boldsymbol{\theta} = \{\boldsymbol{\theta}_1, .., \boldsymbol{\theta}_{t_f}\}$.

The normalizing flow can be trained in two ways: (1) to approximate the distributio of a given dataset; (2) to approximate a target density such as a Boltzmann distributio $\pi_X(\mathbf{x}) = e^{-\mathcal{H}(\mathbf{x})}/Z$, where $\mathcal{H}(\mathbf{x})$ is a Hamiltonian and Z is the partition functio (Boltzmann generators are commonly used to sample from Boltzmann distributions o physical or molecular systems).

When samples $\{\mathbf{x}_s\}_{s=1}^S$ from the target distribution $\pi(\mathbf{x})$ are available (e.g., fro MCMC, molecular dynamics, or for generative modeling where a dataset is available we can train the NF by minimizing the forward KL divergence:

$$D_{\mathrm{KL}}[\pi_X \| p_X] = \mathbb{E}_\pi \left[\log \pi(\mathbf{x}) - \log p_X(\mathbf{x})\right] \tag{8.13}$$

$$\approx -\frac{1}{S}\sum_{s=1}^{S} \log p_X(\mathbf{x}_s) + \text{const}, \tag{8.14}$$

where the constant term includes $\mathbb{E}_\pi [\log \pi(\mathbf{x})]$, which is independent of the parameters $\boldsymbol{\theta}$. This mode is particularly useful when we have direct access to samples from the target distribution and want to learn a model that can generate similar samples.

This is equivalent to maximizing the log-likelihood:

$$\mathcal{L}(\boldsymbol{\theta}) = \frac{1}{S}\sum_{s=1}^{S} \log p_X(\mathbf{x}_s) \tag{8.15}$$

$$= \frac{1}{S}\sum_{s=1}^{S}\left[\log p_{Z_{t_f}}(\mathbf{z}(\mathbf{x}_s;\boldsymbol{\theta})) + \sum_{t=1}^{t_f} \log \left|\det\left(\frac{\partial \mathbf{z}_t^{\theta_t}(\mathbf{z}_{t-1})}{\partial \mathbf{z}_{t-1}}\right)\right|_{\mathbf{z}_{t-1}=\mathbf{z}_{t-1}^{\theta_{t-1}}\circ\cdots\circ\mathbf{z}_1^{\theta_1}(\mathbf{x}_s)}\right], \tag{8.16}$$

where $\mathbf{z}_{t-1}(\mathbf{x}_s)$ denotes the output of the $(t-1)$th transformation evaluated at $\mathbf{x}_s$.

The gradient of the log-likelihood with respect to the parameters can be computed as:

$$\nabla_\theta \mathcal{L}(\boldsymbol{\theta}) = \frac{1}{S}\sum_{s=1}^{S}\left[\nabla_\theta \log p_{Z_{t_f}}(\mathbf{z}(\mathbf{x}_s;\boldsymbol{\theta})) + \sum_{t=1}^{t_f} \nabla_\theta \log \left|\det(\mathbf{J}_t(\mathbf{x}_s;\boldsymbol{\theta}))\right|\right], \tag{8.17}$$

where $\mathbf{J}_t(\mathbf{x}_s;\boldsymbol{\theta})$ is the Jacobian of the tth transformation evaluated at $\mathbf{x}_s$. This gradient can be used in stochastic gradient descent algorithms to optimize the parameters $\boldsymbol{\theta}$. Thanks to the bijectivity of the transformations, after training, we can generate new samples from p_X by sampling from $p_{Z_{t_f}}$ and applying the inverse of the composed transformation.

To train the NF as a Boltzmann generator (Noé et al., 2019) for sampling from a target distribution $\pi_X(\mathbf{x})$, we minimize the reverse KL divergence between $p_X(\mathbf{x})$ and $\pi_X(\mathbf{x})$:

$$D_{\mathrm{KL}}[p_X \| \pi_X] = \mathbb{E}_{p_X}[\log p_X(\mathbf{x}) - \log \pi_X(\mathbf{x})] \tag{8.18}$$

$$= \mathbb{E}_{p_X}[\log p_X(\mathbf{x}) + \mathcal{H}(\mathbf{x})] + \log Z \tag{8.19}$$

$$= -\mathcal{S}[p_X] + \mathbb{E}_{p_X}[\mathcal{H}(\mathbf{x})] + \log Z, \tag{8.20}$$

where $\mathcal{S}[p_X] = -\mathbb{E}_{p_X}[\log p_X(\mathbf{x})]$ is the entropy of p_X. This approach is particularly useful when we have an analytical form of the target distribution (up to a normalization constant) but do not have easy access to samples from it. The $\log Z$ term is a constant and we see again the optimization objective is in the free energy form.

This objective can also be expressed in terms of the latent variables $\mathbf{z}_{t_f}$. From the change of variables formula, we have:

$$D_{\mathrm{KL}}[p_X \| \pi_X] = -\mathbb{E}_{p_{Z_{t_f}}}\left[\log\left|\det(\mathbf{J}(\mathbf{z}_{t_f};\boldsymbol{\theta}))\right|\right] + \mathbb{E}_{p_{Z_{t_f}}}\left[\mathcal{H}\left(\mathbf{x}(\mathbf{z}_{t_f};\boldsymbol{\theta})\right)\right] + \log Z - \mathcal{S}[p_{Z_{t_f}}], \quad (8.21$$

where $\mathbf{J}(\mathbf{z}_{t_f};\boldsymbol{\theta})$ is the Jacobian of the composed transformation at $\mathbf{z}_{t_f}$, and $\mathbf{x}(\mathbf{z}_{t_f};\boldsymbol{\theta})$ i the inverse of the composed transformation.

The gradients with respect to the parameters of the NF can be computed using th change of variables formula and the Jacobian of the NF:

$$\nabla_{\boldsymbol{\theta}} D_{\mathrm{KL}}[p_X \| \pi_X] = -\mathbb{E}_{p_{Z_{t_f}}}\left[\nabla_{\boldsymbol{\theta}}\log\left|\det(\mathbf{J}(\mathbf{z}_{t_f};\boldsymbol{\theta}))\right|\right] + \mathbb{E}_{p_{Z_{t_f}}}\left[\nabla_{\boldsymbol{\theta}}\mathcal{H}\left(\mathbf{x}(\mathbf{z}_{t_f};\boldsymbol{\theta})\right)\right]. \quad (8.22$$

Note that the $\log Z$ term is constant with respect to the parameters and thus disappear in the gradient computation. To compute these gradients, we can use the followin steps:

$$\nabla_{\boldsymbol{\theta}} \log|\det(\mathbf{J}(\mathbf{z}_{t_f};\boldsymbol{\theta}))| = \mathrm{tr}\left(\mathbf{J}(\mathbf{z}_{t_f};\boldsymbol{\theta})^{-1}\nabla_{\boldsymbol{\theta}}\mathbf{J}(\mathbf{z}_{t_f};\boldsymbol{\theta})\right), \quad (8.23$$

$$\nabla_{\boldsymbol{\theta}}\mathcal{H}(\mathbf{x}(\mathbf{z}_{t_f};\boldsymbol{\theta})) = \nabla_{\mathbf{x}}\mathcal{H}(\mathbf{x}(\mathbf{z}_{t_f};\boldsymbol{\theta}))\cdot\nabla_{\boldsymbol{\theta}}\mathbf{x}(\mathbf{z}_{t_f};\boldsymbol{\theta}), \quad (8.24$$

where $\mathrm{tr}(\cdot)$ denotes the trace of a matrix. The term $\nabla_{\boldsymbol{\theta}}\mathbf{J}(\mathbf{z}_{t_f};\boldsymbol{\theta})$ can be computed usin automatic differentiation techniques (i.e., backpropagation; see Section 2.6).

One can also operate in a hybrid mode, where we use MCMC to generate sample from the target density and train the NF on these samples to speed up the MCM sampler. This is sometimes useful when the target distribution is multimodal or has complex structure.

Once trained, the NF as a Boltzmann generator can be used for various tasks, suc as sampling from the target distribution faster using an MCMC operating on the late space $\mathbf{z}_{t_f}$, or estimating expectations or partition functions using importance samplin These have found applications in sampling configurations from biochemical molecul configurations to systems as complex as lattice field theory and gauge theories (Alberg et al., 2021; Abbott et al., 2023). We will explain these in Chapter 11 and Chapter 1

8.5 Invertible Transformations

Having an explicit expression for the log-likelihood is convenient, but we still nee to choose invertible transformations. The invertibility requirement considerably co strains the choice of these maps. Below, we give a few examples of bijective transfo mations. Some of them are illustrated in Figure 8.4.

We begin by splitting the set of variables $\mathbf{x}$ and $\mathbf{z}$ into two (random) subsets, with different split for each layer:

$$\mathbf{x} = \{\mathbf{x}_A, \mathbf{x}_B\}, \quad \mathbf{z} = \{\mathbf{z}_A, \mathbf{z}_B\}. \quad (8.2$$

The *coupling flow transformation* (see Figure 8.4) and its inverse are then given as (Dinh et al., 2017)

$$\mathbf{z}_A = \mathbf{x}_A, \quad \mathbf{z}_B = \exp\left(\mathbf{f}(\mathbf{x}_A)\right) \odot \mathbf{x}_B + \mathbf{g}(\mathbf{x}_A), \tag{8.26}$$

$$\mathbf{x}_A = \mathbf{z}_A, \quad \mathbf{x}_B = \exp\left(-\mathbf{f}(\mathbf{z}_A)\right) \odot \left(\mathbf{z}_B - \mathbf{g}(\mathbf{z}_A)\right), \tag{8.27}$$

where $\odot$ denotes element-wise multiplication, and $\mathbf{f}$, $\mathbf{g}$ are functions (typically neural networks such as the convolutional neural networks in Dinh et al. (2017)) that output scaling and translation parameters based on $\mathbf{x}_A$. This transformation results in a triangular Jacobian that is easy to compute.

A variation on this theme is given by the *residual flow transformation* (Dinh et al., 2014; Gomez et al., 2017):

$$\mathbf{z}_A = \mathbf{x}_A + \mathbf{f}(\mathbf{x}_B), \quad \mathbf{z}_B = \mathbf{x}_B + \mathbf{g}(\mathbf{z}_A) = \mathbf{x}_B + \mathbf{g}(\mathbf{x}_A + \mathbf{f}(\mathbf{x}_B)), \tag{8.28}$$

$$\mathbf{x}_B = \mathbf{z}_B - \mathbf{g}(\mathbf{z}_A), \quad \mathbf{x}_A = \mathbf{z}_A - \mathbf{f}(\mathbf{x}_B) = \mathbf{z}_A - \mathbf{f}(\mathbf{z}_B - \mathbf{g}(\mathbf{z}_A)). \tag{8.29}$$

Finally, we mention the *autoregressive flow transformation* (and its inverse) (Papamakarios et al., 2017):

$$\mathbf{z}_1 = \mathbf{f}_1(\mathbf{x}_1), \tag{8.30}$$

$$\mathbf{z}_2 = \mathbf{f}_2(\mathbf{x}_2|\mathbf{z}_1), \tag{8.31}$$

$$\vdots$$

$$\mathbf{z}_{t_f} = \mathbf{f}_{t_f}(\mathbf{x}_{t_f}|\mathbf{z}_1, .., \mathbf{z}_{t_f-1}), \tag{8.32}$$

$$\mathbf{x}_1 = \mathbf{f}_1^{-1}(\mathbf{z}_1), \tag{8.33}$$

$$\mathbf{x}_2 = \mathbf{f}_2^{-1}(\mathbf{z}_2|\mathbf{x}_1) = \mathbf{f}_2^{-1}(\mathbf{z}_2|\mathbf{f}_1^{-1}(\mathbf{z}_1)), \tag{8.34}$$

$$\vdots$$

$$\mathbf{x}_{t_f} = \mathbf{f}_{t_f}^{-1}(\mathbf{z}_{t_f}|\mathbf{f}_1^{-1}(\mathbf{z}_1), \mathbf{f}_2^{-1}(\mathbf{z}_2|\mathbf{f}_1^{-1}(\mathbf{z}_1)), \ldots), \tag{8.35}$$

where the transformation of each variable depends only on the previous variables. Many more clever invertible transformations have been proposed in the literature, but we leave it to the reader to discover those.

8.6 Decompositions of ELBOs

The ELBO can be decomposed in three distinct ways:

$$\begin{aligned}
\log p_X(\mathbf{x}) &\geq \mathbb{E}_{q_{Z|X}}\left[\log p_{X|Z}(\mathbf{x}|\mathbf{z}) + \log p_Z(\mathbf{z})\right] + S[q_{Z|X}] \\
&= \mathbb{E}_{q_{Z|X}}\left[\log p_{X|Z}(\mathbf{x}|\mathbf{z})\right] - D_{\mathrm{KL}}[q_{Z|X} \| p_Z] \\
&= \mathbb{E}_{q_{Z|X}}\left[\log p_Z(\mathbf{z})\right] + \mathbb{E}_{q_{Z|X}}\left[\log \frac{p_{X|Z}(\mathbf{x}|\mathbf{z})}{q_{Z|X}(\mathbf{z}|\mathbf{x})}\right],
\end{aligned} \tag{8.36}$$

where the first line is the usual (negative) free energy decomposition. The second line is the "rate–distortion" decomposition, with the first term representing the distortion

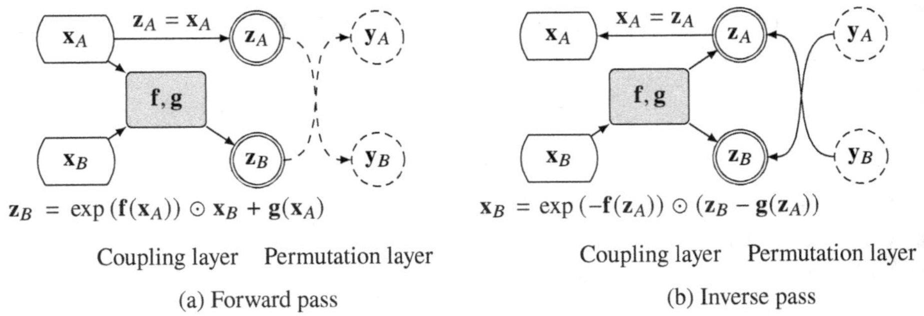

Figure 8.4 Coupling and permutation layers in normalizing flows. (a) Forward pass: The coupling layer applies $\mathbf{f}$ and $\mathbf{g}$ to transform $\mathbf{x}_B$ based on $\mathbf{x}_A$; the permutation layer swaps $\mathbf{z}_A$ an $\mathbf{z}_B$. (b) Inverse pass: The process is reversed using $\mathbf{f}$ and $\mathbf{g}$. This enables invertible transformations between $\mathbf{x}$ and $\mathbf{y}$ spaces with a tractable Jacobian.

(reconstruction error of $\mathbf{x}$) and the second term representing the "rate" or the numbe of bits needed to encode the latent code $\mathbf{z}$ relative to the prior p_Z (assumed known t both sender and receiver). The third line is the most natural one in the context of NFs with the first term being the probability of the transformed input under the prior an the second term representing the Jacobian "scaling factor".

8.7 Thermodynamic Interpretation

Normalizing flows smoothly and invertibly map a state $\mathbf{x}$ to a state $\mathbf{z}$, as shown i Figure 8.3. The only reason we need to use probabilities is that there is initial uncertaint over the value $\mathbf{x}$, which gets propagated to $\mathbf{z}$. In mathematical terms, this is called push-forward map of the probability density p_X, where the probability density of is transformed into the probability density of $\mathbf{z}$ under the invertible map $\mathbf{z}(\mathbf{x})$ (se Figure 8.5(b)). No extra noise (randomness, stochasticity) is added in the map itsel in contrast to stochastic maps of VAEs (Figure 8.5(a)).

The invertibility requirement makes the design of these architectures challengin Also, multiple modes in p_X are harder to model from the unimodal p_Z because th map is smooth, and you will find small bridges of probability connecting the mode in p_X. A solution to this was formulated using stochastic normalizing flows (W et al., 2020) and SurVAE flows (Nielsen et al., 2020), which combine the stochasti and dimension-changing maps typical in a VAE (Figure 8.5(a)) with the deterministi steps of an NF (Figure 8.5(b)). They will be covered in Chapter 20. The great advantag of deterministic NFs, relative to stochastic maps, is that you have access to the exa log-probability instead of a bound.

Because a normalizing flow is a deterministic invertible map where, by definitio no information is lost (we can run the equations backward in time to recover the precis history), the entropy increase is zero. This is similar to saying that at the microscop level, Hamilton's equations are deterministic and invertible, and so no entropy

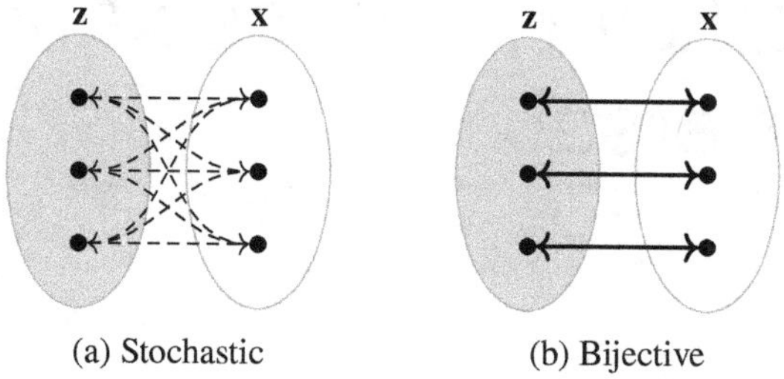

Figure 8.5 Transformations in generative models: (a) Stochastic: Variational autoencoders (VAEs) use probabilistic mappings (dashed arrows) to map between the patterned latent region **z** and the patterned observed region **x**. (b) Bijective: Normalizing flows employ one-to-one deterministic mappings (solid arrows).

generated. Entropy enters the picture when we start to integrate out degrees of freedom (when there are many such discarded degrees of freedom, we call it a "bath"). The analogous concept for NFs is when certain dimensions model the coarse-grained signal of the input, while other dimensions model the noise variables. The remaining dimensions that store the "noisy" bits are required to invert the transformation; however, for tasks such as classification, one might only depend on the coarse-grained concepts. It may even be beneficial in terms of generalization performance to discard noise dimensions. If we forget or delete these noise dimensions, we may interpret this as losing track of details and only keeping track of coarse-grained quantities. We may think of these noise dimensions as a kind of "heat bath". By throwing away (i.e., integrating out) the noise bits, we can no longer invert the transformation, and the transformations become effectively irreversible. We can now introduce an entropy to describe the resultant uncertainty in the system. This entropy counts the number of states of the total system that are consistent with a state in the lower-dimensional system. This is then similar to describing the signal dimensions with irreversible stochastic dynamics such as Brownian motion.

9 Markov Processes and Time Reversal

9.1 Introduction

In this chapter we introduce a key component of studying the nonequilibrium stochasti processes that feature so prominently in stochastic thermodynamics: Markov processe (MPs). A Markov process is a memoryless process where the next state only depend on the previous state but not on states further in the past. In the rest of the book w will need five different related MPs. There is the physical forward process and its tim reversal (nonphysical) "backward" process. The "adjoint" process is very important fc the Markov chain Monte Carlo methods studied in Chapter 11, but also when we deriv fluctuation theorems in Chapter 17. Finally we also add the time-reversed process an the dual process which are all related to fluctuation theorems.

In this chapter we will also dive a little deeper into time reversal symmetry and ho that can be used to relate these various processes.

9.2 Five Markov Kernels

In the following chapters of this book we will encounter a number of complex notation issues. We therefore spend this section on explaining them before we start using then The five kernels defined here will be necessary for understanding Chapters 10 and 1

Assume we have a joint density $\rho_{0:t_f}(\zeta_0, \ldots, \zeta_{t_f})$ for a path, or a marginal densit $\rho_t(\zeta_t)$ for a state at time t in phase space. For convenience we will write $\rho \equiv \rho_{0:}$ in the following. Furthermore, recall that phase space variables ζ consist of bo configuration variables ξ and momentum variables η.

We will consider Markov processes throughout this book. This is an approximatio because if the states that are integrated out are not reaching equilibrium much fast than the variables we consider, there will be memory effects in the sense that the ne state not only depends on the current state plus unpredictable noise, but also predictab depends on a longer history of states. The Markov assumption and the inclusion noise thus model the unpredictable nature of these microscopic degrees of freedo caused by the fast chaotic dynamics of the underlying deterministic processes.

To describe a Markov process mathematically, we use transition kernels to mo a density from one time step to the next. We indicate these with $F_t(\zeta_t|\zeta_{t-1})$. Th physical transition kernel depends on control parameters λ_t:

$$F_t(\zeta_t|\zeta_{t-1}) \equiv F(\zeta_t|\zeta_{t-1}, \lambda_t). \quad (9.$$

Using these transition kernels, the joint probability density $\rho = \rho_{0:t_f}$ for a complete path is given by the following Markov process:

$$\rho(\zeta_0, \zeta_1, \ldots, \zeta_{t_f}) = \rho_0(\zeta_0) \prod_{t=1}^{t_f} F_t(\zeta_t | \zeta_{t-1}), \tag{9.2}$$

where ρ_0 is an arbitrary initial distribution. Because the process is out of equilibrium, the marginal distributions ρ_t will depend on the entire history of control parameters up to that time:

$$\rho_t(\zeta_t) = \rho_t(\zeta_t | \lambda_0, \ldots, \lambda_t). \tag{9.3}$$

Next we want to define time-reversed densities. Even though at a microscopic level nature is time-reversal symmetric, crucially, this does not have to be the case when we describe the world in terms of probability densities over coarse-grained variables. Many key concepts in stochastic thermodynamics are connected to these irreversible processes. For instance, the amount of heat and entropy generated is directly related to the irreversibility of the dynamics. And even more fundamentally, the fact that we perceive time to progress forward and attribute cause and effect to processes that always happen in a certain order is related to the fact that the processes we experience are irreversible. As such, in general, the forward and backward transition kernels in Markov processes as in (9.2) do not have to be the same. For example, the backward kernel of a diffusion process should "antidiffuse" (or "de-noise") a probability distribution, that is, evolve a spread-out distribution into a concentrated one. The fact that this feels nonphysical, in the same sense as unscrambling an omelet into an egg feels nonphysical, is a signal that the evolution law is time-reversal-asymmetric.

Given the forward process in (9.2), we can reparameterize this same joint distribution as a backward process that starts at ρ_{t_f} and transitions backward using another transition kernel B:

$$\rho(\zeta_{0:t_f}) = \rho_{t_f}(\zeta_{t_f}) \prod_{t=1}^{t_f} B_t(\zeta_{t-1} | \zeta_t), \tag{9.4}$$

where $B_t(\zeta_{t-1}|\zeta_t)$ is the backward transition probability density. Note that nonphysical time-reversed processes (e.g., unscrambling an omelet into an egg) are probable under this backward process. We note that (9.4) is simply rewriting (9.2) transitioning in the time-reversed direction.

Forward and backward processes are related through the following "balancing equation":

$$F_t(\zeta_t|\zeta_{t-1})\rho_{t-1}(\zeta_{t-1}) = B_t(\zeta_{t-1}|\zeta_t)\rho_t(\zeta_t) \tag{9.5}$$

$$\Rightarrow \; B_t(\zeta_{t-1}|\zeta_t) = \frac{F_t(\zeta_t|\zeta_{t-1})\rho_{t-1}(\zeta_{t-1})}{\rho_t(\zeta_t)}, \tag{9.6}$$

$$\rho_t(\zeta_t) = \int \mathrm{d}\zeta_{t-1}\, F_t(\zeta_t|\zeta_{t-1})\rho_{t-1}(\zeta_{t-1}), \tag{9.7}$$

$$\rho_{t-1}(\zeta_{t-1}) = \int \mathrm{d}\zeta_t\, B_t(\zeta_{t-1}|\zeta_t)\rho_t(\zeta_t). \tag{9.8}$$

This expresses the fact that B inverts a probability flow that is out of equilibrium (ρ_{t-1} and ρ_t are out-of-equilibrium marginal distributions). The definition of B depends on the (ratio of the) densities ρ_t and ρ_{t-1} (and therefore on $\lambda_0, \dots, \lambda_t$ which does not represent a physical evolution law. (The reason we index B_t with rather than $t-1$ is due to the fact that it depends on all parameters up to and including λ_t.

Besides the nonphysical time-reversed process governed by B, there are a number of other "reverse" Markov chains that we will encounter in the following chapters The first one is a reverse kernel called the adjoint kernel. Given that every irreducible (ergodic, or mixing) Markov chain has a unique stationary distribution, we can alway write

$$\pi_t(\zeta_{t-1}) F_t(\zeta_t|\zeta_{t-1}) = \pi_t(\zeta_t) A_t(\zeta_{t-1}|\zeta_t), \tag{9.9}$$

where π_t represents the stationary (or steady-state) distribution of the transition kernel F_t and therefore depends (only) on λ_t. In fact, the generalized balance equation (GB in (9.9) always holds if π_t is the stationary distribution of F_t and is equivalent to th statement that π_t is invariant under the application of F_t:

$$\int \mathrm{d}\zeta_{t-1}\, \pi_t(\zeta_{t-1}) F_t(\zeta_t|\zeta_{t-1}) = \pi_t(\zeta_t). \tag{9.10}$$

One should therefore view the GB equation,. (9.9), as a definition of A_t:

$$A_t(\zeta_{t-1}|\zeta_t) \equiv \frac{\pi_t(\zeta_{t-1}) F_t(\zeta_t|\zeta_{t-1})}{\pi_t(\zeta_t)}, \tag{9.11}$$

where the subscript t in A_t again indicates that this kernel depends only on λ_t. One ca verify that A_t is non-negative and normalized if π_t is indeed the invariant (stationary distribution of F_t. It can be readily verified that this adjoint kernel also preserves the stationary distribution π_t:

$$\int \mathrm{d}\zeta_t\, A_t(\zeta_{t-1}|\zeta_t)\pi_t(\zeta_t) = \pi_t(\zeta_{t-1}) \int \mathrm{d}\zeta_t\, F_t(\zeta_t|\zeta_{t-1}) = \pi_t(\zeta_{t-1}), \tag{9.12}$$

where we used the normalization of the forward kernel.

Unlike B, which "antidiffuses" (or "denoises" in ML lingo), the kernel A is diffusion process. It differs from F in that it reverses the direction of any remaining probability flow at stationarity.

To illustrate this distinction, we consider the following model (adapted from Spinne and Ford, 2012b; Lee et al., 2013). Consider a circle of L states and two velocitie giving a full state space of dimension $2L$:

$$(\xi, \eta) = \{(0,-1), (0,+1), \dots, (L-1,-1), (L-1,+1)\}. \tag{9.13}$$

We assume the following values for the forward transition kernel, which models mo mentum flips and momentum-dependent spatial hops:

$$F(\xi_i, +1|\xi_i, -1) = a, \quad \text{(momentum flip from } -1 \text{ to } +1\text{)}, \tag{9.14}$$
$$F(\xi_i, -1|\xi_i, +1) = b, \quad \text{(momentum flip from } +1 \text{ to } -1\text{)}, \tag{9.15}$$
$$F(\xi_{i+1}, +1|\xi_i, +1) = c, \quad \text{(hop right for momentum } +1\text{)}, \tag{9.16}$$
$$F(\xi_{i-1}, -1|\xi_i, -1) = d, \quad \text{(hop left for momentum } -1\text{)}, \tag{9.17}$$
$$F(\xi_i, +1|\xi_i, +1) = 1 - b - c, \quad \text{(self-loop)}, \tag{9.18}$$
$$F(\xi_i, -1|\xi_i, -1) = 1 - a - d, \quad \text{(self-loop)}, \tag{9.19}$$

with all other transitions equal to 0. This process is illustrated in Figure 9.1(a).

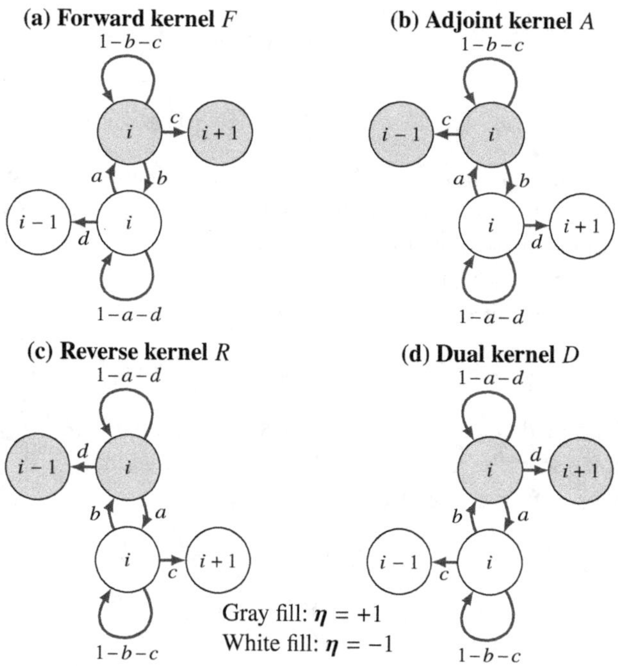

Figure 9.1 Comparison of the four Markov kernels for the circular state space model. States are arranged with $\eta = +1$ in the upper row (gray fill) and $\eta = -1$ in the lower row (white fill). (a) Forward kernel F: the physical evolution with momentum-consistent spatial transitions. (b) Adjoint kernel A: reverses probability flow direction while preserving stationary distribution π_t. (c) Reverse kernel R: obtained by momentum reversal in F, swapping $a \leftrightarrow b$ and $c \leftrightarrow d$. (d) Dual kernel D: combines momentum reversal with adjoint transformation, resulting in forward spatial flow with swapped transition rates.

By translational symmetry the stationary distribution must be uniform over the spatial index i. Let $\pi_+ = \sum_i \pi(\xi_i, +1)$ and $\pi_- = \sum_i \pi(\xi_i, -1)$ denote the total stationary weights of the two velocity sectors; at stationarity the sign-flip fluxes must balance:

$\pi_+ b = \pi_- a$. Together with $\pi_+ + \pi_- = 1$, this yields $\pi_+ = \frac{a}{a+b}$ and $\pi_- = \frac{b}{a+b}$. Hence

$$\pi(\xi_i, +1) = \frac{1}{L}\frac{a}{a+b}, \tag{9.20}$$

$$\pi(\xi_i, -1) = \frac{1}{L}\frac{b}{a+b}. \tag{9.21}$$

We also observe that the distribution is not symmetric under time reversal because i is asymmetric under the transformation $\eta = +1 \leftrightarrow \eta = -1$.

Now let us study what the adjoint kernel A_t looks like in this example. Using th definition of A_t in (9.11) we find

$$A(\xi_i, +1|\xi_i, -1) = a, \tag{9.22}$$

$$A(\xi_i, -1|\xi_i, +1) = b, \tag{9.23}$$

$$A(\xi_{i-1}, +1|\xi_i, +1) = c, \tag{9.24}$$

$$A(\xi_{i+1}, -1|\xi_i, -1) = d, \tag{9.25}$$

$$A(\xi_i, +1|\xi_i, +1) = 1 - b - c, \tag{9.26}$$

$$A(\xi_i, -1|\xi_i, -1) = 1 - a - d. \tag{9.27}$$

As shown in Figure 9.1(b), we find that this kernel only reverses the direction of th probability flow for equal-momentum moves: the spatial movement now flows opposit to the velocity direction! One can verify from (9.10) that, like F_t, the kernel A_t als leaves π_t invariant.

Next we introduce the reverse kernel R_t, defined as

$$R_t(\zeta_{t-1}|\zeta_t) \equiv F_t(\hat{\zeta}_{t-1}|\hat{\zeta}_t). \tag{9.28}$$

The hatted quantities are defined as $\hat{\zeta}_t = (\hat{\xi}_t, \hat{\eta}_t) = (\xi_t, -\eta_t)$; that is, they reverse th direction of the momenta (and any other odd variables). In our example, the kernel R looks as follows (see Figure 9.1(c)):

$$R(\xi_i, +1|\xi_i, -1) = b, \tag{9.29}$$

$$R(\xi_i, -1|\xi_i, +1) = a, \tag{9.30}$$

$$R(\xi_{i-1}, +1|\xi_i, +1) = d, \tag{9.31}$$

$$R(\xi_{i+1}, -1|\xi_i, -1) = c, \tag{9.32}$$

$$R(\xi_i, +1|\xi_i, +1) = 1 - a - d, \tag{9.33}$$

$$R(\xi_i, -1|\xi_i, -1) = 1 - b - c. \tag{9.34}$$

Importantly, the kernel R_t does not leave π_t invariant. Instead, its invariant distributio is given by

$$\pi_R(\xi_i, +1) = \frac{b}{L(a+b)}, \tag{9.35}$$

$$\pi_R(\xi_i, -1) = \frac{a}{L(a+b)}, \tag{9.36}$$

with the roles of a and b reversed.

If we want R_t to also keep the original π_t invariant, we must make it consistent with A_t. From the definition of A_t given by (9.11), this constitutes a constraint on F_t:

$$\begin{aligned} R_t(\zeta_{t-1}|\zeta_t)\pi_t(\zeta_t) &= A_t(\zeta_{t-1}|\zeta_t)\pi_t(\zeta_t) \\ &= F_t(\hat{\zeta}_{t-1}|\hat{\zeta}_t)\pi_t(\zeta_t) \\ &= F_t(\zeta_t|\zeta_{t-1})\pi_t(\zeta_{t-1}). \end{aligned} \tag{9.37}$$

Equating the corresponding terms in the example across A_t and R_t yields $a = b$ and $c = d$.

This constraint is traditionally called detailed balance (DB) in physics, which means that the probability flow between any two ξ states is equal and there are therefore no net probability flows in equilibrium. Note that we do not require that the probability flows between any two states in phase space are equal as this would be impossible due to the deterministic transitions once the velocities are fixed. Instead we want the flows with positive and negative velocities to cancel each other.

In more recent papers (e.g., Spinney and Ford, 2012b; Lee et al., 2013), researchers have argued that the DB condition above can actually be teased apart into two statements: (1) TRS of the stationary distribution under $\zeta \to \hat{\zeta}$ ($a = b$ in the example); and (2) DB given by the condition

$$F_t(\hat{\zeta}_{t-1}|\hat{\zeta}_t)\pi_t(\hat{\zeta}_t) = F_t(\zeta_t|\zeta_{t-1})\pi_t(\zeta_{t-1}), \tag{9.38}$$

which in our example would only require $ac = bd$. We note that this version of DB, by construction – from its definition in (9.38), leads to a balancing of probability flows and therefore to a vanishing net probability flux. However, it does not result in R_t having the same invariant distribution as F_t. Conversely, time-reversal symmetry (TRS) of π indeed leads to R_t having the same stationary distribution as F_t, but not to a balancing of probability flows. We now show that TRS leads to the correct invariant distribution:

$$\begin{aligned} \int \mathrm{d}\zeta_t \, R_t(\zeta_{t-1}|\zeta_t)\pi_t(\zeta_t) &= \int \mathrm{d}\zeta_t \, F_t(\hat{\zeta}_{t-1}|\hat{\zeta}_t)\pi_t(\zeta_t) \\ &= \int \mathrm{d}\hat{\zeta}_t \, F_t(\hat{\zeta}_{t-1}|\hat{\zeta}_t)\pi_t(\hat{\zeta}_t) \\ &\qquad \text{(using TRS of } \pi_t \text{ and Jacobian} = 1 \text{ for } \zeta \to \hat{\zeta}) \\ &= \pi_t(\hat{\zeta}_{t-1}) = \pi_t(\zeta_{t-1}) \quad \text{(using TRS of } \pi_t \text{ again).} \end{aligned} \tag{9.39}$$

9.2.1 Dual Kernel

Finally, we can now define the reverse version of A_t, which we call the dual kernel D_t, defined by flipping the momenta in A_t:

$$\begin{aligned} D_t(\zeta_t|\zeta_{t-1}) &\equiv A_t(\hat{\zeta}_t|\hat{\zeta}_{t-1}) \\ &= \frac{F_t(\hat{\zeta}_{t-1}|\hat{\zeta}_t)\pi_t(\hat{\zeta}_t)}{\pi_t(\hat{\zeta}_{t-1})} \\ &= \frac{R_t(\zeta_{t-1}|\zeta_t)\pi_t(\hat{\zeta}_t)}{\pi_t(\hat{\zeta}_{t-1})}. \end{aligned} \tag{9.40}$$

In terms of our example this gives the transitions shown in Figure 9.1(d):

$$D(\xi_i, +1|\xi_i, -1) = b, \quad (9.41$$

$$D(\xi_i, -1|\xi_i, +1) = a, \quad (9.42$$

$$D(\xi_{i+1}, +1|\xi_i, +1) = d, \quad (9.43$$

$$D(\xi_{i-1}, -1|\xi_i, -1) = c, \quad (9.44$$

$$D(\xi_i, +1|\xi_i, +1) = 1 - a - d, \quad (9.45$$

$$D(\xi_i, -1|\xi_i, -1) = 1 - b - c. \quad (9.46$$

One can again show that the kernels D_t and R_t preserve $\hat{\pi}(\zeta) = \pi(\hat{\zeta})$, and nc necessarily π_t. Under the assumption that the stationary distribution is time-reversa symmetric (i.e., $\pi_t = \hat{\pi}_t$), however, all four kernels F, A, R, D keep π_t invariant.

In summary, we have defined a total of five kernels: B, F, A, R, D. The relationship between these kernels are:

(i) F_t: Forward kernel (physical evolution), preserves π_t.
(ii) B_t: Backward kernel (antidiffusion, (9.6)), depends on (ρ_{t-1}, ρ_t).
(iii) A_t: Adjoint kernel (probability current reversal, (9.11)), preserves π_t.
(iv) R_t: Reverse kernel (momentum reversal, $R_t(\zeta_{t-1}|\zeta_t) = F_t(\hat{\zeta}_{t-1}|\hat{\zeta}_t)$), preserve $\hat{\pi}_t(\zeta) = \pi_t(\hat{\zeta})$.
(v) D_t: Dual kernel (adjoint + momentum reversal, (9.40)), preserves $\hat{\pi}_t$.

The kernel B is the only one in this list that denoises rather than diffuses. The other fou come in pairs: $F \leftrightarrow A$ which leave π invariant and $R \leftrightarrow D$ which leave $\hat{\pi}$ invarian We note that $B \rightarrow A$ when $\rho \rightarrow \pi$; that is, at equilibrium.

To avoid ambiguity later in the book, we will consistently refer to F_t as the *forwar* process and to B_t as the *backward* (variational or inference) process. Whenever we dis cuss the physical time-reversal of a dynamics – including momentum flips and reverse control protocols – we will call it the *time-reversed* process and denote its kernel b R_t. This terminology will be used throughout the book, including our discussions c diffusion models, stochastic thermodynamics, and Monte Carlo methods.

These kernels will come in handy when we study fluctuation theorems in Chapters 1 and 17.

9.3 Time Reversal

Time-reversal symmetry plays a fundamental role in thermodynamics. As we all kno from daily life, our experience of the world is not time-reversal symmetric (the sponta neous formation of an egg from an omelet is a whole lot less likely than the generatio of an omelet from an egg!). Our sense of time as unidirectional comes from this fa of life. How microscopic time-reversal-invariant theories can result in irreversible pro cesses and the notion of a direction of time is a very deep question. Boltzmann himse battled Loschmidt and Zermelo over this question (Boltzmann, 1877, 1896; Brus

1976; Lebowitz, 1993). This became known as the Loschmidt paradox (Loschmidt, 1876).

Therefore TRS is broken at macroscopic scales. Away from equilibrium, reversing the direction of time turns diffusion into denoising and flips the sign of momenta (or velocities). But even a stationary distribution transforms under time reversal as there is net probability flow (or flux) in steady state which will reverse its direction. Only at true equilibrium, with no remaining fluxes at steady state, is the distribution truly time-reversal symmetric.

9.3.1 Time Reversal for Hamiltonian Systems

We will now first look at TRS for Hamiltonian dynamics at the microscopic level. A physical law is said to be time-reversal symmetric if the reversed sequence of states is still a solution to the evolution equations. This property holds for a wide range of physical theories at the microscopic level, including classical and quantum mechanics[1].

For Hamiltonian systems, the Hamiltonian itself remains unchanged under time reversal as does the evolution equation (Hamiltonian dynamics), thus representing the same law of physics in both forward and backward time directions. However, the positions and momenta need to be treated differently. While the positions remain the same under time reversal, the momenta must flip sign; that is, $\eta_\tau \to -\eta_\tau$. This is because position is an even variable under time reversal (even parity), while momentum is an odd variable (odd parity). This result is intuitive, as moving backward in time is like moving in the opposite direction of the velocity vector if we do not flip the sign. However, if we flip the sign of the velocity or momentum vector, the motion becomes physical again, progressing in the direction of the velocity vector. We will also assume time-translation invariance, which means that we can flip the direction of time relative to any fixed time τ.

In the following we will use a tilde to indicate time reversal: $\tilde{\tau} = \tau_f - \tau$ for time reversal relative to a final time τ_f. Since this is an involution, it follows that quantities can only transform in two ways under time reversal: either they stay invariant (*even*), for example $\tilde{\xi}(\tau) = \xi(\tilde{\tau})$, or they flip sign (*odd*): $\tilde{\eta}(\tau) = -\eta(\tilde{\tau})$. As before, we can write this in a unified way as $\tilde{\zeta}(\tau) = \hat{\zeta}(\tilde{\tau})$, where the hat indicates that we should flip the sign of any odd variables. Another example of an odd quantity is a magnetic field: $\tilde{\mathsf{B}}(\xi, \tau) = -\mathsf{B}(\xi, \tilde{\tau})$.

From these transformation rules, we thus find $\tilde{\xi}(\tilde{\tau}) = \xi(\tau)$ and $\tilde{\eta}(\tilde{\tau}) = -\eta(\tau)$, or together $\tilde{\zeta}(\tilde{\tau}) = \hat{\zeta}(\tau)$, which along with the facts that $\partial_{\tilde{\tau}} = -\partial_\tau$ and that the Hamiltonian is even in momentum (i.e., $\mathcal{H}(\xi, -\eta) = \mathcal{H}(\xi, \eta)$), means we can derive

[1] The symmetry that is believed to hold universally at the fundamental level is CPT for charge–parity–time reversal.

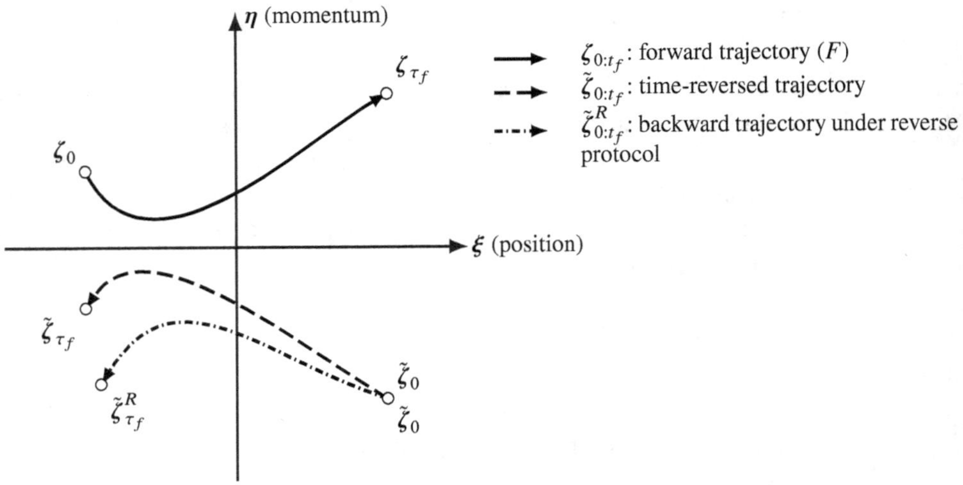

Figure 9.2 Trajectories in phase space. The solid curve $\zeta_{0:t_f}$ illustrates a forward path, the dashed curve $\tilde{\zeta}_{0:t_f}$ shows its exact time reversal, and the dash-dotted curve $\tilde{\zeta}^R_{0:t_f}$ represents a typical backward trajectory generated by the physical reverse protocol (for instance with kerne R_t). Although $\tilde{\zeta}_{0:t_f}$ and $\tilde{\zeta}^R_{0:t_f}$ start from the same state, the latter usually follows a more probable route in the reverse dynamics.

the invariance of the Hamilton equations under time reversal:

$$-\partial_{\tilde{\tau}}\tilde{\xi}(\tilde{\tau}) = \frac{\partial\mathcal{H}(\tilde{\xi},-\tilde{\eta})}{\partial(-\tilde{\eta})}(\tilde{\tau}) \Rightarrow \partial_{\tilde{\tau}}\tilde{\xi}(\tilde{\tau}) = \frac{\partial\mathcal{H}(\tilde{\xi},\tilde{\eta})}{\partial\tilde{\eta}}(\tilde{\tau}), \tag{9.47}$$

$$-\partial_{\tilde{\tau}}(-\tilde{\eta}(\tilde{\tau})) = -\frac{\partial\mathcal{H}(\tilde{\xi},-\tilde{\eta})}{\partial\tilde{\xi}}(\tilde{\tau}) \Rightarrow \partial_{\tilde{\tau}}\tilde{\eta}(\tilde{\tau}) = -\frac{\partial\mathcal{H}(\tilde{\xi},\tilde{\eta})}{\partial\tilde{\xi}}(\tilde{\tau}). \tag{9.48}$$

This expresses the fact that for every forward path, there is a corresponding backwar path if we use the initial conditions $\tilde{\xi}(0) = \xi(\tau_f)$ and $\tilde{\eta}(0) = -\eta(\tau_f)$. So if th distribution over these initial conditions were equal, we would observe as many forwar as backward paths. Apparently, this is not the case because we see a clear differenc between a world evolving forward and backward in time. This is illustrated in Figure 9.:

9.3.2 Time Reversal for Markov Processes

Now let us take a look at TRS for coarse-grained systems described by stochasti Markov chains. In the following we will relate the equations we derived in the previou section to time reversal transformations. First we introduce notation, where we us tilde again to indicate time reversal and hats for sign flipping of odd variables:

$$\begin{aligned}\tilde{\rho}(\zeta_0,\ldots,\zeta_{t_f}) &= \rho(\tilde{\zeta}_0,\ldots,\tilde{\zeta}_{t_f}) = \rho(\hat{\zeta}_{\tilde{0}},\ldots,\hat{\zeta}_{\tilde{t_f}}) = \rho(\hat{\zeta}_{t_f},\ldots,\hat{\zeta}_0)\\ &= \rho(\xi_{t_f},-\eta_{t_f},\ldots,\xi_0,-\eta_0),\end{aligned} \tag{9.49}$$

$$\tilde{\rho}_t(\zeta_t) = \rho_{\tilde{t}}(\tilde{\zeta}_t) = \rho_{\tilde{t}}(\hat{\zeta}_{\tilde{t}}) = \rho_{t_f-t}(\hat{\zeta}_{t_f-t}) = \rho_{t_f-t}(\xi_{t_f-t},-\eta_{t_f-t}). \tag{9.50}$$

The notation we use thus cascades through the arguments, from the density to phase space variables, to time and momentum reversal.

Now, consider the case that the process is controlled by time-dependent parameters $\lambda_0, \ldots, \lambda_{t_f}$. The density $\rho_{0:t_f}$ therefore depends on these parameters. Like momenta, some of these parameters, such as spins or magnetic fields might transform odd under time reversal. However, we will not need this in the following. For the reverse protocol, we use $\hat{\lambda}_t$ to denote the parity-flipped control parameter at time t along the reversed schedule; typically $\tilde{\lambda}_t \equiv \hat{\lambda}_{t_f-t+1}$.

Parameters are associated with the initial distribution (λ_0) and with the transitions, $F(\zeta_t|\zeta_{t-1}, \lambda_t)$. This means that we can also assign them to marginal stationary distributions $\pi(\zeta_t|\lambda_t)$. Because a Markov chain forgets its past, if we run the chain long enough with a fixed parameter value λ_t, the stationary distribution depends on that parameter only. We note, however, that in general marginal distributions that are not in steady state depend on the entire history of all the parameters. In summary, we have

$$F_t(\zeta_t|\zeta_{t-1}) \equiv F(\zeta_t|\zeta_{t-1}, \lambda_t), \tag{9.51}$$

$$\pi_t(\zeta_t) \equiv \pi(\zeta_t|\lambda_t), \tag{9.52}$$

$$\rho_t(\zeta_t) = \rho(\zeta_t|\lambda_0, \ldots, \lambda_t). \tag{9.53}$$

Under time reversal, we now start at the final (marginal) distribution $\rho_{t_f}(\hat{\zeta}_{t_f})$ and apply the control protocol in reverse. We will *not* use B_{t_f} to move backward, which would indeed play the movie backward by antidiffusion. Instead we will use the time-reversed forward process, which for any time t is defined as $F(\hat{\zeta}_{t_f-1}|\hat{\zeta}_{t_f}, \hat{\lambda}_{t_f})$. This is the forward kernel F_{t_f} but with all its arguments reversed (and hatted). More generally, and consistent with the definition in the previous section, we define

$$R_t(\zeta_{t-1}|\zeta_t) \equiv F(\hat{\zeta}_{t-1}|\hat{\zeta}_t, \hat{\lambda}_t), \tag{9.54}$$

where the hat here, and in (9.55), denotes parity-flip only We have chosen to index the kernel R_t with the index t instead of $t-1$ because it depends on λ_t (and not on λ_{t-1}). This makes it consistent with its steady-state distribution $\hat{\pi}_t$, where we have defined the notation

$$\hat{\pi}(\zeta_t) \equiv \pi(\zeta_t|\hat{\lambda}_t). \tag{9.55}$$

We say that a physical process is *time-reversal symmetric* if forward- and time-reversed probabilities are equal. In other words, we want to assert that the probability of observing the process in the time-reversed direction is equally probable as the original process. Any entropy producing process will not satisfy this condition because of the second law of thermodynamics. However, after we have reached a stationary state, this may indeed be true, even macroscopically. We can apply this requirement at any time t, but we have to remember that we use F_t with the same parameters λ_t; that is, π_t is the stationary distribution of F_t by applying it many times with the same parameters λ_t. We then have the following TRS condition:

$$\pi_t(\zeta_{t-1})F_t(\zeta_t|\zeta_{t-1}) = \pi_t(\hat{\zeta}_t)F_t(\hat{\zeta}_{t-1}|\hat{\zeta}_t). \tag{9.56}$$

This says that there is no net probability flow, but it does not imply that π_t is symmetri in the momenta $\boldsymbol{\eta}$. We need to separately enforce that as $\pi(\zeta) = \pi(\hat{\zeta})$.

We will now apply the time reversal operator to (9.9) to get an interesting relation Starting from

$$\pi_{\tilde{t}}(\hat{\zeta}_{\widetilde{t-1}})F_{\tilde{t}}(\hat{\zeta}_{\tilde{t}}|\hat{\zeta}_{\widetilde{t-1}}) = \pi_{\tilde{t}}(\hat{\zeta}_{\tilde{t}})A_{\tilde{t}}(\hat{\zeta}_{\widetilde{t-1}}|\hat{\zeta}_{\tilde{t}}), \quad (9.57$$

which is very messy! To tidy it up, we realize that $\widetilde{t-1} = t_f-(t-1) = (t_f-t)+1 = \tilde{t}+1$ We also realize that the equation holds for arbitrary $\tilde{t}$, and so we can arbitrarily shi time and replace $\tilde{t} \to t-1$ everywhere:

$$\pi_{t-1}(\hat{\zeta}_t)F_{t-1}(\hat{\zeta}_{t-1}|\hat{\zeta}_t) = \pi_{t-1}(\hat{\zeta}_{t-1})A_{t-1}(\hat{\zeta}_t|\hat{\zeta}_{t-1}), \quad (9.58$$

$$\pi_{t-1}(\hat{\zeta}_t)R_{t-1}(\zeta_{t-1}|\zeta_t) = \pi_{t-1}(\hat{\zeta}_{t-1})D_{t-1}(\zeta_t|\zeta_{t-1}), \quad (9.59$$

which is equal to our definition of D_t in (9.40). We thus derived the relation betwee D_t and R_t from the relation between F_t and A_t through time reversal.

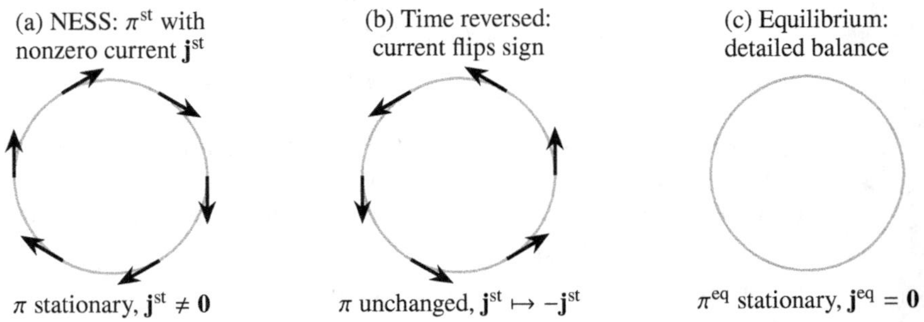

Figure 9.3 Probability currents under time reversal. In a nonequilibrium steady state (NESS), the stationary distribution π^{st} coexists with a nonzero current $\mathbf{j}^{\text{st}}$ around cycles (panel (a), arrows flowing clockwise). Under time reversal, the distribution π is unchanged while the current flips sign (panel (b), arrows flowing counterclockwise). At equilibrium, detailed balance enforces zero net current (panel (c), circle with no arrows).

10 Stochastic Thermodynamics

10.1 Introduction

We have arrived at the heart of the book. In this chapter we will give an overview of the field of stochastic thermodynamics. You will learn about nonequilibrium thermodynamics; it is therefore purely a physics chapter. We will introduce new trajectory-based quantities, for example, the entropy, work, or heat of a single trajectory. We show how heat, work, system entropy, bath entropy, and energy are intimately related even at the trajectory level, and how the second law of thermodynamics emerges as an average result but which can be violated (with very low probability) at the trajectory level. These results are deeply related to concepts such as irreversibility (e.g., the breaking of time-reversal symmetry) and fluctuation theorems. The concepts discussed here will form the foundation of what is going to follow later in the book.

10.2 Stochastic Thermodynamics

Stochastic thermodynamics is a framework that extends the classical thermodynamics we covered in Chapter 3 to small systems where fluctuations play a significant role. It has its roots in the seminal works of Sekimoto (2010), Jarzynski (1997, 2011), Crooks (1998, 1999, 2000), and Seifert (2012), to name a few. They laid the foundation for the modern understanding of thermodynamics at the level of individual trajectories and fluctuations. In this chapter, we will introduce the fundamental concepts and tools of stochastic thermodynamics that are particularly relevant to machine learning.

10.3 Stochastic Processes

Stochastic processes, which are collections of random variables indexed by time, lie at the heart of both stochastic thermodynamics and machine learning. A stochastic process is a mathematical model describing the evolution of a system subject to random fluctuations. In stochastic thermodynamics, they represent the evolution of physical systems subject to random fluctuations and give rise to various nonequilibrium phenomena. Similarly, in machine learning, stochastic processes are used to model the dynamics of various systems, such as the evolution of latent variables in generativ models or the sampling process in MCMC algorithms, as introduced in Chapter 11.

Examples of stochastic processes relevant to both fields include discrete-time an continuous-time Markov processes (such as the Langevin and Hamiltonian Monte Carl dynamics to be discussed in Chapter 11), as well as the dynamics described by maste equations for discrete-state systems. These processes model a wide range of systems from the motion of particles in a fluid to the evolution of latent variables in diffusio models for generating images. To lay the groundwork for exploring the connection between stochastic thermodynamics and machine learning, we will begin by discussin two key examples: Hamiltonian systems and discrete-time Markov processes. The fu continuous-time treatment requires stochastic calculus and will be left for anothe book.

10.3.1 Notation

To maintain clarity and consistency throughout our discussion, we will employ specific notation for physical quantities and variables. Greek letters will be used t represent these entities, with $\zeta_t = (\xi_t, \eta_t)$ denoting the phase space variables at time of a physical dynamics, where ξ_t is the position variable and η_t the momentum variabl at time t. The variables ζ_t are phase space variables at time t along a trajectory fror time $t = 0$ to $t = t_f$ of a dynamical process: $\zeta_{0:t_f} = (\zeta_0, \ldots, \zeta_{t_f})$. Furthermor $\rho_t(\zeta_t)$ represents the (marginal) probability density function in phase space at time Note that ρ_t evolves and therefore changes with time; in other words, it is (usuall not in equilibrium. The joint density over an entire path is indicated with $\rho(\zeta_{0:t_f})$ $\rho(\zeta_0, \ldots, \zeta_{t_f})$. We will also adopt the notation from Chapter 9, where a hat, as i $\hat{\zeta}_t = (\xi_t, -\eta_t)$, denotes the reversal of odd variables (like momentum), and a tild denotes a full time-reversal operation on a path or protocol.

10.3.2 Hamiltonian System

In physics, the dynamics of many systems are governed by a Hamiltonian $\mathcal{H}(\zeta$ where $\zeta = (\xi, \eta)$ represents the state of the system in phase space, with ξ denotin the positions and η denoting the momenta. The Hamiltonian can be thought of a the energy function of the system, which determines how the positions and momen evolve over time. A common form of the Hamiltonian is

$$\mathcal{H}(\zeta) = \mathcal{H}(\xi, \eta) = \frac{1}{2m}\|\eta\|^2 + V(\xi), \tag{10.}$$

where m is the mass of the particles and $V(\xi)$ is the potential energy function. Th first term in the Hamiltonian represents the kinetic energy of the particles, while th second term represents the potential energy due to interactions between the particl and external forces.

The equations of motion are given by Hamilton's equations:

$$\partial_\tau \xi(\tau) = \frac{\partial \mathcal{H}(\xi,\eta)}{\partial \eta}(\tau), \qquad \xi(0) = \xi_0, \tag{10.2}$$

$$\partial_\tau \eta(\tau) = -\frac{\partial \mathcal{H}(\xi,\eta)}{\partial \xi}(\tau), \quad \eta(0) = \eta_0, \tag{10.3}$$

where τ represents physical time.

Hamiltonian evolution is deterministic, meaning that given the initial positions and momenta of the particles, the future state of the system can be precisely determined. However, Hamiltonian systems are still of great interest in stochastic thermodynamics, as they can model the joint system–bath dynamics, introducing stochasticity to the system by integrating out the heat bath variables (Jarzynski, 2000).

Note that Hamiltonian dynamics of many particles is highly chaotic, which means that even if we know the initial state of the entire system to high (but finite) precision, we will inevitably lose track of their precise values due to the sensitivity of the particle trajectories to initial conditions. In the case of a heat bath, whose degrees of freedom we have integrated out, the particles of the system under consideration receive random kicks from particles in the heat bath, making the dynamics stochastic. This is another reason why we, as macroscopic observers, will lose information about the detailed state of system variables ζ_t. It is this process of losing information about the detailed state of the system that leads to the second law of thermodynamics, namely that entropy, which quantifies the amount of information we are losing, always increases on average.

0.3.3 Discrete-Time Markov Process

A discrete-time Markov process is a sequence of random variables $\{\zeta_t\}_{t=0}^{t_f}$, where t represents discrete time steps, and ζ_t takes values from a state space.[1] It is important to realize that "time" t is not physical time but rather a discrete counting index. To distinguish the two, we denote physical time with τ. Every time index t corresponds to some physical time $\tau(t)$, and time evolution maps $\tau(t) \to \tau(t+1) = \tau(t) + \delta\tau$. Figure 10.1 illustrates this discretization of continuous physical time into discrete Markov steps.

The defining property of a (stochastic) Markov process is that the probability distribution of the future state ζ_{t+1} depends only on the current state ζ_t, and not on the history of the process once we know ζ_t (i.e., all information from the past is summarized in the current state ζ_t). This property, known as the Markov property, allows us to describe the evolution of the system using transition probabilities between states, given by the conditional (forward) transition probability distribution $F_t(\zeta_t|\zeta_{t-1})$. This physical transition kernel depends on control parameters λ_t. However, this will generate a lot of clutter in notation because of which we will identify

$$F_t(\zeta_t|\zeta_{t-1}) = F(\zeta_t|\zeta_{t-1}, \lambda_t). \tag{10.4}$$

[1] For discrete state spaces, all integrals over ζ in this chapter should be interpreted as sums.

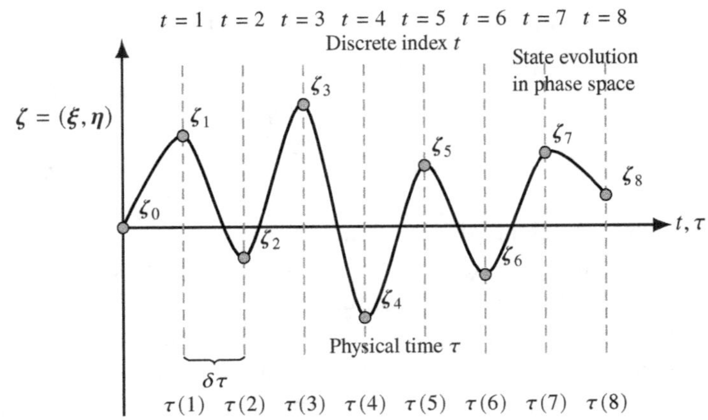

Figure 10.1 Discretization of continuous-time evolution into a Markov process, where each transition depends only on the current state. The smooth solid line shows the evolution of the system state ζ_t in phase space, with circular markers indicating the state at each discrete time step. The states are discretized at regular physical time intervals $\delta\tau$, with the discrete index t shown above and the corresponding physical time $\tau(t)$ shown below.

For thermodynamic consistency, we will later assume that for any fixed control param-eter λ_t, this kernel is ergodic and has a unique stationary distribution π_t correspondin to the Boltzmann distribution for a Hamiltonian $\mathcal{H}_t$.

We can simulate paths according to the Markov chain by following the procedure:

$$\zeta_0 \sim \rho_0(\cdot), \tag{10.5}$$

$$\zeta_1 \sim F_1(\cdot|\zeta_0), \tag{10.6}$$

$$\vdots$$

$$\zeta_{t_f} \sim F_{t_f}(\cdot|\zeta_{t_f-1}). \tag{10.7}$$

The joint probability density of a path $(\zeta_0, \ldots, \zeta_{t_f})$ in the state space is then given b

$$\rho_{0:t_f}(\zeta_0, \zeta_1, \ldots, \zeta_{t_f}) = \rho_0(\zeta_0) \prod_{t=1}^{t_f} F_t(\zeta_t|\zeta_{t-1}), \tag{10.8}$$

where $\rho_0(\zeta_0)$ is the initial probability density of the state ζ_0. In the following we wi often leave out the subscript "0", writing t_f for brevity.

If the Hamiltonian is time independent (i.e., if we do not perform work on the syste by externally controlling it), the transition probability also becomes time independen However, even when the transition probabilities are assumed to be time homogeneou the marginal probability densities $\rho_t(\zeta_t)$ can still depend on t. As mentioned abov the transition kernel F_t can also be time dependent, for instance when the process controlled by an external agent through parameters $\{\lambda_0, \ldots, \lambda_{t_f}\}$.

Markov processes are an approximation when we study probability distributior over coarse-grained variables. Usually, the next state (density) depends on all th states in the past. In that case, we say that the process has "memory". However, the Markov assumption is usually very good if the time scales between fast processes (e.g., collisions) and slow processes (motion of atoms in a molecule) are very different. In that case, random (Brownian) noise provides a very good approximation for modeling complex systems.

10.4 Thermodynamic Quantities

Notation

In the following, we will use square brackets $[\cdot]$ to indicate that a quantity is a functional of a probability distribution, while parentheses $(\cdot)$ denote that the quantity is a function of a specific realization or microstate. For single-time quantities, $\mathcal{A}[\rho]$ represents a functional of the probability distribution $\rho(\zeta)$, and $\mathcal{A}(\zeta)$ or $\mathcal{A}[\rho](\zeta)$ denotes a function of the specific microstate ζ. Similarly, for trajectory-dependent quantities, $\mathcal{A}[\rho_{0:t_f}]$ represents a functional of the probability distribution over trajectories $\rho(\zeta_{0:t_f})$, and $\mathcal{A}(\zeta_{0:t_f})$ or $\mathcal{A}[\rho_{0:t_f}](\zeta_{0:t_f})$ denotes a function of a specific trajectory realization $\zeta_{0:t_f}$. When the context is clear, we may omit the square brackets and simply write $\mathcal{A}$ to refer to the average quantity over the relevant probability distribution, and use $\mathbb{E}[\mathcal{A}(\zeta)] = \mathbb{E}_\rho[\mathcal{A}(\zeta)]$ or $\mathbb{E}[\mathcal{A}(\zeta_{0:t_f})] = \mathbb{E}_\rho[\mathcal{A}(\zeta_{0:t_f})]$.

Internal Energy

The internal energy $\mathcal{U}[\rho]$ is defined as the expectation value of the Hamiltonian $\mathcal{H}(\zeta)$ with respect to the probability density $\rho(\zeta)$:

$$\mathcal{U}[\rho] = \int \mathrm{d}\zeta\, \rho(\zeta)\mathcal{H}(\zeta) = \mathbb{E}_\rho[\mathcal{H}(\zeta)]. \tag{10.9}$$

Here, $\mathcal{H}(\zeta)$ is the internal energy of the system for a specific microstate ζ, sometimes also called the stochastic internal energy.

Entropy

Entropy is a fundamental concept that bridges the worlds of thermodynamics and information theory. It quantifies the amount of uncertainty or surprisal, or unexpectedness, in a system, measuring in bits how much information is hidden or inaccessible. Taking Boltzmann's constant $k_\mathrm{B} = 1$, the stochastic entropy of an event ζ is defined as

$$\mathcal{S}[\rho](\zeta) = -\log \rho(\zeta), \tag{10.10}$$

which measures how surprised we are if the event ζ occurs. The entropy of a probability distribution $\rho(\zeta)$ is then given by the statistical average of the stochastic entropy:

$$\mathcal{S}[\rho] = -\int \mathrm{d}\zeta\, \rho(\zeta) \log \rho(\zeta) = \mathbb{E}_\rho[-\log \rho(\zeta)]. \tag{10.11}$$

In principle, the world is only in one state, but because we cannot model all the degrees of freedom explicitly, we introduce probability distributions over (random) variables.

The entropy is a measure of how much we have forgotten about the actual microscopi state of the system.

In addition to the entropy of a distribution at a specific time, $\mathcal{S}[\rho_t]$ and of state $\mathcal{S}[\rho_t](\zeta_t)$, we can also define the (stochastic) entropy of a trajectory $\zeta_{0:t_f} = (\zeta_0, \ldots, \zeta_{t_f})$ as

$$\mathcal{S}[\rho_{0:t_f}] = -\int \mathrm{d}\zeta_{0:t_f}\, \rho(\zeta_{0:t_f}) \log \rho(\zeta_{0:t_f}) = \mathbb{E}_{\rho_{0:t_f}}[-\log \rho(\zeta_{0:t_f})], \quad (10.12$$

where $\rho(\zeta_{0:t_f})$ is the probability density of the trajectory (given by (10.8) for discrete time Markovian trajectories).

Free Energy

The free energy is a thermodynamic quantity that combines the concepts of energ and entropy. The stochastic free energy $\mathcal{F}(\zeta)$ is defined as

$$\mathcal{F}(\zeta) = \mathcal{H}(\zeta) - T\mathcal{S}(\zeta) = \mathcal{H}(\zeta) + T \log \rho(\zeta), \quad (10.13$$

where T is the temperature of the heat bath. The average free energy functional $\mathcal{F}[\rho$ is then obtained by averaging the stochastic free energy over the probability densit $\rho(\zeta)$:

$$\mathcal{F}[\rho] = \mathbb{E}_\rho[\mathcal{F}(\zeta)] = \mathcal{U}[\rho] - T\mathcal{S}[\rho], \quad (10.14$$

where $\mathcal{U}[\rho] = \mathbb{E}_\rho[\mathcal{H}(\zeta)]$ is the internal energy and $\mathcal{S}[\rho] = -\mathbb{E}_\rho[\log \rho(\zeta)]$ is th entropy.

The free energy functional $\mathcal{F}[\rho]$ is minimized by the equilibrium probability densit $\rho^{\mathrm{eq}}(\zeta)$, which can be obtained by solving the variational problem $\delta\mathcal{F}/\delta\rho = 0$ subje to normalization constraints:

$$\rho^{\mathrm{eq}}(\zeta) = \frac{1}{Z} e^{-\beta\mathcal{H}(\zeta)}, \quad Z = \int \mathrm{d}\zeta\, e^{-\beta\mathcal{H}(\zeta)}, \quad (10.15$$

where $\beta = 1/T$ is the inverse temperature and Z is the partition function. At equilit rium, the free energy reduces to the familiar expression $\mathcal{F}^{\mathrm{eq}} = F = -T \log Z$. Howeve all the quantities $\mathcal{U}[\rho]$, $\mathcal{S}[\rho]$, and $\mathcal{F}[\rho]$ are defined not only for equilibrium system but also for nonequilibrium systems. As such, the nonequilibrium free energy is th natural generalization of the usual definition of free energy for equilibrium systems.

10.5 The First Law of Stochastic Thermodynamics

The first law of thermodynamics states that the change in the internal energy $\Delta\mathcal{U}$ of system equals the sum of the work $\mathcal{W}$ done on the system and the heat Q absorbed t the system:

$$\Delta\mathcal{U} = \mathcal{W} + Q. \quad (10.16$$

In the stochastic thermodynamics setting, the first law is extended to hold for individual trajectories as

$$\Delta\mathcal{U}(\zeta_{0:t_f}) = \mathcal{W}(\zeta_{0:t_f}) + \mathcal{Q}(\zeta_{0:t_f}). \tag{10.17}$$

This extension allows us to analyze the (nonequilibrium) thermodynamic properties of systems at the level of individual fluctuations and rare events.

10.5.1 Hamiltonian System

In a Hamiltonian system, the stochastic work $\mathcal{W}(\zeta_{0:t_f})$ accounts for the change in the Hamiltonian due to the explicit time dependence of the external parameters $\lambda(\tau)$. For a continuous-time Hamiltonian system, the stochastic work is given by the integral of the partial derivative of the Hamiltonian with respect to (physical) time:

$$\mathcal{W}(\zeta_{0\to\tau_f}) = \int \delta\mathcal{W} = \int_0^{\tau_f} \mathrm{d}\tau \, \frac{\partial\mathcal{H}(\zeta,\tau;\lambda)}{\partial\lambda}\frac{\mathrm{d}\lambda}{\mathrm{d}\tau}, \tag{10.18}$$

where λ is the work parameter of the protocol, and $\frac{\mathrm{d}\lambda}{\mathrm{d}\tau}$ is the (physical) time derivative of λ.

For discrete-time processes, the stochastic work and heat can be seen as a discretization of the continuous-time version, (10.18). Consider a system initially in state ζ_0 at time $t = 0$, with a Hamiltonian $\mathcal{H}_0(\zeta_0)$. We can divide the time evolution into two steps, which can be seen as a Trotter–Suzuki or operator splitting of the underlying continuous dynamics:

1. Bring the system out of equilibrium by updating the Hamiltonian to $\mathcal{H}_1$. This step requires work $\delta\mathcal{W}_1 = \mathcal{H}_1(\zeta_0) - \mathcal{H}_0(\zeta_0)$ to be done on the system.
2. Allow the system to relax under the constant Hamiltonian $\mathcal{H}_1$ from ζ_0 to ζ_1. During this step, the system absorbs heat $\delta\mathcal{Q}_1 = \mathcal{H}_1(\zeta_1) - \mathcal{H}_1(\zeta_0)$ from the bath.

By repeating this two-step procedure for t_f steps, we obtain the total work done on the system $\mathcal{W}(\zeta_{0:t_f})$ and the total heat absorbed by the system $\mathcal{Q}(\zeta_{0:t_f})$:

$$\mathcal{W}(\zeta_{0:t_f}) = \sum_{t=1}^{t_f} \delta\mathcal{W}_t = \sum_{t=1}^{t_f} [\mathcal{H}_t(\zeta_{t-1}) - \mathcal{H}_{t-1}(\zeta_{t-1})], \tag{10.19}$$

$$\mathcal{Q}(\zeta_{0:t_f}) = \sum_{t=1}^{t_f} \delta\mathcal{Q}_t = \sum_{t=1}^{t_f} [\mathcal{H}_t(\zeta_t) - \mathcal{H}_t(\zeta_{t-1})]. \tag{10.20}$$

From (10.19) and (10.20), we see that the stochastic work and heat are path-dependent functions. However, their sum gives the total change in the internal energy $\Delta\mathcal{U}(\zeta_{0:t_f})$,

$$\Delta\mathcal{U}(\zeta_{0:t_f}) = \mathcal{Q}(\zeta_{0:t_f}) + \mathcal{W}(\zeta_{0:t_f}) = \mathcal{H}_{t_f}(\zeta_{t_f}) - \mathcal{H}_0(\zeta_0), \tag{10.21}$$

which depends only on the initial and final states of the system, making it a state function.

Equation (10.21) is the stochastic version of the first law of thermodynamics for the discrete-time Hamiltonian system, which holds for each individual trajectory $\zeta_{0:t_f}$. The traditional first law, (10.16), is recovered by averaging the stochastic first law, (10.21), over all possible trajectories:

$$\mathbb{E}_\rho[\Delta\mathcal{U}(\zeta_{0:t_f})] = \mathbb{E}_\rho[\mathcal{Q}(\zeta_{0:t_f})] + \mathbb{E}_\rho[\mathcal{W}(\zeta_{0:t_f})]. \tag{10.22}$$

Time-Reversed Process

To gain further insight into the thermodynamic properties of the system, it is useful to consider the time reversal of the process described above. As stated in Chapter 9 and the Notation subsection, we use hats to flip odd variables and tildes for time reversal, so we will consider time-reversed quantities such as $\tilde{\zeta}_t$, $\tilde{\mathcal{H}}_t$, $\tilde{\mathcal{Q}}_t$, and $\tilde{\mathcal{W}}_t$. In the time-reversed process, we start at $\tilde{t} = \tilde{0}$ with the system in state $\tilde{\zeta}_0 = \hat{\zeta}_{t_f}$ under the Hamiltonian $\tilde{\mathcal{H}}_0 = \mathcal{H}_{t_f}$ (here we assumed that the Hamiltonian $\mathcal{H}$ is even under the flipping of the odd momenta) and then apply the reversed protocol. The first contribution in the time-reversed process is heat, which is equal to the negative of the heat released during relaxation Step 2) in the forward process:

$$\begin{aligned}
\delta\tilde{\mathcal{Q}}_1 &= \tilde{\mathcal{H}}_0(\tilde{\zeta}_1) - \tilde{\mathcal{H}}_0(\tilde{\zeta}_0) \\
&= \mathcal{H}_{t_f}(\hat{\zeta}_{t_f-1}) - \mathcal{H}_{t_f}(\hat{\zeta}_{t_f}) \\
&= \mathcal{H}_{t_f}(\zeta_{t_f-1}) - \mathcal{H}_{t_f}(\zeta_{t_f}) \quad (\text{assuming } \mathcal{H}_{t_f}(\hat{\zeta}) = \mathcal{H}_{t_f}(\zeta)) \\
&= -[\mathcal{H}_{t_f}(\zeta_{t_f}) - \mathcal{H}_{t_f}(\zeta_{t_f-1})] \\
&= -\delta\mathcal{Q}_{t_f}.
\end{aligned} \tag{10.23}$$

The second contribution is work done on the system by updating the Hamiltonian from $\tilde{\mathcal{H}}_0 = \mathcal{H}_{t_f}$ to $\tilde{\mathcal{H}}_1 = \mathcal{H}_{t_f-1}$ at time $\tilde{t} = \tilde{1}$, which is equal to the negative of the work done on the system at time $t = t_f$ in the forward process:

$$\begin{aligned}
\delta\tilde{\mathcal{W}}_1 &= \tilde{\mathcal{H}}_1(\tilde{\zeta}_1) - \tilde{\mathcal{H}}_0(\tilde{\zeta}_1) \\
&= \mathcal{H}_{t_f-1}(\hat{\zeta}_{t_f-1}) - \mathcal{H}_{t_f}(\hat{\zeta}_{t_f-1}) \\
&= \mathcal{H}_{t_f-1}(\zeta_{t_f-1}) - \mathcal{H}_{t_f}(\zeta_{t_f-1}) \quad (\text{assuming } \mathcal{H}(\hat{\zeta}) = \mathcal{H}(\zeta)) \\
&= -[\mathcal{H}_{t_f}(\zeta_{t_f-1}) - \mathcal{H}_{t_f-1}(\zeta_{t_f-1})] \\
&= -\delta\mathcal{W}_{t_f}.
\end{aligned} \tag{10.24}$$

By repeating this procedure for t_f steps until $\tilde{t} = \tilde{t_f}$, we obtain the total stochastic work and heat in the time-reversed process as the negative of the total stochastic work and heat in the forward process:

$$\tilde{\mathcal{Q}}(\zeta_{0:t_f}) = \sum_{t=1}^{t_f} \delta\tilde{\mathcal{Q}}_t = -\mathcal{Q}(\zeta_{0:t_f}), \tag{10.25}$$

$$\tilde{\mathcal{W}}(\zeta_{0:t_f}) = \sum_{t=1}^{t_f} \delta\tilde{\mathcal{W}}_t = -\mathcal{W}(\zeta_{0:t_f}). \tag{10.26}$$

This property of the stochastic work and heat will be crucial in deriving the fluctuation theorems in Chapter 17.

10.5.2 Discrete-Time Markov Process

Now let us consider how stochastic thermodynamics applies to a discrete-time Markov process given by the forward transition kernel $F_t(\zeta_t|\zeta_{t-1})$. We assume that this kernel leaves invariant a distribution $\pi_t(\zeta_t)$ at each time step t:

$$\pi_t(\zeta_t) = \int \mathrm{d}\zeta_{t-1}\, F_t(\zeta_t|\zeta_{t-1})\pi_t(\zeta_{t-1}). \tag{10.27}$$

To connect this process to thermodynamics, we choose the invariant distribution to be the Boltzmann distribution corresponding to a time-dependent Hamiltonian $\mathcal{H}_t(\zeta_t)$:

$$\pi_t(\zeta_t) = \frac{1}{Z_t} e^{-\beta \mathcal{H}_t(\zeta_t)} = e^{\beta \mathcal{F}[\pi_t] - \beta \mathcal{H}_t(\zeta_t)}, \tag{10.28}$$

where β is the inverse temperature, Z_t is the partition function, and $\mathcal{F}[\pi_t] = -T \log Z_t$ is the equilibrium free energy for the distribution π_t.

Detailed Balance Assumption

For the following thermodynamic analysis to be consistent, especially when dealing with momentum variables, we must assume that the system satisfies the detailed balance condition with respect to odd variables (see Chapter 9):

$$F_t(\zeta_t|\zeta_{t-1})\pi_t(\zeta_{t-1}) = F_t(\hat{\zeta}_{t-1}|\hat{\zeta}_t)\pi_t(\zeta_t), \tag{10.29}$$

where $\hat{\zeta} = (\xi, -\eta)$ represents the momentum-reversed state. Additionally, we assume that the stationary distribution is symmetric under momentum reversal (i.e., $\pi_t(\zeta) = \pi_t(\hat{\zeta})$), which means that the equilibrium distribution has zero mean momentum.

From these assumptions and the definitions of π_t, (10.28), and the expression for stochastic heat, (10.20), we can derive the following relation for the stochastic heat in the Markov process. Using the detailed balance condition,

$$\frac{F_t(\zeta_t|\zeta_{t-1})}{F_t(\hat{\zeta}_{t-1}|\hat{\zeta}_t)} = \frac{\pi_t(\zeta_t)}{\pi_t(\zeta_{t-1})} = \frac{F_t(\zeta_t|\zeta_{t-1})}{R_t(\zeta_{t-1}|\zeta_t)}, \tag{10.30}$$

the stochastic heat can be expressed in terms of the transition kernels:

$$\begin{aligned} Q(\zeta_{0:t_f}) &= -T \sum_{t=1}^{t_f} \log \frac{\pi_t(\zeta_t)}{\pi_t(\zeta_{t-1})} \\ &= -T \sum_{t=1}^{t_f} \log \frac{F_t(\zeta_t|\zeta_{t-1})}{R_t(\zeta_{t-1}|\zeta_t)}, \end{aligned} \tag{10.31}$$

where the reverse kernel is defined as $R_t(\zeta_{t-1}|\zeta_t) = F_t(\hat{\zeta}_{t-1}|\hat{\zeta}_t)$ as in Chapter 9.

Using (10.19), the stochastic work can also be expressed as

$$\mathcal{W}(\zeta_{0:t_f}) = \mathcal{F}[\pi_{t_f}] - \mathcal{F}[\pi_0] - \beta^{-1} \sum_{t=1}^{t_f} \log \frac{\pi_t(\zeta_{t-1})}{\pi_{t-1}(\zeta_{t-1})}. \tag{10.32}$$

Consistent with the stochastic first law, (10.21), the total change in the internal energy is thus given as

$$\Delta\mathcal{U}(\zeta_{0:t_f}) = \mathcal{Q}(\zeta_{0:t_f}) + \mathcal{W}(\zeta_{0:t_f}) = -\beta^{-1}\left[\log\frac{Z_{t_f}}{Z_0} + \log\frac{\pi_{t_f}(\zeta_{t_f})}{\pi_0(\zeta_0)}\right], \tag{10.33}$$

which again depends only on the initial and final states of the system and their corresponding equilibrium distributions.

10.6 The Second Law: Thermodynamic and Statistical Irreversibility

Irreversibility in stochastic thermodynamics can be quantified in two ways: *thermodynamic irreversibility*, measured by entropy production or dissipated work, and *statistical irreversibility*, assessed by comparing the probability of observing events in time-reversed order. The interplay between these two forms of irreversibility is a central theme in quantifying the second law of stochastic thermodynamics. The second law of thermodynamics can be stated in two equivalent forms: the Clausius statement and the Kelvin statement. These two statements are related to the concepts of entropy production and dissipated work.

10.6.1 Clausius Statement and Entropy Production

The Clausius statement of the second law asserts that heat cannot spontaneously flow from a colder body to a hotter body. This statement is closely related to the concept of entropy production in irreversible processes. In order for heat to flow from cold to hot, there must be a compensating increase in entropy elsewhere in the system, which is often achieved through the exchange of heat with an external reservoir.

To quantify this idea in the context of stochastic thermodynamics, we introduce the stochastic total entropy production $\Sigma(\zeta_{0:t_f})$ along a trajectory $\zeta_{0:t_f}$ as the sum of the changes in the system entropy and the environmental entropy:

$$\Sigma(\zeta_{0:t_f}) = \Delta\mathcal{S}_{\text{sys}}(\zeta_{0:t_f}) + \Delta\mathcal{S}_{\text{bath}}(\zeta_{0:t_f}), \tag{10.34}$$

where $\Delta\mathcal{S}_{\text{sys}}(\zeta_{0:t_f})$ and $\Delta\mathcal{S}_{\text{bath}}(\zeta_{0:t_f})$ are the changes in the stochastic system and environmental entropy:

$$\Delta\mathcal{S}_{\text{sys}}(\zeta_{0:t_f}) = -\log\rho_{t_f}(\zeta_{t_f}) + \log\rho_0(\zeta_0), \tag{10.35}$$

$$\Delta\mathcal{S}_{\text{bath}}(\zeta_{0:t_f}) = \beta\mathcal{Q}_{\text{bath}}(\zeta_{0:t_f}) = -\beta\mathcal{Q}(\zeta_{0:t_f}). \tag{10.36}$$

Here, $\mathcal{Q}_{\text{bath}}(\zeta_{0:t_f})$ and $\mathcal{Q}(\zeta_{0:t_f})$ are the stochastic heat dissipated to the environment and absorbed by the system along the trajectory, (10.20), and $\beta = 1/T$ is the inverse temperature of the environment. This relation assumes that the heat bath is much larger than the system, so that the temperature change of the bath due to heat exchange is negligible, and the bath quickly relaxes back to equilibrium after any exchange, even if the system itself is out of equilibrium. As heat represents "useless energy", the free energy of the bath will not change. As a result, any changes to the internal energy represented by the heat term will have to be compensated by an equal change in the bath's entropy.

For a discrete-time Markov process with forward path probability $\rho(\zeta_{0:t_f})$, (10.8), and the time-reversed process built from R_t and started at ρ_{t_f}, we can express $\Sigma(\zeta_{0:t_f})$ in terms of the forward and time-reversed path probabilities using (10.35), (10.36), and (10.31):

$$\begin{aligned}\Sigma(\zeta_{0:t_f}) &= \Delta S_{\text{sys}}(\zeta_{0:t_f}) + \Delta S_{\text{bath}}(\zeta_{0:t_f})\\ &= [-\log \rho_{t_f}(\zeta_{t_f}) + \log \rho_0(\zeta_0)] + \sum_{t=1}^{t_f} \log \frac{F_t(\zeta_t|\zeta_{t-1})}{R_t(\zeta_{t-1}|\zeta_t)}\\ &= \log \frac{\rho_0(\zeta_0)\prod_{t=1}^{t_f} F_t(\zeta_t|\zeta_{t-1})}{\rho_{t_f}(\zeta_{t_f})\prod_{t=1}^{t_f} R_t(\zeta_{t-1}|\zeta_t)}\\ &= \log \frac{\rho(\zeta_{0:t_f})}{\rho_R(\zeta_{0:t_f})},\end{aligned} \tag{10.37}$$

where we have used the Markov property for the forward path probability $\rho(\zeta_{0:t_f})$ and defined the time-reversed path probability $\rho_R(\zeta_{0:t_f}) = \rho_{t_f}(\zeta_{t_f})\prod_{t=1}^{t_f} R_t(\zeta_{t-1}|\zeta_t)$.

The stochastic entropy production, (10.37), has a clear interpretation in terms of the statistical irreversibility of the process. It quantifies the difference between the probability of observing a particular forward trajectory and the probability of observing the corresponding time-reversed trajectory. If the process is reversible, the forward and time-reversed path probabilities are equal, and the stochastic entropy production is zero. However, for irreversible processes, the forward path is typically much more likely than the time-reversed path, leading to a positive stochastic entropy production.

It is easy to confuse the time-reversed path probability ρ_R of (10.37) with that of (9.4) in Chapter 9. The latter is the backward process probability that would make the reversed path equally likely. However, please note that the reversed path is exactly equally likely under (9.4) but not under (10.37)!

Averaging the stochastic entropy production over all forward trajectories, the average total entropy production $\mathbb{E}_\rho[\Sigma]$ is expressed as the Kullback–Leibler divergence between the forward and backward path probability distributions:[2]

$$\mathbb{E}_\rho[\Sigma(\zeta_{0:t_f})] = \int d\zeta_{0:t_f}\, \rho(\zeta_{0:t_f}) \log \frac{\rho(\zeta_{0:t_f})}{\rho_R(\zeta_{0:t_f})} = D_{\text{KL}}[\rho \| \rho_R] \geq 0. \tag{10.38}$$

The non-negativity of $\mathbb{E}_\rho[\Sigma]$ follows from the non-negativity of KL divergence, leading

[2] This requires that the path measures ρ and ρ_R are absolutely continuous with respect to each other, so the ratio is well defined.

to the second law[3]:

$$\mathbb{E}_\rho[\Sigma(\zeta_{0:t_f})] = \mathbb{E}_\rho[\Delta S_{\text{sys}}] + \mathbb{E}_\rho[\Delta S_{\text{bath}}] \geq 0. \tag{10.39}$$

Of course, the second law applies not only to the discrete-time Markov process but also to a broad range of physical systems.

In the absence of external work (i.e., when the Hamiltonian is kept constant and every F_t is the same $F_t = F$), we can use the DB condition, (10.29), with the same stationary distribution π,

$$F(\zeta_t|\zeta_{t-1})\pi(\zeta_{t-1}) = R(\zeta_{t-1}|\zeta_t)\pi(\zeta_t), \tag{10.40}$$

to simplify the general expression for the entropy production, (10.37). Starting from that we have

$$\begin{aligned}\Sigma(\zeta_{0:t_f}) &= \log \frac{\rho(\zeta_{0:t_f})}{\rho_R(\zeta_{0:t_f})} \\ &= \log \frac{\rho_0(\zeta_0)\prod_{t=1}^{t_f} F(\zeta_t|\zeta_{t-1})}{\rho_{t_f}(\zeta_{t_f})\prod_{t=1}^{t_f} R(\zeta_{t-1}|\zeta_t)}.\end{aligned} \tag{10.41}$$

Using (10.40) for the stationary distribution, we can rewrite the entropy production as

$$\begin{aligned}\Sigma(\zeta_{0:t_f}) &= \log \frac{\rho_0(\zeta_0)}{\rho_{t_f}(\zeta_{t_f})} + \sum_{t=1}^{t_f} \log \frac{\pi(\zeta_t)}{\pi(\zeta_{t-1})} \\ &= \log \frac{\rho_0(\zeta_0)}{\pi(\zeta_0)} + \log \frac{\pi(\zeta_{t_f})}{\rho_{t_f}(\zeta_{t_f})}.\end{aligned} \tag{10.42}$$

Taking the average over all trajectories, we get

$$\begin{aligned}\mathbb{E}_\rho[\Sigma(\zeta_{0:t_f})] &= \int d\zeta_0\, \rho_0(\zeta_0) \log \frac{\rho_0(\zeta_0)}{\pi(\zeta_0)} + \int d\zeta_{t_f}\, \rho_{t_f}(\zeta_{t_f}) \log \frac{\pi(\zeta_{t_f})}{\rho_{t_f}(\zeta_{t_f})} \\ &= D_{\text{KL}}[\rho_0\|\pi] - D_{\text{KL}}[\rho_{t_f}\|\pi].\end{aligned} \tag{10.43}$$

Because the system has not yet converged to the stationary distribution at time t_f, we get a "refund" for our total entropy production equal to the final term above, which is always smaller than the first term because ρ_{t_f} is closer to stationarity than ρ_0. In fact as the system relaxes towards equilibrium, ρ_{t_f} approaches π. When the process runs for a sufficiently long time to reach equilibrium, we have

$$\lim_{t_f\to\infty} D_{\text{KL}}[\rho_{t_f}\|\pi] = 0, \tag{10.44}$$

$$\lim_{t_f\to\infty} \mathbb{E}_\rho[\Sigma(\zeta_{0:t_f})] = D_{\text{KL}}[\rho_0\|\pi]. \tag{10.45}$$

[3] To complete the derivation, we need to show that the backward path probability density $\rho_R(\zeta_{0:t_f})$ is a valid probability distribution (i.e., it is non-negative and normalized). Non-negativity follows from the definitions, and normalization can be verified by direct integration using the properties of the transition kernels.

That is, the total entropy production is given by the KL divergence between the initial distribution and the final equilibrium distribution.

This also tells us that the entropy production provides a quantitative measure of the "distance" between the initial state of the system and the equilibrium state, and that this distance decreases monotonically as the system evolves towards equilibrium. In fact, Langevin dynamics will follow the path of steepest descent of this objective, where every step is guaranteed to decrease the objective, and as such is also guaranteed to increase the total entropy of the system and the environment.

10.6.2 Kelvin Statement and Dissipated Work

The Kelvin statement of the second law asserts that it is impossible to construct a heat engine that operates in a cycle and produces no other effect than the absorption of heat from a single reservoir and the performance of an equal amount of work. This statement is directly related to the concept of dissipated work in stochastic thermodynamics.

The stochastic dissipated work $\mathcal{W}_{\text{diss}}(\zeta_{0:t_f})$ is defined for a thermodynamic process and quantifies the amount of extra work that is required to perform due to the irreversibility of the process. It is defined as the difference between the stochastic work $\mathcal{W}(\zeta_{0:t_f})$ done on the system, (10.19), and the change in the stochastic free energy $\Delta\mathcal{F} = \mathcal{F}(\zeta_{t_f}) - \mathcal{F}(\zeta_0)$, (10.13):

$$\mathcal{W}_{\text{diss}}(\zeta_{0:t_f}) = \mathcal{W}(\zeta_{0:t_f}) - \Delta\mathcal{F}(\zeta_{0:t_f}). \tag{10.46}$$

Note that while the stochastic work is a path-dependent quantity, the change in free energy only depends on the initial and final states of the system. The dissipated work is a measure of the inefficiency of the process, as it represents the portion of the total work that cannot be recovered as useful work output.

To derive the connection between the dissipated work and the entropy production, we start from the stochastic first law of thermodynamics, (10.17), and the definition of the stochastic free energy, 10.13. For a specific trajectory $\zeta_{0:t_f}$,

$$\Delta\mathcal{U}(\zeta_{0:t_f}) = \mathcal{Q}(\zeta_{0:t_f}) + \mathcal{W}(\zeta_{0:t_f}), \tag{10.47}$$

$$\Delta\mathcal{F}(\zeta_{0:t_f}) = \mathcal{F}(\zeta_{t_f}) - \mathcal{F}(\zeta_0) = \Delta\mathcal{U}(\zeta_{0:t_f}) - T\Delta\mathcal{S}_{\text{sys}}(\zeta_{0:t_f}). \tag{10.48}$$

Substituting the first law into the free energy difference:

$$\Delta\mathcal{F}(\zeta_{0:t_f}) = \mathcal{Q}(\zeta_{0:t_f}) + \mathcal{W}(\zeta_{0:t_f}) - T\Delta\mathcal{S}_{\text{sys}}(\zeta_{0:t_f}). \tag{10.49}$$

Rearranging terms and using the definition of stochastic environmental entropy change, (10.36),

$$T\Delta\mathcal{S}_{\text{sys}}(\zeta_{0:t_f}) + T\Delta\mathcal{S}_{\text{bath}}(\zeta_{0:t_f}) = \mathcal{W}(\zeta_{0:t_f}) - \Delta\mathcal{F}(\zeta_{0:t_f}). \tag{10.50}$$

Using the definition of stochastic total entropy production (10.34), and the stochastic dissipated work, (10.46), we obtain

$$T\Sigma(\zeta_{0:t_f}) = \mathcal{W}_{\text{diss}}(\zeta_{0:t_f}). \tag{10.51}$$

Taking the average over all trajectories, we obtain the second law of thermodynamics in the Kelvin form:

$$T\mathbb{E}_\rho[\Sigma] = \mathbb{E}_\rho[\mathcal{W}_{\mathrm{diss}}] \geq 0. \tag{10.52}$$

The non-negativity of the average dissipated work $\mathbb{E}_\rho[\mathcal{W}_{\mathrm{diss}}]$ is a direct consequence of the second law of thermodynamics (10.39), and it is zero only for reversible processes. However, for individual trajectories, the stochastic dissipated work $\mathcal{W}_{\mathrm{diss}}(\zeta_{0:t_f})$ can be negative, but with low probability, a phenomenon quantified by the fluctuation theorems.

11 Markov Chain Monte Carlo

11.1 Introduction

Following the earlier discussion of Markov processes and kernels in Chapter 4 and the particular challenges surrounding their reversibility in Chapter 9, we will now consider one of their specific application domains: Markov chain Monte Carlo. In addition to variational inference, MCMC is one of the most popular methods for performing posterior inference. It does so by collecting samples from the distribution of interest. MCMC is based on a Markov chain where the transition kernel is designed such that the equilibrium distribution is the distribution of interest. In this chapter we will discuss how to design such kernels and give a few examples, including Metropolis–Hastings, Gibbs sampling, Hamiltonian Monte Carlo, and Langevin sampling. These kernels come in two flavors: those that satisfy detailed balance and those that do not, which is analogous to the kernels we discussed in Chapter 9.

11.2 Markov Chain Monte Carlo

The goal of MCMC is to design an iterative procedure that generates samples from an (unnormalized) probability distribution $q_{\text{target}}(\mathbf{z})$ (or density). MCMC achieves this by designing a Markov kernel $F(\mathbf{z}'|\mathbf{z})$ such that, by iteratively applying the transition

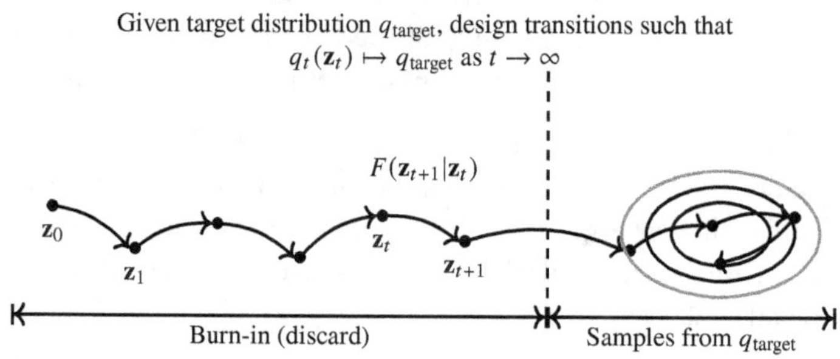

Figure 11.1 The process of a Markov chain Monte Carlo algorithm. The chain starts from an initial state $\mathbf{z}_0$ and evolves through a series of transitions $F(\mathbf{z}_{t+1}|\mathbf{z}_t)$. The burn-in period represents initial samples that are discarded. As $t \to \infty$, the distribution of samples converges to the target distribution q_{target}.

kernel,

$$\begin{aligned} \mathbf{z}_0 &\sim q_0(\mathbf{z}_0), \\ \mathbf{z}_1 &\sim F(\mathbf{z}_1|\mathbf{z}_0), \\ &\vdots \\ \mathbf{z}_t &\sim F(\mathbf{z}_t|\mathbf{z}_{t-1}), \\ &\vdots \end{aligned} \quad (11.1$$

as the consecutive number of applications of the kernel tends to infinity, the margina distribution $q_t(\mathbf{z}_t) = \int d\mathbf{z}_{0:t-1}\, q_0(\mathbf{z}_0) \prod_{j=1}^{t} F(\mathbf{z}_j|\mathbf{z}_{j-1})$, where the integral is over al previous states $\mathbf{z}_0, \ldots, \mathbf{z}_{t-1}$, converges to the target distribution, $q_\infty = q_{\text{target}}$, indepen dent of the initial distribution q_0. This process, which we call ancestral sampling, i illustrated in Figure 11.1.

Formally, this states that as $t \to \infty$, independent of the initial distribution, the tota variation distance between q_t and q_{target} tends to zero:

$$\lim_{t\to\infty} \left\|q_t - q_{\text{target}}\right\|_{\text{TV}} = 0, \quad (11.2$$

which is the desired convergence property for MCMC.

Designing such a transition kernel is nontrivial, but fortunately there is a set c sufficient conditions that let us verify that a kernel does achieve this goal. This is th topic of the next section.

11.3 Designing a Markov Kernel for MCMC

To design a kernel such that we have the convergence property in (11.2), the kern must

(i) have the target distribution as one of its stationary distributions, either by havin the target distribution be invariant with respect to the kernel, or by satisfyin detailed balance with respect to it; and
(ii) be ergodic, meaning that the kernel has a unique stationary distribution and th after repeated application of the kernel the chain converges to this distribution.

Combining these two properties, we can see that the kernel will have the corre stationary distribution, that this stationary distribution will be the only one, and that th chain will converge to this stationary distribution. What being a stationary distributio of a kernel means and what it means for a chain to be ergodic will be discussed in mo detail next.

11.3.1 Stationary Distribution

The first criterion we consider is that the transition kernel F needs to have the targ distribution q_{target} as its stationary distribution. Given a specific q_{target}, many kerne

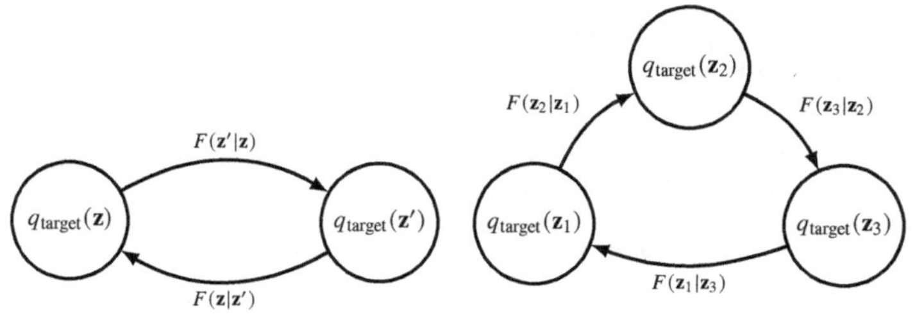

(a) Detailed Balance (b) Invariance Condition

Figure 11.2 Comparison of detailed balance and invariance conditions in MCMC. (a) Detailed balance requires symmetric transitions between states at equilibrium, shown with bidirectional arrows between two states. (b) The invariance condition allows for cyclic flows of probabilities that maintain the overall stationary distribution, illustrated here with a three-state system where probability can flow in a directed cycle while preserving q_{target}.

can achieve this goal, falling into two classes: those satisfying detailed balance and those leaving the target distribution invariant without satisfying detailed balance (see Figure 11.2 for an illustration of both cases).

Invariance Condition

A probability distribution q_{target} is said to be *invariant* under a kernel F if

$$q_{\text{target}}(\mathbf{z}') = \int d\mathbf{z}\ F(\mathbf{z}'|\mathbf{z})q_{\text{target}}(\mathbf{z}) \quad \text{for all } \mathbf{z}'. \tag{11.3}$$

Equivalently, we can say that q_{target} is a *stationary*, or *steady-state*, distribution of F.

One way to think of stationarity/invariance is to imagine a collection of arbitrary volume elements (e.g., various small cubes). Then (11.3) says that at every time step, the kernel F moves the same amount of probability out of each cube as is moved into it. In other words, the probability level in the cubes remains the same. If this is true for all volume elements, we satisfy the condition above.

Notably, however, while the total amount of probability flowing out of a cube and into it is the same, the probability exchanged between two specific cubes does not have to be balanced. This allows for the possibility that probability enters from one side and leaves from another, which can create deterministic flows where probability runs in circles.

Another way to think about this is as a symmetry of the probability distribution. If q_{target} has a symmetry, then there is a vector field that transports probability over equiprobability contours. Per definition, this leaves the distribution invariant.

Adjoint Kernel

We previously discussed the notion of invariant distributions in a physical context in Chapter 9. There we saw an alternative characterization of the invariance condition,

$$\text{there exists } A: \quad F(\mathbf{z}'|\mathbf{z})q_{\text{target}}(\mathbf{z}) = A(\mathbf{z}|\mathbf{z}')q_{\text{target}}(\mathbf{z}') \quad \text{for all } \mathbf{z}, \mathbf{z}', \tag{11.4}$$

which says that there exists a positive and properly normalized adjoint transition kerne A, with $A(\mathbf{z}|\mathbf{z}') \geq 0$ for all $\mathbf{z}, \mathbf{z}'$, and $\int d\mathbf{z}\ A(\mathbf{z}|\mathbf{z}') = 1$ for all $\mathbf{z}'$, such that (11.4) hold true.

It is easily verified that the existence of such an A immediately leads to invariance

$$\int d\mathbf{z}\ F(\mathbf{z}'|\mathbf{z}) q_{\text{target}}(\mathbf{z}) = \int d\mathbf{z}\ A(\mathbf{z}|\mathbf{z}') q_{\text{target}}(\mathbf{z}') = q_{\text{target}}(\mathbf{z}'). \quad (11.5$$

This also highlights that the adjoint kernel A has the same stationary distribution a the forward kernel F.

The reverse implication is slightly more surprising and is proven by constructing a adjoint kernel that satisfies (11.4), namely,

$$A(\mathbf{z}|\mathbf{z}') = \frac{F(\mathbf{z}'|\mathbf{z}) q_{\text{target}}(\mathbf{z})}{q_{\text{target}}(\mathbf{z}')}. \quad (11.6$$

However, this does not guarantee that A is non-negative and properly normalizec For non-negativity, we recall that F and q_{target} are non-negative, so A must also b non-negative. To prove normalization, we use stationarity,

$$\int d\mathbf{z}\ A(\mathbf{z}|\mathbf{z}') = \int d\mathbf{z}\ \frac{F(\mathbf{z}'|\mathbf{z}) q_{\text{target}}(\mathbf{z})}{q_{\text{target}}(\mathbf{z}')} = \frac{q_{\text{target}}(\mathbf{z}')}{q_{\text{target}}(\mathbf{z}')} = 1, \quad (11.7$$

which then proves that (11.3) – invariance of q_{target} under F – and (11.4) – the existenc of A – are in fact equivalent.

The application of the adjoint kernel A to the stationary distribution q_{target} wi reverse the probability flow relative to the forward direction (e.g., probability woul flow into the cube from the right and flow out from the left). For deterministic dynamic applying A to the steady-state distribution q_{target} means we are playing the simulatio of F backward in time. It is therefore perhaps surprising that we refer to a kernel that requires an adjoint kernel A to reverse the flow of probability as "irreversible" The term "nonself-reversible" would have been more descriptive.

Kernels that are "self-reversible" or "self-adjoint," commonly known as "reversible kernels, are discussed next.

Detailed Balance Condition

A stricter condition that we can impose on a kernel F with respect to a target distributio q_{target} is detailed balance:

$$F(\mathbf{z}'|\mathbf{z}) q_{\text{target}}(\mathbf{z}) = F(\mathbf{z}|\mathbf{z}') q_{\text{target}}(\mathbf{z}') \quad \text{for all } \mathbf{z}, \mathbf{z}'. \quad (11.8$$

Comparing this to (11.4), we can directly see the similarity with the adjoint-kerne based definition of the invariance condition. A kernel F satisfies DB if it is "sel adjoint"; that is, $A = F$.

Going back to the analogy of a collection of arbitrary volume elements, we ca now see that DB implies that probability cannot flow into a cube from one end ar flow out from the other end. Instead, for every surface element of any arbitrary volum element, the probability flow into the cube through that surface element must equal tl probability flow out of the cube through that same surface element. So the probability flow is balanced for every pair of points $\mathbf{z}, \mathbf{z}'$.

It is important here to note that, in physics, the notion of DB is defined differently. In the presence of momenta, we define a reverse kernel as $R(\zeta'|\zeta) = F(\hat{\zeta}'|\zeta)$, with $\zeta = (\xi, \eta)$ and $\hat{\zeta} = (\xi, -\eta)$. We now say that DB holds when $A = R$. However, this already involves the inversion of the momenta and so would include probability flow that moves in circles. Within the MCMC definition of DB, if a kernel acts on odd variables, we instead need to explicitly ensure this reversal of the odd variables at the end of the step as part of the kernel to satisfy DB.

For example, below we will discuss Hamiltonian Monte Carlo, where in the MCMC definition we would need to reverse the momenta after every step to obtain DB. However, in the physics definition this would not be necessary to call it DB.

Detailed Balance Implies Invariance

Using the adjoint-kernel-based definition of the invariance condition, showing that DB implies invariance is straightforward, but it is similarly not hard to show that DB implies invariance if we use the definition of invariance in eqn. 11.3:

$$\int d\mathbf{z}\, F(\mathbf{z}'|\mathbf{z}) q_{\text{target}}(\mathbf{z}) = \int d\mathbf{z}\, F(\mathbf{z}|\mathbf{z}') q_{\text{target}}(\mathbf{z}') = q_{\text{target}}(\mathbf{z}'), \quad \text{for all } \mathbf{z}' \\ \left(\text{since} \int d\mathbf{z}\, F(\mathbf{z}|\mathbf{z}') = 1\right). \tag{11.9}$$

Metropolis–Hastings

Considering that DB is a stricter condition than invariance, the question of its relevance arises. After all, we only need our kernel to have the correct stationary distribution for it to be a valid kernel for use in MCMC (in addition to it being ergodic, as we will discuss next). The answer is that for any proposal kernel F, there is an easy trick to construct a new kernel that satisfies DB by using the Metropolis–Hastings (Metropolis et al., 1953; Hastings, 1970) rule to accept or reject proposed samples.

Given a transition kernel F as our proposal distribution, the MH acceptance probability is given by

$$p_{\text{accept}}(\mathbf{z}'|\mathbf{z}) = \min\left[1, \frac{q_{\text{target}}(\mathbf{z}')}{q_{\text{target}}(\mathbf{z})} \cdot \frac{F(\mathbf{z}|\mathbf{z}')}{F(\mathbf{z}'|\mathbf{z})}\right]. \tag{11.10}$$

We can show that the combination of proposing with F and then accepting with p_{accept} will result in the detailed balance condition, (11.8). Specifically, by considering the cases where $\mathbf{z}' = \mathbf{z}$ and $\mathbf{z}' \neq \mathbf{z}$ separately, we find that in both the accepted and the rejected cases,

$$q_{\text{target}}(\mathbf{z}) F(\mathbf{z}'|\mathbf{z}) p_{\text{accept}}(\mathbf{z}'|\mathbf{z}) = q_{\text{target}}(\mathbf{z}') F(\mathbf{z}|\mathbf{z}') p_{\text{accept}}(\mathbf{z}|\mathbf{z}'). \tag{11.11}$$

With this trick, in MCMC the detailed balance condition, 11.8, – plus ergodicity, as we will discuss next – is often used as a convenient (and sufficient) condition for constructing a valid Markov chain that converges to the desired target distribution.

Many popular MCMC algorithms, such as the famous Metropolis–Hastings algorithm (Metropolis et al., 1953; Hastings, 1970), are based on the detailed balance condition.

11.3.2 Ergodicity

In short, a Markov chain constructed with a kernel F is said to be ergodic if it is *irreducible*, *aperiodic*, and *positive Harris recurrent*. We will shortly discuss each of these criteria in more detail, but for a full discussion we refer to dedicated textbooks on this topic (Robert and Casella, 1999; Brooks, 1998). If all three are satisfied, we are guaranteed that the chain will converge to a unique stationary distribution as $t \to \infty$, independent of the initial distribution. As noted before, for this to be the correct stationary distribution q_{target}, the kernel must also satisfy the invariance condition, (11.3). Now to the criteria.

(i) *Positive Harris recurrent*: Positive Harris recurrence means that the chain will return to any state with probability 1 and within a finite mean time. This ensures that the chain will not get stuck in a set of excluded states. Positive recurrence ensures that the kernel has a stationary distribution.
(ii) *Irreducibility*: Every state can be reached from any other state. This is easiest to imagine in a discrete space where it essentially means that if we make a graph of reachable states, there should be a path between any two states. This ensures that the stationary distribution that is guaranteed to exist for positive recurrent kernels is unique.
(iii) *Aperiodicity*: The chain does not contain any fixed cycles. This ensures that at any time t there is not a set of excluded states that the chain cannot reach. Without this criterion, it would be possible for the total variation distance to only converge to 0 for a fixed interval of time steps t. Combined with positive Harris recurrence and irreducibility, this ensures not only the existence of the unique stationary distribution, but also that the chain actually converges to it.[1]

While these three criteria might seem abstract and tough to satisfy, in most cases they can be met by using a kernel that contains some form of stochasticity with sufficient support. We will see some examples of this in the section on notable MCMC algorithms further on in this chapter.

Combining this with the trick to ensure that any kernel has the right stationary distribution through the MH accept–reject step, we now have a full recipe to build a Markov kernel that, after successive applications, converges to our desired target

[1] Notably, there is a second convergence criterion that is often considered for MCMC, which is known as the *ergodic theorem*. The ergodic theorem states that if we take a time average over the samples generated by the chain, the average will converge to the expected value under the target distribution. This is the property we briefly mentioned in Chapter 3 when discussing how to define a probability distribution over a phase space for a dynamical system. Confusingly, despite aperiodicity being a necessary condition for ergodicity of a Markov chain, for the ergodic *theorem* to hold, the chain does not need to be aperiodic.

distribution. In this scenario, where we have a kernel that satisfies DB with respect to our target distribution and is guaranteed to converge to it due to ergodicity, we refer to our target distribution as the *equilibrium distribution* of the kernel.

Mixing Time

In line with the notion of ergodicity, you will often hear books and papers mention the concept of "mixing time". This concept refers to the amount of time, or steps, needed for the chain to converge to an acceptable level of closeness to the target distribution in terms of total variation distance. You will also hear this referred to as the "burn-in period".

Different Markov kernels will have different mixing times. For example, while DB is a convenient condition to satisfy invariance, it tends to mix slowly. In practice, this results in long burn-in periods compared to using irreversible kernels that only satisfy invariance. DB can be compared with mixing the milk in your tea through diffusion, while we really want advection of the milk in the tea by stirring it with a teaspoon, which is achieved by an irreversible MCMC kernel. After all, mixing milk in your tea is much faster if you stir than if you wait for diffusion to distribute the milk!

Figure 11.3 gives a simple two-dimensional illustration of how MCMC samples from a posterior distribution: the chain explores the level sets of $p(\mathbf{z}|\mathbf{x})$ and produces a cloud of samples that can be used to approximate expectations under the posterior.

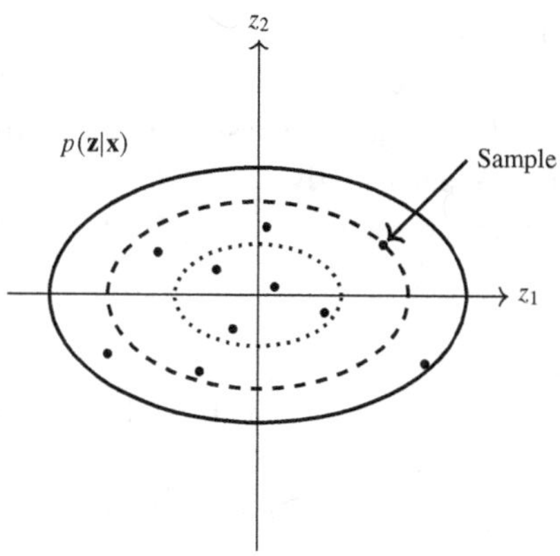

Figure 11.3 Posterior sampling with MCMC. The ellipses represent contours of the posterior distribution $p(\mathbf{z}|\mathbf{x})$. The filled circles represent samples drawn from this distribution using MCMC. The arrow highlights a specific sample $\mathbf{z}_s$. Samples are used to approximate expectations as $\mathbb{E}_{p(\mathbf{z}|\mathbf{x})}[f(\mathbf{z})] \approx \frac{1}{S}\sum_{s=1}^{S} f(\mathbf{z}_s)$, where $\mathbf{z}_s \sim p(\mathbf{z}|\mathbf{x})$.

1.4 Examples of MCMC Kernels

Following our discussion of the requirements for designing valid Markov kernels for MCMC, we now discuss some well-known examples. The kernels we will discuss are

Gibbs sampling, Hamiltonian Monte Carlo, and Langevin dynamics. As you will see while we previously discussed our Markov kernel F as performing a single step in the MCMC process, to satisfy the requirements for being a valid MCMC kernel, most practical kernels – including all of the ones we discuss – require multiple internal steps.

11.4.1 Gibbs Sampling

Gibbs sampling is a useful example of an MCMC method for multivariate random variables. Let the state vector $\mathbf{z}$ be composed of n components; that is, $\mathbf{z} = (\mathbf{z}^1, \mathbf{z}^2, \ldots, \mathbf{z}^n)$. In Gibbs sampling, we update each component $\mathbf{z}^i$ sequentially, conditioned on the current values of all other components $\mathbf{z}^{-i} = (\mathbf{z}^1, \ldots, \mathbf{z}^{i-1}, \mathbf{z}^{i+1}, \ldots, \mathbf{z}^n)$. The order can be either random or fixed. Here we consider a fixed sequential order for the transition from $\mathbf{z}_t$ to $\mathbf{z}_{t+1}$:

$$\mathbf{z}_{t+1}^1 \sim q_{\text{target}}(\mathbf{z}^1 | \mathbf{z}_t^{2:n}), \tag{11.12}$$

$$\mathbf{z}_{t+1}^2 \sim q_{\text{target}}(\mathbf{z}^2 | \mathbf{z}_{t+1}^1, \mathbf{z}_t^{3:n}), \tag{11.13}$$

$$\vdots \tag{11.14}$$

$$\mathbf{z}_{t+1}^n \sim q_{\text{target}}(\mathbf{z}^n | \mathbf{z}_{t+1}^{1:n-1}). \tag{11.15}$$

Here, $q_{\text{target}}(\mathbf{z}^i | \mathbf{z}^{-i})$ denotes the conditional distribution of the ith component, given all other components. This process cycles through all components and defines a transition kernel $F(\mathbf{z}_{t+1} | \mathbf{z}_t)$ as the product of the conditional distributions.

The underlying principle of Gibbs sampling is that sampling from a univariate conditional distribution is often easier than sampling from the full joint distribution. Gibbs sampling is particularly useful for sampling from graphical models, which require only fixing the values of the nodes within the Markov blanket of the node of interest.

Reversibility

One can show that every individual conditional update step of the Gibbs sampling scheme itself satisfies the detailed balance condition, (11.8), with respect to the target distribution q_{target}. However, the composition of all these individual steps into the single Markov kernel F does not. This can easily be seen by considering that the Gibbs sampling algorithm depends on the order in which the variables are updated. This makes the corresponding Markov chain kernel F irreversible; you can check that if you use the same ordering for the forward and backward paths, the detailed balance condition (11.8) is not satisfied.

However, by reversing the ordering of the conditioned variables,

$$\mathbf{z}_t^n \sim q_{\text{target}}(\mathbf{z}^n | \mathbf{z}_{t+1}^{1:n-1}), \tag{11.16}$$

$$\mathbf{z}_t^{n-1} \sim q_{\text{target}}(\mathbf{z}^{n-1} | \mathbf{z}_{t+1}^{1:n-2}, \mathbf{z}_t^n), \tag{11.17}$$

$$\vdots$$

$$\mathbf{z}_t^1 \sim q_{\text{target}}(\mathbf{z}^1 | \mathbf{z}_t^{2:n}), \tag{11.18}$$

a reverse transition kernel $A(\mathbf{z}_t|\mathbf{z}_{t+1})$ can be constructed, and the invariance condition (11.4) holds. As such, both F and A leave the target distribution q_{target} invariant.

Notably, the Gibbs sampling scheme does become reversible if a random ordering is used for the conditional updates, such as in random-scan Gibbs sampling (Tierney, 1994).

11.4.2 Hamiltonian Monte Carlo

A really important MCMC method is called Hamiltonian Monte Carlo (Neal, 2011). It uses Hamiltonian dynamics to propose new samples. The idea behind HMC is to introduce auxiliary momentum variables $\mathbf{p}$ and define a Hamiltonian:

$$\mathcal{H}(\mathbf{z},\mathbf{p}) = \frac{1}{2}||\mathbf{p}||^2 + \mathcal{V}(\mathbf{z}), \tag{11.19}$$

$$\mathcal{V}(\mathbf{z}) = -\log q_{\text{target}}(\mathbf{z}). \tag{11.20}$$

These momentum variables are typically initialized from an isotropic Gaussian distribution,

$$p(\mathbf{p}) \propto e^{-\frac{1}{2}||\mathbf{p}||^2}. \tag{11.21}$$

HMC then constructs a transition kernel $F(\mathbf{x}'|\mathbf{x})$ over the combined phase space $\mathbf{x} = (\mathbf{z},\mathbf{p})$ of the system by simulating the evolution of this physical system using Hamilton's equations,

$$\frac{\mathrm{d}\mathbf{z}}{\mathrm{d}\tau} = \frac{\partial \mathcal{H}}{\partial \mathbf{p}} = \mathbf{p}, \tag{11.22}$$

$$\frac{\mathrm{d}\mathbf{p}}{\mathrm{d}\tau} = -\frac{\partial \mathcal{H}}{\partial \mathbf{z}} = -\frac{\partial \mathcal{V}(\mathbf{z})}{\partial \mathbf{z}} = \frac{\partial \log q_{\text{target}}(\mathbf{z})}{\partial \mathbf{z}}, \tag{11.23}$$

for a fixed amount of time starting from the current sample $\mathbf{x}$ to generate a new sample $\mathbf{x}'$. Here, τ is the fictitious time parameter of the Hamiltonian dynamics. A further discussion on Hamiltonian dynamics can be found in Chapter 3.

As we will confirm in the coming sections, this HMC kernel (including a momentum resampling step that will also be discussed later) has the Boltzmann distribution

$$p(\mathbf{z},\mathbf{p}) \propto \exp(-\mathcal{H}(\mathbf{z},\mathbf{p})) \tag{11.24}$$

as a stationary distribution. Note, however, that we are only interested in the samples $\{\mathbf{z}_n\}$; the momentum variables $\{\mathbf{p}_n\}$ were only added as auxiliary variables to define Hamiltonian dynamics. Fortunately, with $p(\mathbf{p})$ independent of $\mathbf{z}$, the momentum variables are independent of the position variables, and as such the marginal distribution over the original variables $\mathbf{z}$ of the Boltzmann distribution corresponds to our target distribution:

$$\begin{aligned}\int \mathrm{d}\mathbf{p}\, \exp(-\mathcal{H}(\mathbf{z},\mathbf{p})) &= \int \mathrm{d}\mathbf{p}\, \exp\left(-\frac{1}{2}||\mathbf{p}||^2\right) \exp(-\mathcal{V}(\mathbf{z})) \propto \exp(-\mathcal{V}(\mathbf{z})) \\ &= q_{\text{target}}(\mathbf{z}).\end{aligned} \tag{11.25}$$

The only thing we thus have to do is to ignore the samples $\{\mathbf{p}_n\}$, as the samples $\{\mathbf{z}_n\}$ are distributed according to this marginal by definition.

To show this is correct, however, we still need to show that HMC has the Boltzmann distribution $p(\mathbf{z}, \mathbf{p}) \propto \exp(-\mathcal{H}(\mathbf{z}, \mathbf{p}))$ as its unique stationary distribution and converges to it.

Reversibility by Momentum Flip

One can ask if the choice of transition kernel F defined by the Hamiltonian equations of motion satisfies DB with respect to the joint distribution $p(\mathbf{z}, \mathbf{p})$. Similar to the Gibbs sampler, this turns out not to be the case; instead, it satisfies the invariance condition. This can be proven by considering that Hamiltonian dynamics are volume and energy preserving. The conservation of energy can be easily proven by differentiating the Hamiltonian with respect to time:

$$\begin{aligned} \frac{\mathrm{d}\mathcal{H}}{\mathrm{d}\tau} &= \frac{\partial \mathcal{H}}{\partial \mathbf{z}} \frac{\mathrm{d}\mathbf{z}}{\mathrm{d}\tau} + \frac{\partial \mathcal{H}}{\partial \mathbf{p}} \frac{\mathrm{d}\mathbf{p}}{\mathrm{d}\tau} \\ &= \frac{\partial \mathcal{H}}{\partial \mathbf{z}} \frac{\partial \mathcal{H}}{\partial \mathbf{p}} + \frac{\partial \mathcal{H}}{\partial \mathbf{p}} \left(-\frac{\partial \mathcal{H}}{\partial \mathbf{z}} \right) = 0. \end{aligned} \tag{11.26}$$

For volume preservation, we refer to the discussion in Chapter 3.

To see that energy and volume preservation lead to the Boltzmann distribution being a stationary distribution for HMC, we first consider that we can write the Markov kernel defined by the Hamiltonian dynamics as a delta function,

$$F(\mathbf{x}'|\mathbf{x}) = \delta(\mathbf{x}' - \Phi(\mathbf{x})), \tag{11.27}$$

where $\Phi(\mathbf{x})$ defines the solution of running the Hamiltonian dynamics for a fixed time starting from $\mathbf{x}$. If we plug this into the definition of the invariance condition, (11.3) together with the Boltzmann distribution, (11.24), we get

$$\begin{aligned} \int \mathrm{d}\mathbf{x}\, p(\mathbf{x}) F(\mathbf{x}'|\mathbf{x}) &= \int \mathrm{d}\mathbf{x}\, \frac{1}{Z} \exp(-\mathcal{H}(\mathbf{x}))\delta(\mathbf{x}' - \Phi(\mathbf{x})) \\ &= \frac{1}{Z} \exp(-\mathcal{H}(\Phi^{-1}(\mathbf{x}'))) \cdot |\det \mathbf{J}_{\Phi^{-1}}(\mathbf{x}')| \end{aligned} \tag{11.28}$$

where we have used the change of variables formula, (8.2), to rewrite the integral in terms of the inverse transformation $\Phi^{-1}(\mathbf{x}')$. If we now consider that the Hamiltonian dynamics are volume preserving,

$$\exp(-\mathcal{H}(\Phi^{-1}(\mathbf{x}'))) \cdot |\det \mathbf{J}_{\Phi^{-1}}(\mathbf{x}')| = \exp(-\mathcal{H}(\Phi^{-1}(\mathbf{x}'))), \tag{11.29}$$

and energy preserving,

$$\exp(-\mathcal{H}(\Phi^{-1}(\mathbf{x}'))) = \exp(-\mathcal{H}(\mathbf{x}')), \tag{11.30}$$

we indeed find that the invariance condition is satisfied:

$$\int \mathrm{d}\mathbf{x}\, p(\mathbf{x}) F(\mathbf{x}'|\mathbf{x}) = p(\mathbf{x}'). \tag{11.31}$$

The adjoint kernel A can in this case be constructed by traversing the path in reverse order (moving in the opposite direction of $\mathbf{p}$). Without the dynamics conserving energy and volume, the adjoint kernel would also need to account for the Jacobian and the energy difference between the two points.

A naive way of restoring the DB condition would be to simply add a step to the end of each trajectory that flips the momenta. This follows because, with the extra momentum flip, F becomes an involution and can thus be used to both go from $\mathbf{x} \longrightarrow \mathbf{x}'$ and back again. However, while this would formally restore DB, it still has a remaining problem: it simply moves back and forth between two points, and therefore can never satisfy ergodicity.[2]

In general, one can show that deterministic dynamics can only satisfy DB if it is an *involution* (Neklyudov et al., 2020): a map with the property that $f(f(x)) = x$.

Ergodicity by Momentum Resampling

While conservation of energy was a useful property for helping to prove that HMC has the correct stationary distribution through the invariance condition, it unfortunately makes it infeasible for HMC in its simplest form to satisfy ergodicity. Given initial $\mathbf{z}_0$ and $\mathbf{p}_0$ with energy $E_0 = \mathcal{H}(\mathbf{z}_0, \mathbf{p}_0)$, the Markov kernel will only visit states with energy E_0. This makes the Markov kernel non-ergodic, and thus it will not converge towards the joint distribution $p(\mathbf{z}, \mathbf{p})$, which has our target distribution $q_{\text{target}}(\mathbf{z})$ as its marginal.

As briefly mentioned earlier, we can often resolve non-ergodicity by introducing a stochastic step. In the case of HMC, this is achieved by adding a step to the beginning of the HMC kernel where the momenta are reinitialized using a draw from an isotropic Gaussian distribution. This will place the system on a new energy level that will be traversed by the next iteration of the HMC kernel. This is called *momentum resampling*, and it ensures that the kernel is ergodic.

Crucially, we can show that this momentum resampling step will also ensure that the HMC kernel satisfies DB with respect to $p(\mathbf{z}, \mathbf{p})$ if we also include the momentum flip step at the end of the kernel, and thus makes it fully suitable for MCMC, by both having the right stationary distribution and converging to it.

This version of the method, with both the momentum flip and the momentum resampling step, is what is canonically referred to as HMC by the machine learning/MCMC community.

Discretization

Lastly, we make a note on the practical implementation of the HMC kernel, or any other deterministic continuous-time dynamics-based MCMC kernel for that matter. To practically implement the HMC kernel, we need to discretize the dynamics as given in (11.23).

This is typically done by using a reversible and symplectic integrator, such as the leapfrog or Verlet integration, which is used to simulate these equations, updating the

[2] We remind the reader of the comment at the end of Section 11.3.1; namely that physicists do call HMC reversible and say that it satisfies DB due to their different definition of DB.

position and momentum in a series of steps:

$$\mathbf{p}_{\tau+\frac{1}{2}\delta\tau} = \mathbf{p}_\tau - \frac{1}{2}\frac{\partial \mathcal{V}(\mathbf{z}_\tau)}{\partial \mathbf{z}}\delta\tau, \tag{11.32}$$

$$\mathbf{z}_{\tau+\delta\tau} = \mathbf{z}_\tau + \mathbf{p}_{\tau+\frac{1}{2}\delta\tau}\delta\tau, \tag{11.33}$$

$$\mathbf{p}_{\tau+\delta\tau} = \mathbf{p}_{\tau+\frac{1}{2}\delta\tau} - \frac{1}{2}\frac{\partial \mathcal{V}(\mathbf{z}_{\tau+\delta\tau})}{\partial \mathbf{z}}\delta\tau. \tag{11.34}$$

Our Markov kernel $F(\mathbf{x}'|\mathbf{x})$ now thus corresponds to a fixed integration time $T = N\delta\tau$, where both N and $\delta\tau$ are parameters to be tuned. However, this has the effect that the approximate Hamiltonian dynamics are no longer exactly energy preserving and as a result the kernel no longer has the correct stationary distribution. Fortunately we still have our trusted MH acceptance step to reinstate DB. We can show that, when using a reversible and symplectic integrator which retains the volume of the phase space exactly, the acceptance probability for the HMC proposal is given by:

$$p_{\text{accept}}(\mathbf{x}_{\tau+N\delta\tau}|\mathbf{x}_\tau) = \min\left[1, e^{\mathcal{H}(\mathbf{z}_\tau,\mathbf{p}_\tau)-\mathcal{H}(\mathbf{z}_{\tau+N\delta\tau},\mathbf{p}_{\tau+N\delta\tau})}\right]. \tag{11.35}$$

The timestep $\delta\tau$ is typically chosen to be small enough to ensure that the energy is still approximately conserved ($\Delta\mathcal{H} \approx 0$), so that the acceptance rate is close to 1.

With a non-volume-preserving integrator, the acceptance rate would also need to contain a Jacobian factor that corresponds to the change in volume of the phase space. Hamiltonian dynamics also preserves the volume in phase space, as we have shown in Chapter 3.

11.4.3 Langevin Monte Carlo

Finally, we mention the Langevin Monte Carlo (LMC) sampler, which is based on Langevin dynamics:

$$\mathrm{d}\mathbf{z} = \eta\frac{\partial \log q_{\text{target}}(\mathbf{z})}{\partial \mathbf{z}}\,\mathrm{d}\tau + \sqrt{2\eta}\;\mathrm{d}W_\tau, \tag{11.36}$$

where $\mathrm{d}W_\tau$ is a Wiener process and η is a parameter that controls the mobility of the system.

If we construct a Markov kernel $F(\mathbf{z}'|\mathbf{z})$ by running these continuous-time Langevin dynamics for a fixed amount of time, we can show that it satisfies the detailed balance condition with respect to the target distribution $q_{\text{target}}(\mathbf{z})$ and that it is ergodic. These proofs are more involved and require showing stationarity through the Fokker–Planck equation, which is covered in Chapter 21.

Discretization

Similar to HMC, to implement the LMC kernel in practice, we need to discretize the dynamics in (11.36). One approach is to use the Euler–Maruyama method, a simple and widely used numerical method for solving stochastic differential equations. The Euler–Maruyama update is given by:

$$\mathbf{z}_{\tau+\delta\tau} = \mathbf{z}_\tau + \eta\frac{\partial \log q_{\text{target}}(\mathbf{z}_\tau)}{\partial \mathbf{z}}\delta\tau + \sqrt{2\eta\delta\tau}\,\boldsymbol{\epsilon}_\tau, \quad \boldsymbol{\epsilon}_\tau \sim G(\mathbf{0},\mathbf{I}). \tag{11.37}$$

Again, similar to HMC, with discretization the dynamics are no longer exactly reversible and thus do not leave the target distribution $q_{\text{target}}(\mathbf{z})$ invariant. To account for these errors when the step size $\delta\tau$ is not infinitesimally small, we need an additional Metropolis–Hastings correction step. For a single step of the discretized dynamics, the proposal distribution is a Gaussian, and the acceptance probability is given by

$$p_{\text{accept}}(\mathbf{z}_{\mathcal{T}+\delta\mathcal{T}}|\mathbf{z}_{\mathcal{T}}) = \min\left[1, \frac{q_{\text{target}}(\mathbf{z}_{\mathcal{T}+\delta\mathcal{T}})G(\mathbf{z}_{\mathcal{T}}; \boldsymbol{\mu}', 2\eta\delta\mathcal{T}\,\mathbf{I})}{q_{\text{target}}(\mathbf{z}_{\mathcal{T}})G(\mathbf{z}_{\mathcal{T}+\delta\mathcal{T}}; \boldsymbol{\mu}, 2\eta\delta\mathcal{T}\,\mathbf{I})}\right], \tag{11.38}$$

$$\boldsymbol{\mu} = \mathbf{z}_{\mathcal{T}} + \eta\frac{\partial \log q_{\text{target}}(\mathbf{z}_{\mathcal{T}})}{\partial \mathbf{z}}\delta\mathcal{T}, \tag{11.39}$$

$$\boldsymbol{\mu}' = \mathbf{z}_{\mathcal{T}+\delta\mathcal{T}} + \eta\frac{\partial \log q_{\text{target}}(\mathbf{z}_{\mathcal{T}+\delta\mathcal{T}})}{\partial \mathbf{z}}\delta\mathcal{T}. \tag{11.40}$$

This version of Langevin Monte Carlo with an MH correction is commonly referred to as the Metropolis-adjusted Langevin algorithm (MALA). As the step size $\delta\mathcal{T}$ decreases, the acceptance probability approaches 1, and the algorithm reduces to the uncorrected continuous-time Langevin dynamics.

You can show that the Langevin MCMC sampler is a limiting case of HMC where we identify in the first two lines of the leapfrog integrator:

$$\boldsymbol{\epsilon}_{\mathcal{T}} = \mathbf{p}_{\mathcal{T}} \sim G(\mathbf{0}, \mathbf{I}), \tag{11.41}$$

$$\eta = \frac{1}{2}\delta\mathcal{T}. \tag{11.42}$$

However, unlike HMC, which uses deterministic updates for $\mathbf{p}$ during the leapfrog integration, Langevin dynamics introduces stochasticity at each step through the noise term $\sqrt{2\eta\delta\mathcal{T}}\,\boldsymbol{\epsilon}_{\mathcal{T}}$.

In physics, Langevin Monte Carlo methods are widely used to sample from complicated, high-dimensional distributions, from molecules (Frenkel and Smit, 2001), up to problems as complex as lattice gauge theories. In machine learning, Langevin samplers are used to generate samples from the posterior distribution (Salimans et al., 2015), and from energy-based models (EBMs), and also to train them (Du and Mordatch, 2019; Song and Kingma, 2021; Carbone et al., 2023). The log-gradient term also has a close connection to the score-matching objective of diffusion models, which we will discuss in later chapters.

12 Sequential Importance Sampling

12.1 Introduction

In the previous chapter, we looked at the family of MCMC methods, which are designed to sample from a target distribution by constructing a Markov chain that converges to the target distribution. This makes MCMC methods an incredibly powerful tool for sampling from complex distributions. However, MCMC methods are not without their limitations. Most importantly, they can take exponentially long to converge when the target distribution is multimodal with regions of low probability separating the modes, and crucially, while they can even be used to sample from unnormalized distributions, their generated samples cannot be used to approximate the normalizing constant of this unnormalized density.

While it doesn't provide exact samples from the target distribution, unlike MCMC, importance sampling, as discussed in the preliminary chapters, provides a powerful tool for approximating expectations of functions under any target distribution, including multimodal ones. And crucially, IS can be used to approximate the normalizing constant of an unnormalized target distribution, in the form of self-normalized importance sampling.

Unfortunately, however, IS is not a solve-all solution. In order for IS to provide a valid and efficient estimation procedure, the proposal distribution $q(\mathbf{x})$ must satisfy certain requirements. First, it must have support everywhere the target distribution $p_{\text{target}}(\mathbf{x})$ does, meaning that $q(\mathbf{x})$ must be nonzero wherever $p_{\text{target}}(\mathbf{x})$ is nonzero. Second, the proposal distribution should be chosen to be as similar as possible to the target density to reduce the variance of the importance weights, as can be inferred from (12.5). However, in high-dimensional spaces, importance sampling often fails due to the curse of dimensionality: Most samples have negligible weights, with only a few dominating the estimation. This makes it challenging to design effective proposal distributions as dimensionality increases.

This is where sequential importance sampling comes in. Instead of directly sampling from a proposal distribution, similar to MCMC, SIS iteratively updates a set of samples using a Markov kernel. In contrast to MCMC, however, the Markov kernel used is often time dependent, which allows for nontrivial importance weights to be computed. One particularly important SIS method is annealed importance sampling (AIS) (Neal, 2001), which is closely related to concepts from stochastic thermodynamics (ST).

We will start off this chapter with a brief discussion on the variance of the IS and self-normalized importance sampling (SNIS) estimators, and then move on to discuss the sequential importance sampling framework.

12.2 Variance of IS and SNIS

To briefly recap, importance sampling and self-normalized importance sampling are two methods for estimating expectations of functions under a target distribution. Given the objective to estimate the expectation of a function $f(\mathbf{x})$ under a target distribution $p_{\text{target}}(\mathbf{x}) = \frac{1}{Z_p}\gamma(\mathbf{x})$, the IS and SNIS estimators are given by

$$\mathbb{E}_{p_{\text{target}}}[f(\mathbf{x})] \simeq \langle f \rangle_{\text{IS}} = \frac{1}{N}\sum_{n=1}^{N} w(\mathbf{x}_n) f(\mathbf{x}_n), \tag{12.1}$$

$$\mathbb{E}_{p_{\text{target}}}[f(\mathbf{x})] \simeq \langle f \rangle_{\text{SNIS}} = \frac{\frac{1}{N}\sum_{n=1}^{N} \tilde{w}(\mathbf{x}_n) f(\mathbf{x}_n)}{\frac{1}{N}\sum_{n=1}^{N} \tilde{w}(\mathbf{x}_n)}, \tag{12.2}$$

where we have the normalized importance weights and unnormalized importance weights defined as

$$w(\mathbf{x}_n) = \frac{p_{\text{target}}(\mathbf{x}_n)}{q(\mathbf{x}_n)}, \qquad \tilde{w}(\mathbf{x}_n) = \frac{\gamma(\mathbf{x}_n)}{q(\mathbf{x}_n)}. \tag{12.3}$$

Interestingly, for any unnormalized target density $\gamma(\mathbf{x})$, we can use the unnormalized importance weights to estimate the normalization constant Z_p as

$$\mathbb{E}_q[\tilde{w}(\mathbf{x})] = Z_p. \tag{12.4}$$

We can now consider the variance of these two estimators. The variance of the IS estimator is given by

$$\begin{aligned}
\mathbb{V}[\langle f \rangle_{\text{IS}}] &= \mathbb{V}\left[\frac{1}{N}\sum_{n=1}^{N} w(\mathbf{x}_n) f(\mathbf{x}_n)\right] \\
&= \frac{1}{N^2}\sum_{n=1}^{N} \mathbb{V}[w(\mathbf{x}_n) f(\mathbf{x}_n)] \\
&= \frac{1}{N}\mathbb{V}[w(\mathbf{x}) f(\mathbf{x})] \\
&= \frac{1}{N}\left(\mathbb{E}_q[w(\mathbf{x})^2 f(\mathbf{x})^2] - \mathbb{E}_{p_{\text{target}}}[f(\mathbf{x})]^2\right),
\end{aligned} \tag{12.5}$$

where we can generally ignore the constant term containing the true expectation value of $f(\mathbf{x})$, as it is independent of the samples. Similarly, we can derive the asymptotic variance of the SNIS estimator as

$$\mathbb{V}[\langle f \rangle_{\text{SNIS}}] \approx \frac{1}{N}\mathbb{E}_q[w(\mathbf{x})^2 (f(\mathbf{x}) - \mathbb{E}_{p_{\text{target}}}[f(\mathbf{x})])^2], \tag{12.6}$$

which, notably, while having the same leading order $1/N$ as the IS estimator, is often smaller than the variance of the IS estimator due to the centering around the mean.

More fundamentally for the remainder of this chapter, in the case of estimating the normalization constant Z_p, where $f(\mathbf{x}) = 1$, we can see that the variance of the normalizing constant $\mathcal{Z}_p = \frac{1}{N}\sum_{n=1}^{N} \tilde{w}(\mathbf{x}_n)$ is given by

$$\mathbb{V}[\mathcal{Z}_p] = \frac{1}{N}\mathbb{V}[\tilde{w}(\mathbf{x})] = \frac{1}{N}(\mathbb{E}_q[\tilde{w}(\mathbf{x})^2] - Z_p^2), \tag{12.7}$$

which shows that we can minimize the variance of the estimator of the normalization constant Z_p by choosing a proposal distribution $q(\mathbf{x})$ that is as similar as possible to the unnormalized target density $\gamma(\mathbf{x})$, and thus minimizes the expected value of the square of the importance weights (see Figure 12.1).

This idea, of choosing a proposal distribution that is as similar to the target density as possible, and as such, minimizes the variance of the IS estimate of the normalization constant Z_p by minimizing the variance of the weights $\tilde{w}(\mathbf{x})$, is very powerful. As we discuss next, SIS not only overcomes the challenges of importance sampling with regard to how it scales with dimensionality, but also introduces a framework in which there are multiple ways for tuning the weights to minimize the variance.

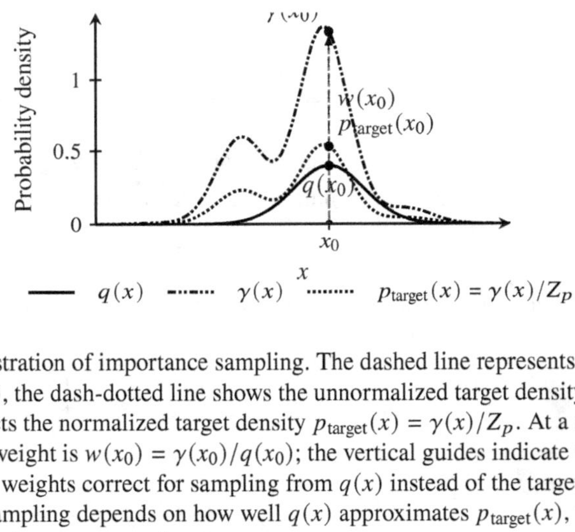

Figure 12.1 Illustration of importance sampling. The dashed line represents the proposal distribution $q(x)$, the dash-dotted line shows the unnormalized target density $\gamma(x)$, and the dotted line depicts the normalized target density $p_{\text{target}}(x) = \gamma(x)/Z_p$. At a specific point x_0, the importance weight is $w(x_0) = \gamma(x_0)/q(x_0)$; the vertical guides indicate the values used in this ratio. These weights correct for sampling from $q(x)$ instead of the target. The effectiveness of importance sampling depends on how well $q(x)$ approximates $p_{\text{target}}(x)$, with the optimal case being when they are proportional.

12.3 Sequential Importance Sampling

To circumvent the issues of IS, sequential importance sampling introduces a sequence of intermediate distributions $\{\pi_t\}$ that bridge from a tractable distribution π_0 to the target distribution $\pi_{t_f} = p_{\text{target}}$. Typically, one chooses

$$\pi_t(\mathbf{x}) = \frac{1}{Z_t}\gamma_t(\mathbf{x}) = \frac{1}{Z_t}\pi_0(\mathbf{x})^{1-\beta_t}\gamma(\mathbf{x})^{\beta_t}, \tag{12.8}$$

with $0 = \beta_0 < \beta_1 < \cdots < \beta_{t_f} = 1$ an annealing schedule and Z_t the normalization constant for the intermediate distribution π_t. Other parameterizations can be considered, and the choice of parameterization plays a crucial role in the variance of the estimator.

Extending the Proposal Distribution Forwards in Time

Additionally, SIS defines a sequence of time-dependent transition kernels F_t. In theory, these can be any valid Markov kernels and do not need to have any specific stationary distributions or satisfy ergodicity, but in practice we will often choose them to leave the corresponding intermediate distributions π_t invariant, satisfying the following condition:

$$F_t(\mathbf{x}_t|\mathbf{x}_{t-1})\pi_t(\mathbf{x}_{t-1}) = A_t(\mathbf{x}_{t-1}|\mathbf{x}_t)\pi_t(\mathbf{x}_t), \tag{12.9}$$

where A_t is the adjoint kernel corresponding to F_t that also leaves the same stationary distribution π_t invariant, following the notation established in Chapter 9.

By sampling $\mathbf{x}_0 \sim \pi_0$ and applying the sequence of transition kernels F_t, SIS constructs an extended joint proposal distribution

$$Q(\mathbf{x}_{0:t_f}) = \pi_0(\mathbf{x}_0) \prod_{t=1}^{t_f} F_t(\mathbf{x}_t|\mathbf{x}_{t-1}). \tag{12.10}$$

The marginal distribution at step t is given by

$$\begin{aligned} q_t(\mathbf{x}_t) &= \int d\mathbf{x}_{0:t-1}\, d\mathbf{x}_{t+1:t_f}\, Q(\mathbf{x}_{0:t_f}) \\ &= \int d\mathbf{x}_{0:t-1}\, \pi_0(\mathbf{x}_0) \prod_{j=1}^{t} F_j(\mathbf{x}_j|\mathbf{x}_{j-1}). \end{aligned} \tag{12.11}$$

Since the transition kernels F_t change at every step, the system has limited time to mix. Consequently, after each sampling step, the marginal distribution of the t-th sample, q_t, is not equal to the equilibrium distribution of the t-th kernel, π_t; that is, $q_t \neq \pi_t$. In thermodynamic terms, we say that the system is out of equilibrium and is not evolving adiabatically (see Figure 12.2).[1]

Extending the Target Distribution Backward in Time

We now introduce a second extended joint distribution, but this time running backward from the target distribution:

$$P(\mathbf{x}_{0:t_f}) = \frac{1}{Z_p}\gamma(\mathbf{x}_{t_f}) \prod_{t=1}^{t_f} K_t(\mathbf{x}_{t-1}|\mathbf{x}_t), \tag{12.12}$$

[1] Note that methods that introduce the extended joint distribution are often referred to in the literature as *sequential Monte Carlo* (SMC) methods (Del Moral et al., 2006) instead of *sequential* or *annealed importance sampling*. We reserve SMC for the more specific case where additional steps (e.g., MCMC steps or reweighting) are introduced to enforce that $q_t \approx \pi_t$.

where K_t are valid Markov transition kernels satisfying $\int d\mathbf{x}_{t-1}\ K_t(\mathbf{x}_{t-1}|\mathbf{x}_t) = 1$. By construction, the marginal distribution at the final step t_f is the target distribution:

$$p_{t_f}(\mathbf{x}_{t_f}) = \int d\mathbf{x}_{0:t_f-1}\ P(\mathbf{x}_{0:t_f}) = \frac{\gamma(\mathbf{x}_{t_f})}{Z_p} = p_{\text{target}}(\mathbf{x}_{t_f}). \qquad (12.13)$$

Using the SIS Framework to Estimate Expectations

For any choice of forward and backward kernels (which do not have to be related to each other), we can devise a procedure to compute approximate averages over functions $h(\mathbf{x})$. First, we identify $\mathbf{x} = \mathbf{x}_{t_f}$ and extend the space of random variables to $\{\mathbf{x}_0, \dots, \mathbf{x}_{t_f}\}$. We then sample from the forward chain (which is tractable by construction) and compute the unnormalized importance weights given by the ratio of the backward and forward joint distributions similar to (12.3):

$$w(\mathbf{x}_{0:t_f}) = Z_p \frac{P(\mathbf{x}_{0:t_f})}{Q(\mathbf{x}_{0:t_f})} = \frac{\gamma(\mathbf{x}_{t_f}) \prod_{t=1}^{t_f} K_t(\mathbf{x}_{t-1}|\mathbf{x}_t)}{\pi_0(\mathbf{x}_0) \prod_{t=1}^{t_f} F_t(\mathbf{x}_t|\mathbf{x}_{t-1})}. \qquad (12.14)$$

Note here that we previously used $\tilde{w}$ to denote the unnormalized importance weight and reserved w for the normalized importance weights. As the remainder of the chapter, and much of the remainder of the book, will primarily work with unnormalized probability distributions, we will use w to denote the unnormalized importance weight for simplicity from now on.

The expectation of a function $h(\mathbf{x})$ under the target distribution can then be estimated in the same way as was IS; that is, by using the importance weights:

$$\mathbb{E}_p[h] \simeq \frac{\sum_{s=1}^S w_s h(\mathbf{x}_{t_f}^s)}{\sum_{s=1}^S w_s}, \qquad w_s \equiv w(\mathbf{x}_0^s, \dots, \mathbf{x}_{t_f}^s), \qquad \mathbf{x}_0^s, \dots, \mathbf{x}_{t_f}^s \sim Q. \quad (12.15)$$

Moreover, if we choose $h = Z_p$ (i.e., a constant) we get

$$Z_p \simeq \frac{1}{S} \sum_{s=1}^S w(\mathbf{x}_0^s, \dots, \mathbf{x}_{t_f}^s) = \frac{1}{S} \sum_{s=1}^S w_s. \qquad (12.16)$$

We remark that we can extend the function h, which is only defined on $\mathbf{x}_{t_f}$, to the whole sequence by simply making it independent of those dimensions.

It is very interesting that these results hold in theory for arbitrary choices of F and K (see the discussion in Section 17.2). However, if we don't choose them wisely, we will face very large variance in our estimates. In the following, we will discuss some choices and relate them back to ST and ML, emphasizing variance-reduction heuristics.

12.3.1 Annealed Importance Sampling

We now consider a specific case of SIS: annealed importance sampling. In AIS, the backward kernels K_t are typically chosen to be the adjoint of the forward kernels F

with respect to the intermediate distributions π_t:

$$K_t(\mathbf{x}_{t-1}|\mathbf{x}_t) = A_t(\mathbf{x}_{t-1}|\mathbf{x}_t) \tag{12.17}$$

$$= \frac{\pi_t(\mathbf{x}_{t-1})F_t(\mathbf{x}_t|\mathbf{x}_{t-1})}{\pi_t(\mathbf{x}_t)}. \tag{12.18}$$

Note here that this kernel must always exist, but that in the case that we choose F_t to leave π_t invariant, we also explicitly know that A_t similarly has the corresponding stationary distribution π_t. This will be useful in the next step. Indeed, with this choice of backward kernels, the importance weights in AIS simplify to

$$\begin{aligned} w(\mathbf{x}_{0:t_f}) &= \frac{\gamma(\mathbf{x}_{t_f})\prod_{t=1}^{t_f} K_t(\mathbf{x}_{t-1}|\mathbf{x}_t)}{\pi_0(\mathbf{x}_0)\prod_{t=1}^{t_f} F_t(\mathbf{x}_t|\mathbf{x}_{t-1})} \\ &= \frac{\gamma(\mathbf{x}_{t_f})\prod_{t=1}^{t_f} A_t(\mathbf{x}_{t-1}|\mathbf{x}_t)}{\pi_0(\mathbf{x}_0)\prod_{t=1}^{t_f} F_t(\mathbf{x}_t|\mathbf{x}_{t-1})} \\ &= \frac{\gamma(\mathbf{x}_{t_f})\prod_{t=1}^{t_f} \frac{\pi_t(\mathbf{x}_{t-1})F_t(\mathbf{x}_t|\mathbf{x}_{t-1})}{\pi_t(\mathbf{x}_t)}}{\pi_0(\mathbf{x}_0)\prod_{t=1}^{t_f} F_t(\mathbf{x}_t|\mathbf{x}_{t-1})} \\ &= Z_0\frac{\gamma(\mathbf{x}_{t_f})}{\gamma_0(\mathbf{x}_0)}\prod_{t=1}^{t_f}\frac{\gamma_t(\mathbf{x}_{t-1})}{\gamma_t(\mathbf{x}_t)} \\ &= Z_0\frac{\gamma(\mathbf{x}_{t_f})}{\gamma_{t_f}(\mathbf{x}_{t_f})}\prod_{t=1}^{t_f}\frac{\gamma_t(\mathbf{x}_{t-1})}{\gamma_{t-1}(\mathbf{x}_{t-1})} \\ &= Z_0\prod_{t=1}^{t_f}\frac{\gamma_t(\mathbf{x}_{t-1})}{\gamma_{t-1}(\mathbf{x}_{t-1})}, \end{aligned} \tag{12.19}$$

which we recognize as the annealed importance weights with Z_0 being the partition function of the initial distribution π_0.

Connection to Stochastic Thermodynamics

If we write $\gamma_t(\mathbf{x}_t) = \exp(-\beta\mathcal{H}_t(\mathbf{x}_t))$,[2] then the weights can be expressed in terms of the work performed during the annealing process:

$$\begin{aligned} w(\mathbf{x}_{0:t_f}) &= Z_0 \exp\left(-\beta\sum_{t=1}^{t_f}[\mathcal{H}_t(\mathbf{x}_{t-1}) - \mathcal{H}_{t-1}(\mathbf{x}_{t-1})]\right) \\ &= Z_0\exp(-\beta\mathcal{W}[\mathbf{x}_0,\ldots,\mathbf{x}_{t_f}]), \end{aligned} \tag{12.20}$$

where, if we assume detailed balance for a moment, the expression in the exponent, $\mathcal{W}[\mathbf{x}_0,\ldots,\mathbf{x}_{t_f}]$, represents work performed in the sequence of steps. If we now use (12.16) and re-express this as work, we find what is known in ST (Chapter 10) as

[2] Note that this inverse temperature β is different from the temperature schedule β_t defined for AIS. Here, β is determined by the heat bath, whereas the sequence above was just to define a sequence of marginal distributions. We have absorbed all the time dependence into the Hamiltonian $\mathcal{H}_t$.

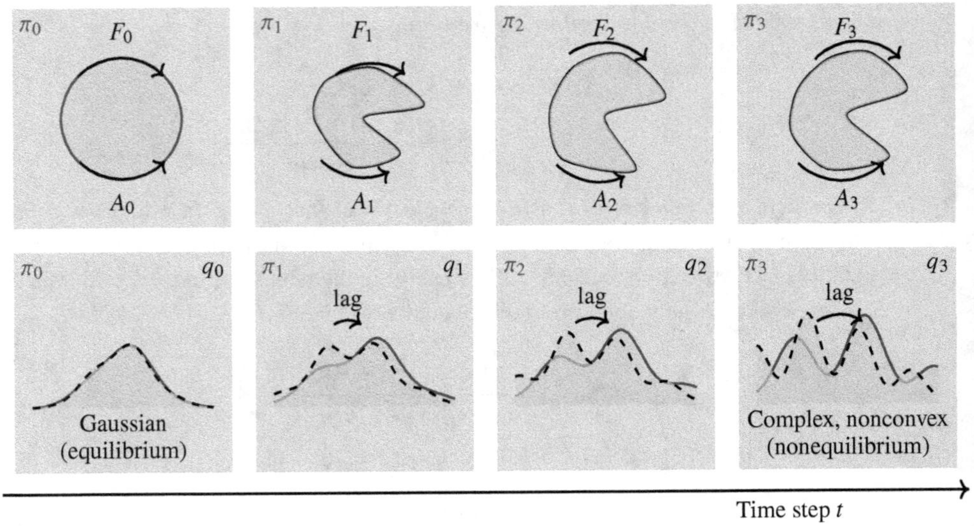

Figure 12.2 Evolution of probability distributions and transition kernels in sequential importance sampling. Each panel represents a time step. Top row: Equilibrium distribution π_t (solid contours) with forward F_t (solid clockwise arrows) and adjoint A_t (solid counterclockwise arrows) kernels that satisfy the balance condition from Chapter 9. Bottom row: Instantaneous equilibrium π_t (solid curves) and marginal q_t (dashed curves) distribution of the forward process, cf. (12.11). The "lag" arrow shows that $q_t \neq \pi_t$ in finite time; that is, the system is driven out of equilibrium and cannot fully relax before the next kernel is applied. The increasing discrepancy from left to right shows how this nonequilibrium lag typically grows as the evolution progresses.

the Jarzynski equality (Jarzynski, 1997) to estimate the free energy:

$$\frac{Z_P}{Z_0} = \mathbb{E}_Q \left[\exp(-\beta \mathcal{W}[\mathbf{x}_0, \ldots, \mathbf{x}_{t_f}]) \right], \tag{12.21}$$

where the average is over sequences sampled from the forward process Q.

Note that this connection to the Jarzynski equality is specific to the case when detailed balance holds and we choose the backward kernels as in (12.17). Without detailed balance, this is connected to the fluctuation theorems of the nonadiabatic entropy production discussed in Chapter 17.

12.3.2 Optimizing Sequential Importance Sampling

The choice we made for K_t in (12.17) for AIS was not optimal in terms of minimizing the variance of the importance weights.

To find the optimal kernel, let us compute the variance of the importance weights. Similar to (12.5), the variance of the importance weights can be decomposed using th law of total variance (Cover and Thomas, 2006):

$$
\begin{aligned}
\mathbb{V}_Q[w(\mathbf{x}_{0:t_f})] &= \mathbb{E}_Q[w(\mathbf{x}_{0:t_f})^2] - \mathbb{E}_Q[w(\mathbf{x}_{0:t_f})]^2 \\
&= \mathbb{E}_{q_{t_f}}[\mathbb{E}_{Q(\cdot|\mathbf{x}_{t_f})}[w(\mathbf{x}_{0:t_f})^2]] - \mathbb{E}_{q_{t_f}}[\mathbb{E}_{Q(\cdot|\mathbf{x}_{t_f})}[w(\mathbf{x}_{0:t_f})]]^2 \\
&= \mathbb{E}_{q_{t_f}}[\mathbb{E}_{Q(\cdot|\mathbf{x}_{t_f})}[w(\mathbf{x}_{0:t_f})^2] - \mathbb{E}_{Q(\cdot|\mathbf{x}_{t_f})}[w(\mathbf{x}_{0:t_f})]^2] \\
&\quad + \mathbb{E}_{q_{t_f}}[\mathbb{E}_{Q(\cdot|\mathbf{x}_{t_f})}[w(\mathbf{x}_{0:t_f})]^2] - \mathbb{E}_{q_{t_f}}[\mathbb{E}_{Q(\cdot|\mathbf{x}_{t_f})}[w(\mathbf{x}_{0:t_f})]]^2 \\
&= \mathbb{E}_{q_{t_f}}[\mathbb{V}_{Q(\cdot|\mathbf{x}_{t_f})}[w(\mathbf{x}_{0:t_f})]] + \mathbb{V}_{q_{t_f}}[\mathbb{E}_{Q(\cdot|\mathbf{x}_{t_f})}[w(\mathbf{x}_{0:t_f})]] \\
&= \mathbb{E}_{q_{t_f}}[\mathbb{V}_{Q(\cdot|\mathbf{x}_{t_f})}[w(\mathbf{x}_{0:t_f})]] + \mathbb{V}_{q_{t_f}}[w_{\text{mar}}(\mathbf{x}_{t_f})],
\end{aligned} \tag{12.22}
$$

where $w_{\text{mar}}(\mathbf{x}_{t_f}) = \gamma(\mathbf{x}_{t_f})/q_{t_f}(\mathbf{x}_{t_f})$ are the marginal importance weights at the final step and the first term can be decomposed into the expected variance of the importance weights at each step, averaged over the marginal distributions, by applying the law of total variance recursively for each step $t = 1, \ldots, t_f$.

A highly related computation can be performed using KL divergences. First, recall from previous chapters that we can invert the forward model using a backward kernel B, defined as

$$
B_t(\mathbf{x}_{t-1}|\mathbf{x}_t) = \frac{F_t(\mathbf{x}_t|\mathbf{x}_{t-1})q_{t-1}(\mathbf{x}_{t-1})}{q_t(\mathbf{x}_t)} \tag{12.23}
$$

$$
\Rightarrow Q(\mathbf{x}_{0:t_f}) = q_{t_f}(\mathbf{x}_{t_f}) \prod_{t=1}^{t_f} B_t(\mathbf{x}_{t-1}|\mathbf{x}_t). \tag{12.24}
$$

Then, the KL divergence between the forward and backward joint distributions can be decomposed using the chain rule as follows:

$$
\begin{aligned}
D_{\text{KL}}[Q\|P] &= \mathbb{E}_Q\left[\log \frac{Q(\mathbf{x}_{0:t_f})}{P(\mathbf{x}_{0:t_f})}\right] \\
&= \mathbb{E}_Q\left[\log \frac{q_{t_f}(\mathbf{x}_{t_f})}{p_{t_f}(\mathbf{x}_{t_f})} + \log \frac{Q(\mathbf{x}_{0:t_f-1}|\mathbf{x}_{t_f})}{P(\mathbf{x}_{0:t_f-1}|\mathbf{x}_{t_f})}\right] \\
&= D_{\text{KL}}[q_{t_f}\|p_{t_f}] + \mathbb{E}_{q_{t_f}}[D_{\text{KL}}[Q(\cdot|\mathbf{x}_{t_f})\|P(\cdot|\mathbf{x}_{t_f})]] \\
&= D_{\text{KL}}[q_{t_f}\|\pi_{t_f}] + \sum_{t=1}^{t_f} \mathbb{E}_{q_t}[D_{\text{KL}}[B_t(\cdot|\mathbf{x}_t)\|K_t(\cdot|\mathbf{x}_t)]].
\end{aligned} \tag{12.25}
$$

The first term in the decomposition represents the KL divergence between the marginal distribution at the final step (q_{t_f}) and the target distribution (π_{t_f}), while the second term is the expected KL divergence between the kernel that inverts F and backward transition kernel K at each step, averaged over the marginal distributions.

For a fixed forward process Q, both the KL divergence and the variance of the importance weights are minimized when the backward kernels are chosen to be the kernel K that gives the inverse of the forward process (Doucet et al., 2022):

$$
K_t^*(\mathbf{x}_{t-1}|\mathbf{x}_t) = B_t(\mathbf{x}_{t-1}|\mathbf{x}_t). \tag{12.26}
$$

At this optimal point, we have

$$D_{\mathrm{KL}}[Q\|P] = D_{\mathrm{KL}}[q_{t_f}\|\pi_{t_f}], \tag{12.27}$$

$$\mathbb{V}_Q[w(\mathbf{x}_{0:t_f})] = \mathbb{V}_{q_{t_f}}[w_{\mathrm{mar}}(\mathbf{x}_{t_f})]. \tag{12.28}$$

We see two differences relative to (12.17): first, we use q instead of π; and second, w use a trajectory balance equation between two subsequent states rather than a conditio for the stationarity of a target distribution at some time t. This equation inverts th process $F_t\colon q_{t-1} \mapsto q_t$. If we view $F_t\colon q_{t-1} \mapsto q_t$ as the map that transforms q_{t-} to q_t, then $K_t^* = B_t$ implements the inverse of that process (like playing the "movie backwards in time); that is, $K_t^*\colon q_t \mapsto q_{t-1}$. Recall the difference between π_t an q_t (see Figure 12.2): the distribution π_t is a fixed, target distribution at time t and i the invariant distribution for F_t, while q_t is the marginal distribution of the forwar process Q at time t.

With this optimal choice of K_t^*, the importance weights simplify to the ratio of th target density and the marginal density at the final step:

$$w(\mathbf{x}_{0:t_f}) = \frac{\gamma(\mathbf{x}_{t_f}) \prod_{t=1}^{t_f} B_t(\mathbf{x}_{t-1}|\mathbf{x}_t)}{\pi_0(\mathbf{x}_0) \prod_{t=1}^{t_f} F_t(\mathbf{x}_t|\mathbf{x}_{t-1})} = \frac{\gamma(\mathbf{x}_{t_f})}{q_{t_f}(\mathbf{x}_{t_f})}. \tag{12.29}$$

While q_{t_f} is not tractable, the expression for the weights in terms of forward an backward kernels is tractable if we have access to K_t^*. One approach is to learn a goo model for K_t^* that approximately inverts F_t and then use this expression to comput the importance weights.

The advantage of (12.29) over the AIS weights in eq12.19 is that it only involve the marginal densities at the final step. However, AIS has the advantage of guiding th forward process Q so that the final marginal $q_{t_f} \approx \pi_{t_f} = p_{\mathrm{target}}$. The low variance c the weights in (12.29) then relies on q_{t_f} being close to $\pi_{t_f} = p_{\mathrm{target}}$.

What we would need is the best of both worlds: if we can design a forward mode with the correct marginal p at time t_f while choosing the backward kernel to be (12.26 this would lead to importance weights that are almost always equal to 1, resulting i very low variance. Let's use the AIS interpolating distributions $\{\pi_t\}$ to guide us to p a before. This sequence determines forward transitions F_t and the adjoint kernel A_t, bot of which leave the distribution π_t invariant. Now, as in (12.26), let's choose the optima kernel K_t^* to extend the distribution p to full sequences. We can rewrite (12.26) as

$$K_t^*(\mathbf{x}_{t-1}|\mathbf{x}_t) = A_t(\mathbf{x}_{t-1}|\mathbf{x}_t)\left[\frac{\pi_t(\mathbf{x}_t)q_{t-1}(\mathbf{x}_{t-1})}{q_t(\mathbf{x}_t)\pi_t(\mathbf{x}_{t-1})}\right], \tag{12.30}$$

where A_t is the adjoint kernel corresponding to F_t with respect to π_t from Chapter The difference between this expression and the AIS backward kernels, 12.17, is sma when $q_t \approx \pi_t$ and $\pi_t \approx q_{t-1}$; that is, when the marginal distributions are close to th equilibrium distributions – the regime where the system is evolving adiabatically. Th importance weights are still given by (12.29), but now we can hope that $q_{t_f} \approx \pi_{t_f}$ p_{target}, leading to more efficient sampling.

While the choice of the backward kernel K can help to reduce the variance of th importance weights, the marginal distributions q_t are ultimately determined by th forward process F. Optimizing both F and K together can lead to even more efficient sampling.

Learning the Optimal Forward and Backward Kernels

We can easily derive a bound on $F_p = -\log Z_p$ by the following derivation (Doucet et al., 2022; Salimans et al., 2015; Ho et al., 2020; Thin et al., 2021). To learn the optimal backward kernels K_t^*, we can formulate a variational objective that minimizes the KL divergence between the forward and backward joint distributions. This produces a lower bound on $\log Z_p$:

$$
\begin{aligned}
& D_{\mathrm{KL}}[Q \| P] \geq 0 \\
\Rightarrow & \sum_{\mathbf{x}_{0:t_f}} Q(\mathbf{x}_{0:t_f}) \log \left(\frac{Q(\mathbf{x}_{0:t_f})}{P(\mathbf{x}_{0:t_f})} \right) \geq 0 \\
\Rightarrow & -\sum_{\mathbf{x}_{0:t_f}} Q(\mathbf{x}_{0:t_f}) \log \left(Z_p \frac{P(\mathbf{x}_{0:t_f})}{Q(\mathbf{x}_{0:t_f})} \right) + \log Z_p \geq 0 \\
\Rightarrow & -\log Z_p = F_p \leq -\sum_{\mathbf{x}_{0:t_f}} Q(\mathbf{x}_{0:t_f}) \log w(\mathbf{x}_{0:t_f}) = \mathcal{F}.
\end{aligned} \tag{12.31}
$$

Of course, we identify this objective as the ELBO we have seen before. For the choice of forward and backward kernels made under AIS, we get

$$
\begin{aligned}
\mathcal{F} &= -\sum_{t=1}^{t_f} \mathbb{E}_{q_{t-1}}[\log(\gamma_t) - \log(\gamma_{t-1})] - \log Z_0 \\
&= \beta \sum_{t=1}^{t_f} (\mathbb{E}_{q_{t-1}}[\mathcal{H}_t] - \mathbb{E}_{q_{t-1}}[\mathcal{H}_{t-1}]) = \beta \mathbb{E}_Q[\mathcal{W}],
\end{aligned} \tag{12.32}
$$

which can be minimized over the intermediate distributions $\{\gamma_t\}$ or the corresponding Hamiltonians $\{\mathcal{H}_t\}$. The $\log Z_0$ term is a constant and can be ignored since π_0 is fixed. The marginals q_t can be obtained by sampling from Q using MCMC samplers that have π_t as their invariant distribution for all t. Uncorrected Langevin samplers with score functions equal to $\nabla \log \pi_t$ can be used for that.

However, the AIS choice of backward kernels is not always optimal. The ELBO objective invites us to optimize both the forward process Q and the backward process P to make the bound as tight as possible, subject to the constraint that the marginal distribution at the final step matches the target distribution; that is, $p_{t_f}(\mathbf{x}_{t_f}) = p_{\text{target}}(\mathbf{x}_{t_f}) = \gamma(\mathbf{x}_{t_f})/Z_p$. We may also want to constrain the initial distribution $\pi_0(\mathbf{x}_0)$ to be at least tractable so we can sample from it efficiently.

The constraint on $p_{t_f} = p_{\text{target}}$ is most conveniently implemented by formulating P in the backward direction:

$$
P(\mathbf{x}_{0:t_f}) = p_{\text{target}}(\mathbf{x}_{t_f}) \prod_{t=1}^{t_f} K_t(\mathbf{x}_{t-1} | \mathbf{x}_t). \tag{12.33}
$$

The optimization problem for learning the optimal kernels can be formulated as

$$\begin{aligned}
&\min_{Q,P} D_{\mathrm{KL}}[Q\|P], \quad \text{subject to:} \\
&Q(\mathbf{x}_{0:t_f}) = q_0(\mathbf{x}_0)\prod_{t=1}^{t_f} F_t(\mathbf{x}_t|\mathbf{x}_{t-1}), \\
&P(\mathbf{x}_{0:t_f}) = p_{t_f}(\mathbf{x}_{t_f})\prod_{t=1}^{t_f} K_t(\mathbf{x}_{t-1}|\mathbf{x}_t), \\
&q_0(\mathbf{x}_0) = \pi_0(\mathbf{x}_0), \qquad p_{t_f}(\mathbf{x}_{t_f}) = p_{\mathrm{target}}(\mathbf{x}_{t_f}),
\end{aligned} \tag{12.34}$$

where we note that due to the parameterization we automatically have that $q_0 = \pi$ and $p_{t_f} = p_{\mathrm{target}}$ are fixed at the distributions we want.

One approach, as proposed by Doucet et al. (2022), is to use a sequence of inte mediate distributions $\{\pi_t\}$ with $\pi_{t_f} = p_{\mathrm{target}}$, and define MCMC kernels F_t that leav π_t invariant. The forward transition kernels are then set to $\{F_t\}$, and both the bac ward kernels $\{K_t\}$ and the intermediate distributions $\{\pi_t\}$ are updated to minimize th ELBO objective.

13 Variational Diffusion Models

13.1 Introduction

In this chapter, we will apply what we have learned from previous chapters about graphical models variational autoencoders, and free energies to a particular architecture called diffusion models (Sohl-Dickstein et al., 2015). Diffusion models are arguably the most popular and successful generative models for image and video generation. They are closely related to stochastic thermodynamics as the title of the first paper (Sohl-Dickstein et al., 2015) on the topic shows: *Deep Unsupervised Learning using Nonequilibrium Thermodynamics*. Diffusion models are also related to VAEs in the sense that they optimize the same objective function (Kingma et al., 2021) but differ from them in the sense that they have many stochastic layers (where the VAE has only a single stochastic layer) and the encoder is fixed to be an Ornstein–Uhlenbeck process (where the encoder is learned in the VAE). In this chapter we derive the standard learning algorithm for diffusion models by minimizing the variational free energy.

13.2 Diffusion Models as Graphical Models

A DM can be understood as a GM with a deep latent variable $\mathbf{z}_{t_f} \sim p_{t_f}(\mathbf{z}_{t_f})$ that is slowly transformed, through many layers of (time-dependent) Markov transitions[1] $p_{t-1|t}(\mathbf{z}_{t-1}|\mathbf{z}_t)$, to generate data-like samples (e.g., images). In the following, we will call $\mathbf{x} = \mathbf{z}_0$ the data layer for which we have observations. All other layers are latent and therefore unobserved. In GM language, the generative model distribution, or decoder in VAE lingo, is given by

$$P(\mathbf{z}_{t_f:0}) \equiv P(\mathbf{z}_{t_f}, \ldots, \mathbf{z}_0) = p_{t_f}(\mathbf{z}_{t_f}) \prod_{t=1}^{t_f} p_{t-1|t}(\mathbf{z}_{t-1}|\mathbf{z}_t), \tag{13.1}$$

where we wrote $\mathbf{z}_{t_f:0}$ to denote the set of all latent and observed variables (including the data layer). This process runs counter to the second law of thermodynamics: it

[1] To avoid confusion and to indicate that each transition probability can be functionally distinct, we explicitly label the probability distribution with the transition it represents; for example, $p_{t-1|t}$ is the distribution from $\mathbf{z}_t \to \mathbf{z}_{t-1}$, or the conditional distribution over $\mathbf{z}_{t-1}$ given $\mathbf{z}_t$.

creates structure (or data) out of noise $\mathbf{z}_{t_f}$, as shown in Figure 13.1:

$$\mathbf{x} = \mathbf{z}_0 \xleftarrow{p_{0|1}} \mathbf{z}_1 \xleftarrow{p_{1|2}} \cdots \xleftarrow{p_{t_f-2|t_f-1}} \mathbf{z}_{t_f-1} \xleftarrow{p_{t_f-1|t_f}} \mathbf{z}_{t_f}. \tag{13.2}$$

It is the proverbial unscrambling of an egg, reducing entropy instead of increasing i Like evolution, learning reduces entropy at the expense of increasing the entropy of it environment, to create pockets of structure (e.g., your body is a great example of suc a low-entropy structure manufactured through many eons of evolution).

The generative process described above is a backward process. We now introduc an inference distribution q, which is the forward process that increases entropy in th way physics naturally evolves. It is given by

$$Q(\mathbf{z}_0, \ldots, \mathbf{z}_{t_f}) = q_0(\mathbf{z}_0) \prod_{t=1}^{t_f} q_{t|t-1}(\mathbf{z}_t|\mathbf{z}_{t-1}), \tag{13.3}$$

which maps the data to the latent space:

$$\mathbf{x} = \mathbf{z}_0 \xrightarrow{q_{1|0}} \mathbf{z}_1 \xrightarrow{q_{2|1}} \cdots \xrightarrow{q_{t_f-1|t_f-2}} \mathbf{z}_{t_f-1} \xrightarrow{q_{t_f|t_f-1}} \mathbf{z}_{t_f}. \tag{13.4}$$

In the general case, we also have time-dependent transitions in the forward proces However, some papers simplify this by using the same transition kernel. For futur reference, we note that

$$q(\mathbf{z}_1, \ldots, \mathbf{z}_{t_f}|\mathbf{z}_0) = \frac{Q(\mathbf{z}_{0:t_f})}{q_0(\mathbf{z}_0)} = \prod_{t=1}^{t_f} q_{t|t-1}(\mathbf{z}_t|\mathbf{z}_{t-1}). \tag{13.5}$$

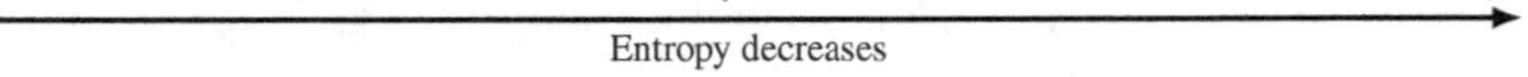

Figure 13.1 The Markov chain of forward and backward diffusion processes for generating a sample by slowly adding or removing noise. The forward process $q_{t|t-1}$ increases entropy (dashed arrows), while the generative process $p_{t-1|t}$ decreases entropy (solid arrows) to creat structure. The annotation highlights that $p_{t-1|t}(\mathbf{z}_{t-1}|\mathbf{z}_t)$ is unknown and must be learned. Latent nodes are shown as double-bordered circles, while the observed node ($\mathbf{z}_0$) is shown as rounded rectangle.

Intuitively, as in a VAE, we want the forward and backward processes to be eac other's inverses. However, there is an important difference: In a VAE, we have a singl latent layer, so the map $q(\mathbf{z}|\mathbf{x})$ acts more like a stochastic embedding of $\mathbf{x}$ in the late space. This means that there is still a lot of correlation between $\mathbf{z}$ and $\mathbf{x}$, implying th regions in latent space encode certain categories. In a diffusion model, the correlatic between **x** and **z** is completely removed, and in principle, any **z** can generate any **x**. All structure in **z** has been removed, and a code for an image of a car could sit right next to a code for a duck. While different from a VAE, both types of models can be successful in generating high-quality data because, for that purpose, you only need all **z** to eventually converge to a good image (or other data-like object). Of course, DMs can be conditioned on information to guide them to data with certain properties, e.g., red cars (Dhariwal and Nichol, 2021). The conditioning information will guide the generation process from an arbitrary sample from the prior to a certain desired region in input space where, for example, images of red cars live.

13.3 Free Energy (Evidence Lower) Bound

The standard free energy bound or the ELBO for a DM is given by

$$\begin{aligned}\mathcal{F} &= -\mathbb{E}_q\left[\log\frac{P(\mathbf{z}_{t_f},\ldots,\mathbf{z}_0)}{Q(\mathbf{z}_1,\ldots,\mathbf{z}_{t_f}|\mathbf{z}_0)}\right]\\ &= -\mathbb{E}_q\left[\log p_{t_f}(\mathbf{z}_{t_f}) + \sum_{t=1}^{t_f}\log\frac{p_{t-1|t}(\mathbf{z}_{t-1}|\mathbf{z}_t)}{q_{t|t-1}(\mathbf{z}_t|\mathbf{z}_{t-1})}\right]\\ &\geq F = \mathbb{E}[-\log p_0(\mathbf{z}_0)].\end{aligned} \tag{13.6}$$

From this free energy bound, we can immediately derive a learning algorithm. Namely, we sample latent variable samples by running the forward process q and then perform gradient updates:

1. Sample a data case: $\mathbf{z}_0 \sim q_0(\mathbf{z}_0)$.
2. Sample latent states: $\mathbf{z}_{s,1},\ldots,\mathbf{z}_{s,t_f} \sim \prod_{t=1}^{t_f} q_{t|t-1}(\mathbf{z}_t|\mathbf{z}_{t-1})$.
3. Perform learning updates:

$$\boldsymbol{\theta}'_{t-1|t} = \boldsymbol{\theta}_{t-1|t} + \eta\frac{1}{S}\sum_{s=1}^{S}\nabla_{\boldsymbol{\theta}_{t-1|t}}\log p_{t-1|t}(\mathbf{z}_{s,t-1}|\mathbf{z}_{s,t};\boldsymbol{\theta}_{t-1|t}),\quad t=1,\ldots,t_f, \tag{13.7}$$

$$\boldsymbol{\theta}'_{t_f} = \boldsymbol{\theta}_{t_f} + \eta\frac{1}{S}\sum_{s=1}^{S}\nabla_{\boldsymbol{\theta}_{t_f}}\log p_{t_f}(\mathbf{z}_{s,t_f}|\boldsymbol{\theta}_{t_f}). \tag{13.8}$$

In Step 2, S samples are drawn and averaged in Step 3 to obtain the gradient estimate. Note that we assume q is fixed, so we don't need to update the parameters of that distribution. While the above learning algorithm can work, it still samples all the latent states over many layers and so will have high variance. The good news is that if we choose all distributions to be normal, we can, in fact, compute many averages in closed form.

13.3.1 Backward Kernel and Flow Balance Equation

Before we do that, let's first rewrite the ELBO a bit by defining a backward kernel for the forward process:

$$q_{t|t-1}(\mathbf{z}_t|\mathbf{z}_{t-1}) = \frac{q_{t-1|t}(\mathbf{z}_{t-1}|\mathbf{z}_t)q_t(\mathbf{z}_t)}{q_{t-1}(\mathbf{z}_{t-1})}. \tag{13.9}$$

This equation does *not* express detailed balance because the marginals $q_t(\mathbf{z}_t)$ and $q_{t-1}(\mathbf{z}_{t-1})$ are different. Instead, it expresses the kernel for running the forward process backward in time. To understand this better, consider the following transition kernel for entire paths $(s, \mathbf{z}_0, \ldots, \mathbf{z}_{t_f})$, with s as an extra source state that can take only one value $s = 1$:

$$T(Z', s'|Z, s) = q_0(\mathbf{z}_0'|s)\left[\prod_{t=1}^{t_f} q_{t|t-1}(\mathbf{z}_t'|\mathbf{z}_{t-1}')\right] T(s'|\mathbf{z}_{t_f}'), \tag{13.10}$$

$$T(s|\mathbf{z}_{t_f}) = \delta_{s,1}, \quad q_0(\mathbf{z}_0|s) = q_0(\mathbf{z}_0). \tag{13.11}$$

This transition matrix is highly constrained in that for each layer, for ancestral updates the next state depends only on the previous state of the layer before. Moreover, the last state deterministically transitions to the source state $s = 1$, and the first state then distributes the source state back into $\mathbf{z}_0$ according to the prior q_0.

If we sample $\mathbf{z}_0 \sim q_0$ and all the subsequent $\mathbf{z}_1, \ldots, \mathbf{z}_{t_f}$ using the forward transition kernel, we sample exactly from the joint $q^{\mathrm{st}}(\mathbf{z}_{0:t_f}) = q(\mathbf{z}_0, \ldots, \mathbf{z}_{t_f})$ in one step (i.e. the Markov chain does not have to converge or "burn in"). Probability flows around in circles, as illustrated in Figure 13.2, and all probabilities are invariant. This gives us a stationary distribution $q^{\mathrm{st}}(\mathbf{z}_{0:t_f})$ and, therefore, also marginals $q_t^{\mathrm{eq}}(\mathbf{z}_t)$, which can differ at different times. These are the marginals in (13.9). The backward kernel $q_{t|t-1}(\mathbf{z}_t|\mathbf{z}_{t-1})$ in that equation is to be understood as generating the transitions if we run time backward, and the flow moves in the opposite direction. When a stationary distribution is reached, the backward kernel clearly also leaves the distribution invariant.

With this interpretation established, we now move on to rework the free energy (negative ELBO):

$$\begin{aligned}
\mathcal{F} &= -\mathbb{E}_q\left[\log p_{t_f}(\mathbf{z}_{t_f}) + \sum_{t=1}^{t_f}\log\frac{p_{t-1|t}(\mathbf{z}_{t-1}|\mathbf{z}_t)}{q_{t|t-1}(\mathbf{z}_t|\mathbf{z}_{t-1})}\right] \\
&= -\mathbb{E}_q\left[\log p_{t_f}(\mathbf{z}_{t_f}) + \sum_{t=1}^{t_f}\log\frac{p_{t-1|t}(\mathbf{z}_{t-1}|\mathbf{z}_t)q_{t-1}(\mathbf{z}_{t-1})}{q_{t-1|t}(\mathbf{z}_{t-1}|\mathbf{z}_t)q_t(\mathbf{z}_t)}\right] \\
&= -\mathbb{E}_q\left[\log\frac{p_{t_f}(\mathbf{z}_{t_f})}{q_{t_f}(\mathbf{z}_{t_f})} + \sum_{t=1}^{t_f}\log\frac{p_{t-1|t}(\mathbf{z}_{t-1}|\mathbf{z}_t)}{q_{t-1|t}(\mathbf{z}_{t-1}|\mathbf{z}_t)} + \log q_0(\mathbf{z}_0)\right] \\
&= D_{\mathrm{KL}}[q_{t_f}\|p_{t_f}] + \sum_{t=1}^{t_f}\mathbb{E}_{q_t}\left[D_{\mathrm{KL}}[q_{t-1|t}\|p_{t-1|t}]\right] + \mathcal{S}[q_0].
\end{aligned} \tag{13.12}$$

This is a nice result: it says that we need to make the prior p_{t_f} of the generative process

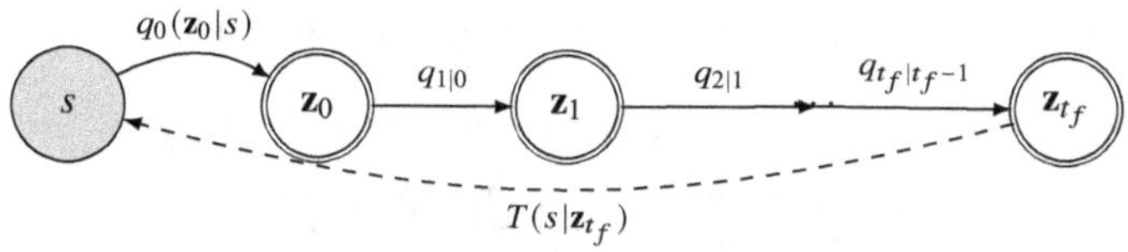

Figure 13.2 Circular flow of probability in the stationary distribution. The process starts from a source state s, goes through all latent states $\mathbf{z}_0, \mathbf{z}_1, \ldots, \mathbf{z}_{t_f}$, and returns to s, forming a closed loop. The probabilities circulate in the system with the forward transitions (solid arrows, $q_{t|t-1}$) and the return transition (dashed arrow, $T(s|\mathbf{z}_{t_f})$) balancing each other, maintaining the stationary distribution.

equal to the aggregated posterior q_{t_f}[2]. Moreover, we want each transition $p_{t-1|t}$ of the generative process to be equal to the inverse of the forward process $q_{t-1|t}$. The entropy term $\mathcal{S}[q_0] = \mathbb{E}_{q_0}[-\log q_0(\mathbf{z}_0)]$ for the data distribution can be ignored for learning as it doesn't depend on parameters.

While elegant, this result is impractical because we do not have access to distributions like $q_{t-1|t}$ or marginals q_t. The reason is that they are averaged over the data distribution and are thus complicated mixtures over all the data (recall that q_0 is the data distribution and is very complex). Distributions that are tractable are conditional distributions of the kind $q_{t|0}(\mathbf{z}_t|\mathbf{z}_0)$ for a specific data case[3]. Below, we will for instance look at the case where we choose Gaussian distributions to define the forward process, in which case we can compute all the necessary distributions when conditioning on one data case. Fortunately, we can also derive an ELBO for this case!

3.3.2 ELBO for Conditional Distributions

We start the derivation as before, but when we arrive at inserting the balance equation, we condition on $\mathbf{z}_0$ and instead use

$$q_{t-1|t,0}(\mathbf{z}_{t-1}|\mathbf{z}_t, \mathbf{z}_0) = \frac{q_{t|t-1}(\mathbf{z}_t|\mathbf{z}_{t-1})q_{t-1|0}(\mathbf{z}_{t-1}|\mathbf{z}_0)}{q_{t|0}(\mathbf{z}_t|\mathbf{z}_0)}, \tag{13.13}$$

where we note that $q_{t|t-1,0}(\mathbf{z}_t|\mathbf{z}_{t-1}, \mathbf{z}_0) = q_{t|t-1}(\mathbf{z}_t|\mathbf{z}_{t-1})$ due to the Markov property. This is the backward kernel for a different flow, namely one that must go through a single state $\mathbf{z}_0 = \mathbf{x}$. We can construct the circular flow again as above, but we need to replace the transition kernel $q_0(\mathbf{z}_0|s)$ with $\delta(\mathbf{z}_0 - \mathbf{x})$. Using this flow balance equation, we can go through a very similar derivation with lots of terms canceling after we apply

[2] The aggregated posterior is the marginal distribution q_{t_f} averaged over all the data. This is intractable because q_0 is a complicated distribution. The tractable distribution is $q_{t_f|0}$, which conditions on a data point.

[3] Note that we are using the notation $q_{t|0}$ to indicate that we are interested in the distribution $q(\mathbf{z}_t|\mathbf{z}_0)$ conditioned on a data case $\mathbf{z}_0 = \mathbf{x}$.

the flow balancing equation in a telescoping sum, to give

$$\mathcal{F} = -\mathbb{E}_q\left[\log \frac{p_{t_f}(\mathbf{z}_{t_f})}{q_{t_f|0}(\mathbf{z}_{t_f}|\mathbf{z}_0)} + \sum_{t=2}^{t_f} \log \frac{p_{t-1|t}(\mathbf{z}_{t-1}|\mathbf{z}_t)}{q_{t-1|t,0}(\mathbf{z}_{t-1}|\mathbf{z}_t, \mathbf{z}_0)} + \log p_{0|1}(\mathbf{z}_0|\mathbf{z}_1)\right]$$
$$= \mathbb{E}_{q_0}\left[D_{\mathrm{KL}}[q_{t_f|0}\|p_{t_f}]\right] + \sum_{t=2}^{t_f} \mathbb{E}_{q_{t|0}}\left[D_{\mathrm{KL}}[q_{t-1|t,0}\|p_{t-1|t}]\right] - \mathbb{E}_{q_{1|0}}[\log p_{0|1}]. \quad (13.14)$$

Again, this decomposition shows that $\mathcal{F}$ can be evaluated using the conditional distributions $q_{t|0}$ and $q_{t-1|t,0}$, which are tractable when conditioning on a specific data point $\mathbf{z}_0$. It is interesting to note that we can define a free energy bound for both unconditional and conditional distributions.

13.4 Training the Decoder Model

To train the decoder model p, we proceed as follows. We sample data cases from q_0. Then, provided we have analytic expressions for all the conditional distributions such as $q_{t_f|0}$ and $q_{t-1|t,0}$, we minimize all terms explicitly. The KL divergence between two Gaussian distributions is given by

$$q = G(\mu_q, \sigma_q), \quad p = G(\mu_p, \sigma_p), \quad (13.15)$$
$$D_{\mathrm{KL}}[q\|p] = \log \frac{\sigma_p}{\sigma_q} + \frac{\sigma_q^2 + (\mu_p - \mu_q)^2}{2\sigma_p^2} - \frac{1}{2}, \quad (13.16)$$

where μ_q and σ_q are given and fixed (see below). We can solve for σ_p by minimizing the KL divergence once we know μ_p:

$$\sigma_p^2 = \sigma_q^2 + (\mu_p - \mu_q)^2. \quad (13.17)$$

To solve for μ_p, we parameterize it as a neural network that tries to predict μ_q.

In the following discussion, we will follow Ho et al. (2020). The first step is to choose a forward process. A good choice is the "variance-preserving" process (which doesn't actually preserve variance, but at least it doesn't explode or implode):

$$\mathbf{z}_t = \sqrt{1 - \beta_t}\, \mathbf{z}_{t-1} + \sqrt{\beta_t}\, \boldsymbol{\epsilon}_t, \quad \boldsymbol{\epsilon}_t \sim G(\mathbf{0}, \mathbf{I}). \quad (13.18)$$

Next, we need explicit expressions for the necessary quantities $q_{t|0}$ and $q_{t-1|t,0}$ that appear in the ELBO. For Gaussians, these are available in closed form. Defining

$\alpha_t \equiv 1 - \beta_t$ and $\bar{\alpha}_t \equiv \prod_{s=1}^{t} \alpha_s$, we get:

$$q_{t|0}(\mathbf{z}_t|\mathbf{z}_0) = G\left(\sqrt{\bar{\alpha}_t}\mathbf{z}_0,\ (1-\bar{\alpha}_t)\mathbf{I}\right) \tag{13.19}$$

$$\Rightarrow\ \mathbf{z}_t(\mathbf{z}_0,\boldsymbol{\epsilon}) = \sqrt{\bar{\alpha}_t}\mathbf{z}_0 + \sqrt{1-\bar{\alpha}_t}\boldsymbol{\epsilon},\quad \boldsymbol{\epsilon}\sim G(\mathbf{0},\mathbf{I}), \tag{13.20}$$

$$q_{t-1|t,0}(\mathbf{z}_{t-1}|\mathbf{z}_t,\mathbf{z}_0) = G\left(\frac{\sqrt{\bar{\alpha}_{t-1}}\beta_t}{1-\bar{\alpha}_t}\mathbf{z}_0 + \frac{\sqrt{\alpha_t}(1-\bar{\alpha}_{t-1})}{1-\bar{\alpha}_t}\mathbf{z}_t,\ \frac{(1-\bar{\alpha}_{t-1})\beta_t}{1-\bar{\alpha}_t}\mathbf{I}\right) \tag{13.21}$$

$$\Rightarrow\ \mathbf{z}_{t-1}(\mathbf{z}_t,\mathbf{z}_0,\boldsymbol{\epsilon}) = \frac{\sqrt{\bar{\alpha}_{t-1}}\beta_t}{1-\bar{\alpha}_t}\mathbf{z}_0 + \frac{\sqrt{\alpha_t}(1-\bar{\alpha}_{t-1})}{1-\bar{\alpha}_t}\mathbf{z}_t + \sqrt{\frac{(1-\bar{\alpha}_{t-1})\beta_t}{1-\bar{\alpha}_t}}\boldsymbol{\epsilon},$$
$$\boldsymbol{\epsilon}\sim G(\mathbf{0},\mathbf{I}). \tag{13.22}$$

These equations are not very easy to derive, but we will give you a taste of how to do it below. Let's look at the mean and variance of a distribution at time t under the above process:

$$\begin{aligned}\mathbb{E}[\mathbf{z}_t] &= \sqrt{1-\beta_t}\,\mathbb{E}[\mathbf{z}_{t-1}] + \sqrt{\beta_t}\,\mathbb{E}[\boldsymbol{\epsilon}_t]\\ &= \prod_{s=1}^{t}\sqrt{1-\beta_s}\,\mathbb{E}[\mathbf{z}_0]\quad (\mathbb{E}[\boldsymbol{\epsilon}_t]=\mathbf{0}\text{ for all }t)\\ &= \sqrt{\bar{\alpha}_t}\mathbf{z}_0,\end{aligned} \tag{13.23}$$

which is indeed the mean of the conditional distribution $q_{t|0}$. For the variance:

$$\begin{aligned}\mathbb{E}[\mathbf{z}_t\mathbf{z}_t^{\top}] &= \mathbb{E}\left[(\sqrt{1-\beta_t}\,\mathbf{z}_{t-1} + \sqrt{\beta_t}\,\boldsymbol{\epsilon}_t)(\sqrt{1-\beta_t}\,\mathbf{z}_{t-1} + \sqrt{\beta_t}\,\boldsymbol{\epsilon}_t)^{\top}\right]\\ &= (1-\beta_t)\mathbb{E}[\mathbf{z}_{t-1}\mathbf{z}_{t-1}^{\top}] + \beta_t\mathbf{I},\quad (\mathbb{E}[\mathbf{z}_{t-1}\boldsymbol{\epsilon}_t^{\top}] = \mathbb{E}[\mathbf{z}_{t-1}]\mathbb{E}[\boldsymbol{\epsilon}_t^{\top}] = \mathbf{0})\\ &= (1-\beta_t)(1-\beta_{t-1})\,\mathbb{E}[\mathbf{z}_{t-2}\mathbf{z}_{t-2}^{\top}] + (\beta_t + (1-\beta_t)\beta_{t-1})\mathbf{I}\\ &= \bar{\alpha}_t\mathbf{z}_0\,\mathbf{z}_0^{\top} + \sum_{s=1}^{t}\left[\prod_{r=1}^{s-1}(1-\beta_{t-r+1})\right]\beta_{t-s+1}\mathbf{I}.\end{aligned} \tag{13.24}$$

This looks more complicated! However, we can interpret the second term as a process where we are flipping a coin and computing the probability that we will see "heads-up" after t trials. But, we are doing the experiment in reverse order, starting our first experiment at time t and working our way back to time 0. The probability of finding heads-up in the "first" trial at time t is β_t. What happens afterwards we don't care about anymore. The probability of seeing heads-up for the first time in the second trial is then $(1-\beta_t)\beta_{t-1}$ (failing has probability $1-\beta_t$), and so on. We know that the total probability of having succeeded in seeing heads-up in those t trials is equal to 1 minus the probability of failing altogether at the task of never seeing heads-up in t trials. That probability is given by $\prod_{s=1}^{t}(1-\beta_s)$. In other words, the complicated sum on the right of (13.24) is given by $1-\prod_{s=1}^{t}(1-\beta_s) = 1-\bar{\alpha}_t$. Also note that we are really interested in the variance and not the covariance – and using (13.23),

$$\begin{aligned}\mathbb{V}[\mathbf{z}_t] &= \mathbb{E}[\mathbf{z}_t\mathbf{z}_t^{\top}] - \mathbb{E}[\mathbf{z}_t]\cdot\mathbb{E}[\mathbf{z}_t^{\top}]\\ &= (1-\bar{\alpha}_t)\,\mathbf{I},\end{aligned} \tag{13.25}$$

which is indeed consistent with (13.19). To derive the equations for the mean and variance of $q_{t-1|t,0}$, we need to recall Bayes' rule, (1.21):

$$q_{t-1|t,0}(\mathbf{z}_{t-1}|\mathbf{z}_t,\mathbf{z}_0) = \frac{q_{t|t-1,0}(\mathbf{z}_t|\mathbf{z}_{t-1},\mathbf{z}_0)\, q_{t-1|0}(\mathbf{z}_{t-1}|\mathbf{z}_0)}{q_{t|0}(\mathbf{z}_t|\mathbf{z}_0)}$$
$$\propto q_{t|t-1}(\mathbf{z}_t|\mathbf{z}_{t-1})q_{t-1|0}(\mathbf{z}_{t-1}|\mathbf{z}_0), \quad (13.26)$$

where we have used $q_{t|t-1,0}(\mathbf{z}_t|\mathbf{z}_{t-1},\mathbf{z}_0) = q_{t|t-1}(\mathbf{z}_t|\mathbf{z}_{t-1})$ since the transitions are Markov and independent of $\mathbf{z}_0$. We have expressions for each of these:

$$q_{t-1|0}(\mathbf{z}_{t-1}|\mathbf{z}_0) = G\left(\sqrt{\bar{\alpha}_{t-1}}\,\mathbf{z}_0,\ (1-\bar{\alpha}_{t-1})\mathbf{I}\right), \quad (13.27)$$

$$q_{t|t-1}(\mathbf{z}_t|\mathbf{z}_{t-1}) = G\left(\sqrt{1-\beta_t}\,\mathbf{z}_{t-1},\ \beta_t\mathbf{I}\right). \quad (13.28)$$

Since everything is Gaussian, we can explicitly write the logarithm of (13.26) and observe that it is a quadratic function in $\mathbf{z}_{t-1}$. Now, we rewrite that quadratic function in terms of a log-Gaussian $-\frac{1}{2}(\mathbf{z}_{t-1}-\mu)^2/\sigma^2 + c$, where the constant does not depend on $\mathbf{z}_{t-1}$. Since we know the end result must be a Gaussian, all constants must, in the end, determine the normalization constant, so you can ignore them and normalize your Gaussian afterward. If you do this, you will get the result in (13.21).

13.5 Variance Reduction Techniques

Like in the VAE, we will now perform a few tricks to reduce the variance of the estimation. The objective we were optimizing had many terms, but let's focus on the most complicated term in our objective, (13.14):

$$\mathbb{E}_{q_{t|0}}\left[D_{\mathrm{KL}}[q_{t-1|t,0}\|p_{t-1|t}]\right]$$
$$= \frac{1}{2(\sigma^p_{t-1|t})^2}\mathbb{E}_{q_{t,0}}\left[\|\boldsymbol{\mu}(\mathbf{z}_t;\boldsymbol{\theta}_t) - \boldsymbol{\mu}_{t-1|t,0}(\mathbf{z}_t,\mathbf{z}_0)\|^2\right] + \text{const}, \quad (13.29)$$

where $\boldsymbol{\mu}(\mathbf{z}_t;\boldsymbol{\theta}_t)$ is the mean of the backward decoder model p that we are trying to learn and which depends only on the state $\mathbf{z}_t$. The mean $\boldsymbol{\mu}_{t-1|t,0}(\mathbf{z}_t,\mathbf{z}_0)$ is the mean of the forward encoder model, which has no free parameters and for which we have an explicit expression.

The first trick is again the "reparameterization trick", based on (13.20). It means that we will replace the random variable $\mathbf{z}_t$ in the expectations with $\boldsymbol{\epsilon} \sim G(\mathbf{0},\mathbf{I})$ and write $\mathbf{z}_t(\mathbf{z}_0,\boldsymbol{\epsilon}_t)$ everywhere:

$$\mathbb{E}_{\mathbf{z}_0\sim q_0,\boldsymbol{\epsilon}_t\sim G_\epsilon}\left[D_{\mathrm{KL}}[q_{t-1|t,0}\|p_{t-1|t}]\right] =$$
$$\frac{1}{2\sigma^2_{t-1|t}}\mathbb{E}_{\mathbf{z}_0\sim q_0,\boldsymbol{\epsilon}_t\sim G_\epsilon}\left[\|\boldsymbol{\mu}(\mathbf{z}_t(\mathbf{z}_0,\boldsymbol{\epsilon}_t);\boldsymbol{\theta}_t) - \boldsymbol{\mu}_{t-1|t,0}(\mathbf{z}_t(\mathbf{z}_0,\boldsymbol{\epsilon}_t),\mathbf{z}_0)\|^2\right] + \text{const}, \quad (13.30)$$

$$\mathbf{z}_t(\mathbf{z}_0,\boldsymbol{\epsilon}) = \sqrt{\bar{\alpha}_t}\mathbf{z}_0 + \sqrt{1-\bar{\alpha}_t}\boldsymbol{\epsilon}, \quad \boldsymbol{\epsilon} \sim G(\mathbf{0},\mathbf{I}). \quad (13.31)$$

We sample a data case $\mathbf{z}_0$ and a random noise vector $\boldsymbol{\epsilon}_t$ from a standard Gaussian, inse them into the expression for $\mathbf{z}_t$, and then into the expressions for the neural network μ^{θ_t} and the mean of q given by (13.21):

$$\mu_{t-1|t,0}(\mathbf{z}_t(\mathbf{z}_0, \epsilon_t), \mathbf{z}_0) = \frac{\sqrt{\bar{\alpha}_{t-1}}\beta_t}{1-\bar{\alpha}_t}\mathbf{z}_0 + \frac{\sqrt{\alpha_t}(1-\bar{\alpha}_{t-1})}{1-\bar{\alpha}_t}\mathbf{z}_t(\mathbf{z}_0, \epsilon_t). \tag{13.32}$$

The second trick is to build a model to predict a zero-mean variable, rather than a variable with a large mean. In particular, if you check the expression for the mean above, you find that the neural network μ^{θ_t} will have access to the value of $\mathbf{z}_t$, so there is no need to predict that. In the expression above, we can first use (13.31) again to write $\mathbf{z}_0$ in terms of $\mathbf{z}_t$ and ϵ_t, which gives, after some simplifications:

$$\mu_{t-1|t,0}(\mathbf{z}_t(\mathbf{z}_0, \epsilon_t), \mathbf{z}_0) = \frac{1}{\sqrt{\alpha_t}}\left(\mathbf{z}_t(\mathbf{z}_0, \epsilon_t) - \frac{\beta_t}{\sqrt{1-\bar{\alpha}_t}}\epsilon_t\right). \tag{13.33}$$

Now we observe that if we parameterize our neural network as

$$\mu(\mathbf{z}_t, \epsilon_t; \theta_t) = \frac{1}{\sqrt{\alpha_t}}\left(\mathbf{z}_t - \frac{\beta_t}{\sqrt{1-\bar{\alpha}_t}}\epsilon(\mathbf{z}_t; \theta_t)\right), \tag{13.34}$$

then after subtracting the two, we get the objective:

$$\mathcal{L}_t = \frac{\beta_t^2}{2\sigma_{t-1|t}^2\alpha_t(1-\bar{\alpha}_t)}\mathbb{E}_{\mathbf{z}_0\sim q_0, \epsilon_t\sim G_\epsilon}\left[\|\epsilon(\mathbf{z}_t(\mathbf{z}_0, \epsilon_t); \theta_t) - \epsilon_t\|^2\right]. \tag{13.35}$$

At first glance, this looks puzzling: How can we ever hope to predict a completely random number, ϵ_t? However, note that the neural network ϵ^{θ_t} itself depends on that same random number through its dependence on $\mathbf{z}_t$. For instance, assume we have a single data case and we are sampling lots of noise vectors. The neural network will receive pairs of $\{\mathbf{z}_n, \epsilon_n\}$ and is asked to predict ϵ from $\mathbf{z}$. Since the noise is symmetrically distributed around $\mathbf{z}_0$, it is easy to learn a map from $\mathbf{z}$ to ϵ and therefore back to $\mathbf{z}_0$. The map is basically the vector $\mathbf{z} \to \mathbf{z}_0 - \mathbf{z}$. One can think of this as denoising: We receive noisy versions of $\mathbf{z}_0$ and are asked to predict the cleaned source $\mathbf{z}_0$. That is why this is sometimes also called denoising score matching (Vincent, 2011).

13.6 Implementation Details

There are some details which we skipped over but are important for a successful implementation. For instance, some have argued that you can simply ignore the weight factors

$$w_t = \frac{\beta_t^2}{2\sigma_{t-1|t}^2\alpha_t(1-\bar{\alpha}_t)} \tag{13.36}$$

because these weights encourage the algorithm to spend a lot of its attention getting the details right close to the data layer. However, while this may be the best way to improve log-likelihood, this is typically less important to us as we can easily train separate models that can generate plausible high-resolution details. Setting all the weights $w_t = 1$ places more emphasis on deeper layers that focus on coarser structures.

Methods like latent diffusion (Tzen and Raginsky, 2019; Rombach et al., 2022) ar trying to take this principle further by training diffusion models for the prior (p_{t_f}) o another model (e.g., a VAE). A generative adversarial network is then used to improv the decoder model of the VAE to generate high-resolution details.

Also, one usually doesn't train the prior p_{t_f} and instead sets it equal to the equilib rium distribution of the forward process. However, that process does not necessaril reach equilibrium after t_f steps, so this is an approximation. One can either train th prior in a similar way as we described here, but then it may be hard to sample fro it during generation. One way to learn the prior is to fit a Gaussian model to sample drawn from $q_0 q_{t_f|0}$.

Another option is to train the encoding forward model alongside the backwar decoder model to try to force q_{t_f} to be a desired (easy to sample from) distributio This is what is called a Schrödinger bridge problem (De Bortoli et al., 2021), whic we will cover in Chapter 14.

Finally, the model $p_{0|1}$ can be trained by sampling $\mathbf{z}_1$ from $q_0 q_{1|0}$ and maximizin

$$\mathcal{L}_0 = \sum_{s=1}^{S} \log p_{0|1}(\mathbf{z}_{0s} = \mathbf{x}_s | \mathbf{z}_{1s}), \quad \mathbf{z}_{1s} \sim q_{1|0}(\mathbf{z}_1 | \mathbf{z}_0 = \mathbf{x}_s), \qquad (13.37$$

by, for example, gradient descent.

14 Schrödinger Bridges

4.1 Introduction

In Chapter 12, we introduced sequential Monte Carlo sampling, where our task was to start from an easy-to-sample initial distribution and then learn to guide the sampling process to sample from the correct target distribution in a finite number of steps. Annealed importance sampling is a well-known instance of that.

In Chapter 13, we minimized a KL divergence between a joint forward distribution $Q(\mathbf{x}, \mathbf{z})$ and a generative distribution $P(\mathbf{x}, \mathbf{z})$ defined jointly over observed variables (a.k.a. data) $\mathbf{x}$ and (many layers of) latent variables $\mathbf{z}$. We assumed access to samples $\{\mathbf{x}_s\}_{s=1}^{S}$ from the data distribution $q_0(\mathbf{x})$ and designed the forward process such that it has a standard normal distribution $q_{t_f}(\mathbf{x}_{t_f})$ as an invariant distribution.

In Chapter 15 we will study controlled processes that start in some initial distribution (typically a delta-peak at a single state) and have a terminal reward proportional to the log-probability (KL control) or to the probability itself (GFlows, see Chapter 16) of the marginal target density at the final time. The task there is to find controls that steer the distribution towards the target distribution. All these problems share a common objective: minimizing a KL divergence between a forward and a backward process subject to marginal constraints on the endpoints.

In this chapter we will describe the general formulation of a Schrödinger Bridge (SB) problem and provide algorithms to solve them. We will also connect this to optimal transport and maximum caliber problems.

4.2 The Schrödinger Bridge

A Schrödinger bridge problem (Schrödinger, 1931; Chetrite et al., 2021) is described by the following mathematical objective:

$$\min_{Q} D_{\mathrm{KL}}[Q\|P] \quad \text{s.t.} \quad q_0(\mathbf{x}_0) = \mu(\mathbf{x}_0), \quad q_{t_f}(\mathbf{x}_{t_f}) = \nu(\mathbf{x}_{t_f}), \tag{14.1}$$

where P is a reference distribution, Q is the distribution we optimize over, μ is the initial distribution, and ν is the target distribution. When choosing P to be the uniform distribution, this becomes a maximum entropy problem over paths, subject to marginal constraints on the start point μ and end point ν. This is sometimes called a maximum caliber (MaxCal) problem (Jaynes, 1980), which we will briefly explain in Section 14.5. The geometric interpretation of the Schrödinger bridge problem i illustrated in Figure 14.1.

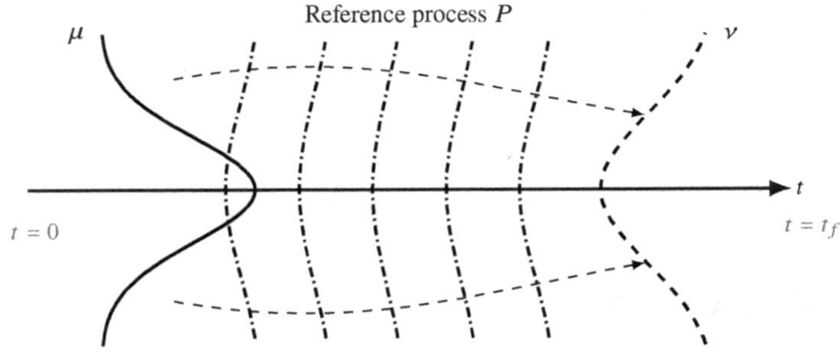

Figure 14.1 Visualization of the Schrödinger bridge problem. The solid curve (μ) represents the initial distribution at $t = 0$, and the dashed curve (ν) represents the target distribution at $t = t_f$. The dash-dotted curves show intermediate distributions of the reference process P. Th dashed arrows indicate possible transport paths between the initial and target distributions. Th Schrödinger bridge problem aims to find the most likely evolution between μ and ν, minimizing the KL divergence between the bridge Q and the reference process P, subject to th marginal constraints $q_0 = \mu$ and $q_{t_f} = \nu$.

To solve the SB problem, we will add Lagrange multiplier terms to enforce bot $q_0 = \mu$ and $q_{t_f} = \nu$:

$$
\begin{aligned}
&\mathcal{L}[Q, \gamma, \lambda] \\
&\quad = D_{\mathrm{KL}}[Q\|P] + \sum_{\mathbf{x}_0} \gamma(\mathbf{x}_0)(q_0(\mathbf{x}_0) - \mu(\mathbf{x}_0)) + \sum_{\mathbf{x}_{t_f}} \lambda(\mathbf{x}_{t_f})(q_{t_f}(\mathbf{x}_{t_f}) - \nu(\mathbf{x}_{t_f})) \\
&\quad = D_{\mathrm{KL}}[Q\|P] + \sum_{\mathbf{x}_{0:t_f}} \gamma(\mathbf{x}_0) Q(\mathbf{x}_{0:t_f}) - \sum_{\mathbf{x}_0} \gamma(\mathbf{x}_0)\mu(\mathbf{x}_0) \\
&\qquad + \sum_{\mathbf{x}_{0:t_f}} \lambda(\mathbf{x}_{t_f}) Q(\mathbf{x}_{0:t_f}) - \sum_{\mathbf{x}_{t_f}} \lambda(\mathbf{x}_{t_f})\nu(\mathbf{x}_{t_f}). \qquad (14.
\end{aligned}
$$

Note that we extended the sum over $Q(\mathbf{x}_{0:t_f})$ to the entire path space to include th Lagrange multipliers at times 0 and t_f, $\gamma(\mathbf{x}_0)$ and $\lambda(\mathbf{x}_{t_f})$. In addition, one can ad constraints to keep Q positive and normalized, but this will happen automatically i the following.

By taking functional derivatives of the Lagrangian $\mathcal{L}$ with respect to Q and settin them to zero, we obtain the optimal solution Q^*:

$$
\begin{aligned}
&\frac{\delta \mathcal{L}}{\delta Q(\mathbf{x}_{0:t_f})} = \log Q(\mathbf{x}_{0:t_f}) - \log P(\mathbf{x}_{0:t_f}) + \gamma(\mathbf{x}_0) + \lambda(\mathbf{x}_{t_f}) + 1 = 0 \\
&\Rightarrow Q^*(\mathbf{x}_{0:t_f}) = \Gamma(\mathbf{x}_{0:t_f}) = \frac{1}{Z_\Gamma} P(\mathbf{x}_{0:t_f}) e^{-\gamma(\mathbf{x}_0) - \lambda(\mathbf{x}_{t_f})}. \qquad (14.
\end{aligned}
$$

This solution can be interpreted as a reweighted version of the reference distribution where the reweighting factors depend on the initial and final states through the Lagrange multipliers.

Let us first try to find an expression for the Lagrange multiplier $\lambda(\mathbf{x}_{t_f})$ that enforces the correct constraint $q_{t_f} = \nu$. This can be done by integrating (14.3) over $\mathbf{x}_0, \ldots, \mathbf{x}_{t_f-1}$ and matching the result to the desired final marginal $\nu(\mathbf{x}_{t_f})$:

$$
\begin{aligned}
q_{t_f}(\mathbf{x}_{t_f}) &= \sum_{\mathbf{x}_{0:t_f-1}} \frac{1}{Z_\Gamma} P(\mathbf{x}_{0:t_f}) e^{-\gamma(\mathbf{x}_0)-\lambda(\mathbf{x}_{t_f})} \\
&= \frac{1}{Z_\Gamma} e^{-\lambda(\mathbf{x}_{t_f})} \tilde{p}_{t_f}(\mathbf{x}_{t_f}|\gamma) \\
&= \nu(\mathbf{x}_{t_f}), \qquad (14.4) \\
\tilde{p}_{t_f}(\mathbf{x}_{t_f}|\gamma) &= \sum_{\mathbf{x}_{0:t_f-1}} P(\mathbf{x}_{0:t_f}) e^{-\gamma(\mathbf{x}_0)} \qquad (14.5) \\
\Rightarrow \ e^{-\lambda(\mathbf{x}_{t_f})} &= \frac{Z_\Gamma \nu(\mathbf{x}_{t_f})}{\tilde{p}_{t_f}(\mathbf{x}_{t_f}|\gamma)}. \qquad (14.6)
\end{aligned}
$$

Plugging this result back into Q^* – see (14.3)) – we obtain a fixed-point equation for the optimal solution Γ:

$$
\Gamma(\mathbf{x}_{0:t_f}) = \frac{P(\mathbf{x}_{0:t_f}) e^{-\gamma(\mathbf{x}_0)} \nu(\mathbf{x}_{t_f})}{\sum_{\mathbf{x}_{0:t_f-1}} P(\mathbf{x}_{0:t_f}) e^{-\gamma(\mathbf{x}_0)}} = \Gamma(\mathbf{x}_{0:t_f-1}|\mathbf{x}_{t_f}) \nu(\mathbf{x}_{t_f}). \qquad (14.7)
$$

This equation has an intuitive interpretation: the Lagrange multiplier $\lambda(\mathbf{x}_{t_f})$ effectively divides the joint distribution by the marginal at time t_f and then replaces it with the desired marginal $\nu(\mathbf{x}_{t_f})$! As such, if this equation holds (with the same Γ on both sides), it definitely solves the constraint on $\mathbf{x}_{t_f}$: the equation then states that $\Gamma(\mathbf{x}_{t_f}) = \nu(\mathbf{x}_{t_f})$. If it does not hold, we can simply treat this as an update to Γ, after which it will hold.

We can repeat the same derivation for the other Lagrange multiplier $\gamma(\mathbf{x}_0)$ to get a fixed-point equation of the form

$$
\Gamma(\mathbf{x}_{0:t_f}) = \frac{P(\mathbf{x}_{0:t_f}) e^{-\lambda(\mathbf{x}_{t_f})} \mu(\mathbf{x}_0)}{\sum_{\mathbf{x}_{1:t_f}} P(\mathbf{x}_{0:t_f}) e^{-\lambda(\mathbf{x}_{t_f})}} = \Gamma(\mathbf{x}_{1:t_f}|\mathbf{x}_0) \mu(\mathbf{x}_0). \qquad (14.8)
$$

Are we done? Unfortunately, after an update like (14.8), it is not guaranteed that (14.7) will still hold. The good news is that we can keep updating these two equations until convergence (which is guaranteed under some conditions) to a fixed point where both conditions are satisfied. This iterative process is called iterative proportional fitting

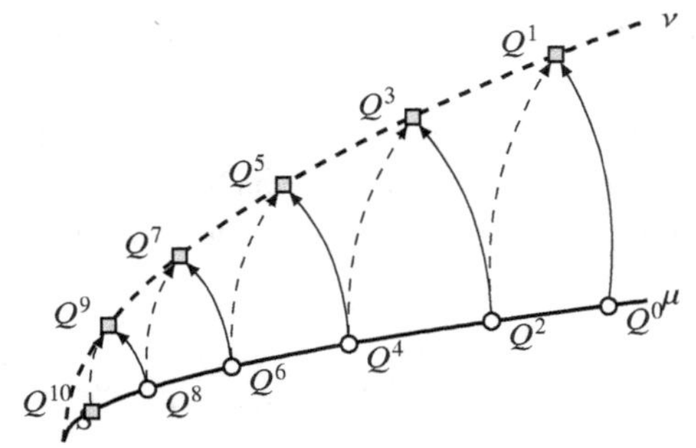

Figure 14.2 Iterative proportional fitting procedure for solving the Schrödinger bridge problem. The dashed curve represents the initial distribution ν and the solid curve represents the target distribution μ. The iterates Q^i show the alternating projections between even iterations (circles, on the μ manifold) and odd iterations (squares, on the ν manifold), converging to the Schrödinger bridge solution S. Solid arrows indicate projection onto the ν constraint; dashed arrows indicate projection onto the μ constraint.

(IPF), which can be formally written as

$$
\begin{aligned}
Q^0 &= Q_{\text{init}}, \\
Q^1 &= \underset{Q}{\operatorname{argmin}}\, D_{\text{KL}}[Q \| Q^0] \quad \text{s.t.} \quad q_0^1 = \nu, \\
Q^2 &= \underset{Q}{\operatorname{argmin}}\, D_{\text{KL}}[Q \| Q^1] \quad \text{s.t.} \quad q_{t_f}^2 = \mu, \\
&\vdots
\end{aligned}
\tag{14.9}
$$

Each subproblem can be solved using the same approach as before, with the referenc distribution being the solution from the previous iteration:

$$
Q^{k+1}(\mathbf{x}_{0:t_f}) = \begin{cases} Q^k(\mathbf{x}_{1:t_f} | \mathbf{x}_0)\mu(\mathbf{x}_0), & \text{if } k \text{ is odd}, \\ Q^k(\mathbf{x}_{0:t_f - 1} | \mathbf{x}_{t_f})\nu(\mathbf{x}_{t_f}), & \text{if } k \text{ is even}. \end{cases}
\tag{14.10}
$$

Computing these conditional distributions can be expensive as it involves sums ove many variables. However, if the distribution is structured as a chain (or a tree), and th number of states $\mathbf{x}$ is not too large, this can be efficiently solved using belief propagatio (see Chapter 6). The alternating projection structure of IPF is illustrated in Figure 14.2

In the previous discussion, we assumed that $q_0(\mathbf{x}_0) = \sum_{\mathbf{x}_{1:t_f}} Q(\mathbf{x}_{0:t_f}) = \mu(\mathbf{x}_0)$ an this prevented us from solving the problem in one shot (without iterations). If we wer to pin down the initial distribution to be a single point – that is, $p_0(\mathbf{x}_0) = \delta(\mathbf{x}_0 - \mathbf{y}_0$ – then solving for the marginal at $\mathbf{x}_{t_f}$ would not change the distribution at $\mathbf{x}_0$. Th can be seen by performing belief propagation (see Chapter 6), starting from the la marginal $\nu(\mathbf{x}_{t_f})$ and propagating back to $t = 0$. After integrating out all the variable

$\{\mathbf{x}_1, \ldots, \mathbf{x}_{t_f}\}$, this would give

$$q_0^*(\mathbf{x}_0) = \frac{\delta(\mathbf{x}_0 - \mathbf{y}_0)m_{1\to 0}(\mathbf{x}_0)}{\sum_{\mathbf{x}'_0} \delta(\mathbf{x}'_0 - \mathbf{y}_0)m_{1\to 0}(\mathbf{x}'_0)} = \delta(\mathbf{x}_0 - \mathbf{y}_0), \tag{14.11}$$

where $m_{t\to t-1}(\mathbf{x}_t)$ is the message as defined in Chapter 6. So we conclude that if we choose $\mu = \delta_{\mathbf{y}_0}$, the Schrödinger bridge problem is solved after one iteration. This will be important in Chapter 15 when we discuss optimal control problems and their relation to SBs (Y. Chen et al., 2020).

Under the constraint above of choosing $\mu = \delta_{\mathbf{y}_0}$, we can rewrite the SB problem by removing the constraint that $q_0 = \mu$, parameterizing P as a forward Markov chain $P = p_0 \prod_t p_{t|t-1}$, choosing $p_0 = \delta_{\mathbf{y}_0}$, and subsequently plugging the solution for λ from (14.6) into the Lagrangian, (14.2), to obtain

$$\begin{aligned}
\mathcal{L} &= D_{\mathrm{KL}}[Q\|P] + \mathbb{E}_Q[\lambda(\mathbf{x}_{t_f})] - \sum_{\mathbf{x}_{t_f}} \lambda(\mathbf{x}_{t_f})\nu(\mathbf{x}_{t_f}) \\
&= D_{\mathrm{KL}}[Q\|P] + \mathbb{E}_Q\left[\log\left(\frac{p_{t_f}}{\nu}\right)\right] + D_{\mathrm{KL}}[\nu\|p_{t_f}] \\
&= D_{\mathrm{KL}}[Q\|P] + \mathbb{E}_Q\left[\log\left(\frac{P(\mathbf{x}_{t_f})}{\nu(\mathbf{x}_{t_f})}\right)\right] + D_{\mathrm{KL}}[\nu\|P_{t_f}] \\
&= D_{\mathrm{KL}}\left[Q(\mathbf{x}_{0:t_f})\|P(\mathbf{x}_{0:t_f-1}|\mathbf{x}_{t_f})\nu(\mathbf{x}_{t_f})\right] + D_{\mathrm{KL}}[\nu\|p_{t_f}].
\end{aligned} \tag{14.12}$$

As we are keeping P (the reference distribution) and ν (the target distribution) fixed, the last term $D_{\mathrm{KL}}[\nu\|p_{t_f}]$ is constant and unimportant for the optimization. We can interpret the term $\mathbb{E}_Q\left[\log\left(\frac{P(\mathbf{x}_{t_f})}{\nu(\mathbf{x}_{t_f})}\right)\right]$ as the terminal cost term of an optimal control problem to solve for a policy Q, which is regularized to stay close to P. This is called KL control, which can be interpreted in thermodynamic terms using free energies. That is the subject of Section 15.4.

4.3 Training Diffusion Schrödinger Bridge

The following is based on De Bortoli et al. (2021).

To implement IPF efficiently, we can represent the joint distributions as Markov chains. For the even ($k = 2n$) and odd ($k = 2n + 1$) iterations, the distributions have the form of the forward and backward processes:

$$Q^{2n}(\mathbf{x}_{0:t_f}) = q_0^n(\mathbf{x}_0) \prod_{t=1}^{t_f} q_{t|t-1}^n(\mathbf{x}_t|\mathbf{x}_{t-1}), \tag{14.13}$$

$$Q^{2n+1}(\mathbf{x}_{0:t_f}) = q_{t_f}^n(\mathbf{x}_{t_f}) \prod_{t=1}^{t_f} q_{t-1|t}^n(\mathbf{x}_{t-1}|\mathbf{x}_t), \tag{14.14}$$

where $q_{t|t-1}^n$ and $q_{t-1|t}^n$ represent the transition kernels from time $t-1$ to t and from time t to $t-1$ at the nth iteration of IPF. To make this more practical for high-dimensional systems, we choose the transition kernels to be Gaussian distributions with learnabl drift functions:

$$q^n_{t|t-1}(\mathbf{x}_t|\mathbf{x}_{t-1}) = G(\mathbf{x}_t; \mathbf{x}_{t-1} + \mathbf{a}^n_{t-1}(\mathbf{x}_{t-1}), \sigma_t^2 \mathbf{I}), \tag{14.15}$$

$$q^n_{t-1|t}(\mathbf{x}_{t-1}|\mathbf{x}_t) = G(\mathbf{x}_{t-1}; \mathbf{x}_t + \mathbf{b}^n_t(\mathbf{x}_t), \sigma_t^2 \mathbf{I}), \tag{14.16}$$

where $\mathbf{a}^n_{t-1}$ and $\mathbf{b}^n_t$ are the forward and backward drift functions at iteration n, and σ are variance parameters that can be fixed or learned.

By minimizing the KL divergence between successive IPF iterations and taking th small step-size limit $\sigma_t^2 \to 0$ (similar to the ELBO decomposition in Chapter 13), th learning objective for the drift functions becomes a regression problem:

$$\hat{\mathbf{b}}^k_t = \underset{\hat{\mathbf{b}}}{\operatorname{argmin}} \mathbb{E}_{p^k_{t-1,t}} [\|\hat{\mathbf{b}}(\mathbf{x}_t) - (\mathbf{x}_t + \hat{\mathbf{a}}^k_{t-1}(\mathbf{x}_{t-1}) - \hat{\mathbf{a}}^k_{t-1}(\mathbf{x}_t))\|^2], \tag{14.17}$$

$$\hat{\mathbf{a}}^{k+1}_{t-1} = \underset{\hat{\mathbf{a}}}{\operatorname{argmin}} \mathbb{E}_{q^k_{t-1,t}} [\|\hat{\mathbf{a}}(\mathbf{x}_{t-1}) - (\mathbf{x}_{t-1} + \hat{\mathbf{b}}^k_t(\mathbf{x}_t) - \hat{\mathbf{b}}^k_t(\mathbf{x}_{t-1}))\|^2], \tag{14.18}$$

where $\hat{\mathbf{b}}^k_t(\mathbf{x}) = \mathbf{x} + \sigma_t \mathbf{b}^k_t(\mathbf{x})$ and $\hat{\mathbf{a}}^k_{t-1}(\mathbf{x}) = \mathbf{x} + \sigma_t \mathbf{a}^k_{t-1}(\mathbf{x})$ are the augmented dri functions including the identity map, and $p^k_{t-1,t}$, $q^k_{t-1,t}$ are the joint densities at step $t-1$ and t. The diffusion Schrödinger bridge (DSB) algorithm then alternates betwee learning the backward drift functions $\hat{\mathbf{b}}^k_t$ and the forward drift functions $\hat{\mathbf{a}}^{k+1}_{t-1}$. Fo learning $\hat{\mathbf{b}}^k_t$, we sample paths from the current forward process starting from μ. Fo learning $\hat{\mathbf{a}}^{k+1}_{t-1}$, we sample paths from the current backward process starting from th prior ν. DSB can be applied to two important scenarios in machine learning. Fo generative modeling, we set $\mu = p_{\text{data}}$ (the data distribution) and $\nu = p_{\text{prior}}$ (typically standard normal distribution). Once the model is trained, we can generate new sample by:

(i) sampling $\mathbf{x}_{t_f} \sim \nu$;
(ii) sequentially sampling $\mathbf{x}_{t-1} \sim q_{t-1|t}(\cdot|\mathbf{x}_t)$ for $t = t_f, t_f - 1, \ldots, 1$ using the learne backward drift function.

This is very similar to the variational diffusion models (Chapter 13), but here w learn both forward and backward transitions, rather than a single forward proces Additionally, the SB ensures that the model matches the desired distributions at bot endpoints in finite time, unlike DMs based on Ornstein–Uhlenbeck processes th require infinite time to converge to the prior.

The DSB can also be applied to sample from unnormalized densities. We may set as an easy-to-sample distribution (e.g., $G(\mathbf{0}, \mathbf{I})$), and take ν to be the target distributio specified up to a normalizing constant; that is, $\nu(\mathbf{x}_{t_f}) \propto \pi(\mathbf{x}_{t_f})$. Training then requir some additional components (see Bernton et al., 2019; Vargas et al., 2022; Hen et al., 2023). For instance, one can incorporate the unnormalized density $\pi(\mathbf{x}_{t_f})$ in the objective function as a terminal cost or reward, connecting to the optimal contr perspective discussed in Chapters 15 and 22. Annealed importance sampling ar eequential Monte Carlo methods may also be used within the IPF iterations (Bernto et al., 2019).

14.4 Relation to Optimal Transport

Optimal transport (Chewi et al., 2024) is another framework that studies how to most efficiently move probability mass from a distribution $\mu = q_0$ to another distribution $\nu = q_{t_f}$. Since this problem is not unique, we define a cost function $C(\mathbf{x}, \mathbf{y})$ to measure the cost of moving a unit of probability mass from $\mathbf{x}$ to $\mathbf{y}$. We then define the problem as

$$\inf_{Q} \mathbb{E}_{Q}\left[C(\mathbf{x}, \mathbf{y})\right] \quad \text{s.t.} \quad q_X = \mu, \quad q_Y = \nu. \tag{14.19}$$

Here, Q is a joint probability distribution over $\mathbf{x}, \mathbf{y}$ with prescribed marginals μ, ν. This formulation of the OT problem is known as the Kantorovich formulation (Kantorovich, 1942). It allows for stochastic maps between $\mathbf{x}$ and $\mathbf{y}$, represented by the joint distribution $Q(\mathbf{x}, \mathbf{y}) = q(\mathbf{x})q(\mathbf{y}|\mathbf{x})$.

A more restricted version of the problem is the Monge formulation (Monge, 1781) – which precedes the Kantorovich formulation – where we only allow deterministic maps: $q(\mathbf{y}|\mathbf{x}) = \delta(\mathbf{y} - f(\mathbf{x}))$. In the Monge formulation, the goal is to find a deterministic map f that minimizes the expected transportation cost $\mathbb{E}_{q_X}\left[C(\mathbf{x}, f(\mathbf{x}))\right]$, subject to the constraint that the pushforward of the initial distribution μ under the map f equals the target distribution ν:

$$\inf_{f} \mathbb{E}_{q_X}\left[C(\mathbf{x}, f(\mathbf{x}))\right] \quad \text{s.t.} \quad q_X = \mu, \quad f_{\#}[q_X] = \nu, \tag{14.20}$$

where $f_{\#}[q_X]$ denotes the *pushforward* of the distribution q_X under the deterministic map f. The pushforward is defined as the transformation of the distribution q_X under the map f, following the transformation rule of densities under deterministic maps:

$$f_{\#}[q_X](\mathbf{y}) = q_X(f^{-1}(\mathbf{y})) \left|\det\left(\frac{\partial f^{-1}(\mathbf{y})}{\partial \mathbf{y}}\right)\right|. \tag{14.21}$$

The classical interpretation of the Monge problem as transporting earth from an excavation to a construction site is illustrated in Figure 14.3.

To connect back to SBs, we add an entropy regularization term to the Kantorovich formulation of the OT problem, (14.19):

$$\inf_{Q} \left\{\mathbb{E}_{Q}\left[C(\mathbf{x}, \mathbf{y})\right] - T\mathcal{S}[Q]\right\} \quad \text{s.t.} \quad q_X = \mu, \quad q_Y = \nu. \tag{14.22}$$

If we now identify $C(\mathbf{x}, \mathbf{y}) = -\log P(\mathbf{x}, \mathbf{y}) = \mathcal{H}(\mathbf{x}, \mathbf{y})$, we are back to a free energy with temperature T, or equivalently an ELBO formulated as the KL divergence between Q and P, subject to marginal constraints:

$$\begin{aligned} &\inf_{Q} D_{\mathrm{KL}}[Q\|P] = \inf_{Q} \mathcal{F}[Q], \quad \mathcal{F}[Q] = \mathbb{E}_{Q}\left[\mathcal{H}\right] - T\mathcal{S}[Q], \\ &\text{s.t.} \quad q_X = \mu, \quad q_Y = \nu. \end{aligned} \tag{14.23}$$

This establishes a clear connection between SB and OT: the Monge problem can be seen as a deterministic limit of the Kantorovich problem, which in turn is a zero-temperature limit of the entropy-regularized Kantorovich problem, which is equivalent to a bivariate SB problem (Léonard, 2014; Y. Chen et al., 2016).

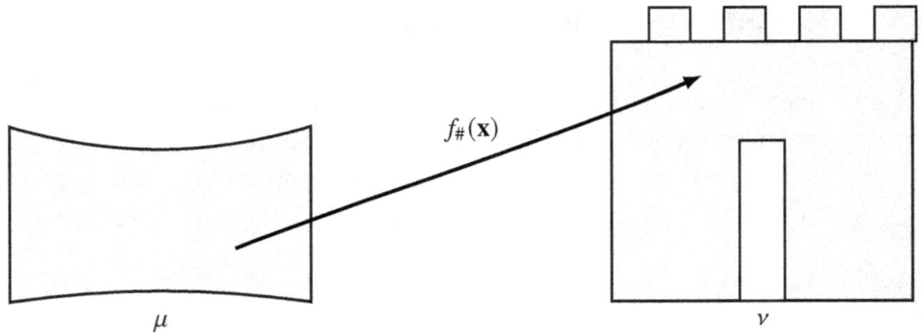

Figure 14.3 Monge formulation of optimal transport. The problem involves finding an optimal map $f_\#(\mathbf{x})$ that transports mass from a source distribution μ (the excavated pit on the left) to a target distribution ν (the walled structure on the right). The arrow indicates the transport map. The map must minimize the expected transportation cost $\mathbb{E}_\mu[C(\mathbf{x}, f(\mathbf{x}))]$ while ensuring that the pushforward of μ under f equals ν.

A similar relationship between stochastic and deterministic maps is also observed in machine learning, where diffusion models (Chapter 13) have stochastic transitions and normalizing flows (Chapter 8) have deterministic transformations.

14.5 Relation to Maximum Caliber

The MaxCal principle was introduced by E. T. Jaynes (1980) as a direct generalization of the maximum entropy principle to path spaces. Its formulation involves maximizing entropy (or more generally minimizing a KL divergence to a reference distribution P) subject to certain expectation constraints on path functionals (see Figure 14.4):

$$\min_Q D_{\mathrm{KL}}[Q\|P] \quad \text{s.t.} \quad \mathbb{E}_Q\left[\mathcal{A}_k(\mathbf{x}_{0:t_f})\right]$$
$$= \sum_{\mathbf{x}_{0:t_f}} Q(\mathbf{x}_{0:t_f})\mathcal{A}_k(\mathbf{x}_{0:t_f}) = a_k, \quad k = 1, \ldots, K, \tag{14.24}$$

where $\mathcal{A}_k(\mathbf{x}_{0:t_f})$ are path functionals, and a_k are their prescribed expectation values.

(a) High caliber: many admissible paths (b) Low caliber: concentrated paths

Figure 14.4 Illustration of the maximum caliber principle comparing high and low entropy path ensembles. (a) High-caliber configuration showing diverse paths (solid curves) between fixed start and end states, corresponding to high path entropy $\mathcal{S}[Q]$. (b) Low-caliber configuration with more concentrated paths (dashed curves), indicating lower path entropy. Both configurations must satisfy the same path functional constraints $\mathcal{A}_k$, but differ in their entropy.

Note that the SB problem can now be viewed as a special case of this MaxCal formalism by choosing specific path functionals that enforce the desired marginal constraints:

$$
\begin{aligned}
&\mathcal{A}_{\mathbf{y}_0}(\mathbf{x}_{0:t_f}) = \delta(\mathbf{x}_0 - \mathbf{y}_0) \times \mathbb{1}(\mathbf{x}_{1:t_f}) \\
\Rightarrow &\sum_{\mathbf{x}_{0:t_f}} Q(\mathbf{x}_{0:t_f})\mathcal{A}_{\mathbf{y}_0}(\mathbf{x}_{0:t_f}) = \mu(\mathbf{y}_0),
\end{aligned}
\tag{14.25}
$$

$$
\begin{aligned}
&\mathcal{A}_{\mathbf{y}_{t_f}}(\mathbf{x}_{0:t_f}) = \mathbb{1}(\mathbf{x}_0, \ldots, \mathbf{x}_{t_f-1}) \times \delta(\mathbf{x}_{t_f} - \mathbf{y}_{t_f}) \\
\Rightarrow &\sum_{\mathbf{x}_{0:t_f}} Q(\mathbf{x}_{0:t_f})\mathcal{A}_{\mathbf{y}_{t_f}}(\mathbf{x}_{0:t_f}) = \nu(\mathbf{y}_{t_f}),
\end{aligned}
\tag{14.26}
$$

where $\mathbb{1}(\cdot)$ is the function that is equal to 1 for all values of its argument.

MaxCal is, however, more general than the SB problem because we can place arbitrary constraints on entire paths. For instance, we may want to control some transition rates or auto-correlation functions. Solving MaxCal problems also proceeds by using Lagrange multipliers to enforce the expectation constraints, very similar to what we did in Chapter 1 for the MaxEnt problem, but now replacing states $\mathbf{x}$ with paths $\mathbf{x}_{0:t_f}$. As such, MaxCal can be considered as a kind of maximum entropy formulation for non-equilibrium thermodynamics!

15 Optimal Control

15.1 Introduction

We may think of a diffusion model as a controlled stochastic process that uses th learned score to steer the diffusion process towards the data distribution. It may there fore not come as a surprise that stochastic control can be formulated in terms of variational free energy minimization. In this chapter we will study KL control, whe we can solve the control problem by performing inference through minimizing a fre energy functional (which we will do by belief propagation). We finish the chapter b relating this back to Schrödinger bridges.

15.2 Model-Based Reinforcement Learning

In model-based reinforcement learning (RL), we want to steer the dynamics of a syste away from its natural dynamics in order to avoid cost or pick up reward (Bellma 1957). This process typically involves defining a dynamical model that describes ho the world evolves under the influence of a control signal. To achieve this, we defi a sequence of external controls $\mathbf{u}_t$ and consider the conditional distribution of stat given the controls:

$$Q(\mathbf{x}|\mathbf{u}) = q_0(\mathbf{x}_0) \prod_{t=1}^{t_f} q_{t|t-1}(\mathbf{x}_t|\mathbf{x}_{t-1}, \mathbf{u}_{t-1}), \qquad (15.1)$$

where $\mathbf{x} = \mathbf{x}_{0:t_f}$ and $\mathbf{u} = \mathbf{u}_{0:t_f-1}$ are the state sequence and the control sequenc respectively. Here, for simplicity, we introduce the shorthand notation $\mathbf{x}$ and $\mathbf{u}$ for $\mathbf{x}_{0:}$ and $\mathbf{u}_{0:t_f-1}$ so that they do not need to be written out every time. The graphical mod representation is shown in Figure 15.1.

Alternatively, we can consider a joint distribution over $\mathbf{x}$ and $\mathbf{u}$ by introducing stochastic policy $\pi_t(\mathbf{u}_{t-1}|\mathbf{x}_{t-1})$:

$$Q(\mathbf{x}, \mathbf{u}) = q_0(\mathbf{x}_0) \prod_{t=1}^{t_f} q_{t|t-1}(\mathbf{x}_t|\mathbf{x}_{t-1}, \mathbf{u}_{t-1})\pi_t(\mathbf{u}_{t-1}|\mathbf{x}_{t-1}). \qquad (15.2)$$

In the limit where π_t is a delta-peak (i.e., a deterministic policy), the two formulatio become equivalent.

In what follows, we will assume that through the control sequence, the agent can manipulate the transition probabilities $q_{t|t-1}(\mathbf{x}_t|\mathbf{x}_{t-1}, \mathbf{u}_{t-1})$ to be any distribution it desires. In other words, it can make the world transition between any two states with the probabilities it desires (at a cost of paying for the effort). For instance, if we restrict ourselves to Gaussian distributions, then the control variable should be able to produce arbitrary mean and covariance structures. This is an approximation, as there are physical limitations to this world that are hard to overcome. However, we will make the agent pay a very large cost for these impossible transitions. The advantage of this approach is that we can treat these probabilities as variational quantities and optimize over them.

In the case of (15.2), the marginal transition probability

$$q_{t|t-1}(\mathbf{x}_t|\mathbf{x}_{t-1}, \pi_t) = \sum_{\mathbf{u}_{t-1}} q_{t|t-1}(\mathbf{x}_t|\mathbf{x}_{t-1}, \mathbf{u}_{t-1})\pi_t(\mathbf{u}_{t-1}|\mathbf{x}_{t-1}) \tag{15.3}$$

can be fully controlled. In the following, for simplicity, we will simply assume the conditional formulation of (15.1).

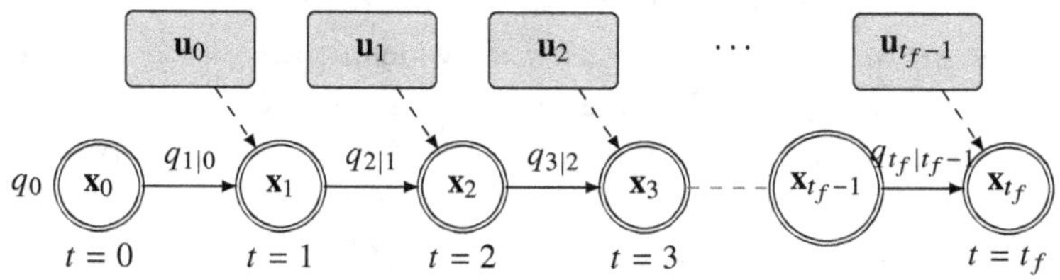

Figure 15.1 Graphical model for model-based reinforcement learning. Circular nodes denote the state trajectory $\mathbf{x}_t$, rectangular nodes denote controls $\mathbf{u}_t$, and the annotated arrows encode the controlled transition densities $q_{t|t-1}(\mathbf{x}_t|\mathbf{x}_{t-1}, \mathbf{u}_{t-1})$ of (15.1).

To complete the formulation of the RL problem, we add a reward (or cost) function. The agent's goal is to compute the best action at each time step t that will maximize the total expected reward. This requires performing inference (or marginalization, as we will see) to compute the optimal action.

We will formulate this problem as a variational inference problem where the optimal policy is the one that maximizes the ELBO or minimizes a variational free energy. To actually solve this inference problem in practice, one needs to assume very small-dimensional state spaces or resort to approximations. In (model-based) RL, one would alternatively stochastically simulate the reward obtained when following a particular policy and then optimize the policy.

15.3 Optimal Control

In optimal control, we distinguish between *planning* and *learning* (Bellman, 1957; Stengel, 1986). In the former case, we have a model of the dynamics of the world, and the agent tries to maximize reward (or minimize cost) by optimizing its actions. Every step thus involves some expensive optimization process. In real life, for example, whe confronted with danger, a fast response can often save your life, so it is no surpris that evolution often tries to replace slow optimization or inference processes with fas reflex-like actions to external stimuli. Daniel Kahneman describes this dichotomy wit his System I and System II modes of thinking to distinguish these fast and slow mode of processing information (Kahneman, 2011).

To emulate this, we can replace the explicit moment-by-moment optimization with learned policy $\pi_t(\mathbf{u}_t|\mathbf{x}_t)$ that one can immediately execute, skipping over the plannin operation. For instance, $\pi_t(\mathbf{u}_t|\mathbf{x}_t;\boldsymbol{\theta})$ or $\mathbf{u}_t = f(\mathbf{x}_t;\boldsymbol{\theta})$ can be parameterized function such as neural networks. This policy function is a form of amortized inference wher by looking at many examples, the agent tries to predict the best action that is a goo approximation to the optimal plan. This amortization is very similar to the variationa autoencoder (VAE), where inference per data case was replaced by a function tha maps the input directly to a distribution over latent factors. Under this definition, i this chapter we will look at planning, where at each step we will optimize for the bes action.

To mathematically formulate the control problem, we define a cost function (or th negative reward function) $C(\mathbf{x},\mathbf{u})$, which depends on both the control sequence an the state sequence. When dealing with stochastic policies or evolution dynamics, it i more meaningful to consider the average cost as an objective to optimize:

$$\mathbb{E}_Q[C] = \sum_{\mathbf{x},\mathbf{u}} Q(\mathbf{x},\mathbf{u})C(\mathbf{x},\mathbf{u}). \qquad (15.4)$$

We can view this average cost as the Hamiltonian of a free energy and add an entrop term that favors high-entropy paths over low-entropy ones:

$$\mathcal{F}[Q] = \mathbb{E}_Q[C] - T\mathcal{S}[Q] = \sum_{\mathbf{x},\mathbf{u}} Q(\mathbf{x},\mathbf{u})\left(C(\mathbf{x},\mathbf{u}) + T\log Q(\mathbf{x},\mathbf{u})\right), \qquad (15.5)$$

where T is a temperature parameter controlling the trade-off between entropy and cos By defining the "Boltzmann distribution" with inverse temperature $\beta = 1/T$,

$$Q^*(\mathbf{x},\mathbf{u}) = \frac{1}{Z_{Q^*}}\exp(-\beta C(\mathbf{x},\mathbf{u})), \qquad (15.6)$$

and using the non-negativity of the KL divergence, $D_{\mathrm{KL}}[Q\|Q^*] \geq 0$, we can deriv the following relation:

$$F_{Q^*} \equiv -T\log Z_{Q^*} \leq \mathcal{F}[Q] = \mathbb{E}_Q[C] - T\mathcal{S}[Q]. \qquad (15.7)$$

From this simple formulation of entropy-regularized control, we reach the conclusio that entropy-regularized control is equivalent to finding an optimal control policy (c sequence of actions) that brings the controlled dynamics Q as close as possible to th Boltzmann distribution Q^*. In other words, we need to minimize (relax) the free energ in (15.5) over Q.

It is interesting that planning now becomes equivalent to performing (approximat inference in the optimal distribution Q^* (Levine, 2018). As we will see in Section 15.4. when only considering a terminal reward, there is a connection with Schröding bridges, which can be solved using iterative proportional fitting, a procedure that replaces the marginal q_{t_f} of some joint distribution Q with a prescribed marginal ν. In the case where the marginal is a delta-peak concentrated on a single state, we revert to conditioning but, in IPF, we can "condition" on an entire marginal.

15.4 Kullback–Leibler Control

The following discussion is based on Kappen et al. (2012). The KL control framework was previously proposed and studied by Todorov (2007, 2008, 2009) and Toussaint and Storkey (2006). To stay consistent with our earlier notation, we use Q to denote the controlled forward process from which we sample trajectories, while P represents our reference process (note that this differs from the notation used in Kappen et al., 2012).

In KL control we introduce a fixed reference process P, typically representing the uncontrolled, "natural" dynamics of the world. This reference process can be expressed as a forward process:

$$P(\mathbf{x}_{0:t_f}) = p_0(\mathbf{x}_0) \prod_{t=1}^{t_f} p_{t|t-1}(\mathbf{x}_t|\mathbf{x}_{t-1}). \tag{15.8}$$

Alternatively, it can be parameterized as a backward process, as done in generative flow networks (see Chapter 16):

$$P(\mathbf{x}_{0:t_f}) = p_{t_f}(\mathbf{x}_{t_f}) \prod_{t=1}^{t_f} p_{t-1|t}(\mathbf{x}_{t-1}|\mathbf{x}_t). \tag{15.9}$$

One can always express one in terms of the other. The relationship between the forward, (15.8), and backward, 15.9, formulations of P is given through the balance equation,

$$p_{t|t-1}(\mathbf{x}_t|\mathbf{x}_{t-1})p_{t-1}(\mathbf{x}_{t-1}) = p_{t-1|t}(\mathbf{x}_{t-1}|\mathbf{x}_t)p_t(\mathbf{x}_t), \tag{15.10}$$

where $p_t(\mathbf{x}_t)$ is the marginal distribution of P at time step t:

$$p_t(\mathbf{x}_t) = \sum_{\mathbf{x}_{0:t-1},\mathbf{x}_{t+1:t_f}} P(\mathbf{x}_{0:t_f}). \tag{15.11}$$

With these definitions, the KL-regularized control problem is formulated as

$$\mathcal{F}[Q,P] = \mathbb{E}_Q[C] + D_{\mathrm{KL}}[Q\|P], \tag{15.12}$$

where we optimize over Q. The KL term in the objective encourages the controlled dynamics Q to stay close to the reference dynamics P, while the expected cost term $\mathbb{E}_Q[C]$ drives Q towards minimizing the cost function. This formulation generalizes the entropy-regularized case we discussed earlier, which can be recovered by choosing P to be uniform. We could have inserted a temperature again, but to keep notation simple, we assume that $\beta = 1/T$ is absorbed in the definition of the cost function C.

By once again defining the guided Boltzmann distribution,

$$Q^*(\mathbf{x}|\mathbf{u}) = \frac{1}{Z_{Q^*}} P(\mathbf{x}) \exp(-C(\mathbf{x},\mathbf{u})), \tag{15.13}$$

we can derive, still starting from the inequality $D_{\mathrm{KL}}[Q||Q^*] \geq 0$, the following bound

$$F_{Q^*} \equiv -\log Z_{Q^*} \leq \mathcal{F}[Q,P] = \mathbb{E}_Q[C] + D_{\mathrm{KL}}[Q||P], \tag{15.14}$$

where the objective is now to find paths that minimize the cost $\mathbb{E}_Q[C]$ on average while being regularized to stay close to the uncontrolled reference path P. This formulation allows again for a free energy interpretation, establishing a direct link to statistical inference. As explained above, we may think of Q^* as a kind of generalized posterior distribution that has incorporated the reward signals.

Typically, we define a cost function that includes both path cost terms and terminal cost terms:

$$C(\mathbf{x},\mathbf{u}) = C_{t_f}(\mathbf{x}_{t_f}) + \sum_{t=1}^{t_f} C_t(\mathbf{x}_t, \mathbf{x}_{t-1}, \mathbf{u}_{t-1}). \tag{15.15}$$

The additional KL term allows us to define a Hamiltonian,

$$\mathcal{H}(\mathbf{x},\mathbf{u}) = C_{t_f}(\mathbf{x}_{t_f}) + \sum_{t=1}^{t_f} \left(C_t(\mathbf{x}_t, \mathbf{x}_{t-1}, \mathbf{u}_{t-1}) - \log p_{t|t-1}(\mathbf{x}_t|\mathbf{x}_{t-1})\right) - \log p_0(\mathbf{x}_0), \tag{15.16}$$

which now combines the cost terms with the negative log-probabilities of the reference process P. These negative log-probabilities can be interpreted as additional costs that penalize deviations from the natural dynamics of the system. Adding an entropy term the free energy can then be written as

$$\mathcal{F} = \mathbb{E}_Q[\mathcal{H}] - \mathcal{S}[Q] = \mathbb{E}_Q\Bigg[C_{t_f}(\mathbf{x}_{t_f}) + \sum_{t=1}^{t_f} \Bigg(C_t(\mathbf{x}_t, \mathbf{x}_{t-1}, \mathbf{u}_{t-1}) + \log \frac{q_{t|t-1}(\mathbf{x}_t|\mathbf{x}_{t-1}, \mathbf{u}_{t-1})}{p_{t|t-1}(\mathbf{x}_t|\mathbf{x}_{t-1})}\Bigg) + \log \frac{q_0(\mathbf{x}_0)}{p_0(\mathbf{x}_0)} \tag{15.17}$$

From the above, we can interpret the problem in two ways. First we can think of it as standard optimal control form that is trying to minimize a cost $\mathbb{E}_Q[C]$ where the cost now also involves Q and P. Alternatively, we can think of this as a statistical inference problem where we want to minimize a free energy over Q by matching it to the guided Boltzmann distribution Q^*, as we further explain in the next section.

15.4.1 Relation to Inference

The KL control problem is connected to statistical inference. To find the optimal action $\mathbf{u}_t$, we need to minimize the free energy in (15.14) over Q. This optimization yields the optimal transitions $q^*_{t|t-1}(\mathbf{x}_t|\mathbf{x}_{t-1}, \mathbf{u}_{t-1})$ for each time step. However, we have alread solved this problem! Namely, the Boltzmann distribution in (15.13) is the optimal solution to the free energy minimization problem. So under the assumption that our control is flexible enough to achieve $Q = Q^*$, we only have to compute (through inference) $q^*_{t|t-1}(\mathbf{x}_t|\mathbf{x}_{t-1}, \mathbf{u}_{t-1})$ to know what our optimal action $\mathbf{u}_{t-1}$ should be.

Note that $Q = Q^*$ is the equilibrium distribution for the control problem in thermodynamic terms. At equilibrium, the controlled dynamics $Q = Q^*$ will be equal to the uncontrolled dynamics P but "guided" by the control cost, where paths with high cost are down-weighted and vice versa. The two procedures defined above will result in the same answer.

How do we compute $q^*_{t|t-1}(\mathbf{x}_t|\mathbf{x}_{t-1}, \mathbf{u}_{t-1})$? To find that, we observe that our task is to compute a conditional distribution from a joint distribution:

$$q^*_{t|t-1}(\mathbf{x}_t|\mathbf{x}_{t-1}, \mathbf{u}_{t-1}) = \frac{q^*_t(\mathbf{x}_t, \mathbf{x}_{t-1}|\mathbf{u}_{t-1})}{\sum_{\mathbf{x}_t} q^*_t(\mathbf{x}_t, \mathbf{x}_{t-1}|\mathbf{u}_{t-1})} \propto \sum_{\mathbf{x}\setminus\{\mathbf{x}_t, \mathbf{x}_{t-1}\}} Q^*(\mathbf{x}|\mathbf{u}), \tag{15.18}$$

$$Q^*(\mathbf{x}|\mathbf{u}) = \frac{1}{Z_{Q^*}} P(\mathbf{x}) \exp(-C(\mathbf{x}, \mathbf{u})). \tag{15.19}$$

This is a standard marginalization problem solvable by dynamic programming (Bellman, 1957) (a.k.a. "belief propagation") as follows (see Chapter 6).

First, observe that Q^* can be written as a product of pairwise potentials:

$$\begin{aligned} Q^*(\mathbf{x}|\mathbf{u}) &\propto p_0(\mathbf{x}_0) e^{-C_{t_f}(x_{t_f})} \prod_{t=1}^{t_f} p_{t|t-1}(\mathbf{x}_t|\mathbf{x}_{t-1}) \exp(-C_t(\mathbf{x}_t, \mathbf{x}_{t-1}, \mathbf{u}_{t-1})) \\ &= \Phi_0(\mathbf{x}_0) \prod_{t=1}^{t_f} \Phi_{t,t-1}(\mathbf{x}_t, \mathbf{x}_{t-1}, \mathbf{u}_{t-1}). \end{aligned} \tag{15.20}$$

Next, marginalize (15.13) and (15.20) over all variables except $\mathbf{x}_t$ and $\mathbf{x}_{t-1}$:

$$\begin{aligned} q^*_t(\mathbf{x}_t, \mathbf{x}_{t-1}|\mathbf{u}_{t-1}) &= \sum_{\mathbf{x}_{0:t-2}, \mathbf{x}_{t+1:t_f}} Q^*(\mathbf{x}|\mathbf{u}) \\ &\propto \Phi_0(\mathbf{x}_0)\Phi_{t,t-1}(\mathbf{x}_t, \mathbf{x}_{t-1}, \mathbf{u}_{t-1}) \left(\sum_{\mathbf{x}_{0:t-2}} \prod_{s=1}^{t-1} \Phi_{s,s-1}(\mathbf{x}_s, \mathbf{x}_{s-1}, \mathbf{u}_{s-1}) \right) \\ &\quad \times \left(\sum_{\mathbf{x}_{t+1:t_f}} \prod_{s=t+1}^{t_f} \Phi_{s,s-1}(\mathbf{x}_s, \mathbf{x}_{s-1}, \mathbf{u}_{s-1}) \right) \\ &= \Phi_{t,t-1}(\mathbf{x}_t, \mathbf{x}_{t-1}, \mathbf{u}_{t-1}) m_{t-1\to t}(\mathbf{x}_{t-1}, \mathbf{u}_{t-1}) m_{t+1\to t}(\mathbf{x}_t, \mathbf{u}_t), \end{aligned} \tag{15.21}$$

where in the final step we have identified the forward and backward messages as

$$m_{t-1\to t}(\mathbf{x}_{t-1}, \mathbf{u}_{t-1}) = \sum_{\mathbf{x}_{0:t-2}} \Phi_0(\mathbf{x}_0) \prod_{s=1}^{t-1} \Phi_{s,s-1}(\mathbf{x}_s, \mathbf{x}_{s-1}, \mathbf{u}_{s-1}), \tag{15.22}$$

$$m_{t+1\to t}(\mathbf{x}_t, \mathbf{u}_t) = \sum_{\mathbf{x}_{t+1:t_f}} \prod_{s=t+1}^{t_f} \Phi_{s,s-1}(\mathbf{x}_s, \mathbf{x}_{s-1}, \mathbf{u}_{s-1}). \tag{15.23}$$

If we initialize the backward messages as $m_{t_f+1\to t_f}(\mathbf{x}_{t_f}, \mathbf{u}_{t_f}) = 1$, then, with th understanding that the message implicitly depends on all future controls, the backwar messages can be computed iteratively as

$$m_{t+1\to t}(\mathbf{x}_t, \mathbf{u}_t) = \sum_{\mathbf{x}_{t+1}} \Phi_{t+1,t}(\mathbf{x}_{t+1}, \mathbf{x}_t, \mathbf{u}_t) m_{t+2\to t+1}(\mathbf{x}_{t+1}, \mathbf{u}_{t+1}). \tag{15.24}$$

Now, to get the conditional probability of the optimal policy, we normalize over $\mathbf{x}$ from (15.21):

$$\begin{aligned} q^*_{t|t-1}(\mathbf{x}_t|\mathbf{x}_{t-1}, \mathbf{u}_{t-1}) &= \frac{q^*_t(\mathbf{x}_t, \mathbf{x}_{t-1}|\mathbf{u}_{t-1})}{\sum_{\mathbf{x}_t} q^*_t(\mathbf{x}_t, \mathbf{x}_{t-1}|\mathbf{u}_{t-1})} \\ &= \frac{\Phi_{t,t-1}(\mathbf{x}_t, \mathbf{x}_{t-1}, \mathbf{u}_{t-1}) m_{t+1\to t}(\mathbf{x}_t, \mathbf{u}_t)}{\sum_{\mathbf{x}_t} \Phi_{t,t-1}(\mathbf{x}_t, \mathbf{x}_{t-1}, \mathbf{u}_{t-1}) m_{t+1\to t}(\mathbf{x}_t, \mathbf{u}_t)}. \end{aligned} \tag{15.25}$$

Interestingly, the forward message $m_{t-1\to t}(\mathbf{x}_{t-1}, \mathbf{u}_{t-1})$ cancels out in the numerato and denominator, meaning we only need to compute backward messages to determin the optimal policy. Intuitively, this follows from the graphical structure of the forwar model Q^*, where the variable $\mathbf{x}_t$ is independent of all variables $\{\mathbf{x}_0, \dots, \mathbf{x}_{t-2}\}$ *give* $\mathbf{x}_{t-1}$. In other words, the variable $\mathbf{x}_{t-1}$ summarizes everything there is to know abou the past, so influences from the past get blocked by knowing $\mathbf{x}_{t-1}$. Thus, our actions a this time do not depend on the rewards we collected (or missed) in the past. Howeve our actions now will obviously influence the rewards we expect to obtain in the future

15.4.2 Learning a Policy

As mentioned, the approach in this chapter is one where, for every time step, we fin the optimal distribution over actions by computing $q^*_{t|t-1}(\mathbf{x}_t|\mathbf{x}_{t-1}, \mathbf{u}_{t-1})$, from whic we compute the optimal actions $\mathbf{u}^*_{t-1}$ that achieve that transition. However, this i computationally expensive, especially in high-dimensional state and action spaces o when dealing with long planning horizons.

An alternative approach is to *amortize* this process by learning a policy $\mathbf{u}^*_t = f(\mathbf{x}_t; \boldsymbol{\theta}$ that approximates the optimal action distribution. This policy can be represented a a function approximator, such as a neural network, that maps states to actions o (probability distributions over) actions. By training this policy offline, we can execut actions quickly without performing expensive optimization at each step.

In practice, learning a policy involves training the function approximator on dat collected from interactions with the environment or simulations using the model. Th objective is to minimize a loss function that measures the discrepancy between th policy's actions and the optimal actions derived from planning, such as

$$\min_{\boldsymbol{\theta}} \mathbb{E}_{\mathbf{x}_t}\left[\|\mathbf{u}^*_t(\mathbf{x}_t) - f(\mathbf{x}_t; \boldsymbol{\theta})\|^2\right]. \tag{15.26}$$

This approach is particularly useful in applications where real-time decision-makin is critical.

The KL control framework has found surprising applications beyond tradition control problems, including in AI alignment. A particularly notable example is reinforcement learning from human feedback (Christiano et al., 2017; Ouyang et al., 2022), where language models are fine-tuned using human preference data. Recent work has shown that RLHF can be elegantly formulated within the KL control framework (Korbak et al., 2022; Yang et al., 2024). In RLHF, the reference process P represents the pretrained language model's distribution over sequences, while the cost function C is derived from a reward model trained on human preferences. The aligned policy then still takes the form of our guided Boltzmann distribution from (15.13). This provides an important insight: RLHF primarily reweights the original distribution rather than introducing genuinely new knowledge, as it can only down-weight undesirable behaviors and up-weight desirable ones present in the pretrained distribution.

We should also mention *model-free* reinforcement learning approaches such as Q-learning (Watkins and Dayan, 1992) and value iteration, which learn value functions or action-value functions without relying on an explicit model of the environment. These methods are outside the scope of this book, but for an interesting perspective on how they relate to free energies and ELBOs, see Levine (2018).

5.4.3 Relation to Schrödinger Bridges

The KL control framework has an interesting connection to Schrödinger bridges, discussed in Chapter 14. Recall the Lagrangian for Schrödinger bridges, (14.12):

$$\mathcal{L} = D_{\mathrm{KL}}[Q\|P] + \mathbb{E}_Q\left[\log\left(\frac{p_{t_f}(\mathbf{x}_{t_f})}{\nu(\mathbf{x}_{t_f})}\right)\right] + \text{const}, \tag{15.27}$$

where we assumed that $q_0 = \delta_{\mathbf{y}_0}$, a delta-peak at $\mathbf{x}_0 = \mathbf{y}_0$. Comparing this to (15.12), we immediately see that with the identification:

$$C(\mathbf{x}) = \mathbb{1}(\mathbf{x}_0, \ldots, \mathbf{x}_{t_f-1}) \log\left(\frac{p_{t_f}(\mathbf{x}_{t_f})}{\nu(\mathbf{x}_{t_f})}\right), \tag{15.28}$$

the KL control objective maps directly to the Schrödinger Bridge Lagrangian. In both frameworks, we're finding a process Q close to a reference process P. The key difference is that in Schrödinger Bridges, we're matching a specified terminal distribution ν, while in KL control we're minimizing a cost function that can depend on the entire trajectory.

16 Generative Flow Networks

16.1 Introduction

Throughout most of the book we have been discussing Markov chains, which ar graphical models that can be depicted as chain graphs. Diffusion models and sequer tial importance sampling methods are good examples of this, and they have bee very successful. In Chapter 4, we also introduced graphical models that can be de picted as directed acyclic graphs (DAGs), and explained how inference and learnin can be executed on them in Chapter 6. In this chapter, we will introduce generativ flow networks (GFlowNets), a class of machine-learning models that are defined o DAGs, introduced by Bengio et al. (2021, 2023). GFlowNets combine ideas from re inforcement learning, graphical probabilistic modeling, and generative AI. They ar particularly useful when we want to sample solution paths proportional to the rewa function. In this chapter we also relate GFlowNets to various other methods describe in this book such as variational inference, annealed importance sampling (AIS), an (entropy-regularized) control.

16.2 Generative Flow Networks

We can formally define a GFlowNet (Bengio et al., 2021, 2023) as a tup $(\mathcal{X}, \mathcal{A}, F, B, R)$, where:

- $\mathcal{X}$ is a set of states, including an initial source state $\mathbf{x}_0$ and a set of terminal state $\mathcal{X}_f \subset \mathcal{X}$, as well as a final sink state $\mathbf{x}_s$.
- $\mathcal{A}$ is a set of actions that define transitions between states.
- $F(\mathbf{x}'|\mathbf{x})$ is a forward policy that specifies the probability of transitioning from sta $\mathbf{x}$ to state $\mathbf{x}'$.
- $B(\mathbf{x}|\mathbf{x}')$ is a backward policy that specifies the probability of transitioning from sta $\mathbf{x}'$ to state $\mathbf{x}$.
- $R(\mathbf{x})$ is a non-negative reward function defined on the terminal states $\mathbf{x} \in \mathcal{X}_f$.

This is depicted in Figure 16.1. If we think of this as a graphical model, then w have a prior distribution at the root node over a single possible source state $\mathbf{x}_0$; th is, $q_0(\mathbf{x}_0) = 1$. We then use transition probabilities $F(\mathbf{x}'|\mathbf{x}_0)$ (where every transitic probability can be different) to spread this probability mass over the next possible state

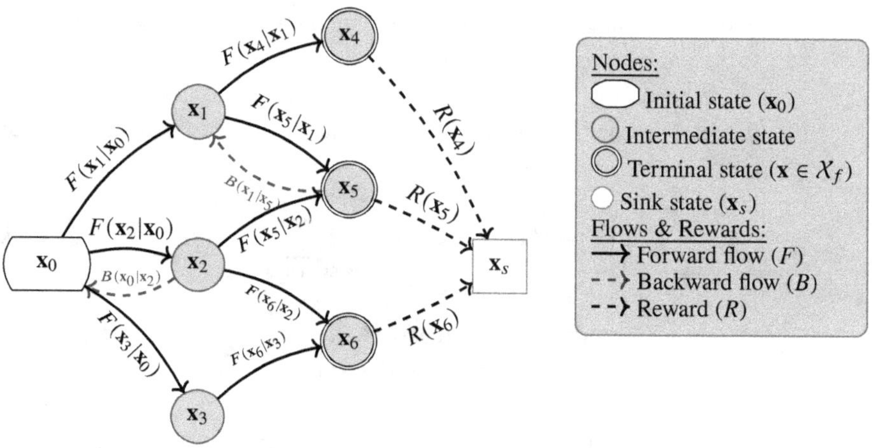

Figure 16.1 Generative flow network (GFlowNet). The network shows the flow of probabilities from the initial state $\mathbf{x}_0$ to the sink state $\mathbf{x}_s$ through various intermediate and terminal states. Forward flows $F(\mathbf{x}'|\mathbf{x})$ (solid arrows) represent transitions between states, while backward flows $B(\mathbf{x}|\mathbf{x}')$ (dashed arrows, only partially drawn) represent reverse transitions. Terminal states (double circles) collect rewards $R(\mathbf{x})$ (dashed arrows to sink).

$\mathbf{x}_1, \mathbf{x}_2, \mathbf{x}_3$, and so on. At the end, we make a transition to a single final "sink" state $\mathbf{x}_s$ with probability 1. The marginal probability of the terminal state (the last state before the sink state) is equal to $q_f(\mathbf{x}_f) \equiv \pi(\mathbf{x}_f) = R(\mathbf{x}_f)/Z_R$, with $Z_R = \sum_{\mathbf{x}' \in \mathcal{X}_f} R(\mathbf{x}')$. Generalizations where one can exit at every state are also easily accommodated; see, for example, Bengio et al. (2023).

If, by designing the transitions F in the appropriate way, we can enforce that the final marginal probability is proportional to $R(\mathbf{x}_f)$, then we can use the GFlowNet to sample states proportional to $R(\mathbf{x}_f)$. In this sense, this is quite similar to reinforcement learning, where we learn a policy that delivers rewards with a probability proportional to $R(\mathbf{x})$. However, note that in RL we learn a policy that maximizes expected reward, whereas here we learn a policy that samples states proportional to their reward.

The key to achieving this goal is to interpret probabilities as flows of a conserved quantity, analogous to particles or probability mass flowing through a network. The original GFlowNet paper used unnormalized "flows" rather than probabilities. However, these two formulations are equivalent. For instance, we can call Z_R the total amount of reward injected at the source, which then redistributes itself over the network and gets collected again at the sink node. We can identify

$$\Gamma(\mathbf{x} \to \mathbf{x}') = Z_R q(\mathbf{x})\, F(\mathbf{x}'|\mathbf{x}) \tag{16.1}$$

as the total reward flowing from node $\mathbf{x}$ to $\mathbf{x}'$, where $\Gamma(\mathbf{x} \to \mathbf{x}')$ denotes flow and $F(\mathbf{x}'|\mathbf{x})$ denotes transition probability (dimensionless). We can think of

$$\gamma(\mathbf{x}) = Z_R q(\mathbf{x}) \tag{16.2}$$

as the total amount of reward residing on node $\mathbf{x}$. When the reward flow has reached the terminal nodes we can "measure" the amount of reward flowing from the terminal nodes to the sink node. The total amount of reward reaching the sink node is then equal to Z_R, which was the total amount of reward injected at the source node.

One can now write down some simple reward conservation laws that express that the total amount of reward flowing into any node must equal the total amount flowing out:

$$\sum_{\mathbf{x} \in \text{Parents}(\mathbf{x}')} \Gamma(\mathbf{x} \to \mathbf{x}') + \mathbb{1}_{\mathbf{x}'=\mathbf{x}_0} Z_R = \sum_{\mathbf{x}'' \in \text{Children}(\mathbf{x}')} \Gamma(\mathbf{x}' \to \mathbf{x}''), \text{ for all } \mathbf{x}' \in \mathcal{X}. \quad (16.3)$$

Dividing both sides by Z_R and using $\Gamma(\mathbf{x} \to \mathbf{x}') = Z_R q(\mathbf{x}) F(\mathbf{x}'|\mathbf{x})$, we obtain the flow conservation equation in probability form:

$$\sum_{\mathbf{x} \in \text{Parents}(\mathbf{x}')} q(\mathbf{x})\, F(\mathbf{x}'|\mathbf{x}) + \mathbb{1}_{\mathbf{x}'=\mathbf{x}_0} = \sum_{\mathbf{x}'' \in \text{Children}(\mathbf{x}')} q(\mathbf{x}') F(\mathbf{x}''|\mathbf{x}'), \text{ for all } \mathbf{x}' \in \mathcal{X}. \quad (16.4)$$

Here, $\mathbb{1}_{\mathbf{x}=\mathbf{y}}$ is an indicator function that is 1 if $\mathbf{x} = \mathbf{y}$ and 0 otherwise. The quantity $Z_R > 0$ is the injected source flow at $\mathbf{x}_0$. We need the extra indicator term when $\mathbf{x}' = \mathbf{x}_0$ because $\mathbf{x}_0$ has no parents in the graph. The set Parents$(\mathbf{x})$ denotes the set of states that can transition to $\mathbf{x}$, and similarly, Children$(\mathbf{x})$ denotes the set of states that $\mathbf{x}$ can transition to. Finally, we note that

$$\Gamma(\mathbf{x}_f \to \mathbf{x}_s) = Z_R\, q_f(\mathbf{x}_f) F(\mathbf{x}_s|\mathbf{x}_f) = Z_R\, \pi(\mathbf{x}_f) \equiv R(\mathbf{x}_f), \quad (16.5)$$

where $F(\mathbf{x}_s|\mathbf{x}_f) = 1$ because there is only one transition possible.

This condition ensures that the flow is conserved throughout the network, except at terminal states where reward is collected (and at the initial state where reward is injected). In physical terms, we can think of this as a physical system with a "particle bath" (reward bath) connected at the source and sink locations (beginning and end of the chain). Reward is injected at the source, then flows through the chain and gets absorbed at the sink. (One can connect the source and sink, in which case reward is flowing around in the system.)

16.3 Relation to Sequential Importance Sampling

GFlowNets can be used to learn a forward policy for sampling from a distribution proportional to a reward function, which can be viewed as a generalization of sequential importance sampling methods, as discussed in Chapter 12. To connect GFlowNets to sequential importance sampling methods from Chapter 12, we now restrict to the special case where the DAG is a chain graph, that is, states are ordered sequentially as $\mathbf{x}_0, \mathbf{x}_1, \ldots, \mathbf{x}_{t_f}$. In a chain, each state $\mathbf{x}_t$ has exactly one parent $\mathbf{x}_{t-1}$ (except $\mathbf{x}_0$) and one child $\mathbf{x}_{t+1}$ (except $\mathbf{x}_{t_f}$).

For the chain case, we define forward and backward models using time-indexed notation:

$$Q(\mathbf{x}_{0:t_f}) = q_0(\mathbf{x}_0)\prod_{t=1}^{t_f} F_t(\mathbf{x}_t|\mathbf{x}_{t-1}), \tag{16.6}$$

$$P(\mathbf{x}_{0:t_f}) = \pi(\mathbf{x}_{t_f})\prod_{t=1}^{t_f} B_t(\mathbf{x}_{t-1}|\mathbf{x}_t). \tag{16.7}$$

Note that we fix $q_{t_f} = \pi = R/Z_R$.

In GFlowNets, the flow balancing equations between forward and backward flows at each timestep are given by

$$q_{t-1}(\mathbf{x}_{t-1})F_t(\mathbf{x}_t|\mathbf{x}_{t-1}) = q_t(\mathbf{x}_t)B_t(\mathbf{x}_{t-1}|\mathbf{x}_t), \tag{16.8}$$

which are enforced using a local consistency objective. This is the chain-graph version of the general flow conservation law in (16.4), specialized to consecutive timesteps. One such objective, proposed by Bengio et al., is sometimes called a "detailed balance" loss:

$$\mathcal{L}_{\mathrm{DB}}(\mathbf{x}_{t-1}, \mathbf{x}_t) = \left(\log \frac{q_{t-1}(\mathbf{x}_{t-1})F_t(\mathbf{x}_t|\mathbf{x}_{t-1})}{q_t(\mathbf{x}_t)B_t(\mathbf{x}_{t-1}|\mathbf{x}_t)}\right)^2. \tag{16.9}$$

We want to stress that, in the context of this book, this equation does *not* enforce detailed balance, as the marginals q_t and q_{t-1} refer to different nodes. Detailed balance is an equilibrium condition, whereas here we simply write a relation between the forward flow F and backward (time-reversed) flow B. We have encountered this subtlety already a few times in this book when talking about Markov chains.

Typically, in the GFlowNet literature, the backward kernels B_t are kept fixed (e.g., uniform over the parents of $\mathbf{x}_t$), although they can also be learned. One can think of this as extending the reward function R back in time by defining a sequence of intermediate reward-like functions that guide the learning process towards the desired terminal reward function, similar to the idea of intermediate distributions in AIS and how diffusion models operate. GFlowNets then learn a forward policy that inversely follows this backward process defined by the extended reward function.

In addition to learning the forward transitions F_t, the marginals q_t must also be learned, as they are tied to the forward transitions through the flow matching condition in (16.4).

Sampling from the target distribution can then be performed using ancestral sampling (forward sampling through F_t) or importance sampling, similar to the approach described in Chapter 12.

Some alternative objectives have been introduced to enforce these flow balancing equations using f-divergences (with some preferred choices of f) (Malkin et al., 2023, 2022) and by matching subtrajectories (Madan et al., 2023) rather than entire trajectories or sequential pairs of timesteps in the chain. Other than that, the framework maps very nicely to the annealed importance sampling discussion of Chapter 12 and is an example of how MCMC-inspired methods can be applied to reinforcement learning problems.

16.4 Relation to Variational Inference

While (16.9) enforces local consistency between flows at each time step, a different objective that enforces trajectory balance over entire trajectories has been shown to perform better and is more intimately connected to variational inference and the ELBO formulations (Malkin et al., 2022, 2023). This objective is based on the following trajectory balance constraint:

$$Z_R\, q_0(\mathbf{x}_0) \prod_{t=1}^{t_f} F_t(\mathbf{x}_t|\mathbf{x}_{t-1}) = R(\mathbf{x}_{t_f}) \prod_{t=1}^{t_f} B_t(\mathbf{x}_{t-1}|\mathbf{x}_t), \tag{16.10}$$

where Z_R is a learnable normalizing constant associated with the source injection.

Recalling that $q_0(\mathbf{x}_0) = 1$, we can define the trajectory balance residual $r(\mathbf{x}_{0:t_f})$ by

$$r(\mathbf{x}_{0:t_f}) = \log Z_R + \sum_{t=1}^{t_f} \log F_t(\mathbf{x}_t|\mathbf{x}_{t-1}) - \log R(\mathbf{x}_{t_f}) - \sum_{t=1}^{t_f} \log B_t(\mathbf{x}_{t-1}|\mathbf{x}_t). \tag{16.11}$$

The trajectory balance objective is then the mean squared residual

$$\mathcal{L}_{\mathrm{TB}}(\mathbf{x}_{0:t_f}) = r(\mathbf{x}_{0:t_f})^2. \tag{16.12}$$

It can be shown that if $r(\mathbf{x}_{0:t_f}) = 0$ for all trajectories $\mathbf{x}_{0:t_f}$, then the corresponding Markovian flow Q satisfies $Q(\mathbf{x}_{t_f}) \propto R(\mathbf{x}_{t_f})$ for all terminal states $\mathbf{x}_{t_f}$, and F_t samples proportionally to the reward.

We now relate this to a KL/ELBO objective. Let $\hat{P}(\mathbf{x}_{0:t_f}) = R(\mathbf{x}_{t_f}) \prod_{t=1}^{t_f} B_t(\mathbf{x}_{t-1}|\mathbf{x}_t)$ be the unnormalized backward path density and $Z_R = \sum_{\mathbf{x}\in\mathcal{X}_f} R(\mathbf{x})$. Then $P(\mathbf{x}_{0:t_f}) = \hat{P}(\mathbf{x}_{0:t_f})/Z_R$ and

$$\mathbb{E}_Q\left[\log \frac{Q(\mathbf{x}_{0:t_f})}{\hat{P}(\mathbf{x}_{0:t_f})}\right] = \mathbb{E}_Q[r(\mathbf{x}_{0:t_f})] - \log Z_R = D_{\mathrm{KL}}[Q\|P] - \log Z_R. \tag{16.13}$$

Assuming B_t is fixed, we can compute a convenient gradient for the residual-based objective:

$$\nabla_\theta \mathbb{E}_Q[r(\mathbf{x}_{0:t_f})] = \mathbb{E}_Q\left[(1 + r(\mathbf{x}_{0:t_f})) \sum_{t=1}^{t_f} \nabla_\theta \log F_t(\mathbf{x}_t|\mathbf{x}_{t-1})\right], \tag{16.14}$$

where θ are the parameters of F_t (and possibly Z_R).

16.5 Relation to AIS

GFlowNets share conceptual similarities with AIS, discussed in Chapter 12. Similar to AIS, GFlowNets operate over a sequence of states or steps, progressively moving from an initial state $\mathbf{x}_0$ to terminal states $\mathbf{x}_f$. Both frameworks aim to compute properties of the target distribution where direct sampling is challenging. Both methods balance forward and reverse transitions to reduce the variance of importance weights or to ensure that the terminal flows align with the desired reward distribution.

AIS is an importance sampling method with carefully designed intermediate distributions to estimate partition functions or expectation values. In AIS, sample trajectories accumulate importance weights based on the ratio of target to intermediate distributions. In contrast, GFlowNets frame the problem as a flow-conserving network that learns policies to sample paths proportionally to rewards. In other words, GFlowNets inherently *construct* a generative model for the entire path.

16.6 Relation to Other Concepts

GFlowNets are also connected to entropy-regularized reinforcement learning as shown in Bengio et al. (2021); Tiapkin et al. (2023).

In entropy-regularized RL, an agent seeks a policy π that maximizes not just the expected reward, but a combination of reward and the policy's entropy:

$$\max_{\pi} \mathbb{E}_{\tau\sim\pi}[R(\tau)] + \alpha\mathcal{S}[\pi], \tag{16.15}$$

where $\mathcal{S}[\pi]$ is the entropy of the policy, which encourages exploration and diversity in the actions taken. GFlowNets can be seen as solving a similar problem.

17 Fluctuation Theorems

17.1 Introduction

Fluctuation theorems (FTs) are a set of equalities that generalize the second law of thermodynamics to small systems where fluctuations are prevalent. They relate the probabilities of observing entropy-producing and entropy-consuming trajectories in nonequilibrium processes. FTs operate at the level of trajectories and they are one of the few exact equalities for nonequilibrium processes. Standard thermodynamic inequalities, such as the second law, follow as approximations from FTs for average quantities. FTs therefore represent a very deep and central theory for nonequilibrium thermodynamics that can be used, for example, when to estimate the free energy (or evidence in ML) of distributions and free energy differences between distributions (e.g., to compute the affinity of a drug to bind to a protein). The next chapter will be entirely dedicated to free energy estimation.

17.2 The Math Behind Fluctuation Theorems

The following exposition is based on the insightful paper by Esposito and Van den Broeck (2010).

Consider a random variable χ distributed according to a probability distribution $P(\chi)$. We say that χ obeys an integral fluctuation theorem (IFT) if

$$\mathbb{E}_P[e^{-\chi}] = \int \mathrm{d}\chi \, P(\chi) e^{-\chi} = 1. \tag{17.1}$$

By Jensen's inequality this implies $\mathbb{E}[\chi] \geq 0$. Equation (17.1) is equivalent to the statement that the non-negative function $P(\chi)e^{-\chi}$ in fact integrates to 1 and is therefore a normalized probability density function. This in turn also implies that the function $Q(\chi) = P(-\chi)e^{\chi}$ is a PDF. Why we choose the latter will become apparent later. This realization leads to the following detailed FT (DFT):

$$\frac{P(\chi)}{Q(-\chi)} = e^{\chi} \quad \text{forall } \chi. \tag{17.2}$$

This means that the integral FT implies the detailed FT. It is easy to see by integration that the DFT also implies the IFT so that in fact these two statements are equivalent.

Moreover, we can also write generalized IFTs as follows: for any function f, we have

$$\begin{aligned}\mathbb{E}_P[f(\chi)e^{-\chi}] &= \int \mathrm{d}\chi\, P(\chi)f(\chi)e^{-\chi} \\ &= \int \mathrm{d}\chi\, Q(-\chi)f(\chi) = \mathbb{E}_Q[f(-\chi)]. \end{aligned} \tag{17.3}$$

We now choose the following dissipation function over thermodynamic paths:

$$\Sigma(\zeta_{0:t_f}) = \log\left[\frac{\rho(\zeta_{0:t_f})}{\omega(\zeta_{0:t_f})}\right], \tag{17.4}$$

where both ρ and ω are two PDFs over paths. We assume these distributions are mutually absolutely continuous (have the same support) so that the log ratio is well-defined. We want to derive an FT for the dissipation function to take a certain value χ; that is, we define

$$P(\chi) = \int \mathrm{d}\zeta_{0:t_f}\, \rho(\zeta_{0:t_f})\, \delta(\Sigma(\zeta_{0:t_f}) - \chi). \tag{17.5}$$

From the definition of the dissipation function in (17.4) we immediately verify the IFT:

$$\begin{aligned}&\int \mathrm{d}\chi\, P(\chi)e^{-\chi} \\ &\quad= \int \mathrm{d}\chi \int \mathrm{d}\zeta_{0:t_f}\, \rho(\zeta_{0:t_f})\, \delta(\Sigma(\zeta_{0:t_f}) - \chi)\, e^{-\chi} \\ &\quad= \int \mathrm{d}\chi \int \mathrm{d}\zeta_{0:t_f}\, \omega(\zeta_{0:t_f})\, e^{\Sigma(\zeta_{0:t_f})}\, \delta(\Sigma(\zeta_{0:t_f}) - \chi)\, e^{-\chi} \\ &\quad= \int \mathrm{d}\zeta_{0:t_f}\, \omega(\zeta_{0:t_f}) = 1 \end{aligned} \tag{17.6}$$

where we have used the property of the delta function $\int \mathrm{d}\chi\, \delta(a - \chi)f(\chi) = f(a)$ and the fact that ω is a normalized PDF. We now know that the IFT must also hold, therefore (changing $\chi \to -\chi$ in (17.1) and using (17.5) and (17.4))

$$\begin{aligned}Q(\chi) &= P(-\chi)\, e^{\chi} \\ &= \int \mathrm{d}\zeta_{0:t_f}\, \rho(\zeta_{0:t_f})\, \delta(\Sigma(\zeta_{0:t_f}) + \chi)\, e^{\chi} \\ &= \int \mathrm{d}\zeta_{0:t_f}\, \omega(\zeta_{0:t_f})\, e^{\Sigma(\zeta_{0:t_f})}\, \delta(\Sigma(\zeta_{0:t_f}) + \chi)\, e^{\chi} \\ &= \int \mathrm{d}\zeta_{0:t_f}\, \omega(\zeta_{0:t_f})\, \delta(\Sigma(\zeta_{0:t_f}) + \chi). \end{aligned} \tag{17.7}$$

We emphasize that so far we have done nothing other than define mathematical objects and relate them to each other. At some level, these are just mathematical tautologies without physical meaning. But in the next steps we make choices that will start to relate back to physics. In particular, we will relate the distribution ω to the distribution ρ through a physical transformation: $\omega = \rho'$. For instance, we may reverse the order of the path, reverse momenta, reverse the control protocol, or apply any arbitrary operation on ρ that transforms one density into another density. We the write:

$$\omega(\zeta_{0:t_f}) = \rho'(\zeta_{0:t_f}). \tag{17.8}$$

By applying the transformation twice, we can derive how the dissipation functio transforms:

$$\begin{aligned}\Sigma'(\zeta_{0:t_f}) &= \log\left[\frac{\rho'(\zeta_{0:t_f})}{\omega'(\zeta_{0:t_f})}\right]\\ &= \log\left[\frac{\omega(\zeta_{0:t_f})}{\omega'(\zeta_{0:t_f})}\right].\end{aligned} \tag{17.9}$$

If we now assume that the operation is an involution; that is, $\rho'' = \omega' = \rho$, we get

$$\Sigma'(\zeta_{0:t_f}) = \log\left[\frac{\omega(\zeta_{0:t_f})}{\rho(\zeta_{0:t_f})}\right] = -\Sigma(\zeta_{0:t_f}). \tag{17.10}$$

From (17.7) we can now further simplify the definition of Q in the FTs:

$$Q(\chi) = \int d\zeta_{0:t_f}\, \rho'(\zeta_{0:t_f})\, \delta(\Sigma'(\zeta_{0:t_f}) - \chi). \tag{17.11}$$

Note that Q now has the same form as (17.5) but with $\rho \to \rho'$ and $\Sigma \to \Sigma'$. these represent physical transformations on the system, the FTs, (17.1) and (17.2 now have interesting physical meaning. In the following sections, we will apply th general framework using three specific transformations: time reversal (giving ρ_R adjoint transformation (giving ρ_A), and dual transformation (giving ρ_D).

17.3 Three Entropy Production Decompositions

As introduced by Esposito and Van den Broeck (2010), the total entropy productio in a nonequilibrium process can be decomposed into adiabatic and nonadiabatic cor tributions, each satisfying its own detailed fluctuation theorem. The case with od variables is more subtle, and in the literature it is treated as a separate case in Spinne and Ford (2012a,b). To avoid these complexities and the associated boundary term we will assume throughout this section that the stationary distribution is symmetric i the momenta; that is, $\hat{\pi} = \pi \Rightarrow \pi(\zeta) = \pi(\hat{\zeta})$.

Consider a forward process with path probability density:

$$\rho(\zeta_{0:t_f}) = \rho_0(\zeta_0) \prod_{t=1}^{t_f} F_t(\zeta_t|\zeta_{t-1}), \tag{17.12}$$

where $F_t(\zeta_t|\zeta_{t-1})$ is the forward transition kernel and $\rho_0(\zeta_0)$ is the initial distributio

Following the notation from Chapter 9, any Markov chain with transition kernel F that has a unique stationary distribution π_t satisfies the following balance equation:

$$F_t(\zeta_t|\zeta_{t-1})\pi_t(\zeta_{t-1}) = A_t(\zeta_{t-1}|\zeta_t)\pi_t(\zeta_t), \tag{17.13}$$

where A_t is the adjoint kernel that leaves the same stationary distribution invariant.

We also define the time-reversed kernel R_t by

$$R_t(\zeta_{t-1}|\zeta_t) = F_t(\hat{\zeta}_{t-1}|\hat{\zeta}_t), \tag{17.14}$$

where $\hat{\zeta}_t = (\xi_t, -\eta_t)$ represents ζ_t with the momenta reversed.

Similarly, we can define the dual kernel D_t by

$$D_t(\zeta_t|\zeta_{t-1}) = A_t(\hat{\zeta}_t|\hat{\zeta}_{t-1}). \tag{17.15}$$

Using these kernels, we define several stochastic processes:

(i) *Time-reversed process with path probability*:

$$\rho_R(\zeta_{0:t_f}) = \rho_{t_f}(\zeta_{t_f}) \prod_{t=1}^{t_f} R_t(\zeta_{t-1}|\zeta_t). \tag{17.16}$$

(ii) *Adjoint process with path probability*:

$$\rho_A(\zeta_{0:t_f}) = \rho_{t_f}(\zeta_{t_f}) \prod_{t=1}^{t_f} A_t(\zeta_{t-1}|\zeta_t). \tag{17.17}$$

(iii) *Dual process with path probability*:

$$\rho_D(\zeta_{0:t_f}) = \rho_0(\zeta_0) \prod_{t=1}^{t_f} D_t(\zeta_t|\zeta_{t-1}). \tag{17.18}$$

These processes allow us to define three trajectory-dependent entropy productions:

$$\Sigma_{\text{tot}}(\zeta_{0:t_f}) = \log \frac{\rho(\zeta_{0:t_f})}{\rho_R(\zeta_{0:t_f})}, \tag{17.19}$$

$$\Sigma_{\text{na}}(\zeta_{0:t_f}) = \log \frac{\rho(\zeta_{0:t_f})}{\rho_A(\zeta_{0:t_f})}, \tag{17.20}$$

$$\Sigma_{\text{a}}(\zeta_{0:t_f}) = \log \frac{\rho(\zeta_{0:t_f})}{\rho_D(\zeta_{0:t_f})}. \tag{17.21}$$

Given our assumption that the stationary distribution is symmetric in the momenta, we can show that these three entropy productions are related as follows:

$$\Sigma_{\text{tot}}(\zeta_{0:t_f}) = \Sigma_{\text{na}}(\zeta_{0:t_f}) + \Sigma_{\text{a}}(\zeta_{0:t_f}). \tag{17.22}$$

However, if we do not assume time-reversal symmetry of the stationary distribution we pick up an extra term which is not necessarily positive, even on average, (Spinney and Ford, 2012b).

The nonadiabatic entropy production Σ_{na} is associated with the relaxation of the system towards its instantaneous stationary state. It quantifies the entropy production due to the system being out of stationary state. This contribution vanishes when the system evolves slowly enough to remain in the instantaneous stationary state throughout the process (a quasi-static or adiabatic process in the thermodynamic sense). If we choose the start and final states to be in equilibrium relative to the parameters λ_0 and

λ_{t_f} – that is, $\rho_0 = \pi_0$ and $\rho_{t_f} = \pi_{t_f}$ – then Σ_{na} corresponds to the dissipated work $\Sigma_{\text{na}} = \beta(W - \Delta F)$.

The adiabatic entropy production Σ_{a} is associated with the maintenance of probability currents in nonequilibrium steady states. It quantifies the entropy production that persists even when the system is in a nonequilibrium steady state due to the breaking of detailed balance. This contribution vanishes for systems that satisfy detailed balance (e.g., systems in equilibrium), but remains nonzero for systems driven by nonconservative forces, even when they have reached a steady state. Note that Σ_{a} is related to the housekeeping heat Q_{hk} as $\Sigma_{\text{a}} = -\beta Q_{\text{hk}}$.

17.3.1 The Proof

To derive the entropy decomposition, (17.22), we substitute the definitions of the entropy productions:

$$\begin{aligned}\Sigma_{\text{na}}(\zeta_{0:t_f}) + \Sigma_{\text{a}}(\zeta_{0:t_f}) &= \log \frac{\rho(\zeta_{0:t_f})}{\rho_A(\zeta_{0:t_f})} + \log \frac{\rho(\zeta_{0:t_f})}{\rho_D(\zeta_{0:t_f})} \\ &= \log \frac{\rho(\zeta_{0:t_f})^2}{\rho_A(\zeta_{0:t_f})\rho_D(\zeta_{0:t_f})}. \end{aligned} \tag{17.23}$$

To proceed, we need to evaluate the product $\rho_A(\zeta_{0:t_f})\rho_D(\zeta_{0:t_f})$. Using the definitions in (17.17) and (17.18) we find:

$$\begin{aligned}\rho_A(\zeta_{0:t_f})\rho_D(\zeta_{0:t_f}) &= \rho_{t_f}(\zeta_{t_f}) \prod_{t=1}^{t_f} A_t(\zeta_{t-1}|\zeta_t) \cdot \rho_0(\zeta_0) \prod_{t=1}^{t_f} D_t(\zeta_t|\zeta_{t-1}) \\ &= \rho_0(\zeta_0)\rho_{t_f}(\zeta_{t_f}) \prod_{t=1}^{t_f} A_t(\zeta_{t-1}|\zeta_t) D_t(\zeta_t|\zeta_{t-1}). \end{aligned} \tag{17.24}$$

Using the definitions of A and D, we can show that:

$$\begin{aligned}A_t(\zeta_{t-1}|\zeta_t)D_t(\zeta_t|\zeta_{t-1}) &= \frac{F_t(\zeta_t|\zeta_{t-1})\pi_t(\zeta_{t-1})}{\pi_t(\zeta_t)} \cdot \frac{R_t(\zeta_{t-1}|\zeta_t)\hat{\pi}_t(\zeta_t)}{\hat{\pi}_t(\zeta_{t-1})} \\ &= R_t(\zeta_{t-1}|\zeta_t)F_t(\zeta_t|\zeta_{t-1}), \end{aligned} \tag{17.25}$$

if we assume $\hat{\pi}_t = \pi_t$. This then results in

$$\rho_A(\zeta_{0:t_f})\rho_D(\zeta_{0:t_f}) = \rho(\zeta_{0:t_f})\rho_R(\zeta_{0:t_f}). \tag{17.26}$$

Therefore

$$\begin{aligned}\Sigma_{\text{na}}(\zeta_{0:t_f}) + \Sigma_{\text{a}}(\zeta_{0:t_f}) &= \log \frac{\rho(\zeta_{0:t_f})^2}{\rho_A(\zeta_{0:t_f})\rho_D(\zeta_{0:t_f})} \\ &= \log \frac{\rho(\zeta_{0:t_f})^2}{\rho(\zeta_{0:t_f})\rho_R(\zeta_{0:t_f})} \\ &= \log \frac{\rho(\zeta_{0:t_f})}{\rho_R(\zeta_{0:t_f})} \\ &= \Sigma_{\text{tot}}(\zeta_{0:t_f}). \end{aligned} \tag{17.27}$$

This proves the decomposition in (17.22).

17.3.2 Explicit Expressions for the Entropy Productions

We can derive explicit expressions for each entropy production in terms of the transition kernels and stationary distributions.

For the total entropy production, starting from the definitions in (17.12) and (17.16):

$$\Sigma_{\text{tot}}(\zeta_{0:t_f}) = \log \frac{\rho_0(\zeta_0)\prod_{t=1}^{t_f} F_t(\zeta_t|\zeta_{t-1})}{\rho_{t_f}(\zeta_{t_f})\prod_{t=1}^{t_f} R_t(\zeta_{t-1}|\zeta_t)} \tag{17.28}$$

$$= \log \frac{\rho_0(\zeta_0)}{\rho_{t_f}(\zeta_{t_f})} + \sum_{t=1}^{t_f} \log \frac{F_t(\zeta_t|\zeta_{t-1})}{R_t(\zeta_{t-1}|\zeta_t)} \tag{17.29}$$

$$= \log \frac{\rho_0(\zeta_0)}{\rho_{t_f}(\zeta_{t_f})} + \sum_{t=1}^{t_f} \log \frac{F_t(\zeta_t|\zeta_{t-1})}{F_t(\hat{\zeta}_{t-1}|\hat{\zeta}_t)}. \tag{17.30}$$

where in the last step we used the definition of R_t from (17.14).

For the adiabatic entropy production, using (17.12), (17.18), and the definition of D_t from (17.15) along with (17.13):

$$\begin{aligned}\Sigma_{\text{a}}(\zeta_{0:t_f}) &= \log \frac{\rho_0(\zeta_0)\prod_{t=1}^{t_f} F_t(\zeta_t|\zeta_{t-1})}{\rho_0(\zeta_0)\prod_{t=1}^{t_f} D_t(\zeta_t|\zeta_{t-1})} \\ &= \sum_{t=1}^{t_f} \log \frac{F_t(\zeta_t|\zeta_{t-1})}{D_t(\zeta_t|\zeta_{t-1})} \\ &= \sum_{t=1}^{t_f} \log \frac{F_t(\zeta_t|\zeta_{t-1})\hat{\pi}_t(\zeta_{t-1})}{F_t(\hat{\zeta}_{t-1}|\hat{\zeta}_t)\hat{\pi}_t(\zeta_t)} \\ &= \sum_{t=1}^{t_f} \log \frac{F_t(\zeta_t|\zeta_{t-1})\pi_t(\zeta_{t-1})}{F_t(\hat{\zeta}_{t-1}|\hat{\zeta}_t)\pi_t(\zeta_t)}, \end{aligned} \tag{17.31}$$

where in the last line we assumed again $\hat{\pi} = \pi$. Observe that Σ_{a} vanishes if detailed balance holds. Therefore Σ_{a} depends solely on the violation of detailed balance at each time step.

For the nonadiabatic entropy production, we get from (17.12) and (17.17),

$$\begin{aligned}\Sigma_{\mathrm{na}}(\zeta_{0:t_f}) &= \log \frac{\rho_0(\zeta_0)\prod_{t=1}^{t_f} F_t(\zeta_t|\zeta_{t-1})}{\rho_{t_f}(\zeta_{t_f})\prod_{t=1}^{t_f} A_t(\zeta_{t-1}|\zeta_t)} \\ &= \log \frac{\rho_0(\zeta_0)}{\rho_{t_f}(\zeta_{t_f})} + \sum_{t=1}^{t_f} \log \frac{F_t(\zeta_t|\zeta_{t-1})}{A_t(\zeta_{t-1}|\zeta_t)} \\ &= \log \frac{\rho_0(\zeta_0)}{\rho_{t_f}(\zeta_{t_f})} + \sum_{t=1}^{t_f} \log \frac{\pi_t(\zeta_t)}{\pi_t(\zeta_{t-1})}. \end{aligned} \tag{17.32}$$

Observe that, as expected,

$$\Sigma_{\mathrm{tot}}(\zeta_{0:t_f}) = \Sigma_{\mathrm{na}}(\zeta_{0:t_f}) + \Sigma_{\mathrm{a}}(\zeta_{0:t_f}). \tag{17.33}$$

Thus, Σ_{na} combines boundary terms with changes in the stationary distribution alon the trajectory, while Σ_{a} captures the detailed balance violations.

17.4 Derivation of Three Fluctuation Theorems

For each entropy production, we can derive a detailed fluctuation theorem. Let's defin the probability distributions for observing specific values of each entropy productior

$$\mathcal{P}_{\mathrm{tot}}(\chi) = \int \mathrm{d}\zeta_{0:t_f}\, \rho(\zeta_{0:t_f})\, \delta(\Sigma_{\mathrm{tot}}(\zeta_{0:t_f}) - \chi), \tag{17.34}$$

$$\mathcal{P}_{\mathrm{na}}(\chi) = \int \mathrm{d}\zeta_{0:t_f}\, \rho(\zeta_{0:t_f})\, \delta(\Sigma_{\mathrm{na}}(\zeta_{0:t_f}) - \chi), \tag{17.35}$$

$$\mathcal{P}_{\mathrm{a}}(\chi) = \int \mathrm{d}\zeta_{0:t_f}\, \rho(\zeta_{0:t_f})\, \delta(\Sigma_{\mathrm{a}}(\zeta_{0:t_f}) - \chi). \tag{17.36}$$

And the corresponding distributions under the respective conjugate processes:

$$\mathcal{P}_R(\chi) = \int \mathrm{d}\zeta_{0:t_f}\, \rho_R(\zeta_{0:t_f})\, \delta(\tilde{\Sigma}_{\mathrm{tot}}(\zeta_{0:t_f}) - \chi), \tag{17.37}$$

$$\mathcal{P}_A(\chi) = \int \mathrm{d}\zeta_{0:t_f}\, \rho_A(\zeta_{0:t_f})\, \delta(\tilde{\Sigma}_{\mathrm{na}}(\zeta_{0:t_f}) - \chi), \tag{17.38}$$

$$\mathcal{P}_D(\chi) = \int \mathrm{d}\zeta_{0:t_f}\, \rho_D(\zeta_{0:t_f})\, \delta(\tilde{\Sigma}_{\mathrm{a}}(\zeta_{0:t_f}) - \chi). \tag{17.39}$$

For the total entropy production, following the approach from Section 17.2, we ca write:

$$\mathcal{P}_{\mathrm{tot}}(\chi) = \int \mathrm{d}\zeta_{0:t_f}\, \rho(\zeta_{0:t_f})\, \delta(\Sigma_{\mathrm{tot}}(\zeta_{0:t_f}) - \chi) \tag{17.40}$$

$$= \int \mathrm{d}\zeta_{0:t_f}\, \rho_R(\zeta_{0:t_f}) e^{\Sigma_{\mathrm{tot}}(\zeta_{0:t_f})}\, \delta(\Sigma_{\mathrm{tot}}(\zeta_{0:t_f}) - \chi)$$

$$= e^{\chi} \int \mathrm{d}\zeta_{0:t_f}\, \rho_R(\zeta_{0:t_f})\, \delta(\Sigma_{\mathrm{tot}}(\zeta_{0:t_f}) - \chi). \tag{17.41}$$

For the time-reversed process, we need to show that the entropy production chang sign. Under the time-reversal transformation $\rho \to \rho_R$, a trajectory $(\zeta_0, \ldots, \zeta_{t_f})$ maps to $(\hat{\zeta}_{t_f}, \ldots, \hat{\zeta}_0)$. The entropy production under this transformation becomes:

$$\tilde{\Sigma}_{\text{tot}}(\zeta_{0:t_f}) = \Sigma_{\text{tot}}(\hat{\zeta}_{t_f}, \ldots, \hat{\zeta}_0) = -\Sigma_{\text{tot}}(\zeta_{0:t_f}), \tag{17.42}$$

where we used $\hat{\pi} = \pi$ and the fact that applying the transformation twice returns the original. This leads to

$$\mathcal{P}_{\text{tot}}(\chi) = e^{\chi} \int \mathrm{d}\zeta_{0:t_f}\, \rho_R(\zeta_{0:t_f})\, \delta(\tilde{\Sigma}_{\text{tot}}(\zeta_{0:t_f}) + \chi) = e^{\chi} \mathcal{P}_R(-\chi). \tag{17.43}$$

Therefore, we arrive at the DFT for total entropy production:

$$\frac{\mathcal{P}_{\text{tot}}(\chi)}{\mathcal{P}_R(-\chi)} = e^{\chi}. \tag{17.44}$$

The derivation for the adiabatic and nonadiabatic entropy productions follows a similar pattern. We have:

$$\tilde{\Sigma}_{\text{na}}(\zeta_{0:t_f}) = -\Sigma_{\text{na}}(\zeta_{0:t_f}), \tag{17.45}$$

$$\tilde{\Sigma}_{\text{a}}(\zeta_{0:t_f}) = -\Sigma_{\text{a}}(\zeta_{0:t_f}). \tag{17.46}$$

This leads to two further detailed fluctuation theorems:

$$\frac{\mathcal{P}_{\text{na}}(\chi)}{\mathcal{P}_A(-\chi)} = e^{\chi}, \tag{17.47}$$

$$\frac{\mathcal{P}_{\text{a}}(\chi)}{\mathcal{P}_D(-\chi)} = e^{\chi}. \tag{17.48}$$

Because each of these entropy productions satisfies its own detailed fluctuation theorem – (17.44), (17.47), and (17.48) – the integral fluctuation theorems follow by integration. This implies that the corresponding average entropy productions are non-negative:

$$\mathbb{E}_\rho\,[\Sigma_{\text{tot}}] \geq 0, \tag{17.49}$$

$$\mathbb{E}_\rho\,[\Sigma_{\text{na}}] \geq 0, \tag{17.50}$$

$$\mathbb{E}_\rho\,[\Sigma_{\text{a}}] \geq 0, \tag{17.51}$$

These inequalities represent three different (generalized) second laws of thermodynamics. For systems approaching equilibrium, the adiabatic contribution vanishes ($\langle \Sigma_{\text{a}} \rangle = 0$), and only the nonadiabatic term contributes to the total entropy production. In contrast, for systems in a nonequilibrium steady state, the nonadiabatic contribution vanishes ($\langle \Sigma_{\text{na}} \rangle = 0$), and only the adiabatic term contributes to the total entropy production.

7.5 Crooks Fluctuation Theorem and the Jarzynski Equality

The Crooks fluctuation theorem (Crooks, 1999) is a special case of the derived FTs in the previous sections. We need two assumptions:

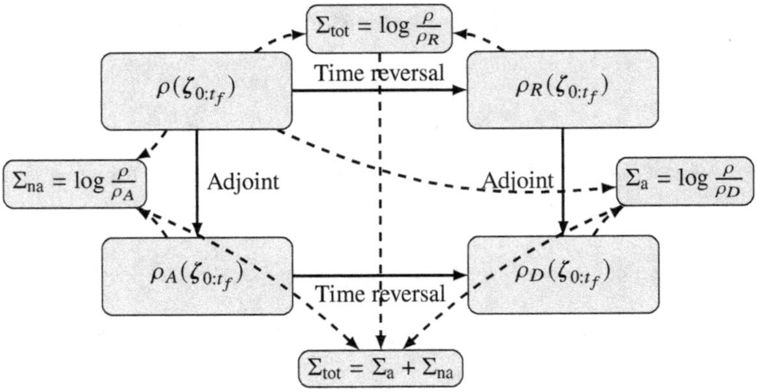

Figure 17.1 Relationship between the forward process and its conjugate processes (time-reversed, adjoint, and time-reversed adjoint), along with the three entropy productions and their decomposition. Each entropy production satisfies its own detailed fluctuation theorem with respect to its conjugate process.

(1) We assume that detailed balance holds at equilibrium; that is, we identify $A_t = R$ and $D_t = F_t$ (see Chapter 9). This makes the adiabatic contribution to the entropy production vanish, as Σ_a measures the violation of detailed balance.

(2) We assume that the initial state and the final state of the Markov chain are the equilibrium distributions of λ_0 and λ_{t_f} respectively:

$$\rho_0(\zeta_0) = \pi_0(\zeta_0) = \frac{1}{Z_0} e^{-\beta \mathcal{H}_0(\zeta_0)}, \tag{17.52}$$

$$\rho_{t_f}(\zeta_{t_f}) = \pi_{t_f}(\zeta_{t_f}) = \frac{1}{Z_{t_f}} e^{-\beta \mathcal{H}_{t_f}(\zeta_{t_f})}, \tag{17.53}$$

where $\mathcal{H}_0(\zeta_0)$ and $\mathcal{H}_{t_f}(\zeta_{t_f})$ are the initial and final Hamiltonians, and $\beta = 1/(k_\text{B}T)$ is the inverse temperature. The initial and final equilibrium free energies are given by

$$\mathcal{F}[\pi_0] = -\frac{1}{\beta} \log Z_0, \tag{17.54}$$

$$\mathcal{F}[\pi_{t_f}] = -\frac{1}{\beta} \log Z_{t_f}. \tag{17.55}$$

Under these assumptions, the stochastic entropy change of the system can be expressed as:

$$\begin{aligned} \Delta S_{\text{sys}}(\zeta_{0:t_f}) &= -\log \frac{\pi_{t_f}(\zeta_{t_f})}{\pi_0(\zeta_0)} \\ &= \beta[\mathcal{H}_{t_f}(\zeta_{t_f}) - \mathcal{H}_0(\zeta_0) - \mathcal{F}[\pi_{t_f}] + \mathcal{F}[\pi_0]] \\ &= \beta[\Delta \mathcal{U}(\zeta_{0:t_f}) - \Delta F], \end{aligned} \tag{17.56}$$

where $\Delta \mathcal{U}(\zeta_{0:t_f}) = \mathcal{H}_{t_f}(\zeta_{t_f}) - \mathcal{H}_0(\zeta_0)$ is the change in internal energy along the trajectory, and $\Delta F = F_{t_f} - F_0 = \mathcal{F}[\pi_{t_f}] - \mathcal{F}[\pi_0]$ is the equilibrium free energy difference.

The stochastic first law, (10.17), from Chapter 10 implies $\mathcal{W}(\zeta_{0:t_f}) = \Delta\mathcal{U}(\zeta_{0:t_f}) - Q(\zeta_{0:t_f})$, and assuming that the entropy change of the environment is given by the heat production in the system, $\Delta\mathcal{S}_{\text{bath}}(\zeta_{0:t_f}) = -\beta Q(\zeta_{0:t_f})$, we can express the total entropy production as:

$$\begin{aligned}\Sigma_{\text{tot}}(\zeta_{0:t_f}) &= \Delta\mathcal{S}_{\text{sys}}(\zeta_{0:t_f}) + \Delta\mathcal{S}_{\text{bath}}(\zeta_{0:t_f}) \\ &= \beta[\Delta\mathcal{U}(\zeta_{0:t_f}) - \Delta F] - \beta Q(\zeta_{0:t_f}) \\ &= \beta[\mathcal{W}(\zeta_{0:t_f}) - \Delta F],\end{aligned} \tag{17.57}$$

where in the last step we used the first law $\Delta\mathcal{U} = \mathcal{W} + Q$, which gives $\Delta\mathcal{U} - Q = \mathcal{W}$. Using (17.19), this gives

$$\frac{\rho(\zeta_{0:t_f})}{\rho_R(\zeta_{0:t_f})} = e^{\Sigma_{\text{tot}}(\zeta_{0:t_f})} = e^{\beta[\mathcal{W}(\zeta_{0:t_f}) - \Delta F]}, \tag{17.58}$$

from which the Crooks detailed FT follows from the general theory of the sections above:

$$\frac{\mathcal{P}(\chi)}{\mathcal{P}_R(-\chi)} = e^{\chi} \quad \Rightarrow \quad \frac{\mathcal{P}(\mathcal{W})}{\mathcal{P}_R(-\mathcal{W})} = e^{\beta[\mathcal{W} - \Delta F]}. \tag{17.59}$$

The crossing point where $\mathcal{P}(\mathcal{W}) = \mathcal{P}_R(-\mathcal{W})$ occurs at $\mathcal{W} = \Delta F$, giving a practical method for estimating free energy differences from nonequilibrium measurements, a topic that we will discuss in more detail in Chapter 18.

The Jarzynski equality (Jarzynski, 1997) can now be trivially derived by integrating both sides of the equation

$$\frac{\rho_R(\zeta_{0:t_f})}{\rho(\zeta_{0:t_f})} = e^{-\Sigma_{\text{tot}}(\zeta_{0:t_f})} = e^{-\beta[\mathcal{W}(\zeta_{0:t_f}) - \Delta F]}, \tag{17.60}$$

derived from (17.58), over ρ:

$$\begin{aligned}1 &= \mathbb{E}_\rho[e^{-\beta[\mathcal{W}(\zeta_{0:t_f}) - \Delta F]}] \\ \Rightarrow \mathbb{E}_\rho[e^{-\beta\mathcal{W}(\zeta_{0:t_f})}] &= e^{-\beta\Delta F}.\end{aligned} \tag{17.61}$$

This is an instance of an integral fluctuation theorem. It establishes a remarkable connection between the work performed on a system during a nonequilibrium process and the equilibrium free energy difference between the initial and final states. For a direct proof via verification of the Jarzynski equality see Chapter 18.

Applying Jensen's inequality to (17.61) leads to the Kelvin statement of the second law of thermodynamics:

$$\mathbb{E}_\rho[\mathcal{W}(\zeta_{0:t_f})] \geq \Delta F. \tag{17.62}$$

18 Free Energy Estimation

18.1 Introduction

Estimating free energy differences is a central problem in physics, machine learning and particularly in the context of biochemistry (Chipot and Pohorille, 2007). Free energy differences between equilibrium states are of great interest in studying dynamical systems, such as small molecules in vacuum or membrane proteins. For instance, drug affinity can be expressed as the free energy difference between the bound and unbound states of a ligand–receptor complex (Kollman et al., 2000), and conformational changes in proteins can be characterized by the free energy landscape along a reaction coordinate (Dellago et al., 2002).

In this chapter we will review a number of popular free energy estimation methods, such as free energy perturbation and thermodynamic integration. We also derive methods based on fluctuation theorems such as the Jarzynski and Crooks FTs. Finally, we will derive the optimal Bennett acceptance ratio method as the minimal variance estimator.

18.2 Free Energy Estimation

In machine learning, the normalization constant of a probabilistic model (the marginal likelihood or model evidence) is mathematically equivalent to the partition function in physics. Its logarithm corresponds to the negative free energy, and methods like annealed importance sampling, discussed in Chapter 12, are direct applications of the physical free energy estimation methods we discuss here.

Let π_A and π_B be two equilibrium distributions defined by their respective Hamiltonians $\mathcal{H}_A$ and $\mathcal{H}_B$. The free energy of a system in equilibrium state A is given by

$$F_A = -k_{\mathrm{B}}T \log Z_A, \tag{18.1}$$

where $Z_A = \int \mathrm{d}\zeta \; e^{-\beta \mathcal{H}_A(\zeta)}$ is the partition function with $\beta = 1/(k_{\mathrm{B}}T)$ the inverse temperature. The free energy difference between equilibrium states A and B is then

$$\Delta F_{AB} = F_B - F_A = -k_{\mathrm{B}}T \log \frac{Z_B}{Z_A}. \tag{18.2}$$

The computational difficulty arises because Z_A and Z_B involve high-dimensional integrals that cannot be computed analytically for realistic systems. Molecular dynamics (MD) simulations are the most common sampling method in biochemistry, where interesting free energy differences are often defined between an easy-to-sample equilibrium state and a more interesting but harder-to-sample state (Karplus and McCammon, 2002). For instance, when studying ligand-gated ion channels, the open state is considered its native state and is significantly easier to sample from than the closed state.

18.2.1 Free Energy Perturbation

The Zwanzig equation, also known as the free energy perturbation theory (Zwanzig, 1954), relates the free energy difference to an ensemble average over the reference equilibrium distribution π_A:

$$\Delta F_{AB} = -\beta^{-1} \log \mathbb{E}_{\pi_A} \left[e^{-\beta[\mathcal{H}_B(\zeta) - \mathcal{H}_A(\zeta)]} \right]. \tag{18.3}$$

This can be understood and derived easily using importance sampling. The ratio of the partition functions can be written as an expectation value with respect to the distribution π_A:

$$\begin{aligned} \frac{Z_B}{Z_A} &= \frac{\int \mathrm{d}\zeta \; e^{-\beta\mathcal{H}_B(\zeta)}}{\int \mathrm{d}\zeta \; e^{-\beta\mathcal{H}_A(\zeta)}} = \frac{\int \mathrm{d}\zeta \; e^{-\beta\mathcal{H}_A(\zeta)} e^{-\beta[\mathcal{H}_B(\zeta) - \mathcal{H}_A(\zeta)]}}{Z_A} \\ &= \int \mathrm{d}\zeta \; \underbrace{\frac{e^{-\beta\mathcal{H}_A(\zeta)}}{Z_A}}_{\pi_A(\zeta)} e^{-\beta[\mathcal{H}_B(\zeta) - \mathcal{H}_A(\zeta)]} \\ &= \mathbb{E}_{\pi_A} \left[e^{-\beta[\mathcal{H}_B(\zeta) - \mathcal{H}_A(\zeta)]} \right]. \end{aligned} \tag{18.4}$$

Taking $-\beta^{-1}$ log of both sides of (18.4) yields the Zwanzig equation, (18.3).

As with any importance sampling estimator, the efficiency of this estimator critically depends on the overlap between the distributions π_A and π_B. If the overlap is small, meaning that typical configurations under π_A are very rare under π_B, the estimator can suffer from high variance and require an impractically large number of samples to converge. Therefore, it is often beneficial to introduce a series of intermediate states to bridge the gap between A and B.

18.2.2 Thermodynamic Integration

An alternative to direct importance sampling is to construct a reversible path connecting the two states. Thermodynamic integration (Kirkwood, 1935; Frenkel and Smit, 2001) offers this approach to estimating free energy differences, based on constructing a path between equilibrium states.

We introduce a continuous parameter $\lambda \in [0, 1]$ to smoothly interpolate between the two Hamiltonians. We define a path-dependent Hamiltonian $\mathcal{H}(\zeta; \lambda)$ that interpolates between $\mathcal{H}_A$ and $\mathcal{H}_B$ as the work parameter λ changes from $\lambda = 0$ to $\lambda = 1$. Fo example, a linear interpolation is often used: $\mathcal{H}(\zeta; \lambda) = (1 - \lambda)\mathcal{H}_A(\zeta) + \lambda\mathcal{H}_B(\zeta)$.

The free energy F_λ is now a function of λ. Its derivative with respect to λ can b computed as follows:

$$F_\lambda = -\beta^{-1} \log Z_\lambda, \qquad Z_\lambda = \int \mathrm{d}\zeta\, e^{-\beta\mathcal{H}(\zeta;\lambda)}, \tag{18.5}$$

$$\frac{\mathrm{d}F_\lambda}{\mathrm{d}\lambda} = -\beta^{-1}\frac{1}{Z_\lambda}\frac{\mathrm{d}Z_\lambda}{\mathrm{d}\lambda} = -\beta^{-1}\frac{1}{Z_\lambda}\int \mathrm{d}\zeta \left(-\beta\frac{\partial\mathcal{H}}{\partial\lambda}(\zeta;\lambda)\right) e^{-\beta\mathcal{H}(\zeta;\lambda)}$$
$$= \int \mathrm{d}\zeta\, \frac{e^{-\beta\mathcal{H}(\zeta;\lambda)}}{Z_\lambda}\frac{\partial\mathcal{H}}{\partial\lambda}(\zeta;\lambda) = \mathbb{E}_{\pi_\lambda}\left[\frac{\partial\mathcal{H}}{\partial\lambda}\right]. \tag{18.6}$$

Integrating this derivative from $\lambda = 0$ to $\lambda = 1$ gives the total free energy difference:

$$\Delta F_{AB} = F_B - F_A = \int_0^1 \mathrm{d}\lambda\, \frac{\mathrm{d}F_\lambda}{\mathrm{d}\lambda}$$
$$= \int_0^1 \mathrm{d}\lambda\, \mathbb{E}_{\pi_\lambda}\left[\frac{\partial\mathcal{H}(\zeta;\lambda)}{\partial\lambda}\right]. \tag{18.7}$$

This shows that the free energy difference can be computed by computing the ensembl average of the total work done in a quasi-static (infinitely slow) or reversible proces where the system remains in equilibrium π_λ at every instant λ. In practice, we cann perform infinitely slow processes. Instead, we discretize λ into t_f steps: a finite numbe of intermediate states defined by λ_t for $t = 0, \ldots, t_f$, where $\lambda_0 = 0$ and $\lambda_{t_f} = 1$. Fo each intermediate state λ_t, an equilibrium simulation (e.g., MD or MCMC) is run t compute the ensemble average $\mathbb{E}_{\pi_{\lambda_t}}\left[\frac{\partial\mathcal{H}}{\partial\lambda}\right]$. The total free energy difference is the obtained by numerically integrating these averages, for instance using the trapezoid rule:

$$\Delta F_{AB} \approx \sum_{t=1}^{t_f} \frac{1}{2}\left(\mathbb{E}_{\pi_{\lambda_t}}\left[\left.\frac{\partial\mathcal{H}}{\partial\lambda}\right|_{\lambda_t}\right] + \mathbb{E}_{\pi_{\lambda_{t-1}}}\left[\left.\frac{\partial\mathcal{H}}{\partial\lambda}\right|_{\lambda_{t-1}}\right]\right)(\lambda_t - \lambda_{t-1}), \tag{18.8}$$

where $\tau(t) = t\delta\tau$ and $\lambda_t = \lambda(\tau(t))$.

This method is distinct from the nonequilibrium work measurements discussed nex which involve a single, finite-time switching process.

18.3 Non-equilibrium Work Measurements

The approach of measuring work during a quasi-static process (where $\mathbb{E}_\rho[\mathcal{W}] = \Delta F$ is often impractical due to the extremely slow process required. Fluctuation theorem provide powerful tools to analyze and improve the estimation of free energy difference from nonequilibrium work measurements, which are more computationally accessibl In this section, we explain how stochastic dynamics can be used to simulate nonequ librium processes and rederive the Jarzynski equality, which relates nonequilibriu work to equilibrium free energy differences.

Consider a system described by a time-dependent Hamiltonian $\mathcal{H}_t(\zeta)$, where th subscript t indicates discrete time steps and the Hamiltonian changes according to a predetermined protocol $\{\lambda_0, \ldots, \lambda_{t_f}\}$. The system evolves under a sequence of Hamiltonians $\{\mathcal{H}_0, \ldots, \mathcal{H}_{t_f}\}$ according to this protocol. At inverse temperature $\beta = 1/(k_\mathrm{B}T)$, the equilibrium distribution corresponding to each Hamiltonian $\mathcal{H}_t$ is given by the Boltzmann distribution:

$$\pi_t(\zeta) = \frac{e^{-\beta\mathcal{H}_t(\zeta)}}{Z_t}, \quad Z_t = \int \mathrm{d}\zeta\, e^{-\beta\mathcal{H}_t(\zeta)}, \tag{18.9}$$

where Z_t is the partition function and $F_t = -\beta^{-1}\log Z_t$ is the equilibrium free energy at time step t.

To simulate the system's evolution, we employ Monte Carlo dynamics. As discussed in Chapter 11, the Monte Carlo algorithm uses a forward transition probability kernel $F_t(\zeta_t|\zeta_{t-1})$ that leaves the distribution π_t invariant:

$$\int \mathrm{d}\zeta_{t-1}\, F_t(\zeta_t|\zeta_{t-1})\, \pi_t(\zeta_{t-1}) = \pi_t(\zeta_t). \tag{18.10}$$

This kernel F_t represents the complete MCMC transition, including any proposal and acceptance–rejection steps. The stationarity condition ensures that if the external driving parameter were held constant at step t, the system would eventually relax to the equilibrium distribution π_t, assuming ergodicity.

Recall from Chapter 9 that we can also define the reverse kernel $R_t(\zeta_{t-1}|\zeta_t) = F_t(\hat{\zeta}_{t-1}|\hat{\zeta}_t)$, where $\hat{\zeta}_t = (\xi_t, -\eta_t)$ represents the momentum-reversed state. This reverse kernel defines the time-reversed process in the context of fluctuation theorems.

In a nonequilibrium switching simulation, we follow a two-step procedure at each time step:

(1) The Hamiltonian is updated from $\mathcal{H}_{t-1}$ to $\mathcal{H}_t$.
(2) A Monte Carlo move is performed using the kernel $F_t(\cdot|\cdot)$, which is constructed to leave π_t invariant, moving the system from state ζ_{t-1} to ζ_t.

We start with the system at equilibrium at $t = 0$, with an initial microstate ζ_0 sampled from the equilibrium distribution $\pi_0(\zeta_0)$. The system then evolves for t_f discrete steps according to this protocol. This process generates a trajectory $\zeta_{0:t_f} = \{\zeta_0, \zeta_1, \ldots, \zeta_{t_f}\}$:

$$\zeta_0 \xrightarrow{F_1} \zeta_1 \xrightarrow{F_2} \zeta_2 \xrightarrow{\cdots} \zeta_{t_f}. \tag{18.11}$$

Following the Markov property, as shown in Chapter 10, the probability density $\rho(\zeta_{0:t_f})$ for generating this trajectory is given by

$$\rho(\zeta_{0:t_f}) = \pi_0(\zeta_0) \prod_{t=1}^{t_f} F_t(\zeta_t|\zeta_{t-1}). \tag{18.12}$$

The amount of stochastic work done on the system is calculated from the energy changes due to the Hamiltonian updates (Step 1) at each time step, before the system relaxes (Step 2):

$$\mathcal{W}(\zeta_{0:t_f}) = \sum_{t=1}^{t_f} \delta\mathcal{W}_t \equiv \sum_{t=1}^{t_f} \left[\mathcal{H}_t(\zeta_{t-1}) - \mathcal{H}_{t-1}(\zeta_{t-1})\right]. \tag{18.13}$$

18.3.1 Jarzynski Estimator

Now, let's verify the Jarzynski equality, (17.61), for this stochastic dynamics by explicitly computing the expectation of the exponential work term over the ensemble of trajectories:

$$\begin{aligned}
&\mathbb{E}_\rho[e^{-\beta\mathcal{W}(\zeta_{0:t_f})}] \\
&= \int d\zeta_{0:t_f}\, \rho(\zeta_{0:t_f})\, e^{-\beta\mathcal{W}(\zeta_{0:t_f})} \\
&= \int d\zeta_{0:t_f}\, \pi_0(\zeta_0) \prod_{t=1}^{t_f} F_t(\zeta_t|\zeta_{t-1})\, \exp\left(-\beta\sum_{t=1}^{t_f}[\mathcal{H}_t(\zeta_{t-1}) - \mathcal{H}_{t-1}(\zeta_{t-1})]\right) \\
&= \int d\zeta_{0:t_f}\, \frac{e^{-\beta\mathcal{H}_0(\zeta_0)}}{Z_0} \prod_{t=1}^{t_f}\left(F_t(\zeta_t|\zeta_{t-1})\, e^{-\beta[\mathcal{H}_t(\zeta_{t-1})-\mathcal{H}_{t-1}(\zeta_{t-1})]}\right).
\end{aligned} \tag{18.14}$$

Focusing on the innermost integral over ζ_0, we can simplify:

$$\begin{aligned}
&\int d\zeta_0\, \frac{e^{-\beta\mathcal{H}_0(\zeta_0)}}{Z_0} F_1(\zeta_1|\zeta_0)\, e^{-\beta[\mathcal{H}_1(\zeta_0)-\mathcal{H}_0(\zeta_0)]} \\
&= \frac{1}{Z_0}\int d\zeta_0\, F_1(\zeta_1|\zeta_0)\, e^{-\beta\mathcal{H}_1(\zeta_0)} \\
&= \frac{Z_1}{Z_0}\int d\zeta_0\, F_1(\zeta_1|\zeta_0)\, \pi_1(\zeta_0) \quad \text{(using (18.9))} \\
&= \frac{Z_1}{Z_0}\pi_1(\zeta_1) \quad \text{(using the invariance property, (18.10)).}
\end{aligned} \tag{18.15}$$

Note, interestingly, we have only used the invariance of each π_t under the corresponding kernel F_t. Detailed balance is not needed for this proof. Substituting this result back the integral over ζ_0 is completed, and the expression now starts with $\frac{Z_1}{Z_0}\pi_1(\zeta_1)$. We can repeat this process for the integrals over $\zeta_1, \zeta_2, \ldots, \zeta_{t_f-1}$. After integrating up to ζ_{t_f-1}, we are left with:

$$\mathbb{E}_\rho[e^{-\beta\mathcal{W}(\zeta_{0:t_f})}] = \frac{Z_1}{Z_0}\frac{Z_2}{Z_1}\cdots\frac{Z_{t_f}}{Z_{t_f-1}}\int d\zeta_{t_f}\, \pi_{t_f}(\zeta_{t_f}) = \frac{Z_{t_f}}{Z_0} = e^{-\beta\Delta F}. \tag{18.16}$$

This Jarzynski equality (Jarzynski, 1997, 2011) allows estimating ΔF from nonequilibrium work measurements. Given S independent work values $\{\mathcal{W}_1, \mathcal{W}_2, \ldots, \mathcal{W}_S\}$ sampled from S independent realizations of the process, the free energy difference can be estimated as:

$$\langle\Delta F\rangle \approx -\frac{1}{\beta}\log\left(\frac{1}{S}\sum_{s=1}^{S} e^{-\beta\mathcal{W}_s}\right). \tag{18.17}$$

The efficiency of this estimator depends on the dissipated work, defined as $\mathcal{W}_{\text{diss}} = \mathcal{W} - \Delta F$. To understand the variance, we need to analyze both the variance of $e^{-\beta\mathcal{W}}$ and the propagated variance to the free energy estimate. First, for the exponential work:

$$\begin{aligned}
\mathbb{V}[e^{-\beta\mathcal{W}}] &= \mathbb{E}_p[e^{-2\beta\mathcal{W}}] - \left(\mathbb{E}_p[e^{-\beta\mathcal{W}}]\right)^2 \\
&= \mathbb{E}_p[e^{-2\beta\mathcal{W}}] - e^{-2\beta\Delta F} \quad \text{(using Jarzynski's equality)} \\
&= e^{-2\beta\Delta F}\left(\mathbb{E}_p[e^{-2\beta(\mathcal{W}-\Delta F)}] - 1\right) \\
&= e^{-2\beta\Delta F}\left(\mathbb{E}_p[e^{-2\beta\mathcal{W}_{\text{diss}}}] - 1\right).
\end{aligned} \tag{18.18}$$

The relative error of the exponential estimator is therefore

$$\frac{\sqrt{\mathbb{V}[e^{-\beta\mathcal{W}}]}}{\mathbb{E}_p[e^{-\beta\mathcal{W}}]} = \sqrt{\mathbb{E}_p[e^{-2\beta\mathcal{W}_{\text{diss}}}] - 1}. \tag{18.19}$$

For the free energy estimate itself, we need to consider the variance of $\langle\Delta F\rangle$. Using the error propagation formula for the logarithm transformation, for large S we get

$$\mathbb{V}[\langle\Delta F\rangle] \approx \frac{1}{\beta^2}\frac{\mathbb{V}[e^{-\beta\mathcal{W}}]}{S\cdot(\mathbb{E}[e^{-\beta\mathcal{W}}])^2} = \frac{1}{\beta^2 S}\left(\mathbb{E}_p[e^{-2\beta\mathcal{W}_{\text{diss}}}] - 1\right). \tag{18.20}$$

To translate this variance into a practical sample size requirement, we use the fact that for S independent samples, the standard error of the sample mean is $\text{SE}[\langle X\rangle] = \sqrt{\mathbb{V}[X]}/\sqrt{S}$. To achieve a desired standard error ε for the estimate, we need a number of samples S such that $\sqrt{\mathbb{V}[\langle\Delta F\rangle]} < \varepsilon$. This implies that

$$S > \frac{1}{\beta^2\varepsilon^2}\left(\mathbb{E}_p[e^{-2\beta\mathcal{W}_{\text{diss}}}] - 1\right). \tag{18.21}$$

Because the average is dominated by rare events where $\mathcal{W}$ is small (i.e., $\mathcal{W}_{\text{diss}}$ is large and negative), this estimator can be inefficient for highly irreversible processes where the average dissipated work is large.

8.4 Bi-directional Estimators: Crooks and Bennett

The efficiency of the Jarzynski estimator can be analyzed (Gore et al., 2003) and often improved by combining data from both a forward process (A to B) and a reverse process (B to A) (Geiger and Dellago, 2010). We now introduce the reverse process and show how it enables more efficient estimators.

The reverse process is defined as follows. Starting from the final equilibrium distribution $\pi_{t_f}(\zeta_{t_f})$, the system evolves under the time-reversed protocol with Hamiltonians applied in reverse order, $\{\mathcal{H}_{t_f}, \mathcal{H}_{t_f-1}, \ldots, \mathcal{H}_0\}$. The transition kernels are also reversed according to the definition from Chapter 9: $R_t(\zeta_{t-1}|\zeta_t) = F_t(\hat{\zeta}_{t-1}|\hat{\zeta}_t)$, where $\hat{\zeta}_t = (\xi_t, -\eta_t)$ represents the state with momenta flipped. The path probability density

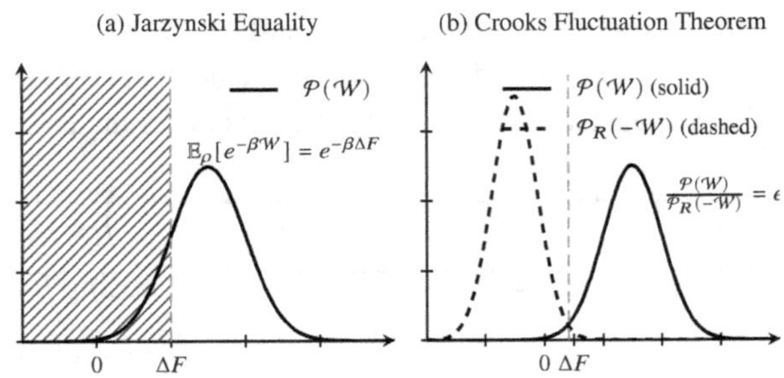

Figure 18.1 Jarzynski's equality and the Crooks fluctuation theorem. (a) The work distributio $\mathcal{P}(\mathcal{W})$ (solid line) for the forward process, with ΔF marked by the vertical dashed guide line. The hatched region represents $\mathcal{W} \leq \Delta F$, corresponding to rare fluctuations where the work performed is less than the free energy difference. The Jarzynski equality relates the average of $e^{-\beta\mathcal{W}}$ to $e^{-\beta\Delta F}$, with the tail of the distribution playing a crucial role. (b) The work distributions for both forward $\mathcal{P}(\mathcal{W})$ (solid line) and reverse $\mathcal{P}_R(-\mathcal{W})$ (dashed line) processe The Crooks fluctuation theorem relates the ratio of these probabilities to $e^{\beta(\mathcal{W}-\Delta F)}$, with the crossing point indicating $\mathcal{W} = \Delta F$. The reverse process typically has a higher probability of work values below ΔF, consistent with the direction of time's arrow in thermodynamics.

for the reverse process is:

$$\rho_R(\zeta_{0:t_f}) = \pi_{t_f}(\zeta_{t_f}) \prod_{t=1}^{t_f} R_t(\zeta_{t-1}|\zeta_t). \quad (18.22$$

For every forward trajectory $\zeta_{0:t_f} = (\zeta_0, \zeta_1, \ldots, \zeta_{t_f})$, we can construct its *conjuga reverse trajectory* by two operations: (1) reversing the time order of states, and (2 flipping all momenta. This gives $\tilde{\zeta}_{0:t_f} = (\hat{\zeta}_{t_f}, \hat{\zeta}_{t_f-1}, \ldots, \hat{\zeta}_0)$. This conjugate trajector represents the exact time-reversal at the trajectory level – it is the specific path tha would be observed if we ran the forward trajectory backward in time with momen reversed. This is distinct from a typical trajectory generated by running the revers protocol starting from a new initial condition sampled from π_{t_f}.

The work functional for the reverse protocol, $\tilde{\mathcal{W}}$, which is by definition applied t the conjugate path $\tilde{\zeta}_{0:t_f}$, yields the negative of the forward work (see Chapter 10):

$$\tilde{\mathcal{W}}(\tilde{\zeta}_{0:t_f}) = -\mathcal{W}(\zeta_{0:t_f}). \quad (18.23$$

This work relation holds for the specific conjugate trajectory. However, in practice w generate independent trajectories from both forward and reverse protocols.

These sample different distributions: forward trajectories follow $\rho(\zeta_{0:t_f})$ with wor distribution $\mathcal{P}(\mathcal{W})$, while reverse trajectories follow $\rho_R(\zeta_{0:t_f})$ with work distributio $\mathcal{P}_R(\tilde{\mathcal{W}})$. These distributions are not simply mirror images of each other. In the fo lowing, we will consider that we have collected S_F forward work values $\{\mathcal{W}_i\}_{i=1}^{S_F}$ an S_R reverse work values $\{\tilde{\mathcal{W}}_j\}_{j=1}^{S_R}$.

As highlighted in Chapter 17, the Crooks fluctuation theorem relates these distrib

tions:

$$\frac{\mathcal{P}(\mathcal{W})}{\mathcal{P}_R(\tilde{\mathcal{W}})} = \frac{\mathcal{P}(\mathcal{W})}{\mathcal{P}_R(-\mathcal{W})} = e^{\beta(\mathcal{W}-\Delta F)}. \tag{18.24}$$

This provides two simple methods for estimating ΔF.

First, ΔF can be determined from the work value $\mathcal{W}^*$ where the forward and reverse work distributions cross: $\mathcal{P}(\mathcal{W}^*) = \mathcal{P}_R(-\mathcal{W}^*)$, yielding $\Delta F = \mathcal{W}^*$ (see Figure 18.1(b)). Second, plotting $\log \frac{\mathcal{P}(\mathcal{W})}{\mathcal{P}_R(-\mathcal{W})}$ against $\mathcal{W}$ should give a line with slope β and y-intercept $-\beta\Delta F$. In practice, we construct histograms or kernel density estimates of the forward and reverse work distributions and find the crossing point or fit a line to the log-ratio. However, both these methods suffer from poor statistics in regions where the distributions have little overlap, limiting their practical utility.

8.4.1 Bennett Acceptance Ratio Method

A statistically optimal way to combine forward and reverse data is the Bennett acceptance ratio (BAR) method (Bennett, 1976; Shirts et al., 2003). There are two complementary derivations: (i) a maximum-likelihood derivation following Shirts et al. (2003), and (ii) the original variance-optimal weighting perspective of Bennett (1976). In this book we will follow the former.

To derive BAR via maximum likelihood, we reformulate the problem as binary classification to be solved with logistic regression. We introduce the following variables:

$$Y = \{F, R\}, \tag{18.25}$$

$$X = \begin{cases} \mathcal{W} & \text{if } Y = F, \\ -\mathcal{W} & \text{if } Y = R, \end{cases} \tag{18.26}$$

$$\theta = \Delta F. \tag{18.27}$$

We can then write a probability distribution for the conditional distribution $P(Y|X,\theta)$ and try to maximize this over samples $\{Y_s, X_s\}$, $s = 1 : N$ by adjusting the parameter $\theta = \Delta F$. In other words, we want to find the value of ΔF that makes the classification probability of predicting whether an observed work value X is from a forward or reverse simulated chain, maximally likely.

The next step is to identify

$$P(X|Y=F) = \mathcal{P}(\mathcal{W}), \tag{18.28}$$

$$P(X|Y=R) = \mathcal{P}_R(-\mathcal{W}) \tag{18.29}$$

so we can use the Crooks fluctuation theorem to relate these two quantities:

$$\frac{P(X|Y=F)}{P(X|Y=R)} = e^{\beta(\mathcal{W}-\Delta F)}. \tag{18.30}$$

We can then use Bayes' rule to write

$$\frac{P(Y=F|X)}{P(Y=R|X)} = \frac{P(Y=F|X)}{1-P(Y=F|X)}, \tag{18.31}$$

since $\sum_Y P(Y|X) = 1$. From (18.28) and (18.29) we can also write

$$\frac{P(Y=F|X)}{P(Y=R|X)} = \frac{P(X|Y=F)P(Y=F)}{P(X|Y=R)P(Y=R)} = e^{\beta(\mathcal{W}-\Delta F)+c}, \tag{18.32}$$

where $c = \log \frac{p(F)}{p(R)}$ is the log prior odds. Since we collect S_F forward and S_R reverse samples, a reasonable choice is the empirical prior $p(F) = \frac{S_F}{S_F+S_R}$, giving $c = \log \frac{S_F}{S_R}$. With these probabilities defined, we can solve for $P(Y = F|X)$ as

$$\begin{aligned} p(Y=F|X) &= \sigma(\beta(\mathcal{W}-\Delta F)+c), && (18.33)\\ p(Y=R|X) &= 1-p(Y=F|X) \\ &= 1-\sigma(\beta(\mathcal{W}-\Delta F)+c) \\ &= \sigma(-\beta(\mathcal{W}-\Delta F)-c), && (18.34) \end{aligned}$$

where $\sigma(x) = \frac{1}{1+e^{-x}}$ is the sigmoid function and we used $1-\sigma(x) = \sigma(-x)$.

With these probabilities defined, we can now write the log-likelihood of our logistic regression classification problem:

$$\begin{aligned} \mathcal{L}(\Delta F) &= \sum_{s=1}^{S_F+S_R} \log p(Y_s|X_s,\Delta F) \\ &= \sum_{s=1}^{S_F} \log p(Y_s=F|X_s,\Delta F) + \sum_{s=1}^{S_R} \log p(Y_s=R|X_s,\Delta F) \\ &= \sum_{s=1}^{S_F} \log \sigma(\beta(\mathcal{W}_s-\Delta F)+c) + \sum_{s=1}^{S_R} \log \sigma(\beta(\tilde{\mathcal{W}}_s+\Delta F)-c). \end{aligned} \tag{18.35}$$

Taking the derivative of the log-likelihood with respect to ΔF and setting it to zero (using $\frac{\mathrm{d}}{\mathrm{d}x}\log\sigma(x) = \sigma(-x)$), we obtain the following equation:

$$\sum_{s=1}^{S_F} \sigma(-\beta(\mathcal{W}_s-\Delta F)-c) = \sum_{s=1}^{S_R} \sigma(-\beta(\tilde{\mathcal{W}}_s+\Delta F)-c) \tag{18.36}$$

$$\Leftrightarrow \sum_{s=1}^{S_F} \frac{1}{1+e^{\beta(\tilde{\mathcal{W}}_s-\Delta F)+c}} = \sum_{s=1}^{S_R} \frac{1}{1+e^{-\beta(\mathcal{W}_s-\Delta F)-c}}, \tag{18.37}$$

which is known as the BAR self-consistency equation and can be solved numerically to find the free energy difference ΔF.

The BAR method is optimal in the sense that it minimizes the asymptotic variance of the free energy estimate among all estimators that combine forward and reverse work values in an unbiased way.

19 Escorted Free Energy Estimations and Fluctuation Theorems

19.1 Introduction

In previous chapters, we have introduced two powerful approaches for building deep hierarchical generative models: normalizing flows (Chapter 8) and variational autoencoders (Chapter 7). Both methods have proven useful for generative modeling, importance sampling, and free energy estimation. However, each approach has its own strengths and limitations. NFs excel at computing exact log-likelihoods, but this advantage comes with the requirement of invertible transformations, which can limit design flexibility. Moreover, the smoothness inherent in invertible architectures makes it challenging to model multimodal distributions, as small probability bridges inevitably connect the modes. VAEs and diffusion models, on the other hand, do not suffer from this limitation and can naturally handle multimodal distributions, but they rely on optimizing variational free energy or ELBOs to approximate the log-likelihood. Additionally, the use of time-dependent and sequential stochastic transformations in these models implies that the system has limited time to equilibrate, potentially leading to highly dissipative processes and inefficient free energy estimation from a thermodynamic perspective.

Given these trade-offs, a natural question arises: Can we combine the strengths of both deterministic and stochastic approaches? In this chapter, we consider this possibility by drawing from advancements in both physics and machine learning. In physics, Vaikuntanathan and Jarzynski (2008, 2011) introduced the escorted free energy estimation method, which employs a sequence of bijective transformations interleaved with stochastic transformations to guide the system along a more efficient path through configuration space. Concurrently, in machine learning, researchers have combined stochastic maps and invertible maps to build more efficient models for generative modeling and importance sampling (Wu et al., 2020; Nielsen et al., 2020). These will be introduced in Chapter 20.

However, a key distinction exists between these approaches in stochastic thermodynamics and machine learning. In ST, the time-reversed process (with transitions R_t) is fixed; the system evolves backward using the same physical laws as in the forward process. In machine learning, the backward process is typically variational, and the free energy bound (or ELBO) must be optimized to make the backward process approximate the inversion of the forward process as closely as possible. For invertible maps, the backward process is deterministic and simply the inverse of the forwar transformations.

In this chapter, we derive the escorted free energy estimation method and connec it to counterdiabatic driving.

19.2 Escorted Simulations for Free Energy Estimation

As discussed in Chapter 17, our goal is to compute the free energy difference betwee two equilibrium states, denoted by $\Delta F = \mathcal{F}[\pi_{t_f}] - \mathcal{F}[\pi_0]$. The simulations start fror the initial equilibrium distribution $\zeta_0 \sim \pi_0(\zeta_0)$ and end by sampling from a proces that will eventually converge to the final equilibrium distribution $\pi_{t_f}(\zeta_{t_f})$. These tw equilibrium states are connected by a sequence of Markov transitions $F_t(\zeta_t|\zeta_{t-1})$ th satisfy the stationarity condition, (9.10):

$$\int \mathrm{d}\zeta_{t-1}\, F_t(\zeta_t|\zeta_{t-1})\, \pi_t(\zeta_{t-1}) = \pi_t(\zeta_t), \tag{19.1}$$

$$\Leftrightarrow \quad F_t(\zeta_t|\zeta_{t-1})\pi_t(\zeta_{t-1}) = A_t(\zeta_{t-1}|\zeta_t)\pi_t(\zeta_t). \tag{19.2}$$

In this chapter, we will assume the stronger condition of detailed balance, which implie that

$$F_t(\zeta_t|\zeta_{t-1})\pi_t(\zeta_{t-1}) = R_t(\zeta_{t-1}|\zeta_t)\pi_t(\zeta_t), \tag{19.3}$$

with $R_t(\zeta_{t-1}|\zeta_t) = F_t(\hat{\zeta}_{t-1}|\hat{\zeta}_t)$. We furthermore define the Boltzmann distribution a

$$\pi_t(\zeta_t) = \frac{\exp[-\beta\mathcal{H}_t(\zeta_t)]}{Z_t}, \tag{19.4}$$

where $\mathcal{H}_t$ are the Hamiltonians at each time step t, β is the inverse temperature, an Z_t is the partition function.

The motivation behind escorted simulations (Vaikuntanathan and Jarzynski, 200 2011) is to address the limitations of traditional nonequilibrium work measuremen for free energy estimation discussed in Chapter 17. These methods often suffer fro slow convergence when dissipation is large, due to the exponential dependence of th variance on the work dissipated. Escorted simulations mitigate this issue by introducin a set of bijective (i.e., one-to-one and onto) mapping functions $\zeta'_t = \zeta'_t(\zeta_t)$ that guid the trajectory along a more adiabatic path.

The escorted trajectory is generated as follows:

$$\begin{aligned}
&\zeta_0 \sim \pi_0(\cdot), \\
&\zeta'_0 = \zeta'_0(\zeta_0), \quad \zeta_1 \sim F_1(\cdot|\zeta'_0), \\
&\zeta'_1 = \zeta'_1(\zeta_1), \quad \zeta_2 \sim F_2(\cdot|\zeta'_1), \\
&\quad\vdots \\
&\zeta'_{t_f-1} = \zeta'_{t_f-1}(\zeta_{t_f-1}), \quad \zeta_{t_f} \sim F_{t_f}(\cdot|\zeta'_{t_f-1}).
\end{aligned} \tag{19.5}$$

Here, we have overloaded the symbol ζ'_t to denote both the mapping function $\zeta'_t(\zeta$

and the resulting microstate ζ'_t. Note that this process does not include a final mapping step on ζ_{t_f}. The process is illustrated in Figure 19.1 for both the forward and time-reversed processes.

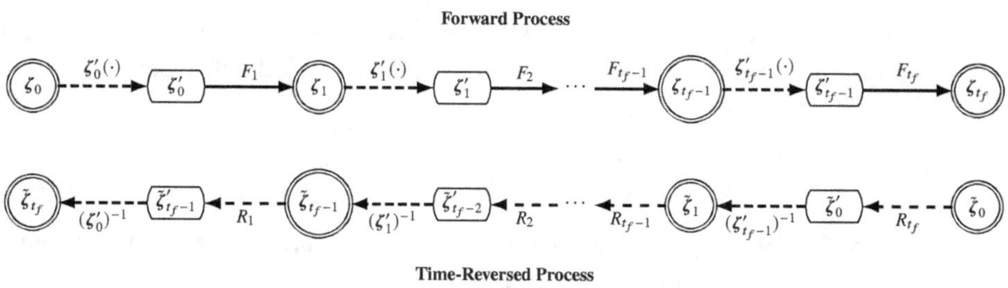

Figure 19.1 Illustration of escorted simulations showing both forward and time-reversed processes. The forward process (top) evolves from ζ_0 to ζ_{t_f} through a series of dashed bijective mappings $\zeta'_t(\cdot)$ (dashed arrows) and solid stochastic transitions F_t (solid arrows). The time-reversed process (bottom) starts from the final state of a corresponding forward path and evolves via transitions R_t and inverse mappings $(\zeta'_t)^{-1}$. This approach improves sampling efficiency by reducing the lag between the system's state and the instantaneous equilibrium state at each step.

The probability of generating the state sequence $\{\zeta_0, \zeta'_0, \ldots, \zeta'_{t_f-1}, \zeta_{t_f}\}$ is given by

$$\rho(\zeta_0, \zeta'_0, \ldots, \zeta_{t_f}) = \pi_0(\zeta_0) \prod_{t=1}^{t_f} F_t(\zeta_t | \zeta'_{t-1}) \delta(\zeta'_{t-1} - \zeta'_{t-1}(\zeta_{t-1})).$$

Since each ζ'_t is uniquely determined by ζ_t, we can write the probability of generating the unprimed state sequence $\zeta_{0:t_f} = \{\zeta_0, \ldots, \zeta_{t_f}\}$ by integrating out the primed variables:

$$\rho(\zeta_{0:t_f}) = \pi_0(\zeta_0) \prod_{t=1}^{t_f} F_t(\zeta_t | \zeta'_{t-1}(\zeta_{t-1})). \tag{19.6}$$

To understand how escorted simulations modify the thermodynamic quantities, let us start from the standard definitions of work, heat, and internal energy changes for the unescorted case from Chapter 10:

$$\mathcal{W}(\zeta_{0:t_f}) = \sum_{t=1}^{t_f} \delta\mathcal{W}_t = \sum_{t=1}^{t_f} [\mathcal{H}_t(\zeta_{t-1}) - \mathcal{H}_{t-1}(\zeta_{t-1})], \tag{19.7}$$

$$\mathcal{Q}(\zeta_{0:t_f}) = \sum_{t=1}^{t_f} \delta\mathcal{Q}_t = \sum_{t=1}^{t_f} [\mathcal{H}_t(\zeta_t) - \mathcal{H}_t(\zeta_{t-1})], \tag{19.8}$$

$$\Delta\mathcal{U}(\zeta_{0:t_f}) = \mathcal{W}(\zeta_{0:t_f}) + \mathcal{Q}(\zeta_{0:t_f}) = \mathcal{H}_{t_f}(\zeta_{t_f}) - \mathcal{H}_0(\zeta_0), \tag{19.9}$$

for which the Jarzynski equality and Crooks fluctuation theorem hold.

In the escorted case, we aim to derive modified versions of these theorems, applicable for more accurate free energy estimation and importance sampling. This challenge was tackled in Vaikuntanathan and Jarzynski (2008, 2011), where a modified wor definition was introduced, and it was shown that a modified Jarzynski equality an Crooks fluctuation theorem hold. Alternatively, we can start from the standard defi nition of work and consider the deterministic limit of the stochastic maps. A simila approach has allowed us to understand how NFs can be seen as a limit of VAEs whe stochastic maps become more deterministic, as discussed in Chapter 8:

$$F'_t(\zeta'_t|\zeta_t) = G(\zeta'_t|\zeta'_t(\zeta_t), \sigma^2\mathbf{I}), \tag{19.10}$$

$$\lim_{\sigma\to 0^+} F'_t(\zeta'_t|\zeta_t) = \delta(\zeta'_t - \zeta'_t(\zeta_t)), \tag{19.11}$$

where $G(\zeta'_t|\zeta'_t(\zeta_t), \sigma^2\mathbf{I})$ denotes a Gaussian distribution for random variable ζ'_t cen tered at value $\zeta'_t(\zeta_t)$ with covariance $\sigma\mathbf{I}$.

It is natural to ask whether we can derive the modified work and fluctuation the orems for the escorted case by starting from the standard definitions and taking th deterministic limit of the stochastic maps.

Let us express the standard work and heat using the escorted sequences,

$$\mathcal{W}'_{t+1} = [\mathcal{H}'_t(\zeta_t) - \mathcal{H}_t(\zeta_t)] + [\mathcal{H}_{t+1}(\zeta'_t) - \mathcal{H}'_t(\zeta'_t)], \tag{19.12}$$

$$\mathcal{Q}'_{t+1} = [\mathcal{H}'_t(\zeta'_t) - \mathcal{H}'_t(\zeta_t)] + [\mathcal{H}_{t+1}(\zeta_{t+1}) - \mathcal{H}_{t+1}(\zeta'_t)]. \tag{19.13}$$

Since the Hamiltonians can be expressed in terms of the equilibrium distribution and th partition function, we also explicitly compare the forward and backward kernels, (19.3

$$\frac{R'_t(\zeta_t|\zeta'_t)}{F'_t(\zeta'_t|\zeta_t)} = \frac{\pi'_t(\zeta_t)}{\pi'_t(\zeta'_t)} = \exp[-\beta(\mathcal{H}'_t(\zeta_t) - \mathcal{H}'_t(\zeta'_t))]. \tag{19.14}$$

Using the stationarity condition (19.4), we can compute these ratios by taking th deterministic limit, (19.10) and (19.11), as follows:

$$\begin{aligned}
\frac{\pi'_t(\zeta_t)}{\pi'_t(\zeta'_t)} &= \frac{\pi'_t(\zeta_t)}{\int d\zeta_t\, F'_t(\zeta'_t|\zeta_t)\pi'_t(\zeta_t)} \\
&= \frac{\pi'_t(\zeta_t)}{\int d\zeta_t\, \delta(\zeta'_t - \zeta'_t(\zeta_t))\pi'_t(\zeta_t)} \\
&= \frac{\pi'_t(\zeta_t)}{\int d\zeta'_t \left|\det\left(\frac{\partial\zeta'_t(\zeta_t)}{\partial\zeta_t}\right)\right|^{-1} \delta(\zeta'_t - \zeta'_t(\zeta_t))\pi'_t(\zeta_t)} \\
&= \frac{\left|\det\left(\frac{\partial\zeta'_t(\zeta_t)}{\partial\zeta_t}\right)\right| \pi'_t(\zeta_t)}{\pi'_t(\zeta_t)} \\
&= \left|\det\left(\frac{\partial\zeta'_t(\zeta_t)}{\partial\zeta_t}\right)\right|,
\end{aligned} \tag{19.15}$$

which is, of course, just the transformation law for probability densities under dete ministic invertible (bijective) transformations of the random variables. By taking th logarithm of the above equations, we note the contributions to the stochastic work:

$$\mathcal{H}'_t(\zeta'_t) - \mathcal{H}'_t(\zeta_t) = T\log\frac{R'_t(\zeta_t|\zeta'_t)}{F'_t(\zeta'_t|\zeta_t)} = T\log\left|\det\left(\frac{\partial\zeta'_t}{\partial\zeta_t}\right)\right|. \tag{19.16}$$

In the end, we arrive at the modified work definition that is the same as in Vaikuntanathan and Jarzynski (2011):

$$\mathcal{W}'(\zeta_{0:t_f}) = \sum_{t=1}^{t_f} \delta\mathcal{W}'_t \equiv \sum_{t=1}^{t_f} \left[\mathcal{H}_t(\zeta'_{t-1}) - \mathcal{H}_{t-1}(\zeta_{t-1}) - T \log \left| \det \left(\frac{\partial \zeta'_{t-1}}{\partial \zeta_{t-1}} \right) \right| \right] \tag{19.17}$$

$$\equiv \Delta\mathcal{U}(\zeta_{0:t_f}) - \mathcal{Q}'(\zeta_{0:t_f}), \tag{19.18}$$

where

$$\Delta\mathcal{U}(\zeta_{0:t_f}) \equiv \mathcal{H}_{t_f}(\zeta_{t_f}) - \mathcal{H}_0(\zeta_0), \tag{19.19}$$

$$\mathcal{Q}'(\zeta_{0:t_f}) = \sum_{t=1}^{t_f} \left[\mathcal{H}_t(\zeta_t) - \mathcal{H}_t(\zeta'_{t-1}) \right] + T \sum_{t=1}^{t_f} \log \left| \det \left(\frac{\partial \zeta'_{t-1}}{\partial \zeta_{t-1}} \right) \right|$$

$$\equiv \mathcal{Q}(\zeta_{0:t_f}) + T \sum_{t=1}^{t_f} \log \left| \det \left(\frac{\partial \zeta'_{t-1}}{\partial \zeta_{t-1}} \right) \right|. \tag{19.20}$$

Here, $\Delta\mathcal{U}$ is the total energy change, and $\mathcal{Q}'$ is the heat transferred from the reservoir during the stochastic updates with an additional Jacobian determinant term that accounts for the volume changes induced by the mapping (note that compared to Vaikuntanathan and Jarzynski (2011), we opted to absorb these Jacobian terms into the definition of heat). Note also that the definition of $\mathcal{Q}$ is now slightly modified relative to the original one in (19.8).

Using the detailed balance condition, (19.3), and the definition of the Boltzmann distribution, (19.4), we can establish two key relations. First, the ratio of forward to backward transition probabilities for the stochastic steps is related to the heat exchanged:

$$\prod_{t=1}^{t_f} \frac{F_t(\zeta_t|\zeta'_{t-1})}{R_t(\zeta'_{t-1}|\zeta_t)} = \prod_{t=1}^{t_f} \frac{\pi_t(\zeta_t)}{\pi_t(\zeta'_{t-1})} = e^{-\beta\mathcal{Q}(\zeta_{0:t_f})}. \tag{19.21}$$

Second, the ratio of the initial and final equilibrium distributions is related to the change in internal energy and free energy:

$$\frac{\pi_0(\zeta_0)}{\pi_{t_f}(\zeta_{t_f})} = \frac{Z_{t_f}}{Z_0} e^{-\beta(\mathcal{H}_0(\zeta_0) - \mathcal{H}_{t_f}(\zeta_{t_f}))} = e^{\beta(\Delta\mathcal{U}(\zeta_{0:t_f}) - \Delta F)}. \tag{19.22}$$

It then automatically follows that the Jarzynski equality and Crooks fluctuation theorem hold for the escorted case with the modified work definition. For the Crooks fluctuation theorem

$$\frac{\mathcal{P}(\mathcal{W}')}{\mathcal{P}_R(-\mathcal{W}')} = e^{\beta[\mathcal{W}' - \Delta F]}, \tag{19.23}$$

we need to specify the time-reversed process further.

Let us compute the forward–backward path ratio for the escorted case (which should also give the total entropy production) and take the deterministic limit:

$$\begin{aligned}
&\lim_{\sigma\to 0^+} \frac{\rho(\zeta_0, \zeta_0', \ldots, \zeta_{t_f})}{\rho_R(\zeta_0, \zeta_0', \ldots, \zeta_{t_f})} \\
&= \lim_{\sigma\to 0^+} \frac{\pi_0(\zeta_0) \prod_{t=1}^{t_f} F_t(\zeta_t|\zeta_{t-1}') F_{t-1}'(\zeta_{t-1}'|\zeta_{t-1})}{\pi_{t_f}(\zeta_{t_f}) \prod_{t=1}^{t_f} R_t(\zeta_{t-1}'|\zeta_t) R_{t-1}'(\zeta_{t-1}|\zeta_{t-1}')} \\
&= \frac{\pi_0(\zeta_0)}{\pi_{t_f}(\zeta_{t_f})} \prod_{t=1}^{t_f} \frac{F_t(\zeta_t|\zeta_{t-1}')}{R_t(\zeta_{t-1}'|\zeta_t)} \cdot \lim_{\sigma\to 0^+} \prod_{t=0}^{t_f-1} \frac{F_t'(\zeta_t'|\zeta_t)}{R_t'(\zeta_t|\zeta_t')} \\
&= \frac{\pi_0(\zeta_0)}{\pi_{t_f}(\zeta_{t_f})} \prod_{t=1}^{t_f} \frac{F_t(\zeta_t|\zeta_{t-1}')}{R_t(\zeta_{t-1}'|\zeta_t)} \left|\det\left(\frac{\partial \zeta_{0:t_f-1}'}{\partial \zeta_{0:t_f-1}}\right)\right|^{-1} \\
&= \exp[\beta(\Delta\mathcal{U}(\zeta_{0:t_f}) - \Delta F - \mathcal{Q}'(\zeta_{0:t_f}))] \\
&= \exp[\beta(\mathcal{W}'(\zeta_{0:t_f}) - \Delta F)].
\end{aligned} \tag{19.24}$$

We obtain a generalization of the trajectory probability ratio in (17.28) to the case c escorted simulations. Note that the continuous-time version of this escorted Crook fluctuation theorem was recently investigated in Zhong et al. (2024); Vargas et a (2024).

Then we can apply the generalized Crooks fluctuation theorem back to the fre energy estimation problem using all the tricks we learned in Section 18.3.

19.3 Escorted Jarzynski Equality

We can verify the Jarzynski equality for the escorted case by computing the averag of the exponential negative work $\exp(-\beta\mathcal{W}'(\zeta_{0:t_f}))$ over the ensemble of escorte trajectories. We will prove this equality by starting with its definition and recursivel integrating out the variables $\zeta_0, \zeta_1, \ldots, \zeta_{t_f-1}$.

$$\mathbb{E}_\rho[e^{-\beta\mathcal{W}'(\zeta_{0:t_f})}] = \int \mathrm{d}\zeta_{0:t_f}\, e^{-\beta\mathcal{W}'(\zeta_{0:t_f})} \rho(\zeta_{0:t_f}) \tag{19.25}$$

$$= \frac{1}{Z_0} \int \mathrm{d}\zeta_0 \cdots \mathrm{d}\zeta_{t_f}\, e^{-\beta\mathcal{H}_0(\zeta_0)} \left(\prod_{t=1}^{t_f} F_t(\zeta_t|\zeta_{t-1}')\right) e^{-\beta\sum_{t=1}^{t_f}\delta\mathcal{W}_t'}. \tag{19.26}$$

To evaluate this expression, we proceed by successive integration, starting from ζ_0 and moving forward. Let's first integrate over ζ_0:

$$\begin{aligned}
&\int \mathrm{d}\zeta_0\, e^{-\beta\mathcal{H}_0(\zeta_0)} F_1(\zeta_1|\zeta_0')e^{-\beta\delta\mathcal{W}_1'} \\
&= \int \mathrm{d}\zeta_0\, e^{-\beta\mathcal{H}_0(\zeta_0)} F_1(\zeta_1|\zeta_0')e^{-\beta[\mathcal{H}_1(\zeta_0')-\mathcal{H}_0(\zeta_0)-T\log\left|\det\left(\frac{\partial\zeta_0'}{\partial\zeta_0}\right)\right|]} \\
&= \int \mathrm{d}\zeta_0\, F_1(\zeta_1|\zeta_0')e^{-\beta\mathcal{H}_1(\zeta_0')}\left|\det\left(\frac{\partial\zeta_0'}{\partial\zeta_0}\right)\right| \\
&= \int \mathrm{d}\zeta_0'\, F_1(\zeta_1|\zeta_0')e^{-\beta\mathcal{H}_1(\zeta_0')} \quad \text{(change of variables: } \zeta_0' = \zeta_0'(\zeta_0)\text{)}. \qquad (19.27)
\end{aligned}$$

Now, using the stationarity condition from (19.4), where $\pi_1(\zeta_0') = e^{-\beta\mathcal{H}_1(\zeta_0')}/Z_1$, the integral becomes:

$$\int \mathrm{d}\zeta_0'\, F_1(\zeta_1|\zeta_0')Z_1\pi_1(\zeta_0') = Z_1 \int \mathrm{d}\zeta_0'\, F_1(\zeta_1|\zeta_0')\pi_1(\zeta_0') = Z_1\pi_1(\zeta_1) = e^{-\beta\mathcal{H}_1(\zeta_1)}. \qquad (19.28)$$

After integrating out ζ_0, the original expression simplifies to:

$$\mathbb{E}_\rho[e^{-\beta\mathcal{W}'}] = \frac{1}{Z_0}\int \mathrm{d}\zeta_1\cdots\mathrm{d}\zeta_{t_f}\, e^{-\beta\mathcal{H}_1(\zeta_1)}\left(\prod_{t=2}^{t_f} F_t(\zeta_t|\zeta_{t-1}')\right)e^{-\beta\sum_{t=2}^{t_f}\delta\mathcal{W}_t'}. \qquad (19.29)$$

We can repeat this process for $\zeta_1, \zeta_2, \ldots, \zeta_{t_f-2}$. At each step k, the integral over ζ_{k-1} yields $e^{-\beta\mathcal{H}_k(\zeta_k)}$. After integrating up to ζ_{t_f-2}, we are left with:

$$\mathbb{E}_\rho[e^{-\beta\mathcal{W}'}] = \frac{1}{Z_0}\int \mathrm{d}\zeta_{t_f-1}\,\mathrm{d}\zeta_{t_f}\, e^{-\beta\mathcal{H}_{t_f-1}(\zeta_{t_f-1})} F_{t_f}(\zeta_{t_f}|\zeta_{t_f-1}')e^{-\beta\delta\mathcal{W}_{t_f}'}. \qquad (19.30)$$

Next, we integrate over ζ_{t_f-1}:

$$\begin{aligned}
&\int \mathrm{d}\zeta_{t_f-1}\, e^{-\beta\mathcal{H}_{t_f-1}(\zeta_{t_f-1})} F_{t_f}(\zeta_{t_f}|\zeta_{t_f-1}')e^{-\beta\delta\mathcal{W}_{t_f}'} \\
&= \int \mathrm{d}\zeta_{t_f-1}\, F_{t_f}(\zeta_{t_f}|\zeta_{t_f-1}')e^{-\beta\mathcal{H}_{t_f}(\zeta_{t_f-1}')}\left|\det\left(\frac{\partial\zeta_{t_f-1}'}{\partial\zeta_{t_f-1}}\right)\right| \\
&= \int \mathrm{d}\zeta_{t_f-1}'\, F_{t_f}(\zeta_{t_f}|\zeta_{t_f-1}')e^{-\beta\mathcal{H}_{t_f}(\zeta_{t_f-1}')}. \qquad (19.31)
\end{aligned}$$

Substituting this back and using the stationarity condition for the final step:

$$\begin{aligned}
\mathbb{E}_\rho[e^{-\beta\mathcal{W}'}] &= \frac{1}{Z_0}\int \mathrm{d}\zeta_{t_f}\left[\int \mathrm{d}\zeta_{t_f-1}'\, F_{t_f}(\zeta_{t_f}|\zeta_{t_f-1}')e^{-\beta\mathcal{H}_{t_f}(\zeta_{t_f-1}')}\right] \\
&= \frac{1}{Z_0}\int \mathrm{d}\zeta_{t_f}\left[Z_{t_f}\int \mathrm{d}\zeta_{t_f-1}'\, F_{t_f}(\zeta_{t_f}|\zeta_{t_f-1}')\pi_{t_f}(\zeta_{t_f-1}')\right] \\
&= \frac{Z_{t_f}}{Z_0}\int \mathrm{d}\zeta_{t_f}\,\pi_{t_f}(\zeta_{t_f}) = \frac{Z_{t_f}}{Z_0} = e^{-\beta\Delta F}. \qquad (19.32)
\end{aligned}$$

Therefore, we have derived the escorted version of the Jarzynski equality:

$$\mathbb{E}_\rho[e^{-\beta \mathcal{W}'(\zeta_{0:t_f})}] = e^{-\beta \Delta F}. \tag{19.33}$$

This identity holds for any choice of bijective mapping functions $\{\zeta_t'(\zeta_t)\}$. When each $\zeta_t'(\zeta_t)$ is the identity map, we recover the original Jarzynski equality in (17.61).

19.4 Counterdiabatic Driving

The efficiency of estimating ΔF using (19.33) depends critically on the choice of mapping functions $\{\zeta_t'(\zeta_t)\}$. The key to improving convergence lies in reducing the lag between the system's state and the equilibrium state of the instantaneous Hamiltonian at each step. Here, the "lag" refers to the difference between the current distribution of the system $\rho_t(\zeta_t)$ and the equilibrium distribution of the instantaneous Hamiltonian $\pi_t(\zeta_t)$.

If we could find perfect mappings $\{\zeta_{t-1}'^{*}(\zeta_{t-1})\}$ that eliminate the lag entirely, they would transform the equilibrium distribution at one step to the next:

$$\pi_t(\zeta_{t-1}') = \frac{\pi_{t-1}(\zeta_{t-1})}{\left|\det\left(\frac{\partial \zeta_{t-1}'^{*}(\zeta_{t-1})}{\partial \zeta_{t-1}}\right)\right|}, \tag{19.34}$$

where the denominator accounts for the change of variables. For such a perfect mapping the corresponding work increment $\delta\mathcal{W}_t'$ becomes deterministic:

$$\begin{aligned}
\delta\mathcal{W}_t' &= \mathcal{H}_t(\zeta_{t-1}') - \mathcal{H}_{t-1}(\zeta_{t-1}) - T\log\left|\det\left(\frac{\partial \zeta_{t-1}'^{*}(\zeta_{t-1})}{\partial \zeta_{t-1}}\right)\right| \\
&= -T\log(Z_t\pi_t(\zeta_{t-1}')) + T\log(Z_{t-1}\pi_{t-1}(\zeta_{t-1})) - T\log\left|\det\left(\frac{\partial \zeta_{t-1}'^{*}(\zeta_{t-1})}{\partial \zeta_{t-1}}\right)\right| \\
&= -T\log\frac{Z_t}{Z_{t-1}} - T\log\left(\frac{\pi_t(\zeta_{t-1}')}{\pi_{t-1}(\zeta_{t-1})}\left|\det\left(\frac{\partial \zeta_{t-1}'^{*}(\zeta_{t-1})}{\partial \zeta_{t-1}}\right)\right|\right) \\
&= \mathcal{F}[\pi_t] - \mathcal{F}[\pi_{t-1}],
\end{aligned} \tag{19.35}$$

where we have used (19.34) in the last step. Summing over all steps, the total modified work for any trajectory becomes exactly the free energy difference:

$$\mathcal{W}'(\zeta_{0:t_f}) = \sum_{t=1}^{t_f}(\mathcal{F}[\pi_t] - \mathcal{F}[\pi_{t-1}]) = \mathcal{F}[\pi_{t_f}] - \mathcal{F}[\pi_0] = \Delta F. \tag{19.36}$$

This result implies that with perfect mappings, every trajectory yields the exact free energy difference, regardless of the initial microstate or the specific path taken. Consequently, we obtain a zero-variance estimate of ΔF. Intuitively, perfect mappings guide the system along a path that maintains equilibrium at each step, eliminating dissipation and ensuring that the work performed matches the free energy difference.

Such perfect mappings are also known in the literature as *counterdiabatic driving* or *shortcuts to adiabaticity* (Li et al., 2017). We will explain a continuous-time version using the Fokker–Planck equations in Chapter 22.

While perfect mappings are generally impractical to achieve in complex systems, mappings that substantially reduce the lag can still significantly improve convergence. To find better mappings, we can formulate this as a learning problem and try to minimize the KL divergence between the target equilibrium distribution π_t and the distribution obtained by mapping the previous equilibrium distribution π_{t-1}:

$$\min_{\zeta'_{t-1}} D_{\mathrm{KL}}[\pi_t \| (\zeta'_{t-1})_{\#}\pi_{t-1}], \tag{19.37}$$

where $(\zeta'_{t-1})_{\#}\pi_{t-1}$ is the pushforward of π_{t-1} by the map ζ'_{t-1}. This is equivalent to training a normalizing flow to transform samples from π_{t-1} to samples from π_t. Samples from the equilibrium distributions $\pi_t(\zeta)$ can be generated by repeated application of the respective Markovian kernel F_t. This is related to the approach taken by Arbel et al. (2021).

20 Hybrid Stochastic Flows and Surjective Flows

20.1 Introduction

We have seen VAEs with a single stochastic map but with the flexibility to chang the number of dimensions between input and output. We have used the ELBO boun to train them. We have also studied deterministic transformations in NFs where w have exact expressions for the model probability of the data, but we cannot easil change dimensions between layers and the maps need to be invertible. In this chapte we combine these into one architecture, which are either called stochastic normalizin flows (Wu et al., 2020) or surjective VAEs (Nielsen et al., 2020). We present a gener framework for this more general class of models and discuss some illustrative exam ples such as tensor slicing and augmentation, rounding and sorting. We emphasize th fascinating convergence of these ideas in both modern ML and stochastic thermody namics because the escorted free energy estimation method from the previous chapte is indeed an example of an alternating invertible (reversible) and irreversible processe as described in this chapter.

20.2 Stochastic Normalizing Flows

Normalizing flows (Chapter 8) are built using a series of bijective transformatior starting from a base distribution. Hierarchical VAEs (or diffusion models, Chapter 1 can also be formulated by applying a series of stochastic transformations to a bas distribution. In Section 8.1, we mentioned how the change-of-variable formulas use in NFs can be equated to Bayes' rule:

$$p_X(\mathbf{x}) = p_Z(\mathbf{z})\frac{p_{X|Z}(\mathbf{x}|\mathbf{z})}{p_{Z|X}(\mathbf{z}|\mathbf{x})} \quad \Rightarrow \tag{20.1}$$

$$p_X(\mathbf{x}) = p_Z(\mathbf{z}(\mathbf{x}))\,|\det(\mathbf{J})|\,, \tag{20.2}$$

if we use a stochastic transformation $p(\mathbf{x}|\mathbf{z}) = G(\mathbf{x}|\mathbf{x}(\mathbf{z}), \sigma^2\mathbf{I})$ and take the determi istic limit $\sigma \to 0^+$.

In Section 19.2, we saw how free energy estimations can be improved by combi ing stochastic and deterministic transformations, with additional Jacobian determina corrections. These observations naturally lead to the question: Can we systematicall combine VAEs and NFs into a single framework that learns both stochastic and deterministic transformations? This is precisely the idea behind stochastic flow models (Wu et al., 2020; Nielsen et al., 2020).

20.2.1 General Framework for Hybrid Layers

Consider a general framework where each layer in a model is defined by a forward transformation that takes an input $\mathbf{z}$ and produces an output $\mathbf{x}$, and an inverse transformation that takes $\mathbf{x}$ and produces $\mathbf{z}$. Both can be stochastic or deterministic. We write a stochastic forward transformation as $p_{X|Z}(\mathbf{x}|\mathbf{z})$ and a deterministic forward transformation can be written as $p_{X|Z}(\mathbf{x}|\mathbf{z}) = \delta(\mathbf{x} - \mathbf{x}(\mathbf{z}))$ or simply $\mathbf{x} = \mathbf{x}(\mathbf{z})$ where $\mathbf{x}$ can be both a random variable and a function. The deterministic inverse transformation is simply given by $\mathbf{z} = \mathbf{z}(\mathbf{x})$. The true stochastic inverse transformation should be given by Bayes' rule

$$p_{Z|X}(\mathbf{z}|\mathbf{x}) = \frac{p_{X|Z}(\mathbf{x}|\mathbf{z})p_Z(\mathbf{z})}{p_X(\mathbf{x})}, \tag{20.3}$$

but this is often intractable. Instead, a learnable variational approximation $q_{Z|X}(\mathbf{z}|\mathbf{x})$ is used, which differs from the inverse transformation used in stochastic thermodynamics.

Given this variational approximation, we can now derive bounds on the likelihood. For both deterministic and stochastic layers, we can formulate the ELBO (Evidence Lower Bound) or free energy bounds. We decompose the log-likelihood into three terms: a base distribution contribution, a likelihood contribution $\mathcal{V}(\mathbf{x}, \mathbf{z})$, and a variational gap $\mathcal{E}(\mathbf{x}, \mathbf{z})$:

$$\begin{aligned} \log p_X(\mathbf{x}) =& \mathbb{E}_{q_{Z|X}}\left[\log p_Z(\mathbf{z})\right] + \mathbb{E}_{q_{Z|X}}\left[\log \frac{p_{X|Z}(\mathbf{x}|\mathbf{z})}{q_{Z|X}(\mathbf{z}|\mathbf{x})}\right] \\ &+ D_{\mathrm{KL}}\left[q_{Z|X}(\mathbf{z}|\mathbf{x}) \| p_{Z|X}(\mathbf{z}|\mathbf{x})\right] \\ \simeq& \log p_Z(\mathbf{z}) + \mathcal{V}(\mathbf{x}, \mathbf{z}) + \mathcal{E}(\mathbf{x}, \mathbf{z}), \quad \mathbf{z} \sim q_{Z|X}(\mathbf{z}|\mathbf{x}), \end{aligned} \tag{20.4}$$

for a single Monte Carlo sample from $q_{Z|X}(\mathbf{z}|\mathbf{x})$. The approximation $\simeq$ denotes a single-sample Monte Carlo estimate of the expectation. The precise forms of $\mathcal{V}$ and $\mathcal{E}$ depend on whether the layer is bijective or stochastic, as we detail below. Later, in Section 20.3, we extend this framework to accommodate surjective layers.

For bijective transformations, the likelihood evaluation is exact ($\mathcal{E} = 0$); for stochastic maps, the bound has a finite gap:

$$\text{for bijections:} \quad \mathcal{V}(\mathbf{x}, \mathbf{z}) = \log\left|\det\left(\frac{\partial \mathbf{z}(\mathbf{x})}{\partial \mathbf{x}}\right)\right|, \quad \mathcal{E}(\mathbf{x}, \mathbf{z}) = 0; \tag{20.5}$$

$$\text{for stochastic maps:} \quad \mathcal{V}(\mathbf{x}, \mathbf{z}) = \log \frac{p_{X|Z}(\mathbf{x}|\mathbf{z})}{q_{Z|X}(\mathbf{z}|\mathbf{x})}, \quad \mathcal{E}(\mathbf{x}, \mathbf{z}) = \log \frac{q_{Z|X}(\mathbf{z}|\mathbf{x})}{p_{Z|X}(\mathbf{z}|\mathbf{x})}. \tag{20.6}$$

Composing Hybrid Layers

Now we can compose these deterministic and stochastic layers to form a deep mode $\{\mathbf{z}_{t_f}, \mathbf{z}_{t_f-1}, \ldots, \mathbf{z}_1, \mathbf{x}\}$, with the negative log-likelihood bounded by

$$-\log p_X(\mathbf{x}) \leq \mathcal{F}[\mathbf{x}] = -\log p_Z(\mathbf{z}_{t_f}) - \sum_{t=1}^{t_f} \mathcal{V}_t(\mathbf{z}_{t-1}, \mathbf{z}_t), \tag{20.7}$$

where,

$$\text{for bijections:} \quad \mathcal{V}_t = \log \left| \det \left(\frac{\partial \mathbf{z}_t(\mathbf{z}_{t-1})}{\partial \mathbf{z}_{t-1}} \right) \right|; \tag{20.8}$$

$$\text{for stochastic maps:} \quad \mathcal{V}_t = \log \frac{p_{t-1|t}(\mathbf{z}_{t-1}|\mathbf{z}_t)}{q_{t|t-1}(\mathbf{z}_t|\mathbf{z}_{t-1})}, \tag{20.9}$$

and $p_Z(\mathbf{z}_{t_f})$ is the base distribution.

Similar to Chapter 13, if we wish to use the model for generative purposes, w can use a backward (generative) model $p_{t-1|t}$ to generate samples from the bas distribution $\mathbf{z}_{t_f}$. To find better generative models, we would optimize the ELBO or fre energy bound (20.7).

20.2.2 Application to Importance Sampling

Beyond generative modeling, these hybrid flows enable improved importance samplin schemes that combine the strengths of deterministic and stochastic transformation Consider intermediate distributions $\pi_t(\mathbf{z}_t) = \gamma_t(\mathbf{z}_t)/Z_t = \pi_0(\mathbf{z}_t)^{1-\beta_t}\gamma(\mathbf{z})^{\beta_t}$ that bridg a tractable distribution π_0 to the target distribution $\pi_{t_f} = p_{\text{target}}$. Note that now $\mathbf{z}$ rather than $\mathbf{z}_{t_f}$, is drawn from the simpler distribution, different from the conventio of variational diffusion models. The expression for the importance weight is given b

$$w(\mathbf{z}_{0:t_f}) = Z_P \frac{P(\mathbf{z}_{0:t_f})}{Q(\mathbf{z}_{0:t_f})} = \frac{\gamma(\mathbf{z}_{t_f})}{\pi_0(\mathbf{z}_0)} \prod_{t=1}^{t_f} \exp(\mathcal{V}_t). \tag{20.10}$$

Then, expectation values can be estimated as

$$\mathbb{E}_{\mathbf{z}_{t_f} \sim \pi_{t_f}}[f(\mathbf{z}_{t_f})] \approx \frac{\sum_{s=1}^{S} w(\mathbf{z}_0^s, \ldots, \mathbf{z}_{t_f}^s) f(\mathbf{z}_{t_f}^s)}{\sum_{s=1}^{S} w(\mathbf{z}_0^s, \ldots, \mathbf{z}_{t_f}^s)}, \tag{20.11}$$

where paths are drawn from the forward path distribution $Q(\mathbf{z}_{0:t_f})$. To reduce the var ance of the estimator – for example, the variance in estimating the partition functior $\mathbb{V}[w(\mathbf{z}_{0:t_f})]$ – we would optimize the same ELBO again.

The accuracy of this estimator depends on how well Q approximates P. As we sa in Chapter 12, the variance of the estimator is eventually determined by how the fin distribution lags behind the equilibrium distributions. If the bijective transformatior can be learned to reduce this lag, the variance of the estimator can be reduced. Whe the deterministic transformations are perfect, the variance of the estimator becom zero.

If annealed importance sampling is used for the stochastic transformations, and an intertwined structure between deterministic and stochastic transformations is employed – much like the setup of the escorted simulations – then the importance sampling identity reduces to the escorted Jarzynski equality, (19.33). More generally, for other choices of the forward Q, an escorted generalization of the integral fluctuation theorem is used as the importance sampling identity, similar to Chapter 17 and Section 19.2.

20.3 Surjective Flows

While bijective and stochastic layers provide great flexibility, certain operations natural for generative modeling are inherently surjective (many-to-one). For instance, dimensionality reduction, quantization, or enforcing permutation invariance all involve mappings where multiple inputs can produce the same output. Surjective flows extend our framework to handle these operations while maintaining tractable likelihood bounds. The key innovation of SurVAE flows (Nielsen et al., 2020) is showing that these surjective transformations are fully composable with bijective and stochastic transformations, enabling richer model architectures.

The key idea is to introduce surjective transformations that are deterministic in one direction but stochastic in the reverse direction. Figure 20.1 illustrates the surjective mappings for both the generative direction (a) and the inference direction (b), where solid arrows indicate the deterministic direction and dashed arrows show the stochastic direction.

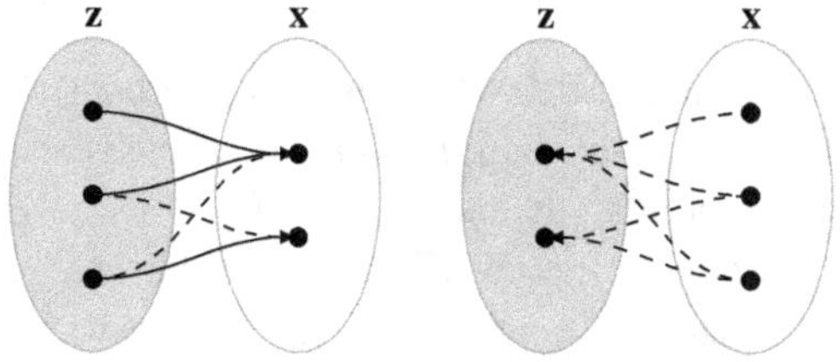

(a) Surjective (Gen.) (b) Surjective (Inf.)

Figure 20.1 Surjective transformations in hybrid models. (a) Surjective (Generative): Many-to-one mappings where multiple $\mathbf{z}$ values map to the same $\mathbf{x}$. Solid arrows show the deterministic forward direction; dashed arrows show possible stochastic inverse paths. (b) Surjective (Inference): One-to-many mappings, inverse of (a), where one $\mathbf{x}$ can map stochastically to multiple $\mathbf{z}$ values. Input space $\mathbf{z}$ is shown with a shaded backdrop, output space $\mathbf{x}$ is unfilled.

Let $\mathcal{X}$ and $\mathcal{Z}$ be two spaces. A surjective mapping $f: \mathcal{Z} \to \mathcal{X}$ satisfies that for all $\mathbf{x} \in \mathcal{X}$, there exists a $\mathbf{z} \in \mathcal{Z}$ such that $\mathbf{x} = f(\mathbf{z})$. While not necessarily invertible, surjective mappings possess right inverses $g: \mathcal{X} \to \mathcal{Z}$ such that $f \circ g(\mathbf{x}) = \mathbf{x}$ for all $\mathbf{x} \in \mathcal{X}$.

We distinguish between generative surjections (surjective in $\mathcal{Z} \to \mathcal{X}$) and inference surjections (surjective in $\mathcal{X} \to \mathcal{Z}$). For a generative surjection $f: \mathcal{Z} \to \mathcal{X}$, we define

$$\text{forward (deterministic):} \quad p(\mathbf{x}|\mathbf{z}) = \delta(\mathbf{x} - f(\mathbf{z})); \tag{20.12}$$

$$\text{inverse (stochastic):} \quad q(\mathbf{z}|\mathbf{x}) \text{ with support over } \mathcal{B}(\mathbf{x}) = \{\mathbf{z}|\mathbf{x} = f(\mathbf{z})\}. \tag{20.13}$$

Here, $\delta(\cdot)$ is the Dirac delta function, and $\mathcal{B}(\mathbf{x})$ is the preimage of $\mathbf{x}$ – the set of all that map to $\mathbf{x}$ under f. For an inference surjection $g: \mathcal{X} \to \mathcal{Z}$, we have:

$$\text{forward (stochastic):} \quad p(\mathbf{x}|\mathbf{z}) \text{ with support over } \mathcal{B}(\mathbf{z}) = \{\mathbf{x}|\mathbf{z} = g(\mathbf{x})\}; \tag{20.14}$$

$$\text{inverse (deterministic):} \quad q(\mathbf{z}|\mathbf{x}) = \delta(\mathbf{z} - g(\mathbf{x})). \tag{20.15}$$

The likelihood contribution term for continuous surjections is given by

$$\mathcal{V}(\mathbf{x}, \mathbf{z}) = \mathbb{E}_{q(\mathbf{z}|\mathbf{x})}\left[\log \frac{p(\mathbf{x}|\mathbf{z})}{q(\mathbf{z}|\mathbf{x})}\right], \tag{20.16}$$

where

$$\begin{cases} p(\mathbf{x}|\mathbf{z}) \to \delta(\mathbf{x} - f(\mathbf{z})), & \text{for generative surjections,} \\ q(\mathbf{z}|\mathbf{x}) \to \delta(\mathbf{z} - g(\mathbf{x})), & \text{for inference surjections,} \end{cases} \tag{20.17}$$

where we will soon see that the logarithm of a delta function in the case of surjective transformations can be properly defined if we take proper limits.

For inference surjections we moreover have that the ELBO bound is tight; that is $\mathcal{E}(\mathbf{x}, \mathbf{z}) = 0$. This can be shown by writing

$$p(\mathbf{z}|\mathbf{x}) \propto p(\mathbf{x}|\mathbf{z})p(\mathbf{z}) = \delta(\mathbf{x} \in \mathcal{B}(\mathbf{z}))s(\mathbf{x}|\mathbf{z})p(\mathbf{z}), \tag{20.18}$$

and observing that there is only one single $\mathbf{z}$ consistent with any particular $\mathbf{x}$, which implies (after normalization) $p(\mathbf{z}|\mathbf{x}) = \delta(\mathbf{z} - g(\mathbf{x})) = q(\mathbf{z}|\mathbf{x})$. For generative surjections the bound is not tight; that is, $\mathbb{E}_q[\mathcal{E}] > 0$.

A fully composable SurVAE flow is given by a sequence of transformations, including bijective, surjective, and stochastic transformations. Bijectors often struggle with multimodal data or distributions with topological obstructions. Surjective transformations can be used for generative modeling of both continuous (Nielsen et al., 2020) and discrete data, or even multimodal data (Hoogeboom et al., 2021), and for sampling from complex discrete distributions (Jaini et al., 2021).

To illustrate the application of SurVAE flows, let us consider a few examples.

20.3.1 Tensor Slicing and Augmentation

One of the simplest types of surjection involves changing the dimensionality of the space by either discarding (slicing) or adding (augmenting) variables. These two operations are inverses of each other and form the basis for many advanced generative models.

Consider a generative tensor slicing surjection f that takes input $\mathbf{z} = (\mathbf{z}_a, \mathbf{z}_b) \in \mathbb{R}^d$

and returns a subset of its components, $\mathbf{x} = f(\mathbf{z}) = \mathbf{z}_a$. We define the stochastic forward and inverse transformations as:

$$\text{forward (deterministic):} \quad p(\mathbf{x}|\mathbf{z}) = \lim_{\sigma \to 0^+} G(\mathbf{x}|\mathbf{z}_a, \sigma^2 \mathbf{I}); \tag{20.19}$$

$$\text{inverse (stochastic):} \quad q(\mathbf{z}|\mathbf{x}) = \lim_{\sigma \to 0^+} G(\mathbf{z}_a|\mathbf{x}, \sigma^2 \mathbf{I}) q(\mathbf{z}_b|\mathbf{x}). \tag{20.20}$$

The likelihood contribution term is derived as:

$$\begin{aligned}
\mathcal{V}(\mathbf{x}, \mathbf{z}) &= \lim_{\sigma \to 0^+} \mathbb{E}_{q(\mathbf{z}|\mathbf{x})} \left[\log \frac{p(\mathbf{x}|\mathbf{z})}{q(\mathbf{z}|\mathbf{x})} \right] \\
&= \lim_{\sigma \to 0^+} \mathbb{E}_{q(\mathbf{z}|\mathbf{x})} \left[\log \frac{G(\mathbf{x}|\mathbf{z}_a, \sigma^2 \mathbf{I})}{G(\mathbf{z}_a|\mathbf{x}, \sigma^2 \mathbf{I}) q(\mathbf{z}_b|\mathbf{x})} \right] \\
&= \lim_{\sigma \to 0^+} \mathbb{E}_{q(\mathbf{z}|\mathbf{x})} \left[\log \frac{G(\mathbf{x}|\mathbf{z}_a, \sigma^2 \mathbf{I})}{G(\mathbf{z}_a|\mathbf{x}, \sigma^2 \mathbf{I})} - \log q(\mathbf{z}_b|\mathbf{x}) \right] \\
&= \mathbb{E}_{q(\mathbf{z}_b|\mathbf{x})} \left[- \log q(\mathbf{z}_b|\mathbf{x}) \right].
\end{aligned} \tag{20.21}$$

In the final step, as $\sigma \to 0^+$, the Gaussian distributions become delta functions, and their ratio approaches 1, leaving only the term involving $q(\mathbf{z}_b|\mathbf{x})$. This transformation clearly loses information by discarding the $\mathbf{z}_b$ components.

The inverse operation of tensor slicing is augmentation, an inference surjection that increases the dimensionality by appending additional random variables. Consider a mapping $g\colon \mathcal{X} \to \mathcal{Z}$ where $\mathbf{x} \in \mathbb{R}^d$ is the original data and $\mathbf{z} = g(\mathbf{x}) = (\mathbf{x}, \mathbf{u}) \in \mathbb{R}^{d+k}$ is the augmented data, with $\mathbf{u} \in \mathbb{R}^k$ being the appended random variable. The stochastic forward and deterministic inverse transformations are:

$$\text{orward (stochastic):} \quad p(\mathbf{z}|\mathbf{x}) = p(\mathbf{u}|\mathbf{x}) \delta(\mathbf{z}_{1:d} - \mathbf{x}); \tag{20.22}$$

$$\text{inverse (deterministic):} \quad q(\mathbf{x}|\mathbf{z}) = \delta(\mathbf{x} - \mathbf{z}_{1:d}), \tag{20.23}$$

where $\mathbf{z}_{1:d}$ denotes the first d components of $\mathbf{z}$. The likelihood contribution term can be derived as for tensor slicing, given by $\mathcal{V}(\mathbf{x}, \mathbf{z}) = \mathbb{E}_{p(\mathbf{u}|\mathbf{x})} [\log p(\mathbf{u}|\mathbf{x})]$. Since this is an inference surjection, the ELBO bound is tight ($\mathcal{E}(\mathbf{x}, \mathbf{z}) = 0$), as the true posterior $p(\mathbf{x}|\mathbf{z})$ equals the variational approximation $q(\mathbf{x}|\mathbf{z}) = \delta(\mathbf{x} - \mathbf{z}_{1:d})$.

When composed together, augmentation and tensor slicing are particularly useful in SurVAE flows for increasing model expressiveness. For example, in multiscale architectures, augmentation can introduce additional latent variables at different scales, allowing the model to capture hierarchical structures in the data. By augmenting the latent space, the model can learn more complex dependencies and represent a wider range of distributions. This is what was used in augmented normalizing flows (Huang et al., 2020) and VFlow (J. Chen et al., 2020), whose forward transformations involve augmenting the data space with additional dimensions, followed by a bijective transformation, and can be equivalently expressed as a bijection composed with a generative slicing surjection that discards the augmented dimensions.

Thermodynamic Interpretation

From a thermodynamic perspective, the tensor slicing operation can be interpreted as a coarse-graining process, where information about $\mathbf{z}_b$ is discarded. This process is analogous to the coarse-graining discussed by Kawai et al. (2007) and Gomez-Mari et al. (2008). In stochastic thermodynamics (Chapter 10), let ρ denote the forward pat probability and ρ_R the time-reversed path probability. The KL divergence betwee these path probabilities is related to the average total entropy production $\mathbb{E}[\Sigma]$:

$$D_{\mathrm{KL}}[\rho \| \rho_R] = \mathbb{E}[\Sigma]. \tag{20.24}$$

In the context of tensor slicing, we can apply this concept to both the full system an the coarse-grained (sliced) system:

$$\begin{aligned} \mathbb{E}[\Sigma^{\text{full}}] &= D_{\mathrm{KL}}[\rho_{Z_a,Z_b} \| \rho_{R\,Z_a,Z_b}] \\ &= D_{\mathrm{KL}}[\rho_{Z_a} \| \rho_{R\,Z_a}] + \mathbb{E}_{\rho_{Z_a}}\left[D_{\mathrm{KL}}[\rho_{Z_b|Z_a} \| \rho_{R\,Z_b|Z_a}]\right] \\ &\geq D_{\mathrm{KL}}[\rho_{Z_a} \| \rho_{R\,Z_a}] = \mathbb{E}[\Sigma^{\text{observed}}]. \end{aligned} \tag{20.25}$$

Here, ρ_{Z_a,Z_b} and $\rho_{R\,Z_a,Z_b}$ are the joint distributions of the full system in the forwar and time-reversed processes, respectively; ρ_{Z_a} and $\rho_{R\,Z_a}$ are the marginal distribution of the observed (sliced) variable.

This inequality provides a lower bound on the dissipation in the full system based o what we observe in the coarse-grained system. The difference $\mathbb{E}[\Sigma^{\text{full}}] - \mathbb{E}[\Sigma^{\text{observed}}]$ represents the "hidden" entropy production due to the discarded information. Physi cally, this means that coarse-graining (tensor slicing) leads to an apparent reduction i the observed dissipation or entropy production of the system. However, this reductio is a consequence of our limited observation (slicing) rather than a true decrease in th system's entropy.

In physical systems, the time-reversed path is obtained by time reversal using th same physical laws. In SurVAE flows, the stochastic inverse $q(\mathbf{z}|\mathbf{x})$ is not necessaril defined in this way. While it is tempting to interpret the bound looseness term $\mathcal{E}(\mathbf{x}, \mathbf{z})$ log $\frac{q(\mathbf{z}|\mathbf{x})}{p(\mathbf{z}|\mathbf{x})}$ in SurVAE flows as the hidden extra work, this interpretation is not strictl accurate due to differences in how the reverse process is defined in these contexts.

20.3.2 Rounding

Beyond continuous dimensionality changes, surjections naturally model discretizatio operations arising from finite resolutions. The rounding surjection is a transformatio that rounds the elements of an input vector to the nearest integer values. Let f be rounding surjection that takes an input $\mathbf{z} \in \mathbb{R}^{d_z}$ and returns the rounded $\mathbf{x} := \lfloor \mathbf{z} \rfloor$, whe $\lfloor \cdot \rfloor$ denotes the floor function applied elementwise. We define:

$$\text{forward (deterministic):} \quad p(\mathbf{x}|\mathbf{z}) = \mathbb{1}(\mathbf{z} \in \mathcal{B}(\mathbf{x})), \ \text{for } \mathcal{B}(\mathbf{x}) = \{\mathbf{x} + \mathbf{u} | \mathbf{u} \in [0,1)^d\}; \tag{20.26}$$

$$\text{inverse (stochastic):} \quad q(\mathbf{z}|\mathbf{x}) = r(\mathbf{z}|\mathbf{x}) \mathbb{1}(\mathbf{z} \in \mathcal{B}(\mathbf{x})). \tag{20.27}$$

Here, $\mathbb{1}(\cdot)$ is the indicator function, and $\mathcal{B}(\mathbf{x})$ represents the unit cube of possible values that round to $\mathbf{x}$. In physics, such an operation would originate from the limite precision of measurement devices, such as the pixelation in a camera.

The likelihood contribution term for the rounding operation is derived as follows:

$$\begin{aligned}\mathcal{V}(\mathbf{x},\mathbf{z}) &= \mathbb{E}_{q(\mathbf{z}|\mathbf{x})}\left[\log\frac{p(\mathbf{x}|\mathbf{z})}{q(\mathbf{z}|\mathbf{x})}\right]\\ &= \mathbb{E}_{q(\mathbf{z}|\mathbf{x})}\left[\log\frac{\mathbb{1}(\mathbf{z}\in\mathcal{B}(\mathbf{x}))}{r(\mathbf{z}|\mathbf{x})\mathbb{1}(\mathbf{z}\in\mathcal{B}(\mathbf{x}))}\right]\\ &= \mathbb{E}_{q(\mathbf{z}|\mathbf{x})}\left[-\log r(\mathbf{z}|\mathbf{x})\right]. \end{aligned} \tag{20.28}$$

The indicator function $\mathbb{1}(\mathbf{z}\in\mathcal{B}(\mathbf{x}))$ is always 1 for $\mathbf{z}$ sampled from $q(\mathbf{z}|\mathbf{x})$, so it disappears in the final expression. The result shows that the likelihood contribution is the differential entropy of the inverse distribution $q(\mathbf{z}|\mathbf{x})$.

Both uniform (Uria et al., 2014) and variational dequantization (Ho et al., 2019) can be viewed as inverse operations to the rounding surjection (see Figure 20.2 for an illustration). Uniform dequantization corresponds to a generative rounding surjection with a uniform stochastic inverse $q(\mathbf{z}|\mathbf{x})$, while variational dequantization uses a more flexible flow-based distribution for $q(\mathbf{z}|\mathbf{x})$. Mathematically, we can express this connection as:

$$f(\mathbf{z}) = \lfloor \mathbf{z} \rfloor \qquad \text{(rounding)}, \tag{20.29}$$

$$g(\mathbf{x}) = \mathbf{x}+\mathbf{u}, \quad \mathbf{u}\sim q(\mathbf{u}|\mathbf{x}) \qquad \text{(dequantization)}. \tag{20.30}$$

These techniques allow for modeling discrete data with continuous distributions by introducing a continuous latent variable that is rounded to obtain the discrete observation. The choice of the dequantization distribution $q(\mathbf{u}|\mathbf{x})$ determines the expressiveness of the model, with more flexible distributions leading to better approximations of the true discrete distribution.

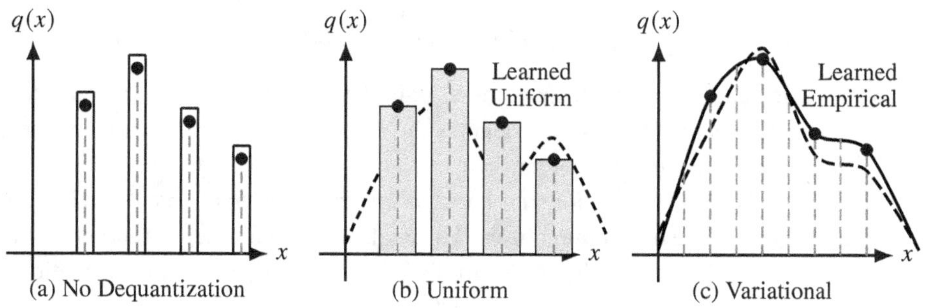

Figure 20.2 Comparison of dequantization methods. (a) Without dequantization the data remain spike measures, making continuous fits difficult. (b) Uniform dequantization pads each sample with symmetric noise bands, yielding a smoothed surrogate density. (c) Variational dequantization learns a flow-based $q(x)$ (dashed) that more closely follows the empirical spikes while remaining continuous.

20.3.3 Sort Surjection

A more sophisticated surjection arises when we want to model permutation-invariant distributions or distributions over order statistics. The sort surjection is a transformation that orders the elements of an input vector in ascending order. Let $\mathbf{x} \in \mathbb{R}^d$ be the input vector and $\mathbf{z} = \text{sort}(\mathbf{x})$ be the sorted output. This is a many-to-one mapping, since any permutation of a given vector $\mathbf{x}$ results in the same sorted vector $\mathbf{z}$. We define S_d as the set of all permutations of d elements.

We can represent this inference surjection as:

$$\begin{aligned} \text{forward (stochastic):} \quad p(\mathbf{x}|\mathbf{z}) &= \sum_{\pi \in S_d} p(\mathbf{x}|\mathbf{z}, \pi) p(\pi|\mathbf{z}) \\ &= \sum_{\pi \in S_d} \delta(\mathbf{x} - \pi^{-1}(\mathbf{z})) p(\pi|\mathbf{z}); \quad (20.31) \\ \text{inverse (deterministic):} \quad q(\mathbf{z}|\mathbf{x}) &= \delta(\mathbf{z} - \text{sort}(\mathbf{x})), \quad (20.32) \end{aligned}$$

where π^{-1} is the inverse permutation of π, and $p(\pi|\mathbf{z})$ is a learnable categorical distribution over permutations, conditioned on the sorted vector $\mathbf{z}$. The forward process generates an unsorted vector $\mathbf{x}$ by picking a permutation π and applying its inverse to the sorted vector $\mathbf{z}$.

The likelihood contribution term for the sort surjection is derived as:

$$\begin{aligned} \mathcal{V}(\mathbf{x}, \mathbf{z}) &= \mathbb{E}_{q(\mathbf{z}|\mathbf{x})} \left[\log \frac{p(\mathbf{x}|\mathbf{z})}{q(\mathbf{z}|\mathbf{x})} \right] \\ &= \mathbb{E}_{q(\mathbf{z}|\mathbf{x})} \left[\log \frac{\sum_{\pi \in S_d} \delta(\mathbf{x} - \pi^{-1}(\mathbf{z})) p(\pi|\mathbf{z})}{\delta(\mathbf{z} - \text{sort}(\mathbf{x}))} \right] \\ &= \log \frac{\sum_{\pi \in S_d} \delta(\mathbf{x} - \pi^{-1}(\text{sort}(\mathbf{x}))) p(\pi|\,\text{sort}(\mathbf{x}))}{\delta(\text{sort}(\mathbf{x}) - \text{sort}(\mathbf{x}))} \\ &= \log[\delta(\mathbf{x} - \text{sort}^{-1}(\text{sort}(\mathbf{x}))) p(\text{sort}\,|\,\text{sort}(\mathbf{x}))] \\ &= \log p(\text{sort}\,|\,\text{sort}(\mathbf{x})); \quad (20.33) \end{aligned}$$

for each $\mathbf{x}$ and corresponding $\mathbf{z}$, only the permutation π that sorts $\mathbf{x}$ to $\mathbf{z}$ contributes to the sum. Here, sort^{-1} denotes the inverse permutation that maps the sorted vector back to the original order.

The sort surjection can be used to model distributions involving order statistics, such as the distribution of the kth smallest value in a set of random variables.

We leave it to the reader to discover more surjective transformations proposed in the literature (Nielsen et al., 2020).

Part III

Continuous-Time Probabilistic Dynamics

In this part, we take the limit of discrete-time dynamics in which the time step shrinks to zero, so that the dynamics become continuous in time. Chapter 21 extends the free energy narrative of Chapter 5 and the diffusion view of Chapter 13 into Fokker–Planck dynamics, and Chapter 22 ties this dynamics to optimal transport and Schrödinger bridges. Chapter 23 links the discrete normalizing and stochastic flows of Chapter 8 and Chapter 20 to continuous (optimal) transport. We also revisit time reversal, entropy production, and control explained in the discrete Markov-process view from the Fokker–Planck probabilistic perspective.

21 Stochastic Thermodynamics from the Fokker–Planck Equation

21.1 Introduction

In most of this book, we have followed the discrete formulation of the problem to describe the time evolution of the physical system. This involved an index-time variable t that progressed in unit steps: $t = 0, 1, 2, \ldots$ However, physics (at least at the classical level) is continuous; as such, we need to introduce physical time τ that progresses in infinitesimal steps $\tau = \tau_0, \tau_0 + \delta\tau$, and so on. Additionally, we must replace sums with integrals over time and adjust other relevant expressions accordingly. In this chapter, we will use τ to denote physical time to maintain consistent notation across the chapter.

In stochastic systems with Brownian motion, integrating over random paths is actually tricky and requires Itô calculus. This advanced topic will be addressed in a subsequent volume. Nevertheless, many of the results we have discovered in this book can be elegantly derived through the introduction of Fokker–Planck equations, first formulated in the seminal works of Fokker (1914), Planck (1917), and Kolmogorov (1931). We could not resist the temptation to give you a taste of this elegant alternative framework to understand the rich field of stochastic thermodynamics.

In this chapter we revisit many of the thermodynamic relations discussed in Part II, such as the first and second laws of thermodynamics connecting energy, work, heat, and (system and bath) entropy. We also derive Fokker–Planck dynamics as the gradient flow of the variational free energy and generalize the Fokker–Planck equation to include momenta and nonconservative rotational components, which leads to the Klein–Kramers equation. We then once again derive the second law and finally derive a quite general equation for the excess work necessary to transform one distribution into another.

21.2 The Continuity Equation

In this chapter, we aim for generality by using phase space variables $\zeta = (\xi, \eta)$, while noting that some results simplify considerably in the overdamped limit where $\zeta = \xi$. In the next chapter we will focus on this overdamped limit, working in configuration space rather than full phase space, which provides a natural bridge to machine learning applications.

We begin this chapter by deriving the continuity equation. This is a very intuitive, general, and natural law, namely the law that mass does not get lost or tele-transportec If we have some mass and we flow that mass under some velocity field, all the mass wi still be there; it is just moved. In other words, no new mass is created anywhere, an no mass is destroyed anywhere. Another way of making that intuition more concrete i to consider an arbitrary volume in space $\mathcal{V}$. By the definition of conservation of mas we conclude that the increase of the amount of mass inside $\mathcal{V}$ must be given by th amount of mass that flows in minus the amount of mass that flows out.

Let ζ denote a phase space variable and $\rho(\zeta, \tau)$ be the probability density at point and time τ. Let $\mathcal{B}(\mathcal{V})$ denote the boundary of the volume $\mathcal{V}$, and $\hat{\mathbf{n}}$ be the unit surface normal vector pointing outwards. Then, the integral $\oiint_{\mathcal{B}(\mathcal{V})} \rho\mathbf{v} \cdot \hat{\mathbf{n}}\ \mathrm{d}\mathcal{B}$ represents th outward flow of probability through the surface, where $\mathbf{v}(\zeta, \tau)$ is the velocity fiel Applying the conservation of mass, we have

$$
\begin{aligned}
\partial_\tau \iiint_{\mathcal{V}} \rho(\zeta, \tau)\ \mathrm{d}\mathcal{V} &= -\oiint_{\mathcal{B}(\mathcal{V})} \rho(\zeta, \tau)\mathbf{v}(\zeta, \tau) \cdot \hat{\mathbf{n}}(\zeta)\ \mathrm{d}\mathcal{B} \\
&= -\iiint_{\mathcal{V}} \mathbf{div}(\rho(\zeta, \tau)\mathbf{v}(\zeta, \tau))\ \mathrm{d}\mathcal{V} \\
&\Rightarrow \iiint_{\mathcal{V}} (\partial_\tau \rho(\zeta, \tau) + \mathbf{div}(\rho(\zeta, \tau)\mathbf{v}(\zeta, \tau)))\ \mathrm{d}\mathcal{V} = 0, \qquad (21.1)
\end{aligned}
$$

where we have used Gauss's theorem to convert the surface integral into a volum integral. By observing that this identity needs to hold for every arbitrary volume $\mathcal{V}$ we arrive at the conclusion that this can only be true if the integrand vanishes:

$$
\partial_\tau \rho(\zeta, \tau) + \boldsymbol{\nabla} \cdot (\rho(\zeta, \tau)\mathbf{v}(\zeta, \tau)) = 0. \qquad (21.2)
$$

This is the continuity equation, and it is a very general result. It holds for any probabilit density that gets transported along a (possibly time-dependent) vector field $\mathbf{v}$, provide that probability mass cannot be created, destroyed, or tele-transported, which is usuall true in physics (see Figure 21.1).

Let's also derive the result in a slightly different manner and connect it back t concepts we have already seen in previous chapters. Assume that we start with density $\rho(\zeta, \tau)$ and evolve it under deterministic dynamics (a.k.a. "push forward") th density under the flow

$$
\begin{aligned}
\tau &\mapsto \tau' = \tau + \delta\tau, \qquad (21.3) \\
\zeta &\mapsto \zeta' = \zeta + \mathbf{v}(\zeta, \tau)\delta\tau. \qquad (21.4)
\end{aligned}
$$

This evolution can be viewed as a coordinate transformation. Consequently, the densi transforms according to

$$
\rho(\zeta, \tau) = \rho(\zeta', \tau') \left| \det \left(\frac{\partial \zeta'}{\partial \zeta} \right) \right|. \qquad (21.5)
$$

Expanding to first order in $\delta\tau$, we have

$$\begin{aligned}
&\rho(\zeta,\tau) \approx (\rho(\zeta,\tau) + \partial_\tau\rho(\zeta,\tau)\delta\tau + \mathbf{v}(\zeta,\tau)\cdot\nabla\rho(\zeta,\tau)\delta\tau)\,(\mathbf{I} + \nabla\cdot\mathbf{v}(\zeta,\tau)\delta\tau)\\
&\Rightarrow \rho(\zeta,\tau) + \partial_\tau\rho(\zeta,\tau)\delta\tau + \mathbf{v}(\zeta,\tau)\cdot\nabla\rho(\zeta,\tau)\delta\tau + \rho(\zeta,\tau)\nabla\cdot\mathbf{v}(\zeta,\tau)\delta\tau \approx \rho(\zeta,\tau)\\
&\Rightarrow \partial_\tau\rho(\zeta,\tau) + \mathbf{v}(\zeta,\tau)\cdot\nabla\rho(\zeta,\tau) + \rho(\zeta,\tau)\nabla\cdot\mathbf{v}(\zeta,\tau) = 0\\
&\Rightarrow \partial_\tau\rho(\zeta,\tau) + \nabla\cdot(\rho(\zeta,\tau)\mathbf{v}(\zeta,\tau)) = 0.
\end{aligned} \tag{21.6}$$

Thus, we see that the continuity equation is simply the result of applying the transformation rule for densities. Given the continuity equation, one can ask when the density ρ is stationary. This is similar to the condition of stationarity in the context of MCMC algorithms (see Chapter 11). To achieve stationarity, we need that ρ does not change with time:

$$\partial_\tau\rho(\zeta,\tau) = 0, \;\Rightarrow\; \mathbf{div}(\rho(\zeta,\tau)\mathbf{v}(\zeta,\tau)) = 0. \tag{21.7}$$

In other words, we are looking for a vector field for which, at any fixed point ζ, the density $\rho(\zeta,\tau)$ does not change with time. Such a vector field guarantees that the inflow of probability into any region in space equals the outflow of probability out of that region, which implies that the total probability in that region remains invariant, in other words stationarity. If we want the more restrictive condition of detailed balance, then we require that for every surface element of every volume, the inward and outward flow must be the same. In the overdamped case, where $\zeta = \xi$, detailed balance implies $\mathbf{v} = 0$ everywhere.

This may not have to be a trivial solution because, as we will see, $\mathbf{v}$ may consist of drift and diffusion terms. In particular, when there are drift and diffusion terms, the detailed balance condition will reduce to

$$\nabla\mathcal{H}(\zeta) = -T\nabla\log\rho(\zeta), \tag{21.8}$$

with $\mathcal{H}$ the Hamiltonian, which is of course equivalent to the statement that ρ^{eq} should be the Boltzmann distribution:

$$\rho^{\mathrm{eq}}(\zeta) = \frac{1}{Z}\exp(-\beta\mathcal{H}(\zeta)). \tag{21.9}$$

1.3 Energy Change and the First Law

In previous chapters, we have defined the internal energy of a thermodynamic system as

$$\mathcal{U}[\rho] = \int \mathrm{d}\zeta\,\rho(\zeta,\tau)\mathcal{H}(\zeta,\tau), \tag{21.10}$$

with $\mathcal{H}$ the Hamiltonian of the system. We now calculate the energy change as a function of time. In these computations, it is important to realize that we adopt the Eulerian formalism, where ζ is a fixed random variable over which we integrate, and both the density ρ and the Hamiltonian $\mathcal{H}$ (or any other function) explicitly vary with time. Importantly, the variable ζ itself does not depend on time.

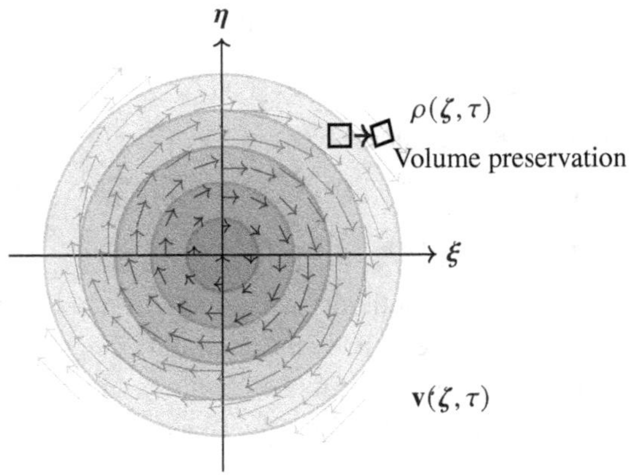

Figure 21.1 Visualization of the continuity equation in phase space. The concentric contours represent the probability density $\rho(\zeta,\tau)$, with darker shading indicating higher density near the center. The arrows show the velocity field $\mathbf{v}(\zeta,\tau)$, with arrow intensity proportional to fiel strength. The inset (upper right, square transforming to parallelogram) demonstrates volume element deformation under the flow, illustrating the conservation of probability mass as expressed in (21.2).

Alternatively, we can adopt the Lagrangian perspective, analogous to the repa rameterization trick used in VAEs discussed in Chapter 7. In this view, the rando variable $\zeta_\tau = g(\zeta_0,\tau)$ becomes an explicit function of time, while the measu $\rho(\zeta_\tau,\tau)\,\mathrm{d}\zeta_\tau = \rho(\zeta_0,0)\,\mathrm{d}\zeta_0$ remains invariant, independent of time. We give an illus tration of both perspectives in Figure 21.2. It should be noted that these two views ar equivalent and can be mapped into each other by a change of variables $\zeta_0 \mapsto \zeta_\tau$.

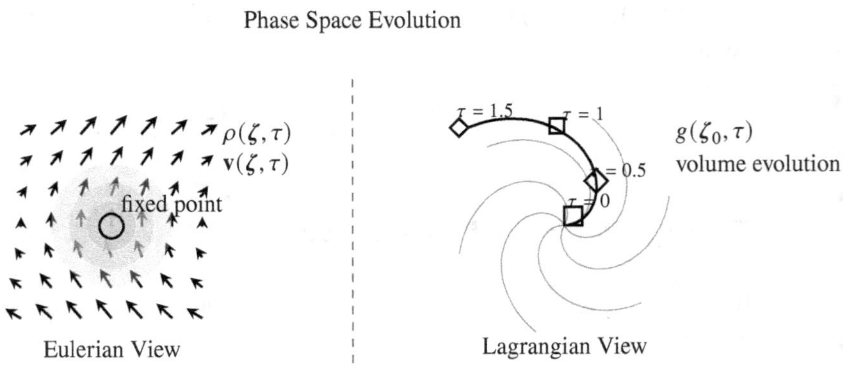

Figure 21.2 Comparison of Eulerian and Lagrangian perspectives in phase space dynamics. Left: Fixed-point view showing density field $\rho(\zeta,\tau)$ (shaded contours) and velocity field $\mathbf{v}(\zeta,\tau)$ (arrows), with a fixed reference point (circle). Right: Particle-following view showing how volume elements (squares) deform along the trajectory $g(\zeta_0,\tau)$ (solid curve), with time labels $\tau = 0, 0.5, 1, 1.5$ marking positions along the path; background streamlines indicate th flow field.

The rate of change of energy is now given by

$$\begin{aligned}\frac{\mathrm{d}}{\mathrm{d}\tau}\mathcal{U}[\rho](\tau) &= \partial_\tau \mathcal{U}[\rho](\tau)\\ &= \int \mathrm{d}\zeta\, (\partial_\tau \rho(\zeta,\tau))\mathcal{H}(\zeta,\tau) + \int \mathrm{d}\zeta\, \rho(\zeta,\tau)\partial_\tau \mathcal{H}(\zeta,\tau)\\ &= \int \mathrm{d}\zeta\, (-\mathbf{div}(\rho(\zeta,\tau)\mathbf{v}(\zeta,\tau)))\,\mathcal{H}(\zeta,\tau) + \int \mathrm{d}\zeta\, \rho(\zeta,\tau)\partial_\tau \mathcal{H}(\zeta,\tau),\end{aligned} \tag{21.11}$$

where we used the continuity equation in the last line. By integrating by parts, we continue to find

$$\begin{aligned}\frac{\mathrm{d}}{\mathrm{d}\tau}\mathcal{U}[\rho](\tau) &= \int \mathrm{d}\zeta\, \rho(\zeta,\tau)\mathbf{v}(\zeta,\tau)\cdot\nabla\mathcal{H}(\zeta,\tau) + \int \mathrm{d}\zeta\, \rho(\zeta,\tau)\partial_\tau\mathcal{H}(\zeta,\tau)\\ &= \int \mathrm{d}\zeta\, \rho(\zeta,\tau)\,(\partial_\tau\mathcal{H}(\zeta,\tau) + \mathbf{v}(\zeta,\tau)\cdot\nabla\mathcal{H}(\zeta,\tau))\\ &= \int \mathrm{d}\zeta\, \rho(\zeta,\tau)\, \mathcal{D}_\tau\mathcal{H}(\zeta,\tau),\end{aligned} \tag{21.12}$$

where we have defined $\mathcal{D}_\tau = \partial_\tau + \mathbf{v}(\zeta,\tau)\cdot\nabla$ as the *material derivative* (or comoving derivative). Here, it describes how $\mathcal{H}$ changes when moving with the velocity field. In this derivation, we employed the continuity equation and integrated by parts, assuming that the density ρ vanishes at the boundary of the integration volume.

From this expression, we can identify the changes in heat and work as follows:

$$\partial_\tau\mathcal{U}[\rho](\tau) = \partial_\tau Q(\tau) + \partial_\tau \mathcal{W}(\tau), \tag{21.13}$$

$$\partial_\tau \mathcal{W}(\tau) = \int \mathrm{d}\zeta\, \rho(\zeta,\tau)\, \partial_\tau\mathcal{H}(\zeta,\tau), \tag{21.14}$$

$$\partial_\tau Q(\tau) = \int \mathrm{d}\zeta\, \rho(\zeta,\tau)\, \mathbf{v}(\zeta,\tau)\cdot\nabla\mathcal{H}(\zeta,\tau). \tag{21.15}$$

Here, $\partial_\tau \mathcal{W}(\tau)$ represents the rate of work done on the system, and $\partial_\tau Q(\tau)$ represents the rate of heat transfer into the system. This is the first law of thermodynamics.

21.4 Entropy Production and the Second Law

Now let's have a look at how the continuity equation changes the entropy of a system. The entropy at any time τ is defined as

$$\mathcal{S}[\rho](\tau) = -\int \mathrm{d}\zeta\, \rho(\zeta,\tau)\log\rho(\zeta,\tau). \tag{21.16}$$

The entropy production rate is therefore given by

$$\begin{aligned}\frac{\mathrm{d}}{\mathrm{d}\tau}\mathcal{S}[\rho](\tau) &= \partial_\tau \mathcal{S}[\rho](\tau)\\ &= -\int \mathrm{d}\zeta\ (\partial_\tau \rho(\zeta,\tau)) \log \rho(\zeta,\tau) - \int \mathrm{d}\zeta\ \rho(\zeta,\tau)\partial_\tau \log \rho(\zeta,\tau)\\ &= \int \mathrm{d}\zeta\ \boldsymbol{\nabla}\cdot(\rho(\zeta,\tau)\mathbf{v}(\zeta,\tau)) \log \rho(\zeta,\tau) - \int \mathrm{d}\zeta\ \partial_\tau \rho(\zeta,\tau).\end{aligned} \tag{21.17}$$

In the second equality, we used the continuity equation, (21.2), to substitute for $\partial_\tau \rho$. Integrating by parts and assuming that $\rho(\zeta,\tau)$ vanishes at the boundary, the expression simplifies to

$$\begin{aligned}\frac{\mathrm{d}}{\mathrm{d}\tau}\mathcal{S}[\rho](\tau) &= -\int \mathrm{d}\zeta\ \rho(\zeta,\tau)\mathbf{v}(\zeta,\tau)\cdot\boldsymbol{\nabla}\log\rho(\zeta,\tau) - \partial_\tau \int \mathrm{d}\zeta\ \rho(\zeta,\tau)\\ &= -\int \mathrm{d}\zeta\ \mathbf{v}(\zeta,\tau)\cdot\boldsymbol{\nabla}\rho(\zeta,\tau) - 0\\ &= \int \mathrm{d}\zeta\ \rho(\zeta,\tau)\mathbf{div}(\mathbf{v}(\zeta,\tau)).\end{aligned} \tag{21.18}$$

The final line follows by applying integration by parts once again. This result implies that, in the absence of compression in phase space (i.e., when $\mathbf{div}(\mathbf{v}) = 0$), there is no entropy production. As we will see below, Hamiltonian dynamics has no compression (preserves volume) and therefore does not produce entropy. We also observe from the above derivation that the component of the vector field $\mathbf{v}$ in the direction of the negative score function $-\boldsymbol{\nabla}\log\rho$ is responsible for generating entropy.

21.4.1 Hamiltonian Flows are Incompressible

Next, let's use Hamilton's equations to generate the vector field. For a phase space system with variables $\boldsymbol{\zeta} = (\boldsymbol{\xi}, \boldsymbol{\eta})$, Hamilton's equations give us

$$\mathbf{v}_\xi(\zeta,\tau) = \boldsymbol{\nabla}_\eta \mathcal{H}(\zeta,\tau), \tag{21.19}$$

$$\mathbf{v}_\eta(\zeta,\tau) = -\boldsymbol{\nabla}_\xi \mathcal{H}(\zeta,\tau). \tag{21.20}$$

These equations can be written more compactly using the symplectic matrix $\mathbf{J}$:

$$\mathbf{v}(\zeta,\tau) = \mathbf{J}\boldsymbol{\nabla}_\zeta \mathcal{H}(\zeta,\tau), \quad \text{where} \quad \mathbf{J} = \begin{pmatrix} 0 & \mathbf{I} \\ -\mathbf{I} & 0 \end{pmatrix}, \tag{21.21}$$

with $\mathbf{I}$ the identity matrix. Here, $\boldsymbol{\nabla}_\zeta$ denotes the gradient with respect to all phase space variables $\boldsymbol{\zeta} = (\boldsymbol{\xi}, \boldsymbol{\eta})$.

The divergence is given by

$$\begin{aligned}\mathbf{div}(\mathbf{v}(\zeta,\tau)) = \boldsymbol{\nabla}\cdot\mathbf{v}(\zeta,\tau) &= \boldsymbol{\nabla}_\xi\cdot\mathbf{v}_\xi(\zeta,\tau) + \boldsymbol{\nabla}_\eta\cdot\mathbf{v}_\eta(\zeta,\tau)\\ &= \boldsymbol{\nabla}_\xi\cdot\boldsymbol{\nabla}_\eta\mathcal{H}(\zeta,\tau) - \boldsymbol{\nabla}_\eta\cdot\boldsymbol{\nabla}_\xi\mathcal{H}(\zeta,\tau)\\ &= 0,\end{aligned} \tag{21.22}$$

since mixed partial derivatives are symmetric. So we see that Hamiltonian flows are incompressible and do not generate entropy (see Figure 21.3). This is indeed a reasonable result. Remember that we are describing all degrees of freedom in the system, and not coarse-grained or effective degrees of freedom. This means that under evolution, the number of bits we need to describe the system remains the same (that is, $6N$ real numbers), which implies that there is no loss of information the observer has about the system. In fact, the preservation of information is a fundamental assumption about physical laws that is deeply tied to the fact that our physical laws are time-reversible. In other words, at any point in time, we have enough information to trace the trajectory of our system exactly back in time. This is only possible when no information is lost during time evolution.

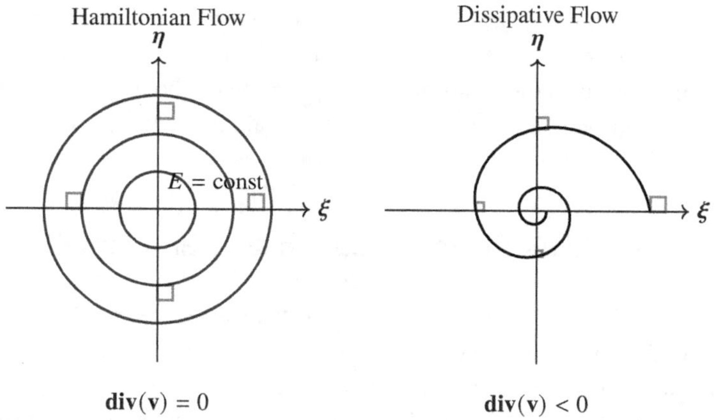

Figure 21.3 Comparison of phase space flows. Left: Hamiltonian flow preserves phase space volume ($\mathbf{div}(\mathbf{v}) = 0$) as shown by the constant-sized squares placed along concentric constant-energy contours. Right: Dissipative flow contracts phase space volume ($\mathbf{div}(\mathbf{v}) < 0$), illustrated by shrinking squares along the inward spiral trajectory.

21.4.2 Dissipation

Now let's look at an example where we add a dissipative term to the Hamiltonian equations:

$$\mathbf{v}_\xi(\zeta, \tau) = \nabla_\eta \mathcal{H}(\zeta, \tau), \tag{21.23}$$

$$\mathbf{v}_\eta(\zeta, \tau) = -\nabla_\xi \mathcal{H}(\zeta, \tau) - \gamma \boldsymbol{\eta}, \quad \gamma > 0. \tag{21.24}$$

Here, γ is the damping constant, which determines the strength of the dissipation. This form of equation was extensively studied by Kramers (1940) in his groundbreaking work on Brownian motion in a force field. In this case, the divergence is given by

$$\begin{aligned}\mathbf{div}(\mathbf{v}(\zeta, \tau)) &= \nabla_\xi \cdot \mathbf{v}_\xi(\zeta, \tau) + \nabla_\eta \cdot \mathbf{v}_\eta(\zeta, \tau)\\ &= \nabla_\xi \cdot \nabla_\eta \mathcal{H}(\zeta, \tau) - \nabla_\eta \cdot \nabla_\xi \mathcal{H}(\zeta, \tau) - 3N\gamma\\ &= -3N\gamma, \quad \gamma > 0.\end{aligned} \tag{21.25}$$

The negative divergence means that phase space is contracting under evolution (se
Figure 21.3). We can compute the entropy production as in Section 21.4:

$$\frac{\mathrm{d}}{\mathrm{d}\tau}\mathcal{S}[\rho](\tau) = \int \mathrm{d}\zeta\ \rho(\zeta,\tau)\mathbf{div}(\mathbf{v}(\zeta,\tau)) = -3N\gamma. \quad (21.26$$

Thus, we see that the entropy of the *system* decreases! This makes sense as we ar bleeding energy out of the system, and in the absence of entropy-producing randor collisions, all N particles will eventually reside in a state without kinetic energy an at the minimum of the potential $\mathcal{V}(\boldsymbol{\xi})$. That is a truly simple state to describe in on sentence, and so its complexity is very low; that is, it has low entropy.

Is this a violation of the second law of thermodynamics then, which states th entropy must always increase? No, because the friction term represents an interactio with an external environment (a heat bath) that is absorbing the energy and thu increasing its own entropy. The total entropy of both systems together (the system an its environment) should increase or remain the same, consistent with the second law.

21.5 The Fokker–Planck Equation as a Gradient Flow

Next, we derive the famous Fokker–Planck (FP) equation, also known as the drift diffusion or Smoluchowski equation. It is the equation that governs the dynamics c gases and fluids in the overdamped limit (Risken, 1996). We will derive the equation b finding the velocity field that results in the minimization of the free energy "as quickl as possible", which is called a gradient flow (Jordan et al., 1998). We will also directl relate this to a seminal result in mathematics derived by Benamou and Brenier th connects the FP equation to optimal transport theory (Benamou and Brenier, 2000).

First, let's define a functional $\mathcal{F}: \rho \mapsto \mathbb{R}$ that maps densities to a real number (fc example, the energy or the free energy). The one we will be most interested in is th free energy functional:

$$\mathcal{F}[\rho] = \int \mathrm{d}\zeta\ \rho(\zeta,\tau)\left(\mathcal{H}(\zeta,\tau) + T\log\rho(\zeta,\tau)\right) + \lambda\left(\int \mathrm{d}\zeta\ \rho(\zeta,\tau) - 1\right), \quad (21.2$$

with $\mathcal{H}$ a Hamiltonian function and the second term representing the entropy c the distribution ρ (we have set the Boltzmann constant $k_{\mathrm{B}} = 1$). The last term a Lagrange multiplier term that enforces the constraint that ρ must be normalize $\int \mathrm{d}\zeta\ \rho(\zeta,\tau) = 1$. We emphasize that this is only one possibility. In fact, classic density functional theory poses a much more general and complex term to replace th entropy term above (Evans, 1979; Dijkman et al., 2025).

Let's first take the functional derivative of $\mathcal{F}$ with respect to ρ to give

$$\frac{\delta\mathcal{F}}{\delta\rho(\zeta,\tau)} = \mathcal{H}(\zeta,\tau) + T\log\rho(\zeta,\tau) + T + \lambda. \quad (21.2$$

We immediately see that setting this derivative to zero and solving for ρ gives us th

Boltzmann distribution at time τ:

$$\rho^{\mathrm{eq}}(\zeta,\tau) = \frac{1}{Z}\exp(-\beta\mathcal{H}(\zeta,\tau)). \tag{21.29}$$

We emphasize that while this is the equilibrium distribution for each time τ, in general $\rho(\zeta,\tau)$ is not in equilibrium and therefore not equal to $\rho^{\mathrm{eq}}(\zeta,\tau)$ (hence the term non-equilibrium thermodynamics).

How does $\mathcal{F}$ change if we change the density $\rho(\zeta,\tau)$?

$$\begin{aligned}\partial_\tau\mathcal{F} &= \int \mathrm{d}\zeta\,\frac{\delta\mathcal{F}}{\delta\rho(\zeta,\tau)}\partial_\tau\rho(\zeta,\tau)\\ &= -\int \mathrm{d}\zeta\,\frac{\delta\mathcal{F}}{\delta\rho(\zeta,\tau)}\boldsymbol{\nabla}\cdot(\rho(\zeta,\tau)\mathbf{v}(\zeta,\tau))\\ &= \int \mathrm{d}\zeta\,\rho(\zeta,\tau)\boldsymbol{\nabla}\left(\frac{\delta\mathcal{F}}{\delta\rho(\zeta,\tau)}\right)\cdot\mathbf{v}(\zeta,\tau).\end{aligned} \tag{21.30}$$

Here we have integrated by parts and assumed that boundary terms vanish. So the change in $\mathcal{F}$ is proportional to the inner product of $\boldsymbol{\nabla}\left(\frac{\delta\mathcal{F}}{\delta\rho}\right)$ and $\mathbf{v}$. It becomes clear that the fastest way to descend on the free energy is to choose, at every time τ, the vector field $\mathbf{v}$ to be

$$\mathbf{v}(\zeta,\tau) \propto -\boldsymbol{\nabla}\left(\frac{\delta\mathcal{F}}{\delta\rho(\zeta,\tau)}\right). \tag{21.31}$$

With that choice, the FP equation is given by

$$\partial_\tau\rho(\zeta,\tau) = \gamma\boldsymbol{\nabla}\cdot\left(\rho(\zeta,\tau)\boldsymbol{\nabla}\left(\frac{\delta\mathcal{F}}{\delta\rho(\zeta,\tau)}\right)\right), \tag{21.32}$$

where the constant of proportionality γ is called the "mobility". We can absorb this constant by rescaling time (i.e., changing the mobility constant is equivalent to speeding up or slowing down time). For that reason, we will set $\gamma = 1$ in the following.

Note that under this choice, the change in $\mathcal{F}$ can also be computed and is always nonpositive:

$$\partial_\tau\mathcal{F} = -\int \mathrm{d}\zeta\,\rho(\zeta,\tau)\left\|\boldsymbol{\nabla}\left(\frac{\delta\mathcal{F}}{\delta\rho(\zeta,\tau)}\right)\right\|^2 \leq 0. \tag{21.33}$$

For the special case of (21.27), the continuity equation reduces to

$$\begin{aligned}\partial_\tau\rho(\zeta,\tau) &= \boldsymbol{\nabla}\cdot(\rho(\zeta,\tau)\,(\boldsymbol{\nabla}\mathcal{H}(\zeta,\tau) + T\boldsymbol{\nabla}\log\rho(\zeta,\tau)))\\ &= \boldsymbol{\nabla}\cdot(\rho(\zeta,\tau)\boldsymbol{\nabla}\mathcal{H}(\zeta,\tau)) + T\boldsymbol{\nabla}^2\rho(\zeta,\tau).\end{aligned} \tag{21.34}$$

The identification of the FP equation as a gradient flow provides a powerful framework for understanding the evolution of probability distributions in thermodynamic systems. In the next section, we will revisit the second law of thermodynamics in light of this formulation.

21.6 Generalized Fokker–Planck Equation

While the FP equation was derived in the previous section as the gradient flow of th free energy, this is not the most general FP equation that is guaranteed to minimize th free energy. For instance, we can replace the velocity with the following expressio and still guarantee a decrease of the free energy at every step:

$$\mathbf{v}' = \mathbf{M}\mathbf{v} = (\mathbf{D}+\mathbf{A})\mathbf{v}, \quad \mathbf{D}^\top = \mathbf{D}, \ \mathbf{A}^\top = -\mathbf{A}, \tag{21.35}$$

with $\mathbf{M}$ an arbitrary matrix which gets decomposed into a symmetric (diffusion) matri and an antisymmetric matrix $\mathbf{A}$. Because any psymmetric positive-semidefinite matri can be written as $\mathbf{D} = \mathbf{G}^\top\mathbf{G}$ and, for any antisymmetric matrix, we have $\mathrm{tr}(\mathbf{SA}) = 0$ where $\mathbf{S}$ is an arbitrary symmetric matrix and $\mathrm{tr}(\cdot)$ indicates the trace of a matrix, w have

$$\begin{aligned}
\partial_\tau \mathcal{F} &= \int \mathrm{d}\zeta\ \rho(\zeta,\tau)\boldsymbol{\nabla}\left(\frac{\delta\mathcal{F}}{\delta\rho(\zeta,\tau)}\right)\cdot\mathbf{v}(\zeta,\tau) \\
&= -\int \mathrm{d}\zeta\ \rho(\zeta,\tau)\boldsymbol{\nabla}^\top\left(\frac{\delta\mathcal{F}}{\delta\rho(\zeta,\tau)}\right)(\mathbf{D}+\mathbf{A})\boldsymbol{\nabla}\left(\frac{\delta\mathcal{F}}{\delta\rho(\zeta,\tau)}\right) \\
&= -\int \mathrm{d}\zeta\ \rho(\zeta,\tau)\left(\mathbf{G}\boldsymbol{\nabla}\left(\frac{\delta\mathcal{F}}{\delta\rho(\zeta,\tau)}\right)\right)^\top\left(\mathbf{G}\boldsymbol{\nabla}\left(\frac{\delta\mathcal{F}}{\delta\rho(\zeta,\tau)}\right)\right) \leq 0.
\end{aligned}\tag{21.36}$$

Let's now apply this more general form of the FP equation to the free energy a in (21.27). Starting from the continuity equation we find

$$\begin{aligned}
\partial_\tau\rho(\zeta,\tau) &= \boldsymbol{\nabla}\cdot\left(\rho(\zeta,\tau)(\mathbf{D}+\mathbf{A})\left(\boldsymbol{\nabla}\mathcal{H}(\zeta,\tau) + T\boldsymbol{\nabla}\log\rho(\zeta,\tau)\right)\right) \\
&= \boldsymbol{\nabla}\cdot\left(\rho(\zeta,\tau)(\mathbf{D}+\mathbf{A})\boldsymbol{\nabla}\mathcal{H}(\zeta,\tau)\right) + T\Delta_{\mathbf{D}}\rho(\zeta,\tau),
\end{aligned}\tag{21.37}$$

where $\Delta_{\mathbf{D}} = \boldsymbol{\nabla}^\top\mathbf{D}\boldsymbol{\nabla}$ is the generalized Laplacian operator.

Next, we choose to make an explicit choice for $\mathcal{H}$, $\mathbf{D}$, and $\mathbf{A}$:

$$\mathcal{H}(\zeta,\tau) = \frac{\eta^2}{2m} + \mathcal{V}(\xi,\tau), \tag{21.38}$$

$$\mathbf{A} = \mathbf{J} \equiv \begin{bmatrix} 0 & \mathbf{I} \\ -\mathbf{I} & 0 \end{bmatrix}, \tag{21.39}$$

$$\mathbf{D} = \begin{bmatrix} 0 & 0 \\ 0 & \gamma\mathbf{I} \end{bmatrix}, \tag{21.40}$$

which leads to the equation

$$\begin{aligned}
\partial_\tau\rho(\zeta,\tau) &= \frac{\gamma}{m}\boldsymbol{\nabla}_\eta\cdot(\rho(\zeta,\tau)\boldsymbol{\eta}) - \frac{\eta}{m}\cdot\boldsymbol{\nabla}_\xi\rho(\zeta,\tau) + \boldsymbol{\nabla}_\eta\cdot(\rho(\zeta,\tau)\boldsymbol{\nabla}_\xi\mathcal{V}(\xi,\tau)) \\
&\quad + \gamma T\boldsymbol{\nabla}_\eta^2\rho(\zeta,\tau).
\end{aligned}\tag{21.41}$$

This is the famous Klein–Kramers equation once we identify

$$T \to k_{\mathrm{B}}T, \tag{21.42}$$

$$\gamma = m\mu, \tag{21.43}$$

with k_{B} the Boltzmann constant and μ the friction or drag coefficient.

Other choices for $\mathbf{A}$ and $\mathbf{D}$ lead to different well-known approximations. For instance, setting $\mathbf{A} = 0$ and

$$\mathbf{D} = \begin{bmatrix} \alpha\mathbf{I} & 0 \\ 0 & 0 \end{bmatrix} \tag{21.44}$$

leads to the overdamped Langevin equation:

$$\partial_\tau \rho(\zeta, \tau) = \alpha \boldsymbol{\nabla}_\xi \cdot (\rho(\zeta, \tau)\boldsymbol{\nabla}_\xi \mathcal{V}(\xi, \tau)) + \alpha T \Delta_\xi \rho(\zeta, \tau). \tag{21.45}$$

We note that we have chosen $\mathbf{M} = \mathbf{D} + \mathbf{A}$ to be constant (independent of space and time). We can make both functions of space and time but that would create more terms in the FP equations, which we have avoided for the purpose of readability. But see, for example, Ma et al. (2015) for the more general construction.

21.7 Corresponding SDEs

Each FP equation corresponds to a stochastic differential equation that can be used to efficiently simulate $\rho(\zeta, \tau)$ by drawing samples. The most general SDE corresponding to the FP equation treated in the previous section is given by (without proof)

$$\mathrm{d}\zeta(\tau) = -\mathbf{M}\boldsymbol{\nabla}\mathcal{H}(\zeta, \tau)\,\mathrm{d}\tau + \mathrm{d}\varepsilon(\tau), \quad \mathrm{d}\varepsilon(\tau) \sim G(0, 2T\mathbf{D}\,\mathrm{d}\tau), \tag{21.46}$$

where $\mathrm{d}\varepsilon$ is sampled from a normal distribution with covariance equal to $\boldsymbol{\Sigma} = 2T\mathbf{D}\,\mathrm{d}\tau$.

For the Langevin case, this reduces to

$$\mathrm{d}\boldsymbol{\xi}(\tau) = \frac{\boldsymbol{\eta}}{m}\,\mathrm{d}\tau, \tag{21.47}$$

$$\mathrm{d}\boldsymbol{\eta}(\tau) = -(\boldsymbol{\nabla}_\xi \mathcal{V}(\xi, \tau) + \mu\boldsymbol{\eta})\,\mathrm{d}\tau + \sqrt{2\mu m k_B T}\,\mathrm{d}\varepsilon(\tau), \quad \mathrm{d}\varepsilon(\tau) \sim G(0, \mathrm{d}\tau). \tag{21.48}$$

Here, the first terms in both equations are the Hamiltonian equations of motion while the equation for the momentum also has a friction term and a noise term. The Hamiltonian equations correspond to the asymmetric part of the update and conserve energy. The friction and noise terms change energy, but keep each other in balance: the friction term transfers energy from the system to the bath, while the noise term transfers energy from the bath into the system.

Finally, for Brownian motion we have the simpler SDE

$$\mathrm{d}\boldsymbol{\xi}(\tau) = -\alpha\boldsymbol{\nabla}_\xi \mathcal{V}(\xi, \tau)\,\mathrm{d}\tau + \sqrt{2\alpha T}\,\mathrm{d}\varepsilon(\tau). \tag{21.49}$$

These SDEs have been employed to do MCMC sampling. To achieve that we need to choose $\beta\mathcal{V}(\boldsymbol{\xi}) = -\log p_{\text{target}}(\boldsymbol{\xi})$ (up to a constant), and possibly introduce auxiliary momentum variables to improve mixing efficiency.

21.8 The Second Law (Again)

With the choice of the velocity field as given in (21.31), we can now revisit th definitions of the heat generation rate, (21.15), and the entropy production rate, (21.18)

$$\partial_\tau \mathcal{Q}(\tau) = \int \mathrm{d}\zeta \; \rho(\zeta,\tau)\, \mathbf{v}(\zeta,\tau) \cdot \nabla \mathcal{H}(\zeta,\tau), \tag{21.50}$$

$$\partial_\tau \mathcal{S}(\tau) = -\int \mathrm{d}\zeta \; \rho(\zeta,\tau)\, \mathbf{v}(\zeta,\tau) \cdot \nabla \log \rho(\zeta,\tau), \tag{21.51}$$

$$\begin{aligned} \Rightarrow \; \partial_\tau \mathcal{Q}(\tau) - T\partial_\tau \mathcal{S}(\tau) &= \int \mathrm{d}\zeta \; \rho(\zeta,\tau)\, \mathbf{v}(\zeta,\tau) \cdot \left(\nabla \mathcal{H}(\zeta,\tau) + T\nabla \log \rho(\zeta,\tau)\right) \\ &= -\int \mathrm{d}\zeta \; \rho(\zeta,\tau)\, \|\nabla \mathcal{H}(\zeta,\tau) + T\nabla \log \rho(\zeta,\tau)\|_{\mathbf{D}}^2 \\ &\le 0, \end{aligned} \tag{21.52}$$

where $\|\mathbf{v}\|_{\mathbf{D}}^2 \equiv \mathbf{v}^\top \mathbf{D} \mathbf{v}$. We conclude that the second law is once again obeyed if w assume that the heat bath is at a constant temperature and in equilibrium, which lead to $T\partial_\tau \mathcal{S}_{\text{bath}}(\tau) = -\partial_\tau \mathcal{Q}(\tau)$ and thus

$$T\partial_\tau \Sigma(\tau) = T\partial_\tau \mathcal{S}(\tau) + T\partial_\tau \mathcal{S}_{\text{bath}}(\tau) = T\partial_\tau \mathcal{S}(\tau) - \partial_\tau \mathcal{Q}(\tau) \ge 0, \tag{21.53}$$

where $\Sigma(\tau)$ is the total entropy production of the system and its environment up t time τ.

We can relate the entropy production to the change in the KL divergence betwee the current density and the equilibrium density. Recall that the Fokker–Planck equatio with a time-independent drift and diffusion is given by

$$\partial_\tau \rho(\zeta,\tau) = -\nabla \cdot \left(\rho(\zeta,\tau)\mathbf{v}(\zeta,\tau)\right), \tag{21.54}$$

$$\mathbf{v}(\zeta,\tau) = -\mathbf{M}\nabla\left[\mathcal{H}(\zeta) + T\log \rho(\zeta,\tau)\right]. \tag{21.55}$$

The equilibrium distribution $\rho^{\text{eq}}(\zeta)$ satisfies $\nabla\left[\mathcal{H}(\zeta) + T\log \rho^{\text{eq}}(\zeta)\right] = 0$, whic leads to the canonical distribution:

$$\rho^{\text{eq}}(\zeta) = \frac{\exp[-\beta\mathcal{H}(\zeta)]}{Z}, \quad Z = \int \mathrm{d}\zeta' \exp[-\beta\mathcal{H}(\zeta')]. \tag{21.56}$$

We can now express the entropy production rate $\sigma(\tau) = \partial_\tau \Sigma(\tau)$ in terms of the tim derivative of the KL divergence between $\rho(\zeta,\tau)$ and $\rho^{\text{eq}}(\zeta)$:

$$\begin{aligned} \partial_\tau D_{\text{KL}}\left[\rho(\tau)\|\rho^{\text{eq}}\right] &= \int \mathrm{d}\zeta \; \left(\partial_\tau \rho(\zeta,\tau)\right) \log \frac{\rho(\zeta,\tau)}{\rho^{\text{eq}}(\zeta)} - \partial_\tau \int \mathrm{d}\zeta \; \rho^{\text{eq}}(\zeta) \\ &= -\int \mathrm{d}\zeta \; \nabla \cdot \left(\rho(\zeta,\tau)\mathbf{v}(\zeta,\tau)\right) \log \frac{\rho(\zeta,\tau)}{\rho^{\text{eq}}(\zeta)} \\ &= \int \mathrm{d}\zeta \; \rho(\zeta,\tau)\mathbf{v}(\zeta,\tau) \cdot \nabla \log \frac{\rho(\zeta,\tau)}{\rho^{\text{eq}}(\zeta)}. \end{aligned} \tag{21.57}$$

Recalling that $\log \frac{\rho(\zeta,\tau)}{\rho^{\text{eq}}(\zeta)} = \log \rho(\zeta,\tau) + \beta\mathcal{H}(\zeta) + \log Z$, and noting that $\nabla \log \rho^{\text{eq}}(\zeta)$

$-\beta\nabla\mathcal{H}(\zeta)$, we obtain

$$\begin{aligned}\partial_\tau D_{\mathrm{KL}}\left[\rho(\tau)\|\rho^{\mathrm{eq}}\right] &= \int \mathrm{d}\zeta\, \rho(\zeta,\tau)\mathbf{v}(\zeta,\tau)\cdot(\nabla\log\rho(\zeta,\tau)+\beta\nabla\mathcal{H}(\zeta)) \\ &= -\beta\int \mathrm{d}\zeta\, \rho(\zeta,\tau)\left\|\nabla\mathcal{H}(\zeta)+T\nabla\log\rho(\zeta,\tau)\right\|_{\mathbf{D}}^2 \\ &= -\partial_\tau\Sigma(\tau). \end{aligned} \tag{21.58}$$

Therefore, the entropy production rate is related to the decrease of the KL divergence:

$$\sigma(\tau) = -\partial_\tau D_{\mathrm{KL}}\left[\rho(\tau)\|\rho^{\mathrm{eq}}\right] \geq 0. \tag{21.59}$$

This shows that the KL divergence between $\rho(\tau)$ and ρ^{eq} decreases over time, which is consistent with the second law of thermodynamics.

21.9 Free Energy Change and Excess Work

Combining the results from the previous sections, we derive

$$\begin{aligned}\partial_\tau\mathcal{F}(\tau) &= \partial_\tau\mathcal{U}(\tau) - T\partial_\tau\mathcal{S}(\tau) \\ &= \partial_\tau\mathcal{W}(\tau) + \partial_\tau\mathcal{Q}(\tau) - T\partial_\tau\mathcal{S}(\tau) \\ &= \partial_\tau\mathcal{W}(\tau) - T\partial_\tau\Sigma(\tau), \end{aligned} \tag{21.60}$$

where $\partial_\tau\mathcal{W}(\tau)$ is the rate of work done on the system, and $\partial_\tau\Sigma(\tau)$ represents the total entropy production rate. From the above equations, we identify the rate at which work is dissipated:

$$\partial_\tau\mathcal{W}_{\mathrm{diss}}(\tau) \equiv \partial_\tau\mathcal{W}(\tau) - \partial_\tau\mathcal{F}(\tau) = T\partial_\tau\Sigma(\tau) \geq 0, \tag{21.61}$$

which is equal to the total entropy production rate (multiplied by T).

Integrating over time from $\tau = 0$ to $\tau = \tau_f$ gives the total dissipated work:

$$\begin{aligned}\mathcal{W}_{\mathrm{diss}} &\equiv \mathcal{W} - \Delta\mathcal{F} = T\Sigma \\ &= \int_0^{\tau_f}\mathrm{d}\tau \int \mathrm{d}\zeta\, \rho(\zeta,\tau)\left\|\nabla\mathcal{H}(\zeta,\tau)+T\nabla\log\rho(\zeta,\tau)\right\|_{\mathbf{D}}^2 \geq 0, \end{aligned} \tag{21.62}$$

where we note that quantities $\mathcal{W}_{\mathrm{diss}}$, $\mathcal{W}$, and Σ are path-dependent, while $\Delta\mathcal{F} = \mathcal{F}_{\tau_f} - \mathcal{F}_0$ is a state function and thus independent of the chosen path.

We are often interested in quantifying the total amount of dissipated work between $\tau = 0$ and $\tau = \infty$, when the system is completely equilibrated. We call this the *excess work*, $\mathcal{W}_{\mathrm{exc}}$. We assume that we can control the system until $\tau = \tau_f$, after which it equilibrates without any external influences:

$$\mathcal{H}(\zeta,\tau) = \mathcal{H}_\infty(\zeta) + \mathcal{H}_\lambda(\zeta;\lambda(\tau)), \quad \tau\in[0,\tau_f), \tag{21.63}$$

$$\mathcal{H}(\zeta,\tau) = \mathcal{H}_\infty(\zeta), \quad \tau\in[\tau_f,\infty). \tag{21.64}$$

This means that (21.62) still holds, but now with the integration from $\tau = 0$ to ∞ an using the Hamiltonian defined above. We can also rewrite this as follows:

$$\mathcal{W}_{\text{exc}} = \mathcal{W}_{\text{diss}} - (\mathcal{F}_\infty - \mathcal{F}_{\tau_f}), \tag{21.65}$$

where we have identified that in the last part for $\tau \geq \tau_f$, the work $\mathcal{W} = 0$ becaus $\partial_\tau \mathcal{H}_\infty(\zeta) = 0$. We also note that $\mathcal{F}_\infty = F_\infty = -T \log Z_\infty$. Moreover,

$$TD_{\text{KL}}[\rho_{\tau_f} \| \rho_\infty] = -TS[\rho_{\tau_f}] + \mathbb{E}_{\rho_{\tau_f}}[\mathcal{H}_\infty] + T \log Z_\infty = \mathcal{F}_{\tau_f} - \mathcal{F}_\infty. \tag{21.66}$$

Taking these together, we find the following useful identity:

$$\begin{aligned} \mathcal{W}_{\text{exc}} &= \int_0^{\tau_f} \mathrm{d}\tau \int \mathrm{d}\zeta\, \rho(\zeta, \tau) \|\nabla \mathcal{H}(\zeta, \tau) + T \nabla \log \rho(\zeta, \tau)\|_{\mathbf{D}}^2 + TD_{\text{KL}}[\rho_{\tau_f} \| \rho_\infty] \\ &\geq 0. \end{aligned} \tag{21.67}$$

The above equation is valid for any controlled Hamiltonian $\mathcal{H}_\lambda$. We can now ask th important question: What is the optimal control sequence, $\lambda(\tau)$, that minimizes th total dissipated energy (or $\mathcal{W}_{\text{exc}}$) if we are given a time τ_f to control the system an we start from a distribution ρ_0 and wish to arrive at a distribution ρ_∞? We will "solve this in the next chapter.

22 Optimal Transport and Schrödinger Bridge

22.1 Introduction

In this chapter we will switch notation from phase space to configuration space., $\zeta \to \xi$, and from a full Hamiltonian to a potential function, $\mathcal{H} \to \mathcal{V}$. This corresponds to working in the overdamped (Brownian motion) limit of thermodynamics, which we introduced at the end of Chapter 21. The reason for this simplification is twofold: first, some results are not known or much more difficult to derive in full phase space; second, this configuration space formulation provides a natural bridge to machine learning applications, where we typically work with distributions over observable variables rather than full phase space trajectories.

In this chapter we look more closely at optimal transport and Wasserstein distances and how they relate to the minimal (excess) work needed to change one distribution to another. We study counterdiabatic driving, which is a form of optimal control for minimizing the work needed for transporting a distribution, of which the optimal transport solution is one example. We revisit Schrödinger bridges, optimal control, and diffusion models in this new language of Fokker–Planck equations. In passing we explain the JKO scheme for numerically solving FP equations, and look at more general actions for deriving differential equations relevant to physics.

22.2 Optimal Transport and Wasserstein Distances

In a cornerstone paper, Benamou and Brenier reformulated the optimal transport problem as a Lagrange problem and related it to fluid dynamics (Benamou and Brenier, 2000). We will first formulate the standard OT problem due to Monge (see Figure 22.1).

We assume that we have a map f that transports probability mass: $\xi' = f(\xi)$. We define the cost of moving probability mass by

$$C[f,\rho_0,\rho_{\tau_f}] = \int d\xi\ \rho_0(\xi)c(\xi, f(\xi)), \quad \text{s.t. } \rho_{\tau_f} = f_\#[\rho_0], \tag{22.1}$$

where $c(\xi,\xi')$ is a cost function measuring the "effort" required to move mass from ξ to ξ', and $f_\#[\rho_0]$ denotes the pushforward measure of ρ_0 under the map f. The

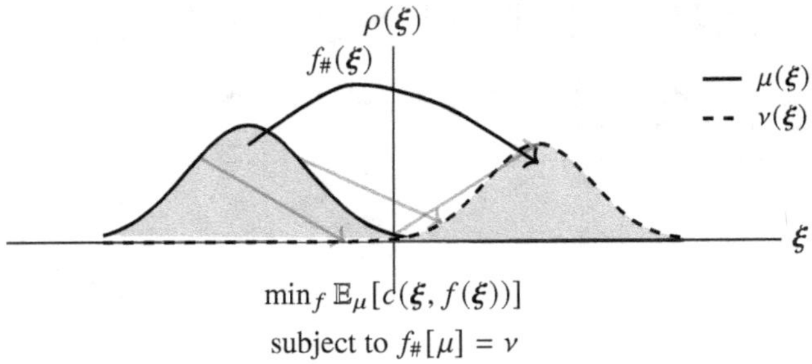

Figure 22.1 Monge formulation of optimal transport showing the transformation of source distribution $\mu(\xi)$ (left peak) to target distribution $\nu(\xi)$ (right peak) through the optimal transport map $f_\#(\xi)$ (solid curve with arrow connecting the peaks). The faint arrows indicate mass flow from source to target positions. The pushforward measure constraint $f_\#[\mu] = \nu$ ensures mass conservation.

pushforward measure is defined by

$$\rho_{\tau_f}(\xi') = \int \mathrm{d}\xi\, \delta(\xi' - f(\xi))\, \rho_0(\xi). \qquad (22.2$$

In other words, the map f is required to transform ρ_0 to ρ_{τ_f}. The cost of the trans formation is given by $c(\xi, \xi')$, where $\xi' = f(\xi)$ in our case. In the following, we wi restrict our attention to the 2-Wasserstein distance, which uses the L_2 distance for Given this cost, we can now ask ourselves which map f among all maps that fulfill th constraint of moving between ρ_0 and ρ_{τ_f}, minimizes this cost. And we can call th cost the distance between the distributions ρ_0 and ρ_{τ_f} by taking the infimum over a possible maps f:

$$W_2[\rho_0, \rho_{\tau_f}] = \left(\inf_{f:\, f_\#[\rho_0] = \rho_{\tau_f}} \int \|\xi - f(\xi)\|^2 \rho_0(\xi)\, \mathrm{d}\xi \right)^{1/2}. \qquad (22.3$$

In the Monge formulation, there may not exist a map that satisfies the constrain (e.g., when mass has to split). However, Kantorovich's relaxation of the proble guarantees the existence of a solution by considering probability measures on th product space:

$$\mathcal{D}_{\mathrm{MK}}[\rho_0, \rho_{\tau_f}] = \inf_{\gamma \in \Gamma(\rho_0, \rho_{\tau_f})} \int \mathrm{d}\xi_0\, \mathrm{d}\xi_{\tau_f}\, \gamma(\xi_0, \xi_{\tau_f})\, c(\xi_0, \xi_{\tau_f}), \qquad (22.4$$

where we average over joint distributions $\gamma(\xi_0, \xi_{\tau_f})$ such that this joint has the pr scribed marginals ρ_0 and ρ_{τ_f}.

The formulation that Benamou and Brenier proposed, which they proved to be equi alent to the Kantorovich OT formulation, is to introduce a Markov process betwee ρ_0 and ρ_{τ_f}, described in the continuum limit by a continuity equation with a veloci field $\mathbf{v}$. Our task is to find the densities and velocity fields over time that satisfy th continuity equation and the constraints on ρ_0 and ρ_{τ_f}, minimizing the total expecte kinetic energy (or control cost)[1]:

$$\mathcal{D}_{\mathrm{OT}}[\rho_0, \rho_{\tau_f}] = \inf_{\rho, \mathbf{v}} \tau_f \int_0^{\tau_f} \mathrm{d}\tau \int \mathrm{d}\xi \, \rho(\xi, \tau) \|\mathbf{v}(\xi, \tau)\|^2, \tag{22.5}$$

$$\text{s.t. } \partial_\tau \rho(\xi, \tau) = -\mathbf{div}(\rho(\xi, \tau)\mathbf{v}(\xi, \tau)), \tag{22.6}$$

$$\text{s.t. } \rho(\xi, 0) = \rho_0, \quad \rho(\xi, \tau_f) = \rho_{\tau_f}. \tag{22.7}$$

We first observe that the continuity equation guarantees that a properly normalized and non-negative density at $\tau = 0$ will remain normalized and non-negative at all $\tau > 0$, so we do not have to add that as a separate constraint. We can now formulate a Lagrangian that adds the continuity equation as a constraint to the objective (we use $2\phi(\xi, \tau)$ instead of $\phi(\xi, \tau)$ as a Lagrange multiplier for later convenience). To keep the equations manageable, we will omit the constraints that impose the boundary conditions at $\tau = 0$ and $\tau = \tau_f$ from the following derivation:

$$\begin{aligned}
\mathcal{L}_{\mathrm{BB}}[\rho, \mathbf{v}, \phi] &= \inf_{\rho, \mathbf{v}} \sup_{\phi} \tau_f \int_0^{\tau_f} \mathrm{d}\tau \int \mathrm{d}\xi \Big[\rho(\xi, \tau)\|\mathbf{v}(\xi, \tau)\|^2 \\
&\quad + 2\phi(\xi, \tau)\left(\partial_\tau \rho(\xi, \tau) + \mathbf{div}(\rho(\xi, \tau)\mathbf{v}(\xi, \tau))\right)\Big] \\
&= \inf_{\rho, \mathbf{v}} \sup_{\phi} \tau_f \int_0^{\tau_f} \mathrm{d}\tau \int \mathrm{d}\xi \Big[\rho(\xi, \tau)\|\mathbf{v}(\xi, \tau)\|^2 - 2\rho(\xi, \tau)\partial_\tau \phi(\xi, \tau) \\
&\quad - 2\rho(\xi, \tau)\mathbf{v}(\xi, \tau) \cdot \nabla\phi(\xi, \tau)\Big] \\
&\quad + \int \mathrm{d}\xi \, 2\rho(\xi, \tau_f)\phi(\xi, \tau_f) - 2\rho(\xi, 0)\phi(\xi, 0).
\end{aligned} \tag{22.8}$$

Here we have integrated by parts and rearranged terms. We now demand stationarity of the Lagrangian under variations of $\mathbf{v}$ and ρ, subject to boundary conditions:

$$\begin{aligned}
\frac{\delta}{\delta \mathbf{v}(\xi, \tau)} \mathcal{L}_{\mathrm{BB}} &= 2\rho(\xi, \tau)\mathbf{v}(\xi, \tau) - 2\rho(\xi, \tau)\nabla\phi(\xi, \tau) = 0 \\
&\Rightarrow \ \mathbf{v}(\xi, \tau) = \nabla\phi(\xi, \tau), \ \text{ if } \ \rho(\xi, \tau) > 0,
\end{aligned} \tag{22.9}$$

$$\begin{aligned}
\frac{\delta}{\delta \rho(\xi, \tau)} \mathcal{L}_{\mathrm{BB}} &= \|\mathbf{v}(\xi, \tau)\|^2 - 2\partial_\tau \phi(\xi, \tau) - 2\mathbf{v}(\xi, \tau) \cdot \nabla\phi(\xi, \tau) \\
&= -\|\nabla\phi(\xi, \tau)\|^2 - 2\partial_\tau \phi(\xi, \tau) = 0 \\
&\Rightarrow \ \partial_\tau \phi(\xi, \tau) = -\frac{1}{2}\|\nabla\phi(\xi, \tau)\|^2.
\end{aligned} \tag{22.10}$$

By inserting these equations into the Lagrangian, we obtain the dual Lagrangian:

$$\mathcal{D}[\phi, \rho_0, \rho_{\tau_f}] = 2\int \mathrm{d}\xi \, \rho_{\tau_f}(\xi)\phi(\xi, \tau_f) - 2\int \mathrm{d}\xi \, \rho_0(\xi)\phi(\xi, 0). \tag{22.11}$$

The dual optimization problem maximizes this objective subject to the Hamilton–Jacobi–Bellman (HJB) equation, (22.10).

[1] One can also define the same distance in a more standardized form by transforming $s = \tau/\tau_f$. Acknowledging that the measure transforms as $\mathrm{d}\tau = \tau_f \, \mathrm{d}s$, and that $\mathbf{v}(\xi, \tau) = \tau_f{}^{-1}\mathbf{v}'(\xi, s)$, we can transform $\tau_f \int_0^{\tau_f} \mathrm{d}\tau \int \mathrm{d}\xi \, \rho(\xi, \tau)\|\mathbf{v}(\xi, \tau)\|^2 \to \int_0^1 \mathrm{d}s \int \mathrm{d}\xi \, \rho(\xi, s)\|\mathbf{v}'(\xi, s)\|^2$.

It is instructive to verify how the individual paths of a solution to the OT problem behave. Paths follow the ordinary differential equation

$$\frac{\mathrm{d}}{\mathrm{d}\tau}\boldsymbol{\xi}(\tau) = \mathbf{v}(\boldsymbol{\xi}(\tau), \tau) = \boldsymbol{\nabla}\phi(\boldsymbol{\xi}(\tau), \tau), \tag{22.12}$$

which implies that the acceleration is given by

$$\begin{aligned}\frac{\mathrm{d}^2}{\mathrm{d}\tau^2}\boldsymbol{\xi}(\tau) &= \frac{\mathrm{d}}{\mathrm{d}\tau}\mathbf{v}(\boldsymbol{\xi}(\tau), \tau) = \partial_\tau \mathbf{v}(\boldsymbol{\xi}(\tau), \tau) + (\mathbf{v}(\boldsymbol{\xi}(\tau), \tau) \cdot \boldsymbol{\nabla})\, \mathbf{v}(\boldsymbol{\xi}(\tau), \tau) \\ &= \boldsymbol{\nabla}\left(\partial_\tau \phi(\boldsymbol{\xi}(\tau), \tau) + \frac{1}{2}\|\boldsymbol{\nabla}\phi(\boldsymbol{\xi}(\tau), \tau)\|^2\right) = 0,\end{aligned} \tag{22.13}$$

where we used the (22.10) in the last equality. This shows that particles following the OT solution move along straight lines with constant velocity. This deterministic straight-line structure will be significant when we talk, in Chapter 23, about a specific instance of a machine-learning model called OT flow matching.

The Wasserstein distance W_2 is a proper distance measure on the space of sufficiently well-behaved probability distributions. The path in probability space $\rho(\boldsymbol{\xi}, \tau)$ that represents the OT solution is the shortest path (geodesic) in the Wasserstein metric between two distributions. The Wasserstein distance also satisfies the triangle inequality:

$$W_2[\rho_1, \rho_3] \leq W_2[\rho_1, \rho_2] + W_2[\rho_2, \rho_3]. \tag{22.14}$$

Moreover, the OT problem is a convex optimization problem, and therefore the dual problem is equivalent to the primal problem with no duality gap.

22.3 Minimal Dissipated Work

The Benamou–Brenier formulation (Benamou and Brenier, 2000) of optimal transport leads to a natural connection with the concept of minimal dissipated work in stochastic thermodynamics. Recall from (21.62) in Chapter 21 that the total dissipated work between time 0 and τ_f is given by

$$\mathcal{W}_{\text{diss}} = \int_0^{\tau_f} \mathrm{d}\tau \int \mathrm{d}\boldsymbol{\xi}\, \rho(\boldsymbol{\xi}, \tau)\, \|\boldsymbol{\nabla}\mathcal{V}(\boldsymbol{\xi}, \tau) + T\boldsymbol{\nabla}\log\rho(\boldsymbol{\xi}, \tau)\|^2. \tag{22.15}$$

By comparing this with the Benamou–Brenier formulation of optimal transport, (22.5) we observe that by identifying

$$\begin{aligned}\phi(\boldsymbol{\xi}, \tau) &= -\mathcal{V}(\boldsymbol{\xi}, \tau) - T\log\rho(\boldsymbol{\xi}, \tau) \\ &= -\mathcal{V}_\infty(\boldsymbol{\xi}) - \mathcal{V}_\lambda(\boldsymbol{\xi}; \lambda(\tau)) - T\log\rho(\boldsymbol{\xi}, \tau),\end{aligned} \tag{22.16}$$

where $\lambda(\tau)$ is the time-dependent control parameter introduced in (21.67)), minimizing $\mathcal{W}_{\text{diss}}$ precisely maps to the OT problem. In fact, if we assume that $\mathcal{V}_\lambda$ is powerful enough to transform ρ_0 to ρ_{τ_f} in a finite time τ_f, then, if we respect the corre- dynamical equation, the minimal possible dissipated work is given by the pair $\rho^*(\boldsymbol{\xi}, \tau$

and $\phi^*(\xi,\tau)$ that solve the OT problem. To find the actual control Hamiltonian, we solve

$$\mathcal{V}_{\lambda^*}(\xi,\tau) = -\phi^*(\xi,\tau) - \mathcal{V}_\infty(\xi) - T\log\rho^*(\xi,\tau). \tag{22.17}$$

To interpret this, we note that this means that the control λ^* needs to first cancel the terms $\mathcal{V}_\infty$ and $T\log\rho^*$ and then add back the optimal potential ϕ^*. Canceling the osmotic force term $T\log\rho^*$ effectively denoises (or antidiffuses) the flow. This makes sense because diffusion is the main culprit for irreversible dynamics and heat generation. To corroborate this interpretation, recall from the previous section that particles that solve the OT problem move deterministically along straight lines and have thus denoised their intrinsically noisy trajectories (see Figure 22.2).

Thus, to denoise the flow, work must be performed on the system, generating its own heat. As such, if we want to transform the distribution from ρ_0 to ρ_{τ_f} in finite time, there is an absolute minimum to the entropy production given by the Wasserstein distance between the two distributions (Aurell et al., 2012; Dechant and Sakurai, 2019; Nakazato and Ito, 2021):

$$\Sigma_{\tau_f} \geq \frac{W_2^2[\rho_0,\rho_{\tau_f}]}{T\tau_f}. \tag{22.18}$$

This inequality can be interpreted as a thermodynamic speed limit (Aurell et al., 2012), stating that, given a budget on entropy production, a minimal amount of time is required to move ρ_0 to ρ_{τ_f}:

$$\tau_f \geq \frac{W_2^2[\rho_0,\rho_{\tau_f}]}{T\Sigma_{\tau_f}}. \tag{22.19}$$

This bound is tight and can be saturated for any choice of initial and final distributions (Aurell et al., 2012; Nakazato and Ito, 2021). In addition, this principle can be applied to derive a finite-time correction to the Landauer bound of information erasure (Landauer, 1961; Proesmans et al., 2020), which bounds the thermodynamic cost of erasing one bit of classical information under a finite time process.

So far, we have assumed that our controller is powerful enough to reach the target distribution. However, this is not always the case. Suppose the distribution reaches ρ_{τ_f} after time τ_f, but it naturally tends to relax towards ρ_∞. From the decomposition of the potential, it is clear that the only thing we have to do is wait until the system has relaxed to equilibrium. If we want to minimize the amount of dissipated work over the entire trajectory, both controlled ($\tau \in [0,\tau_f]$) and uncontrolled ($\tau > \tau_f$), then we recall that the expression is given by the excess work – see (21.67) – and now we want to minimize its value over all distributions ρ_{τ_f}:

$$\mathcal{W}_{\text{exc}} \geq \inf_{\rho_{\tau_f}}\left(\frac{W_2^2[\rho_0,\rho_{\tau_f}]}{\tau_f} + TD_{\text{KL}}[\rho_{\tau_f}\|\rho_\infty]\right). \tag{22.20}$$

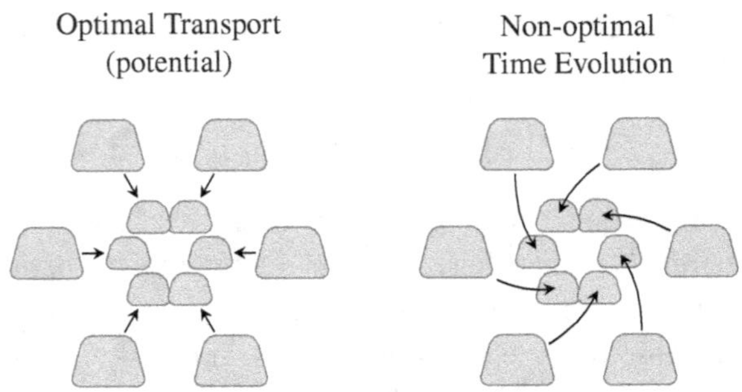

Figure 22.2 Comparison of optimal and nonoptimal transport. Left: Optimal transport (gradient flow) moves mass along direct radial paths (straight arrows) from outer trapezoids tc inner trapezoids, minimizing dissipation. Right: Nonoptimal time evolution follows curved paths (bent arrows) that result in higher dissipation. The trapezoid shapes represent probabilit mass at outer (source) and inner (target) positions.

22.4 Counterdiabatic Driving

In the previous section, we solved for both the density flow $\rho^*(\boldsymbol{\xi}, \tau)$ and the veloc ity/control vector $\mathbf{v}^*(\boldsymbol{\xi}, \tau)$ to minimize the total entropy production. We found th the control potential needed to cancel the flow due to the natural potential and th diffusion. In this section, we will discuss a related method, called *counterdiabati driving*, where we choose the sequence of densities $\rho^\#(\boldsymbol{\xi}, \tau)$ ourselves and solve fc the control potential that makes the system follow this prescribed path. Each densit is parameterized by a potential through the Boltzmann distribution (which is alway possible):

$$\rho^\#(\boldsymbol{\xi}, \tau) = \frac{1}{Z^\#_\tau} \exp(-\beta \mathcal{V}_\#(\boldsymbol{\xi}, \tau)). \tag{22.21}$$

We assume that the system is evolving according to the sum of the natural and th controlled potential,

$$\partial_\tau \rho(\boldsymbol{\xi}, \tau) = \mathbf{div}\,(\rho(\boldsymbol{\xi}, \tau)\,(\boldsymbol{\nabla}\mathcal{V}_\infty(\boldsymbol{\xi}) + \boldsymbol{\nabla}\mathcal{V}_\lambda(\boldsymbol{\xi}, \tau))) + T\boldsymbol{\nabla}^2\rho(\boldsymbol{\xi}, \tau), \tag{22.22}$$

and we demand that $\rho = \rho^\#$. This leads to

$$\begin{aligned}\beta\partial_\tau F_\#(\tau) &= \beta\partial_\tau \mathcal{V}_\#(\boldsymbol{\xi}, \tau) - \boldsymbol{\nabla}\mathcal{V}_\#(\boldsymbol{\xi}, \tau) \cdot (\boldsymbol{\nabla}\mathcal{V}_\infty(\boldsymbol{\xi}) + \boldsymbol{\nabla}\mathcal{V}_\lambda(\boldsymbol{\xi}, \tau) - \boldsymbol{\nabla}\mathcal{V}_\#(\boldsymbol{\xi}, \tau)) \\ &\quad + \boldsymbol{\nabla}^2\mathcal{V}_\infty(\boldsymbol{\xi}) + \boldsymbol{\nabla}^2\mathcal{V}_\lambda(\boldsymbol{\xi}, \tau) - \boldsymbol{\nabla}^2\mathcal{V}_\#(\boldsymbol{\xi}, \tau) \\ &= \beta\partial_\tau \mathcal{V}_\#(\boldsymbol{\xi}, \tau) - \boldsymbol{\nabla}\mathcal{V}_\#(\boldsymbol{\xi}, \tau) \cdot \boldsymbol{\nabla}\phi(\boldsymbol{\xi}, \tau) + \boldsymbol{\nabla}^2\phi(\boldsymbol{\xi}, \tau),\end{aligned} \tag{22.23}$$

where we recall that $F_\# = -T \log Z_\#$ and we have defined $\phi(\boldsymbol{\xi}, \tau) = \mathcal{V}_\infty(\boldsymbol{\xi}) + \mathcal{V}_\lambda(\boldsymbol{\xi}, \tau)$ $\mathcal{V}_\#(\boldsymbol{\xi}, \tau)$. If we solve the above equation for ϕ, we can then extract the control potenti from the relation

$$\mathcal{V}_{\lambda^*}(\boldsymbol{\xi}, \tau) = \phi^*(\boldsymbol{\xi}, \tau) - \mathcal{V}_\infty(\boldsymbol{\xi}) + \mathcal{V}_\#(\boldsymbol{\xi}, \tau). \tag{22.24}$$

This is clearly very similar in spirit to the reasoning we had in the previous sectio However, instead of solving the OT problem for both ϕ and ρ, we have fixed th density path $\rho^{\#}$ here and only solve for ϕ. However, solving (22.23) seems harder than solving the OT problem, since we do not have an expression for $F_{\#}(\tau)$ which is hard to compute.

However, from (22.23) it becomes clear that once we do have an expression for ϕ (e.g., by solving the OT problem, which also then determines $\mathcal{V}_{\#}$), we have a new way to compute free energy differences. Making sure that $\mathcal{V}_{\#}$ such that $\mathcal{V}_{\#}(\boldsymbol{\xi}, 0)$ and $\mathcal{V}_{\#}(\boldsymbol{\xi}, \tau_f)$ correspond to the desired initial and final Boltzmann distributions, we can compute,

$$\Delta F_{\#} = \int_0^{\tau_f} \mathrm{d}\tau \, \Big(\partial_\tau \mathcal{V}_{\#}(\boldsymbol{\xi}, \tau) - \boldsymbol{\nabla}\mathcal{V}_{\#}(\boldsymbol{\xi}, \tau) \cdot \boldsymbol{\nabla}\phi(\boldsymbol{\xi}, \tau) + T\boldsymbol{\nabla}^2\phi(\boldsymbol{\xi}, \tau)\Big). \tag{22.25}$$

This is a rather special result because the left-hand side does not depend on $\boldsymbol{\xi}$, while the right-hand side does! This means that the equation holds for every value of $\boldsymbol{\xi}$, and indeed for every trajectory $\boldsymbol{\xi}(\tau) = \psi(\boldsymbol{\xi}_0, \tau)$. To see this, we can write

$$\begin{aligned}
&\int_0^{\tau_f} \mathrm{d}\tau \int \mathrm{d}\boldsymbol{\xi}_0 \, \rho(\boldsymbol{\xi}_0)\big(\partial_\tau \mathcal{V}_{\#}(\psi(\boldsymbol{\xi}_0, \tau), \tau) - \boldsymbol{\nabla}\mathcal{V}_{\#}(\psi(\boldsymbol{\xi}_0, \tau), \tau) \cdot \boldsymbol{\nabla}\phi(\psi(\boldsymbol{\xi}_0, \tau), \tau) \\
&\qquad + T\boldsymbol{\nabla}^2\phi(\psi(\boldsymbol{\xi}_0, \tau), \tau)\big) \\
&= \int_0^{\tau_f} \mathrm{d}\tau \int \mathrm{d}\boldsymbol{\xi} \, \rho(\boldsymbol{\xi}, \tau)\big(\partial_\tau \mathcal{V}_{\#}(\boldsymbol{\xi}, \tau) - \boldsymbol{\nabla}\mathcal{V}_{\#}(\boldsymbol{\xi}, \tau) \cdot \boldsymbol{\nabla}\phi(\boldsymbol{\xi}, \tau) + T\boldsymbol{\nabla}^2\phi(\boldsymbol{\xi}, \tau)\big) \\
&= \int_0^{\tau_f} \mathrm{d}\tau \int \mathrm{d}\boldsymbol{\xi} \, \rho(\boldsymbol{\xi}, \tau)\partial_\tau F_{\#}(\tau) \\
&= \int_0^{\tau_f} \mathrm{d}\tau \, \partial_\tau F_{\#}(\tau) \\
&= \Delta F_{\#},
\end{aligned} \tag{22.26}$$

where in the first line we write the Lagrangian expression for integrating the expression in brackets over paths, in the second line we switch to the Eulerian view, and in the third line we use (22.25). The result in (22.26) holds for any arbitrary initial ρ_0 and trajectory $\psi(\boldsymbol{\xi}_0, \tau)$, which therefore means that the result holds for any path or distribution over paths. This, in turn, means that any fluctuations due to randomness from sampling paths are nullified, and as such, the estimator for $\Delta F_{\#}$ has zero variance.

Moreover, because $\mathcal{V}_{\#}$ is invariant under time reversal and ϕ flips sign under time reversal (since its gradient is a velocity), the integrand also flips sign under time reversal. This has led to the definition of the right-hand side as a new expression for work, from which new fluctuation theorems and thus new ways to estimate free energy differences through Jarzynski-type equations can be derived (Zhong et al., 2024; Vargas et al., 2024).

22.5 The Jordan–Kinderlehrer–Otto Scheme

In Section 21.5 we saw that the Fokker–Planck equation can be derived as the negative gradient of the functional derivative of the free energy, representing a gradient flow of the free energy. Intuitively, this means that we are performing gradient descent in the space of probability distributions with respect to the free energy. In that derivation, w assumed the continuity equation to hold for some velocity field. In this section, we g one level deeper and derive the result that the FP equation is a gradient flow of the fre energy functional by assuming only that distances between probability measures ar measured by the Wasserstein metric on the space of probability densities. The resultin algorithm numerically "solves" the FP equation by discretizing time and is called th Jordan–Kinderlehrer–Otto (JKO) scheme (Jordan et al., 1998). It is an instance of proximal gradient method or minimal movement scheme.

The method is usually presented as the following iterative optimization method:

$$\rho_{\mathcal{T}+\delta\mathcal{T}} = \underset{\rho}{\operatorname{argmin}} \left\{ \mathcal{F}[\rho] + \frac{1}{2\lambda} W_2^2[\rho_{\mathcal{T}}, \rho] \right\}, \tag{22.27}$$

where $\lambda > 0$ is a time-step parameter. However, to build geometric intuition, we wi represent this problem in an alternative form using Lagrange multipliers. Geometri cally, we define a small "sphere" of radius ε around the current density $\rho_{\mathcal{T}}$. To defin a radius, we require a metric on probability measures, which we choose to be th Wasserstein metric. We now search on the surface of this sphere for the density th has the smallest free energy

$$\rho_{\mathcal{T}+\delta\mathcal{T}} = \underset{\rho}{\operatorname{argmin}} \left\{ \mathcal{F}[\rho] + \mu \left(W_2^2[\rho_{\mathcal{T}}, \rho] - \varepsilon^2 \right) \right\}, \tag{22.28}$$

where we think of the Wasserstein metric as the square of the distance. The Lagrang multiplier μ is there to ensure that ρ is on the sphere and represents a force that counter the force coming from the free energy.

The equation that characterizes the solution is given by taking the functional deriva tive of the objective above:

$$\frac{\delta \mathcal{F}[\rho^*]}{\delta \rho} + \mu \frac{\delta W_2^2[\rho_{\mathcal{T}}, \rho^*]}{\delta \rho} = 0. \tag{22.29}$$

From the dual formulation of the OT problem, (22.11), we find that

$$\frac{\delta W_2^2[\rho_{\mathcal{T}}, \rho]}{\delta \rho}(\boldsymbol{\xi}) = 2\phi(\boldsymbol{\xi}, \mathcal{T}) \tag{22.30}$$

$$\Rightarrow \frac{\delta \mathcal{F}[\rho^*]}{\delta \rho}(\boldsymbol{\xi}) = -2\mu\phi^*(\boldsymbol{\xi}, \mathcal{T}) \tag{22.31}$$

$$\Rightarrow \boldsymbol{\nabla} \frac{\delta \mathcal{F}[\rho^*]}{\delta \rho}(\boldsymbol{\xi}) = -2\mu \boldsymbol{\nabla}\phi^*(\boldsymbol{\xi}, \mathcal{T}) = -2\mu \mathbf{v}^*(\boldsymbol{\xi}, \mathcal{T}). \tag{22.32}$$

Since the Benamou–Brenier formulation of the OT problem involves the continuit equation with velocity $\mathbf{v}^*$, we have now shown that indeed the solution to the constraine optimization problem defined above is an FP-like equation with a velocity field give by

$$\mathbf{v}^*(\boldsymbol{\xi}, \mathcal{T}) = -\frac{1}{2\mu} \boldsymbol{\nabla} \frac{\delta \mathcal{F}[\rho^*]}{\delta \rho}(\boldsymbol{\xi}). \tag{22.33}$$

This is consistent with (21.31) in Section 21.5.

Our final task is to relate μ to ε. For a given ρ_τ and some $\mathbf{v}^*$, flowing for a very short time $\delta\tau$ using the continuity equation yields $\rho^{\text{new}}_{\tau+\delta\tau}$, while the squared Wasserstein distance in this case is given by

$$\begin{aligned}
W_2^2[\rho_\tau, \rho_{\tau+\delta\tau}] &= \delta\tau \int_\tau^{\tau+\delta\tau} \mathrm{d}\tau \int \mathrm{d}\boldsymbol{\xi}\, \rho^*(\boldsymbol{\xi},\tau)\|\mathbf{v}^*(\boldsymbol{\xi},\tau)\|^2 \\
&= \frac{\delta\tau}{4\mu^2}\int_\tau^{\tau+\delta\tau} \mathrm{d}\tau \int \mathrm{d}\boldsymbol{\xi}\, \rho^*(\boldsymbol{\xi},\tau) \left\| \boldsymbol{\nabla}\frac{\delta\mathcal{F}[\rho^*]}{\delta\rho}(\boldsymbol{\xi},\tau)\right\|^2 \\
&= \frac{\delta\tau T\Sigma_{\delta\tau}}{4\mu^2} = \varepsilon^2, \\
&\Rightarrow \mu = \frac{\sqrt{\delta\tau T\Sigma_{\delta\tau}}}{2\varepsilon}, \quad \Rightarrow \lambda = \frac{\varepsilon}{\sqrt{\delta\tau T\Sigma_{\tau_f}}}.
\end{aligned} \tag{22.34}$$

The JKO scheme not only shows that the FP equation is a gradient flow of the free energy on the Wasserstein metric, but it also happens to be a stable numerical method to solve the FP equation by iteratively solving a series of OT problems.

22.6 Schrödinger Bridges

The Schrödinger bridge problem is only slightly different from the OT problem in that we assume diffusive dynamics instead of merely the continuity equation:

$$\mathcal{D}_{\text{SB}}[\rho_0, \rho_{\tau_f}] = \inf_{\rho,\mathbf{v}} \tau_f \int_0^{\tau_f} \mathrm{d}\tau \int \mathrm{d}\boldsymbol{\xi}\, \rho(\boldsymbol{\xi},\tau)\|\mathbf{v}(\boldsymbol{\xi},\tau)\|^2, \tag{22.35}$$

$$\text{s.t.} \quad \partial_\tau\rho(\boldsymbol{\xi},\tau) = -\mathbf{div}(\rho(\boldsymbol{\xi},\tau)\mathbf{v}(\boldsymbol{\xi},\tau)) + \nu\boldsymbol{\nabla}^2\rho(\boldsymbol{\xi},\tau), \tag{22.36}$$

$$\text{s.t.} \quad \rho(\boldsymbol{\xi},0) = \rho_0, \quad \rho(\boldsymbol{\xi},\tau_f) = \rho_{\tau_f}. \tag{22.37}$$

Here, ν is the diffusion constant. By constructing the Lagrangian similarly to previous sections, we derive the Hamilton–Jacobi–Bellman equation:

$$\begin{aligned}
\mathcal{L}_{\text{SB}}(\rho,\mathbf{v},\phi) &= \inf_{\rho,\mathbf{v}}\sup_{\phi} \tau_f \int_0^{\tau_f} \mathrm{d}\tau \int \mathrm{d}\boldsymbol{\xi} \Big[\rho(\boldsymbol{\xi},\tau)\|\mathbf{v}(\boldsymbol{\xi},\tau)\|^2 \\
&\quad + 2\phi(\boldsymbol{\xi},\tau)\left(\partial_\tau\rho(\boldsymbol{\xi},\tau) + \mathbf{div}(\rho(\boldsymbol{\xi},\tau)[\mathbf{v}(\boldsymbol{\xi},\tau) - \nu\boldsymbol{\nabla}\log\rho(\boldsymbol{\xi},\tau)])\right)\Big] \\
&= \inf_{\rho,\mathbf{v}}\sup_{\phi} \tau_f \int_0^{\tau_f} \mathrm{d}\tau \int \mathrm{d}\boldsymbol{\xi} \Big[\rho(\boldsymbol{\xi},\tau)\|\mathbf{v}(\boldsymbol{\xi},\tau)\|^2 - 2\rho(\boldsymbol{\xi},\tau)\partial_\tau\phi(\boldsymbol{\xi},\tau) \\
&\quad - 2\rho(\boldsymbol{\xi},\tau)[\mathbf{v}(\boldsymbol{\xi},\tau) - \nu\boldsymbol{\nabla}\log\rho(\boldsymbol{\xi},\tau)]\cdot\boldsymbol{\nabla}\phi(\boldsymbol{\xi},\tau)\Big] \\
&\quad + \int \mathrm{d}\boldsymbol{\xi}\, 2\rho(\boldsymbol{\xi},\tau_f)\phi(\boldsymbol{\xi},\tau_f) - 2\rho(\boldsymbol{\xi},0)\phi(\boldsymbol{\xi},0).
\end{aligned} \tag{22.38}$$

The variational derivative with respect to $\mathbf{v}$ will result in exactly the same equation as for the OT problem, namely: $\mathbf{v}(\boldsymbol{\xi},\tau) = \boldsymbol{\nabla}\phi(\boldsymbol{\xi},\tau)$. Substituting this into the Lagrangian and performing the variation with respect to ρ, we obtain

$$\partial_\tau \phi(\boldsymbol{\xi},\tau) = -\frac{1}{2}\|\boldsymbol{\nabla}\phi(\boldsymbol{\xi},\tau)\|^2 - \nu\boldsymbol{\nabla}^2\phi(\boldsymbol{\xi},\tau). \tag{22.39}$$

We note that the dual Lagrangian has the same simple form as the OT optimization problem, consisting of only two boundary terms, but of course now subject to the HJB equation above, which has an additional diffusion-like term for ϕ. The SB problem can therefore be interpreted as a stochastic optimal control problem where the dynamics are governed by the Fokker–Planck equation with diffusion.

22.6.1 Relation between OT and SB

Starting from the SB problem, it is instructive to use the transformation

$$\mathbf{w}(\boldsymbol{\xi},\tau) = \mathbf{v}(\boldsymbol{\xi},\tau) - \nu\boldsymbol{\nabla}\log\rho(\boldsymbol{\xi},\tau), \tag{22.40}$$

with $\mathbf{w} = \boldsymbol{\nabla}\psi$. This transforms the diffusive dynamics into a continuity equation:,

$$\partial_\tau \rho(\boldsymbol{\xi},\tau) = -\mathbf{div}(\rho(\boldsymbol{\xi},\tau)\mathbf{w}(\boldsymbol{\xi},\tau)), \tag{22.41}$$

while the distance (or action) is now transformed to

$$\begin{aligned}\mathcal{D}_{\mathrm{SB}}[\rho_0,\rho_{\tau_f}] = \inf_{\rho,\mathbf{w}} \tau_f \int_0^{\tau_f} \mathrm{d}\tau \int \mathrm{d}\boldsymbol{\xi}\; \rho(\boldsymbol{\xi},\tau)\big[\|\mathbf{w}(\boldsymbol{\xi},\tau)\|^2 + \nu^2\|\boldsymbol{\nabla}\log\rho(\boldsymbol{\xi},\tau)\|^2 \\ + 2\nu\mathbf{w}(\boldsymbol{\xi},\tau)\cdot\boldsymbol{\nabla}\log\rho(\boldsymbol{\xi},\tau)\big].\end{aligned} \tag{22.42}$$

The final term can be rewritten as a boundary term using (21.18):

$$\begin{aligned}&\tau_f \int_0^{\tau_f} \mathrm{d}\tau \int \mathrm{d}\boldsymbol{\xi}\; \rho(\boldsymbol{\xi},\tau)\, 2\nu\mathbf{w}(\boldsymbol{\xi},\tau)\cdot\boldsymbol{\nabla}\log\rho(\boldsymbol{\xi},\tau) \\ &\quad = -2\nu\,\tau_f \int_0^{\tau_f} \mathrm{d}\tau\, \partial_\tau \mathcal{S}[\rho_\tau] = -2\nu\,\tau_f(\mathcal{S}[\rho_{\tau_f}] - \mathcal{S}[\rho_0]),\end{aligned} \tag{22.43}$$

which is constant due to the marginal constraints on the boundaries. This results in the important conclusion that the difference between the OT and the SB problems is an extra term in the action, which we identify as the Fisher information, the same as the energy due to the osmotic force $\boldsymbol{\nabla}\log\rho$. Taken together, we thus have the following equivalent formulation of the SB problem, known as the Yasue problem (Léger, 2019)

$$\mathcal{D}_{\mathrm{Y}}[\rho_0,\rho_{\tau_f}] = \inf_{\rho,\mathbf{w}} \tau_f \int_0^{\tau_f} \mathrm{d}\tau \int \mathrm{d}\boldsymbol{\xi}\; \rho(\boldsymbol{\xi},\tau)\left[\|\mathbf{w}(\boldsymbol{\xi},\tau)\|^2 + \nu^2\|\boldsymbol{\nabla}\log\rho(\boldsymbol{\xi},\tau)\|^2\right], \tag{22.44}$$

$$\text{s.t. } \partial_\tau \rho(\boldsymbol{\xi},\tau) = -\mathbf{div}(\rho(\boldsymbol{\xi},\tau)\mathbf{w}(\boldsymbol{\xi},\tau)), \tag{22.45}$$

$$\text{s.t. } \rho(\boldsymbol{\xi},0) = \rho_0, \quad \rho(\boldsymbol{\xi},\tau_f) = \rho_{\tau_f}, \tag{22.46}$$

resulting in the following Hamilton–Jacobi–Bellman equation (using the usual relation $\mathbf{w} = \boldsymbol{\nabla}\psi$, with ψ a Lagrange multiplier, obtained from stationarity under variation of $\mathbf{w}$

$$\partial_\tau \psi(\boldsymbol{\xi},\tau) = -\frac{1}{2}\|\boldsymbol{\nabla}\psi(\boldsymbol{\xi},\tau)\|^2 - \frac{1}{2}\nu^2\|\boldsymbol{\nabla}\log\rho(\boldsymbol{\xi},\tau)\|^2 - \nu^2\boldsymbol{\nabla}^2\log\rho(\boldsymbol{\xi},\tau). \tag{22.47}$$

The relationship between the Lagrange multipliers is given by

$$\psi(\xi,\tau) = \phi(\xi,\tau) - \nu \log \rho(\xi,\tau). \tag{22.48}$$

22.6.2 Time Reversal

In the previous chapters, we have seen the fundamental role played by time reversal symmetry. It was the asymmetry between forward and backward processes that could tell us how much entropy a process is generating. So how do the various OT and SB problems behave under time reversal?

Let's first look at the OT problem:

$$\partial_\tau \rho(\xi,\tau) = -\nabla \cdot (\rho(\xi,\tau)\nabla\phi(\xi,\tau)), \tag{22.49}$$

$$\partial_\tau \phi(\xi,\tau) = -\frac{1}{2}\|\nabla\phi(\xi,\tau)\|^2. \tag{22.50}$$

Now apply the transformation $\tau \to \tilde{\tau} = \tau_f - \tau$:

$$\partial_{\tau_f-\tilde{\tau}} \rho(\xi,\tau_f-\tilde{\tau}) = -\nabla \cdot (\rho(\xi,\tau_f-\tilde{\tau})\nabla\phi(\xi,\tau_f-\tilde{\tau})), \tag{22.51}$$

$$\partial_{\tau_f-\tilde{\tau}} \phi(\xi,\tau_f-\tilde{\tau}) = -\frac{1}{2}\|\nabla\phi(\xi,\tau_f-\tilde{\tau})\|^2. \tag{22.52}$$

Next, we use $\partial_{\tau_f-\tilde{\tau}} = -\partial_{\tilde{\tau}}$ and call $\rho(\xi,\tau_f-\tilde{\tau}) = \tilde{\rho}(\zeta,\tilde{\tau})$ with $\zeta = (\xi,-\eta)$. As we do not yet know the transformation rule for ϕ, we write $\phi(\xi,\tau_f-\tilde{\tau}) = \alpha\tilde{\phi}(\zeta,\tilde{\tau})$:

$$-\partial_{\tilde{\tau}}\tilde{\rho}(\zeta,\tilde{\tau}) = -\alpha\nabla \cdot (\tilde{\rho}(\zeta,\tilde{\tau})\nabla\tilde{\phi}(\zeta,\tilde{\tau})), \tag{22.53}$$

$$-\alpha\partial_{\tilde{\tau}}\tilde{\phi}(\zeta,\tilde{\tau}) = -\frac{1}{2}\alpha^2\|\nabla\tilde{\phi}(\zeta,\tilde{\tau})\|^2. \tag{22.54}$$

In transformed variables we want the evolution equations to maintain the form of the original equations, from which we read out $\alpha = 1$ and

$$\tilde{\phi}(\zeta,\tilde{\tau}) = -\phi(\zeta,\tilde{\tau}). \tag{22.55}$$

For the SB problem, the situation is slightly more complex. However, the Yasue formulation of the SB problem is explicitly time symmetric. In other words, following the same reasoning as above, we can also simply set

$$\begin{aligned}
&\tilde{\psi}(\zeta,\tilde{\tau}) = -\psi(\zeta,\tilde{\tau}) \\
&\Rightarrow\ \tilde{\phi}(\zeta,\tilde{\tau}) - \nu\log\tilde{\rho}(\zeta,\tilde{\tau}) = -\phi(\zeta,\tilde{\tau}) + \nu\log\rho(\zeta,\tilde{\tau}) \\
&\Rightarrow\ \tilde{\phi}(\zeta,\tilde{\tau}) = -\phi(\zeta,\tilde{\tau}) + 2\nu\ \log\rho(\zeta,\tilde{\tau}).
\end{aligned} \tag{22.56}$$

This somewhat strange-looking transformation law under time reversal for the potential ϕ is necessary to keep the propagation laws invariant under time reversal.

22.7 More General Actions

Physicists have discovered that almost all fundamental physical laws can be derived from a variational principle (Goldstein, 1950; Landau and Lifshitz, 1976), very similar to the one we employed for the OT and SB problems. In variational problems, th initial and final states of the system are constrained, and the solution path is derived b extremizing an action functional which is given by the integral of a Lagrangian ove the path (see Figure 22.3):

$$\mathcal{A}[\boldsymbol{\xi}] = \int_{\tau_0}^{\tau_f} \mathcal{L}(\boldsymbol{\xi}(\tau), \boldsymbol{\eta}(\tau), \tau)\,\mathrm{d}\tau, \tag{22.57}$$

where $\boldsymbol{\xi}(\tau)$ is the position coordinate and $\boldsymbol{\eta}(\tau) = \partial_\tau \boldsymbol{\xi}(\tau)$.

Consider an infinitesimal variation in the path, $\boldsymbol{\xi}(\tau) \to \boldsymbol{\xi}(\tau) + \delta\boldsymbol{\xi}(\tau)$, with th variation satisfying the boundary conditions $\delta\boldsymbol{\xi}(\tau_0) = \mathbf{0}$ and $\delta\boldsymbol{\xi}(\tau_f) = \mathbf{0}$. The corre sponding variation in the velocity is given by $\delta\boldsymbol{\eta}(\tau) = \partial_\tau \delta\boldsymbol{\xi}(\tau)$. The variation of th action (by expanding to first order in $\delta\boldsymbol{\xi}$ and $\delta\boldsymbol{\eta}$) is

$$\begin{aligned}
\delta\mathcal{A} &= \mathcal{A}[\boldsymbol{\xi} + \delta\boldsymbol{\xi}] - \mathcal{A}[\boldsymbol{\xi}] \\
&= \int_{\tau_0}^{\tau_f} \mathrm{d}\tau \left\{\mathcal{L}(\boldsymbol{\xi} + \delta\boldsymbol{\xi}, \boldsymbol{\eta} + \delta\boldsymbol{\eta}, \tau) - \mathcal{L}(\boldsymbol{\xi}, \boldsymbol{\eta}, \tau)\right\} \\
&= \int_{\tau_0}^{\tau_f} \mathrm{d}\tau \left\{\frac{\delta\mathcal{L}}{\delta\boldsymbol{\xi}} \cdot \delta\boldsymbol{\xi}(\tau) + \frac{\delta\mathcal{L}}{\delta\boldsymbol{\eta}} \cdot \delta\boldsymbol{\eta}(\tau)\right\}.
\end{aligned} \tag{22.58}$$

Since $\delta\boldsymbol{\eta}(\tau) = \partial_\tau \delta\boldsymbol{\xi}(\tau)$, we rewrite the second term using integration by parts:

$$\int_{\tau_0}^{\tau_f} \mathrm{d}\tau\, \frac{\delta\mathcal{L}}{\delta\boldsymbol{\eta}} \cdot \partial_\tau \delta\boldsymbol{\xi}(\tau) = \frac{\delta\mathcal{L}}{\delta\boldsymbol{\eta}} \cdot \delta\boldsymbol{\xi}(\tau)\Big|_{\tau_0}^{\tau_f} - \int_{\tau_0}^{\tau_f} \mathrm{d}\tau\, \partial_\tau \left(\frac{\delta\mathcal{L}}{\delta\boldsymbol{\eta}}\right) \cdot \delta\boldsymbol{\xi}(\tau). \tag{22.59}$$

Due to the boundary conditions $\delta\boldsymbol{\xi}(\tau_0) = \delta\boldsymbol{\xi}(\tau_f) = \mathbf{0}$, the boundary term vanishe Therefore, from the extremal condition $\delta\mathcal{A} = 0$ under arbitrary variations $\delta\boldsymbol{\xi}(\tau)$, w obtain the Euler–Lagrange equation:

$$\begin{aligned}
\delta\mathcal{A} &= \int_{\tau_0}^{\tau_f} \mathrm{d}\tau \left[\frac{\delta\mathcal{L}}{\delta\boldsymbol{\xi}} - \partial_\tau \left(\frac{\delta\mathcal{L}}{\delta\boldsymbol{\eta}}\right)\right] \cdot \delta\boldsymbol{\xi}(\tau) \\
&\Rightarrow \frac{\delta\mathcal{L}}{\delta\boldsymbol{\xi}} - \partial_\tau \left(\frac{\delta\mathcal{L}}{\delta\boldsymbol{\eta}}\right) = \mathbf{0}.
\end{aligned} \tag{22.60}$$

In deterministic classical systems, the Lagrangian is given by the kinetic energ minus the potential energy, $\mathcal{L}(\boldsymbol{\xi}, \boldsymbol{\eta}, \tau) = \frac{1}{2}\|\boldsymbol{\eta}(\tau)\|^2 - \mathcal{V}(\boldsymbol{\xi})$. The solutions given b Newton's laws of mechanics are obtained by substituting this into the Euler–Lagrang equation, (22.60):

$$\partial_\tau \boldsymbol{\eta}(\tau) + \frac{\delta\mathcal{V}}{\delta\boldsymbol{\xi}}(\boldsymbol{\xi}(\tau)) = \mathbf{0} \Rightarrow \frac{\mathrm{d}^2\boldsymbol{\xi}(\tau)}{\mathrm{d}\tau^2} = -\boldsymbol{\nabla}\mathcal{V}(\boldsymbol{\xi}(\tau)). \tag{22.61}$$

We note that this minimal action setup is slightly different than the usual caus formulation of Newton's laws, where one is given an initial location and velocity fro which the future follows. In a variational formulation, we are given some informatio in the future (initial and final location) while the velocity field in the beginning nee to be derived.

This variational principle also applies to probability densities (and even quantu mechanical wave functions Feynman et al., 2010). By specifying the initial and fin

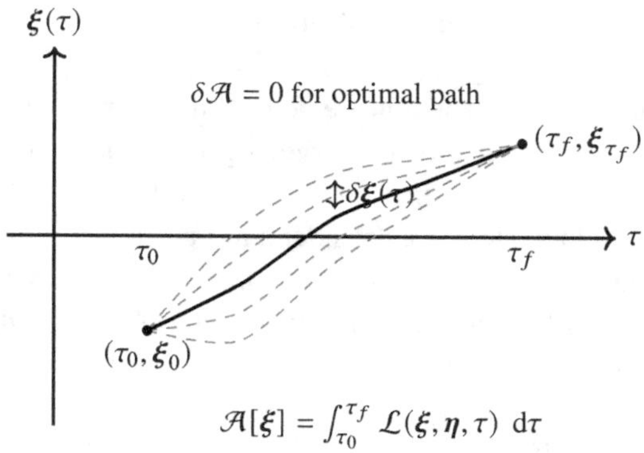

Figure 22.3 The principle of least action states that the physical path $\xi(\tau)$ (solid curve) between fixed endpoints (τ_0, ξ_0) and (τ_f, ξ_{τ_f}) (filled circles) is the one that extremizes the action functional $\mathcal{A}[\xi]$. Any variation $\delta\xi(\tau)$ around this optimal path (with $\delta\xi(\tau_0) = \delta\xi(\tau_f) = 0$) results in $\delta\mathcal{A} = 0$ to first order. The dashed curves represent possible path variations that satisfy the endpoint constraints.

probability densities (without specifying the velocity fields), one can write down an action, such as those in the OT or SB problems, and determine the optimal path by finding the saddle point of that action (i.e., the path that extremizes the action). This is precisely what we have done so far in the case of OT and SB but for rather simple actions.

In general, we can consider a more flexible action functional:

$$\begin{aligned}
&\mathcal{A}[\rho_0, \rho_{\tau_f}] = \inf_{\rho, \mathbf{v}} \int_0^{\tau_f} \mathrm{d}\tau \int \mathrm{d}\xi\, \rho(\xi, \tau) \left(\frac{1}{2} \|\mathbf{v}(\xi, \tau)\|^2 - \mathcal{V}(\xi, \tau) \right), \\
&\text{s.t. } \partial_\tau \rho(\xi, \tau) = -\mathbf{div}(\rho(\xi, \tau)\mathbf{v}(\xi, \tau)) + \nu \nabla^2 \rho(\xi, \tau), \\
&\text{s.t. } \rho(\xi, 0) = \rho_0, \quad \rho(\xi, \tau_f) = \rho_{\tau_f}.
\end{aligned} \tag{22.62}$$

Here, the first term represents the kinetic energy density, and the second term is the negative potential energy density. One can add again the FP equation with a Lagrange multiplier to derive the HJB equation:

$$\partial_\tau \phi(\xi, \tau) = -\frac{1}{2} \|\nabla \phi(\xi, \tau)\|^2 - \mathcal{V}(\xi, \tau) - \nu \nabla^2 \phi(\xi, \tau) \tag{22.63}$$

$$\Rightarrow \partial_\tau \mathbf{v}(\xi, \tau) + \frac{1}{2} \mathbf{v}(\xi, \tau) \cdot \nabla \mathbf{v}(\xi, \tau) = -\nabla \mathcal{V}(\xi, \tau) - \nu \nabla^2 \mathbf{v}(\xi, \tau), \tag{22.64}$$

where $\mathbf{f} = -\nabla \mathcal{V}$ can be identified with a force field. The equation states that the comoving derivative of the velocity field is proportional to the force field plus an additional diffusive term. This is a hydrodynamic generalization of Newton's law!

22.8 Relation to Optimal Control

One can think of the action we defined in the previous sections as a cost function fc a controlled system aimed at achieving a specific goal. In the case of the SB problen the goal is to reach a final probability distribution $\rho(\boldsymbol{\xi}, \tau_f) = \rho_{\tau_f}(\boldsymbol{\xi})$ by controllin the flow field $\mathbf{v}$. Here, we consider a more general terminal cost for time τ_f.

Assume we are at time τ in a definite state $\boldsymbol{\xi}_\tau = \mathbf{y}_\tau$; that is, $\rho(\boldsymbol{\xi}, \tau) = \delta(\boldsymbol{\xi} - \mathbf{y}_\tau$ Then the "cost-to-go" is the minimal achievable cost when acting optimally from thi point onward, defined as:

$$\mathcal{J}(\mathbf{y}_\tau, \tau) = \inf_{\rho, \mathbf{v}} \left\{ \int_\tau^{\tau_f} \mathrm{d}\tau \int \mathrm{d}\boldsymbol{\xi}\, \rho(\boldsymbol{\xi}, \tau) \left(\frac{1}{2} \|\mathbf{v}(\boldsymbol{\xi}, \tau)\|^2 - \mathcal{V}(\boldsymbol{\xi}, \tau) \right) + \mathcal{K}_{\tau_f} \right\}, \quad (22.65)$$

$$\text{s.t. } \partial_\tau \rho(\boldsymbol{\xi}, \tau) = -\mathbf{div}(\rho(\boldsymbol{\xi}, \tau)\mathbf{v}(\boldsymbol{\xi}, \tau)) + \nu \boldsymbol{\nabla}^2 \rho(\boldsymbol{\xi}, \tau), \quad (22.66)$$

$$\text{s.t. } \rho(\boldsymbol{\xi}, \tau) = \delta(\boldsymbol{\xi} - \mathbf{y}_\tau). \quad (22.67)$$

Here, $\mathcal{K}_{\tau_f}$ represents the terminal cost at time τ_f. The term $\mathcal{V}$ is interpreted as th reward for being in state $\boldsymbol{\xi}$ at time τ. Due to the negative sign, the system aims t maximize this function along the traversed path to accumulate as much reward a possible.

To find the optimal solution, we minimize this cost over both ρ and $\mathbf{v}$, subject t the FP equation and the constraint on the current state $\rho(\boldsymbol{\xi}, \tau)$. Of course, we alread know that this results in the HJB equations. But let's interpret this in a slightly differe way. If we add the constraints as Lagrange multipliers and solve them, as before, w can rewrite the cost as (this is formally the dual)

$$\begin{aligned}\mathcal{J}(\mathbf{y}_\tau, \tau) &= \int \mathrm{d}\boldsymbol{\xi}\, \rho(\boldsymbol{\xi}, \tau_f)\phi(\boldsymbol{\xi}, \tau_f) - \int \mathrm{d}\boldsymbol{\xi}\, \rho(\boldsymbol{\xi}, \tau)\phi(\boldsymbol{\xi}, \tau) + \mathcal{K}_{\tau_f}[\rho_{\tau_f}] \\ &= \mathcal{K}'_{\tau_f}[\rho_{\tau_f}] - \phi(\mathbf{y}_\tau, \tau), \end{aligned} \quad (22.68)$$

where $\mathcal{K}'_{\tau_f}$ collects the first and last terms and is a constant independent of $\mathbf{y}_\tau$ $\tau \neq \tau_f$. We also used (22.67) to derive the second term. In other words, the cost-to-g is proportional to the negative of the Lagrange multiplier. The HJB equations for th control problem are an expression for $\partial_\tau \mathcal{J}(\mathbf{y}_\tau, \tau)$. Since we made the identificatio of the cost-to-go with the negative potential ϕ, we know that the answer should b equal (22.63). But let's derive this in an analogous way to how the HJB equation usually derived in optimal control theory. We observe that the total cost from time to the end time τ_f is given by the cost to go from τ to $\tau + \delta\tau$ plus the remaining co at time $\tau + \delta\tau$:

$$\begin{aligned}\mathcal{J}(\mathbf{y}_\tau, \tau) &= \mathcal{J}(\mathbf{y}_\tau, \tau + \delta\tau) + \delta\tau \int \mathrm{d}\boldsymbol{\xi}\, \rho(\boldsymbol{\xi}, \tau) \left(\frac{1}{2} \|\mathbf{v}(\boldsymbol{\xi}, \tau)\|^2 - \mathcal{V}(\boldsymbol{\xi}, \tau) \right) \\ &= \mathcal{J}(\mathbf{y}_\tau, \tau) - \delta\tau \int \mathrm{d}\boldsymbol{\xi}\, (\rho(\boldsymbol{\xi}, \tau)\partial_\tau \phi(\boldsymbol{\xi}, \tau) + \phi(\boldsymbol{\xi}, \tau)\partial_\tau \rho(\boldsymbol{\xi}, \tau)) \\ &\quad + \delta\tau \int \mathrm{d}\boldsymbol{\xi}\, \rho(\boldsymbol{\xi}, \tau) \left(\frac{1}{2} \|\boldsymbol{\nabla}\phi(\boldsymbol{\xi}, \tau)\|^2 - \mathcal{V}(\boldsymbol{\xi}, \tau) \right), \end{aligned} \quad (22.69)$$

where in the second line we used (22.68) and a Taylor expansion in $\delta\tau$. From this w derive

$$\int \mathrm{d}\xi\, \rho(\xi,\tau)\partial_\tau \phi(\xi,\tau) = \int \mathrm{d}\xi\, \rho(\xi,\tau)\left(-\frac{1}{2}\|\nabla\phi(\xi,\tau)\|^2 - \mathcal{V}(\xi,\tau) - \nu\nabla^2\phi(\xi,\tau)\right), \tag{22.70}$$

which is indeed consistent with (22.63). Now, using the fact that $\rho(\xi,\tau) = \delta(\xi - \mathbf{y}_\tau)$ and using (22.68), we find the usual HJB equation derived in optimal control theory for stochastic Brownian dynamics and quadratic control:

$$\begin{aligned} \frac{\partial \mathcal{J}(\mathbf{y}_\tau,\tau)}{\partial \tau} &= \frac{1}{2}\|\nabla\mathcal{J}(\mathbf{y}_\tau,\tau)\|^2 + \mathcal{V}(\mathbf{y}_\tau,\tau) - \nu\nabla^2\mathcal{J}(\mathbf{y}_\tau,\tau), \\ \text{s.t.}\quad \mathcal{J}(\mathbf{y}_{\tau_f},\tau_f) &= \mathcal{K}_{\tau_f}(\mathbf{y}_{\tau_f}). \end{aligned} \tag{22.71}$$

This equation is also known as the Riccati equation; it must be solved backward in time because of the boundary condition at $\tau = \tau_f$.

To summarize, we have shown that an extension of the SB problem (with stochastic dynamics) with an additional reward term $\mathcal{V}$ and an initial state distribution $\delta(\xi - \mathbf{y}_\tau)$ is precisely equivalent to an optimal control (OC) problem. The HJB equation acts as an ODE to compute the cost-to-go. This once again beautifully links OC to SBs and OT problems.

22.9 Back to Diffusion Models

Recall that to train a diffusion model, we defined both forward and backward processes (see Chapter 13). The forward process typically employs a simple Ornstein–Uhlenbeck process that initiates at the data distribution and converges to a standard normal distribution as its fixed point. This process, first analyzed by Uhlenbeck and Ornstein (1930) in their seminal work on Brownian motion, provides a mathematically tractable framework for modeling stochastic dynamics. The backward process is trained to invert the forward process, transforming the prior standard normal distribution back to the data distribution.

In this chapter, we approached stochastic processes through the lens of Fokker–Planck equations (see also Chapter 13 for the discrete-time perspective). Hence, the forward process takes the form

$$\begin{aligned} &\partial_\tau \rho(\xi,\tau) = -\mathbf{div}(\rho(\xi,\tau)\mathbf{v}(\xi,\tau)) + \nu\nabla^2\rho(\xi,\tau), \\ &\text{s.t.}\quad \rho(\xi,0) = \rho_{\text{data}}. \end{aligned} \tag{22.72}$$

The time-reversed process can be directly derived by applying the time reversal transformation. Specifically, by using $\tilde{\tau} = \tau_f - \tau$, $\tilde{\zeta} = (\xi, -\boldsymbol{\eta})$, $\tilde{\rho}(\tilde{\zeta},\tilde{\tau}) = \rho(\xi,\tau)$, and $\tilde{\mathbf{v}}(\tilde{\zeta},\tilde{\tau}) = -\mathbf{v}(\xi,\tau)$, the time-reversed equations become

$$\begin{aligned} &\partial_{\tilde{\tau}} \tilde{\rho}(\tilde{\zeta},\tilde{\tau}) = -\mathbf{div}(\tilde{\rho}(\tilde{\zeta},\tilde{\tau})\tilde{\mathbf{v}}(\tilde{\zeta},\tilde{\tau})) - \nu\nabla^2\tilde{\rho}(\tilde{\zeta},\tilde{\tau}), \\ &\text{s.t.}\quad \tilde{\rho}(\tilde{\zeta},0) = \rho_{\text{prior}}. \end{aligned} \tag{22.73}$$

From these transformations, we read off that the diffusion term acquires a negative sign. This reduces the entropy of the system, transitioning from noise to structure (a.k.a., denoising), mirroring the behavior discussed in Chapter 13.

To obtain an equation with a positive diffusion term, we move the diffusion term inside the divergence:

$$\partial_{\tilde{\tau}}\tilde{\rho}(\tilde{\zeta},\tilde{\tau}) = -\mathbf{div}\left(\tilde{\rho}(\tilde{\zeta},\tilde{\tau})\left[\tilde{\mathbf{v}}(\tilde{\zeta},\tilde{\tau}) + 2\nu\boldsymbol{\nabla}\log\tilde{\rho}(\tilde{\zeta},\tilde{\tau})\right]\right) + \nu\boldsymbol{\nabla}^2\tilde{\rho}(\tilde{\zeta},\tilde{\tau}). \tag{22.74}$$

This suggests that the effective reverse drift velocity field is (Anderson, 1982; Nelson, 1967)

$$\begin{aligned}\mathbf{v}_R(\boldsymbol{\xi},\tilde{\tau}) &= \tilde{\mathbf{v}}(\tilde{\zeta},\tilde{\tau}) + 2\nu\boldsymbol{\nabla}\log\tilde{\rho}(\tilde{\zeta},\tilde{\tau}) \\ &= -\mathbf{v}(\boldsymbol{\xi},\tau) + 2\nu\boldsymbol{\nabla}\log\rho(\boldsymbol{\xi},\tau).\end{aligned} \tag{22.75}$$

Thus, the reverse-time dynamics are governed by a drift term that involves both the negative of the forward drift and an additional term proportional to the gradient of the log density, known as the *score function*:

$$\mathbf{s}(\boldsymbol{\xi},\tau) := \boldsymbol{\nabla}\log\rho(\boldsymbol{\xi},\tau). \tag{22.76}$$

However, in practice, the marginal distribution $\rho(\boldsymbol{\xi},\tau)$ is unknown. Instead, we rely on sample paths to train a velocity field that can invert this dynamics. The idea is to parameterize the score function using a neural network $\mathbf{s}_\theta(\boldsymbol{\xi},\tau)$[2]. To learn the parameters $\boldsymbol{\theta}$, we formulate a score-matching objective that minimizes the difference between the neural network's output and the true score function:

$$\mathcal{L}(\boldsymbol{\theta}) = \mathbb{E}_{\tau\sim\mathrm{Unif}[0,\tau_f]}\left[\lambda(\tau)\,\mathbb{E}_{\rho(\boldsymbol{\xi},\tau)}\left[\frac{1}{2}\left\|\mathbf{s}_\theta(\boldsymbol{\xi},\tau) - \mathbf{s}(\boldsymbol{\xi},\tau)\right\|^2\right]\right], \tag{22.77}$$

where $\lambda(\tau)$ is a time-dependent weighting function. This objective can be challenging to compute directly due to the unknown score function $\mathbf{s}(\boldsymbol{\xi},\tau)$ (see Song and Ermon, 2019 for a discussion). A further simplification comes with the use of the *denoising score matching* objective (Vincent, 2011; Song et al., 2021). If we perturb the data distribution with Gaussian noise at multiple noise levels, the score function can be estimated by minimizing

$$\begin{aligned}\mathcal{L}(\boldsymbol{\theta}) = \mathbb{E}_{\tau\sim\mathrm{Unif}[0,\tau_f]}\Bigg[&\lambda(\tau)\,\mathbb{E}_{\rho(\boldsymbol{\xi}(0))}\mathbb{E}_{\rho(\boldsymbol{\xi}(\tau)|\boldsymbol{\xi}(0))} \\ &\left[\frac{1}{2}\left\|\mathbf{s}_\theta(\boldsymbol{\xi}(\tau),\tau) - \boldsymbol{\nabla}_{\boldsymbol{\xi}(\tau)}\log\rho(\boldsymbol{\xi}(\tau)|\boldsymbol{\xi}(0))\right\|^2\right]\Bigg],\end{aligned} \tag{22.78}$$

where $\rho(\boldsymbol{\xi}(\tau)|\boldsymbol{\xi}(0))$ is the transition kernel of the forward process. When the forward process is chosen to be Ornstein–Uhlenbeck; that is, when the velocity field $\mathbf{v}(\boldsymbol{\xi},\tau)$ is affine in $\boldsymbol{\xi}$, the transition kernel $\rho(\boldsymbol{\xi}(\tau)|\boldsymbol{\xi}(0))$ is Gaussian and has a closed-form solution, which can be used for training. When the score network is perfectly trained, the backward process will exactly reverse the forward diffusion almost everywhere.

[2] For simplicity and common practice in diffusion models, we often consider the overdamped case where $\zeta = \xi$, although the general formulation remains valid.

For the Fokker–Planck equations given in (22.72) and (22.74), they are paired with the stochastic differential equations

$$d\boldsymbol{\xi} = \mathbf{v}(\boldsymbol{\xi}, \tau)\, d\tau + \sqrt{2\nu}\, d\mathbf{w}_\tau, \tag{22.79}$$

$$d\boldsymbol{\xi} = [-\mathbf{v}(\boldsymbol{\xi}, \tau) + 2\nu\boldsymbol{\nabla} \log \rho(\boldsymbol{\xi}, \tau)]\, d\tau + \sqrt{2\nu}\, d\tilde{\mathbf{w}}_\tau, \tag{22.80}$$

where $d\mathbf{w}_\tau$ and $d\tilde{\mathbf{w}}_\tau$ are standard and reverse-time Wiener processes, respectively. The concept of the Wiener process is based on the mathematical foundation laid by Norbert Wiener (1930), who formalized Brownian motion within a rigorous mathematical framework. After training the neural network $\mathbf{s}_\theta(\boldsymbol{\xi}, \tau)$ to approximate the score function, an approximate reverse SDE can be used to generate new samples starting from the prior distribution ρ_{prior} at $\tau = \tau_f$, by integrating backward in time to $\tau = 0$:

$$d\boldsymbol{\xi} = [-\mathbf{v}(\boldsymbol{\xi}, \tau) + 2\nu\mathbf{s}_\theta(\boldsymbol{\xi}, \tau)]\, d\tau + \sqrt{2\nu}\, d\tilde{\mathbf{w}}_\tau. \tag{22.81}$$

In this book, we have not treated SDEs and Brownian motion in detail, so we refer readers to Song and Ermon (2019); Song et al. (2021); Kingma et al. (2021); Gardiner (2009) for more detailed discussions on score matching and its applications in SDE-based diffusion models. Gardiner (2009) provides an especially comprehensive treatment of stochastic methods in both physical and computational contexts.

In the next chapter, we will apply a lesson we have learned in this chapter: namely, that instead of evolving using diffusion, we can solve the optimal transport problem (see Section 22.2). This has the advantage that paths between the prior and data distributions are simpler (straight-line paths) and therefore easier to learn. Also, the Ornstein–Uhlenbeck process only reaches its fixed point (our prior) after infinitely many steps, while solving the OT problem guarantees that we map between the data distribution and prior in a finite number of steps. This is important because when we generate samples, we assume that we have reached that fixed point as we draw our initial sample from this prior.

Several works in the generative AI literature have explored numerical solutions to the OT problem. The Sinkhorn autoencoder (Patrini et al., 2020) is a notable example. It implements a one-step deterministic map (a.k.a., push-forward) from the data distribution to a chosen prior by posing an objective based on matching samples from both distributions to train both an encoder and a decoder model.

More recent attempts to use continuous deterministic maps (or continuous normalizing flows (CNFs)) as generative models are flow matching (FM Lipman et al., 2023) and its derivatives, conditional flow matching (CFM) and optimal transport conditional flow matching (OT-CFM Tong et al., 2023). We will explore these methods in more detail in Chapter 23. All of these models are methods to learn push-forward maps from a prior to the data distribution.

23 Continuous Normalizing Flows and Flow Matching

23.1 Introduction

Following the previous chapter, where we discussed diffusion models through th lens of stochastic processes and Fokker–Planck equations, we now turn to generativ models defined through deterministic rather than stochastic maps. We will discuss th various flavors of flow matching, such as conditional flow matching and variation flow matching and how optimal transport theory can provide a flow field to solve th flow matching problem. Finally, we interpret this in light of a physical system th would have to invest minimal work to transform the distribution from the prior to th data distribution.

23.2 Continuous Normalizing Flows

Deterministic maps offer the advantage of exact likelihoods without requiring vari tional bounds, though they impose stronger constraints on model architecture. Thes models are governed by the continuity equation (introduced in Chapter 21)

$$\partial_\tau p(\mathbf{x}, \tau) = -\mathbf{div}(p(\mathbf{x}, \tau)\mathbf{v}(\mathbf{x}, \tau)) \quad (23.1)$$

$$\text{s.t.} \;\; p(\mathbf{x}, \tau = 0) = p_{\text{data}}. \quad (23.2)$$

To generate samples from a prior distribution p_{prior} to the data distribution p_{data}, w need the time-reversed process. Let us define $\tilde{\tau} = \tau_f - \tau$ as the reversed time variabl The time-reversed density $\tilde{p}(\mathbf{x}, \tilde{\tau}) = p(\mathbf{x}, \tau_f - \tilde{\tau})$ then evolves according to

$$\partial_{\tilde{\tau}} \tilde{p}(\mathbf{x}, \tilde{\tau}) = -\mathbf{div}(\tilde{p}(\mathbf{x}, \tilde{\tau})\tilde{\mathbf{v}}(\mathbf{x}, \tilde{\tau})) \quad (23.3)$$

$$\text{s.t.} \;\; \tilde{p}(\mathbf{x}, \tilde{\tau} = 0) = p_{\text{prior}}, \quad (23.4)$$

with the time-reversal relationships

$$\tilde{p}(\mathbf{x}, \tilde{\tau}) = p(\mathbf{x}, \tau) = p(\mathbf{x}, \tau_f - \tilde{\tau}), \quad (23.5)$$

$$\tilde{\mathbf{v}}(\mathbf{x}, \tilde{\tau}) = -\mathbf{v}(\mathbf{x}, \tau) = -\mathbf{v}(\mathbf{x}, \tau_f - \tilde{\tau}). \quad (23.6)$$

Given an arbitrarily chosen p_{prior}, the main objective is now to find the determinist time-inverted velocity field $\tilde{\mathbf{v}}(\mathbf{x}, \tilde{\tau}) = -\mathbf{v}(\mathbf{x}, \tau)$ that maps our p_{prior} at $\tilde{\tau} = 0$ (whic corresponds to $\tau = \tau_f$) to the data distribution p_{data} at $\tilde{\tau} = \tau_f$ (which corresponds

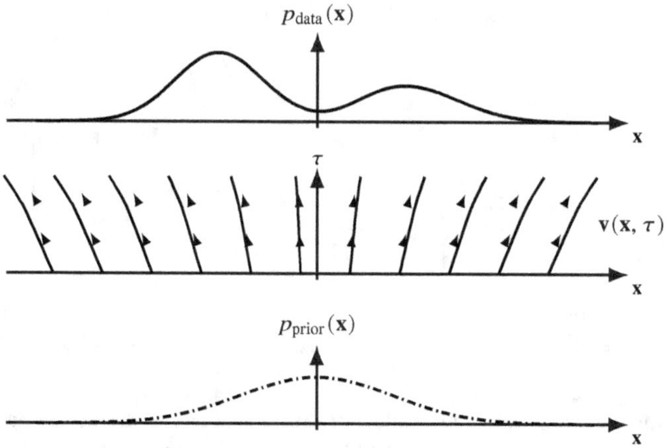

Figure 23.1 Continuous-time flow viewed from three perspectives. The top panel shows the complex data density $p_{\text{data}}(\mathbf{x})$, the middle panel depicts the velocity field $\mathbf{v}(\mathbf{x}, \tau)$ that drives trajectories, and the bottom panel shows the simplified prior $p_{\text{prior}}(\mathbf{x})$. Integrating the field forward in τ morphs the data into the prior, while reversing the field recovers the data for generation.

$\tau = 0)$[1] that maps our p_{prior} to the data distribution p_{data}. However, we do not have direct access to either $\mathbf{v}(\mathbf{x}, \tau)$ or its time inverse $-\mathbf{v}(\mathbf{x}, \tau)$, and will thus have to learn them from data.

A first approach to learning the velocity field extends the discrete normalizing flows from Chapter 8 to continuous time. This approach is known as continuous normalizing flows (CNFs; R. Chen et al., 2018; Grathwohl et al., 2018).

Instead of directly defining a sequence of parameterized bijective transformations $\mathbf{x}_t^{\theta}(\mathbf{x}_{t-1})$ that are at the core of discrete NFs, CNFs consider the ordinary differential equation

$$\mathrm{d}\mathbf{x} = \mathbf{v}(\mathbf{x}, \tau)\, \mathrm{d}\tau, \tag{23.7}$$

and define $\mathbf{x}(\mathbf{x}_0, \tau)$ as the solution to this ODE with the initial condition $\mathbf{x}(\mathbf{x}_0, 0) = \mathbf{x}_0$. In other words, $\mathbf{x}(\mathbf{x}_0, \tau)$ is the sample $\mathbf{x}_0$ transported along $\mathbf{v}$ from time 0 to time τ. Figure 23.1 illustrates how a CNF transforms a complex data distribution through a sequence of continuous transformations to a simple prior.

Change of Density Along the Flow

We now examine how the probability density $p(\mathbf{x}, \tau)$ evolves as we follow individual trajectories (the Lagrangian perspective). For this, consider the total derivative of

[1] Note that this is inverted from most other definitions of the problem, which aim to find simply $\mathbf{v}(\mathbf{x}, \tau)$ that maps our p_{prior} to the data distribution p_{data}.

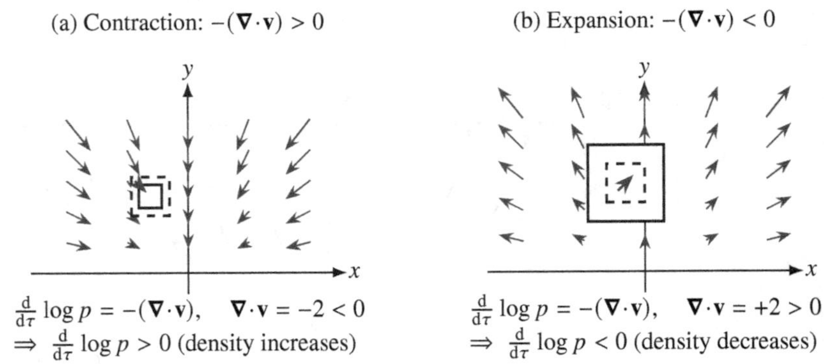

Figure 23.2 Local volume effect of divergence on log-density along characteristics. (a) Contracting flow $\mathbf{v} = -(x, y)$ has $\nabla\cdot\mathbf{v} = -2$, hence $-(\nabla\cdot\mathbf{v}) > 0$ and $\frac{d}{d\tau}\log p > 0$. (b) Expanding flow $\mathbf{v} = (x, y)$ has $\nabla\cdot\mathbf{v} = +2$, hence $-(\nabla\cdot\mathbf{v}) < 0$ and $\frac{d}{d\tau}\log p < 0$.

$\log p(\mathbf{x}, \tau)$ with respect to time:

$$\begin{aligned}\frac{d}{d\tau}\log p(\mathbf{x}, \tau) &= \partial_\tau \log p(\mathbf{x}, \tau) + \frac{d\mathbf{x}}{d\tau}\cdot\nabla_{\mathbf{x}}\log p(\mathbf{x}, \tau)\\ &= \partial_\tau \log p(\mathbf{x}, \tau) + \mathbf{v}(\mathbf{x}, \tau)\cdot\nabla_{\mathbf{x}}\log p(\mathbf{x}, \tau),\end{aligned} \tag{23.8}$$

where we substituted $\frac{d\mathbf{x}}{d\tau} = \mathbf{v}(\mathbf{x}, \tau)$ according to the ODE in (23.7).

Now consider the continuity equation restated in terms of the flow $\mathbf{x}$, $\partial_\tau p(\mathbf{x}, \tau) = -\mathbf{div}(p(\mathbf{x}, \tau)\mathbf{v}(\mathbf{x}, \tau))$, and expand the divergence using the product rule $\mathbf{div}(fg) = f\mathbf{div}(g) + g\cdot\nabla f$. We have

$$\frac{1}{p(\mathbf{x}, \tau)}\partial_\tau p(\mathbf{x}, \tau) = -\frac{1}{p(\mathbf{x}, \tau)}\mathbf{div}(p(\mathbf{x}, \tau)\mathbf{v}(\mathbf{x}, \tau)) \tag{23.9}$$

$$\Rightarrow \quad \partial_\tau \log p(\mathbf{x}, \tau) = -\frac{1}{p(\mathbf{x}, \tau)}\mathbf{div}(p(\mathbf{x}, \tau)\mathbf{v}(\mathbf{x}, \tau)) \tag{23.10}$$

$$\Rightarrow \quad \partial_\tau \log p(\mathbf{x}, \tau) + \mathbf{v}(\mathbf{x}, \tau)\cdot\nabla_{\mathbf{x}}\log p(\mathbf{x}, \tau) = -\mathbf{div}(\mathbf{v}(\mathbf{x}, \tau)). \tag{23.11}$$

Substituting (23.8), we find

$$\frac{d}{d\tau}\log p(\mathbf{x}, \tau) = -\mathbf{div}(\mathbf{v}(\mathbf{x}, \tau)), \tag{23.12}$$

showing that the rate of change of the log density along trajectories is given by th negative divergence of the vector field $\mathbf{v}$. This shows that density changes arise fro contraction and expansion of the flow in phase space, as illustrated in Figure 23.2.

Change of Variables in Continuous Time

This result allows us to derive the continuous-time analog of the change-of-variabl formula from discrete normalizing flows. To establish this connection, we integra both sides of (23.12) from time τ_0 to time τ_1,

$$\int_{\tau_0}^{\tau_1} \frac{\mathrm{d}}{\mathrm{d}\tau} \log p(\mathbf{x}, \tau)\, \mathrm{d}\tau = -\int_{\tau_0}^{\tau_1} \mathbf{div}(\mathbf{v}(\mathbf{x}, \tau))\, \mathrm{d}\tau, \tag{23.13}$$

for initial condition $\mathbf{x}(\mathbf{x}_0, \tau_0) = \mathbf{x}_0$

$$\Rightarrow \log \frac{p(\mathbf{x}(\mathbf{x}_0, \tau_1), \tau_1)}{p(\mathbf{x}(\mathbf{x}_0, \tau_0), \tau_0)} = -\int_{\tau_0}^{\tau_1} \mathbf{div}(\mathbf{v}(\mathbf{x}(\mathbf{x}_0, \tau), \tau))\, \mathrm{d}\tau \tag{23.14}$$

Exponentiating both sides

$$\Rightarrow \frac{p(\mathbf{x}(\mathbf{x}_0, \tau_1), \tau_1)}{p(\mathbf{x}(\mathbf{x}_0, \tau_0), \tau_0)} = \exp\left(-\int_{\tau_0}^{\tau_1} \mathbf{div}(\mathbf{v}(\mathbf{x}(\mathbf{x}_0, \tau), \tau))\, \mathrm{d}\tau\right). \tag{23.15}$$

This defines the push-forward density $p_{\tau_1} := \mathbf{x}(\cdot, \tau_1)_\#[p_{\tau_0}]$ (where $[\cdot]_\#$ denotes the push-forward of a measure by a map) in terms of the flow $\mathbf{x}$. Comparing this back to the definition of the normalizing flow and the transformation rule of probability densities in (8.2), we observe that by considering the transformation $\mathbf{x}$ in continuous time, we significantly simplify the computation of the Jacobian determinant. For multilayer normalizing flows, the invertibility constraint on each layer is restrictive, while in CNFs the ODE is invertible by construction for well-posed ODEs.

Training CNFs

We can parameterize the velocity field $\mathbf{v}$ using neural networks and train them using the same forward and reverse KL approaches as used for training normalizing flows in Chapter 8. The goal is to learn a velocity field $\mathbf{v}_\theta$ such that the push-forward density $p_{\tau_f} := \mathbf{x}(\cdot, \tau_f)_\#[p_{\tau_0}]$ matches the prior distribution p_{prior} at time τ_f for $p_{\tau_0} = p_{\text{data}}$, see Figure 23.1. The resulting model is referred to as a CNF. To generate new samples from the data distribution, we use our time-reversal relationship to obtain the velocity field $\tilde{\mathbf{v}}_\theta = -\mathbf{v}_\theta$ that transports the prior p_{prior} at time $\tilde{\tau} = 0$ to the data distribution p_{data} at time $\tilde{\tau} = \tau_f$.

However, this approach requires simulation of the forward ODE during training to evaluate the push-forward density, which becomes computationally expensive due to the accumulation of numerical integration errors and memory requirements for backpropagation through the ODE solver (R. Chen et al., 2018). Recent work has therefore explored simulation-free approaches to training CNFs. The predominant family of such methods is referred to as *flow matching*, which we discuss next.

3.3 Flow Matching

To avoid the computational cost of ODE simulation during training, Flow matching takes a different approach: directly regressing the velocity field using tractable conditional flows. The key insight is that we can construct conditional flows whose marginal behavior matches the desired velocity field, without requiring direct access to it. This simulation-free approach dramatically reduces computational and memory costs compared to CNFs. Flow matching was first introduced by Lipman et al. (2023). In this chapter, we closely follow the exposition from Tong et al. (2023), which provides unifying view of several related methods.

In this section we use a time direction opposite to that used in most of the flo matching literature, but consistent with the direction used in the other chapters of th book. The formulas would match the literature if we use the tilded variables. We us $\tilde{\tau} = \tau_f - \tau$ for reversed time throughout.

To reiterate, our aim is to learn the reverse time-inverted velocity field $\tilde{\mathbf{v}}$ such that transports the prior $\tilde{p}(\mathbf{x}, \tilde{\tau} = 0) = p_{\text{prior}}$ to the data distribution $\tilde{p}(\mathbf{x}, \tilde{\tau} = \tau_f) = p_{\text{dat}}$ From a supervised learning perspective, a natural approach would be to directly regres the parameterized vector field $\tilde{\mathbf{v}}^{\theta}$ onto the true vector field $\tilde{\mathbf{v}}$ using the flow matchin loss

$$\mathcal{L}_{\text{FM}} := \mathbb{E}_{\tilde{\tau} \sim \text{Unif}[0, \tau_f], \mathbf{x} \sim \tilde{p}(\mathbf{x}, \tilde{\tau})} \left[||\tilde{\mathbf{v}}^{\theta}(\mathbf{x}, \tilde{\tau}) - \tilde{\mathbf{v}}(\mathbf{x}, \tilde{\tau})||^2 \right]. \quad (23.16$$

If we had access to $\tilde{p}(\mathbf{x}, \tilde{\tau})$ and $\tilde{\mathbf{v}}(\mathbf{x}, \tilde{\tau})$, this would provide a simulation-free approac to learn $\tilde{\mathbf{v}}^{\theta}(\mathbf{x}, \tilde{\tau})$ – we wouldn't need to simulate the ODE in (23.7) during trainin However, this objective assumes access to the very quantity we wish to learn, name $\tilde{\mathbf{v}}(\mathbf{x}, \tilde{\tau})$. The key insight of flow matching is to construct an alternative objective usin tractable conditional flows whose marginal behavior matches the desired velocity fiel without requiring direct access to it.

23.3.1 Conditional Flow Matching

The key observation is that by introducing a conditioning variable, we can constru tractable conditional flows whose marginal matches the desired distribution. For th purpose we introduce a conditioning latent variable $\mathbf{z}$, governed by some distribution our choice $q(\mathbf{z})$, that together with a conditional density $\tilde{p}(\mathbf{x}, \tilde{\tau}|\mathbf{z})$ defines the margin $\tilde{p}(\mathbf{x}, \tilde{\tau})$ as

$$\tilde{p}(\mathbf{x}, \tilde{\tau}) = \int d\mathbf{z}\; \tilde{p}(\mathbf{x}, \tilde{\tau}|\mathbf{z}) q(\mathbf{z}). \quad (23.17)$$

If we consider $\tilde{\mathbf{v}}(\mathbf{x}, \tilde{\tau}|\mathbf{z})$ to be the conditional vector field that generates the condition density $\tilde{p}(\mathbf{x}, \tilde{\tau}|\mathbf{z})$; that is, it solves the conditional continuity equation for every valu of $\mathbf{z}$ separately,

$$\partial_{\tilde{\tau}} \tilde{p}(\mathbf{x}, \tilde{\tau}|\mathbf{z}) = -\mathbf{div}(\tilde{p}(\mathbf{x}, \tilde{\tau}|\mathbf{z}) \tilde{\mathbf{v}}(\mathbf{x}, \tilde{\tau}|\mathbf{z})), \quad (23.18)$$

then the marginal velocity field defined as

$$\tilde{\mathbf{v}}(\mathbf{x}, \tilde{\tau}) := \frac{1}{\tilde{p}(\mathbf{x}, \tilde{\tau})} \mathbb{E}_{q(\mathbf{z})} \left[\tilde{\mathbf{v}}(\mathbf{x}, \tilde{\tau}|\mathbf{z}) \tilde{p}(\mathbf{x}, \tilde{\tau}|\mathbf{z}) \right] \quad (23.19)$$

will generate the marginal density $\tilde{p}(\mathbf{x}, \tilde{\tau})$. To verify this, we take the time derivati of (23.17):

$$\partial_{\tilde{\tau}} \tilde{p}(\mathbf{x}, \tilde{\tau}) = \int d\mathbf{z}\; \partial_{\tilde{\tau}} \tilde{p}(\mathbf{x}, \tilde{\tau}|\mathbf{z})\, q(\mathbf{z}). \quad (23.20)$$

Combining with the conditional continuity equation in (23.18) and moving the integral inside the divergence gives

$$\partial_{\tilde{\tau}} \tilde{p}(\mathbf{x}, \tilde{\tau}) = -\int d\mathbf{z}\, \mathbf{div}(\tilde{p}(\mathbf{x}, \tilde{\tau}|\mathbf{z})\tilde{\mathbf{v}}(\mathbf{x}, \tilde{\tau}|\mathbf{z}))q(\mathbf{z})$$

$$= -\mathbf{div}\left(\int d\mathbf{z}\, \tilde{p}(\mathbf{x}, \tilde{\tau}|\mathbf{z})\tilde{\mathbf{v}}(\mathbf{x}, \tilde{\tau}|\mathbf{z})q(\mathbf{z})\right) \quad \text{(using (23.19))} \tag{23.21}$$

$$\Rightarrow \quad \partial_{\tilde{\tau}} \tilde{p}(\mathbf{x}, \tilde{\tau}) = -\mathbf{div}(\tilde{p}(\mathbf{x}, \tilde{\tau})\tilde{\mathbf{v}}(\mathbf{x}, \tilde{\tau})), \tag{23.22}$$

we obtain the continuity equation relating the marginals $\tilde{p}(\mathbf{x}, \tilde{\tau})$ and $\tilde{\mathbf{v}}(\mathbf{x}, \tilde{\tau})$.

Conditional Flow Matching Loss

Unfortunately, the marginal density $\tilde{p}(\mathbf{x}, \tilde{\tau})$ in (23.17), as used in the definition of the marginal velocity field in (23.19), remains an intractable integral. We therefore cannot directly evaluate the original flow matching objective in (23.16). Nevertheless, we can construct an alternative per-sample objective based on conditional flows that has the same gradient. A second auxiliary conditional flow matching loss is defined as

$$\mathcal{L}_{\text{CFM}} := \mathbb{E}_{\tilde{\tau}\sim\text{Unif}[0,\tau_f],\mathbf{x}\sim\tilde{p}(\mathbf{x},\tilde{\tau}|\mathbf{z}),\mathbf{z}\sim q(\mathbf{z})}\left[||\tilde{\mathbf{v}}^{\theta}(\mathbf{x}, \tilde{\tau}) - \tilde{\mathbf{v}}(\mathbf{x}, \tilde{\tau}|\mathbf{z})||^2\right], \tag{23.23}$$

where, crucially, the learned velocity field $\tilde{\mathbf{v}}^{\theta}(\mathbf{x}, \tilde{\tau})$ is *not* conditioned on $\mathbf{z}$, even though we regress against the conditional field $\tilde{\mathbf{v}}(\mathbf{x}, \tilde{\tau}|\mathbf{z})$.

The remarkable result is that the gradients of the two losses are equivalent:

$$\nabla_{\theta}\mathcal{L}_{\text{CFM}} = \nabla_{\theta}\mathcal{L}_{\text{FM}}. \tag{23.24}$$

This can be shown by splitting the gradient into three terms:

$$\nabla_{\theta}\mathcal{L}_{\text{CFM}} = \nabla_{\theta}\mathbb{E}_{\tilde{\tau}\sim\text{Unif}[0,\tau_f],\mathbf{x}\sim\tilde{p}(\mathbf{x},\tilde{\tau}|\mathbf{z}),\mathbf{z}\sim q(\mathbf{z})}\Big[||\tilde{\mathbf{v}}^{\theta}(\mathbf{x}, \tilde{\tau})||^2 - 2\tilde{\mathbf{v}}^{\theta}(\mathbf{x}, \tilde{\tau})^{\top}\tilde{\mathbf{v}}(\mathbf{x}, \tilde{\tau}|\mathbf{z}) + ||\tilde{\mathbf{v}}(\mathbf{x}, \tilde{\tau}|\mathbf{z})||^2\Big]. \tag{23.25}$$

The key observation is that in each term, we can marginalize over $\mathbf{z}$ to show that the dependence on $\mathbf{z}$ cancels out. We leave this to the reader as an exercise and refer to Tong et al. (2023) for details.

Thus, having a tractable conditional vector field $\tilde{\mathbf{v}}(\mathbf{x}, \tilde{\tau}|\mathbf{z})$ is sufficient to regress our parameterized vector field $\tilde{\mathbf{v}}^{\theta}(\mathbf{x}, \tilde{\tau})$ to the marginal vector field $\tilde{\mathbf{v}}(\mathbf{x}, \tilde{\tau})$, even though this marginal velocity field itself remains intractable. The conditional formulation enables stochastic (batch) learning by sampling a small number of $(\tilde{\tau}, \mathbf{z}, \mathbf{x})$ triplets for gradient updates. While this is approximate, we know from stochastic gradient descent in deep learning that such mini-batch training is key to successfully training models at scale.

23.3.2 Variational Flow Matching

Alternatively, to learn the vector field $\tilde{\mathbf{v}}^{\theta}$ we can recast flow matching as a variational inference problem over endpoint labels of conditional trajectories, as introduced by Eijkelboom et al. (2024). This variational perspective provides an alternative parameterization and naturally connects flow matching to score-based models. For this purpose, consider the following rewriting of the marginal velocity field in (23.19):

$$\begin{aligned}\tilde{\mathbf{v}}(\mathbf{x},\tilde{\tau}) &= \int \mathrm{d}\mathbf{z}\, q(\mathbf{z})\tilde{\mathbf{v}}(\mathbf{x},\tilde{\tau}|\mathbf{z})\frac{\tilde{p}(\mathbf{x},\tilde{\tau}|\mathbf{z})}{\tilde{p}(\mathbf{x},\tilde{\tau})} \\ &= \int \mathrm{d}\mathbf{z}\, \tilde{\mathbf{v}}(\mathbf{x},\tilde{\tau}|\mathbf{z})\tilde{p}(\mathbf{z}|\mathbf{x},\tilde{\tau}) \\ &= \mathbb{E}_{\tilde{p}(\mathbf{z}|\mathbf{x},\tilde{\tau})}[\tilde{\mathbf{v}}(\mathbf{x},\tilde{\tau}|\mathbf{z})], \end{aligned} \tag{23.26}$$

where $\tilde{p}(\mathbf{z}|\mathbf{x},\tilde{\tau})$ is the posterior over conditioning variables given the current state.

Instead of parametrizing the marginal $\tilde{\mathbf{v}}^{\theta}(\mathbf{x},\tilde{\tau})$ directly, we can equivalently introduce a variational approximation $q^{\theta}(\mathbf{z}|\mathbf{x},\tilde{\tau})$ for $\mathbf{z}$ and tie the predictor to the variational expectation:

$$\tilde{\mathbf{v}}^{\theta}(\mathbf{x},\tilde{\tau}) := \int \tilde{\mathbf{v}}(\mathbf{x},\tilde{\tau}|\mathbf{z})q^{\theta}(\mathbf{z}|\mathbf{x},\tilde{\tau})\,\mathrm{d}\mathbf{z} = \mathbb{E}_{q^{\theta}(\mathbf{z}|\mathbf{x},\tilde{\tau})}[\tilde{\mathbf{v}}(\mathbf{x},\tilde{\tau}|\mathbf{z})]. \tag{23.27}$$

Training then proceeds by minimizing the KL divergence in expectation over $\tilde{\tau}$ and $\mathbf{x}$:

$$\begin{aligned}\mathcal{L}_{\mathrm{VFM}}(\boldsymbol{\theta}) &:= \mathbb{E}_{\tilde{\tau}\sim\mathrm{Unif}[0,\tau_f],\mathbf{x}\sim\tilde{p}(\mathbf{x},\tilde{\tau}|\mathbf{z}),\mathbf{z}\sim q(\mathbf{z})}\left[D_{\mathrm{KL}}[\tilde{p}(\mathbf{z}|\mathbf{x},\tilde{\tau})\|q^{\theta}(\mathbf{z}|\mathbf{x},\tilde{\tau})]\right] \\ &= -\mathbb{E}_{\tilde{\tau}\sim\mathrm{Unif}[0,\tau_f],\mathbf{x}\sim\tilde{p}(\mathbf{x},\tilde{\tau}|\mathbf{z}),\mathbf{z}\sim q(\mathbf{z})}[\log q^{\theta}(\mathbf{z}|\mathbf{x},\tilde{\tau})] + \text{const}, \end{aligned} \tag{23.28}$$

which, similar to the CFM loss, yields a simulation-free objective using samples $(\tilde{\tau},\mathbf{z},\mathbf{x})$ with $\mathbf{z}\sim q(\mathbf{z})$ and $\mathbf{x}\sim\tilde{p}(\mathbf{x},\tilde{\tau}|\mathbf{z})$. A key benefit of this variational perspective is that the learned variational approximation naturally parameterizes the score of the marginal distribution based on the score of the conditional distribution. To see this note that

$$\begin{aligned}\nabla_{\mathbf{x}}\log\tilde{p}(\mathbf{x},\tilde{\tau}) &= \frac{1}{\tilde{p}(\mathbf{x},\tilde{\tau})}\nabla_{\mathbf{x}}\tilde{p}(\mathbf{x},\tilde{\tau}) \\ &= \frac{1}{\tilde{p}(\mathbf{x},\tilde{\tau})}\nabla_{\mathbf{x}}\int \mathrm{d}\mathbf{z}\,\tilde{p}(\mathbf{x},\tilde{\tau}|\mathbf{z})q(\mathbf{z}) \\ &= \int \mathrm{d}\mathbf{z}\,\frac{\tilde{p}(\mathbf{x},\tilde{\tau}|\mathbf{z})q(\mathbf{z})}{\tilde{p}(\mathbf{x},\tilde{\tau})}\frac{\nabla_{\mathbf{x}}\tilde{p}(\mathbf{x},\tilde{\tau}|\mathbf{z})}{\tilde{p}(\mathbf{x},\tilde{\tau}|\mathbf{z})} \\ &= \int \mathrm{d}\mathbf{z}\,\tilde{p}(\mathbf{z}|\mathbf{x},\tilde{\tau})\nabla_{\mathbf{x}}\log\tilde{p}(\mathbf{x},\tilde{\tau}|\mathbf{z}) \\ &\approx \mathbb{E}_{q^{\theta}(\mathbf{z}|\mathbf{x},\tilde{\tau})}\left[\nabla_{\mathbf{x}}\log\tilde{p}(\mathbf{x},\tilde{\tau}|\mathbf{z})\right], \end{aligned} \tag{23.29}$$

where we have marginalized over $\mathbf{z}$ and then approximated the true posterior with its variational approximation. Variational flow matching (VFM) thus provides an intuitive bridge between deterministic flow-based generative models and stochastic generative models based on score estimation, such as diffusion models. This perspective has also led to generalizations that can work for categorical data (Eijkelboom et al., 2024).

23.3.3 Conditional Probability Paths

Having established the CFM and VFM frameworks, we now examine three specific choices of conditional probability paths that showcase these methods in practice.

Different choices lead to different marginal probability paths $\tilde{p}(\mathbf{x}, \tilde{\tau})$ and corresponding marginal vector fields $\tilde{\mathbf{v}}(\mathbf{x}, \tilde{\tau})$, each with distinct properties. Figure 23.3 illustrates the differences between these three approaches to conditional probability paths.

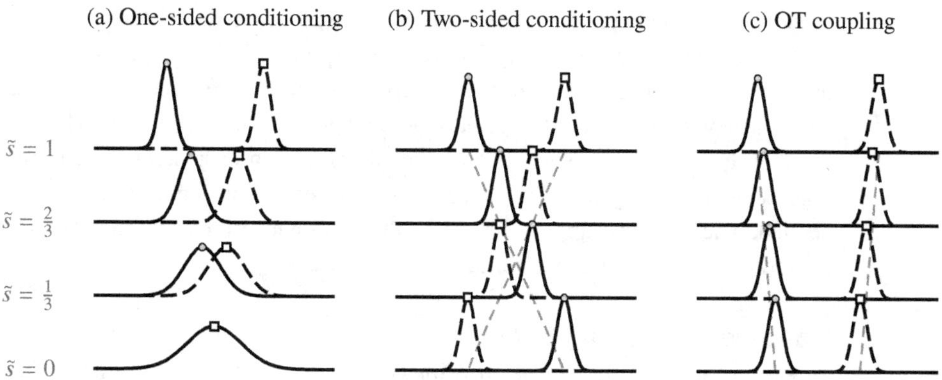

Figure 23.3 Comparison of flow matching approaches showing the evolution of probability distributions. Time increases upward and the tick labels indicate the rescaled time $\tilde{s} = \tilde{\tau}/\tau_f$. Solid curves with circular markers indicate the source/prior density, while dashed curves with square markers denote the target/data density. (a) One-sided conditioning (Gaussian CFM) merges two peaks into one. (b) Two-sided conditioning with an independent coupling exhibits straight crossing trajectories. (c) OT coupling yields parallel, noncrossing paths with minimal movement, reflecting the optimal transport displacement interpolation. Dotted guides mark representative transport paths. Figure adapted from Tong et al. (2023).

The discussion above is valid for any choice of $q(\mathbf{z})$, $\tilde{p}(\mathbf{x}, \tilde{\tau}|\mathbf{z})$, and $\tilde{\mathbf{v}}(\mathbf{x}, \tilde{\tau}|\mathbf{z})$ as long as $\tilde{\mathbf{v}}(\mathbf{x}, \tilde{\tau}|\mathbf{z})$ generates $\tilde{p}(\mathbf{x}, \tilde{\tau}|\mathbf{z})$.

To simplify the notation in what follows, we work with rescaled time $\tilde{s} \in [0, 1]$ where $\tilde{s} = \tilde{\tau}/\tau_f$. This makes the conditional paths easier to parameterize, and time derivatives transform as $\mathrm{d}\tilde{\tau} = \tau_f \, \mathrm{d}\tilde{s}$.

Gaussian CFM

In Gaussian CFM, we specialize by identifying the conditioning variable with data points: $\mathbf{z} = \mathbf{x}_1 \sim p_{\text{data}}$. Thus the conditioning distribution is $q(\mathbf{z}) = p_{\text{data}}(\mathbf{z})$. We consider a conditional probability path of the form

$$\tilde{p}(\mathbf{x}, \tilde{\tau}|\mathbf{z}) = G(\mathbf{x}|\tilde{s}\mathbf{x}_1, (\tilde{s}\sigma - \tilde{s} + 1)^2\mathbf{I}), \tag{23.30}$$

where $\sigma \in (0, 1)$ is a hyperparameter. The corresponding conditional velocity field is

$$\tilde{\mathbf{v}}(\mathbf{x}, \tilde{\tau}|\mathbf{z}) = \frac{1}{t_f} \cdot \frac{\mathbf{x}_1 - (1 - \sigma)\mathbf{x}}{1 - (1 - \sigma)\tilde{s}}. \tag{23.31}$$

We can verify that this is a valid choice of conditional density and velocity field by showing that $\partial_{\tilde{\tau}} \tilde{p}(\mathbf{x}, \tilde{\tau}|\mathbf{z})$ and $-\mathbf{div}(\tilde{p}(\mathbf{x}, \tilde{\tau}|\mathbf{z})\tilde{\mathbf{v}}(\mathbf{x}, \tilde{\tau}|\mathbf{z}))$ are equal, thereby satisfying the conditional continuity equation in (23.18). However, as this is a rather laborious task, we leave the verification to the reader.

This setup restricts the marginal at time $\tilde{\tau} = 0$ of the conditional density to be standard Gaussian with unit variance, $\tilde{p}(\mathbf{x}, 0) = G(\mathbf{0}, \mathbf{I})$, which we can subsequentl choose as our prior density $p_{\text{prior}}(\mathbf{x})$. This allows for efficient sampling from our prio similar to what is done in diffusion models. Note, however, that in contrast to diffusio models, this is an explicit choice of the prior distribution, and not a requirement.

This approach was originally proposed in Lipman et al. (2023), a seminal work o using flow matching for generative modeling. If one is purely interested in learning t generate new samples, using a simple Gaussian prior suffices. However, when intereste in other auxiliary tasks, such as conditional generation or generation with optimalit objectives over the generating trajectories, different conditional probability paths ar needed. The next two approaches relax the Gaussian prior constraint and ultimatel lead to thermodynamically optimal paths.

Independent Coupling CFM

To step away from the Gaussian prior constraint, we now generalize by letting th conditioning variable $\mathbf{z}$ represent a pair of points: $\mathbf{z} = (\mathbf{x}_0, \mathbf{x}_1)$, where $\mathbf{x}_0$ is a sourc point and $\mathbf{x}_1$ is a target point. We will consider general joint distributions $q(\mathbf{x}_0, \mathbf{x}_1$ next, but first we consider the case where $q(\mathbf{z}) = q(\mathbf{x}_0, \mathbf{x}_1) = p_{\text{prior}}(\mathbf{x}_0) p_{\text{data}}(\mathbf{x}_1)$ is a independent coupling between the prior and data distribution.

The conditional distribution and velocity field are defined as

$$\tilde{p}(\mathbf{x}, \tilde{\tau} | \mathbf{x}_0, \mathbf{x}_1) = G(\mathbf{x} | \tilde{s}\mathbf{x}_1 + (1 - \tilde{s})\mathbf{x}_0, \sigma^2 \mathbf{I}), \tag{23.32}$$

$$\tilde{\mathbf{v}}(\mathbf{x}, \tilde{\tau} | \mathbf{x}_0, \mathbf{x}_1) = \frac{1}{\tau_f}(\mathbf{x}_1 - \mathbf{x}_0), \tag{23.33}$$

recalling that $\tilde{s} = \tilde{\tau}/\tau_f$. This path linearly interpolates between source $\mathbf{x}_0$ and target $\mathbf{x}$ with Gaussian noise, giving constant velocity along each conditional trajectory.

The marginal at time $\tilde{\tau}$ is

$$\begin{aligned} \tilde{p}(\mathbf{x}, \tilde{\tau}) &= \iint d\mathbf{x}_0 \ d\mathbf{x}_1 \ \tilde{p}(\mathbf{x}, \tilde{\tau} | \mathbf{x}_0, \mathbf{x}_1) q(\mathbf{x}_0, \mathbf{x}_1) \\ &= \iint d\mathbf{x}_0 \ d\mathbf{x}_1 \ G(\mathbf{x} | \tilde{s}\mathbf{x}_1 + (1 - \tilde{s})\mathbf{x}_0, \sigma^2 \mathbf{I}) p_{\text{prior}}(\mathbf{x}_0) p_{\text{data}}(\mathbf{x}_1). \end{aligned} \tag{23.34}$$

When evaluated at time $\tilde{\tau} = 0$, this corresponds to the prior distribution convolve with a Gaussian (where $(f * g)(\mathbf{x}) = \int f(\mathbf{x} - \mathbf{y}) g(\mathbf{y}) \, d\mathbf{y}$ denotes convolution):

$$\begin{aligned} \tilde{p}(\mathbf{x}, 0) &= \iint d\mathbf{x}_0 \ d\mathbf{x}_1 \ G(\mathbf{x} | \mathbf{x}_0, \sigma^2 \mathbf{I}) p_{\text{prior}}(\mathbf{x}_0) p_{\text{data}}(\mathbf{x}_1) \\ &= \int d\mathbf{x}_0 \ G(\mathbf{x} | \mathbf{x}_0, \sigma^2 \mathbf{I}) p_{\text{prior}}(\mathbf{x}_0) \\ &= (p_{\text{prior}} * G(\mathbf{0}, \sigma^2 \mathbf{I}))(\mathbf{x}). \end{aligned} \tag{23.35}$$

Similarly, for $\tilde{\tau} = \tau_f \Rightarrow \tilde{s} = 1$, we have $\tilde{p}(\mathbf{x}, \tau_f) = (p_{\text{data}} * G(\mathbf{0}, \sigma^2 \mathbf{I}))(\mathbf{x})$. As approaches 0, the marginal velocity field $\tilde{\mathbf{v}}(\mathbf{x}, \tilde{\tau})$ thus maps samples from the pri distribution to the target distribution. This is a key limitation: unlike Gaussian CF we cannot write down the marginal path $\tilde{p}(\mathbf{x}, \tilde{\tau})$ in closed form except at the endpoint

For any time $\tilde{\tau}$ not equal to 0 or τ_f, we remain with an intractable integral over source and target samples.

Crucially, this prior itself does not need to be a Gaussian distribution, despite the conditional probability path being Gaussian. Including the conditioning on $\mathbf{x}_0$ allows for generalizing the flow matching approach to any set of source and target distributions.

One thing we have not yet validated is that (23.32) and (23.33) are a valid conditional density and velocity field pair satisfying the conditional continuity equation. Fortunately, if we define

$$\mu(\tilde{\tau}) = \tilde{s}\mathbf{x}_1 + (1 - \tilde{s})\mathbf{x}_0 \quad \text{with} \quad \frac{\mathrm{d}}{\mathrm{d}\tilde{\tau}}\mu(\tilde{\tau}) = \frac{1}{\tau_f}(\mathbf{x}_1 - \mathbf{x}_0), \tag{23.36}$$

we quickly see that with

$$\partial_{\tilde{\tau}}\tilde{p}(\mathbf{x}, \tilde{\tau}|\mathbf{x}_0, \mathbf{x}_1) = \frac{\tilde{p}(\mathbf{x}, \tilde{\tau}|\mathbf{x}_0, \mathbf{x}_1)}{\tau_f \sigma^2}(\mathbf{x} - \mu(\tilde{\tau}))^\top(\mathbf{x}_1 - \mathbf{x}_0), \tag{23.37}$$

and, noting that $\mathbf{div}(\tilde{\mathbf{v}}) = 0$ since $\tilde{\mathbf{v}}$ is constant in space (depends only on $\mathbf{x}_0, \mathbf{x}_1$, not on $\mathbf{x}$),

$$\begin{aligned} \mathbf{div}(\tilde{p}(\mathbf{x}, \tilde{\tau}|\mathbf{x}_0, \mathbf{x}_1)\tilde{\mathbf{v}}(\mathbf{x}, \tilde{\tau}|\mathbf{x}_0, \mathbf{x}_1)) &= \nabla\tilde{p}(\mathbf{x}, \tilde{\tau}|\mathbf{x}_0, \mathbf{x}_1) \cdot \tilde{\mathbf{v}}(\mathbf{x}, \tilde{\tau}|\mathbf{x}_0, \mathbf{x}_1) \\ &= -\frac{\tilde{p}(\mathbf{x}, \tilde{\tau}|\mathbf{x}_0, \mathbf{x}_1)}{\tau_f \sigma^2}(\mathbf{x} - \mu(\tilde{\tau}))^\top(\mathbf{x}_1 - \mathbf{x}_0), \end{aligned} \tag{23.38}$$

confirming that (23.18) is satisfied.

Optimal Transport CFM

The independent coupling treats all source–target pairs equally, but we can do better by preferring pairs that are close together, minimizing transport cost. This is the optimal transport coupling. We can further generalize the independent coupling CFM to joint distributions $q(\mathbf{z}) = q(\mathbf{x}_0, \mathbf{x}_1)$ that do not factorize. A particularly interesting choice is to take $q(\mathbf{z}) := \gamma(\mathbf{x}_0, \mathbf{x}_1) = p_{\text{prior}}(\mathbf{x}_0)\gamma(\mathbf{x}_1|\mathbf{x}_0)$, where γ is the deterministic invertible Monge map that solves the optimal transport problem (which minimizes expected transport cost between p_{prior} and p_{data}).

What's interesting to see is that changing the coupling $q(\mathbf{z})$ will change the marginal density path $\tilde{p}(\mathbf{x}, \tilde{\tau})$ even when the conditional density path $\tilde{p}(\mathbf{x}, \tilde{\tau}|\mathbf{z})$ remains the same. With the OT coupling $\gamma(\mathbf{x}_0, \mathbf{x}_1)$ and the conditional density as in (23.32), our marginal at time $\tilde{\tau}$ is now

$$\begin{aligned} \tilde{p}(\mathbf{x}, \tilde{\tau}) &= \iint \mathrm{d}\mathbf{x}_0\ \mathrm{d}\mathbf{x}_1\ G(\mathbf{x}|\tilde{s}\mathbf{x}_1 + (1 - \tilde{s})\mathbf{x}_0, \sigma^2\mathbf{I})\gamma(\mathbf{x}_0, \mathbf{x}_1) \\ &= \iint \mathrm{d}\mathbf{x}_0\ \mathrm{d}\mathbf{x}_1\ G(\mathbf{x}|\tilde{s}\mathbf{x}_1 + (1 - \tilde{s})\mathbf{x}_0, \sigma^2\mathbf{I})p_{\text{prior}}(\mathbf{x}_0)\gamma(\mathbf{x}_1|\mathbf{x}_0) \\ &= \iint \mathrm{d}\mathbf{x}_0\ \mathrm{d}\mathbf{x}_1\ G(\mathbf{x}|\tilde{s}\mathbf{x}_1 + (1 - \tilde{s})\mathbf{x}_0, \sigma^2\mathbf{I})p_{\text{prior}}(\mathbf{x}_0)\delta(\mathbf{x}_1 - T_\gamma(\mathbf{x}_0)) \\ &= \int \mathrm{d}\mathbf{x}_0\ G(\mathbf{x}|\tilde{s}T_\gamma(\mathbf{x}_0) + (1 - \tilde{s})\mathbf{x}_0, \sigma^2\mathbf{I})p_{\text{prior}}(\mathbf{x}_0), \end{aligned} \tag{23.39}$$

where $T_\gamma\colon \mathbf{x}_0 \mapsto \mathbf{x}_1$ is the Monge map (deterministic optimal transport map).

While for the independent coupling we were able to define the marginal densit path $\tilde{p}(\mathbf{x}, \tilde{\tau})$ as a simple convolution at times $\tilde{\tau} = 0$ and $\tilde{\tau} = \tau_f$ at intermediate times we remained limited by having to marginalize over both the source and target samples Now that we have used an OT-coupling, (23.39) gives us an expression for the margina density path as a convolution at any time $\tilde{\tau}$,

$$\tilde{p}(\mathbf{x}, \tilde{\tau}) = ([\mu_{\tilde{\tau}}]_{\#} p_{\text{prior}} * G(\mathbf{0}, \sigma^2 \mathbf{I}))(\mathbf{x}), \tag{23.40}$$

where $\mu_{\tilde{\tau}}(\mathbf{x}) = \mu(\mathbf{x}, \tilde{\tau}) = \tilde{s} T_\gamma(\mathbf{x}) + (1 - \tilde{s})\mathbf{x}$ is the displacement interpolation an $[\mu_{\tilde{\tau}}]_{\#}$ denotes the push-forward by the map $\mu_{\tilde{\tau}}$. When $\sigma \to 0$, this converges t simply $[\mu_{\tilde{\tau}}]_{\#} p_{\text{prior}}(\mathbf{x})$, known as McCann interpolation (Gangbo and McCann, 1996 McCann, 1997).

So far we have assumed that the Monge map was given to us. But solving fo the OT solution is a nontrivial problem in its own right. Interestingly, Benamou an Brenier (2000) showed that the Monge map can be found by solving a variationa fluid mechanics problem, which was discussed in Chapter 22. This then also forge a connection between flow matching and solving the OT problem, as we will discus next.

In the next paragraph we will show the following. If we assume (23.32) and (23.33 hold for the marginal density and the velocity field, and we furthermore assume tha the map $T_\gamma(\cdot)$ is invertible, then it minimizes the kinetic energy functional that define Benamou and Brenier's dynamical fluid dynamics description of the OT problem.

Solving the Dynamical OT Problem

To show this we have to consider two things. First, we must show that for the con ditional density (23.32), conditional velocity field 23.33, and coupling $\gamma(\mathbf{x}_0, \mathbf{x}_1)$, th corresponding marginal density path $\tilde{p}(\mathbf{x}, \tilde{\tau})$ and conditional velocity field $\tilde{\mathbf{v}}(\mathbf{x}, \tilde{\tau}$ satisfy the continuity equation, as required for them to be a solution to the dynami cal OT problem. This can be proven by considering that in Section 23.3.3 we hav already shown for the independent coupling case, that the conditional density pat $\tilde{p}(\mathbf{x}, \tilde{\tau}|\mathbf{x}_0, \mathbf{x}_1)$ and marginal velocity field $\tilde{\mathbf{v}}(\mathbf{x}, \tilde{\tau}|\mathbf{x}_0, \mathbf{x}_1)$ satisfy the conditional continu ity equation. Since we are conditioning on $\mathbf{z} = \{\mathbf{x}_0, \mathbf{x}_1\}$, the derivation is the same fc the OT coupling case. Then, using (23.22) we can conclude that the marginal densit path $\tilde{p}(\mathbf{x}, \tilde{\tau})$ and marginal velocity field $\tilde{\mathbf{v}}(\mathbf{x}, \tilde{\tau})$ also satisfy the continuity equation.

Second, and slightly more complicated, we must show that the marginal densit path $\tilde{p}(\mathbf{x}, \tilde{\tau})$ and corresponding velocity field $\tilde{\mathbf{v}}(\mathbf{x}, \tilde{\tau})$ also minimize the kinetic energ over the path defined by the OT solution:

$$\tilde{\mathbf{v}}(\mathbf{x}, \tilde{\tau}) = \underset{\tilde{\mathbf{v}}'(\mathbf{x}, \tilde{\tau}) :\, \partial_{\tilde{\tau}} \tilde{p} = -\mathbf{div}(\tilde{p}\tilde{\mathbf{v}}')}{\operatorname{argmin}} \tau_f \int_0^{\tau_f} d\tilde{\tau} \int d\mathbf{x}\, \tilde{p}(\mathbf{x}, \tilde{\tau}) ||\tilde{\mathbf{v}}'(\mathbf{x}, \tilde{\tau})||^2. \tag{23.41}$$

For this purpose we first need to derive the marginal velocity field $\tilde{\mathbf{v}}(\mathbf{x}, \tilde{\tau})$ that corre sponds to the OT coupling, starting with the observation that using the Monge map T the conditional velocity field $\tilde{\mathbf{v}}(\mathbf{x}, \tilde{\tau}|\mathbf{x}_0, \mathbf{x}_1)$ is only dependent on the term $\mathbf{x}_0$ and ca thus be rewritten for simplicity as

$$\tilde{\mathbf{v}}(\mathbf{x}, \tilde{\tau}|\mathbf{x}_0, \mathbf{x}_1) = \frac{1}{\tau_f}(\mathbf{x}_1 - \mathbf{x}_0) = \frac{1}{\tau_f}(T_\gamma(\mathbf{x}_0) - \mathbf{x}_0) = \hat{\mathbf{v}}(\mathbf{x}_0), \tag{23.42}$$

where we introduce the shorthand $\hat{\mathbf{v}}(\mathbf{x}_0) := (T_\gamma(\mathbf{x}_0) - \mathbf{x}_0)/\tau_f$. Similarly,

$$\tilde{p}(\mathbf{x}, \tilde{\tau}|\mathbf{x}_0, \mathbf{x}_1) = \tilde{p}(\mathbf{x}, \tilde{\tau}|\mathbf{x}_0, T_\gamma(\mathbf{x}_0)) = \tilde{p}(\mathbf{x}, \tilde{\tau}|\mathbf{x}_0). \tag{23.43}$$

Now, from the definition of the marginal velocity field given the conditional density and velocity field in (23.19), we rewrite the expectation as

$$\begin{aligned}
&\mathbb{E}_{\gamma(\mathbf{x}_0,\mathbf{x}_1)}\left[\tilde{\mathbf{v}}(\mathbf{x}, \tilde{\tau}|\mathbf{x}_0, \mathbf{x}_1)\tilde{p}(\mathbf{x}, \tilde{\tau}|\mathbf{x}_0, \mathbf{x}_1)\right] \\
&= \iint d\mathbf{x}_0 \; d\mathbf{x}_1 \; \tilde{\mathbf{v}}(\mathbf{x}, \tilde{\tau}|\mathbf{x}_0, \mathbf{x}_1)\tilde{p}(\mathbf{x}, \tilde{\tau}|\mathbf{x}_0, \mathbf{x}_1)\gamma(\mathbf{x}_0, \mathbf{x}_1) \\
&= \iint d\mathbf{x}_0 \; d\mathbf{x}_1 \; \hat{\mathbf{v}}(\mathbf{x}_0)\tilde{p}(\mathbf{x}, \tilde{\tau}|\mathbf{x}_0)\gamma(\mathbf{x}_1|\mathbf{x}_0)p_{\text{prior}}(\mathbf{x}_0) \\
&= \int d\mathbf{x}_0 \; \hat{\mathbf{v}}(\mathbf{x}_0)\tilde{p}(\mathbf{x}, \tilde{\tau}|\mathbf{x}_0)p_{\text{prior}}(\mathbf{x}_0) \\
&= \int d\mathbf{x}_0 \; \hat{\mathbf{v}}(\mathbf{x}_0)G(\mathbf{x}|\mu(\mathbf{x}_0, \tilde{\tau}), \sigma^2\mathbf{I})p_{\text{prior}}(\mathbf{x}_0).
\end{aligned} \tag{23.44}$$

Plugging this into the definition of the marginal velocity field in (23.19), we find

$$\begin{aligned}
\tilde{\mathbf{v}}(\mathbf{x}, \tilde{\tau}) &:= \frac{1}{\tilde{p}(\mathbf{x}, \tilde{\tau})}\mathbb{E}_{\gamma(\mathbf{x}_0,\mathbf{x}_1)}\left[\tilde{\mathbf{v}}(\mathbf{x}, \tilde{\tau}|\mathbf{x}_0, \mathbf{x}_1)\tilde{p}(\mathbf{x}, \tilde{\tau}|\mathbf{x}_0, \mathbf{x}_1)\right] \\
&= \int d\mathbf{x}_0 \; \hat{\mathbf{v}}(\mathbf{x}_0)\frac{G(\mathbf{x}|\mu(\mathbf{x}_0, \tilde{\tau}), \sigma^2\mathbf{I})p_{\text{prior}}(\mathbf{x}_0)}{\tilde{p}(\mathbf{x}, \tilde{\tau})} \\
&= \int d\mathbf{x}_0 \; \hat{\mathbf{v}}(\mathbf{x}_0)\tilde{p}(\mathbf{x}_0|\mathbf{x}, \tilde{\tau}),
\end{aligned} \tag{23.45}$$

where $\tilde{p}(\mathbf{x}_0|\mathbf{x}, \tilde{\tau})$ is the posterior over source points given the current state. As $\sigma \to 0$, the posterior concentrates: $\tilde{p}(\mathbf{x}_0|\mathbf{x}, \tilde{\tau}) \to \delta(\mathbf{x}_0 - \mu^{-1}(\mathbf{x}, \tilde{\tau}))$. Thus, we find that

$$\begin{aligned}
\tilde{\mathbf{v}}(\mathbf{x}, \tilde{\tau}) &= \int d\mathbf{x}_0 \; \hat{\mathbf{v}}(\mathbf{x}_0)\delta(\mathbf{x}_0 - \mu^{-1}(\mathbf{x}, \tilde{\tau})) \\
&= \hat{\mathbf{v}}(\mu^{-1}(\mathbf{x}, \tilde{\tau})) \\
&= \frac{1}{\tau_f}\left(T_\gamma(\mu^{-1}(\mathbf{x}, \tilde{\tau})) - \mu^{-1}(\mathbf{x}, \tilde{\tau})\right),
\end{aligned} \tag{23.46}$$

which corresponds to moving samples along a straight line at constant speed between initial and target distributions. This is the velocity field that minimizes the kinetic energy, and we can thus conclude that with an invertible map $T_\gamma(\cdot)$ and the conditional density and velocity field as defined in (23.32) and (23.33), CFM learns a velocity field $\tilde{\mathbf{v}}^\theta(\mathbf{x}, \tilde{\tau})$ that solves the Benamou–Brenier dynamical OT problem.

In the derivation, we did not seem to have used the properties of the Monge map $T_\gamma(\cdot)$ at all, except for invertibility. The proof appeared to depend only on mapping all points from the initial distribution to the final distribution with straight lines at constant velocity. However, finding such a map that is invertible (i.e., no lines are crossing) is no small feat and indeed solves the OT problem. In fact, solving the static OT proble to obtain this map is computationally expensive, scaling cubically in the number samples ($O(n^3)$ time) and quadratically in memory ($O(n^2)$) (Villani, 2003, 2008).

In practice, we have a collection of data points. A practical algorithm to find the m is to also sample an equal number of points from the prior and match them accordir to the Sinkhorn algorithm. Practical algorithms to achieve that can be found in, f example, Peyré and Cuturi (2019). We then connect these matching points by straig lines and assume constant velocities for them. We then use these lines to learn t marginal velocity field $\tilde{\mathbf{v}}^{\theta}(\mathbf{x}, \tilde{\tau})$ by minimizing the loss in (23.23). This then represen a practical procedure to map any point from the prior to the data distribution.

In practice, solving the OT matching problem for all data-points (e.g., with t Sinkhorn algorithm) can be prohibitively slow. Instead, it is often combined wi a mini-batching approach where the matching problem is solved only for sampl included in the batch. This has been shown empirically to give good performance ev for small batch sizes.

Minimal Dissipated Work Conditional Flow Matching

While certainly theoretically interesting, the answer to "why" we would want to learn velocity field $\tilde{\mathbf{v}}^{\theta}(\mathbf{x}, \tilde{\tau})$ that solves the Benamou–Brenier dynamical OT problem is n immediately apparent. Strictly for the purpose of generating new samples $\mathbf{x}$, any pa of conditional densities and velocity fields that have p_{prior} as their initial distributi would suffice. Having straight integration lines for our ODE to solve as provided t the OT–CFM solution does have some numerical benefits, such as requiring few integration steps, but it does not immediately increase the quality of the samples.

The benefit of using optimal oransport paths in our sampling procedure becom clear only when we start considering tasks where not only the terminal marginals a of interest but also the path we took to get there. Not coincidentally, this is exactly t same consideration as made in the field of stochastic thermodynamics. In this conte the use of optimal transport paths in CFM can be nicely coupled back to the discussi of work dissipation minimization and counterdiabatic driving in the previous chapte

In learning a velocity field $\tilde{\mathbf{v}}^{\theta}(\mathbf{x}, \tilde{\tau})$ that solves the Benamou–Brenier dynamical O problem, trajectories sampled using OT-CFM have minimal work dissipation. As suc it is the solution that increases the total entropy of the system the least and, as such, w lose as little information about the system as possible . The intriguing insight is th solutions with the minimal heat generation are also the ones that result in the best (e.g lowest variance) estimators, for example, estimating free energy differences (Geig and Dellago, 2010). This can be easily understood from the Jarzynski equality, whe the fluctuations in work across paths cause the variance in computing free energ differences.

Other combinations of conditional velocity field, density, and coupling do not pr vide this guarantee. The learned velocity fields for these approaches still descri counterdiabatic driving protocols, but dissipate more work. Control protocols simil to counterdiabatic driving were used in the controlled Monte Carlo diffusion sa pler (Vargas et al., 2024) to improve sampling performance and reduce variance computing marginal log-likelihoods (a.k.a., free energies). Principles from stochastic thermodynamics were also used in Ikeda et al. (2025) to improve diffusion sampler performance.

Part IV

Epilogue

24 Unification: Free Energy is All You Need

Congratulations, you have made it to the end! I hope you got the main message of this book: that there is a remarkable connection between the field of nonequilibrium thermodynamics (or a subfield known as stochastic thermodynamics) and probabilistic machine learning (and its subfield now known as generative AI). The mathematics that is used to generate beautiful videos of dogs playing in the snow is the same as that of describing thermodynamic systems such as solids, liquids, and gases out of equilibrium.

At the core of this connection sits the variational free energy, also known as the (negative) evidence lower bound in ML. In physics, the variational free energy serves as a generalization of the equilibrium free energy used to describe nonequilibrium systems. This variational free energy upper bounds the equilibrium free energy. In fact, physical systems can be understood as descending on this free energy, following the steepest descent direction at all times. In probabilistic (generative) ML, we also minimize the free energy when we perform inference or when we learn. As such, we discovered a deep connection between thermodynamic concepts such as work, heat, and entropy production and the expectation-maximization algorithm in statistics and ML.

We would like to call out, in particular, the role of entropy in both theories. In physics, entropy could be thought of as an ontological property of the system. However, we would like to argue (alongside many others, most prominently E. T. Jaynes) that entropy is to be interpreted as "lost information" or "lack of knowledge" about the system. This aligns perfectly with the role of probability and entropy in AI: these are mathematical tools to deal with the lack of detailed information of the system. Entropy quantifies how much information we have lost access to. An alien species with much more advanced measuring tools that could track individual particles might reduce entropy to almost zero in their description of the world!

But the connection runs much deeper. Diffusion-based generative AI models can be viewed as systems that evolve towards equilibrium in the encoder direction while being controlled to evolve away from equilibrium in the generative, decoder direction. We believe that the mathematics of these two fields transcends these applications, and we can fruitfully think of generative AI as a form of nonequilibrium thermodynamics. At the deepest level, both can be considered information processing systems, or "it from bit" as J. A. Wheeler famously said. In this sense, we believe that the 2024 Nobel Prize in Physics awarded to Hopfield and Hinton couldn't have been more appropriate.

Besides diffusion models, in this book we connected many different tools in the MI community to concepts of nonequilibrium thermodynamics, ranging from Schrödinge bridges, maximum caliber methods, optimal transport theory, Markov chain Mont Carlo sampling methods, to variational learning, normalizing flows, flow-based model optimal control theory, reinforcement learning, and GFlowNets. At their core, they ca all be described by an encoder Markov chain Q and a decoder Markov chain P. Th former, Q, is the chain that runs in the natural, physical forward direction, increasin entropy, while P runs in the backward, controlled direction, reducing entropy b denoising dynamics and creating structure out of noise.

Differences among all these methods can be attributed to certain choices we mak about these distributions. For example, do we assume that we have an expressio for the distribution Q_0, or do we assume that we only have access to data? Do w parameterize the decoder in the direction starting at $t = t_f$ and iterating backward (generative models), or do we parameterize them in the same direction as a polic (optimal control methods)? Do we treat the dynamics as stochastic (diffusion) or do w make them deterministic (flows)? Do we optimize the forces to guide the generativ model through learning from data or from a reward function (reinforcement)? Wha unifies all these methods are these two Markov chains, with one being the approximat inverse of the other, and the concept of the free energy objective that underlies it al This book truly is a "Tale of Free Energies".

A hallmark result of the theory of stochastic thermodynamics is fluctuation theo rems, which state that exponential averages of thermodynamic quantities over sampl paths satisfy exact relations even out of equilibrium. For instance, the famous Jarzynsk equality relates the exponential average of total (negative) work over sample paths to th exponential of the (negative) free energy difference between two distributions (Jarzyn ski, 1997). This equality is, in fact, equivalent to the one used in annealed importanc sampling as developed by Radford Neal in the context of MCMC sampling. Crook fluctuation theorem is even more general in that it relates the expected probability o entropy production to the irreversibility of the underlying physical process (Crook 1999). This connects to a very deep philosophical discussion among scientists lik Gibbs and Boltzmann – which became known as the Loschmidt paradox – about wh we observe an asymmetry in the way the world evolves – we never see an egg tha unscrambles itself. If the underlying laws of physics are in fact time-reversal sym metric, why do we see, at a coarse-grained level, a direction of time defined by a ever-increasing entropy? While the fluctuation theorems seem to provide an answe Loschmidt argued that the problem has not truly been resolved. Somehow, the prob ability of initial conditions that lead to increasing entropy of the type of variable we like to (or can) measure is much higher than the probability of initial conditio that evolve in the direction of decreasing entropy. Some argue this asymmetry mu have been encoded in the initial condition of the universe at the time of the big ban However, it would not surprise us if a deeper theory will still be needed that mode the role of information processing observers in a universe.

Related to time reversal is the second fundamental concept discussed in this book: th concept of "balancing equations". Detailed balance is the simplest of these, stating th the probability flow between any two states is equal (Metropolis et al., 1953). This can be used to derive fluctuation theorems and is also key to designing MCMC algorithms. A generalization of these equations only demands invariance (or stationarity) of a distribution where the forward and reversed kernels can be different but share the same invariant distribution. This generalizes fluctuation theorems to this case and also leads to irreversible MCMC methods that tend to mix faster than those based on detailed balance. Irreversible kernels can even be used for fully deterministic systems and are ultimately a reflection of the continuity equation – that probability should be preserved. There are many opportunities to get confused about terminology: a time-reversed Markov chain based on an irreversible kernel still follows physical dynamics where the entropy increases and has the same equilibrium distribution as the forward dynamics. It's like seeing the dynamics in a mirror where all velocities are reversed. The time-reversed dynamics P generated by the backward transitions B (see Figure 24.1) is, however, nonphysical and tends to reduce entropy. It performs denoising on the system, which can only occur when it is controlled by external (learned) forces.

We acknowledge that in this book we have not covered some pretty important theories. In particular, you may have noticed that we have avoided stochastic calculus altogether. This is the theory behind "stochastic differential equations", e.g., Brownian motion and the Langevin equation, for which one needs Itô calculus. This describes how to take the limit $\delta\tau \to 0$ for particles experiencing random dynamics caused by collisions. We are currently working on a separate book (or an edition of this book) to describe stochastic thermodynamics in this language. This involves the continuous-time description of random individual sample paths and the theory of path integrals.

In this book, we described stochastic thermodynamics in terms of discrete time increments – avoiding the nasty limits as $\delta\tau \to 0$ – both at the level of probability densities and in terms of individual sample paths. In addition, in the final chapters we also covered the (mean field) continuous-time limit of the description of time-evolving probability densities (but not of individual sample paths). Unlike individual sample paths, probability densities can be assumed smooth at all times and so the limit $\delta\tau \to 0$ is standard.

This then paints an interesting picture: we can describe stochastic thermodynamics in terms of four distinct mathematical frameworks: at the level of probability distributions in discrete time (Markov chains), probability distributions in continuous time (Fokker–Planck partial differential equations), at the level of individual sample paths in discrete time (e.g., MCMC-like sampling algorithms), and individual sample paths in continuous time (stochastic differential equations and Brownian motion). Additionally, there is the path integral formulation, which assigns probability to individual sample paths in continuous time.

Both discrete-time and continuous-time frameworks have their limitations: discrete-time dynamics implicitly make an approximation by breaking up time into finite increments but can describe arbitrary (non-Gaussian) dynamics, while continuous-time dynamics are usually limited to Gaussian noise (e.g., Brownian motion). There is an interesting parallel between probability-level and path-level descriptions of a

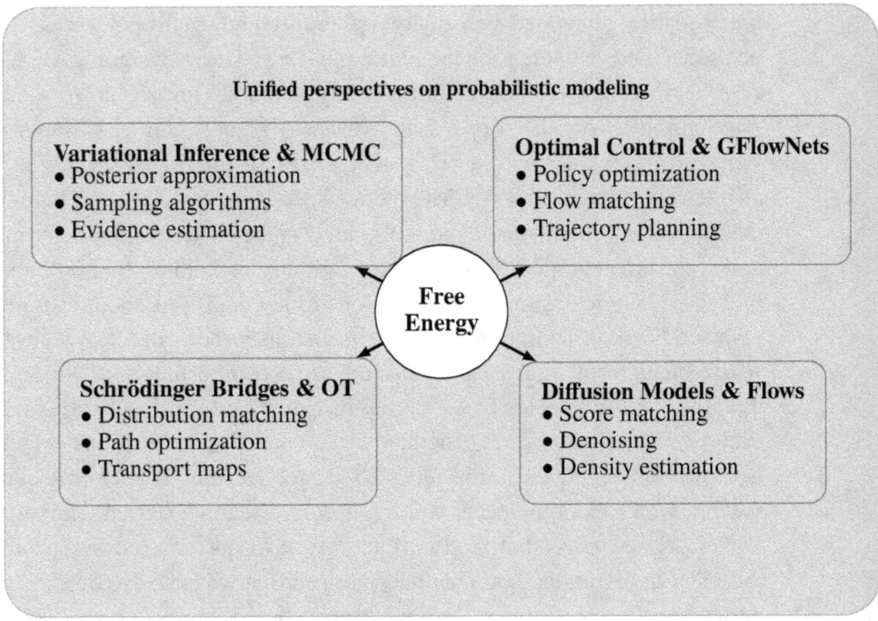

Figure 24.1 A conceptual overview of how free energy unifies different areas of probabilistic machine learning. The expression of the free energy objective (to be minimized) is given by: $D_{\mathrm{KL}}[Q||P] + F[P, \mathbf{x}] = \mathcal{F}(Q, P, \mathbf{x}) \equiv \mathbb{E}_Q\left[-\log\left(P(\mathbf{x}|\mathbf{z})P(\mathbf{z})\right)\right] - \mathcal{S}[Q]$, where Q, P are Markov chains: $Q(\mathbf{z}_{0:t_f}) = Q_0(\mathbf{z}_0)\prod_{t=1}^{t_f} F_{t|t-1}(\mathbf{z}_t|\mathbf{z}_{t-1})$ and $P(\mathbf{z}_{0:t_f}) = P_{t_f}(\mathbf{z}_{t_f})\prod_{t=1}^{t_f} B_{t-1|t}(\mathbf{z}_{t-1}|\mathbf{z}_t)$. Various ML methods that can be described in this framework are: (1) Variational inference and MCMC: optimizing variational distributions anc designing efficient samplers; (2) Optimal control and GFlowNets: mapping control problems probabilistic inference and flow-balancing; (3) Schrödinger bridges and optimal transport: minimizing KL divergence between forward and backward processes under marginal constraints; (4) Diffusion models and normalizing flows: learning generative models via score matching and change of variables.

thermodynamic system in ML when we think about probabilities or individual sample For instance, the reparameterization trick in VAEs can be thought of as a transitic from probability distributions to sample paths. Note that this is also related to tl distinction between the Eulerian view, where we think of time-evolving probabili distributions, $\rho(\zeta, t)$, and the Lagrangian view, where we think of evolving individu sample paths and describe their probability as $\rho(\zeta(t))$.

All methods in this book assume "memoryless" dynamics, implied by the fa that collisions occur on much shorter timescales than the dynamics of the molecule However, this is an approximation that does not necessarily hold in all cases. In fac when the "separation of timescales" does not occur, one needs to add memory to tl dynamics of the system under study. Memoryful extensions (e.g., for the Langevi equation) do exist but are not treated in this book. The reason that memory appea when integrating out degrees of freedom is well known in ML: when marginalizing ov variables that influence multiple downstream variables, these latter variables become correlated.

The laws of physics at their fundamental (classical) level are second-order in nature. That means we have positions and momenta, and particles follow Hamilton's equations of motion. Throughout the book, we used the notation $\zeta = (\xi, \eta)$ to indicate that we want to develop our theory in the full phase space. Sometimes, however, we have assumed overdamped dynamics, where the timescale at which velocity changes is much shorter than the timescale at which position changes. In such cases, we can set $\dot{\eta} = 0$, which results in the usual drift–diffusion SDE on the position variable. Many results in the stochastic thermodynamics literature are derived in this overdamped limit (with the more complicated underdamped system in the SI section).

You may have noticed that in the physics chapters we always talk about thermal baths and their temperature, but these were conspicuously absent when we discussed ML. It is true that in stochastic thermodynamics we make an extra assumption that the latent degrees of freedom are coupled to an infinitely large thermal bath with which they exchange energy. This is not the most general problem of a system where part of the information is integrated (or marginalized) out, for instance when that very large bath is absent. The ML formulation is therefore slightly more general in that sense, but we have found that the concepts of variational free energy, work, heat, and entropy still meaningfully apply.

We believe that we have only witnessed the tip of an iceberg. With two Nobel Prizes awarded to this field in 2024, and driven by its mathematical elegance and important applications in drug development and sustainability, we expect this field to grow rapidly. It is beautiful that two very different fields, rooted in perhaps an even more fundamental theory of information processing, have begun to cross-fertilize each other: new ML methods are developed based on physics principles, and new ML tools are built to accelerate the physical sciences. We hope that we have provided a taste of this elegant new field and that this was enticing enough to pique your interest.

Bibliography

R. Abbott, M. S. Albergo, A. Botev, D. Boyda, K. Cranmer, D. C. Hackett, G. Kanwar, A. G. D. G. Matthews, S. Racanière, A. Razavi, D. J. Rezende, F. Romero-López, P. E. Shanahan, and J. M. Urban (2023). Normalizing flows for lattice gauge theory in arbitrary space-time dimension, ArXiv preprint 2305.02402. (Cited on p. 92).

M. S. Albergo, D. Boyda, D. C. Hackett, G. Kanwar, K. Cranmer, S. Racanière, D. J. Rezende, and P. E. Shanahan (2021). Introduction to normalizing flows for lattice field theory, ArXiv preprint 2101.08176. (Cited on p. 92).

B. D. Anderson. Reverse-time diffusion equation models (1982). *Stoch. Proc. and their Appl.*, 12(3):313–326. (Cited on p. 246).

M. Arbel, A. G. de G. Matthews, and A. Doucet (2021). Annealed flow transport Monte Carlo. Pages 318–330 in *Proc. of ICML*, M. Meila and T. Zhang, editors, volume 139 of *Proceedings of Machine Learning Research*. (Cited on p. 205).

E. Aurell, K. Gawędzki, C. Mejía-Monasterio, R. Mohayaee, and P. Muratore-Ginanneschi (2012). Refined second law of thermodynamics for fast random processes. *J. Stat. Phys.*, 147(3):487–505. (Cited on p. 235).

J. L. Ba, J. R. Kiros, and G. E. Hinton. Layer normalization, ArXiv preprint 1607.06450, July 2016. (Cited on p. 28).

M. J. Beal. *Variational Algorithms for Approximate Bayesian Inference*. PhD thesis, University College London, 2003. (Cited on p. 68).

R. E. Bellman. *Dynamic Programming*. Princeton University Press, 1957. (Cited on pp. 164, 165, and 169).

J.-D. Benamou and Y. Brenier (2000). A computational fluid mechanics solution to the Monge–Kantorovich mass transfer problem. *Numer. Math.*, 84:375–393. (Cited on pp. 224, 231, 234, and 258).

E. Bengio, M. Jain, M. Korablyov, D. Precup, and Y. Bengio (2021). Flow network based generative models for non-iterative diverse candidate generation. pages 27381–27394 in *Adv. Neural Inf. Process. Syst.*, volume 34, Curran Associates, Inc. (Cited on pp. 172 and 177).

Y. Bengio, S. Lahlou, T. Deleu, E. J. Hu, M. Tiwari, and E. Bengio (2023). GFlowNet Foundations, ArXiV preprint, 2111.09266. (Cited on pp. 172 and 173).

C. H. Bennett (1976). Efficient estimation of free energy differences from Monte Carlo data. *J. Computat. Phys.*, 22(2):245–268. (Cited on p. 195).

C. H. Bennett (1982). The thermodynamics of computation – A review. *Int. J. Theor. Phys.*, 21(12):905–940. (Cited on p. 52).

E. Bernton, J. Heng, A. Doucet, and P. E. Jacob (2019). Schrödinger bridge samplers ArXiv preprint, 1912.13170. (Cited on p. 160).

C. M. Bishop (2006). *Pattern Recognition and Machine Learning*. Springer. (Cite on pp. xviii, 23, and 82).

D. M. Blei, A. Kucukelbir, and J. D. McAuliffe (2017). Variational inference: A review for statisticians. *J. Amer. Stat. Assoc.*, 112(518):859–877. (Cited on pp. xvi and 81).

L. Boltzmann (1877). Über die Beziehung zwischen dem zweiten Hauptsatze de mechanischen Wärmetheorie und der Wahrscheinlichkeitsrechnung respecktive de Sätzen über das Wärmegleichgewicht. *Wiener Berichte*, 2:373–435. (Cited on p 102).

L. Boltzmann (1896). Entgegnung auf die wärmetheoretischen Betrachtungen de Hrn. E. Zermelo. *Ann. der Phys.*, 293(4):773–784. (Cited on p. 102).

S. Boyd and L. Vandenberghe (2004). *Convex Optimization*. Cambridge Universit Press. (Cited on pp. 16, 17, and 18).

M. Braun and J. McAuliffe (2010). Variational inference for large-scale models o discrete choice. *J. Amer. Stat. Assoc.*, 105(489): 324–335. (Cited on p. xviii).

S. Brooks (1998). Markov chain Monte Carlo method and its application. *J. R. Sta Soc. D*, 47(1):69–100. (Cited on p. 126).

S. G. Brush (1976). *The Kind of Motion We Call Heat: A History of the Kinetic Theor of Gases in the 19th Century*, volume 1–2. North-Holland Publishing Compan (Cited on p. 102).

H. B. Callen (1985). *Thermodynamics and an Introduction to Thermostatistics*, Secon edition. Wiley. (Cited on p. 48).

D. Carbone, M. Hua, S. Coste, and E. Vanden-Eijnden (2023). Efficient training o energy-based models using Jarzynski's equality. Pages 52583–52614 in *Advances i Neural Information Processing Systems*, volume 36, A. Oh, T. Naumann, A. Globe son, K. Saenko, M. Hardt, and S. Levine, editors, Curran Associates, Inc. (Cited o p. 133).

J. Chen, C. Lu, B. Chenli, J. Zhu, and T. Tian (2020). VFlow: More expressive gene ative flows with variational data augmentation. Pages 1660–1669 in *Proceedings o the 37th ICML*. (Cited on p. 211).

R. T. Q. Chen, Y. Rubanova, J. Bettencourt, and D. K. Duvenaud (2018). Neur ordinary differential equations. In *Adv. Neural Inf. Process. Syst.*, Vol. 31. Curra Associates, Inc. (Cited on pp. 249 and 251).

T. Chen, B. Xu, C. Zhang, and C. Guestrin (2016). Training deep nets with subline memory cost, ArXiv preprint, 1604.06174. No citations.

T. Q. Chen, J. Behrmann, D. Duvenaud, and J.-H. Jacobsen (2019). Residual flows fo invertible generative modeling. Pages pages 9913–9923 in *Adv. Neural Inf. Proces Syst.* 32, H. M. Wallach, H. Larochelle, A. Beygelzimer, F. d'Alché-Buc, E. B. Fo and R. Garnett, editors. No citations.

Y. Chen, T. T. Georgiou, and M. Pavon (2016). On the relation between optim transport and Schrödinger bridges: A stochastic control viewpoint. *J. Optim. Theor Appl.*, 169(2):671–691, 2016b. (Cited on p. 161).

Y. Chen, T. T. Georgiou, and A. Tannenbaum (2020). Stochastic control and nonequilibrium thermodynamics: Fundamental limits. *IEEE Trans. Automat. Contr.*, 65(7): 2979–2991. (Cited on p. 159).

R. Chetrite, P. Muratore-Ginanneschi, and K. Schwieger (2021). E. Schrödinger's 1931 paper "On the reversal of the laws of nature" ["Über die umkehrung der naturgesetze", *Sitzungsberichte der Preussischen Akademie der Wissenschaften, Physikalische Mathematische Klasse*, 8 N9 144–153]. *Eur. Phys. J. H*, 46(1):28–57. (Cited on p. 155).

S. Chewi, J. Niles-Weed, and P. Rigollet (2024). Statistical optimal transport, ArXiv preprint 2407.18163. (Cited on p. 161).

C. Chipot and A. Pohorille (2007). *Free Energy Calculations: Theory and Applications in Chemistry and Biology*. Springer. (Cited on p. 188).

P. F. Christiano, J. Leike, T. Brown, M. Martic, S. Legg, and D. Amodei (2017). Deep reinforcement learning from human preferences. In *Adv. Neural Inf. Process. Syst.*, volume 30. Curran Associates, Inc. (Cited on p. 171).

T. S. Cohen and M. Welling (2016). Group equivariant convolutional networks. Pages 2990–2999 in *Proceedings of the 33rd International Conference on Machine Learning*, M. F. Balcan and K. Q. Weinberger, editors, volume 48 of *Proceedings of Machine Learning Research.* (Cited on p. 26).

T. S. Cohen, M. Geiger, J. Köhler, and M. Welling (2018). Spherical CNNs. In *Proc. of ICLR.* OpenReview.net. (Cited on p. 27).

T. Cover and J. Thomas (2006). *Elements of Information Theory*. Wiley–Interscience. (Cited on pp. 9 and 141).

G. E. Crooks (1998). Nonequilibrium measurements of free energy differences for microscopically reversible Markovian systems. *J. Stat. Phys.*, 90(5):1481–1487. (Cited on p. 107).

G. E. Crooks (1999). Entropy production fluctuation theorem and the nonequilibrium work relation for free energy differences. *Phys. Rev. E*, 60(3):2721–2726. (Cited on pp. 107, 185, and 266).

G. E. Crooks (2000). Path-ensemble averages in systems driven far from equilibrium. *Phys. Rev. E*, 61(3):2361–2366. (Cited on p. 107).

P. Dayan, G. E. Hinton, R. M. Neal, and R. S. Zemel (1995). The Helmholtz machine. *Neural Comput.*, 7(5):889–904. (Cited on p. 66).

V. De Bortoli, J. Thornton, J. Heng, and A. Doucet. Diffusion Schrödinger bridge with applications to score-based generative modeling (2021). Pages 17695–17709 in *Adv. Neural Inf. Process. Syst.* 34, M. Ranzato, A. Beygelzimer, Y. N. Dauphin, P. Liang, and J. W. Vaughan, editors. (Cited on pp. 154 and 159).

A. Dechant and Y. Sakurai (2019). Thermodynamic interpretation of Wasserstein distance, ArXiv preprint 1912.08405. (Cited on p. 235).

P. Del Moral, A. Doucet, and A. Jasra (2006). Sequential Monte Carlo samplers. *J. Roy. Stat. Soc. Series B (Statistical Methodology)*, 68(3):411–436. (Cited on p. 137).

C. Dellago, P. G. Bolhuis, and P. L. Geissler (2002). Transition path sampling and the calculation of rate constants. *Advances in Chemical Physics*, 123:1–78. (Cited on p. 188).

P. Dhariwal and A. Q. Nichol. Diffusion models beat GANs on image synthesis. I *Advances in Neural Information Processing Systems*, volume 34. Curran Associates Inc., Nov. 2021. (Cited on p. 147).

J. Dijkman, M. Dijkstra, R. van Roij, M. Welling, J.-W. van de Meent, and B. Ensin (2025). Learning neural free-energy functionals with pair-correlation matching *Phys. Rev. Lett.*, 134(5):056103. (Cited on p. 224).

L. Dinh, D. Sohl-Dickstein, and Y. Bengio (2014). Nice: non-linear independen components estimation, ArXiv preprint 1410.8516. (Cited on p. 93).

L. Dinh, J. Sohl-Dickstein, and S. Bengio (2017). Density estimation using real NVF In *Proc. of ICLR*. OpenReview.net. (Cited on p. 93).

A. Dosovitskiy, L. Beyer, A. Kolesnikov, D. Weissenborn, X. Zhai, T. Unterthine M. Dehghani, M. Minderer, G. Heigold, S. Gelly, J. Uszkoreit, and N. Houlsb (2021). An image is worth 16 × 16 words: Transformers for image recognition a scale. In *Proc. of ICLR*. OpenReview.net. (Cited on p. 30).

A. Doucet, W. S. Grathwohl, A. G. D. G. Matthews, and H. Strathmann (2022 Score-based diffusion meets annealed importance sampling. In *Advances in Neura Information Processing Systems*. (Cited on pp. 141, 143, and 144).

Y. Du and I. Mordatch. Implicit generation and modeling with energy -based mode (2019). In *Adv. Neural Inf. Process. Syst.*, volume 32. Curran Associates, Inc. (Cite on p. 133).

F. Eijkelboom, G. Bartosh, C. A. Naesseth, M. Welling, and J.-W. van de Meent (2024 Variational flow matching for graph generation. *Advances in Neural Informatio Processing Systems*, 37:11735–11764. (Cited on p. 254).

M. Esposito and C. Van den Broeck. Three detailed fluctuation theorems. *Phys. Re Lett.*, 104(9):090601, 2010. (Cited on pp. 178 and 180).

R. Evans (1979). The nature of the liquid–vapour interface and other topics in th statistical mechanics of non-uniform, classical fluids. *Advances in Physics*, 28(2 143–200. (Cited on p. 224).

R. P. Feynman, R. B. Leighton, and M. Sands (1963). *The Feynman Lectures o Physics, Vol. I: Mainly Mechanics, Radiation, and Heat*. Addison-Wesley. (Cite on p. 48).

R. P. Feynman, Albert R. Hibbs, and Daniel F. Styer (2010). *Quantum Mechanics an Path Integrals*, Emended edition. Dover Publications. (Cited on p. 242).

A. D. Fokker (1914). Die mittlere Energie rotierender elektrischer Dipole i Strahlungsfeld. *Ann, der Phys.*, 348(5):810–820. (Cited on p. 217).

D. Frenkel and B. Smit (2001). *Understanding Molecular Simulation: From Algorithn to Applications*, Second edition. Academic Press. (Cited on pp. 133 and 189).

K. Fukushima (1969). Visual feature extraction by a multilayered network of analo threshold elements. *IEEE Transactions on Systems Science and Cybernetics*, SSC- (4):322–333. (Cited on p. 24).

W. Gangbo and R. J. McCann (1996). The geometry of optimal transportation. *Ac Mathematica*, 177(2):113–161. (Cited on p. 258).

C. W. Gardiner (2009). *Stochastic Methods: A Handbook for the Natural and Soci Sciences*. Springer. (Cited on p. 247).

P. Geiger and C. Dellago (2010). Optimum protocol for fast-switching free-energy calculations. *Phys. Rev. E*, 81(2):021127. (Cited on pp. 193 and 260).

A. Gelman, J. B. Carlin, H. S. Stern, D. B. Dunson, A. Vehtari, and D. B. Rubin (2013). *Bayesian Data Analysis*, Third edition. Chapman and Hall/CRC. (Cited on p. 67).

Z. Ghahramani and M. I. Jordan (1997). Factorial hidden Markov models. *Machine Learning*, 29(2-3):245–273. (Cited on p. xvii).

J. W. Gibbs (1902). *Elementary Principles in Statistical Mechanics*. Charles Scribner's Sons. (Cited on p. 35).

X. Glorot, A. Bordes, and Y. Bengio (2011). Deep sparse rectifier neural networks. Pages 315–323 in *Proceedings of the 14th International Conference on Artificial Intelligence and Statistics*, G. Gordon, D. Dunson, and M. Dudík, editors, vol. 15 of *Proceedings of Machine Learning Research*. (Cited on p. 24).

H. Goldstein (1950). *Classical Mechanics*. Addison-Wesley. (Cited on p. 241).

A. N. Gomez, M. Ren, R. Urtasun, and R. B. Grosse (2017). The reversible residual network: backpropagation without storing activations. Pages 2211–2221 in *Proceedings of the 31st International Conference on Neural Information Processing Systems*. (Cited on p. 93).

A. Gomez-Marin, J. M. R. Parrondo, and C. Van den Broeck (2008). Lower bounds on dissipation upon coarse graining. *Phys. Rev. E*, 78(1):011107. (Cited on p. 212).

I. Goodfellow, Y. Bengio, and A. Courville (2016). *Deep Learning*. MIT Press, 2016. (Cited on p. 23).

J. Gore, F. Ritort, and C. Bustamante (2003). Bias and error in estimates of equilibrium free-energy differences from nonequilibrium measurements. *Proc. Natl. Acad. Sci. USA.*, 100(22):12564–12569. (Cited on p. 193).

W. Grathwohl, R. T. Q. Chen, J. Bettencourt, I. Sutskever, and D. Duvenaud (2018). FFJORD: Free-form continuous dynamics for scalable reversible generative models. In *Proc. of ICLR*. (Cited on p. 249).

J. Hadamard (1945). *An Essay on the Psychology of Invention in the Mathematical Field*. Princeton University Press. (Cited on p. xiii).

W. K. Hastings (1970). Monte Carlo sampling methods using Markov chains and their applications. *Biometrika*, 57(1):97–109. (Cited on pp. 125 and 126).

K. He, X. Zhang, S. Ren, and J. Sun (2016). Deep residual learning for image recognition. Pages 770–778 in *Proceedings of the IEEE Conference on Computer Vision and Pattern Recognition*. (Cited on p. 29).

J. Heng, V. De Bortoli, and A. Doucet (2023). Diffusion Schrödinger bridges for Bayesian computation, ArXiv preprint 2308.14106. (Cited on p. 160).

T. Heskes (2002). Stable fixed points of loopy belief propagation are local minima of the Bethe free energy. In *Adv. Neural Inf. Process. Syst.*, Vol. 15. MIT Press. (Cited on p. 78).

I. Higgins, L. Matthey, A. Pal, C. Burgess, X. Glorot, M. Botvinick, S. Mohamed, and A. Lerchner (2017). Beta-VAE: Learning basic visual concepts with a constrained variational pramework. In *Proc. of ICLR*. (Cited on p. 71).

G. E. Hinton and D. van Camp (1993). Keeping the neural networks simple b minimizing the description length of the weights. Pages 5–13, in *Proceedings of th Sixth Annual Conference on Computational Learning Theory*. ACM. (Cited on pp xvii and 68).

G. E. Hinton and R. Zemel (1993). Autoencoders, minimum description length an Helmholtz free energy. In *Adv. Neural Inf. Process. Syst.*, Vol. 6. Morgan–Kaufmann (Cited on p. xvii).

J. Ho, X. Chen, A. Srinivas, Y. Duan, and P. Abbeel (2019). Flow++: Improvin flow-based generative models with variational dequantization and architecture de sign. Pages 2722–2730 in *Proc. of the 36th International Conference on Machin Learning*. (Cited on p. 213).

J. Ho, A. Jain, and P. Abbeel (2020). Denoising diffusion probabilistic models. Page 6840–6851 in *Adv. Neural Inf. Process. Syst.*, Vol. 33. Curran Associates, Inc. (Cite on pp. xviii, 84, 143, and 150).

E. Hoogeboom, D. Nielsen, P. Jaini, P. Forré, and M. Welling (2021). Argmax flows an multinomial diffusion: Learning categorical distributions. Pages 12454–12465 i *Adv. Neural Inf. Process. Syst.* Vol. 34. M. Ranzato, A. Beygelzimer, Y. N. Dauphi P. Liang, and J. W. Vaughan, editors, NeurIPS. (Cited on p. 210).

K. Hornik, M. Stinchcombe, and H. White (1989). Multilayer feedforward network are universal approximators. *Neural Networks*, 2(5):359–366. (Cited on p. 25).

C.-W. Huang, L. Dinh, and A. Courville (2020). Augmented Normalizing flows: Brid ing the gap between generative flows and latent variable models, ArXiv prepri 2002.07101. (Cited on p. 211).

C.-W. Huang, J. H. Lim, and A. C. Courville (2021). A variational perspective o diffusion-based generative models and score matching. Pages 22863–22876 in *Ad Neural Inf. Process. Syst.*, Vol. 34, Curran Associates, Inc. (Cited on p. xviii).

K. Huang (1987). *Statistical Mechanics*, Second edition. Wiley. (Cited on p. 35).

K. Ikeda, T. Uda, D. Okanohara, and S. Ito (2025). Speed–accuracy relations for diffu sion models: Wisdom from nonequilibrium thermodynamics and optimal transpor *Phys. Rev. X*, 15(3):031031. (Cited on p. 261).

S. Ioffe and C. Szegedy (2015). Batch normalization: Accelerating deep networ training by reducing internal covariate shift. Pages 448–456 in *Proc. of the 32n International Conference on Machine Learning*, F. Bach and D. Blei, editors, Vol. 3 of *Proceedings of Machine Learning Research*. (Cited on p. 28).

T. S. Jaakkola and M. I. Jordan (1996). Recursive algorithms for approximatin probabilities in graphical models. Pages 487–493 in *Adv. Neural Inf. Process. Syst.* Vol. 9, MIT Press. (Cited on p. xvii).

T. S. Jaakkola and M. I. Jordan (1997). A variational approach to Bayesian logi tic regression models and their extensions. Pages 283–294 in *Sixth Internationa Workshop on Artificial Intelligence and Statistics*, Vol. R1, *Proceedings of Machin Learning Research*. (Cited on p. xvii).

P. Jaini, D. Nielsen, and M. Welling (2021). Sampling in combinatorial spaces wi

SurVAE flow augmented MCMC. Pages 3349–3357 in *Proceedings of The 24th International Conference on Artificial Intelligence and Statistics*, Vol. 130*Proceedings of Machine Learning Research*. (Cited on p. 210).

C. Jarzynski. Nonequilibrium equality for free energy differences (1997). *Phys. Rev. Lett.*, 78(14):2690–2693. (Cited on pp. 107, 140, 187, 192, and 266).

C. Jarzynski (2000). Hamiltonian derivation of a detailed fluctuation theorem. *J. Stat. Phys.*, 98(1/2):77–102. (Cited on p. 109).

C. Jarzynski (2011). Equalities and inequalities: Irreversibility and the second law of thermodynamics at the nanoscale. *Annu. Rev. Condens. Matter Phys.*, 2(1):329–351. (Cited on pp. 13, 107, and 192).

E. T. Jaynes (1957a). Information theory and statistical mechanics. *Phys. Rev.*, 106 (4):620–630. (Cited on pp. 19, 36, and 40).

E. T. Jaynes (1957b). Information theory and statistical mechanics. II. *Phys. Rev.*, 108 (2):171–190. (Cited on pp. 19 and 36).

E. T. Jaynes (1980). The minimum entropy production principle. *Annu. Rev. Phys. Chem.*, 31(1):579–601, 1980. (Cited on pp. 155 and 162).

E. T. Jaynes (2003). *Probability Theory: The Logic of Science*. Cambridge University Press. (Cited on pp. 19 and 67).

M. I. Jordan, Z. Ghahramani, T. S. Jaakkola, and L. K. Saul (1999). An introduction to variational methods for graphical models. *Machine Learning*, 37(2):183–233. (Cited on p. xvii).

R. Jordan, D. Kinderlehrer, and F. Otto (1998). The variational formulation of the Fokker–Planck equation. *SIAM J. Math. Anal.*, 29(1):1–17. (Cited on pp. 224 and 238).

D. Kahneman (2011). *Thinking, Fast and Slow*. Farrar, Straus and Giroux. (Cited on p. 166).

L. Kantorovich (1942). On the translocation of masses. *Doklady Akademii Nauk SSSR*, 37(7-8):199–201. (Cited on p. 161).

H. J. Kappen, V. Gómez, and M. Opper (2012). Optimal control as a graphical model inference problem. *Machine Learning*, 87(2):159–182. (Cited on p. 167).

M. Karplus and J. A. McCammon (2002). Molecular dynamics simulations of biomolecules. *Nature Structural Biology*, 9(9):646–652. (Cited on p. 189).

R. Kawai, J. M. R. Parrondo, and C. Van den Broeck (2007). Dissipation: The phase-space perspective. *Phys. Rev. Lett.*, 98(8):080602. (Cited on p. 212).

R. Kindermann and J. L. Snell (1980). *Markov Random Fields and Their Applications*. American Mathematical Society. (Cited on p. 60).

D. Kingma, T. Salimans, B. Poole, and J. Ho (2021). Variational diffusion models. Pages 21696–21707 in *Adv. Neural Inf. Process. Syst.*, Vol. 34, Curran Associates, Inc. (Cited on pp. xviii, 145, and 247).

D. P. Kingma and J. Ba (2014). Adam: A method for stochastic optimization, ArXiv preprint 1412.6980. (Cited on p. 33).

D. P. Kingma and M. Welling (2014). Auto-encoding variational Bayes. In *Proc. of ICLR, 2014*, Y. Bengio and Y. LeCun, editors. (Cited on pp. xviii, 63, 65, 83, and 86).

D. P. Kingma and M. Welling (2019). An introduction to variational autoencoders *Found. Trends® Mach. Learn.*, 12(4):307–392. (Cited on p. 86).

D. P. Kingma, T. Salimans, R. Jozefowicz, X. Chen, I. Sutskever, and M. Wellin (2016). Improved variational inference with inverse autoregressive flow. In *Adv Neural Inf. Process. Syst.*, Vol. 29. Curran Associates, Inc. (Cited on p. 84).

J. G. Kirkwood (1935). Statistical mechanics of fluid mixtures. *J. Chem. Phys.*, 3(5) 300–313. (Cited on p. 189).

C. Kittel and H. Kroemer (1980). *Thermal Physics*, Second edition. W. H. Freeman (Cited on p. 48).

D. Koller and N. Friedman (2009). *Probabilistic Graphical Models: Principles an Techniques*. MIT Press. (Cited on p. 59).

P. A. Kollman, I. Massova, C. Reyes, B. Kuhn, S. Huo, L. Chong, M. Lee, T. Lee Y. Duan, W. Wang, O. Donini, P. Cieplak, J. Srinivasan, D. A. Case, and T. E Cheatham (2000). Calculating structures and free energies of complex molecules Combining molecular mechanics and continuum models. *Accounts of Chem. Res* 33(12):889–897. (Cited on p. 188).

A. N. Kolmogorov (1931). Über die analytischen Methoden in der Wahrscheinlichkeit srechnung. *Math. Ann.*, 104(1):415–458. (Cited on p. 217).

T. Korbak, E. Perez, and C. Buckley (2022). RL with KL penalties is better viewed a Bayesian inference. Pages 1083–1091 in *Findings of the Association for Computa tional Linguistics: EMNLP 2022, Abu Dhabi, UAE*, Y. Goldberg, Z. Kozareva, an Y. Zhang, editors. Association for Computational Linguistics. (Cited on p. 171).

H. A. Kramers (1940). Brownian motion in a field of force and the diffusion model c chemical reactions. *Physica*, 7(4):284–304. (Cited on p. 223).

L. D. Landau and E. M. Lifshitz (1976). *Mechanics*, Third edition. Butterworth Heinemann. (Cited on pp. 37 and 241).

L. D. Landau and E. M. Lifshitz (1980). *Statistical Physics*, Third edition. Butterworth Heinemann. (Cited on p. 35).

R. Landauer (1961). Irreversibility and heat generation in the computing process. *IBM J. Research and Development*, 5(3):183–191. (Cited on pp. 52 and 235).

J. L. Lebowitz. Boltzmann's entropy and time's arrow (1993). *Phys. Today*, 46(9 32–38. (Cited on p. 103).

Y. LeCun (1987). *Modèles Connexionnistes de l'Apprentissage*. PhD thesis, Universit Pierre et Marie Curie, Paris. (Cited on p. 32).

Y. LeCun (1988). A theoretical framework for back-propagation. Pages 21–28 i *Proceedings of the Connectionist Models Summer School*, D. Touretzky, and C Hinton, and T. Sejnowski, editors. Morgan Kaufmann. (Cited on p. 32).

Y. LeCun, L. Bottou, Y. Bengio, and P. Haffner (1998). Gradient-based learnin applied to document recognition. *Proc. IEEE*, 86(11):2278–2324. (Cited on p. 26

H. K. Lee, C. Kwon, and H. Park (2013). Fluctuation theorems and entropy productic with odd-parity variables. *Phys. Rev. Lett.*, 110(5):050602. (Cited on pp. 98 and 101

F. Léger (2019). A geometric perspective on regularized optimal transport. *J. Dy Diff. Equat.*, 31(4):1777–1791. (Cited on p. 240).

C. Léonard (2014). A survey of the Schrödinger problem and some of its connections with optimal transport. *DCDS*, 34(4):1533–1574. (Cited on p. 161).

S. Levine (2018). Reinforcement learning and control as probabilistic inference: Tutorial and review, ArXiv preprint 1805.00909. (Cited on pp. 166 and 171).

G. Li, H. T. Quan, and Z. C. Tu (2017). Shortcuts to isothermality and nonequilibrium work relations. *Phys. Rev. E*, 96(1):012144. (Cited on p. 204).

Y. Lipman, R. T. Q. Chen, H. Ben-Hamu, M. Nickel, and M. Le (2023). Flow matching for generative modeling. In *The 11th International Conference on Learning Representations*. (Cited on pp. 247, 251, and 256).

J. Loschmidt (1876). Über den Zustand des Wärmegleichgewichtes eines Systems von Körpern mit Rücksicht auf die Schwerkraft. *Sitzungsberichte der Akademie der Wissenschaften in Wien*, 73:128–142. (Cited on p. 103).

Y.-A. Ma, T. Chen, and E. Fox (2015). A complete recipe for stochastic gradient MCMC. In *Adv. Neural Inf. Process. Syst.*, Vol. 28. Curran Associates, Inc.. (Cited on p. 227).

A. L. Maas, A. Y. Hannun, and A. Y. Ng (2013). Rectifier nonlinearities improve neural network acoustic models. *Proc. 30th International Conference on Machine Learning*, 28(3):1–6. (Cited on p. 25).

K. Madan, J. Rector-Brooks, M. Korablyov, E. Bengio, M. Jain, A. C. Nica, T. Bosc, Y. Bengio, and N. Malkin (2023). Learning GFlowNets from partial episodes for improved convergence and stability. Pages 23467–23483 in *Proc. of ICML*, PMLR. (Cited on p. 175).

N. Malkin, M. Jain, E. Bengio, C. Sun, and Y. Bengio (2022). Trajectory balance: Improved credit assignment in GFlowNets. *Advances in Neural Information Processing Systems*, 35:5955–5967. (Cited on pp. 175 and 176).

N. Malkin, S. Lahlou, T. Deleu, X. Ji, E. J. Hu, K. E. Everett, D. Zhang, and Y. Bengio (2023). GFlowNets and variational inference. In *Proc. of ICLR, 2023*. (Cited on pp. 175 and 176).

R. J. McCann (1997). A convexity principle for interacting gases. *Adv. in. Math.*, 128 (1):153–179. (Cited on p. 258).

N. Metropolis, A. W. Rosenbluth, M. N. Rosenbluth, A. H. Teller, and E. Teller (1953). Equation of state calculations by fast computing machines. *J. Chem. Phys.*, 21(6): 1087–1092. (Cited on pp. 125, 126, and 267).

T. P. Minka (2001). Expectation propagation for approximate Bayesian inference. Pages 362–369 in *Proc. 17th Conference on Uncertainty in Artificial Intelligence*. (Cited on p. 78).

G. Monge (1781). *Mémoire sur la Théorie des Déblais et des Remblais*, De l'Imprimerie Royale, Paris. (Cited on p. 161).

T. Morita (1990). Cluster variation method and Moebius inversion formula. *J. Stat. Phys.*, 59(3):819–825. (Cited on p. 75).

K. P. Murphy (2012). *Machine Learning: A Probabilistic Perspective*. MIT Press. (Cited on p. 23).

M. Nakazato and S. Ito (2021). Geometrical aspects of entropy production in stochastic thermodynamics based on Wasserstein distance. *Phys. Rev. Research*, 3(4):04309 (Cited on p. 235).

R. M. Neal (2001). Annealed importance sampling, *Statistics and Computing* 11(2):125–139. (Cited on p. 134).

R. M. Neal (2011). MCMC using Hamiltonian dynamics. Chapter 5, pages 113–16 in *Handbook of Markov Chain Monte Carlo*, S. Brooks, A. Gelman, G. L. Jones and X.-L. Meng, editors. Chapman and Hall/CRC. (Cited on p. 129).

R. M. Neal and G. E. Hinton (1998). A view of the EM algorithm that justifie incremental, sparse, and other variants. Pages 355–368 in *Learning in Graphica Models*, M. I. Jordan, editor, Springer. (Cited on pp. xvii and 83).

K. Neklyudov, M. Welling, E. Egorov, and D. Vetrov (2020). Involutive MCMC: unifying framework. Pages 7273–7282 in *International Conference on Machin Learning*, PMLR. (Cited on p. 131).

E. Nelson (1967). *Dynamical Theories of Brownian Motion*. Princeton Universit Press. (Cited on p. 246).

D. Nielsen, P. Jaini, E. Hoogeboom, O. Winther, and M. Welling (2020). SurVA Flows: Surjections to bridge the gap between VAEs and flows. Pages 12685–1269 in *Adv. Neural Inf. Process. Syst.*, Vol. 33, Curran Associates, Inc. (Cited on pp. 9 197, 206, 207, 209, 210, and 214).

F. Noé, S. Olsson, J. Köhler, and H. Wu (2019). Boltzmann generators: Samplin equilibrium states of many-body systems with deep learning. *Science*, 365(6457 eaaw1147. (Cited on p. 91).

L. Ouyang, J. Wu, X. Jiang, D. Almeida, C. Wainwright, P. Mishkin, C. Zhang S. Agarwal, K. Slama, A. Ray, J. Schulman, J. Hilton, F. Kelton, L. Miller, M. Simen A. Askell, P. Welinder, P. F. Christiano, J. Leike, and R. Lowe (2022). Trainin language models to follow instructions with human feedback. Pages 27730–2774 in *Advances in Neural Information Processing Systems*, Vol. 35. (Cited on p. 171

G. Papamakarios, T. Pavlakou, and I. Murray (2017). Masked autoregressive flow f density estimation. In *Adv. Neural Inf. Process. Syst.*, Vol. 30. Curran Associate Inc. (Cited on p. 93).

G. Parisi (1988). *Statistical Field Theory*. Addison-Wesley. (Cited on p. 66).

J. M. R. Parrondo, J. M. Horowitz, and T. Sagawa (2015). Thermodynamics information. *Nat. Phys.*, 11(2):131–139. (Cited on p. 52).

G. Patrini, R. van den Berg, P. Forré, M. Carioni, S. Bhargav, M. Welling, T. Genewei and F. Nielsen (2020). Sinkhorn AutoEncoders. Pages 733–743 in *Proc. 35 Uncertainty in Artificial Intelligence Conference*, PMLR. (Cited on p. 247).

W. Peebles and S. Xie (2023). Scalable diffusion models with transformers. Pag 4172–4182 in *IEEE/CVF International Conference on Computer Vision (ICCV Paris*. IEEE. (Cited on pp. 30 and 32).

L. Peliti and S. Pigolotti (2021). *Stochastic Thermodynamics: An Introduction*. Princ ton University Press. (Cited on p. xviii).

C. Peterson and J. R. Anderson (1987). A mean field theory learning algorithm f neural networks. *Complex Systems*, 1:995–1019. (Cited on p. xvii).

G. Peyré and M. Cuturi. Computational optimal transport: With applications to data science. *Found. Trends® Mach. Learn.*, 11(5-6):355–607, Feb. 2019. (Cited on p. 260).

M. Planck. Über einen Satz der statistichen Dynamik und seine Erweiterung in der Quantentheorie. *Sitzungsberichte der Preussischen Akademie der Wissenschaften*, 324–341, 1917. (Cited on p. 217).

K. Proesmans, J. Ehrich, and J. Bechhoefer (2020). Finite-time Landauer principle. *Phys. Rev. Lett.*, 125(10):100602. (Cited on p. 235).

L. R. Rabiner (1989). A tutorial on hidden Markov models and selected applications in speech recognition. *Proceedings of the IEEE*, 77(2):257–286. (Cited on p. 60).

D. J. Rezende and S. Mohamed (2015). Variational inference with normalizing flows. Pages 1530–1538 in *Proc. of ICML*, F. R. Bach and D. M. Blei, editors, Vol. 37 of JMLR Workshop and Conference Proceedings. (Cited on p. 89).

D. J. Rezende, S. Mohamed, and D. Wierstra (2014). Stochastic backpropagation and approximate inference in deep generative models. Pages 1278–1286 in *Proc. of ICML*, Vol. 32 of JMLR Workshop and Conference Proceedings, 2014. (Cited on pp. xviii, 65, and 83).

H. Risken (1996). *The Fokker–Planck Equation: Methods of Solution and Applications*. Springer. (Cited on p. 224).

C. P. Robert and G. Casella (1999). *Monte Carlo Statistical Methods*. Springer. (Cited on p. 126).

R. Rombach, A. Blattmann, D. Lorenz, P. Esser, and B. Ommer (2022). High-resolution image synthesis with latent diffusion models. Pages 10684–10695 in *Proc. IEEE/CVF Conference on Computer Vision and Pattern Recognition (CVPR), 2022*. (Cited on p. 154).

O. Ronneberger, P. Fischer, and T. Brox (2015). U-Net: Convolutional networks for biomedical image segmentation. Pages 234–241 in *Medical Image Computing and Computer-Assisted Intervention – MICCAI 2015*, N. Navab, J. Hornegger, W. M. Wells, and A. F. Frangi, editors, Springer International Publishing. (Cited on p. 29).

T. Salimans, D. P. Kingma, and M. Welling (2015). Markov chain Monte Carlo and variational inference: Bridging the gap. Pages 1218–1226 in *Proc. of ICML*, F. R. Bach and D. M. Blei, editors, Vol. 37 of JMLR Workshop and Conference Proceedings. (Cited on pp. 133 and 143).

L. K. Saul, T. Jaakkola, and M. I. Jordan (1996). Mean field theory for sigmoid belief networks. *J. Artif. Intell. Res.*, 4: 61–76. (Cited on p. xvii).

D. Scherer, A. Müller, and S. Behnke (2010). Evaluation of pooling operations in convolutional architectures for object recognition. Pages 92–101 in *Artificial Neural Networks – ICANN*, Springer. (Cited on p. 27).

E. Schrödinger (1931). Über die Umkehrung der Naturgesetze. *Sitzungsberichte der Preussischen Akademie der Wissenschaften, Physikalisch-mathematische Klasse*, 8(9): 144–153. (Cited on p. 155).

U. Seifert. Stochastic thermodynamics, fluctuation theorems and molecular machines (2012). *Rep. Prog. Phys.*, 75(12):126001. (Cited on pp. 13 and 107).

K. Sekimoto (2010). *Stochastic Energetics*. Springer. (Cited on pp. xviii and 107).

N. Shiraishi (2021). *Stochastic Thermodynamics: From Basic to Advanced.* Springe Briefs in Physics. Springer. (Cited on p. xviii).

M. R. Shirts, E. Bair, G. Hooker, and V. S. Pande (2003). Equilibrium free energie from nonequilibrium measurements using maximum-likelihood methods. *Phys. Re Lett.*, 91(14):140601. (Cited on p. 195).

J. Sohl-Dickstein, E. A. Weiss, N. Maheswaranathan, and S. Ganguli (2015). Dee unsupervised learning using nonequilibrium thermodynamics. Pages 2256–2265 i *Proc. of ICML*, F. R. Bach and D. M. Blei, editors, Vol. 37 of *JMLR Workshop an Conference Proceedings*. (Cited on pp. xviii, 84, and 145).

Y. Song and S. Ermon (2019). Generative modeling by estimating gradients of th data distribution. Pages 11895–11907 in *Adv. Neural Inf. Process. Syst. 32nd An nual Conference on Neural Information Processing Systems (NeurIPS) 2019*, H. M Wallach, H. Larochelle, A. Beygelzimer, F. d'Alché-Buc, E. B. Fox, and R. Garnet editors. (Cited on pp. 246 and 247).

Y. Song and D. P. Kingma (2021). How to train your energy-based models, ArXi preprint 2101.03288. (Cited on p. 133).

Y. Song, J. Sohl-Dickstein, D. P. Kingma, A. Kumar, S. Ermon, and B. Poole (2021 Score-based generative modeling through stochastic differential equations. In *Pro of ICLR*. OpenReview.net. (Cited on pp. xviii, 246, and 247).

R. E. Spinney and I. J. Ford (2012a). Entropy production in full phase space fc continuous stochastic dynamics. *Phys. Rev. E*, 85(5):051113. (Cited on p. 180).

R. E. Spinney and I. J. Ford (2012b). Nonequilibrium thermodynamics of stochasti systems with odd and even variables. *Phys. Rev. Lett.*, 108(17):170603. (Cited o pp. 98, 101, 180, and 181).

N. Srivastava, G. Hinton, A. Krizhevsky, I. Sutskever, and R. Salakhutdinov (2014 Dropout: A simple way to prevent neural networks from overfitting. *J. Mach. Lear Res.*, 15:1929–1958. (Cited on p. 28).

R. F. Stengel (1986). *Stochastic Optimal Control: Theory and Application.* Wile (Cited on p. 165).

A. Thin, N. Kotelevskii, A. Doucet, A. Durmus, E. Moulines, and M. Panov (2021 Monte Carlo variational auto-encoders. Pages 10247–10257 in *Proc. of ICM* M. Meila and T. Zhang, editors, Vol. 139 of *Proceedings of Machine Learnin Research*. (Cited on p. 143).

D. Tiapkin, N. Morozov, A. Naumov, and D. Vetrov (2023). Generative flow network as entropy-regularized RL, ArXiv preprint 2310.12934. (Cited on p. 177).

L. Tierney (1994). Markov chains for exploring posterior distributions. *Ann. Sta* 22 (4): 1701–1762. (Cited on p. 129).

E. Todorov (2007). Linearly-solvable Markov decision problems. Pages 1369–1376 i *Adv. Neural Inf. Process. Syst.* Vol. 19, MIT Press. (Cited on p. 167).

E. Todorov (2008). General duality between optimal control and estimation. Pag 4286–4292 in *47th IEEE Conference on Decision and Control*. IEEE. (Cited on 167).

E. Todorov (2009). Efficient computation of optimal actions. *Proc. Natl. Acad. Sc* 106(28):11478–11483. (Cited on p. 167).

A. Tong, N. Malkin, G. Huguet, Y. Zhang, J. Rector-Brooks, K. Fatras, G. Wolf, and Y. Bengio (2023). Improving and generalizing flow-based generative models with minibatch optimal transport, ArXiV preprint 2302.00482. (Cited on pp. 247, 252, 253, and 255).

M. Toussaint and A. Storkey (2006). Probabilistic inference for solving discrete and continuous state Markov decision processes. Pages 945–952 in *ICML '06: Proc. 23rd Int. Conf. Machine Learning*, ACM. (Cited on p. 167).

B. Tzen and M. Raginsky (2019). Theoretical guarantees for sampling and inference in generative models with latent diffusions. Pages 3084–3114 in *Proc. 32nd Conf. on Learning Theory*, PMLR. (Cited on p. 154).

G. E. Uhlenbeck and L. S. Ornstein (1930). On the theory of the Brownian motion. *Phys. Rev.*, 36(5):823–841. (Cited on p. 245).

B. Uria, I. Murray, and H. Larochelle (2014). A deep and tractable density estimator. Pages 467–475 in *Proc. 31st Int. Conf. on Machine Learning*, PMLR. (Cited on p. 213).

S. Vaikuntanathan and C. Jarzynski (2008). Escorted Free energy dimulations: Improving convergence by reducing dissipation. *Phys. Rev. Lett.*, 100(19):190601. (Cited on pp. 197, 198, and 200).

S. Vaikuntanathan and C. Jarzynski (2011). Escorted free energy simulations. *J. Chem. Phys.*, 134(5):054107. (Cited on pp. 197, 198, 200, and 201).

C. Van den Broeck and M. Esposito (2013). Ensemble and trajectory thermodynamics: A brief introduction. *Physica A*, 418: 6–16. (Cited on p. xviii).

F. Vargas, A. Ovsianas, D. Fernandes, M. Girolami, N. D. Lawrence, and N. Nüsken (2022). Bayesian learning via neural Schrödinger–Föllmer flows. *Stat Comput*, 33 (1):3. ISSN 1573-1375. (Cited on p. 160).

F. Vargas, S. Padhy, D. Blessing, and N. Nüsken (2024). Transport meets variational inference: Controlled Monte Carlo diffusions. In *Proc. of ICLR*. (Cited on pp. 202, 237, and 260).

A. Vaswani, N. Shazeer, N. Parmar, J. Uszkoreit, L. Jones, A. N. Gomez, L. Kaiser, and I. Polosukhin (2017). Attention is all you need. Pages 5998–6008 in *Adv. Neural Inf. Process. Syst.*, volume 30, I. Guyon, U. V. Luxburg, S. Bengio, H. Wallach, R. Fergus, S. Vishwanathan, and R. Garnett, editors. Curran Associates, Inc. (Cited on pp. 29 and 30).

C. Villani (2003). *Topics in Optimal Transportation*, American Mathematical Society. (Cited on p. 260).

C. Villani (2008). *Optimal Transport: Old and New*. Springer. (Cited on p. 260).

P. Vincent (2011). A connection between score matching and denoising autoencoders. *Neural Comput.*, 23(7):1661–1674. (Cited on pp. 153 and 246).

M. J. Wainwright and M. I. Jordan (2007). Graphical models, exponential families, and variational inference. *Found. Trends Mach. Learn.*, 1(1–2):1–305. (Cited on p. 5).

C. J. C. H. Watkins and P. Dayan (1992). Q-learning. *Mach. Learn*, 8(3):279–292. (Cited on p. 171).

N. Wiener (1930). Generalized harmonic analysis. *Acta Mathematica*, 55(1):117–25
(Cited on p. 247).

R. J. Williams (1992). Simple statistical gradient-following algorithms for connec
tionist reinforcement learning. *Machine Learning*, 8:229–256. (Cited on pp. 6
and 83).

A. Winter (2021). A genuinely natural information measure, ArXiv preprir
2103.16662. (Cited on p. 7).

H. Wu, J. Köhler, and F. Noé (2020). Stochastic normalizing flows. In *Adv. Neural In
Process. Syst 33*, H. Larochelle, M. Ranzato, R. Hadsell, M.-F. Balcan, and H.-
Lin, editors. (Cited on pp. 94, 197, 206, and 207).

J. Q. Yang, S. Salamatian, Z. Sun, A. T. Suresh, and A. Beirami (2024). Asymp
totics of language model alignment. Pages 2027–2032 in *2024 IEEE Internationa
Symposium on Information Theory (ISIT)*. (Cited on p. 171).

J. Yedidia, W. Freeman, and Y. Weiss (2005). Constructing free-energy approximation
and generalized belief propagation algorithms. *IEEE Trans. Inf. Theory*, 51(7
2282–2312. (Cited on pp. 75 and 78).

A. Zhong, B. Kuznets-Speck, and M. R. DeWeese (2024). Time-asymmetric fluctuatio
theorem and efficient free-energy estimation. *Phys. Rev. E*, 110(3):034121. (Cite
on pp. 202 and 237).

R. Zwanzig (2001). *Nonequilibrium Statistical Mechanics*. Oxford University Pres
(Cited on p. xviii).

R. W. Zwanzig (1954). High-temperature equation of state by a perturbation metho
I. Nonpolar gases. *J. Chem. Phys.*, 22(8):1420–1426. (Cited on p. 189).

Index

For EU product safety concerns, contact us at Calle de José Abascal, 56–1°,
28003 Madrid, Spain or eugpsr@cambridge.org.

www.ingramcontent.com/pod-product-compliance
Lightning Source LLC
LaVergne TN
LVHW080029210926
848481LV00011B/3135

* 9 7 8 1 0 0 9 7 0 9 0 3 3 *